ENGLISH PROSE
1600—1660

ENGLISH PROSE
1600–1660

EDITED BY

CECIL A. MOORE

PROFESSOR OF ENGLISH IN THE
UNIVERSITY OF MINNESOTA

AND

DOUGLAS BUSH

ASSOCIATE PROFESSOR OF ENGLISH
IN THE UNIVERSITY OF
MINNESOTA

GARDEN CITY, NEW YORK
DOUBLEDAY, DORAN & COMPANY, INC.

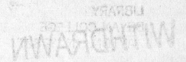

PREFACE

WHILE it is axiomatic that anthologies never please anyone
except the compilers (and not always them), a few words may
be given to explaining the aims and the plan of this book.
The chief objection lodged against the innumerable college
texts of this sort is that a collection of snippets leads students to
forget that the authors wrote whole books, which need to be read
as wholes. The argument is a *non sequitur*, of course, for the aim
of volumes like this is not to provide, as it were, the whole duty
of man, but merely to put into the hands of every student, as an
aid to discussion in class, as large a body of significant material
as possible. Complete units are given here wherever they can
be, but obviously the nature of the material very often forbids
that. In addition to complete units and long extracts we have
sometimes incorporated important short passages which every
student ought to know, and which might better be under his eye
than buried in various books. For instance, it is a doubtful kind
of rigor which would omit the last page of *The Garden of Cyrus*,
though the rest of that discourse can hardly appeal to students,
or would pass by famous purple patches in Donne because the
contexts are too full of arid divinity to be printed *in extenso*.
But such brief excerpts form a very small proportion of the
whole book.

Literary criticism had either to be represented adequately
or omitted altogether. As the bulky volumes of Mr. Gregory
Smith and Mr. Spingarn testify, the former alternative was
impossible, and to the latter we have had to submit, except
in the case of Jonson, who—apart from a few "characters"—
could be represented only by critical prose. The greatest work of
Tudor-Stuart prose has been passed over, on the perhaps rash
assumption that every student possesses a copy. Some early
specimens of translation have been given, partly for their own
sake, but mainly because they constitute important models for

v

the developing essay; space forbade the representation of other translators, such as Shelton and the unique Urquhart. We hope that the copious selections from Bacon, from the *Novum Organum* as well as the English works, may be justified by consideration of the immense importance of science in the period. And selections from certain lesser authors may help to show that the age had its light and humorous as well as its cathedral (and controversial) moods.

The texts have been modernized in spelling, and sometimes, necessarily, in punctuation; in a volume of this sort absolute fidelity to original punctuation (in some authors at least) would only achieve the somewhat pedantic merit of puzzling the reader. No liberties have been taken with the text, of course, except that in a few cases topical headings (enclosed in square brackets) have been added. Since frankness is the boast of our age, it has not seemed necessary to delete occasional robust phrases. It has been thought generally inadvisable to include authors' footnotes in the few pieces where they occur. While the arrangement by types is not wholly satisfactory, it seems the only possible one; arrangement according to authors or to dates of published works would mean chaos. The categories used are naturally broad.

We hope that the brief introductory notes, however heterodox in a volume designed mainly for the classroom, may not be considered impertinent in either sense of the word. They are given partly for biographical facts, where such are essential, partly for the purpose of explaining the choice of selections and to some degree relating them. If some remarks do not fall into either category it may be because—to admit still graver heterodoxy—editorial enthusiasm has got slightly out of hand. In any case the notes are not intended either to affront or to embarrass a teacher. Annotation of the text, in a volume of this kind, would double its size, and has not been attempted, though a glossary is provided.

It remains to acknowledge the generosity of publishers and editors who have kindly allowed us to include extracts from copyright books. We return thanks to Messrs. Jackson, Wylie & Co., Glasgow, for permission to use their edition of Moryson; to G. Routledge & Ampersand Sons and E. P. Dutton & Co., for selections from Lord Herbert's *Autobiography*; to F. P. Wilson, Esq., and Basil Blackwell, Oxford, for selections from Dekker's *Four Birds of Noah's Ark;* to F. P. Wilson, Esq., and the Oxford Press, for selections from *Dekker's Plague Pamphlets;* to R. B. McKerrow, Esq., for the use of his edition of *The Gull's Hornbook;* to the Oxford Press for selections from Clarendon's *History* (ed. Macray); to William Edwin Rudge and Geoffrey Keynes, Esq., for several corrected readings in Mr. Keynes's edition of Browne.

C. A. M.
D. B.

CONTENTS

TRANSLATIONS

ESSAYS

ix

CONTENTS

HISTORY

CONTENTS

BIOGRAPHY

PHILOSOPHY AND SCIENCE

CONTENTS

CONTENTS

CONTENTS

TRANSLATIONS

THOMAS LODGE (?1558–1625)

Two specimens of translation from Latin and Greek are given here, as we said in the preface, partly because they illustrate a fine art much practised in the period, still more because the development of the essay owed so much in form and substance to the ancients. Seneca's *Epistles to Lucilius* embody in an epistolary form akin to the essay the observation and thought of a philosopher whose moral commonplaces were tested not merely in the study but in the dangers of public life—very real dangers, for Seneca fell a victim to Nero in 65 A.D. Seneca's Stoicism was of a liberal and eclectic cast, as the quotation from Epicurus in this essay testifies. His style was that of an age which had turned away from the rolling periods of Cicero and delighted in prose compact, epigrammatic, aphoristic.

Thomas Lodge, after a varied life and varied contributions to Elizabethan literature, settled down as a physician, and his translation of Seneca's prose was one of the avocations of his professional career.

SENECA'S *EPISTLES* (Translated 1614)

EPISTLE XII

OF OLD AGE

ON WHICH side soever I turn myself I perceive the proofs of mine old age. I repaired lately to my country farm, which adjoineth the city, and complained of my daily expense in reparations, and my bailiff that had the keeping thereof answered me that it was not his fault, alleging that he had done the best that he could, but that the building was over-old and ruinous. Yet notwithstanding it was I myself that builded it! I leave it to thee to judge of me, since the stones of mine age decay so much through antiquity. Being touched herewith I took occasion to be displeased with him upon every first thing that encountereth me in my walk. "It well appeareth," said I, "that these plane trees are not well labored, they are altogether

3

leafless, their boughs are knotty and withered, and their stocks covered with moss and filthiness: this would not happen if any man had digged about them and watered them as they ought to be." He sweareth by my Genius that he doth his uttermost endeavor, and that he hath neglected them in no manner, but that the trees were old. Then remembered I myself that I had planted them with mine own hands, and seen them bear their first leaf. Turning myself to the door, "What decrepit fellow is that," said I, "that for his age is left at the gate as dead bodies are wont to be, for he looketh outward? Whence came he? What pleasure hast thou to carry forth the carcass of a strange man?" "Knowest thou me not?" saith he, "I am Felicio to whom thou wert wont to bring childish gifts; I am the son of Philositus thy bailiff, thy playfellow." "Undoubtedly," said I, "this man doteth. My darling then is become an infant; undoubtedly it may so be, for he is almost toothless."

This owe I to my farm, that my old age appeareth unto me which way soever I turn myself. Let us then embrace and love the same: it is wholly replenished with agreeable delights, if a man know how to make use of it. The apples are never so good than when they begin to wither and ripen. Infancy is most agreeable in the end thereof. To those that delight in carousing, the last draught is most pleasant, that which drowneth him in wine and consummateth his drunkenness. Whatsoever most contenting all pleasure hath contained in herself, is deferred till the end. The age that declineth is also most agreeable, when as yet it is not wholly decrepit and spent; neither judge I that age without his particular pleasure whose foot is almost in the grave, or thus succeedeth in place of pleasure that he needeth none. O how sweet and pleasant a thing is it to see man's self discharged of all covetousness! But thou mayest say that it is a tedious thing to have death always before a man's eyes. First of all this ought as well to be presented to a young as to an old man's eyes. For we are not called by the Censor according to our estate, and there is none so old that hopeth not to live at least one day longer; and one day is a degree of life.

For all our age consisteth of many parts, and is a sphere that hath divers circles, the one inclosed within the other. And one there is that incloseth and comprehendeth all the rest, which is that of the nativity until death; another that excludeth the years of youth, another that containeth all childhood; after these succeedeth the year, which incloseth all, the time by the multiplication whereof life is composed. In the circle of the year is the month, and in that of the month is the day, which is the least of all; yet notwithstanding he hath his beginning and his end, his rise and his set. And for this cause Heraclitus, that was called Scotinus by reason of the obscurity of his speech, said that one day is like to all; which another hath interpreted after another manner, to wit, that one day is like to all in number of hours. And he said true, for if a day be the time of four and twenty hours, it is necessary that they should be all alike, because the night hath that which the day hath lost. Another said that one day was like to all by reason of the conformity and resemblance, for there is nothing in the space of a very long time that thou shalt not find in one day, the light and the night, the turns and returns of the heavens. The shortness and length of the nights make these things more plainly appear. Therefore ought we to dispose of every day in such sort as if it did lead up the rearward of our time and should consummate our lives.

Pacuvius, he that usurped over Syria, being buried in the evening, being buried in his wine and those meats which he had caused to be richly and sumptuously prepared for him, as if he himself had solemnized his own obsequies, caused himself to be transported from his banquet to his bed, in such manner that amidst the dances and clapping of hands of his courtesans it was sung to the music, *He hath lived, he hath lived*; and no day over-passed his head wherein he buried not himself after this manner. That which he did of an evil conscience let us perform with a good, and addressing ourselves to our rest, let us joyfully and contentedly say,

"I have lived, and ended the course that fortune gave me."

If God vouchsafe us the next morrow, let us receive the same with thanksgiving. He is thrice happy and assuredly possessed of himself that expecteth the next day without care. Whosoever hath said "I have lived" doth daily rise to his profit.

But now I must close my letter. "What," sayest thou, "shall it come to me without any present?" Do not fear, it shall bring somewhat with it. Why said I somewhat? It will be a great deal. For what can be more excellent than this sentence it bringeth unto thee? *It is an evil thing to live in necessity, but there is no necessity to live in necessity,* for the way that leadeth unto liberty is on every side open, short, and easy to keep. Let us give God thanks for this, that no man can be constrained to live, and that it is lawful for everyone to tread necessity under his feet. Thou wilt say that these words are of Epicurus,—"what hast thou to do with another man's?" That which is true is mine. I will persevere to urge Epicurus unto thee, that they who swear and consent to the words, and consider not what is spoken but by whom, let them know that those things are best that are common.

PHILEMON HOLLAND (1552–1637)

Plutarch was one of the relatively few Greek authors who were really read by men of the Renaissance, and to witness the nature and extent of his influence we have only to turn to Montaigne, who was proud to call him master. The *Morals* was virtually a collection of essays, and, if it lacks the unique virtues of the *Lives*, its sober sense and rational habit of mind appealed greatly to men who were trying to order a new world in the dry light of ancient wisdom. This essay may well be compared with Bacon's "Of Envy."

Plutarch has been uncommonly fortunate in his translators. North had turned the *Lives* from Amyot's French, which Montaigne read, into the racy English that Shakespeare studied. Philemon Holland belonged to a younger generation than North, with more scholarship and stricter notions of a translator's function, but he achieved fair fidelity to his originals without losing a noble Elizabethan amplitude of style. Like Lodge he was a physician, but, happily, he had a small practice and much time; he lives, in Fuller's historic appellation, as "the translator general in his age."

PLUTARCH'S *MORALS* (Translated 1603)

OF ENVY AND HATRED

It seemeth at the first sight that there is no difference between envy and hatred, but that they be both one. For vice, to speak in general, having as it were many hooks or crotchets, by means thereof, as it stirreth to and fro, it yieldeth unto those passions which hang thereto many occasions and opportunities to catch hold one of another, and so to be knit and interlaced one within the other; and the same verily, like unto diseases of the body, have a sympathy and fellow-feeling one of another's distemperature and inflammation. For thus it cometh to pass that a malicious and spiteful man is as much grieved

7

and offended at the prosperity of another as the envious person; and so we hold that benevolence and goodwill is opposite unto them both, for that it is an affection of a man wishing good unto his neighbor; and envy in this respect resembleth hatred, for that they have both a will and intention quite contrary unto love. But forasmuch as no things be the same, and the resemblances between them be not so effectual to make them all one, as the differences to distinguish them asunder, let us search and examine the said differences, beginning at the very source and original of these passions.

Hatred, then, is engendered and ariseth in our heart upon an imagination and deep apprehension that we conceive of him whom we hate, that either he is naught and wicked in general to every man, or else intending mischief particularly unto ourselves. For commonly it falleth out that those who think they have received some injury at such an one's hand are disposed to hate him, yea, and those whom otherwise they know to be maliciously bent and wont to hurt others, although they have not wronged them, yet they hate and cannot abide to look upon them with patience; whereas ordinarily they bear envy unto such only as seem to prosper and to live in better state than their neighbors: by which reckoning it should seem that envy is a thing indefinite, much like unto the disease of the eyes, ophthalmia, which is offended with the brightness of any light whatsoever, whereas hatred is determinate, being always grounded upon some certain subject matters respective to itself, and on them it worketh. Secondly, our hatred doth extend even to brute beasts, for some you shall have who naturally abhor and cannot abide to see cats nor the flies cantharides, nor toads, nor yet snakes and any such serpents. As for Germanicus Cæsar, he could not of all things abide either to see a cock or to hear him crow. The sages of Persia, called their Magi, killed all their mice and rats, as well for that themselves could not away with them but detested them, as also because the god, forsooth, whom they worshipped had them in horror. And, in truth, all the Arabians and Ethiopians generally hold them abominable. But envy properly is between man and man, neither is there any likelihood at all that there should be imprinted envy in savage creatures one against another, because they have not this imagination and apprehension that another is either fortunate or unfortunate, neither be they touched with any sense of honor or dishonor; which is the one thing that principally and most of all other giveth an edge and whetteth on envy; whereas it is evident that they hate one another, they bear malice and maintain enmity; nay, they go to war as against those that be disloyal, treacherous, and such as are not to be trusted. For in this wise do eagles war with dragons, crows with owls, and the little nonnet or titmouse fighteth with the linnet, insomuch as by report the very blood of them after they be killed will not mingle together; and that which is more, if you seem to mix them, they will separate and run apart again one from the other. And, by all likelihood, the hatred that the lion hath to the cock, and the elephant also unto an hog, proceedeth from fear, for lightly that which creatures naturally fear, the same they also hate; so that herein also a man may assign and note the difference between envy and hatred, for that the nature of beasts is capable of the one but not of the other.

Over and besides, no man deserveth justly to be envied, for to be in prosperity and in better state than another is no wrong or injury offered to any person, and yet this is it for which men be envied; whereas, contrariwise, many are hated worthily, such as those whom in Greek we call ἀξιομισήτους, that is to say, worthy of public hatred, as also as many as do not fly from such, detest them not nor abhor their company. And a great argument to verify this point may be gathered from hence, namely, in that some there be who confess and take it upon them that they hate many, but no man will be known that he envieth any; for in truth the hatred of wicked persons and of wickedness is commended as a quality in men praiseworthy. And to this purpose serveth well that which was said of Charillus, who reigned in Sparta and was Lycurgus his brother's son, whom when there were certain that commended for a man of mild behavior and of a relenting and gentle nature,—"And how can it be," quoth he who was joined with him in the royal government, "that Charillus should be good, seeing he is not sharp and rigorous to the wicked?" And the poet Homer, describing the deformity of Thersites his body, depainted his defects and imperfections in sundry parts of his person and by many circumlocutions, but his perverse nature and crooked conditions he set down briefly and in one word, in this wise:

> Worthy Achilles of all the host
> And sage Ulysses, he hated most,

for he could not choose but be stark naught and wicked in the highest degree who was so full of hatred unto the best men.

As for those who deny that they are envious, in case they be convinced manifestly therein, they have a thousand pretences and excuses therefor, alleging that they are angry with the man, or stand in fear of him whom indeed they bear envy unto, or that they hate him, coloring and cloaking this passion of envy with the veil of any other whatsoever for to hide and cover it, as if it were the only malady of the soul that would be concealed and dissembled. It cannot choose, therefore, but that these two passions be nourished and grow as plants of one kind, by the same means, considering that naturally they succeed one the other: howbeit, we rather hate those that be given more to lewdness and wickedness, and we envy such rather who seem to excel others in virtue. And therefore Themistocles, being but a youth, gave out and said that he had done nothing notable, because as yet he was not envied: for like as the flies cantharides settle principally upon that wheat which is the fairest and come to full perfection, and likewise stick unto the roses that are most out, and in the very pride of their flowering, even so envy taketh commonly unto the best-conditioned persons, and to such as are growing to the height of virtue and honor: whereas contrariwise the lewdest qualities that be, and wicked in the highest degree, do mightily move and augment hatred. And hereupon it was that the Athenians had them in such detestable hatred, and abhorred them so deadly, who by their slanderous imputations brought good Socrates their fellow-citizen to his death, insomuch as they would not vouchsafe either to give them a coal or two of fire, or light their candles, or deign them an answer when they asked a question; nay, they would not wash or bathe together with them in the same water, but commanded those servitors in the bains which were called Parachytæ, that is to say, drawers and laders of water into the bathing vessels, to let forth that as polluted and defiled wherein they had washed, whereupon they, seeing themselves thus excommunicate and not able to endure this public hatred which they had incurred, being weary of their lives, hung and strangled themselves.

On the contrary side, it is often seen that the excellency of virtue, honor, and glory, and the extraordinary success of men, is so much that it doth extinguish and quench all envy. For it is not a likely or credible matter that any man bare envy unto Cyrus or Alexander the Great, after they were become the only lords and monarchs of the whole world: but like as the sun, when he is directly and plumb over the head or top of anything, causeth either no shadow at all, or the same very small and short, by the reason that his light overspreadeth round about; even so, when the prosperity of a man is come to the highest point and have gotten over the head of envy, then the said envy retireth and is either gone altogether, or else drawn within a little room by reason of that brightness overspreading it. But contrariwise the grandence of fortune and puissance in the enemies doth not one jot abbreviate or allay the hatred of their evil-willers; and that this is true may appear by the example of Alexander above named, who had not one that envied him, but many enemies he found, and those malicious, and by them in the end he was traitorously forelaid and murdered.

Semblably, adversities may well stay envy and cause it cease, but enmity and hatred they do not abolish; for men never give over to despite their enemies, no, not when they are brought low and oppressed with calamities; whereas you shall not see one in misery envied. But most true is that saying found of a certain sophister or great professor in our days: that envious persons of all other be ever pitiful and delight most in commiseration: so that herein lieth one of the greatest differences between these two passions, that hatred departeth not from those persons of whom it hath once taken hold, neither in the prosperity nor adversity of those whom they hate, whereas envy doth avoid and vanish away to nothing upon extremity as well of the one as the other.

Over and besides, we may the better discover the difference also of them by the contraries: for hatred, enmity, and malice cease presently so soon as a man is persuaded that he hath caught no harm nor sustained injury by the party; or when he hath conceived an opinion that such as he hated for their lewdness are reformed and become honest men; or thirdly, if he have received some pleasure or good turn at their hand: for evermore the last favor that is showed, as Thucydides saith, though it be less than many others, yet if it come in season and a good time is able to do out a greater offence taken before. Now of these three causes before specified, the first doth not wash away envy: for say that men were persuaded at the first that they received no wrong at all, yet they give not over for all that to bear envy still: and as for the two later, they do irritate and provoke it the rather, for such as they esteem men of quality and good worth, those they do eyebite more than before, as having virtue, the greatest good that is; and notwithstanding that they do reap commodity and find favor at their hands who prosper more than they, yet they grieve and vex thereat, envying them still both for their good mind to benefit them, and for their might and ability to perform the same, for that the one proceedeth from virtue, and the other from an happy estate, both which are good things.

We may therefore conclude that envy is a passion far different from hatred, since it is so that wherewith the one is appeased and mollified, the other is made more exasperate and grievous. But let us consider a little in the end the scope and intention as well of the one as the other. Certes, the man that is malicious purposeth fully to do him a mischief whom he hateth, so that this passion is defined to be a disposition and forward will to spy out an occasion and opportunity to wait another a shrewd turn; but surely this is not in envy, for many there be who have an envious eye to their kinsfolk and companions, whom they would not for all the good in the world see either to perish or to fall into any grievous calamity, only they are grieved to see them in such prosperity, and would impeach what they can their power, and eclipse the brightness of their glory; marry, they would not procure nor desire their utter overthrow, nor any distresses remediless or extreme miseries, but it would content and suffice them to take down their height, and as it were the upmost garret or turret of an high house which overlooketh them.

JOHN FLORIO (?1553–1625)

Montaigne (1533–1592) spent most of his life as a quiet country gentleman. Accepting his family with remarkable detachment, he did experience one supreme personal relation, friendship with La Boétie, who, though he soon died, remained a passionate memory for the survivor. In the seclusion of his beloved tower Montaigne absorbed and re-expressed the wisdom of the ancients on the conduct of life, and, whatever disturbing modern currents touched him, he seldom lost the clear-eyed sanity and reasonableness of his masters. His *Essays* (1580 *et seq.*), beginning in *marginalia*, grew, through several philosophic phases, into rich and independent analyses of almost the whole of man's world. Always applying literature to life and life to literature, and above all studying the inexhaustible subject he knew best, himself, he produced one of the ripest and wisest of books. No less full and frank than Pepys in his self-revelations, Montaigne went on to interpret his experience, and, as Hazlitt finely declared, "he may be said to have been the first who had the courage to say as an author what he felt as a man."

The Jacobean age, turning to reflection and self-scrutiny, found in Montaigne an inviting if inimitable model for the developing essay, and his influence ran alongside the very different influence of Bacon. The translation of the *Essays* by "resolute John Florio," which Shakespeare read to good account, is a living book, though its Elizabethan virtues of juiciness and verve exact a price of more than the usual Elizabethan freedom of treatment—a qualification which Florio might dismiss as "verbal wily-beguilies whereat I shake mine ears."

MONTAIGNE'S *ESSAYS* (Translated 1603)

OF REPENTING

III. 2

OTHERS fashion man, I repeat him; and represent a particular one, but ill made; and whom were I to form anew, he should be far other than he is; but he is now made. And though the lines

13

of my picture change and vary, yet lose they not themselves. The world runs all on wheels. All things therein move without intermission, yea, the earth, the rocks of Caucasus, and the pyramids of Egypt, both with the public and their own motion. Constancy itself is nothing but a languishing and wavering dance. I cannot settle my object; it goeth so unquietly and staggering, with a natural drunkenness. I take it in this plight, as it is at th' instant I amuse myself about it. I describe not the essence, but the passage; not a passage from age to age, or as the people reckon, from seven years to seven, but from day to day, from minute to minute. My history must be fitted to the present. I may soon change not only fortune, but intention. It is a counter-roll of divers and variable accidents, and irresolute imaginations, and sometimes contrary: whether it be that myself am other, or that I apprehend subjects by other circumstances and considerations. Howsoever, I may perhaps gainsay myself, but truth (as Demades said) I never gainsay. Were my mind settled, I would not essay, but resolve myself. It is still a prentice and a probationer. I propose a mean life, and without luster; 'tis all one. They fasten all moral philosophy as well to a popular and private life as to one of richer stuff. Every man beareth the whole stamp of human condition. Authors communicate themselves unto the world by some special and strange mark; I the first, by my general disposition, as Michael de Montaigne; not as a grammarian, or a poet, or a lawyer. If the world complain I speak too much of myself, I complain it thinks no more of itself. But is it reason, that being so private in use, I should pretend to make myself public in knowledge? Or is it reason I should produce into the world, where fashion and art have such sway and command, the raw and simple effects of nature, and of a nature as yet exceeding weak? To write books without learning, is it not to make a wall without stone or such like thing? Conceits of music are directed by art, mine by hap. Yet have I this according to learning, that never man handled subject he understood or knew better than I do this I have undertaken, being therein the cunningest man alive.

Secondly, that never man waded further into his matter, nor more distinctly sifted the parts and dependences of it, nor arrived more exactly and fully to the end he proposed unto himself. To finish the same I have need of naught but faithfulness, which is therein as sincere and pure as may be found. I speak truth, not my bellyful, but as much as I dare; and I dare the more, the more I grow into years; for it seemeth custom alloweth old age more liberty to babble and indiscretion to talk of itself. It cannot herein be as in trades, where the craftsman and his work do often differ. Being a man of so sound and honest conversation, writ he so foolishly? Are such learned writings come from a man of so weak a conversation? Who hath but an ordinary conceit, and writeth excellently, one may say his capacity is borrowed, not of himself. A skilful man is not skilful in all things; but a sufficient man is sufficient everywhere, even unto ignorance. Here my book and myself march together and keep one pace. Elsewhere one may commend or condemn the work without the workman, here not; who toucheth one toucheth the other. He who shall judge of it without knowing him shall wrong himself more than me; he that knows it hath wholly satisfied me. Happy beyond my merit, if I get this only portion of public approbation, as I may cause men of understanding to think I had been able to make use and benefit of learning, had I been endowed with any; and deserved better help of memory. Excuse we here what I often say, that I seldom repent myself, and that my conscience is contented with itself, not of an angel's or a horse's conscience, but as of a man's conscience. Adding ever this clause, not of ceremony, but of true and essential submission, that I speak inquiring and doubting, merely and simply referring myself, from resolution, unto common and lawful opinions. I teach not, I report. No vice is absolutely vice, which offendeth not, and a sound judgment accuseth not. For the deformity and incommodity thereof is so palpable, as peradventure they have reason who say it is chiefly produced by sottishness and brought forth by ignorance; so hard is it to imagine one should know it without hating it. Malice sucks up the greatest part of her own venom, and therewith impoisoneth herself. Vice leaveth, as an ulcer in the flesh, a repentance in the soul, which still scratcheth and bloodieth itself. For reason effaceth other griefs and sorrows, but engendereth those of repentance, the more irksome, because inward, as the cold and heat of agues is more offensive than that which comes outward. I account vice (but each according to their measure) not only those which reason disallows, and nature condemns, but such as man's opinion hath forged as false and erroneous, if laws and custom authorize the same. In like manner there is no goodness but gladdeth an honest disposition. There is truly I wot not what kind of congratulation of well doing, which rejoiceth in ourselves, and a generous jollity that accompanieth a good conscience. A mind courageously vicious may happily furnish itself with security, but she cannot be fraught with this self-joying delight and satisfaction. It is no small pleasure for one to feel himself preserved from the contagion of an age so infected as ours, and to say to himself, "Could a man enter and see even into my soul, yet should he not find me guilty, either of the affliction or ruin of anybody, nor culpable of envy or revenge, nor of public offence against the laws, nor tainted with innovation, trouble or sedition; nor spotted with falsifying of my word: and although the liberty of times allowed and taught it every man, yet could I never be induced to touch the goods or dive into the purse of any Frenchman, and have always lived upon mine own, as well in time of war as peace; nor did I ever make use of any poor man's labor without reward." These testimonies of an unspotted conscience are very pleasing, which natural joy is a great benefit unto us, and the only payment never faileth us. To ground the recompense of virtuous actions upon the approbation of others is to undertake a most uncertain or troubled foundation, namely in an age so corrupt and times so ignorant as this is; the vulgar people's good opinion is injurious. Whom trust you in seeing what is commendable? God keep me from being an honest man, according to the description I daily see made of honor, each one by himself. *Quæ fuerant vitia, mores sunt.* What erst were vices are now grown fashions. Some of my friends have sometimes attempted to school me roundly, and sift me plainly, either of their own motion or invited by me, as to an office which to a well composed mind, both in profit and lovingness, exceedeth all the duties of sincere amity. Such have I ever entertained with open arms of courtesy and kind acknowledgment. But now to speak from my conscience I often found so much false measure in their reproaches and praises that I had not greatly erred if I had rather erred than done well after their fashion. Such as we especially, who live a private life not exposed to any gaze but our own, ought in our hearts establish a touchstone, and there to touch our deeds and try our actions, and accordingly now cherish and now chastise ourselves.   I have my own laws and tribunal to judge of me, whither I address myself more than anywhere else.   I restrain my actions according to other but extend them according to myself.   None but yourself knows rightly whether you be demiss and cruel or loyal and devout.   Others see you not, but guess you by uncertain conjectures. They see not so much your nature as your art.   Adhere not then to their opinion, but hold unto your own.   *Tuo tibi judicio est utendum. Virtutis et viciorum grave ipsius conscientiæ pondus est; qua sublata jacent omnia* (CIC. *Nat. Deor.* iii.).   You must use your own judgment.   The weight of the very conscience of vice and virtues is heavy: take that away, and all is down. But whereas it is said that repentance nearly followeth sin, seemeth not to imply sin placed in his rich array, which lodgeth in us as in his proper mansion.   One may disavow and disclaim vices that surprise us, and whereto our passions transport us; but those, which by long habit are rooted in a strong, and anchored in a powerful will, are not subject to contradiction.   Repentance is but a denying of our will, and an opposition of our fantasies which diverts us here and there.   It makes some disavow his former virtue and continency.

> *Quæ mens est hodie, cur eadem non puero fuit,*
> *Vel cur his animis incolumes non redeunt genæ?*
>   HOR. *Car.* iv. *Od.* x. 7.

Why was not in a youth same mind as now?
Or why bears not this mind a youthful brow?

That is an exquisite life which even in his own private keepeth itself in awe and order.   Every one may play the juggler, and represent an honest man upon the stage; but within, and in bosom, where all things are lawful, where all is concealed, to keep a due rule or formal decorum, that's the point.   The next degree is to be so in one's own home and in his ordinary actions, whereof we are to give account to nobody, wherein is no study nor art. And therefore Bias describing the perfect state of a family, whereof (saith he) the master be such inwardly by himself, as he is outwardly, for fear of the laws, and respect of men's speeches.

And it was a worthy saying of Julius Drusus, to those workmen which for three thousand crowns offered so to reform his house that his neighbors should no more overlook into it: "I will give you six thousand," said he, "and contrive it so that on all sides every man may look into it." The custom of Agesilaus is remembered with honor, who in his travel was wont to take up his lodging in churches, that the people and gods themselves might pry into his private actions. Some have been admirable to the world, in whom nor his wife nor his servants ever noted anything remarkable. Few men have been admired of their familiars. No man hath been a prophet, not only in his house, but in his own country, saith the experience of histories. Even so in things of naught. And in this base example is the image of greatness discerned. In my climate of Gascoigne they deem it a jest to see me in print. The further the knowledge which is taken of me is from my home, of so much more worth am I. In Guienne I pay printers; in other places they pay me. Upon this accident they ground, who living and present keep close-lurking, to purchase credit when they shall be dead and absent. I had rather have less. And I cast not myself into the world but for the portion I draw from it. That done, I quit it. The people attend on such a man with wonderment, from a public act unto his own doors; together with his robes he leaves off his part; falling so much the lower, by how much higher he was mounted. View him within, there all is turbulent, disordered, and vile. And were order and formality found in him, a lively, impartial, and well-sorted judgment is required to perceive and fully to discern him in these base and private actions. Considering that order is but a dumpish and drowsy virtue, to gain a battle, perform an ambassage, and govern a people, are noble and worthy actions; to chide, laugh, sell, pay, love, hate, and mildly and justly to converse both with his own and with himself, not to relent, and not gainsay himself, are things more rare, more difficult, and less remarkable.

Retired lives sustain that way, whatever some say, offices as much more crabbed and extended than other lives do. And private men (saith Aristotle) serve virtue more hardly, and more highly attend her, than those which are magistrates or placed in authority. We prepare ourselves unto eminent occasions more for glory than for conscience. The nearest way to come unto glory were to do that for conscience which we do for glory. And meseemeth the virtue of Alexander representeth much less vigor in her large theatre than that of Socrates in his base and obscure excrcitation. I easily conceive Socrates in the room of Alexander; Alexander in that of Socrates I cannot. If any ask the one what he can do, he will answer, "Conquer the world"; let the same question be demanded of the other, he will say, "Lead my life conformably to its natural condition,"—a science much more generous, more important, and more lawful.

The worth of the mind consisteth not in going high, but in marching orderly. Her greatness is not exercised in greatness, in mediocrity it is. As those which judge and touch us inwardly make no great account of the brightness of our public actions, and see they are but streaks and points of clear water, surging from a bottom otherwise slimy and full of mud, so those who judge us by this gay outward appearance conclude the same of our inward constitution, and cannot couple popular faculties as theirs are, unto these other faculties, which amaze them so far from their level. So do we attribute savage shapes and ugly forms unto devils. As who doth not ascribe high-raised eyebrows, open nostrils, a stern, frightful visage, and a huge body unto Tamburlaine, as is the form or shape of the imagination we have fore-conceived by the bruit of his name? Had any heretofore showed me Erasmus, I could hardly had been induced to think but whatsoever he had said to his boy or hostess, had been adages and apothegms. We imagine much more fitly an artificer upon his close-stool or on his wife, than a great judge, reverend for his carriage and regardful for his sufficiency; we think that from those high thrones they should not abase themselves so low as to live. As vicious minds are often incited to do well by some strange impulsion, so are virtuous spirits moved to do ill. They must then be judged by their settled estate, when they are near themselves, and as we say, at home, if at any time they be so, or when they are nearest unto rest, and in their natural seat. Natural inclinations are by institution helped and strengthened, but they neither change nor exceed. A thousand natures in my time have athwart a contrary discipline escaped toward virtue or toward vice.

> *Sic ubi desuetæ silvis in carcere clausæ,*
> *Mansuevere feræ, et vultus posuere minaces,*
> *Atque hominem didicere pati, si torrida parvus*
> *Venit in ora cruor, redeunt rabiesque furorque,*
> *Admonitæque tument gustato sanguine fauces,*
> *Fervet, et a trepido vix abstinet iræ magistro.*
>
> LUCAN, iv. 237.

So when wild beasts, disused from the wood,
Fierce looks laid down, grow tame, closed in a cage,
Taught to bear man, if then a little blood
Touch their hot lips, fury returns and rage;
Their jaws by taste admonished swell with veins,
Rage boils, and from faint keeper scarce abstains.

These original qualities are not grubbed out, they are but covered and hidden. The Latin tongue is to me in a manner natural, I understand it better than French; but it is now forty years I have not made use of it to speak, nor much to write. Yet in some extreme emotions and sudden passions, wherein I have twice or thrice fallen since my years of discretion, and namely once, when my father, being in perfect health, fell all along upon me in a swoon, I have ever even from my very heart uttered my first words in Latin—nature rushing and by force expressing itself, against so long a custom; the like example is alleged of divers others. Those which in my time have attempted to correct the fashions of the world by new opinions, reform the vices of appearance, those of essence they leave untouched if they increase them not; and their increase is much to be feared. We willingly protract all other well-doing upon these external reformations, of less cost, and of greater merit; whereby we satisfy good cheap other natural, consubstantial, and intestine vices. Look a little into the course of our experience. There is no man (if he listen to himself) that doth not discover in himself a peculiar form of his, a swaying form, which wrestleth against the institution, and against the tempests of passions, which are contrary unto him. As for me, I feel not myself much agitated by a shock; I commonly find myself in mine own

place, as are sluggish and lumpish bodies.   If I am not close
and near unto myself, I am never far off; my debauches or excesses transport me not much.   There is nothing extreme and
strange; yet have I sound fits and vigorous lusts.   The true
condemnation, and which toucheth the common fashion of our
men, is that their very retreat is full of corruption and filth,
the idea of their amendment blurred and deformed, their repentance crazed and faulty very near as much as their sin.   Some,
either because they are so fast and naturally joined unto vice,
or through long custom, have lost all sense of its ugliness.   To
others (of whose rank I am) vice is burthenous, but they counter-
balance it with pleasure or other occasions; and suffer it, and at a
certain rate lend themselves unto it, though basely and viciously.
Yet might happily so remote a disproportion of measure be
imagined, where with justice the pleasure might excuse the offence, as we say of profit.   Not only being accidental, and out of
sin, as in thefts, but even in the very exercise of it, as in the acquaintance or copulation with women, where the provocation is
so violent, and as they say, sometime unresistable.   In a
town of a kinsman of mine, the other day, being in Armignac, I
saw a countryman, commonly surnamed the thief, who himself
reported his life to have been thus.   Being born a beggar, and
perceiving that to get his bread by the sweat of his brow and
labor of his hands would never sufficiently arm him against
penury, he resolved to become a thief, and that trade had employed all his youth safely, by means of his bodily strength; for
he ever made up harvest and vintage in other men's grounds,
but so far off, and in so great heaps, that it was beyond imagination one man should in one night carry away so much upon his
shoulders; and was so careful to equal the prey, and disperse the
mischief he did, that the spoil was of less import to every
particular man.
     He is now in old years indifferently rich for a man of his
condition (Godamercy his trade), which he is not ashamed to
confess openly.   And to reconcile himself with God he affirmeth
to be daily ready, with his gettings and other good turns, to
satisfy the posterity of those he hath heretofore wronged or
robbed; which if himself be not of ability to perform (for he
cannot do all at once) he will charge his heirs withal, according
to the knowledge he hath, of the wrongs by him done to every

man. By this description, be it true or false, he respecteth theft as a dishonest and unlawful action, and hateth the same: yet less than pinching want; he repents but simply, for in regard it was so counterbalanced and recompensed, he repenteth not. That is not that habit which incorporates us unto vice and confirmeth our understanding in it; nor is it that boisterous wind which by violent blasts dazzleth and troubleth our minds, and at that time confounds and overwhelms both us, our judgment, and all, into the power of vice. What I do is ordinarily full and complete, and I march (as we say) all in one pace; I have not many motions that hide themselves and slink away from my reason, or which very near are not guided by the consent of all my parts, without division or intestine sedition; my judgment hath the whole blame or commendation, and the blame it hath once, it hath ever; for, almost from its birth, it hath been one of the same inclination, course, and force. And in matters of general opinions, even from my infancy, I ranged myself to the point I was to hold. Some sins there are outrageous, violent, and sudden; leave we them.

But those other sins, so often reassumed, determined, and advised upon, whether they be of complexion, or of profession and calling, I cannot conceive how they should so long be settled in one same courage, unless the reason and conscience of the sinner were thereunto inwardly privy and constantly willing. And how to imagine or fashion the repentance thereof, which he vaunteth doth sometimes visit him, seemeth somewhat hard unto me. I am not of Pythagoras' sect, that men take a new soul, when to receive oracles they approach the images of gods, unless he would say withal that it must be a strange one, new, and lent him for the time, our own giving so little sign of purification and cleanness worthy of that office. They do altogether against the Stoical precepts, which appoint us to correct the imperfections and vices we find in ourselves, but withal forbid us to disturb the quiet of our mind. They make us believe they feel great remorse, and are inwardly much displeased with sin, but of amendment, correction, or intermission, they show us none. Surely there can be no perfect health where the disease is not perfectly removed. Were repentance put in the scale of the balance, it would weigh down sin. I find no humor so easy to be counterfeited as devotion. If one conform not his life and conditions to it, her essence is abstruse and concealed, her appearance gentle and stately.

For my part, I may in general wish to be other than I am, I may condemn and mislike my universal form, I may beseech God to grant me an undefiled reformation, and excuse my natural weakness; but meseemeth I ought not to term this repentance no more than the displeasure of being neither angel nor Cato. My actions are squared to what I am and conformed to my condition. I cannot do better. And repentance doth not properly concern what is not in our power, sorrow doth. I may imagine infinite dispositions of a higher pitch, and better governed than mine, yet do I nothing better my faculties; no more than mine arm becometh stronger, or my wit more excellent, by conceiving some others to be so. If to suppose and wish a more nobler working than ours might produce the repentance of our own, we should then repent us of our most innocent actions, for so much as we judge that in a more excellent nature, they had been directed with greater perfection and dignity, and ourselves would do the like. When I consult with my age of my youth's proceedings, I find that commonly (according to my opinion) I managed them in order. This is all my resistance is able to perform. I flatter not myself; in like circumstances I should ever be the same. It is not a spot but a whole dye that stains me. I acknowledge no repentance, [that] is superficial, mean, and ceremonious. It must touch me on all sides before I can term it repentance. It must pinch my entrails and afflict them as deeply and thoroughly as God himself beholds me. When in negotiating many good fortunes have slipped me for want of good discretion, yet did my projects make good choice according to the occurrences presented unto them. Their manner is ever to take the easier and surer side. I find that in my former deliberations I proceeded, after my rules, discreetly for the subject's state propounded to me; and in like occasions would proceed alike a hundred years hence. I respect not what now it is, but what it was, when I consulted of it. The consequence of all designs consists in the seasons; occasions pass, and matters change incessantly. I have in my time run into some gross, absurd, and important errors, not for want of good advice, but of good hap. There are secret and indivinable parts in the objects men do handle, especially in the nature of men

and mute conditions, without show, and sometimes unknown
of the very possessors, produced and stirred up by sudden
occasions. If my wit could neither find nor presage them, I am
not offended with it; the function thereof is contained within its
own limits. If the success beat me and favor the side I refused,
there is no remedy; I fall not out with myself; I accuse my fortune, not my endeavor: that's not called repentance. Phocion
had given the Athenians some counsel, which was not followed;
the matter, against his opinion, succeeding happily: "How now,
Phocion," quoth one, "art thou pleased the matter hath thrived
so well?" "Yea," said he, "and I am glad of it, yet repent not
the advice I gave."

When any of my friends come to me for counsel, I bestow it
frankly and clearly, not (as well-nigh all the world doth),
wavering at the hazard of the matter, whereby the contrary of
my meaning may happen, that so they may justly find fault
with my advice, for which I care not greatly. For they shall
do me wrong, and it became not me to refuse them that duty. I
have nobody to blame for my faults or misfortunes but myself.
For in effect I seldom use the advice of other unless it be for
compliment sake, and where I have need of instruction or
knowledge of the fact. Marry, in things wherein naught but
judgment is to be employed, strange reasons may serve to sustain but not to divert me. I lend a favorable and courteous
ear unto them all. But (to my remembrance) I never believed
any but mine own. With me they are but flies and moths, which
distract my will. I little regard mine own opinions, other men's
I esteem as little; fortune pays me accordingly. If I take no
counsel I give as little. I am not much sought after for it, and
less credited when I give it; neither know I any enterprise, either
private or public, that my advice hath directed and brought to
conclusion. Even those whom fortune had some way tied
thereunto have more willingly admitted the direction of others'
conceits than mine. As one that am as jealous of the rights of
my quiet, as of those of my authority, I would rather have it
thus.

Where leaving me, they jump with my profession, which is
wholly to settle and contain me in myself. It is a pleasure unto
me to be disinterested of other men's affairs, and disengaged
from their contentions. When suits or businesses be over-past,

howsoever it be, I grieve little at them. For the imagination that they must necessarily happen so puts me out of pain; behold them in the course of the universe, and enchained in Stoical causes. Your fantasy cannot by wish or imagination remove one point of them, but the whole order of things must reverse both what is past and what is to come. Moreover, I hate that accidental repentance which old age brings with it.

He that in ancient times said he was beholden to years, because they had rid him of voluptuousness, was not of mine opinion. I shall never give impuissance thanks for any good it can do me. *Nec tam aversa unquam videbitur ab opere suo providentia, ut debilitas inter optima inventa sit.* Nor shall foresight ever be seen so averse from her own work, that weakness be found to be one of the best things. Our appetites are rare in old age; the blow over-passed, a deep satiety seizeth upon us; therein I see no conscience. Fretting care and weakness imprint in us an effeminate and drowsy virtue.

We must not suffer ourselves so fully to be carried into natural alterations as to corrupt or adulterate our judgment by them. Youth and pleasure have not heretofore prevailed so much over me but I could ever (even in the midst of sensualities) discern the ugly face of sin; nor can the distaste which years bring on me, at this instant, keep me from discerning that of voluptuousness in vice. Now I am no longer in it, I judge of it as if I were still there. I, who lively and attentively examine my reason, find it to be the same that possessed me in my most dissolute and licentious age, unless perhaps they being enfeebled and impaired by years do make some difference: and find, that what delight it refuseth to afford me in regard of my bodily health, it would no more deny me than in times past for the health of my soul. To see it out of combat, I hold it not the more courageous. My temptations are so mortified and crazed, as they are not worthy of its oppositions; holding but my hand before me, I becalm them. Should one present that former concupiscence unto it, I fear it would be of less power to sustain it than heretofore it hath been. I see in it by itself no increase of judgment, nor access of brightness; what it now judgeth, it did then. Wherefore if there be any amendment, 'tis but diseased. Oh miserable kind of remedy, to be beholden unto sickness for our health. It is not for our mishap, but for the good success of our judgment, to perform this office. Crosses and afflictions make me do nothing but curse them. They are for people that cannot be awaked but by the whip; the course of my reason is the nimbler in prosperity, it is much more distracted and busied in the digesting of mischiefs than of delights. I see much clearer in fair weather. Health forewarneth me, as with more pleasure, so to better purpose, than sickness. I approached the nearest I could unto amendment and regularity when I should have enjoyed the same. I should be ashamed and vexed that the misery and mishap of my old age could exceed the health, attention, and vigor of my youth; and that I should be esteemed, not for what I have been, but for what I am left to be. The happy life, in my opinion, not (as said Antisthenes) the happy death, is it that makes man's happiness in this world.

I have not preposterously busied myself to tie the tail of a philosopher unto the head and body of a varlet; nor that this paltry end should disavow and belie the fairest, soundest, and longest part of my life. I will present myself, and make a general muster of my whole, everywhere uniformally. Were I to live again, it should be as I have already lived. I neither deplore what is past, nor dread what is to come; and if I be not deceived, the inward parts have nearly resembled the outward. It is one of the chiefest points wherein I am beholden to fortune, that in the course of my body's estate each thing hath been carried in season. I have seen the leaves, the blossoms, and the fruit; and now see the drooping and withering of it. Happily, because naturally, I bear my present miseries the more gently because they are in season, and with greater favor make me remember the long happiness of my former life. In like manner, my discretion may well be of like proportion in the one and the other time; but sure it was of much more performance, and had a better grace, being fresh, jolly and full of spirit, than now that it is worn, decrepit and toilsome.

I therefore renounce these casual and dolorous reformations. God must touch our hearts, our conscience must amend of itself, and not by reinforcement of our reason, nor by the enfeebling of our appetites. Voluptuousness in itself is neither pale nor discolored, to be discerned by blear and troubled eyes. We should affect temperance and chastity for itself, and for God's cause, who hath ordained them unto us; that which catarrhs bestow upon us, and which I am beholden to my colic for, is neither temperance nor chastity. A man cannot boast of contemning or combating sensuality, if he see her not, or know not her grace, her force, and most attractive beauties. I know them both, and therefore may speak it. But methinks our souls in age are subject unto more importunate diseases and imperfections than they are in youth. I said so being young, when my beardless chin was upbraided me, and I say it again, now that my gray beard gives me authority. We entitle wisdom the frowardness of our humors, and the distaste of present things; but in truth we abandon not vices, so much as we change them, and in mine opinion for the worse. Besides a silly and ruinous pride, cumbersome tattle, wayward and unsociable humors, superstition and a ridiculous carking for wealth, when the use of it is well-nigh lost, I find the more envy, injustice, and lewdness in it. It sets more wrinkles in our minds than on our foreheads; nor are there any spirits, or very rare ones, which in growing old taste not sourly and mustily. Man marcheth entirely towards his increase and decrease. View but the wisdom of Socrates, and divers circumstances of his condemnation; I dare say he something lent himself unto it by prevarication of purpose, being so near, and at the age of seventy, to endure the benumbing of his spirit's richest pace, and the dimming of his accustomed brightness. What metamorphoses have I seen it daily make in divers of mine acquaintances? It is a powerful malady, which naturally and imperceptibly glideth into us. There is required great provision of study, heed, and precaution, to avoid the imperfections wherewith it chargeth us, or at least to weaken their further progress. I find that notwithstanding all my entrenchings, by little and little it getteth ground upon me; I hold out as long as I can, but know not whither at length it will bring me. Hap what hap will, I am pleased the world know from what height I tumbled.

ESSAYS

FRANCIS BACON (1561–1626)

The slow, tortuous rise and the sudden fall of Bacon, which might have been a theme for a dramatist, are too familiar to need a summary here. Comments upon him by Ben Jonson and James Howell are reprinted on pages 580 and 591. The *Essays* of 1597 were little more than strings of aphorisms—as the specimen below illustrates—but in the editions of 1612 and 1625 these were expanded and many others were added. The style of the later essays was more akin to that of the *Advancement of Learning*, relatively loose and flexible, though it did not cease to show the influence of the sententious Seneca and the books of maxims so popular in the sixteenth century. To the *Advancement* also one may go for the best account of the technique and the aims and scope of the *Essays*. (See pp. 219, 220, under the headings "The Aphoristic Method" and "Points of Nature and Fortune, etc."). In order to gain space for the less commonly read and reprinted pieces, we have included only a few of Bacon's essays.

ESSAYS (1597; 1612; 1625)

OF DISCOURSE (1597)

SOME in their discourse desire rather commendation of wit in being able to hold all arguments, than of judgment in discerning what is true; as if it were a praise to know what might be said, and not what should be thought. Some have certain commonplaces and themes wherein they are good, and want variety; which kind of poverty is for the most part tedious, and now and then ridiculous. The honorablest part of talk is to give the occasion, and again to moderate and pass to somewhat else. It is good to vary, and mix speech of the present occasion with arguments, tales with reasons, asking of questions with telling of opinions, and jest with earnest; but some things are privileged from jest, namely, religion, matters of state, great persons, all men's present business of importance, and any case that deserveth pity. He that questioneth much shall learn much, and content much, especially if he apply his questions to the skill of the party of whom he asketh; for he shall give them occasion to please themselves in speaking, and himself shall continually gather knowledge. If sometimes you dissemble your knowledge of that you are thought to know, you shall be thought another time to know that which you know not. Speech of a man's self is not good often; and there is but one thing wherein a man may commend himself with good grace, and that is commending virtue in another, especially if it be such a virtue as whereunto himself pretendeth. Discretion of speech is more than eloquence, and to speak agreeably to him with whom we deal is more than to speak in good words or in good order. A good continued speech, without a good speech of interlocution, showeth slowness; and a good second speech without a good set speech showeth shallowness. To use too many circumstances ere one come to the matter is wearisome, and to use none at all is blunt.

DEDICATION OF 1612 MS. TO PRINCE HENRY

HAVING divided my life into the contemplative and active part, I am desirous to give His Majesty and Your Highness of the fruit of both, simple though they be. To write just treatises requireth leisure in the writer, and leisure in the reader, and therefore are not so fit, neither in regard of Your Highness' princely affairs, nor in regard of my continual service, which is the cause that hath made me choose to write certain brief notes, set down rather significantly than curiously, which I have called Essays. The word is late, but the thing is ancient. For Seneca's *Epistles to Lucilius*, if one mark them well, are but essays—that is, dispersed meditations, though conveyed in the form of epistles. These labors of mine I know cannot be worthy of Your Highness, for what can be worthy of you? But my hope is they may be as grains of salt, that will rather give you an appetite than offend you with satiety. And although they handle those things wherein both men's lives and their pens are most conversant yet (what I have attained I know not) but I have endeavored to make them not vulgar; but of a nature whereof a man shall find much in experience, little in books, so as they are neither repetitions nor fancies. . . .

OF TRUTH (1625)

WHAT IS TRUTH? said jesting Pilate, and would not stay for an answer. Certainly there be that delight in giddiness, and count it a bondage to fix a belief, affecting free-will in thinking as well as in acting. And though the sects of philosophers of that kind be gone, yet there remain certain discoursing wits which are of the same veins, though there be not so much blood in them as was in those of the ancients. But it is not only the difficulty and labor which men take in finding out of truth, nor again that when it is found it imposeth upon men's thoughts, that doth bring lies in favor, but a natural though corrupt love of the lie itself. One of the later school of the Grecians examineth the matter, and is at a stand to think what should be in it that men should love lies, where neither they make for pleasure as with poets, nor for advantage as with the merchant, but for the lie's sake. But I cannot tell; this same truth is a naked and open daylight that doth not show the masks and mummeries and triumphs of the world half so stately and daintily as candlelights. Truth may, perhaps, come to the price of a pearl that showeth best by day, but it will not rise to the price of a diamond or carbuncle that showeth best in varied lights. A mixture of a lie doth ever add pleasure. Doth any man doubt that if there were taken out of men's minds vain opinions, flattering hopes, false valuations, imaginations as one would, and the like, but it would leave the minds of a number of men poor shrunken things, full of melancholy and indisposition, and unpleasing to themselves? One of the Fathers, in great severity, called poesy *vinum dæmonum*,[1] because it filleth the imagination, and yet it is but with the shadow of a lie. But it is not the lie that passeth through the mind, but the lie that sinketh in and settleth in it, that doth the hurt, such as we spake of before. But howsoever these things are thus in men's depraved judgments and affections, yet truth, which only doth judge itself, teacheth that the inquiry of truth, which is the love-making or wooing of it, the knowledge of truth, which is the presence of it, and the belief of truth, which is the enjoying of it, is the sovereign good of human nature. The first creature of God, in

---

[1] Wine of devils.

the works of the days, was the light of the sense; the last was the light of reason; and his sabbath work ever since is the illumination of his Spirit. First he breathed light upon the face of the matter or chaos, then he breathed light into the face of man, and still he breatheth and inspireth light into the face of his chosen. The poet that beautified the sect that was otherwise inferior to the rest, saith yet excellently well: *It is a pleasure to stand upon the shore and to see ships tossed upon the sea; a pleasure to stand in the window of a castle and to see a battle and the adventures thereof below; but no pleasure is comparable to the standing upon the vantage ground of truth* (a hill not to be commanded, and where the air is always clear and serene), *and to see the errors, and wanderings, and mists, and tempests in the vale below;* so always that this prospect be with pity, and not with swelling or pride. Certainly it is heaven upon earth to have a man's mind move in charity, rest in providence, and turn upon the poles of truth.

To pass from theological and philosophical truth to the truth of civil business, it will be acknowledged, even by those that practise it not, that clear and round dealing is the honor of man's nature; and that mixture of falsehood is like alloy in coin of gold and silver, which may make the metal work the better, but it embaseth it. For these winding and crooked courses are the goings of the serpent, which goeth basely upon the belly, and not upon the feet. There is no vice that doth so cover a man with shame as to be found false and perfidious. And therefore Montaigne saith prettily, when he inquired the reason why the word of the lie should be such a disgrace and such an odious charge? Saith he, *If it be well weighed, to say that a man lieth is as much to say as that he is brave towards God and a coward towards men.* For a lie faces God and shrinks from man. Surely the wickedness of falsehood and breach of faith cannot possibly be so highly expressed as in that it shall be the last peal to call the judgments of God upon the generations of men, it being foretold that when Christ cometh, *he shall not find faith upon the earth.*

OF DEATH (1612; 1625)

MEN fear death as children fear to go in the dark; and as that natural fear in children is increased with tales, so is the other.

Certainly the contemplation of death as the wages of sin and passage to another world, is holy and religious; but the fear of it, as a tribute due unto nature, is weak. Yet in religious meditations there is sometimes mixture of vanity and of superstition. You shall read in some of the friars' books of mortification that a man should think with himself what the pain is if he have but his finger's end pressed or tortured, and thereby imagine what the pains of death are, when the whole body is corrupted and dissolved; when many times death passeth with less pain than the torture of a limb; for the most vital parts are not the quickest of sense. And by him that spake only as a philosopher and natural man it was well said: *Pompa mortis magis terret, quam mors ipsa.*[1] Groans and convulsions, and a discolored face, and friends weeping, and blacks, and obsequies and the like, show death terrible. It is worthy the observing that there is no passion in the mind of man so weak but it mates and masters the fear of death; and therefore death is no such terrible enemy when a man hath so many attendants about him that can win the combat of him. Revenge triumphs over death, love slights it, honor aspireth to it, grief flieth to it, fear preoccupateth it; nay, we read, after Otho the emperor had slain himself, pity, which is the tenderest of affections, provoked many to die out of mere compassion to their sovereign, and as the truest sort of followers. Nay, Seneca adds niceness and satiety: *Cogita quamdiu eadem feceris; mori velle, non tantum fortis, aut miser, sed etiam fastidiosus potest.* A man would die, though he were neither valiant nor miserable, only upon a weariness to do the same thing so oft over and over. It is no less worthy to observe, how little alteration in good spirits the approaches of death make; for they appear to be the same men till the last instant. Augustus Cæsar died in a compliment, *Livia, conjugii nostri memor, vive et vale;*[2] Tiberius in dissimulation, as Tacitus saith of him, *Jam Tiberium vires et corpus, non dissimulatio, deserebant;*[3] Vespasian in a jest, sitting upon the stool, *Ut puto Deus fio;*[4] Galba with a sentence, *Feri, si ex re sit populi*

---

[1] It is the accompaniments of death that are frightful rather than death itself.

[2] Farewell, Livia, and forget not the days of our marriage.

[3] His strength of body left Tiberius, not his dissimulation.

[4] As I think, I am becoming a god.

Romani,[1] holding forth his neck; Septimius Severus in dispatch, *Adeste, si quid mihi restat agendum;*[2] and the like. Certainly the Stoics bestowed too much cost upon death, and by their great preparations made it appear more fearful. Better saith he, *Qui finem vitæ extremum inter munera ponat naturæ.*[3] It is as natural to die as to be born, and to a little infant perhaps the one is as painful as the other. He that dies in an earnest pursuit is like one that is wounded in hot blood, who for the time scarce feels the hurt; and therefore a mind fixed and bent upon somewhat that is good, doth avert the dolors of death. But above all, believe it, the sweetest canticle is, *Nunc dimittis*,[4] when a man hath obtained worthy ends and expectations. Death hath this also, that it openeth the gate to good fame and extinguisheth envy, *Extinctus amabitur idem.*[5]

OF ADVERSITY (1625)

IT WAS an high speech of Seneca (after the manner of the Stoics), that the good things which belong to prosperity are to be wished; but the good things that belong to adversity are to be admired: *Bona rerum secundarum optabilia; adversarum mirabilia.* Certainly if miracles be the command over nature, they appear most in adversity. It is yet a higher speech of his than the other (much too high for a heathen): *It is true greatness to have in one the frailty of a man and the security of a God, Vere magnum habere fragilitatem hominis, securitatem Dei.* This would have done better in poesy, where transcendences are more allowed. And the poets, indeed, have been busy with it; for it is in effect the thing which is figured in that strange fiction of the ancient poets, which seemeth not to be without mystery; nay, and to have some approach to the state of a Christian: that *Hercules, when he went to unbind Prometheus* (by whom human nature is represented), *sailed the length of the great ocean in an earthen pot or pitcher;* lively describing Christian resolution, that saileth in the frail bark of the flesh through the waves of the

---

[1] Strike, if it be for the good of Rome.

[2] Make haste, if there is anything more for me to do.

[3] Who regards the close of life as one of the benefits of nature.

[4] Lord, now lettest thou thy servant depart in peace.

[5] The man who was envied while he lived shall be loved when he is dead.

world. But to speak in a mean, the virtue of prosperity is temperance; the virtue of adversity is fortitude, which in morals is the more heroical virtue. Prosperity is the blessing of the Old Testament; adversity is the blessing of the New, which carrieth the greater benediction, and the clearer revelation of God's favor. Yet, even in the Old Testament, if you listen to David's harp, you shall hear as many hearse-like airs as carols; and the pencil of the Holy Ghost hath labored more in describing the afflictions of Job than the felicities of Salomon. Prosperity is not without many fears and distastes; and adversity is not without comforts and hopes. We see in needle-works and embroideries, it is more pleasing to have a lively work upon a sad and solemn ground than to have a dark and melancholy work upon a lightsome ground. Judge, therefore, of the pleasure of the heart by the pleasure of the eye. Certainly virtue is like precious odors, most fragrant when they are incensed or crushed; for prosperity doth best discover vice, but adversity doth best discover virtue.

OF MARRIAGE AND SINGLE LIFE (1612; 1625)

HE THAT hath wife and children hath given hostages to fortune, for they are impediments to great enterprises, either of virtue or mischief. Certainly the best works and of greatest merit for the public have proceeded from the unmarried or childless men, which both in affection and means have married and endowed the public. Yet it were great reason that those that have children should have greatest care of future times, unto which they know they must transmit their dearest pledges. Some there are who, though they lead a single life, yet their thoughts do end with themselves, and account future times impertinences. Nay, there are some other that account wife and children but as bills of charges. Nay more, there are some foolish rich covetous men that take a pride in having no children, because they may be thought so much the richer. For perhaps they have heard some talk, *Such an one is a great rich man*, and another except to it, *Yea, but he hath a great charge of children*, as if it were an abatement to his riches. But the most ordinary cause of a single life is liberty, especially in certain self-pleasing and humorous minds, which are so sensible of every restraint, as they will go near to think their girdles and garters to be bonds and shackles. Unmarried men are best friends, best masters, best servants, but not always best subjects; for they are light to run away, and almost all fugitives are of that condition. A single life doth well with churchmen, for charity will hardly water the ground where it must first fill a pool. It is indifferent for judges and magistrates, for if they be facile and corrupt, you shall have a servant five times worse than a wife. For soldiers, I find the generals commonly in their hortatives put men in mind of their wives and children. And I think the despising of marriage amongst the Turks maketh the vulgar soldier more base. Certainly, wife and children are a kind of discipline of humanity; and single men, though they be many times more charitable, because their means are less exhaust, yet, on the other side, they are more cruel and hard-hearted (good to make severe inquisitors), because their tenderness is not so oft called upon. Grave natures, led by custom, and therefore constant, are commonly loving husbands; as was said of Ulysses, *Vetulam suam prætulit immortalitati*.[1] Chaste women are often proud and froward, as presuming upon the merit of their chastity. It is one of the best bonds both of chastity and obedience in the wife, if she think her husband wise; which she will never do if she find him jealous. Wives are young men's mistresses, companions for middle age, and old men's nurses; so as a man may have a quarrel to marry when he will. But yet he was reputed one of the wise men that made answer to the question, when a man should marry, *A young man not yet, an elder man not at all*. It is often seen that bad husbands have very good wives; whether it be that it raiseth the price of their husband's kindness when it comes, or that the wives take a pride in their patience. But this never fails, if the bad husbands were of their own choosing, against their friends' consent; for then they will be sure to make good their own folly.

OF ENVY (1625)

THERE be none of the affections which have been noted to fascinate or bewitch, but love and envy. They both have ve-

---

[1] He preferred his old wife to immortality.

hement wishes; they frame themselves readily into imaginations and suggestions; and they come easily into the eye, especially upon the presence of the objects; which are the points that conduce to fascination, if any such thing there be. We see likewise the Scripture calleth envy an *evil eye;* and the astrologers call the evil influences of the stars *evil aspects;* so that still there seemeth to be acknowledged, in the act of envy, an ejaculation or irradiation of the eye. Nay some have been so curious as to note that the times when the stroke or percussion of an envious eye doth most hurt, are when the party envied is beheld in glory or triumph; for that sets an edge upon envy: and besides, at such times the spirits of the person envied do come forth most into the outward parts, and so meet the blow.

But leaving these curiosities (though not unworthy to be thought on in fit place), we will handle what persons are apt to envy others; what persons are most subject to be envied themselves; and what is the difference between public and private envy.

A man that hath no virtue in himself ever envieth virtue in others. For men's minds will either feed upon their own good or upon others' evil; and who wanteth the one will prey upon the other; and whoso is out of hope to attain to another's virtue will seek to come at even hand by depressing another's fortune.

A man that is busy and inquisitive is commonly envious. For to know much of other men's matters cannot be because all that ado may concern his own estate; therefore it must needs be that he taketh a kind of play-pleasure in looking upon the fortunes of others. Neither can he that mindeth but his own business find much matter for envy. For envy is a gadding passion, and walketh the streets, and doth not keep home: *Non est curiosus, quin idem sit malevolus.*[1]

Men of noble birth are noted to be envious towards new men when they rise. For the distance is altered, and it is like a deceit of the eye, that when others come on they think themselves go back.

Deformed persons, and eunuchs, and old men, and bastards, are envious; for he that cannot possibly mend his own case will do what he can to impair another's; except these defects light

---

[1]No one is curious without also being malevolent.

upon a very brave and heroical nature, which thinketh to make his natural wants part of his honor; in that it should be said that an eunuch or a lame man did such great matters; affecting the honor of a miracle: as it was in Narses the eunuch, and Agesilaus and Tamberlanes, that were lame men.

The same is the case of men that rise after calamities and misfortunes; for they are as men fallen out with the times, and think other men's harms a redemption of their own sufferings.

They that desire to excel in too many matters, out of levity and vain glory, are ever envious; for they cannot want work, it being impossible but many in some one of those things should surpass them. Which was the character of Adrian, the emperor, that mortally envied poets and painters and artificers, in works wherein he had a vein to excel.

Lastly, near kinsfolks, and fellows in office, and those that have been bred together, are more apt to envy their equals when they are raised. For it doth upbraid unto them their own fortunes, and pointeth at them, and cometh oftener into their remembrance, and incurreth likewise more into the note of others; and envy ever redoubleth from speech and fame. Cain's envy was the more vile and malignant towards his brother Abel because, when his sacrifice was better accepted, there was nobody to look on. Thus much for those that are apt to envy.

Concerning those that are more or less subject to envy:— first, persons of eminent virtue when they are advanced are less envied, for their fortune seemeth but due unto them; and no man envieth the payment of a debt, but rewards and liberality rather. Again, envy is ever joined with the comparing of a man's self, and where there is no comparison, no envy; and therefore kings are not envied but by kings. Nevertheless, it is to be noted that unworthy persons are most envied at their first coming in, and afterwards overcome it better; whereas contrariwise, persons of worth and merit are most envied when their fortune continueth long. For by that time, though their virtue be the same, yet it hath not the same lustre, for fresh men grow up that darken it.

Persons of noble blood are less envied in their rising, for it seemeth but right done to their birth; besides, there seemeth not much added to their fortune, and envy is as the sunbeams, that beat hotter upon a bank or steep rising ground than upon a flat. And for the same reason, those that are advanced by degrees are less envied than those that are advanced suddenly, and *per saltum*.[1]

Those that have joined with their honor great travels, cares, or perils are less subject to envy, for men think that they earn their honors hardly, and pity them sometimes; and pity ever healeth envy. Wherefore you shall observe that the more deep and sober sort of politic persons, in their greatness, are ever bemoaning themselves what a life they lead, chanting a *Quanta patimur*;[2] not that they feel it so, but only to abate the edge of envy. But this is to be understood of business that is laid upon men, and not such as they call unto themselves. For nothing increaseth envy more than an unnecessary and ambitious engrossing of business; and nothing doth extinguish envy more than for a great person to preserve all other inferior officers in their full rights and pre-eminences of their places: for by that means there be so many screens between him and envy.

Above all, those are most subject to envy which carry the greatness of their fortunes in an insolent and proud manner, being never well but while they are showing how great they are, either by outward pomp, or by triumphing over all opposition or competition; whereas wise men will rather do sacrifice to envy, in suffering themselves sometimes of purpose to be crossed and overborne in things that do not much concern them. Notwithstanding, so much is true, that the carriage of greatness in a plain and open manner (so it be without arrogancy and vain glory) doth draw less envy than if it be in a more crafty and cunning fashion. For in that course a man doth but disavow fortune, and seemeth to be conscious of his own want in worth, and doth but teach others to envy him.

Lastly, to conclude this part, as we said in the beginning that the act of envy had somewhat in it of witchcraft, so there is no other cure of envy but the cure of witchcraft; and that is to remove the lot (as they call it) and to lay it upon another. For which purpose the wiser sort of great persons bring in ever upon the stage somebody upon whom to derive the envy that would

---

[1] At a bound.
[2] How much we suffer!

come upon themselves; sometimes upon ministers and servants, sometimes upon colleagues and associates, and the like; and for that turn there are never wanting some persons of violent and undertaking natures, who, so they may have power and business, will take it at any cost.

Now to speak of public envy. There is yet some good in public envy, whereas in private there is none. For public envy is as an ostracism, that eclipseth men when they grow too great; and therefore it is a bridle also to great ones, to keep them within bounds.

This envy, being in the Latin word *invidia*, goeth in the modern languages by the name of *discontentment*, of which we shall speak in handling sedition. It is a disease in a state like to infection. For as infection spreadeth upon that which is sound, and tainteth it, so when envy is gotten once into a state, it traduceth even the best actions thereof, and turneth them into an ill odor. And therefore there is little won by intermingling of plausible actions; for that doth argue but a weakness and fear of envy, which hurteth so much the more; as it is likewise usual in infections, which, if you fear them, you call them upon you.

This public envy seemeth to beat chiefly upon principal officers or ministers, rather than upon kings and estates themselves. But this is a sure rule, that if the envy upon the minister be great when the cause of it in him is small, or if the envy be general in a manner upon all the ministers of an estate, then the envy (though hidden) is truly upon the state itself. And so much of public envy or discontentment, and the difference thereof from private envy, which was handled in the first place.

We will add this in general, touching the affection of envy, that of all other affections it is the most importune and continual; for of other affections there is occasion given but now and then, and therefore it was well said, *Invidia festos dies non agit*,[1] for it is ever working upon some or other. And it is also noted that love and envy do make a man pine, which other affections do not, because they are not so continual. It is also the vilest affection and the most depraved, for which cause it is the proper attribute of the devil, who is called *the envious man, that soweth tares amongst the wheat by night;* as it always cometh to pass that

---

[1]Envy keeps no holidays.

envy worketh subtilly and in the dark, and to the prejudice of good things, such as is the wheat.

OF GREAT PLACE (1612; 1625)

MEN in great place are thrice servants: servants of the sovereign or state, servants of fame, and servants of business. So as they have no freedom, neither in their persons, nor in their actions, nor in their times. It is a strange desire, to seek power and to lose liberty, or to seek power over others and to lose power over a man's self. The rising unto place is laborious, and by pains men come to greater pains; and it is sometimes base, and by indignities men come to dignities. The standing is slippery, and the regress is either a downfall or at least an eclipse, which is a melancholy thing: *Cum non sis qui fueris, non esse cur velis vivere.*[1] Nay, retire men cannot when they would, neither will they when it were reason; but are impatient of privateness, even in age and sickness, which require the shadow; like old townsmen, that will be still sitting at their street door, though thereby they offer age to scorn. Certainly, great persons had need to borrow other men's opinions to think themselves happy; for if they judge by their own feeling, they cannot find it; but if they think with themselves what other men think of them, and that other men would fain be as they are, then they are happy, as it were by report; when perhaps they find the contrary within. For they are the first that find their own griefs, though they be the last that find their own faults. Certainly men in great fortunes are strangers to themselves, and while they are in the puzzle of business they have no time to tend their health, either of body or mind. *Illi mors gravis incubat, qui notus nimis omnibus, ignotus moritur sibi.*[2] In place there is license to do good and evil, whereof the latter is a curse; for in evil the best condition is not to will, the second not to can. But power to do good is the true and lawful end of aspiring; for good thoughts (though God accept them) yet towards men are little better than good dreams, except they be put in act; and that cannot be without power and place, as the vantage and

---

[1] When you are not what you were, you have no reason to wish to live longer.

[2] It is a sad fate for a man to die too well known to everybody else, and still unknown to himself.

commanding ground. Merit and good works is the end of man's motion, and conscience of the same is the accomplishment of man's rest; for if a man can be partaker of God's theatre, he shall likewise be partaker of God's rest. *Et conversus Deus, ut aspiceret opera quæ fecerunt manus suæ, vidit quod omnia essent bona nimis;*[1] and then the sabbath. In the discharge of thy place set before thee the best examples, for imitation is a globe of precepts. And after a time set before thee thine own example; and examine thyself strictly, whether thou didst not best at first. Neglect not also the examples of those that have carried themselves ill in the same place; not to set off thyself by taxing their memory, but to direct thyself what to avoid. Reform, therefore, without bravery, or scandal of former times and persons; but yet set it down to thyself as well to create good precedents as to follow them. Reduce things to the first institution, and observe wherein and how they have degenerate; but yet ask counsel of both times; of the ancient time what is best, and of the latter time what is fittest. Seek to make thy course regular, that men may know beforehand what they may expect; but be not too positive and peremptory, and express thyself well when thou digressest from thy rule. Preserve the right of thy place, but stir not questions of jurisdiction; and rather assume thy right in silence and *de facto*, than voice it with claims and challenges. Preserve likewise the rights of inferior places, and think it more honor to direct in chief than to be busy in all. Embrace and invite helps and advices touching the execution of thy place, and do not drive away such as bring thee information as meddlers, but accept of them in good part. The vices of authority are chiefly four: delays, corruption, roughness, and facility. For delays, give easy access, keep times appointed, go through with that which is in hand, and interlace not business but of necessity. For corruption, do not only bind thine own hands or thy servants' hands from taking, but bind the hands of suitors also from offering. For integrity used doth the one; but integrity professed, and with a manifest detestation of bribery, doth the other. And avoid not only the fault, but the suspicion. Whosoever is found variable and changeth manifestly, without manifest cause, giveth suspicion of corruption. Therefore,

---

[1]And God turned to look upon the works which his hands had made and saw that all were very good.

always when thou changest thine opinion or course, profess it plainly and declare it, together with the reasons that move thee to change; and do not think to steal it. A servant or a favorite, if he be inward, and no other apparent cause of esteem, is commonly thought but a by-way to close corruption. For roughness, it is a needless cause of discontent; severity breedeth fear, but roughness breedeth hate. Even reproofs from authority ought to be grave, and not taunting. As for facility, it is worse than bribery; for bribes come but now and then; but if importunity or idle respects lead a man, he shall never be without. As Salomon saith, *To respect persons is not good, for such a man will transgress for a piece of bread.* It is most true that was anciently spoken, *A place showeth the man;* and it showeth some to the better and some to the worse. *Omnium consensu capax imperii, nisi imperasset*[1], saith Tacitus of Galba; but of Vespasian he saith, *Solus imperantium Vespasianus mutatus in melius:*[2] though the one was meant of sufficiency, the other of manners and affection. It is an assured sign of a worthy and generous spirit, whom honor amends. For honor is, or should be, the place of virtue; and as in nature things move violently to their place and calmly in their place, so virtue in ambition is violent, in authority settled and calm. All rising to great place is by a winding stair; and if there be factions, it is good to side a man's self whilst he is in the rising, and to balance himself when he is placed. Use the memory of thy predecessor fairly and tenderly; for if thou dost not, it is a debt will sure be paid when thou art gone. If thou have colleagues, respect them, and rather call them when they look not for it, than exclude them when they have reason to look to be called. Be not too sensible or too remembering of thy place in conversation and private answers to suitors; but let it rather be said, *When he sits in place he is another man.*

OF CUNNING (1612; 1625)

WE TAKE cunning for a sinister or crooked wisdom. And certainly there is a great difference between a cunning man and a

[1] A man whom everyone would have thought fit for empire, if he had not been emperor.

[2] He was the only emperor whom the possession of sovereignty changed for the better.

wise man, not only in point of honesty, but in point of ability. There be that can pack the cards, and yet cannot play well; so there are some that are good in canvasses and factions, that are otherwise weak men. Again, it is one thing to understand persons and another thing to understand matters; for many are perfect in men's humors that are not greatly capable of the real part of business, which is the constitution of one that hath studied men more than books. Such men are fitter for practice than for counsel, and they are good but in their own alley; turn them to new men and they have lost their aim. So as the old rule, to know a fool from a wise man, *Mitte ambos nudos ad ignotos, et videbis*,[1] doth scarce hold for them. And because these cunning men are like haberdashers of small wares, it is not amiss to set forth their shop.

It is a point of cunning to wait upon him with whom you speak, with your eye, as the Jesuits give it in precept, for there be many wise men that have secret hearts and transparent countenances. Yet this would be done with a demure abasing of your eye sometimes, as the Jesuits also do use.

Another is, that when you have anything to obtain of present dispatch, you entertain and amuse the party with whom you deal with some other discourse, that he be not too much awake to make objections. I knew a counsellor and secretary that never came to Queen Elizabeth of England with bills to sign but he would always first put her into some discourse of estate, that she mought the less mind the bills.

The like surprise may be made by moving things when the party is in haste, and cannot stay to consider advisedly of that is moved.

If a man would cross a business that he doubts some other would handsomely and effectually move, let him pretend to wish it well, and move it himself, in such sort as may foil it.

The breaking off in the midst of that one was about to say, as if he took himself up, breeds a greater appetite in him with whom you confer to know more.

And because it works better when anything seemeth to be gotten from you by question than if you offer it of yourself, you may lay a bait for a question by showing another visage

---

[1] Send them both naked to those they know not, and you will see.

and countenance than you are wont, to the end to give occasion for the party to ask what the matter is of the change? As Nehemias did: *And I had not before that time been sad before the king.*

In things that are tender and unpleasing, it is good to break the ice by some whose words are of less weight, and to reserve the more weighty voice to come in as by chance, so that he may be asked the question upon the other's speech; as Narcissus did, in relating to Claudius the marriage of Messalina and Silius.

In things that a man would not be seen in himself, it is a point of cunning to borrow the name of the world, as to say, *The world says,* or *There is a speech abroad.*

I knew one that when he wrote a letter he would put that which was most material in the postscript, as if it had been a by-matter.

I knew another, that when he came to have speech he would pass over that that he intended most, and go forth, and come back again, and speak of it as of a thing that he had almost forgot.

Some procure themselves to be surprised at such times as it is like the party that they work upon will suddenly come upon them, and to be found with a letter in their hand, or doing something which they are not accustomed, to the end they may be apposed of those things which of themselves they are desirous to utter.

It is a point of cunning to let fall those words in a man's own name which he would have another man learn and use, and thereupon take advantage. I knew two that were competitors for the secretary's place in Queen Elizabeth's time, and yet kept good quarter between themselves, and would confer one with another upon the business; and the one of them said, that to be a secretary *in the declination of a monarchy* was a ticklish thing, and that he did not affect it; the other straight caught up those words, and discoursed with divers of his friends that he had no reason to desire to be secretary in the declination of a monarchy. The first man took hold of it, and found means it was told the queen, who hearing of *a declination of a monarchy,* took it so ill as she would never after hear of the other's suit.

There is a cunning which we in England call *the turning of the cat in the pan;* which is, when that which a man says to another, he lays it as if another had said it to him.   And to say truth, it is not easy when such a matter passed between two to make it appear from which of them it first moved and began.

It is a way that some men have, to glance and dart at others by justifying themselves by negatives, as to say: *This I do not;* as Tigellinus did towards Burrhus, *Se non diversas spes, sed incolumitatem imperatoris simpliciter spectare.*[1]

Some have in readiness so many tales and stories, as there is nothing they would insinuate but they can wrap it into a tale, which serveth both to keep themselves more in guard, and to make others carry it with more pleasure.

It is a good point of cunning for a man to shape the answer he would have in his own words and propositions; for it makes the other party stick the less.

It is strange how long some men will lie in wait to speak somewhat they desire to say, and how far about they will fetch, and how many other matters they will beat over to come near it. It is a thing of great patience, but yet of much use.

A sudden, bold, and unexpected question doth many times surprise a man and lay him open.   Like to him that having changed his name, and walking in Paul's, another suddenly came behind him, and called him by his true name, whereat straightways he looked back.

But these small wares and petty points of cunning are infinite. And it were a good deed to make a list of them; for that nothing doth more hurt in a state than that cunning men pass for wise.

But certainly some there are that know the resorts and falls of business, that cannot sink into the main of it; like a house that hath convenient stairs and entries, but never a fair room. Therefore, you shall see them find out pretty looses in the conclusion, but are no ways able to examine or debate matters. And yet commonly they take advantage of their inability, and would be thought wits of direction.   Some build rather upon the abusing of others, and, as we now say, *putting tricks upon them,* than upon soundness of their own proceedings.   But Salomon saith, *Prudens advertit ad gressus suos: stultus divertit ad dolos.*[2]

---

[1] That he had not several hopes to rest on, but looked simply to the safety of the emperor.

[2] The wise man taketh heed to his steps, the fool turneth aside to deceits.

OF DISCOURSE (1597; 1612; 1625)

SOME in their discourse desire rather commendation of wit, in being able to hold all arguments, than of judgment, in discerning what is true; as if it were a praise to know what might be said, and not what should be thought. Some have certain commonplaces and themes wherein they are good, and want variety; which kind of poverty is for the most part tedious, and when it is once perceived, ridiculous. The honorablest part of talk is to give the occasion, and again to moderate and pass to somewhat else; for then a man leads the dance. It is good in discourse and speech of conversation to vary and intermingle speech of the present occasion with arguments, tales with reasons, asking of questions with telling of opinions, and jest with earnest; for it is a dull thing to tire, and as we say now, to jade, anything too far. As for jest, there be certain things which ought to be privileged from it; namely, religion, matters of state, great persons, any man's present business of importance, and any case that deserveth pity. Yet there be some that think their wits have been asleep, except they dart out somewhat that is piquant and to the quick; that is a vein which would be bridled.

Parce, puer, stimulis, et fortius utere loris.[1]

And, generally, men ought to find the difference between saltness and bitterness. Certainly he that hath a satirical vein, as he maketh others afraid of his wit, so he had need be afraid of others' memory. He that questioneth much shall learn much, and content much; but especially if he apply his questions to the skill of the persons whom he asketh; for he shall give them occasion to please themselves in speaking, and himself shall continually gather knowledge. But let his questions not be troublesome, for that is fit for a poser; and let him be sure to leave other men their turns to speak. Nay, if there be any that would reign and take up all the time, let him find means to take them off, and to bring others on; as musicians use to do with those that dance too long galliards. If you dissemble sometimes your knowledge of that you are thought to

---

[1] Boy, spare the whip, and hold the reins more firmly.

know, you shall be thought another time to know that you know not. Speech of a man's self ought to be seldom, and well chosen. I knew one was wont to say in scorn, *He must needs be a wise man, he speaks so much of himself.* And there is but one case wherein a man may commend himself with good grace, and that is in commending virtue in another; especially if it be such a virtue whereunto himself pretendeth. Speech of touch towards others should be sparingly used; for discourse ought to be as a field, without coming home to any man. I knew two noblemen of the west part of England, whereof the one was given to scoff, but kept ever royal cheer in his house; the other would ask of those that had been at the other's table, *Tell truly, was there never a flout or dry blow given?* To which the guest would answer, *Such and such a thing passed.* The lord would say, *I thought he would mar a good dinner.* Discretion of speech is more than eloquence; and to speak agreeably to him with whom we deal is more than to speak in good words or in good order. A good continued speech, without a good speech of interlocution, shows slowness; and a good reply or second speech, without a good settled speech, showeth shallowness and weakness. As we see in beasts, that those that are weakest in the course are yet nimblest in the turn; as it is betwixt the greyhound and the hare. To use too many circumstances ere one come to the matter is wearisome; to use none at all is blunt.

OF NATURE IN MEN (1612; 1625)

NATURE is often hidden, sometimes overcome, seldom extinguished. Force maketh nature more violent in the return; doctrine and discourse maketh nature less importune; but custom only doth alter and subdue nature. He that seeketh victory over his nature, let him not set himself too great nor too small tasks; for the first will make him dejected by often failings, and the second will make him a small proceeder, though by often prevailings. And, at the first, let him practise with helps, as swimmers do with bladders or rushes; but after a time let him practise with disadvantages, as dancers do with thick shoes. For it breeds great perfection if the practice be harder than the use. Where nature is mighty, and therefore the victory hard, the degrees had need be: first, to stay and arrest nature in

time, like to him that would say over the four-and-twenty letters when he was angry; then, to go less in quantity, as if one
should, in forbearing wine, come from drinking healths to a
draught at a meal; and lastly, to discontinue altogether. But if
a man have the fortitude and resolution to enfranchise himself
at once, that is the best.

> *Optimus ille animi vindex lædentia pectus*
> *Vincula qui rupit, dedoluitque semel.*[1]

Neither is the ancient rule amiss, to bend nature as a wand to a
contrary extreme, whereby to set it right; understanding it,
where the contrary extreme is no vice. Let not a man force a
habit upon himself with a perpetual continuance, but with some
intermission. For both the pause reinforceth the new onset;
and if a man that is not perfect be ever in practice, he shall
as well practise his errors as his abilities, and induce one habit of
both; and there is no means to help this, but by seasonable inter-
missions. But let not a man trust his victory over his nature
too far; for nature will lay buried a great time, and yet revive
upon the occasion or temptation. Like as it was with Æsop's
damosel, turned from a cat to a woman; who sat very demurely
at the board's end till a mouse ran before her. Therefore, let a
man either avoid the occasion altogether, or put himself often to
it, that he may be little moved with it. A man's nature is best
perceived in privateness, for there is no affectation; in passion,
for that putteth a man out of his precepts; and in a new case or
experiment, for there custom leaveth him. They are happy
men whose natures sort with their vocations; otherwise they may
say, *Multum incola fuit anima mea*,[2] when they converse in those
things they do not affect. In studies, whatsoever a man com-
mandeth upon himself, let him set hours for it; but whatsoever
is agreeable to his nature, let him take no care for any set times;
for his thoughts will fly to it of themselves, so as the spaces of
other business or studies will suffice. A man's nature runs either
to herbs or weeds; therefore let him seasonably water the one,
and destroy the other.

---

[1]Wouldst thou be free? The chains that gall thy breast
  With one strong effort burst, and be at rest.
[2]My soul hath been a stranger and sojourner.

OF STUDIES (1597; 1612; 1625)

STUDIES serve for delight, for ornament, and for ability. Their chief use for delight is in privateness and retiring; for ornament, is in discourse; and for ability, is in the judgment and disposition of business. For expert men can execute, and perhaps judge of particulars, one by one; but the general counsels, and the plots and marshalling of affairs, come best from those that are learned. To spend too much time in studies is sloth; to use them too much for ornament is affectation; to make judgment wholly by their rules is the humor of a scholar. They perfect nature, and are perfected by experience; for natural abilities are like natural plants, that need proyning by study; and studies themselves do give forth directions too much at large, except they be bounded in by experience. Crafty men contemn studies, simple men admire them, and wise men use them; for they teach not their own use; but that is a wisdom without them, and above them, won by observation. Read not to contradict and confute, nor to believe and take for granted, nor to find talk and discourse, but to weigh and consider. Some books are to be tasted, others to be swallowed, and some few to be chewed and digested: that is, some books are to be read only in parts; others to be read, but not curiously; and some few to be read wholly, and with diligence and attention. Some books also may be read by deputy, and extracts made of them by others; but that would be only in the less important arguments and the meaner sort of books; else distilled books are like common distilled waters, flashy things. Reading maketh a full man, conference a ready man, and writing an exact man. And therefore if a man write little, he had need have a great memory; if he confer little, he had need have a present wit; and if he read little, he had need have much cunning to seem to know that he doth not. Histories make men wise, poets witty, the mathematics subtle, natural philosophy deep, moral grave, logic and rhetoric able to contend. *Abeunt studia in mores.*[1] Nay, there is no stond or impediment in the wit but may be wrought out by fit studies, like as diseases of the body may have appropriate exercises. Bowling is good for the stone and reins,

---

[1] Studies mould character.

shooting for the lungs and breast, gentle walking for the stomach, riding for the head, and the like. So if a man's wit be wandering, let him study the mathematics; for in demonstrations, if his wit be called away never so little, he must begin again. If his wit be not apt to distinguish or find differences, let him study the schoolmen, for they are *cymini sectores*.[1] If he be not apt to beat over matters, and to call up one thing to prove and illustrate another, let him study the lawyers' cases. So every defect of the mind may have a special receipt.

[1]Splitters of hairs.

SIR WILLIAM CORNWALLIS (? —1631?)

Although this book seeks to avoid writing that is "historically important" rather than alive, Cornwallis's essays are one exception. His first collection appeared in 1600, and the last enlarged edition in 1610. When one recalls the character and chronology of Bacon's essays Cornwallis takes rank as a pioneer. By following Montaigne—at a considerable distance—in subject-matter and in a discursive, personal style, Cornwallis, though quite lacking Montaigne's critical mind and rich flavor, gave direction to the English essay. His essays are significant also in presenting, in an age beginning to take stock of itself, a liberal if somewhat pallid ideal of the civilized, cultivated gentleman. Two extracts, from essays too long to print entire, throw light on Cornwallis's conception of the essay.

ESSAYS (1600 *et seq.*)

OF ADVICE

If we could persuade the first taste to respect the operation, or the operation to leave some part of the sweetness to the first taste, our lives should be long, happy, and safe: for we should begin to live when we begin to breathe, whereas we begin not to live before we are ready to die: still defective—if having strength, wanting judgment; if wise, decrepit; Fate, Destiny, and Fortune are the goddesses of Sloth, Negligence, and Pleasure. These warrant our deafness and promise a sanctuary to privilege us from infamy, beggary, and misery, but, alas, they cannot: wisdom and virtue prevails, and before them these names of shelter are but the surnames to our folly. Our actions are in our own hands, and it were pity else, for virtue and vice should be confounded, were our deeds necessited. The world were no world if they could not be cut asunder by a distinction: there were no pains, no hire, there were no virtue, no glory, all were one, and this one were a chaos. But there are differences: there are good, and they are to be praised; bad, the example for them yet indifferent, to eschew badness by their punishment;

54

youth ready for impression; age wherein may be read the journey of youth; times christened by our use; ages past, to light us the way; others to come, the judges of our deserts. If the end of life be to be good, if the safest purchase of goodness be counsel, if counsel without scars be most profitable, why eschew we the blessing of advice? Let us alter this tradition, let us not be so tender; let us make our beauties, our strengths, our abilities complete, with making the proportion of the mind answerable to the beauty of the body, with giving strength direction, ability judgment.

Wars and states and councils choose men practised in wars, in states, and in councils. We are to ask counsel for the passage of our circuit of them that have passed it, of age, and books. We ask to know; we cannot know except we believe; we must ask if we will know; we must believe or else our asking is vain. We give and rightly give pre-eminence to age; we have found out a word to beautify the wrinkles and hoariness thereof. We call it venerable. Why? Merely in respect of the appearance? No, but in respect of the annection; because wisdom commonly accompanies such a presence: for should we see it in any other thing, it would be despised and called rivelled and ill-favored.

Let them in God's name then show us their inward excellencies, and as our eyes believe them to be old, let our minds believe them to be wise: I see nothing more decay the fairest branches of our commonwealth than this neglect: either we will not endure advice, or not believe it, until our own perils and over-throws make us see it, to our shame.

We are inquisitive of travelers concerning strange countries, our ears stand wide open for news, and sometimes we swallow matters unprobable: but when we are advised for our own sakes, persuaded by virtue, told the passages of the world truly, and have all this sealed up with the assurance of a father's or a friend's love, whom we have no cause to suspect as speaking either for ostentation or flattery, yet we believe not. Let us supple our affections with reverence and regard of their words: let us prepare ourselves to receive this inheritance, which feeds the mind, though it doth not dirtily pamper our bodies; it fortifieth all, and costs nothing; with safety it gives you that which another perhaps purchased with danger, in an hour his collection of years. It would doubly bless you with youth and judgment, which seldom happen in our age, because our age is so obstinate as not to be capable of advice.

Let us ask and follow. The life of industry's first fruit is somewhat sweaty and painful, but then pleasant, and ever pleasant. A memory stored with the performance of gallant actions is only rich; it is a sweet meditation that may be often read over without tediousness. The most leaden spirit that ever was, at the hearing a relation of an unusual excellency, though he be more beholding to his ears than his head, yet feels emulation tickle him, and wishes his brand were set upon those riches. Wish and spare not, but let not laziness make thy wishes vain.

First, let us proclaim war against delicious niceness, and either turn our affections to a good use or turn them out of doors, —*semen laboris, honoris seges*.[1] It was pity Pyrrhus had no more to give, he knew so well to whom to give, naming him his heir whose sword was sharpest, the height of whose spirit should carry him to the conversation of actions stuffed with magnanimity and judgment. Yea, here is the life; whether he win or lose, he is happy. Hannibal, being demanded who were the worthiest captains that ever were, names Alexander, himself, and some other: Scipio demands where he would have stood if he had conquered? He answers, "First." It was well answered, and he meant well; his attempt shined too gloriously to be dusked by misfortune.

I would allow a man to keep the house no longer than till he be able to fly, until his mind and body are able to carry themselves without falling, not until he be past reeling and staggering, for that ability we never have: but in this time let books and advice rectify and prepare us fit for the entertaining of all fortunes, victories, and overthrows, calamity, and happiness. Let us rob and suck from our parents' experience and judgment: let us be acquainted with the successes and sequences of the world, track their observations, be acquainted with the minds of times past, and let their bodies go, if we have the best part of them: for the work is commonly better than the manual instruments effecting it, for they are the servants of direction, the

---

[1] The seed of toil brings the harvest of honor.

thing performed the issue both of mind and hand. Fie upon these engrossing senses of ours, that make all fare the worse for the satisfaction of one, and yet limit their objects, and carry level but certain distances. The mind, the mind is the magazine of contentment, it is the mind that can distil the whole world, all ages, all acts, all human knowledges, within the little, little compass of a brain, and yet with the force of that little treasure command, dispose, censure, and determine states, actions, kingdoms, wars, overthrows, and all the acts and actors busied upon our human theatre. To this mind, to this cistern of preciousness, let us attribute all, and not suffer the weight of our affections to disorder this goodly frame, this clock of Time and Reason. *O quam contempta res est homo, nisi supra humana se erexerit.*[1]

These licorous humors and affections are the out-offices of our mansion, and the respect ought to be given to the director, whose high-erected situation witnesseth his prerogative; from the rays of this sun proceed all blessings, advice is the medium transporting them, our brains like a sense able to perform good offices, if employed. Let us receive and utter, be capable, and return increase of this fruit. What a precious sight it is to see a temperate young man, how he shines: glory and admiration attends all his actions. It is good in age, because the contrary were abominable; but it is common, and, their night being almost come, they cannot but look gravely, and live temperately, as well to preserve them from pain as to eschew shame and reproach. I thank not Alexander for conquering the world, but for performing it before thirty years old. Augustus commands admiration of me for nothing so much as his beginning enterprises of high moment very young, and yet with that youth reducing the whole world under his subjection. I often hear old men wish themselves young, which though I allow not, as being wishes of impossibility, yet hoping their intent is to trace their course moderately, and to unite the blessings of youth and judgment, I think it tolerable: but we that are yet young need not wish youth, for we possess it, but judgment, that may make us worthy to possess it. Then begin with hearing, next

---

[1] O how contemptible a thing is man, unless he raise himself above the level of man.

with following advice and counsel: let us begin with ourselves, and marshal and dispose our own course; let us determine it and leave nothing to uncertainties, but, drawing out our intents regularly, follow that delineated and weighed manner. Here lives happiness, for here lives wisdom: this music of two strings is the most delightful harmony, for the world affords not a more admirable excellency than youth and judgment included in one substance: both parts show their richest treasure, the soul judgment, the body youth. Let us then enfranchise advice and persuade our ears to become good commonwealth's men, to respect the general profit. Counsel and advice are the parents of government: what can I reckon then more worthy, more safe, more excellent in institution, than counsel and advice?

OF DISCOURSE

It is a pitiful thing at great assemblies to see how the rich and gay will engross their talk, and how basely they use that commodity, not a word able to profit a hackney-man: they send away Time worse appareled than their horse-keepers, poor and naked of what is precious, but loaden with straw and dirt, good only for thatchers and daubers. At this time I suffer much, specially if I would choose rather to fill my ears than my belly. I wish for fiddlers to confound them, or any noise saving theirs. I would at this time lose my memory, for she is covetous and takes all, and with this she will pollute all, making all taste of barbarism.

In this time my eye, wandering to find a handsome cause of interruption, meets with a fellow in black; back again they come with their intelligence and tell me they have found a scholar. I go to this vessel, and, thirsting after some good liquor, hastily pierce it, when there issueth medicines or law terms: alas, it is either a surgeon or an attorney, my expectation hath broken her neck. Well, these are places to grow fat in, not wise. Let us travel somewhither else, to the university: their discourse is good, but too finical; you undo them if you suffer them not to go methodically to work. *Nego maiorem, aut minorem; probo; ipse dixit,* etc.[1] I like not this; except his adversary be a fencer too, there is no understanding one another. It is a general fault

---

[1] I deny the major, or the minor; I approve; his own authority.

among the best professions. For mercenary and mechanical it skills not: it becomes them well to discover themselves by their speech: but a gentleman should talk like a gentleman, which is, like a wise man: his knowledge ought to be general, it becomes him not to talk of one thing too much, or to be weighed down with any particular profession. Herein I admire Plato his description of Socrates, who, although a soldier and a scholar, yet he discoursed still like wisdom, which commands over all. One knowledge is but one part of the house, a baywindow or a gable-end: who builds his house so maimed, much less himself? No, be complete. If thy guests be weary of thy parlor, carry them into thy gallery: be thus, but yet if thou meetest with a fellow that would fain show thee he is a mathematician or a navigator, be content to talk with him of circles and quadrangles, of the poles and navigating stars.

There is another creature that weighs every word and will be sure to turn the verb behind, affects elegancy, and to be thought learned: this fellow is formal, he robs himself of his commendations with this premeditated course. Men look for much where they discern such a preparation: besides, methinks he dresses truth and wisdom too gaudily. It is the country fashion to sugar over what is naturally sweet; he profits not his auditory.

I knew a country church furnished with a clock whose hammer was stricken by an image like a man; upon the wheels stood a cat, which, when the image strook, made much haste away: as the parishioners when they should have wept for their sins, and were moved thereunto by the preacher, laughed at the cat's nimbleness, so is it with this man's hearers; they catch at some pretty sounding words, and let the matter slip without any attention. Let ape-keepers and players catch the ears of their auditory and spectators with fair bombast words and set speeches: it shall be my course when I must discourse (but I had rather hear) not to lose myself in my tale, to speak words that may be understood, and to my power to mean wisely rather than to speak eloquently.

OF CENSURING

. . . ALL this time I have built but the bridge I mean to travel upon, and not that anointed with a finical exordium. I travel where I list, and when I list, and will not bind myself to more than I list. Let my feet be bound to come into the hall before the great chamber, my head shall see which I list first.

I hate the dullness of my own feet, and my horse, when I travel, and cherish the nimbleness of my thoughts which can fly over the world in an afternoon.

I am determined to speak of books next, to whom, if you would not say I were too bookish, I should give the first place of all things here. The best wit of man that ever was, not assisted by such helps as may make my comparison blasphemy, never brought so much into the world as by their assistance he hath had. When I hear a natural man speak in his best, I can say but witty: my commendations are at the farthest; but the tongue steeped in the true understanding incident to learning hath wisdom for his reward. Experience doth much, but it is too full of scars and wounds, and is bought with gray hairs and danger: when the other hath no less that hath traveled but in his study. In a word, propound any course saving eating and sleeping, and, wanting this, you are maimed: even in the life of blows and wars, where strength seems to bear more sway than understanding, yet armor, discipline, marshal-advantage of number, and situation of the place, ends with the well-tuned harmony of an oration, whose force hath often been as much as all the rest, and with the sweetness added vigor to the harshness of valor. Of books, for both philosophies I only esteem Plato, who doth so cunningly weave them together, as (methinks) he saith he is content to give you knowledge on condition you should be honest. In the person of his Socrates he setteth down one of the most absolute forms of life that is possible to be imagined. I doubt whether he were so well as his picture, yet Plato tells it so with the circumstances as I am afraid sometimes by doubting to do him wrong. If he wanted not very much, he is worthy of admiration; if very much, of applause, being the only man that ever I heard of most innocent of entertaining a forced grace for some second cause.

Of history if you will have me show you the best first, I must begin and end with Tacitus. So grave a style, so judicial a censure, and so piercing an eye into the designs of princes and states, never met in one man: he is so worthy that I wish he were as rare, for I hold no eye meet to wade in him that is not at the helm of a state.

For profitable recreation, that noble French knight, the Lord de Montaigne, is most excellent, whom though I have not been so much beholding to the French as to see in his original, yet divers of his pieces I have seen translated: they that understand both languages say very well done, and I am able to say (if you will take the word of ignorance) translated into a style admitting as few idle words as our language will endure. It is well fitted in this new garment, and Montaigne speaks now good English. It is done by a fellow less beholding to nature for his fortune than wit, yet lesser for his face than fortune; the truth is, he looks more like a good fellow than a wise man, and yet he is wise, beyond either his fortune or education: but his author speaks nobly, honestly, and wisely, with little method, but with much judgment. Learned he was, and often shows it, but with such a happiness as his own following is not disgraced by his own reading. He speaks freely, and yet wisely; censures and determines many things judicially, and yet forceth you not to attention with a "Hem" and a spitting exordium. In a word, he hath made moral philosophy speak courageously, and instead of her gown given her an armor; he hath put pedantical scholarism out of countenance, and made manifest that learning mingled with nobility shines most clearly. . . .

OF IMITATION

THE first times had a great advantage of us; all came from them we must now say, because they got the start, spake before us, and lived before us. In truth I think they were more industrious; for out of their natural wits and observations they founded arts and sciences in which they were much more profound than latter times, though we are assisted by their travels, and know whither we should go, and how to go by their methodical courses. We must lay the fault to covetousness and pleasure, with whose enticements we are diverted, so that we choose now rather to be rich men than wise men. In these trades they have not outrun us; our times may safely brag with them that we have hunted out more fashions to please the senses, and to get riches: the age after us, that shall see both, and must be our judges, I am afraid will determine the times of old times begetting philosophers and wise men, ours an age of cooks and tailors.

I wonder not that virtue is so out of regard: for we imitate nothing but what we see. Plato his Socrates, and Xenophon his Cyrus, are things to be talked of, not to be worn. I should be sorry for our times (but that it is out of fashion to be sorrowful for others) to see how willingly we put on all habits saving virtues: our hair shall go off, or on, as occasion serves, we will pull our brows and endure any pain to imitate the fashion, but not entertain the least virtue, though she offer herself and would be ours with less pains and expense. All this time we are free from imitation, yea, from following the good, but in the apish kind we are exact: for a new congee or protestation we swallow presently, and the fashions of our apparel run among us like a plague. I observe a people that will tell you where they were last by their behavior and table-talk, as well as upon the inwardest acquaintance. If he hath but seen Callis, he cries out of the English beer, and that with a shrug and shaking of the head, as if he knew more than he durst utter. A year in Italy makes him forget his English, and speak it broken and lisping: they run away with all villainous customs, and think it fine to talk of Giulia and Lucretia, the famous courtesans. Methinks these fellows are like snowballs, that carry away part of the dirt they are rolled upon. These are base imitations begotten between the senses and the fantasy, bastards unknown to the inward, true-discerning soul.

There are another kind that will hold their necks awry with Alexander, these are not wanton but subtle apes, which seek to creep into princes and great men with putting on their habits; they are the dangerousest flatterers. Come, I will make an end with these fantastics, they go against my stomach, they are worse than onions, I can commend them for nothing: sometimes perhaps the stuff they wear is good, and the stockings, and the hat and the rest, all saving the man: they are like hatters' blocks, that wear what is worthier than themselves. But now to a worthier subject, I will not reject imitation, yet I will hardly imitate any man living, especially in things apparently his, as his behavior and accustomed phrases: in virtue it is very lawful, for that is neither his nor mine, it carries no mark of any owner, but of the real possessor of eternity, whom if we could imitate in the least perfection we were blessed.

There are a great sort past, as worthy as any living, among

whom I will choose some one, by whom I would be most governed, yet not in all things, for I would not license myself to put on his imperfections: I have too many of mine own that were born with me, I have no need of his: but when he speaks well and virtuously, I would think he speaks to me and do my endeavor to execute his advice: the actions performed by him I hold like the vaulter's instructions, done first to show me how to perform them with greatest facility.

We are beholding to times past, they have showed us the ends of all courses: we may know virtues and vices as lively by their example as Lycurgus taught it the Lacedæmonians in the persons of their *ephori*, and the helots, their slaves. If I find my strength able to follow one of these, and to get his virtues by heart, I will take out a new lesson, and buy some perfections of others, wherein he was wanting. Thus is imitation ennobled, and well becomes the worthiest; so shall he enjoy abundance when he hath his own store multiplied with gathering from the[m] stored with virtue.

OF ESSAYS AND BOOKS

I HOLD neither Plutarch's, nor none of these ancient short manner of writings, nor Montaigne's, nor such of this latter time, to be rightly termed "essays," for though they be short, yet they are strong and able to endure the sharpest trial: but mine are essays, who am but newly bound prentice to the inquisition of knowledge, and use these papers as a painter's boy a board, that is trying to bring his hand and his fancy acquainted. It is a manner of writing well befitting undigested motions, or a head not knowing his strength, like a circumspect runner trying for a start, or providence that tastes before she buys: for it is easier to think well than to do well, and no trial to have handsome dapper conceits run invisibly in a brain, but to put them out, and then look upon them. If they prove nothing but words, yet they break not promise with the world, for they say but an essay, like a scrivener trying his pen before he engrosseth his work. Nor, to speak plainly, are they more to blame than many other that promise more, for the most that I have yet touched have millions of words, to the bringing forth one reason; and when a reason is gotten, there is such borrowing it one of another that in a multitude of books still that conceit, or some issued out of that, appears so belabored and worn, as in the end it is good for nothing but for a proverb. When I think of the abilities of man I promise myself much out of my reading, but it proves not so. Time goeth, and I turn leaves, yet still find myself in the state of ignorance, wherefore I have thought better of honesty than of knowledge: what I may know I will convert to that use, and what I write I mean so, for I will choose rather to be an honest man than a good logician. There was never art yet that laid so fast hold on me that she might justly call me her servant. I never knew them but superficially, nor indeed will not, though I might; for they swallow their subject, and make him as Ovid said of himself:

Quicquid conabar dicere versus erat.[1]

I would earn none of these so dearly as to tie up the mind to think only of one thing; her best power by this means is taken from her, for so her circuit is limited to a distance which should walk universally. Moreover, there grows pride and a self-opinion out of this which devours wisdom.

Mark but a grammarian, whose occupation, well examined, is but a single-souled trade, for his subject is but words, and yet his construction is of great matters resting in himself. Socrates was the wisest man of his time, and his ground for that was his turning all his acquired knowledge into morality; of whom one said he fetched philosophy from heaven and placed her in cities. Plato laughs at those commonwealth's men that intend only the enlarging and enriching of their countries and in the meantime they suffer the enjoyers of their labors to be vicious and dishonest: even so of these thirsters after knowledge, for hath he all that man possibly may have, and then enclose it in the chest of a dishonest breast, it but corrupts him and makes the poison of his viciousness more forcible. . . .

---

[1] Whatever I tried to utter turned into verse.

OWEN FELLTHAM (?1602–1668)

Little is known of Felltham's life—like almost everyone of a literary turn he was acquainted with Ben Jonson—but his *Resolves* reveal many facets of a serious and attractive character. His book first appeared about 1620, and was enlarged and re-arranged in many later editions. As the title implies, Felltham's essays are didactic and sententious, but he has enough personality and literary talent to shun the merely platitudinous. Some of the pieces given here show the pronounced Stoic vein in his philosophy. They also show the breadth of interest and the *amateur* spirit which gentlemen like Felltham and Cornwallis possessed and labored to cultivate in others—an aim somewhat akin to that of Addison and Steele a century later, the instructing and civilizing of the *bourgeoisie*.

RESOLVES (1620 *et seq.*)

TO THE READERS

I AM to answer two objections, one, that I have made use of story, yet not quoted my authorities; and this I have purposely done. It had been all one labor, inserting the matter, to give them, both the author and place. But, while I am not controversial, I should only have troubled the text, or spotted a margent, which I always wish to leave free, for the comments of the man that reads. Besides, I do not profess myself a scholar, and for a gentleman I hold it a little pedantical. He should use them rather as brought in by memory, *raptim*, and occasional, than by study, search, or strict collection, especially in essay, which, of all writing, is the nearest to a running discourse. I have so used them as you may see I do not steal but borrow. . . . What you find here, if you please, like: but remember always, to censure a Resolve in the middle is to give your judgment a possibility of erring. If you ask why I writ them, 'twas because I loved my study; if why I publish them, know that, having no other means to show myself to the world so well, I chose this, not to boast, but because I would not deceive.

OF PURITANS

I FIND many that are called puritans, yet few or none that will own the name. Whereof the reason sure is this, that 'tis for the most part held a name of infamy, and is so new that it hath scarcely yet obtained a definition; nor is it an appellation derived from one man's name, whose tenents we may find digested into a volume, whereby we do much err in the application. It imports a kind of excellency above another, which man (being conscious of his own frail bendings) is ashamed to assume to himself. So that I believe there are men which would be puritans, but indeed not any that are. One will have him one that lives religiously, and will not revel it in a shoreless excess. Another, him that separates from our divine assemblies. Another, him that in some tenents only is peculiar. Another, him that will not swear. Absolutely to define him is a work, I think, of difficulty; some I know that rejoice in the name, but sure they be such as least understand it. As he is more generally in these times taken, I suppose we may call him a Church-rebel, or one that would exclude order, that his brain might rule. To decline offences, to be careful and conscionable in our several actions, is a purity that every man ought to labor for, which we may well do without a sullen segregation from all society. If there be any privileges, they are surely granted to the children of the king, which are those that are the children of heaven. If mirth and recreations be lawful, sure such a one may lawfully use it. If wine were given to cheer the heart, why should I fear to use it for that end? Surely the merry soul is freer from intended mischief than the thoughtful man. A bounded mirth is a patent adding time and happiness to the crazed life of man. Yet, if Laertius reports him rightly, Plato deserves a censure for allowing drunkenness at festivals; because, says he, as then, the gods themselves reach wines to present men. God delights in nothing more than in a cheerful heart, careful to perform him service. What parent is it that rejoiceth not to see his child pleasant, in the limits of a filial duty? I know, we read of Christ's weeping, not of his laughter: yet we see he graceth a feast with his first miracle, and that a feast of joy; and can we think that such a meeting could pass without the noise of laughter? What a lump of quickened care is the melancholic man! Change anger into mirth, and the precept will hold good still: be merry but sin not. As there be many that in their life assume too great a liberty, so I believe there are some that abridge themselves of what they might lawfully use. Ignorance is an ill steward to provide for either soul or body. A man that submits to reverent order, that sometimes unbends himself in a moderate relaxation, and in all, labors to approve himself in the sereneness of a healthful conscience, such a puritan I will love immutably. But when a man, in things but ceremonial, shall spurn at the grave authority of the Church, and out of a needless nicety be a thief to himself of those benefits which God hath allowed him, or out of a blind and uncharitable pride censure and scorn others as reprobates, or out of obstinacy fill the world with brawls about undeterminable tenents, I shall think him one of those whose opinion hath fevered his zeal to madness and distraction. I have more faith in one Salomon than in a thousand Dutch parlors of such opinionists. "Behold then, what I have seen good!—That it is comely to eat, and to drink, and to take pleasure in all his labor wherein he travaileth under the sun, the whole number of the days of his life, which God giveth him. For this is his portion. Nay, there is no profit to man, but that he eat, and drink, and delight his soul with the profit of his labor." For he that saw other things but vanity saw this also, that it was the hand of God. Methinks the reading of *Ecclesiastes* should make a puritan undress his brain, and lay off all those fanatic toys that jingle about his understanding. For my own part, I think the world hath not better men than some that suffer under that name; nor withal, more *scelestique* villains. For when they are once elated with that pride, they so contemn others that they infringe the laws of all human society.

OF THE TEMPER OF AFFECTIONS

Every man is a vast and spacious sea; his passions are the winds, that swell him in disturbant waves. How he tumbles, and roars, and foams, when they in their fury trouble him! Sometimes the west of pleasure, fanning in luxurious gales;

sometimes the madded south, sorrowful and full of tears; sometimes the sharp east, piercing with a testy spleen; sometimes
the violent and blustering north, swelling the cheek with the
angler's boiling blood.   Any of these, in extremes, make it become unnavigable, and full of danger to the vessel that shall
coast upon it.   When these are too loud, 'tis perilous, but when
again they are all laid in the stillness of an immotive calm, 'tis
useless: and though it be not so ready to hurt, yet it is far from
availing to the profit of a voyage, and the passengers may
sooner famish by being becalmed than coast it over for the
advantage of their mart.   Surely the man that is always still
and reposed in his own thoughts, though they be good, is but a
piece of deadened charity.   I care not for the planed Stoic; there
is a sect between him and the Epicure.   An unmoved man is
but a motive statue, harmless and unprofitable.   Indeed fury
is far the worser extreme, for, besides the trouble it puts on the
company, it always delivers the author into successive mischiefs.   He that is raging in one thing feeds his business with
many inconveniencies.   Fury is like false position in a verse,
at least nine faults together.   Says Claudian,

Caret eventu nimius furor—

Rage knows not when nor how to end.

I like neither a devouring stork nor a Jupiter's log.   Man
is not fit for conversation neither when his passions hurry him
in a hideous distemper, nor when they are all laid in a silent
and unstirring calm.   The sea is best in a pretty pleasant gale;
and so is man, when his passions are alive, without raging.   God
implanted passions in the soul, as he gave his talents in the gospel, neither to be lavished out impetuously, nor to be buried in
napkins.   We may warm us at these fires, though we burn not.
Man without any is no better than a speaking stone.   Cato's
best emperor was *qui potuit imperare affectus;* he does not say
deponere.[1]   Moderate passions are the most affable expressions
of humanity, without which the soul finds nothing like itself to
love.   A horse too hot and fiery is the danger of his rider, one too
dull is his trouble; and as the first will not endure any man, so

---

[1] One who could govern his passions; he does not say "banish them."

the last will be endured by no man. One will suffer none to
back him, the other admits each child to abuse him. A good
temper is a sure expression of a well-composed soul. Our wild
passions are like so many lawyers wrangling and bawling at a
bar; discretion is the Lord Keeper of man, that sits as judge,
and moderates their contestations. Too great a spirit in a man
born to poor means is like a high-heeled shoe to one of mean
stature; it advanceth his proportion, but is ready to fit him
with falls. The flat sole walks more sure, though it abates his
gracefulness; yet, being too low, it is subject to bemire the foot.
A little elevation is the best mediocrity, 'tis both raised from
the earth and sure; and for his tallness, it disposeth it to an equal
competency. I will neither walk so lifted as to occasion falling,
nor so dejected as at every step to take soil. As I care not for
being powder, or the cap of the company, so I would not be
earth, or the fool's football.

OF POETS AND POETRY

SURELY he was a little wanton with his leisure that first invented poetry. 'Tis but a play which makes words dance in the
evenness of a cadency; yet without doubt, being a harmony, it is
nearer to the mind than prose, for that itself is a harmony in
height. But the words being rather the drossy part, conceit I
take to be the principal. And here, though it disgresseth from
truth, it flies above her, making her more rare by giving curious
raiment to her nakedness. The name the Grecians gave the
men that wrote thus, showed how much they honored it; they
called them *makers*. And had some of them had power to put
their conceits in act, how near would they have come to deity!
And for the virtues of men, they rest not on the bare demeanor,
but slide into imagination; so proposing things above us, they
kindle the reader to wonder and imitation. And certainly, poets
that write thus Plato never meant to banish. His own practice
shows he excluded not all. He was content to hear Antimachus
recite his poem, when all the herd had left him; and he himself
wrote both tragedies and other pieces. Perhaps he found them
a little too busy with his gods; and he, being the first that made
philosophy divine and rational, was modest in his own beginnings. Another name they had of honor, too, and that was

vates. Nor know I how to distinguish between the prophets and poets of Israel. What is Jeremiah's *Lamentation*, but a kind of Sapphic elegy? David's *Psalms* are not only poems but songs, snatches and raptures of a flaming spirit. And this indeed I observe to the honor of poets; I never found them covetous or scrapingly base. The Jews had not two such kings in all their catalogue as Salomon and his father, poets both. There is a largeness in their souls beyond the narrowness of other men; and why may we not then think this may embrace more both of heaven and God? I cannot but conjecture this to be the reason that they, most of them, are poor; they find their minds so solaced with their own flights that they neglect the study of growing rich; and this, I confess again, I think turns them to vice and unmanly courses. Besides, they are for the most part mighty lovers of their palates, and this is known an impoverisher. Antigonus, in the tented field, found Antagoras cooking of a conger himself. And they all are friends to the grape and liquor, though I think many, more out of a ductible nature and their love to pleasant company, than their affection to the juice alone. They are all of free natures, and are the truest definition of that philosopher's man, which gives him *animal risibile.* Their grossest fault is that you may conclude them sensual, yet this does not touch them all. Ingenious for the most part they are. I know there be some rhyming fools; but what have they to do with poetry? When Sallust would tell us, that Sempronia's wit was not ill, says he,—*Potuit versus facere, et jocum movere;* she could make a verse and break a jest. Something there is in it more than ordinary in that it is all in such measured language as may be marred by reading. I laugh heartily at Philoxenus his jest, who passing by, and hearing some masons mis-sensing his lines (with their ignorant sawing of them) falls to breaking their bricks amain; they ask the cause, and he replies, they spoil his work, and he theirs. Certainly, a worthy poet is so far from being a fool that there is some wit required in him that shall be able to read him well; and without the true accent numbered poetry does lose of the gloss. It was a speech becoming an able poet of our own, when a lord read his verses crookedly, and he beseeched his lordship not to murder him in his own lines. He that speaks false Latin breaks Priscian's head: but he that repeats a verse ill puts Homer out of joint. One thing commends it beyond oratory, it ever complieth to the sharpest judgments. He is the best orator that pleaseth all, even the crowd and clowns. But poetry would be poor that they should all approve of. If the learned and judicious like it, let the throng bray. These, when 'tis best, will like it the least. So they contemn what they understand not, and the neglected poet falls by want. Calpurnius makes one complain the misfortune,

Frange, puer, calamos, et inanes desere Musas:
Et potius glandes, rubicundaque collige corna.
Duc ad mulctra greges, et lac venale per urbem
Non tacitus porta: Quid enim tibi fistula reddet,
Quo tutere famem? certe, mea carmina nemo
Præter ab his scopulis ventosa remurmurat Echo.

Boy, break thy pipes, leave, leave thy fruitless Muse:
Rather the mast, and blood-red cornel choose.
Go lead thy flocks to milking; sell and cry
Milk through the city: what can learning buy,
To keep back hunger? None my verses mind,
But Echo, babbling from these rocks and wind.

Two things are commonly blamed in poetry; nay, you take away that, if them; and these are lies and flatteries. But I have told them in the worst words; for 'tis only to the shallow insight that they appear thus. Truth may dwell more clearly in an allegory, or a moralled fable, than in a bare narration. And for flattery, no man will take poetry literal; since in commendations it rather shows what men should be than what they are. If this were not, it would appear uncomely. But we all know hyperboles in poetry do bear a decency, nay, a grace along with them. The greatest danger that I find in it is that it wantons the blood and imagination, as carrying a man in too high a delight. To prevent these, let the wise poet strive to be modest in his lines. First, that he dash not the gods; next, that he injure not chastity nor corrupt the ear with lasciviousness. When these are declined, I think a grave poem the deepest kind of writing. It wings the soul up higher than the slacked pace of prose. Flashes that do follow the cup, I fear me, are too sprightly to be solid; they run smartly upon the loose for a distance or two, but then, being foul, they give in and tire. I confess I love the sober muse and fasting; from the other, matter cannot come so clear but that it will be misted with the fumes of wine. Long poetry some cannot be friends withal; and indeed, it palls upon the reading. The wittiest poets have been all short and changing soon their subject, as Horace, Martial, Juvenal, Seneca and the two comedians. Poetry should be rather like a coranto, short and nimbly-lofty, than a dull lesson of a day long. Nor can it be but deadish, if distended; for when 'tis right, it centers conceit and takes but the spirit of things, and therefore foolish poesy is of all writing the most ridiculous. When a goose dances and a fool versifies, there is sport alike. He is twice an ass that is a rhyming one. He is something the less unwise that is unwise but in prose. If the subject be history or con-texted fable, then I hold it better put in prose or blanks; for ordinary discourse never shows so well in meter as in the strain that it may seem to be spoken in; the commendation is to do it to the life, nor is this any other than poetry in prose. Surely, though the world think not so, he is happy to himself that can play the poet. He shall vent his passions by his pen, and ease his heart of their weight; and he shall often raise himself a joy in his raptures which no man can perceive but he. Sure Ovid found a pleasure in't, even when he writ his *Tristia*. It gently delivers the mind of distempers and works the thoughts to a sweetness in their searching conceit. I would not love it for a profession, and I would not want it for a recreation. I can make myself harmless, nay, amending mirth with it, while I should, perhaps, be trying of a worser pastime. And this I believe in it further, unless conversation corrupts his easiness, it lifts a man to nobleness, and is never in any rightly but it makes him of a royal and capacious soul.

HOW HE MUST LIVE THAT LIVES WELL

Whosoever neglects his duty to himself, his neighbor, or his God, halts in something that should make life commendable. For ourselves we need order, for our neighbor charity, and for our God our reverence and humility; and these are so certainly linked one to another as he that lives orderly cannot but be acceptable both to God and the world. Nothing jars the world's harmony like men that break their ranks. One turbulent spirit will dissentiate even the calmest kingdom. We may see the beauty of order in nothing more than in some princely procession, and though indeed the circumstances and complements belonging to state be nothing to better governments, yet by a secret working in the minds of men they add a reverence to state, and awe the else loose rabble. See a king in parliament, and his nobles set about him, and see how mad he shows that wildly dances out of his room. Such is man, when he spurns at the law he lives under. Nay, when he gives himself leave to transgress, he must needs put others out of their way, and he that disorders himself first shall trouble all the company. Did every man keep his own life, what a concord in music would a world, a kingdom, a city, a family, be! But being so infinitely disjointed, it is necessary some should help it, and be charitable. If no man should repair the breaches, how soon would all lie flatted in demolishments? Love is so excellent that, though it be but to one's self alone, yet others shall partake and find the benefit. Posterity will be the better for the bags that the covetous hoarded up for himself. But when a man shall be ever striving to do the world a courtesy, his love is so much the more thankworthy by how much the good is larger. Without charity a man cannot be sociable: and take away that, and there is little else that a man has to do in the world. How pleasant can good company make his life beneath? Certainly if there be anything sweet in mere humanity it is in the intercourses of beloved society, when everyone shall be each other's counsellor, each other's friend and mine, and solace. And such a pleasant life as this I take to be best pleasing, both to God and man. Nor yet can this be truly pleasant unless a man be careful to give to God the honor that he owes him. When a man shall do these, and perform his duty to his Maker, he shall find a peace within that shall fit him for whatsoever falls. He shall not fear himself, for he knows his course is order. He shall not fear the world, for he knows he hath done nothing that has angered it. He shall not be afraid of heaven, for he knows he there shall find the favor of a servant, of a son, and be protected against the malice and the spleen of hell. Let me live thus, and I care not, though the world should flout my innocence; I wish but to obey Saint Bernard, then I know I cannot but be happy, both below and after. *Tu qui in congregatione es, bene vive, ordinabiliter, sociabiliter, et humiliter: ordinabiliter tibi, sociabiliter proximo, humiliter Deo.*[1]

OF IDLE BOOKS

IDLE books are nothing else but corrupted tales in ink and paper, or indeed vice sent abroad with a license, which makes him that reads them conscious of a double injury, they being in effect like that sin of brutish adultery. For if one reads, two are catched; he that angles in these waters is sure to strike the torpedo, that instead of being his food confounds him. Besides the time ill spent in them, a two-fold reason shall make me refrain, both in regard of my love to my own soul, and pity unto his that made them. For if I be corrupted by them, the compriser of them is mediately a cause of my ill; and at the day of reckoning, though now dead, must give an account for't, because I am corrupted by his bad example which he leaves behind him. So I become guilty by receiving, and he by thus conveying this lewdness unto me; he is the thief, I the receiver, and what difference makes our law betwixt them? If one be but off, the other dies; both I am sure perish alike. I will write none, lest I hurt them that come after me. I will read none, lest I augment his mulct that is gone before me: neither write nor read, lest I prove a foe to myself. A lame hand is better than a lewd pen. While I live, I sin too much; let me not continue longer in wickedness than life. If I write aught, it shall be both on a good subject, and from a deliberate pen; for a foolish sentence dropped upon paper sets folly on a hill, and is a monument to make infamy eternal.

THE MISERY OF BEING OLD AND IGNORANT

'TIS a capital misery for a man to be at once both old and ignorant. If he were only old, and had some knowledge, he might abate the tediousness of decrepit age by the divine raptures of contemplation. If he were young, though he knew

---

[1]You who are here present, live well, in a manner orderly, friendly, and humble; orderly as regards yourself, friendly to your neighbor, humble toward God.

nothing, yet his years would serve him to labor and learn; whereby in the winter of his time he might beguile the weariness of his pillow and chair.   But now his body being withered by the stealing length of his days, and his limbs wholly disabled for either motion or exercise, these, together with a mind unfur-nished of those contenting speculations of admired science, cannot but delineate the portraiture of a man wretched.   A gray head with a wise mind is a treasury of grave precepts, experience, and judgment.   But foolish old age is a barren vine in autumn, or an university to study folly in: every action is a pattern of infirmity: while his body sits still he knows not how to find his mind action: and tell me if there be any life more irksome than idleness.   I have numbered yet but a few days, and those, I know, I have neglected; I am not sure they shall be more, nor can I promise my head it shall have a snowy hair. What then? Knowledge is not hurtful, but helps a good mind; anything that is laudable I desire to learn.   If I die to-morrow, my life to-day shall be somewhat the sweeter for knowledge: and if my day prove a summer one, it shall not be amiss to have provided something that in the evening of my age may make my mind my companion.   Notable was the answer that Antisthenes gave when he was asked what fruit he had reaped of all his studies.   "By them," saith he, "I have learned both to live and to talk with myself."

CONTENT MAKES RICH

EVERY man either is rich or may be so, though not all in one and the same wealth.   Some have abundance, and rejoice in't; some a competency, and are content; some, having nothing, have a mind desiring nothing.   He that hath most wants some-thing; he that hath least is in something supplied, wherein the mind which maketh rich may well possess him with the thought of store.   Who whistles out more content than the low-fortuned ploughman, or sings more merrily than the abject cobbler that sits under the stall?   Content dwells with those that are out of the eye of the world, whom she hath never trained with her gauds, her toils, her lures.   Wealth is like learning, wherein our greater knowledge is only a larger sight of our wants. Desires fulfilled teach us to desire more: so we that at first were pleased, by removing from that, are now grown insatiable. Wishes have neither End, nor end. So in the midst of affluency we complain of penury, which, not finding, we make. For to possess the whole world with a grumbling mind is but a little more specious poverty. If I be not outwardly rich, I will labor to be poor in craving desires; but in the virtues of the mind, the best riches, I would not have a man exceed me. He that hath a mind contentedly good enjoyeth in it boundless possessions. If I be pleased in myself, who can add to my happiness? As no man lives so happy but to some his life would be burdensome, so we shall find none so miserable but we shall hear of another that would change calamities.

CHARACTERS

THEOPHRASTUS

Theophrastus, disciple and successor of Aristotle at the Lyceum, stepped off the rostrum, as it were, to write a series of character sketches —he may have done Virtues as well as Vices, but only the latter have come down to us. The literature of his age was devoted largely to the minute study of manners, of man as a social being, and Theophrastus, observing deflections from the norm or mean of conduct, produced satirical, objective portraits which are at once ethically typical and individual. The early seventeenth century took the Theophrastian formula to its heart, or rather its head, and quickly developed it. The chief direct influence of Theophrastus upon the English character-writers had been exerted before the appearance of Healey's translation. Of course character-drawing on a less rigid pattern had long been, and continued to be, very popular; compare, for instance, Dekker's "politician." (See p. 545.)

CHARACTERES ETHICÆ

(Translation of John Healey, 1616)

OF FLATTERY

FLATTERY may be said to be a foul deformed custom in common life, making for the advantage of the flatterer. A flatterer is such a one as, if he walk or converse with you, will thus say unto you: "Do you observe how all men's eyes are upon you? I have not noted any in this town to be so much beheld. Yesterday in the gallery you had reason to be proud of your reputation. For there being at that time assembled more than thirty persons, and question being made which should be the worthiest citizen, the company, being very impatient it should be disputed, concluded all upon you." These and such like he putteth upon him. If there be the least mote upon his clothes, or if there be none, he maketh a show to take it off; or if any small straw or feather be gotten into his locks, the flatterer taketh it away, and smiling saith, "You are grown gray within

79

these few days for want of my company, and yet your hair is naturally as black as any man of your years." If he reply, the flatterer proclaimeth silence, praiseth him palpably and profusely to his face. When he hath spoken, he breaketh out into an exclamation, with an "O well spoken!" And if he break a jest upon any, the flatterer laughs as if he were tickled, muffling himself in his cloak, as if he could not possibly forbear. As he meeteth any, he playeth the gentleman-usher, praying them to give way, as if his patron were a very great person. He buys pears and apples, and bears them home to his children, and gives them, for the most part, in his presence; and kissing them, crieth out, "O the worthy father's lively picture!" If he buy a shoe, if he be present, he swears his foot is far handsomer, and that the shoe mis-shapes it. If at any time he repair to visit a friend, the flatterer plays the harbinger, runs before and advertiseth them of his coming, and speedily returning back again telleth him that he hath given them notice thereof. Whatsoever belongeth to the women's academy, as paintings, preservings, needle-works, and such like, he discourseth of them like my lady's woman. Of all the guests he first commends the wine, and always sitting by his ingle, courts him, asking him how sparingly he feeds, and how he bridles it; and, taking some special dish from the table, taketh occasion to commend it. He is busy and full of questions—whether this man be not cold? why he goes so thin, and why he will not go better clothed? Then he whispers in his patron's ear, and, while others speak, his eye is still upon him. At the theatre, taking the cushions from the boy, he setteth them up himself; he commendeth the situation and building of the house, the well tilling and husbanding of the ground. In conclusion, you shall always note a flatterer to speak and do what he presumeth will be most pleasing and agreeable.

BEN JONSON (1572-1637)

Ben Jonson, equally great in liquor and in scholarship, was the first English imitator of Theophrastus, whom he read in Casaubon's edition of 1592. But he altered the method considerably, and in so doing led the way for other English practitioners. His characters have less universality than those of Theophrastus, and he works from the outside in, piling up item after item of concrete fact—doing, in fact, in these miniatures what he does on a large scale in the plays themselves. The ethical interest of his model, therefore, may be more or less hidden behind a mass of external observation.

For a not unfriendly glimpse of Ben in a convivial hour, see Howell's letter, p. 595.

_____

EVERY MAN OUT OF HIS HUMOR (1600)

CHARACTERS OF THE PERSONS

PUNTARVOLO, a vain-glorious knight, over-Englishing his travels, and wholly consecrated to singularity; the very Jacob's staff of compliment; a Sir that hath lived to see the revolution of time in most of his apparel: of presence good enough, but so palpably affected to his own praise that for want of flatterers he commends himself, to the floutage of his own family. He deals upon returns, and strange performances, resolving, in despite of public derision, to stick to his own fashion, phrase, and gesture.

CARLO BUFFONE, a public, scurrilous, and profane jester, that, more swift than Circe, with absurd similes will transform any person into deformity. A good feast-hound or banquet-beagle, that will scent you out a supper some three mile off, and swear to his patrons, "damn him! he came in oars," when he was but wafted over in a sculler. A slave that hath an extraordinary gift in pleasing his palate, and will swill up more sack at a sitting than would make all the guard a posset. His religion is railing, and his discourse ribaldry. They stand highest in his respect whom he studies most to reproach.

FASTIDIUS BRISK, a neat, spruce, affecting courtier, one that wears clothes well and in fashion; practiseth by his glass how to salute; speaks good remnants, notwithstanding the base viol and tobacco; swears tersely and with variety; cares not what lady's favor he belies, or great man's familiarity: a good property to perfume the boot of a coach. He will borrow another man's horse to praise, and backs him as his own; or, for a need, on foot can post himself into credit with his merchant, only with the jingle of his spur and the jerk of his wand.

CYNTHIA'S REVELS (1601)

[A TRAVELER]

ACT II, SCENE I

HE THAT is with him is Amorphus, a traveler, one so made out of the mixture and shreds of forms that himself is truly deformed. He walks most commonly with a clove or pick-tooth in his mouth; he is the very mint of compliment; all his behaviors are printed; his face is another volume of essays, and his beard is an Aristarchus. He speaks all cream, skimmed, and more affected than a dozen of waiting-women. He is his own promoter in every place. The wife of the ordinary gives him his diet to maintain her table in discourse; which, indeed, is a mere tyranny over her other guests, for he will usurp all the talk; ten constables are not so tedious. He is no great shifter; once a year his apparel is ready to revolt. He doth use much to arbitrate quarrels, and fights himself exceeding well, out at a window. He will lie cheaper than any beggar, and louder than most clocks; for which he is right properly accommodated to the whetstone, his page. The other gallant is his zany, and doth most of these tricks after him; sweats to imitate him in everything to a hair except a beard, which is not yet extant. He doth learn to make strange sauces, to eat anchovies, macaroni, bovoli, fagioli, and caviare, because he loves them; speaks as he speaks, looks, walks, goes so in clothes and fashion; is in all as if he were moulded of him. Marry, before they met he had other very pretty sufficiencies, which yet he retains some light impression of; as frequenting a dancing-school, and grievously torturing strangers with inquisition after his grace in his galliard. He buys a fresh acquaintance at any rate. His eye and his raiment confer much together as he goes in the street. He treads nicely, like the fellow that walks upon ropes, especially the first Sunday of his silk stockings; and when he is most neat and new, you shall strip him with commendations.

JOSEPH HALL (1574–1656)

Hall's Virtues were quite abstract and didactic, as became a clergyman. His Vices are nearer the Theophrastian model, though Hall has a heavier touch. He is, also, nearer to Theophrastus than many of his English successors in having a serious ethical interest, but naturally that of a Christian rather than of a pagan philosopher.

CHARACTERS OF VIRTUES AND VICES (1608)

THE HUMBLE MAN

He is a friendly enemy to himself, for, though he be not out of his own favor, no man sets so low a value of his worth as himself; not out of ignorance or carelessness, but of a voluntary and meek dejectedness. He admires everything in another, while the same or better in himself he thinks not unworthily contemned; his eyes are full of his own wants and others' perfections. He loves rather to give than to take honor, not in a fashion of complimental courtesy, but in simplicity of his judgment: neither doth he fret at those on whom he forceth precedency, as one that hoped their modesty would have refused; but holds his mind unfeignedly below his place, and is ready to go lower, if need be, without discontentment. When he hath but his due he magnifieth courtesy and disclaims his deserts. He can be more ashamed of honor than grieved with contempt, because he thinks that causeless, this deserved. His face, his carriage, his habit, savor of lowliness without affectation, and yet he is much under that he seemeth. His words are few and soft, never either peremptory or censorious, because he thinks both each man more wise and none more faulty than himself; and when he approacheth to the throne of God he is so taken up with the divine greatness that in his own eyes he is either vile or nothing. Places of public charge are fain to sue to him and hale him out of his chosen obscurity; which he holds off, not cunningly, to cause importunity, but sincerely, in the conscience of

84

his defects. He frequenteth not the stages of common resorts, and then alone thinks himself in his natural element when he is shrouded within his own walls. He is ever jealous over himself, and still suspecteth that which others applaud. There is no better object of beneficence, for what he receives he ascribes merely to the bounty of the giver, nothing to merit. He emulates no man in anything but goodness, and that with more desire than hope to overtake. No man is so contented with his little, and so patient under miseries, because he knows the greatest evils are below his sins, and the least favors above his deservings. He walks ever in awe, and dare not but subject every word and action to a high and just censure. He is a lowly valley, sweetly planted and well watered; the proud man's earth, whereon he trampleth; but secretly full of wealthy mines, more worth than he that walks over them; a rich stone, set in lead; and, lastly, a true temple of God, built with a low roof.

THE HYPOCRITE

AN HYPOCRITE is the worst kind of player, by so much as he acts the better part, which hath always two faces, ofttimes two hearts; that can compose his forehead to sadness and gravity, while he bids his heart be wanton and careless within, and in the meantime laughs within himself to think how smoothly he hath cozened the beholder: in whose silent face are written the characters of religion, which his tongue and gestures pronounce but his hands recant: that hath a clean face and garment, with a foul soul, whose mouth belies his heart, and his fingers belie his mouth. Walking early up into the city, he turns into the great church, and salutes one of the pillars on one knee, worshipping that God which at home he cares not for, while his eye is fixed on some window, on some passenger, and his heart knows not whither his lips go. He rises, and looking about with admiration, complains of our frozen charity, commends the ancient. At church he will ever sit where he may be seen best, and in the midst of the sermon pulls out his tables in haste, as if he feared to lose that note; when he writes either his forgotten errand or nothing: then he turns his Bible with a noise to seek an omitted quotation, and folds the leaf as if he had found it, and asks aloud the name of the preacher, and repeats it, whom

he publicly salutes, thanks, praises, invites, entertains with tedious good counsel, with good discourse, if it had come from an
honester mouth. He can command tears when he speaks of his
youth, indeed because it is past, not because it was sinful; himself
is now better, but the times are worse. All other sins he reckons
up with detestation, while he loves and hides his darling in his
bosom. All his speech returns to himself, and every occurrent
draws in a story to his own praise. When he should give, he
looks about him and says, "Who sees me?" No alms, no
prayers, fall from him without a witness, belike lest God should
deny that he hath received them; and when he hath done
(lest the world should not know it) his own mouth is his trumpet
to proclaim it. With the superfluity of his usury he builds an
hospital, and harbors them whom his extortion hath spoiled;
so, while he makes many beggars he keeps some. He turneth
all gnats into camels, and cares not to undo the world for a
circumstance. Flesh on a Friday is more abomination to him
than his neighbor's bed: he abhors more not to uncover at the
name of Jesus than to swear by the name of God. When a
rhymer reads his poem to him he begs a copy, and persuades the
press: there is nothing that he dislikes in presence that in absence
he censures not. He comes to the sick-bed of his stepmother,
and weeps, when he secretly fears her recovery. He greets his
friend in the street with so clear a countenance, so fast a closure,
that the other thinks he reads his heart in his face, and shakes
hands with an indefinite invitation of "When will you come?"
and when his back is turned, joys that he is so well rid of a guest;
yet if that guest visit him unfeared, he counterfeits a smiling
welcome, and excuses his cheer, when closely he frowns on his
wife for too much. He shows well, and says well, and himself
is the worst thing he hath. In brief, he is the stranger's saint,
the neighbor's disease, the blot of goodness, a rotten stick in a
dark night, a poppy in a corn-field, an ill-tempered candle with
a great snuff that in going out smells ill; an angel abroad, a
devil at home, and worse when an angel than when a devil.

THE BUSYBODY

HIS estate is too narrow for his mind, and therefore he is fain
to make himself room in others' affairs; yet ever in pretence of

love. No news can stir but by his door; neither can he know that which he must not tell. What every man ventures in Guiana voyage, and what they gained, he knows to a hair. Whether Holland will have peace, he knows; and on what conditions, and with what success, is familiar to him ere it be concluded. No post can pass him without a question; and rather than he will lose the news, he rides back with him to appose him of tidings: and then to the next man he meets he supplies the wants of his hasty intelligence, and makes up a perfect tale; wherewith he so haunteth the patient auditor, that, after many excuses, he is fain to endure rather the censure of his manners in running away, than the tediousness of an impertinent discourse. His speech is oft broken off with a succession of long parentheses, which he ever vows to fill up ere the conclusion; and perhaps would effect it, if the other's ear were as unweariable as his tongue. If he sees but two men talk, and read a letter in the street, he runs to them, and asks if he may not be partner of that secret relation; and if they deny it, he offers to tell, since he may not hear, wonders; and then falls upon the report of the Scottish mine, or of the great fish taken up at Lynn, or of the freezing of the Thames; and, after many thanks and dismissions, is hardly entreated silence. He undertakes as much as he performs little. This man will thrust himself forward, to be the guide of the way he knows not; and calls at his neighbor's window and asks why his servants are not at work. The market hath no commodity which he prizeth not, and which the next table shall not hear recited. His tongue, like the tail of Samson's foxes, carries firebrands, and is enough to set the whole field of the world on a flame. Himself begins table-talk of his neighbor at another's board; to whom he bears the first news, and adjures him to conceal the reporter: whose choleric answer he returns to his first host, enlarged with a second edition: so, as it uses to be done in the fight of unwilling mastiffs, he claps each on the side apart, and provokes them to an eager conflict. There can no act pass without his comment, which is ever far-fetched, rash, suspicious, dilatory. His ears are long, and his eyes quick, but most of all to imperfections, which as he easily sees, so he increases with intermeddling. He harbors another man's servant, and, amidst his entertainment, asks what fare is usual at home, what hours are kept, what talk passeth their meals, what his master's disposition is, what his government, what his guests: and when he hath by curious inquiries extracted all the juice and spirit of hoped intelligence, turns him off whence he came, and works on a new. He hates constancy as an earthen dullness, unfit for men of spirit, and loves to change his work and his place: neither yet can he be so soon weary of any place as every place is weary of him: for as he sets himself on work, so others pay him with hatred; and look, how many masters he hath, so many enemies; neither is it possible that any should not hate him but who know him not. So then he labors without thanks, talks without credit, lives without love, dies without tears, without pity, save that some say, "It was pity he died no sooner."

SIR THOMAS OVERBURY (1581-1613)

After studying at Oxford and the Middle Temple, Overbury commenced a prosperous career under the wing of Robert Carr, later Earl of Somerset. As the intimate of the royal favorite Overbury was in an excellent situation for observing the life of the court and the city—and no such observer, in the time of James I, was likely to be a naïve idealist. But the period of sunshine came to an end when plans developed for the marriage of Carr and the notorious Frances Howard, Countess of Essex. The net-work of intrigue and crime woven around that match is far too intricate to be unraveled here. Overbury's opposition led to his being imprisoned and then poisoned. A number of heads fell, but not those of the principals. (See Howell's account, p. 588.)

Overbury's *Characters* were written perhaps as early as Hall's, though they were not published until 1614. They were very popular, and the twenty-one characters of the first edition (composed by Overbury and others) were increased—of course not by Overbury—until the final edition contained over eighty. The Overbury *Characters*, while following the Greek model in many obvious respects, depart from it in many others. There is a wider range of themes, a style which prefers constant cleverness to simplicity; ethical traits receive less attention than external facts.

(CHARACTERS, 1614)

AN AMORIST

Is a man blasted or planet-strooken, and is the dog that leads blind Cupid; when he is at the best his fashion exceeds the worth of his weight. He is never without verses and musk confects, and sighs to the hazard of his buttons. His eyes are all white, either to wear the livery of his mistress' complexion or to keep Cupid from hitting the black. He fights with passion, and loseth much of his blood by his weapon; dreams, thence his paleness. His arms are carelessly used, as if their best use was nothing but embracements. He is untrussed, unbuttoned, and ungartered, not out of carelessness, but care; his farthest end being but going to bed. Sometimes he wraps his petition in neatness, but he goeth not alone; for then he makes some other quality moralize his affection, and his trimness is the grace of that grace. Her favor lifts him up as the sun moisture; when she disfavors, unable to hold that happiness, it falls down in tears. His fingers are his orators, and he expresseth much of himself upon some instrument. He answers not, or not to the purpose, and no marvel, for he is not at home. He scotcheth time with dancing with his mistress, taking up of her glove, and wearing her feather; he is confined to her color, and dares not pass out of the circuit of her memory. His imagination is a fool, and it goeth in a pied coat of red and white. Shortly, he is translated out of a man into folly; his imagination is the glass of lust, and himself the traitor to his own discretion.

AN AFFECTATE TRAVELER

Is A speaking fashion; he hath taken pains to be ridiculous, and hath seen more than he hath perceived. His attire speaks French or Italian, and his gait cries, "Behold me." He censures all things by countenances and shrugs, and speaks his own language with shame and lisping; he will choke rather than confess beer good drink, and his pick-tooth is a main part of his behavior. He chooseth rather to be counted a spy than not a politician, and maintains his reputation by naming great men familiarly. He chooseth rather to tell lies than not wonders, and talks with men singly; his discourse sounds big, but means nothing; and his boy is bound to admire him howsoever. He comes still from great personages, but goes with mean. He takes occasion to show jewels given him in regard of his virtue, that were bought in St. Martin's; and not long after having with a mountebank's method pronounced them worth thousands, impawneth them for a few shillings. Upon festival days he goes to court, and salutes without resaluting; at night in an ordinary he canvasseth the business in hand, and seems as conversant with all intents and plots as if he begot them. His extraordinary account of men is, first to tell them the ends of all matters of consequence, and then to borrow money of them; he

offers courtesies to show them, rather than himself, humble.
He disdains all things above his reach, and preferreth all countries before his own. He imputeth his want and poverty to the
ignorance of the time, not his own unworthiness; and concludes
his discourse with half a period, or a word, and leaves the
rest to imagination. In a word, his religion is fashion, and
both body and soul are governed by fame; he loves most voices
above truth.

A COURTIER

To ALL men's thinking is a man, and to most men the finest;
all things else are defined by the understanding, but this by
the senses; but his surest mark is that he is to be found only
about princes. He smells, and putteth away much of his
judgment about the situation of his clothes. He knows no man
that is not generally known. His wit, like the marigold, openeth
with the sun, and therefore he riseth not before ten of the clock.
He puts more confidence in his words than meaning, and more in
his pronunciation than his words. Occasion is his Cupid, and
he hath but one receipt of making love. He follows nothing
but inconstancy, admires nothing but beauty, honors nothing
but fortune; loves nothing. The sustenance of his discourse is
news, and his censure, like a shot, depends upon the charging.
He is not, if he be out of court, but fish-like breathes destruction
if out of his own element. Neither his motion or aspect are
regular, but he moves by the upper spheres, and is the reflection
of higher substances.

If you find him not here, you shall in Paul's, with a pick-tooth
in his hat, a cape-cloak, and a long stocking.

AN OLD MAN

Is A thing that hath been a man in his days. Old men are to
be known blindfolded, for their talk is as terrible as their resemblance. They praise their own times as vehemently as if
they would sell them. They become wrinkled with frowning
and facing youth; they admire their old customs, even to the
eating of red herring and going wetshod. They call the thumb
under the girdle, gravity; and because they can hardly smell at
all their posies are under their girdles. They count it an ornament of speech to close the period with a cough; and it is vener-

able (they say) to spend time in wiping their drivelled beards. Their discourse is unanswerable, by reason of their obstinacy; their speech is much, though little to the purpose. Truths and lies pass with an equal affirmation; for their memories several are won into one receptacle, and so they come out with one sense. They teach their servants their duties with as much scorn and tyranny as some people teach their dogs to fetch. Their envy is one of their diseases. They put off and on their clothes with that certainty as if they knew their heads would not direct them and therefore custom should. They take a pride in halting and going stiffly, and therefore their staves are carved and tipped; they trust their attire with much of their gravity; and they dare not go without a gown in summer. Their hats are brushed, to draw men's eyes off from their faces; but of all, their pomanders are worn to most purpose, for their putrefied breath ought not to want either a smell to defend or a dog to excuse.

A MELANCHOLY MAN

Is A strayer from the drove; one that nature made a sociable, because she made him man, and a crazed disposition hath altered. Impleasing to all, as all to him; straggling thoughts are his content, they make him dream waking; there's his pleasure. His imagination is never idle, it keeps his mind in a continual motion, as the poise the clock: he winds up his thoughts often, and as often unwinds them; Penelope's web thrives faster. He'll seldom be found without the shade of some grove, in whose bottom a river dwells. He carries a cloud in his face, never fair weather; his outside is framed to his inside, in that he keeps a decorum, both unseemly. Speak to him; he hears with his eyes, ears follow his mind, and that's not at leisure. He thinks business, but never does any; he is all contemplation, no action. He hews and fashions his thoughts, as if he meant them to some purpose, but they prove unprofitable, as a piece of wrought timber to no use. His spirits and the sun are enemies, the sun bright and warm, his humor black and cold; variety of foolish apparitions people his head, they suffer him not to breathe according to the necessities of nature, which makes him sup up a draught of as much air at once as would serve at thrice. He denies nature her due in sleep, and overpays her

with watchfulness; nothing pleaseth him long, but that which
pleaseth his own fantasies; they are the consuming evils, and evil
consumptions that consume him alive. Lastly, he is a man
only in show; but comes short of the better part, a whole reasonable soul, which is man's chief pre-eminence and sole mark from
creatures sensible.

A MERE SCHOLAR

A MERE scholar is an intelligible ass, or a silly fellow in black
that speaks sentences more familiarly than sense. The antiquity of his university is his creed, and the excellency of his
college (though but for a match at football) an article of his
faith. He speaks Latin better than his mother-tongue, and is a
stranger in no part of the world but in his own country. He does
usually tell great stories of himself to small purpose, for they
are commonly ridiculous, be they true or false. His ambition
is that he either is or shall be a graduate, but if ever he get a
fellowship, he has then no fellow. In spite of all logic he dares
swear and maintain it, that a cuckold and a townsman are
termini convertibiles,[1] though his mother's husband be an alderman. He was never begotten (as it seems) without much
wrangling, for his whole life is spent in *pro* and *contra*. His
tongue goes always before his wit, like gentleman-usher, but
somewhat faster. That he is a complete gallant in all points,
cap-à-pie, witness his horsemanship and the wearing of his
weapons. He is commonly long-winded, able to speak more
with ease than any man can endure to hear with patience.
University jests are his universal discourse, and his news the
demeanor of the proctors. His phrase, the apparel of his mind,
is made of divers shreds, like a cushion, and when it goes plainest
it hath a rash outside and fustian linings. The current of his
speech is closed with an *ergo;* and, whatever be the question, the
truth is on his side. 'Tis a wrong to his reputation to be ignorant of anything; and yet he knows not that he knows nothing.
He gives directions for husbandry from Vergil's *Georgics;* for
cattle, from his *Bucolics;* for warlike stratagems, from his
Æneids or Cæsar's *Commentaries*. He orders all things by the
book, is skilful in all trades and thrives in none. He is led
more by his ears than his understanding, taking the sound of

---

[1] Interchangeable terms.

words for their true sense, and does therefore confidently believe that Erra Pater was the father of heretics, Rodolphus Agricola a substantial farmer, and will not stick to aver that Systema's Logic doth excel Keckerman's. His ill luck is not so much in being a fool, as in being put to such pains to express it to the world, for what in others is natural, in him (with much ado) is artificial. His poverty is his happiness, for it makes some men believe that he is none of fortune's favorites. That learning which he hath was in nonage put in backward like a glister, and 'tis now like ware mislaid in a pedlar's pack; a has it, but knows not where it is. In a word, he is the index of a man and the title-page of a scholar, or a puritan in morality; much in profession, nothing in practice.

A TINKER

Is A movable, for he hath no abiding-place; by his motion he gathers heat, thence his choleric nature. He seems to be very devout, for his life is a continual pilgrimage, and sometimes in humility goes barefoot, therein making necessity a virtue. His house is as ancient as Tubal Cain's, and so is a runagate by antiquity: yet he proves himself a gallant, for he carries all his wealth upon his back; or a philosopher, for he bears all his substance about him. From his art was music first invented, and therefore is he always furnished with a song; to which his hammer keeping tune, proves that he was the first founder of the kettledrum. Note that where the best ale is, there stands his music most upon crotchets. The companion of his travels is some foul sun-burnt quean that, since the terrible statute, recanted gipsyism and is turned pedlaress. So marches he all over England with his bag and baggage. His conversation is unreprovable, for he is ever mending. He observes truly the statutes, and therefore he had rather steal than beg, in which he is unremovably constant, in spite of whips or imprisonment: and so a strong enemy to idleness, that in mending one hole he had rather make three than want work, and when he hath done he throws the wallet of his faults behind him. He embraceth naturally ancient customs, conversing in open fields and lowly cottages. If he visit cities or towns, 'tis but to deal upon the imperfections of our weaker vessels. His tongue is very voluble, which with canting proves him a linguist. He is entertained in every place, but enters no further than the door, to avoid suspicion. Some would take him to be a coward; but believe it, he is a lad of mettle; his valor is commonly three or four yards long, fastened to a pike in the end for flying off. He is very provident, for he will fight but with one at once, and then also he had rather submit than be counted obstinate. To conclude, if he 'scape Tyburn and Banbury, he dies a beggar.

A FAIR AND HAPPY MILKMAID

Is a country wench, that is so far from making herself beautiful by art that one look of hers is able to put all face-physic out of countenance. She knows a fair look is but a dumb orator to commend virtue, therefore minds it not. All her excellencies stand in her so silently, as if they had stolen upon her without her knowledge. The lining of her apparel (which is herself) is far better than outsides of tissue: for though she be not arrayed in the spoil of the silkworm, she is decked in innocency, a far better wearing. She doth not, with lying long abed, spoil both her complexion and conditions; nature hath taught her too immoderate sleep is rust to the soul: she rises therefore with chanticleer, her dame's cock, and at night makes the lamb her curfew. In milking a cow, and straining the teats through her fingers, it seems that so sweet a milk-press makes the milk the whiter or sweeter; for never came almond glove or aromatic ointment on her palm to taint it. The golden ears of corn fall and kiss her feet when she reaps them, as if they wished to be bound and led prisoners by the same hand that felled them. Her breath is her own, which scents all the year long of June, like a new-made haycock. She makes her hand hard with labor, and her heart soft with pity; and when winter evenings fall early (sitting at her merry wheel), she sings a defiance to the giddy wheel of fortune. She doth all things with so sweet a grace, it seems ignorance will not suffer her to do ill, being her mind is to do well. She bestows her year's wages at next fair; and in choosing her garments counts no bravery in the world like decency. The garden and beehive are all her physic and chirurgery, and she lives the longer for it. She dares go alone and unfold sheep in the night, and fears no manner of ill because she means none: yet to say truth, she is never alone, for she is still accompanied with old songs, honest thoughts, and prayers, but short ones; yet they have their efficacy, in that they are not palled with ensuing idle cogitations. Lastly, her dreams are so chaste that she dare tell them; only a Friday's dream is all her superstition: that she conceals for fear of anger. Thus lives she, and all her care is she may die in the springtime, to have store of flowers stuck upon her winding-sheet.

AN EXCELLENT ACTOR

WHATSOEVER is commendable to the grave orator is most exquisitely perfect in him, for by a full and significant action of body he charms our attention. Sit in a full theatre and you will think you see so many lines drawn from the circumference of so many ears, whiles the actor is the center. He doth not strive to make nature monstrous; she is often seen in the same scene with him, but neither on stilts nor crutches; and for his voice, 'tis not lower than the prompter, nor louder than the foil and target. By his action he fortifies moral precepts with examples, for what we see him personate we think truly done before us: a man of a deep thought might apprehend the ghost of our ancient heroes walked again, and take him at several times for many of them. He is much affected to painting, and 'tis a question whether that make him an excellent player, or his playing an exquisite painter. He adds grace to the poet's labors, for what in the poet is but ditty in him is both ditty and music. He entertains us in the best leisure of our life, that is, between meals, the most unfit time either for study or bodily exercise. The flight of hawks and chase of wild beasts, either of them are delights noble; but some think this sport of men the worthier, despite all calumny. All men have been of his occupation; and indeed, what he doth feignedly, that do others essentially. This day one plays a monarch, the next a private person; here one acts a tyrant, on the morrow an exile; a parasite this man to-night, to-morrow a precisian; and so of divers others. I observe of all men living a worthy actor in one kind is the strongest motive of affection that can be; for, when he dies, we cannot be persuaded any man can do his parts like him. But, to conclude, I value a worthy actor by the corruption of some few of the quality as I would do gold in the ore; I should not mind the dross but the purity of the metal.

A FRANKLIN

His outside is an ancient yeoman of England, though his inside may give arms (with the best gentleman) and ne'er see the herald. There is no truer servant in the house than himself. Though he be master, he says not to his servants, "Go to field," but, "Let us go"; and with his own eye doth both fatten his flock and set forward all manner of husbandry. He is taught by nature to be contented with a little; his own fold yields him both food and raiment: he is pleased with any nourishment God sends, whilst curious gluttony ransacks, as it were, Noah's ark for food, only to feed the riot of one meal. He is never known to go to law; understanding to be law-bound among men is like to be hide-bound among his beasts; they thrive not under it: and that such men sleep as unquietly as if their pillows were stuffed with lawyers' penknives. When he builds, no poor tenant's cottage hinders his prospect: they are indeed his alms-houses, though there be painted on them no such superscription. He never sits up late, but when he hunts the badger, the vowed foe of his lambs: nor uses he any cruelty, but when he hunts the hare; nor subtlety, but when he setteth snares for the snipe or pitfalls for the blackbird; nor oppression, but when in the month of July he goes to the next river and shears his sheep. He allows of honest pastime, and thinks not the bones of the dead anything bruised, or the worse for it, though the country lasses dance in the churchyard after evensong. Rock Monday, and the wake in summer, shrovings, the wakeful catches on Christmas Eve, the hockey or seed-cake, these he yearly keeps, yet holds them no relics of popery. He is not so inquisitive after news derived from the privy closet, when the finding of an eyry of hawks in his own ground, or the foaling of a colt come of a good strain, are tidings more pleasant, more profitable. He is lord paramount within himself, though he hold by never so mean a tenure; and dies the more contentedly (though he leave his heir young), in regard he leaves him not liable to a covetous guardian. Lastly, to end him: he cares not when his end comes, he needs not fear his audit, for his quietus is in heaven.

JOHN EARLE (?1601-1665)

John Earle was distinguished at Oxford and rose to be Bishop of Salisbury. "He was very dear to the Lord Falkland," says Clarendon, and the words are perhaps a sufficient tribute. And one can believe Clarendon's statement that "he was amongst the few excellent men who never had, nor ever could have an enemy, but such a one who was an enemy to all learning and virtue, and therefore would never make himself known."

Earle's *Microcosmography*, which appeared in 1628 and was augmented in later editions, is the most agreeable to modern taste among all the character-books. His wit is a sauce, not a meal; his satire is not a constant crackle, but cuts deep. His appeal, however, is rather in his sympathetic treatment of subjects slighted or roughly handled by others —witness such replies to the Overbury sketches as his *Downright Scholar* and *Good Old Man*. With no lower standards of liberal culture than those of the Overbury group, and with no less dislike of ignorance and illiberality, Earle sees more in average human beings, in trivial incidents, than objects for attack or contempt. Earle's head and his heart work together.

MICROCOSMOGRAPHY (1628-9)

A CHILD

Is a man in a small letter, yet the best copy of Adam before he tasted of Eve or the apple; and he is happy whose small practice in the world can only write this character. He is nature's fresh picture newly drawn in oil, which time and much handling dims and defaces. His soul is yet a white paper unscribbled with observations of the world, wherewith at length it becomes a blurred notebook. He is purely happy, because he knows no evil, nor hath made means by sin to be acquainted with misery. He arrives not at the mischief of being wise, nor endures evils to come by foreseeing them. He kisses and loves all, and when the smart of the rod is past smiles on his beater. Nature and his parents alike dandle him, and tice him on with a bait of sugar to a draught of wormwood. He plays yet like a young prentice the first day, and is not yet come to his task of melancholy. All the language he speaks yet is tears, and they serve him well enough to express his necessity. His hardest labor is his tongue, as if he were loth to use so deceitful an organ; and he is best company with it when he can but prattle. We laugh at his foolish sports, but his game is our earnest; and his drums, rattles, and hobby-horses, but the emblems and mocking of man's business. His father hath writ him as his own little story, wherein he reads those days of his life that he cannot remember, and sighs to see what innocence he has outlived. The elder he grows he is a stair lower from God, and, like his first father, much worse in his breeches. He is the Christian's example, and the old man's relapse; the one imitates his pureness, and the other falls into his simplicity. Could he put off his body with his little coat, he had got eternity without a burthen, and exchanged but one heaven for another.

A DISCONTENTED MAN

Is ONE that is fallen out with the world, and will be revenged on himself. Fortune has denied him in something, and he now takes pet, and will be miserable in spite. The root of his disease is a self-humoring pride, and an accustomed tenderness not to be crossed in his fancy: and the occasions commonly one of these three, a hard father, a peevish wench, or his ambition thwarted. He considered not the nature of the world till he felt it, and all blows fall on him heavier, because they light not first on his expectation. He has now forgone all but his pride, and is yet vain-glorious in the ostentation of his melancholy. His composure of himself is a studied carelessness, with his arms across, and a neglected hanging of his head and cloak, and he is as great an enemy to an hatband as fortune. He quarrels at the time and upstarts, and sighs at the neglect of men of parts, that is, such as himself. His life is a perpetual satire, and he is still girding the age's vanity, when this very anger shows he too much esteems it. He is much displeased co see men merry, and wonders what they can find to laugh at. He never draws his own lips higher than a smile, and frowns wrinkle him before forty. He at the last falls into that deadly melancholy to be a bitter hater of men, and is the most apt companion for any mischief. He is the spark that kindles the commonwealth, and the bellows himself to blow it: and if he turn anything, it is commonly one of these, either friar, traitor, or madman.

A DOWNRIGHT SCHOLAR

Is ONE that has much learning in the ore, unwrought and untried, which time and experience fashions and refines. He is good metal in the inside, though rough and unscoured without, and therefore hated of the courtier, that is quite contrary. The time has got a vein of making him ridiculous, and men laugh at him by tradition, and no unlucky absurdity but is put upon his profession, and done like a scholar. But his fault is only this, that his mind is somewhat too much taken up with his mind, and his thoughts not loaden with any carriage besides. He has not put on the quaint garb of the age, which is now a man's *imprimis* and all the *item*. He has not humbled his meditations to the industry of compliment, nor afflicted his brain in an elaborate leg. His body is not set upon nice pins, to be turning and flexible for every motion, but his scrape is homely and his nod worse. He cannot kiss his hand and cry, "Madam," nor talk idly enough to bear her company. His smacking of a gentlewoman is somewhat too savory, and he mistakes her nose for her lip. A very woodcock would puzzle him in carving, and he wants the logic of a capon. He has not the glib faculty of sliding over a tale, but his words come squeamishly out of his mouth, and the laughter commonly before the jest. He names this word college too often, and his discourse bears too much on the university. The perplexity of mannerliness will not let him feed, and he is sharp set at an argument when he should cut his meat. He is discarded for a gamester at all games but one and thirty, and at tables he reaches not beyond doublets. His fingers are not long and drawn out to handle a fiddle, but his fist is clunched with the habit of disputing. He ascends a horse somewhat sinisterly, though not on the left side, and they both go jogging in grief together. He is exceedingly censured by the Inns a Court men for that heinous vice, being out of fashion. He cannot speak to a dog in his own dialect, and understands Greek better than the language of a falconer. He has been used to a dark room, and dark clothes, and his eyes dazzle at a satin doublet. The hermitage of his study has made him somewhat uncouth in the world, and men make him worse by staring on him. Thus is he silly and ridiculous, and it continues with him for some quarter of a year out of the university. But practise him a little in men, and brush him o'er with good company, and he shall outbalance those glisterers as far as a solid substance does a feather, or gold, gold-lace.

A MERE YOUNG GENTLEMAN OF THE UNIVERSITY

Is ONE that comes there to wear a gown, and to say hereafter he has been at the university. His father sent him thither because he heard there were the best fencing and dancing schools; from these he has his education, from his tutor the oversight. The first element of his knowledge is to be shown the colleges, and initiated in a tavern by the way, which hereafter he will learn of himself. The two marks of his seniority is the bare velvet of his gown and his proficiency at tennis, where when he can once play a set he is a freshman no more. His study has commonly handsome shelves, his books neat silk strings, which he shows to his father's man, and is loth to untie or take down for fear of misplacing. Upon foul days for recreation he retires thither and looks over the pretty book his tutor reads to him, which is commonly some short history, or a piece of Euphormio; for which his tutor gives him money to spend next day. His main loitering is at the library, where he studies arms and books of honor, and turns a gentleman-critic in pedigrees. Of all things he endures not to be mistaken for a scholar, and hates a black suit though it be of satin. His companion is ordinarily some stale fellow, that has been notorious for an ingle to gold hatbands, whom he admires at first, afterward scorns. If he have spirit or wit he may light of better company, and may learn some flashes of wit, which may do him knight's service in the country hereafter. But he is now gone to the Inns of Court, where he studies to forget what he learned before, his acquaintance and the fashion.

A POT-POET

Is THE dregs of wit, yet mingled with good drink may have some relish. His inspirations are more real than others', for they do but feign a god, but he has his by him. His verses run like the tap, and his invention as the barrel ebbs and flows at the mercy of the spigot. In thin drink he aspires not above a ballad, but a cup of sack inflames him, and sets his muse and nose afire together. The press is his mint, and stamps him now and then a sixpence or two in reward of the baser coin his pamphlet. His works would scarce sell for three halfpence, though they are given oft for three shillings, but for the pretty title that allures the country gentleman; and for which the printer maintains him in ale a fortnight. His verses are like his clothes, miserable centos and patches, yet their pace is not altogether so hobbling as an almanac's. The death of a great man or the burning of a house furnish him with an argument, and the nine Muses are out straight in mourning gown, and Melpomene cries "Fire! Fire!" His other poems are but briefs in rhyme, and like the poor Greek's collections to redeem him from captivity. He is a man now much employed in commendations of our navy, and a bitter inveigher against the Spaniard. His frequentest works go out in single sheets, and are chanted from market to market, to a vile tune and a worse throat; whilst the poor country wench melts like her butter to hear them. And these are the stories of some men of Tyburn, or a strange monster out of Germany; or, sitting in a bawdy-house, he writes God's judgments. He ends at last in some obscure painted cloth, to which himself made the verses, and his life like a can too full spills upon the bench. He leaves twenty shillings on the score, which my hostess loses.

A PLAIN COUNTRY FELLOW

Is ONE that manures his ground well, but lets himself lie fallow and untilled. He has reason enough to do his business, and not enough to be idle or melancholy. He seems to have the judgment of Nebuchadnezzar; for his conversation is among beasts, and his talons none of the shortest, only he eats not grass, because he loves not sallets. His hand guides the plough, and the plough his thoughts, and his ditch and landmark is the very mound of his meditations. He expostulates with his oxen very understandingly, and speaks *gee* and *ree* better than English. His mind is not much distracted with objects: but if a good fat cow come in his way, he stands dumb and astonished, and though his haste be never so great, will fix here half an hour's contemplation. His habitation is some poor thatched roof, distinguished from his barn by the loop-holes that let out smoke, which the rain had long since washed through, but for the double ceiling of bacon on the inside, which has hung there from his grandsire's time, and is yet to make rashers for posterity. His dinner is his other work, for he sweats at it as much as at his labor; he is a terrible fastener on a piece of beef, and you may hope to stave the guard off sooner. His religion is a part of his copyhold, which he takes from his landlord, and refers it wholly to his discretion. Yet if he give him leave, he is a good Christian to his power; that is, comes to church in his best clothes, and sits there with his neighbors, where he is capable only of two prayers, for rain and fair weather. He apprehends God's blessings only in a good year, or a fat pasture, and never praises him but on good ground. Sunday he esteems a day to make merry in, and thinks a bagpipe as essential to it as evening prayer, where he walks very solemnly after service with his hands coupled behind him, and censures the dancing of his parish. His compliment with his neighbor is a good thump on the back, and his salutation commonly some blunt curse. He thinks nothing to be vices but pride and ill husbandry, from which he will gravely dissuade youth, and has some thrifty hobnail proverbs to clout his discourse. He is a niggard all the week except only market-day, where if his corn sell well, he thinks he may be drunk with a good conscience. His feet never stink so unbecomingly, as when he trots after a lawyer in Westminster-hall, and even cleaves the ground with hard scraping, in beseeching his worship to take his money. He is sensible of no calamity but the burning of a stack of corn, or the overflowing of a meadow, and thinks Noah's Flood the greatest plague that ever was, not because it drowned the world, but spoiled the grass. For death he is never troubled, and if he get in but his harvest before, let it come when it will he cares not.

A PRETENDER TO LEARNING

Is ONE that would make others more fools than himself, for though he know nothing, he would not have the world know so much. He conceits nothing in learning but the opinion, which he seeks to purchase without it, though he might with less labor cure his ignorance than hide it. He is indeed a kind of scholar-mountebank, and his art our delusion. He is tricked out in all the accoutrements of learning, and at the first encounter none passes better. He is oftener in his study than at his book, and you cannot pleasure him better than to deprehend him. Yet he hears you not till the third knock, and then comes out very angry, as interrupted. You find him in his slippers and a pen in his ear, in which formality he was asleep. His table is spread wide with some classic folio, which is as constant to it as the carpet, and hath laid open in the same page this half year. His candle is always a longer sitter up than himself, and the boast of his window at midnight. He walks much alone in the posture of meditation, and has a book still before his face in the fields. His pocket is seldom without a Greek Testament or Hebrew Bible, which he opens only in the church, and that when some stander-by looks over. He has his sentences for company, some scatterings of Seneca and Tacitus, which are good upon all occasions. If he read anything in the morning, it comes up all at dinner; and as long as that lasts, the discourse is his. He is a great plagiary of tavern wit, and comes to sermons only that he may talk of Austin. His parcels are the mere scrapings from company, yet he complains at parting what time he has lost. He is wondrously capricious to seem a judgment, and listens with a sour attention to what he understands not He talks much of Scaliger, and Casaubon, and the Jesuits and prefers some unheard-of Dutch name before them all. He has verses to bring in upon these and these hints, and it shall go hard but he will wind in his opportunity. He is critical in a language he cannot conster, and speaks seldom under Arminius in divinity. His business and retirement and caller away is his study, and he protests no delight to it comparable. He is a great nomenclator of authors, which he has read in general in the catalogue, and in particular in the title, and goes seldom so far as the dedication. He never talks of anything but learning, and learns all from talking. Three encounters with the same men pump him, and then he only puts in or gravely says nothing. He has taken pains to be an ass, though not to be a scholar, and is at length discovered and laughed at.

A VULGAR-SPIRITED MAN

Is ONE of the herd of the world. One that follows merely the common cry, and makes it louder by one. A man that loves none but who are publicly affected, and he will not be wiser than the rest of the town. That never owns a friend after an ill name, or some general imputation, though he knows it most unworthy. That opposes to reason "thus men say," and "thus most do," and "thus the world goes," and thinks this enough to poise the other. That worships men in place, and those only, and thinks all a great man speaks oracles. Much taken with my lord's jest, and repeats you it all to a syllable. One that justifies nothing out of fashion, nor any opinion out of the applauded way. That thinks certainly all Spaniards and Jesuits very villains, and is still cursing the Pope and Spinola. One that thinks the gravest cassock the best scholar, and the best clothes the finest man. That is taken only with broad and obscene wit, and hisses anything too deep for him. That cries Chaucer for his money above all our English poets, because the voice has gone so, and he has read none. That is much ravished with such a nobleman's courtesy, and would venture his life for him, because he put off his hat. One that is foremost still to kiss the king's hand, and cries, "God bless His Majesty!" loudest. That rails on all men condemned and out of favor, and the first that says "Away with the traitors!"—yet struck with much ruth at executions, and, for pity to see a man die, could kill the hangman. That comes to London to see it, and the pretty things in it, and the chief cause of his journey the bears. That measures the happiness of the kingdom by the cheapness of corn, and conceives no harm of state but ill trading. Within this compass, too, come those that are too much wedged into the world, and have no lifting thoughts above those things that call to thrive, to do well, and preferment only the grace of God. That aim all studies at this mark, and show you poor scholars as an example to take heed by. That think the prison and want a judgment for some sin, and never like well hereafter of a jailbird. That know no other content but wealth, bravery, and the town-pleasures; that think all else but idle speculation, and the philosophers mad-men. In short, men that are carried away with all outwardnesses, shows, appearances, the stream, the people; for there is no man of worth but has a piece of singularity, and scorns something.

A PLODDING STUDENT

Is A kind of alchemist or persecutor of nature, that would change the dull lead of his brain into finer metal, with success many times as unprosperous, or at least not quitting the cost, to wit, of his own oil and candles. He has a strange forced appetite to learning, and to achieve it brings nothing but patience and a body. His study is not great but continual, and consists much in the sitting up till after midnight in a rug-gown and a night-cap, to the vanquishing perhaps of some six lines; yet what he has, he has perfect, for he reads it so long to understand it till he gets it without book. He may with much industry make a breach into logic, and arrive at some ability in an argument; but for politer studies he dare not skirmish with them, and for poetry accounts it impregnable. His invention is no more than the finding out of his papers, and his few gleanings there; and his disposition of them is as just as the book-binder's, a setting or gluing of them together. He is a great discomforter of young students, by telling them what travail it has cost him, and how often his brain turned at philosophy, and makes others fear studying as a cause of duncery. He is a man much given to apothegms which serve him for wit, and seldom breaks any jest but which belonged to some Lacedæmonian or Roman in Lycosthenes. He is like a dull carrier's horse, that will go a whole week together, but never out of a foot-pace; and he that sets forth on the Saturday shall overtake him.

PAUL'S WALK

Is THE land's epitome, or you may call it the lesser isle of Great Britain. It is more than this, the whole world's map, which you may here discern in its perfectest motion, justling and turning. It is a heap of stones and men, with a vast confusion of languages, and, were the steeple not sanctified, nothing liker Babel. The noise in it is like that of bees, a strange humming or buzz mixed of walking tongues and feet; it is a kind of still roar or loud whisper. It is the great exchange of all discourse, and no business whatsoever but is here stirring and afoot. It is the synod of all pates politic, jointed and laid together in most serious posture, and they are not half so busy at the Parliament. It is the antic of tails to tails, and backs to backs, and for vizards you need go no further than faces. It is the market of young lecturers, whom you may cheapen here at all rates and sizes. It is the general mint of all famous lies, which are here like the legends of popery, first coined and stamped in the church. All inventions are emptied here, and not few pockets. The best sign of a temple in it is, that it is the thieves' sanctuary, which rob more safely in the crowd than a wilderness, whilst every searcher is a bush to hide them. It is the other expense of the day, after plays, tavern, and a bawdy-house; and men have still some oaths left to swear here. It is the ears' brothel, and satisfies their lust and itch. The visitants are all men without exceptions, but the principal inhabitants and possessors are stale knights and captains out of service, men of long rapiers and breeches, which after all turn merchants here and traffic for news. Some make it a preface to their dinner, and travel for a stomach; but thriftier men make it their ordinary, and board here very cheap. Of all such places it is least haunted with hobgoblins, for if a ghost would walk more, he could not.

A STAID MAN

Is A man. One that has taken order with himself, and set a rule to those lawlessnesses within him; whose life is distinct and in method, and his actions as it were cast up before; not loosed into the world's vanities, but gathered up and contracted in his station; not scattered into many pieces of businesses, but that one course he takes goes through with. A man firm and standing in his purposes, nor heaved off with each wind and passion; that squares his expense to his coffers, and makes the total first, and then the items. One that thinks what he does, and does what he says, and foresees what he may do before he purposes. One whose "if I can" is more than another's assurance, and his doubtful tale before some men's protestations; that is confident of nothing in futurity, yet his conjectures oft true prophecies; that makes a pause still betwixt his ear and belief, and is not too hasty to say after others. One whose tongue is strung up like a clock till the time, and then strikes, and says much when he talks little; that can see the truth betwixt two wranglers, and sees them agree even in that they fall out upon; that speaks no rebellion in a bravery, or talks big from the spirit of sack. A man cool and temperate in his passions, not easily betrayed by his choler; that vies not oath with oath, nor heat with heat, but replies calmly to an angry man, and is too hard for him too; that can come fairly off from captains' companies, and neither drink nor quarrel. One whom no ill hunting sends home discontented and makes him swear at his dogs and family. One not hasty to pursue the new fashion, nor yet affectedly true to his old round breeches; but gravely handsome, and to his place, which suits him better than his tailor; active in the world without disquiet, and careful without misery; yet neither engulfed in his pleasures, nor a seeker of business, but has his hours for both. A man that seldom laughs violently, but his mirth is a cheerful look; of a composed and settled countenance, not set, nor much alterable with sadness or joy. He affects nothing so wholly that he must be a miserable man when he loses it; but forethinks what will come hereafter, and spares fortune his thanks and curses. One that loves his credit, not this word reputation; yet can save both without a duel; whose entertainments to greater men are respectful, not complimentary, and to his friends plain, not rude. A good husband, father, master; that is, without doting, pampering, familiarity. A man well poised in all humors, in whom nature showed most geometry, and he has not spoiled the work. A man of more wisdom than wittiness, and brain than fancy; and abler to anything than to make verses.

A GOOD OLD MAN

Is THE best antiquity, and which we may with least vanity admire. One whom Time hath been thus long a-working, and like winter fruit ripened when others are shaken down. He hath taken out as many lessons of the world as days, and learned the best thing in it, the vanity of it. He looks o'er his former life as a danger well past, and would not hazard himself to begin again. His lust was long broken before his body, yet he is glad this temptation is broke too, and that he is fortified from it by this weakness. The next door of death sads him not, but he expects it calmly as his turn in nature, and fears more his recoiling back to childishness than dust. All men look on him as a common father, and on old age for his sake as a reverent thing. His very presence and face puts vice out of countenance, and makes it an indecorum in a vicious man. He practises his experience on youth without the harshness of reproof, and in his counsel is good company. He has some old stories still of his own seeing to confirm what he says, and makes them better in the telling; yet is not troublesome neither with the same tale again, but remembers with them how oft he has told them. His old sayings and morals seem proper to his beard; and the poetry of *Cato* does well out of his mouth, and he speaks it as if he were the author. He is not apt to put the boy on a younger man, nor the fool on a boy, but can distinguish gravity from a sour look, and the less testy he is, the more regarded. You must pardon him if he like his own times better than these, because those things are follies to him now that were wisdom then; yet he makes us of that opinion too, when we see him and conjecture those times by so good a relic. He is a man capable of a dearness with the youngest men, yet he not youthfuller for them, but they older for him, and no man credits more his acquaintance. He goes away at last too soon whensoever, with all men's sorrow but his own, and his memory is fresh when it is twice as old.

THOMAS FULLER (1608–1661)

Fuller received degrees from Cambridge in 1625 and 1628, and he was a contemporary there of Milton, Jeremy Taylor, and other young men destined to greatness. Though his royalist sympathies and activities involved him in difficulties during the war, he enjoyed peace and happiness in London when he returned to the pulpit. No reader of his writings needs to be told that he was a popular preacher—so popular, indeed, that he had two congregations, one inside and one listening through the windows. And many greater masters of prose—though his style is an easy and natural medium—have not attracted Fuller's generations of devotees, who relish his manly sense and spirit, and his incomparable humor. There was not a drop of acid in Fuller, but there was plenty of ginger. He himself would not have relished the epithet "quaint." His *Holy and Profane State* (1642) was a collection of characters and brief biographies. The following well-known specimen of the former indicates how far the character had departed from the Theophrastian model.

THE HOLY AND PROFANE STATE (1642)

THE GOOD SCHOOLMASTER

There is scarce any profession in the commonwealth more necessary, which is so slightly performed. The reasons whereof I conceive to be these: first, young scholars make this calling their refuge, yea, perchance, before they have taken any degree in the university, commence schoolmasters in the country, as if nothing else were required to set up this profession but only a rod and a ferula. Secondly, others who are able, use it only as a passage to better preferment, to patch the rents in their present fortune, till they can provide a new one and betake themselves to some more gainful calling. Thirdly, they are disheartened from doing their best with the miserable reward which in some places they receive, being masters to the children and slaves to their parents.   Fourthly, being grown rich, they grow negligent, and scorn to touch the school, but by the proxy of an usher. But see how well our schoolmaster behaves himself.

1. *His genius inclines him with delight to his profession.*   Some men had as lief be schoolboys as schoolmasters, to be tied to the school as Cooper's *Dictionary* and Scapula's *Lexicon* are chained to the desk therein; and though great scholars, and skilful in other arts, are bunglers in this: but God of his goodness hath fitted several men for several callings, that the necessity of church and state, in all conditions, may be provided for.   So that he who beholds the fabric thereof may say, God hewed out this stone, and appointed it to lie in this very place, for it would fit none other so well, and here it doth most excellent. And thus God mouldeth some for a schoolmaster's life, undertaking it with desire and delight, and discharging it with dexterity and happy success.

2. *He studies his scholars' natures as carefully as they their books;* and ranks their dispositions into several forms.   And though it may seem difficult for him in a great school to descend to all particulars, yet experienced schoolmasters may quickly make a grammar of boys' natures, and reduce them all, saving some few exceptions, to these general rules:

(1) Those that are ingenious and industrious.   The conjunction of two such planets in a youth presage much good unto him.   To such a lad a frown may be a whipping, and a whipping a death; yea, where their master whips them once, shame whips them all the week after.   Such natures he useth with all gentleness.

(2) Those that are ingenious and idle.   These think, with the hare in the fable, that, running with snails (so they count the rest of their schoolfellows), they shall come soon enough to the post, though sleeping a good while before their starting. Oh, a good rod would finely take them napping!

(3) Those that are dull and diligent.   Wines, the stronger they be, the more lees they have when they are new.   Many boys are muddy-headed till they be clarified with age, and such afterwards prove the best.   Bristol diamonds are both bright, and squared and pointed by nature, and yet are soft and worthless; whereas orient ones in India are rough and rugged naturally. Hard, rugged, and dull natures of youth acquit themselves

afterwards the jewels of the country, and therefore their dullness at first is to be borne with, if they be diligent. That schoolmaster deserves to be beaten himself, who beats nature in a boy for a fault. And I question whether all the whipping in the world can make their parts, which are naturally sluggish, rise one minute before the hour nature hath appointed.

(4) Those that are invincibly dull and negligent also. Correction may reform the latter, not amend the former. All the whetting in the world can never set a razor's edge on that which hath no steel in it. Such boys he consigneth over to other professions. Shipwrights and boatmakers will choose those crooked pieces of timber which other carpenters refuse. Those may .make excellent merchants and mechanics which will not serve for scholars.

3. *He is able, diligent, and methodical in his teaching;* not leading them rather in a circle than forwards. He minces his precepts for children to swallow, hanging clogs on the nimbleness of his own soul, that his scholars may go along with him.

4. *He is and will be known to be an absolute monarch in his school.* If cockering mothers proffer him money to purchase their sons an exemption from his rod (to live as it were in a peculiar, out of their master's jurisdiction), with disdain he refuseth it, and scorns the late custom, in some places, of commuting whipping into money, and ransoming boys from the rod at a set price. If he hath a stubborn youth, correction-proof, he debaseth not his authority by contesting with him, but fairly, if he can, puts him away before his obstinacy hath infected others.

5. *He is moderate in inflicting deserved correction.* Many a schoolmaster better answereth the name παιδοτρίβης than παιδαγωγός, rather tearing his scholars' flesh with whipping, than giving them good education. No wonder if his scholars hate the Muses, being presented unto them in the shapes of fiends and furies. Junius complains *de insolenti carnificina*[1] of his schoolmaster, by whom *conscindebatur flagris septies aut octies in dies singulos.*[2] Yea, hear the lamentable verses of poor Tusser, in his own Life:

---

[1] About the harsh cruelty.

[2] He was flogged seven or eight times a day.

From Paul's I went, to Eton sent,
To learn straightways the Latin phrase,
Where fifty-three stripes given to me
    At once I had.
For fault but small, or none at all,
It came to pass thus beat I was;
See, Udal, see the mercy of thee
    To me, poor lad.

Such an Orbilius mars more scholars than he makes: their
tyranny hath caused many tongues to stammer, which spake
plain by nature, and whose stuttering at first was nothing
else but fears quavering on their speech at their master's presence; and whose mauling them about their heads hath dulled
those who in quickness exceeded their master.

6. *He makes his school free to him who sues to him in forma
pauperis.*[1] And surely learning is the greatest alms that can
be given. But he is a beast who, because the poor scholar can
not pay him his wages, pays the scholar in his whipping. Rather
are diligent lads to be encouraged with all excitements to learning. This minds me of what I have heard concerning Mr. Bust,
the worthy late schoolmaster of Eton, who would never suffer
any wandering begging scholar (such as justly the statute hath
ranked in the forefront of rogues), to come into his school, but
would thrust him out with earnestness (however privately
charitable unto him), lest his schoolboys should be disheartened
from their books, by seeing some scholars, after their studying in
the university, preferred to beggary.

7. *He spoils not a good school to make thereof a bad college,*
therein to teach his scholars logic. For besides that logic may
have an action of trespass against grammar for encroaching on
her liberties, syllogisms are solecisms taught in the school, and
oftentimes they are forced afterwards in the university to unlearn
the fumbling skill they had before.

8. *Out of his school he is no whit pedantical in carriage or discourse;* contenting himself to be rich in Latin, though he doth
not jingle with it in every company wherein he comes.

To conclude, let this amongst other motives make schoolmasters careful in their place, that the eminencies of their

---

[1]As one too poor to pay.

scholars have commended the memories of their schoolmasters to posterity, who otherwise in obscurity had altogether been forgotten. Who had ever heard of R. Bond in Lancashire, but for the breeding of learned Ascham his scholar; or of Hartgrave in Brundley school, in the same county, but because he was the first did teach worthy Dr. Whitaker? Nor do I honor the memory of Mulcaster for anything so much as for his scholar, that gulf of learning, Bishop Andrewes. This made the Athenians, the day before the great feast of Theseus their founder, to sacrifice a ram to the memory of Conidas his schoolmaster that first instructed him.

HISTORY

SIR WALTER RALEIGH (?1552–1618)

The life of Raleigh, soldier, sailor, explorer, statesman, courtier, scientific amateur, scholar, poet, is not to be compressed within a few lines. In an age of energy and versatility he was the most energetic and the most versatile. His restless body might be forced into inactivity, but never his restless mind. His character and career are a web of enigmatic contradictions. A sudden and bewildering planet in the Elizabethan firmament, the supreme actor on a glamorous stage, Raleigh dragged out years in the Tower under James. Released to make a last voyage (see Howell, page 590), he returned to be betrayed to Spain by his royal master, and the fifth act, as in so many actual dramas of the time, ended on the scaffold, where "all the far-stretched greatness, all the pride, cruelty, and ambition" of his life was drawn together in a gesture at once theatrical and sincere.

In the Tower, prematurely old and broken, Raleigh set about a task conceivable only to a man of Elizabethan vitality, a *History of the World*, designed to show the rise and fall of empires and justify the ways of God to man. His knowledge was really great, and if his critical standards are not those of a modern historian his book is literature, that fine prose of a man of action who is also a poet.

HISTORY OF THE WORLD (1614)

PREFACE

How unfit and how unworthy a choice I have made of myself to undertake a work of this mixture mine own reason, though exceeding weak, hath sufficiently resolved me. For had it been begotten then with my first dawn of day, when the light of common knowledge began to open itself to my younger years, and before any wound received either from fortune or time, I might yet well have doubted that the darkness of age and death would have covered over both it and me long before the performance. For, beginning with the creation, I have proceeded with the history of the world, and lastly purposed, some few

sallies excepted, to confine my discourse with this our renowned
island of Great Britain. I confess that it had better sorted with
my disability, the better part of whose times are run out in other
travails, to have set together, as I could, the unjointed and scattered frame of our English affairs than of the universal; in whom
had there been no other defect (who am all defect), than the time
of the day, it were enough, the day of a tempestuous life drawn
on to the very evening ere I began. But those inmost and soul-
piercing wounds, which are ever aching while uncured, with the
desire to satisfy those few friends which I have tried by the fire
of adversity, the former enforcing, the latter persuading, have
caused me to make my thoughts legible, and myself the subject
of every opinion, wise or weak.

To the world I present them, to which I am nothing indebted;
neither have others that were, fortune changing, sped much better in any age. . . .

For myself, if I have in anything served my country, and
prized it before my private, the general acceptation can yield
me no other profit at this time than doth a fair sunshine day
to a seaman after shipwreck; and the contrary no other harm
than an outrageous tempest after the port attained. I know
that I lost the love of many for my fidelity towards her whom
I must still honor in the dust, though further than the defence
of her excellent person I never persecuted any man. Of those
that did it, and by what device they did it, he that is the
Supreme Judge of all the world hath taken the accompt, so as
for this kind of suffering I must say with Seneca, *Mala opinio*,
bene parta, delectat. . . .[1]

To me it belongs in the first part of this preface, following the
common and approved custom of those who have left the
memories of time past to after ages, to give, as near as I can,
the same right to history which they have done. Yet seeing
therein I should but borrow other men's words, I will not trouble
the reader with the repetition. True it is that among many
other benefits for which it hath been honored, in this one it
triumpheth over all human knowledge, that it hath given us
life in our understanding, since the world itself had life and beginning, even to this day. Yea, it hath triumphed over time,

---

[1]Evil opinion, honorably gained, is welcome.

which besides it nothing but eternity hath triumphed over: for it hath carried our knowledge over the vast and devouring space of many thousands of years, and given so fair and piercing eyes to our mind that we plainly behold living now, as if we had lived then, that great world, *magni Dei sapiens opus*, the wise work (saith Hermes) of a great God, as it was then, when but new to itself. By it I say it is that we live in the very time when it was created; we behold how it was governed, how it was covered with waters, and again repeopled; how kings and kingdoms have flourished and fallen; and for what virtue and piety God made prosperous, and for what vice and deformity he made wretched, both the one and the other. And it is not the least debt which we owe unto history, that it hath made us acquainted with our dead ancestors, and, out of the depth and darkness of the earth, delivered us their memory and fame. In a word, we may gather out of history a policy no less wise than eternal, by the comparison and application of other men's forepast miseries with our own like errors and ill deservings.

But it is neither of examples the most lively instructions, nor the words of the wisest men, nor the terror of future torments, that hath yet so wrought in our blind and stupefied minds as to make us remember that the infinite eye and wisdom of God doth pierce through all our pretences; as to make us remember that the justice of God doth require none other accuser than our own consciences, which neither the false beauty of our apparent actions, nor all the formality which (to pacify the opinions of men) we put on, can in any or the least kind cover from his knowledge. And so much did that heathen wisdom confess, no way as yet qualified by the knowledge of a true God. If any, saith Euripides, having in his life committed wickedness, think he can hide it from the everlasting gods, he thinks not well.

To repeat God's judgments in particular upon those of all degrees which have played with his mercies, would require a volume apart, for the sea of examples hath no bottom. The marks set on private men are with their bodies cast into the earth, and their fortunes written only in the memories of those that lived with them, so as they who succeed, and have not seen the fall of others, do not fear their own faults. God's judgments upon the greater and greatest have been left to posterity, first, by those happy hands which the Holy Ghost hath guided, and

secondly, by their virtue who have gathered the acts and ends
of men mighty and remarkable in the world. Now to point
far off and to speak of the conversion of angels into devils, for
ambition; or of the greatest and most glorious kings, who have
gnawn the grass of the earth with beasts, for pride and ingrati-
tude towards God; or of that wise working of Pharaoh when he
slew the infants of Israel ere they had recovered their cradles; or
of the policy of Jezebel in covering the murder of Naboth by a
trial of the elders, according to the law; with many thousands of
the like: what were it other than to make an hopeless proof that
far-off examples would not be left to the same far-off respects
as heretofore? For who hath not observed what labor, practice, peril, bloodshed, and cruelty the kings and princes of the
world have undergone, exercised, taken on them, and committed, to make themselves and their issues masters of the world?
And yet hath Babylon, Persia, Egypt, Syria, Macedon, Carthage,
Rome, and the rest, no fruit, no flower, grass, nor leaf springing
upon the face of the earth of those seeds: no, their very roots and
ruins do hardly remain. *Omnia quaemanu hominum facta sunt,
vel manu hominum evertuntur, vel stando et durando deficiunt:* all
that the hand of man can make is either overturned by the hand
of man, or at length by standing and continuing consumed. . . .

For seeing God, who is the author of all our tragedies, hath
written out for us and appointed us all the parts we are to play,
and hath not, in their distribution, been partial to the most
mighty princes of the world—that gave unto Darius the part
of the greatest emperor and the part of the most miserable
beggar, a beggar begging water of an enemy to quench the great
drought of death; that appointed Bajazet to play the Grand
Signior of the Turks in the morning, and in the same day the
footstool of Tamerlane (both which parts Valerian had also
played, being taken by Sapores); that made Belisarius play the
most victorious captain, and lastly the part of a blind beggar;
of which examples many thousands may be produced—why
should other men, who are but as the least worms, complain
of wrongs? Certainly there is no other account to be made of
this ridiculous world than to resolve that the change of fortune
on the great theatre is but as the change of garments on the
less. For when on the one and the other every man wears but
his own skin, the players are all alike. . . .

Howsoever, I know that it will be said by many that I might have been more pleasing to the reader if I had written the story of mine own times, having been permitted to draw water as near the well-head as another. To this I answer that whosoever, in writing a modern history, shall follow truth too near the heels, it may happily strike out his teeth. . . .

For it was for the service of that inestimable Prince Henry, the successive hope, and one of the greatest of the Christian world, that I undertook this work. It pleased him to peruse some part thereof, and to pardon what was amiss. It is now left to the world without a master: from which all that is presented hath received both blows and thanks. . . .

[INFLUENCE OF THE STARS]

BOOK I, C. I, SEC. XI.

. . . And if we cannot deny but that God hath given virtues to springs and fountains, to cold earth, to plants and stones, minerals, and to the excremental parts of the basest living creatures, why should we rob the beautiful stars of their working powers? For, seeing they are many in number, and of eminent beauty and magnitude, we may not think that in the treasury of his wisdom, who is infinite, there can be wanting (even for every star) a peculiar virtue and operation; as every herb, plant, fruit, and flower adorning the face of the earth hath the like. For, as these were not created to beautify the earth alone, and to cover and shadow her dusty face, but otherwise for the use of man and beast, to feed them and cure them, so were not those uncountable glorious bodies set in the firmament to no other end than to adorn it, but for instruments and organs of his divine providence, so far as it hath pleased his just will to determine. . . . And though, for the capacity of men, we know somewhat, yet in the true and uttermost virtues of herbs and plants, which ourselves sow and set, and which grow under our feet, we are in effect ignorant; much more in the powers and workings of celestial bodies. For hardly, saith Salomon, can we discern the things that are upon the earth, and with great labor find we out those things that are before us: who can then investigate the things that are in heaven? *Multum est de rebus cælestibus aliquid cognoscere:* it is much to know a little of heavenly things. But in this question of fate the middle course is to be followed; that, as with the heathen, we do not bind God to his creatures in this supposed necessity of destiny, so on the contrary we do not rob those beautiful creatures of their powers and offices. . . .

But that the stars and other celestial bodies incline the will by mediation of the sensitive appetite, which is also stirred by the constitution and complexion, it cannot be doubted. *Corpora cælestia*, saith Damascene, *constituunt in nobis habitus, complexiones, et dispositiones:* the heavenly bodies, saith he, make in us habits, complexions, and dispositions. For the body (though Galen enforce it further) hath undoubtedly a kind of drawing after it the affections of the mind, especially bodies strong in humor, and minds weak in virtues: for those of choleric complexion are subject to anger and the furious effects thereof, by which they suffer themselves to be transported, where the mind hath not reason to remember that passions ought to be her vassals, not her masters. And that they wholly direct the reasonless mind, I am resolved; for all those which were created mortal, as birds, beasts, and the like, are left to their natural appetites; over all which, celestial bodies (as instruments and executioners of God's providence) have absolute dominion. . .

But that either the stars or the sun have any power over the minds of men immediately, it is absurd to think, other than as aforesaid, as the same by the body's temper may be affected.

[MAN THE MICROCOSM]
BOOK I, C. 2, SEC. V.

MAN, thus compounded and formed by God, was an abstract or model or brief story of the universal, in whom God concluded the creation and work of the world, and whom he made the last and most excellent of his creatures, being internally endued with a divine understanding, by which he might contemplate and serve his Creator, after whose image he was formed, and endued with the powers and faculties of reason and other abilities, that thereby also he might govern and rule the world and all other God's creatures therein. . . . And because in the little frame of man's body there is a representation of the universal, and (by allusion) a kind of participation of all the parts

thereof, therefore was man called *microcosmos*, or the little world.
. . . His blood, which disperseth itself by the branches of
veins through all the body, may be resembled to those waters
which are carried by brooks and rivers over all the earth; his
breath to the air; his natural heat to the enclosed warmth which
the earth hath in itself, which, stirred up by the heat of the sun,
assisteth nature in the speedier procreation of those varieties
which the earth bringeth forth; our radical moisture, oil or
balsamum (whereon the natural heat feedeth and is maintained),
is resembled to the fat and fertility of the earth; the hairs of man's
body, which adorns or overshadows it, to the grass which
covereth the upper face and skin of the earth; our generative
power, to nature, which produceth all things; our determina-
tions, to the light, wandering, and unstable clouds, carried everywhere with uncertain winds; our eyes, to the light of the sun and
moon; and the beauty of our youth, to the flowers of the spring,
which, either in a very short time, or with the sun's heat, dry up
and wither away, or the fierce puffs of wind blow them from the
stalks; the thoughts of our mind, to the motion of angels; and our
pure understanding (formerly called *mens*, and that which always looketh upwards), to those intellectual natures which are
always present with God; and lastly, our immortal souls (while
they are righteous) are by God himself beautified with the title
of his own image and similitude. . . .

Our infancy is compared to the moon, in which we seem only
to live and grow as plants; the second age to Mercury, wherein
we are taught and instructed; our third age to Venus, the days of
love, desire, and vanity; the fourth to the sun, the strong, flourishing, and beautiful age of man's life; the fifth to Mars, in
which we seek honor and victory, and in which our thoughts
travel to ambitious ends; the sixth age is ascribed to Jupiter,
in which we begin to take account of our times, judge of ourselves
and grow to the perfection of our understanding; the last and
seventh to Saturn, wherein our days are sad and overcast, and
in which we find by dear and lamentable experience, and by the
loss which can never be repaired, that of all our vain passions
and affections past the sorrow only abideth; our attendants are
sicknesses and variable infirmities; and by how much the more
we are accompanied with plenty, by so much the more greedily
is our end desired, whom when time hath made unsociable to

others, we become a burden to ourselves, being of no other use than to hold the riches we have from our successors. In this time it is, when (as aforesaid) we, for the most part, and never before, prepare for our eternal habitation, which we pass on unto with many sighs, groans, and sad thoughts, and in the end, by the workmanship of death, finish the sorrowful business of a wretched life; towards which we always travel, both sleeping and waking; neither have those beloved companions of honor and riches any power at all to hold us any one day by the glorious promise of entertainments; but by what crooked path soever we walk, the same leadeth on directly to the house of death, whose doors lie open at all hours, and to all persons. For this tide of man's life, after it once turneth and declineth, ever runneth with a perpetual ebb and falling stream, but never floweth again; our leaf, once fallen, springeth no more; neither doth the sun or the summer adorn us again, with the garments of new leaves and flowers. . .

THE CONCLUSION OF THE WORK

By this which we have already set down is seen the beginning and end of the three first monarchies of the world, whereof the founders and erectors thought that they could never have ended. That of Rome, which made the fourth, was also at this time almost at the highest. We have left it flourishing in the middle of the field, having rooted up, or cut down, all that kept it from the eyes and admiration of the world: but after some continuance it shall begin to lose the beauty it had; the storms of ambition shall beat her great boughs and branches one against another; her leaves shall fall off, her limbs wither, and a rabble of barbarous nations enter the field and cut her down.

Now these great kings and conquering nations have been the subject of those ancient histories which have been preserved and yet remain among us; and withal of so many tragical poets, as in the persons of powerful princes and other mighty men have complained against infidelity, time, destiny, and most of all against the variable success of worldly things and instability of fortune. To these undertakings the greatest lords of the world have been stirred up, rather by the desire of fame, which ploweth up the air and soweth in the wind, than by the affection of bearing rule, which draweth after it so much vexation and so many cares. And that this is true the good advice of Cineas to Pyrrhus proves. And certainly, as fame hath often been dangerous to the living, so is it to the dead of no use at all, because separate from knowledge. Which were it otherwise, and the extreme ill bargain of buying this lasting discourse understood by them which are dissolved, they themselves would then rather have wished to have stolen out of the world without noise, than to be put in mind that they have purchased the report of their actions in the world by rapine, oppression, and cruelty, by giving in spoil the innocent and laboring soul to the idle and insolent, and by having emptied the cities of the world of their ancient inhabitants, and filled them again with so many and so variable sorts of sorrows.

Since the fall of the Roman Empire (omitting that of the Germans, which had neither greatness nor continuance), there hath been no state fearful in the east but that of the Turk; nor in the west any prince that hath spread his wings far over his nest but the Spaniard, who, since the time that Ferdinand expelled the Moors out of Granada, have made many attempts to make themselves masters of all Europe. And it is true that by the treasures of both Indies, and by the many kingdoms which they possess in Europe, they are at this day the most powerful. But as the Turk is now counterpoised by the Persian, so instead of so many millions as have been spent by the English, French, and Netherlands in a defensive war and in diversions against them, it is easy to demonstrate that with the charge of two hundred thousand pound, continued but for two years or three at the most, they may not only be persuaded to live in peace, but all their swelling and overflowing streams may be brought back into their natural channels and old banks. These two nations, I say, are at this day the most eminent, and to be regarded; the one seeking to root out the Christian religion altogether, the other the truth and sincere profession thereof, the one to join all Europe to Asia, the other the rest of all Europe to Spain.

For the rest, if we seek a reason of the succession and continuance of this boundless ambition in mortal men, we may add to that which hath already been said, that the kings and princes of the world have always laid before them the actions, but not the ends, of those great ones which preceded them. They are always transported with the glory of the one, but they never mind the misery of the other, till they find the experience in themselves. They neglect the advice of God while they enjoy life, or hope it, but they follow the counsel of Death upon his first approach. It is he that puts into man all the wisdom of the world, without speaking a word, which God with all the words of his law, promises, or threats, doth not infuse. Death, which hateth and destroyeth man, is believed; God, which hath made him and loves him, is always deferred. *I have considered,* saith Salomon, *all the works that are under the sun, and behold, all is vanity and vexation of spirit:* but who believes it, till Death tells it us? It was Death which, opening the conscience of Charles the Fifth, made him enjoin his son Philip to restore Navarre; and King Francis the First of France to command that justice should be done upon the murderers of the Protestants in Merindol and Cabrieres, which till then he neglected. It is therefore Death alone that can suddenly make man to know himself. He tells the proud and insolent that they are but abjects, and humbles them at the instant; makes them cry, complain, and repent, yea, even to hate their forepast happiness. He takes the account of the rich, and proves him a beggar, a naked beggar, which hath interest in nothing but in the gravel that fills his mouth. He holds a glass before the eyes of the most beautiful, and makes them see therein their deformity and rottenness, and they acknowledge it.

O eloquent, just, and mighty Death! whom none could advise, thou hast persuaded, what none hath dared, thou hast done, and whom all the world hath flattered, thou only hast cast out of the world and despised; thou hast drawn together all the far-stretched greatness, all the pride, cruelty, and ambition of man, and covered it all over with these two narrow words, *Hic jacet.*

THOMAS FULLER (1608–1661)

Where Bacon and others had led the way in the writing of sober scientific history Thomas Fuller was not likely to follow. He had a fund of information, relevant and irrelevant, sometimes valuable as history, often irresistible as anecdote, and he makes many a shrewd and deceptively simple comment, but his *Church History* defies the anthologist—unless one were following the suggestion of the caustic Peter Heylyn and collecting Fuller's "merry tales, and scraps of trencher-jests, frequently interlaced in all parts of the history." The only way to appreciate Fuller's book is to turn over its voluminous pages and relish those unexpected things which, says the indignant Heylyn, "neither do become the gravity of a Church-historian, nor are consistent with the nature of a sober argument." However, the following passages, with their account of a famous scene, help to dramatize the all-important problem of Church and State.

THE CHURCH HISTORY OF BRITAIN (1655)

THE DEATH OF QUEEN ELIZABETH

QUEEN ELIZABETH, the mirror of her sex and age, having, above forty years, to the admiration of envy itself, managed this kingdom, finding, when she began, few friends that durst help, and leaving no foes that could hurt her, exchanged her earthly for a heavenly crown; who, as she lived and died an unspotted virgin, so her maiden memory is likely, in this respect, to remain sole and single; seeing history affords no prince to be matched to her fame in all considerable particulars. Her corpse was solemnly interred under a fair tomb in Westminster; the lively draught whereof is pictured in most London—and many country—churches; every parish being proud of the shadow of her tomb: and no wonder, when each loyal subject erected a mournful monument for her in his heart. But, soon

after, all English souls were employed equally to divide themselves betwixt exclamations of sorrow for her death and acclamations of joy for King James succeeding her.

EPISCOPAL AND PRESBYTERIAN AFFAIRS

AND now it is strange with what assiduity and diligence the
two potent parties, the defenders of episcopacy and presbytery,
with equal hopes of success, made, beside private and particular
addresses, public and visible applications to King James, the
first to continue, the latter to restore, or rather set up, their government; so that whilst each side was jealous his rival should
get the start by early stirring, and rise first in the King's favor,
such was their vigilancy that neither may seem to go to bed;
incessantly diligent both before and since the Queen's death, in
dispatching posts and messages into Scotland to advance their
several designs.   We take notice of two principal:—Mr. Lewis
Pickering, a Northamptonshire gentleman, and zealous for the
presbyterian party, was the third person of quality who, riding
incredibly swift (good news makes good horsemen), brought
King James the tidings of Queen Elizabeth's death.   But how
far, and with what answer, he moved the King in that cause,
is uncertain.   Dr. Thomas Nevill, Dean of Canterbury, came
into Scotland some days after him (except any will say that he
comes first that comes really to effect what he was sent for),
being solemnly employed by Archbishop Whitgift to His Majesty
in the name of the bishops and clergy of England, to tender their
bounden duties and to understand His Highness's pleasure for
the ordering and guiding of ecclesiastical causes.   He brought
back a welcome answer to such as sent him, of His Highness's
purpose, which was to uphold and maintain the government of
the late Queen as she left it settled.   . . .

MR. CARTWRIGHT DEDICATES A BOOK TO KING JAMES. MR. CARTWRIGHT'S DEATH

No SOONER was King James settled on the English throne
but Mr. Cartwright presented unto him his Latin comment on

Ecclesiastes, thankfully mentioning in his dedication how he had, some twenty years before, been chosen to be professor in a Scotch university, though declining the acceptance thereof because of his pastoral charge, being then minister of the English congregation at Antwerp: thanks, perchance, not so proper to the person of King James (though in loyalty and good manners justly tendered unto him) as due rather to those who in his minority steered the affairs of Scotland. Nor let any wonder that an Englishman should be proffered preferment in Scotland, seeing it was but one for another, remembering that I have read in the Life of Mr. Knox that he was offered an English bishopric in the reign (as I take it) of King Edward VI, and likewise refused the same.

But Mr. Cartwright survived not long after (otherwise, no doubt, we should have heard of him in Hampton Court Conference as the champion of his party), who died at the age of sixty, on the 27th of December following. To what we have formerly largely written of his character we now only add that he was born in Hertfordshire and married the sister of Mr. Stubbs whose hand was struck off for writing an interpreted libel against Queen Elizabeth's marriage with Monsieur. This I dare boldly say, she was a most excellent wife if she proved like her brother, whom Mr. Camden (no great friend of puritans) cordially commendeth for a right honest man, generally beloved whilst living and lamented when dead. He was afflicted towards his old age with many infirmities, insomuch that he was forced continually to study upon his knees. My ears shall be deaf to the uncharitable inference of those who impute this extraordinary painful posture as a just punishment upon him, in that he had so bitterly inveighed against the gesture of those as superstitious who reverently received the sacrament on their knees. Mr. Dod preached his funeral sermon.

THE PRESBYTERIAN PETITION TO THE KING AND PARLIAMENT

AND now, because there was a general expectation of a parliament suddenly to succeed, the presbyterian party, that they might not be surprised before they had their tackling about them, went about to get hands of the ministers to a petition, which they intended seasonably to present to the King and Parliament. Mr. Arthur Hildersham, and Mr. Stephen Egerton, with some others, were chosen, and chiefly intrusted to manage this important business. This was called "the Millenary Petition," as *one of a thousand:* though indeed there were but seven hundred and fifty preachers' hands set thereunto: but those all collected only out of five-and-twenty counties. However, for the more rotundity of the number, and grace of the matter, it passeth for a full thousand; which, no doubt, the collectors of the names (if so pleased) might easily have completed. I dare not guess what made them desist before their number was finished; whether they thought that these were enough to do the deed and more were rather for ostentation than use, or, because disheartened by the intervening of the Hampton Court Conference, they thought that these were even too many to petition for a denial. It is left as yet uncertain, whether this Conference was by the King's favor graciously tendered or by the mediation of the lords of his Council powerfully procured, or by the bishops, as confident of their cause, voluntarily proffered, or by the ministers' importunity effectually obtained. Each opinion pretends to probability, but the last most likely. And, by what means soever this Conference was compassed, Hampton Court was the place, the 14th of January the time, and the following names the persons which were employed therein. . . .

THE SECOND DAY'S CONFERENCE AT HAMPTON COURT

. . . DR. REYNOLDS.—I desire that, according to certain provincial constitutions, the clergy may have meetings every three weeks:—

1. First, in rural deaneries, therein to have prophesying, as Archbishop Grindal and other bishops desired of her late majesty.

2. That such things as could not be resolved on there might be referred to the archdeacons' visitations.

3. And so to the episcopal synod, to determine such points before not decided.

HIS MAJESTY.—If you aim at a Scottish presbytery, it agreeth as well with monarchy as God and the devil. Then Jack and Tom and Will and Dick shall meet and censure me and my

Council. Therefore I reiterate my former speech, *Le roy s'avisera.* Stay, I pray, for one seven years, before you demand; and then if you find me grow pursy and fat, I may, perchance, hearken unto you; for that government will keep me in breath, and give me work enough. I shall speak of one matter more, somewhat out of order, but it skilleth not. Dr. Reynolds, you have often spoken for my supremacy, and it is well. But know you any here or elsewhere who like of the present government ecclesiastical and dislike my supremacy?

DR. REYNOLDS.—I know none.

HIS MAJESTY.—Why, then, I will tell you a tale: After that the religion restored by King Edward VI was soon overthrown by Queen Mary here in England, we in Scotland felt the effect of it. For, thereupon, Mr. Knox writes to the queen regent, a virtuous and moderate lady, telling her that she was the supreme head of the church, and charged her, as she would answer it at God's tribunal, to take care of Christ's Evangel, in suppressing the popish prelates who withstood the same. But how long, trow you, did this continue? Even till, by her authority, the popish bishops were repressed and Knox, with his adherents, being brought in, made strong enough. Then began they to make small account of her supremacy, when, according to that *more light* wherewith they were illuminated, they made a farther reformation of themselves. How they used the poor lady my mother is not unknown, and how they dealt with me in my minority. I thus apply it: my Lords the Bishops (this he said, putting his hand to his hat), I may thank you that these men plead thus for my supremacy. They think they cannot make their party good against you but by appealing unto it. But if once you were out and they in, I know what would become of my supremacy; for, "No bishop, no king!" I have learned of what cut they have been, who, preaching before me since my coming into England, passed over, with silence, my being supreme governor in causes ecclesiastical. Well, doctor, have you anything else to say?

DR. REYNOLDS.—No more, if it please Your Majesty.

HIS MAJESTY.—If this be all your party hath to say, I will make them conform themselves, or else I will harry them out of the land, or else do worse. . . .

THE GENERAL CENSURE OF THE CONFERENCERS. THE
NONCONFORMISTS' COMPLAINT. THE PRODUCT OF THIS
CONFERENCE

THUS ended the three days' Conference; wherein how discreetly the King carried himself, posterity, out of the reach of flattery, is the most competent judge—such matters being most truly discerned at a distance. It is generally said that herein he went *above* himself; that the Bishop of London appeared *even with* himself; and Dr. Reynolds fell much *beneath* himself. Others observed that Archbishop Whitgift spake most gravely; Bancroft, when out of passion, most politicly; Bilson, most learnedly; and of the divines, Mr. Reynolds, most largely; Knewstubs, most affectionately; Chaderton, most sparingly. In this scene only Dr. Sparks was κωφὸν πρόσωπον,[1] making use of his hearing, not speech, converted (it seems) to the truth of what was spoken, and soon after setting forth a treatise of unity and uniformity.

But the nonconformists complained that the King sent for their divines, not to have their scruples satisfied, but his pleasure propounded; not that he might know what they could *say*, but they what he would *do* in the matter. Besides, no wonder if Dr. Reynolds a little lost himself, whose eyes were partly dazzled with the light of the King's majesty, partly daunted with the heat of his displeasure. Others complain that this Conference is partially set forth only by Dr. Barlow, Dean of Chester, their professed adversary, to the great disadvantage of their divines. And when the Israelites go down to the Philistines to whet all their iron tools, no wonder if they set a sharp edge on their own and a blunt one on their enemies' weapons.

This Conference produced some alterations in the Liturgy; women's baptizing of infants, formerly frequent, hereafter forbidden; in the rubric of absolution, "remission of sins" inserted, confirmation termed also "an examination" of children; and some words altered in the Dominical Gospels, with a resolution for a new translation of the Bible. But whereas it was hitherto disputable whether the north, where he long lived, or the south, whither he lately came, should prevail most on the King's

[1] A dumb mask.

judgment in Church government, this doubt was now clearly decided. Henceforward many cripples in conformity were cured of their former halting therein, and such who knew not their own till they knew the King's mind in this matter for the future quietly digested the ceremonies of the Church.

LORD CLARENDON (1609–1674)

Edward Hyde had a more notable share in the making of history than any other great English historian. Becoming a successful lawyer, he sympathized at first with the parliamentary struggle against the operations of unconstitutional courts. But parliamentary hostility to the Church caused a change of allegiance, and he became a royalist. In 1643 he was made Chancellor of the Exchequer. After the last Royalist defeat in 1646 he escorted the Prince of Wales to Scilly, and, a few weeks later, to Jersey. With extraordinary powers of detachment from the troubles of the moment, he commenced his *History* in Scilly. His motive, he says in a letter of 1646, was "to provide myself for new business against the time I should be called to it" by looking over "the faults of the old." But, though he wished both to vindicate and to advise the King and the King's party, he had his eye upon posterity, and reflected much upon the art of historical writing. His return to public activity in 1648 broke off his work. Coming back to England in 1660, he was Lord Chancellor until 1667, when he was forced into exile. In France he resumed his *History of the Rebellion*, but it was really a new work, his *Life*; not a tract for the times now, but a frank and voluminous autobiography. He also revised the earlier work. Needless to say, he has a realistic grasp of men and affairs. His reputation has always rested mainly on his personal portraits, most of which occur in the *Life*. The following extracts reveal his sense of drama and character, and his command of massive, sinewy prose that is intricate but not difficult.

HISTORY OF THE REBELLION

(1646 *et seq.*; *pub.* 1702)

BOOK I

[CHARACTER OF THE DUKE OF BUCKINGHAM]

AFTER all this, and such a transcendent mixture of ill fortune, of which as ill conduct and great infirmities seem to be the foundation and source, this great man was a person of a noble nature and generous disposition, and of such other endowments as made him very capable of being a great favorite to a great King. He understood the arts and artifices of a court, and all the learning that is professed there, exactly well: by long practice in business, under a master that discoursed excellently and surely knew all things wonderfully, and took much delight in indoctrinating his young unexperienced favorite, who, he knew, would be always looked upon as the workmanship of his own hands, he had obtained a quick conception and apprehension of business, and had the habit of speaking very gracefully and pertinently. He was of a most flowing courtesy and affability to all men who made any address to him, and so desirous to oblige them that he did not enough consider the value of the obligation, or the merit of the person he chose to oblige; from which much of his misfortune resulted. He was of a courage not to be daunted, which was manifested in all his actions, and his contests with particular persons of the greatest reputation; and especially in his whole demeanor at the Isle of Rees, both at the landing and upon the retreat, in both which no man was more fearless, or more ready to expose himself to the brightest dangers. His kindness and affection to his friends was so vehement, that it was as so many marriages, for better and worse, and so many leagues offensive and defensive; as if he thought himself obliged to love all his friends, and to make war upon all they were angry with, let the cause be what it would. And it cannot be denied that he was an enemy in the same excess, and prosecuted those he looked upon as his enemies with the utmost rigor and animosity, and was not easily induced to a reconciliation; and yet there were some examples of his receding in that particular; and in highest passion, he was so far from stooping to any dissimulation, whereby his displeasure might be concealed and covered till he had attained his revenge (the low method of courts), that he never endeavored to do any man an ill office, before he first told him what he was to expect from him, and reproached him with the injuries he had done, with so much generosity, that the person found it in his power to receive further satisfaction, in the way he would choose for himself.

And in this manner he proceeded with the Earl of Oxford, a man of great name in that time, and whom he had endeavored

by many civil offices to make his friend, and who seemed equally
to incline to the friendship: when he discovered (or, as many
thought, but suspected) that the earl was entered into some cabal
in Parliament against him; he could not be dissuaded by any
of his friends to whom he imparted his resolution; but meeting
the earl the next day, he took him aside, and after many reproaches for such and such ill offices he had done, and for breaking his word towards him, he told him, he would rely no longer
on his friendship, nor should he expect any farther friendship
from him, but, on the contrary, he would be for ever his enemy,
and do him all the mischief he could. The earl (who, as many
thought, had not been faulty towards him), was as great-
hearted as he, and thought the very suspecting him to be an
injury unpardonable, [and] without any reply to the particulars,
declared that he neither cared for his friendship nor feared his
hatred; and from thence avowedly entered into the conversation and confidence of those who were always awake to discover
and solicitous to pursue anything that might prove to his disadvantage; which was of evil consequence to the duke, the earl
being of the most ancient of the nobility, and a man of great
courage, and of a family which had in no time swerved from
its fidelity to the Crown.

Sir Francis Cottington, who was secretary to the Prince,
and not grown courtier enough to dissemble well his opinion,
had given the duke offence before the journey into Spain, as is
before touched upon, and improved that prejudice after his
coming thither, by disposing the Prince all he could to the
marriage of the Infanta; and by his behavior after his return in
justifying to King James, who had a very good opinion of him,
the sincerity of the Spaniard in the treaty of the marriage, that
they did in truth desire it, and were fully resolved to gratify His
Majesty in the business of the Palatinate, and only desired, in
the manner of it, to gratify the Emperor and the Duke of Bavaria
all he could, which would take up very little time. All
which being so contrary to the duke's positions and purposes,
his displeasure to Cottington was sufficiently manifest, and
King James was no sooner dead, and the new officers and orders
made, but the profits and privileges which had used to be continued to him who had been secretary, till some other promotion,
were all retrenched. And when he was one morning attending

in the privy lodgings, as he was accustomed to do, one of the secretaries of state came to him, and told him that it was the King's pleasure that he should no more presume to come into those rooms (which was the first instance he had received of the King's disfavor). And at the same instant the duke entered into that quarter, upon which Sir Francis Cottington addressed himself towards [him,] and desired he would give him leave to speak to him: upon which the duke inclining his ear, moved to a window from the company; and the other told him, that he received every day fresh marks of his severity; mentioned the message which had been then delivered to him, and desired only to know, whether it could not be in his power, by all dutiful application, and all possible service, to be restored to the good opinion his grace had once vouchsafed to have of him, and to be admitted to serve him? The duke heard him without the least commotion, and with a countenance serene enough, and then answered him, that he would deal very clearly with him; that it was utterly impossible to bring that to pass which he had proposed: that he was not only firmly resolved never to trust him, or to have to do with [him,] but that he was, and would be always, his declared enemy; and that he would do always whatever should be in his power to ruin and destroy him, and of this he might be most assured; without mentioning any particular ground for his so heightened displeasure.

The other very calmly replied to him (as he was master of an incomparable temper), that since he was resolved never to do him good, that he hoped, from his justice and generosity, that he would not suffer himself to gain by his loss; that he had laid out by his command so much money for jewels and pictures, which he had received: and that, in hope of his future favor, he had once presented a suit of hangings to him, which cost him £800, which he hoped he would cause to be restored to him, and that he would not let him be so great a loser by him. The duke answered, he was in the right; that he should the next morning go to Oliver (who was his receiver), and give him a particular account of all the money due to him, and he should presently pay him; which was done the next morning accordingly, without the least abatement of any of his demands. And he was so far reconciled to him before his death that being resolved to make a peace with Spain, to the end he might more vigorously pursue the war with France (to which his heart was most passionately fixed), he sent for Cottington to come to him, and after conference with him, told him the King would send him ambassador thither, and that he should attend him at Portsmouth for his despatch.

His single misfortune was (which indeed was productive of many greater) that he never made a noble and a worthy friendship with a man so near his equal that he would frankly advise him, for his honor and true interest, against the current, or rather the torrent, of his impetuous passions; which was partly the vice of the time, when the Court was not replenished with great choice of excellent men, and partly the vice of the persons who were most worthy to be applied to, and looked upon his youth and his obscurity as obligations upon him to gain their friendships by extraordinary application. Then his ascent was so quick that it seemed rather a flight than a growth, and he was such a darling of fortune that he was at the top before he was seen at the bottom, for the gradation of his titles was the effect, not cause, of his first promotion; and, as if he had been born a favorite, he was supreme the first month he came to Court; and it was want of confidence, not of credit, that he had not all at first which he obtained afterwards, never meeting with the least obstruction from his setting out till he was as great as he could be: so that he wanted dependants before he thought he could want coadjutors. Nor was he very fortunate in the election of those dependants, very few of his servants having been ever qualified enough to assist or advise him, and were intent only upon growing rich under [him], not upon their master's growing good as well as great: insomuch as he was throughout his fortune a much wiser man than any servant or friend he had.

Let the fault or misfortune be what or whence it will, it may very reasonably be believed that, if he had been blessed with one faithful friend, who had been qualified with wisdom and integrity, that great person would have committed as few faults, and done as transcendent worthy actions, as any man who shined in such a sphere in that age in Europe. For he was of an excellent nature, and of a capacity very capable of advice and counsel; he was in his nature just and candid, liberal, generous, and bountiful; nor was it ever known, that the temptation of money swayed him to do an unjust or unkind thing; and though he left a very great inheritance to his heirs, considering the vast fortune he inherited by his wife (the sole daughter and heir of Francis Earl of Rutland), he owed no part of it to his own industry or solicitation, but to the impatient humor of two kings his masters, who would make his fortune equal to his titles, and the one above other men as the other was; and he considered it no otherwise than as theirs, and left it at his death engaged for the Crown, almost to the value of it, as is touched upon before.

If he had an immoderate ambition, with which he was charged, and is a weed (if it be a weed) apt to grow in the best soils, it does not appear that it was in his nature, or that he brought it with him to the Court, but rather found it there, and was a garment necessary for that air; nor was it more in his power to be without promotion, and titles, and wealth, than for a healthy man to sit in the sun in the brightest dog-days, and remain without any warmth. He needed no ambition, who was so seated in the hearts of two such masters.

BOOK III

[THE FALL OF STRAFFORD]

DURING these perplexities, the Earl of Strafford, taking notice of the straits the King was in, the rage of the people still increasing (from whence he might expect a certain outrage and ruin, how constant soever the King continued to him); and, it may be, knowing of an undertaking (for such an undertaking there was) by a great person, who then had a command in the Tower, that if the King refused to pass the bill, to free the kingdom from the hazard it seemed to be in, he would cause his head to be strucken off in the Tower, writ a most pathetical letter to the King, full of acknowledgment of his favors, but lively presenting the dangers, which threatened himself and his posterity by his obstinacy in those favors; and therefore by many arguments conjuring him no longer to defer his assent to the bill, that so his death might free the kingdom from the many troubles it apprehended.

The delivery of this letter being quickly known, new arguments were applied; that this free consent of his own clearly absolved the King from any scruple that could remain with him; and so in the end they extorted from him to sign a commission to some lords to pass the bill, which was as valid as if he had signed it himself; though they comforted him even with that circumstance, that his own hand was not in it.

It may easily be said that, the freedom of the Parliament and his own negative voice being thus barbarously invaded, if His Majesty had, instead of passing that act, come to the House and dissolved the Parliament, or if he had withdrawn himself from that seditious city, and put himself in the head of his own army, much of the mischief which hath since happened would have been prevented. But whoever truly considers the state of affairs at that time: the prevalency of that faction in both Houses; the rage and fury of the people; the use that was made by the schismatical preachers (by whom all the orthodox were silenced) of the late protestation in their pulpits; the fears and jealousies they had infused into the minds of many sober men upon the discourse of the late plot; the constitution of the council-table, that there was not an honest man durst speak his conscience to the King, for fear of his ruin; and that those whom he thought most true to him betrayed him every hour, insomuch as his whispers in his bedchamber were instantly conveyed to those against whom those whispers were; so that he had very few men to whom he could breathe his conscience and complaint that were not suborned against him, or averse to his opinions: that, on the other side, if some expedient were not speedily found out to allay that frantic rage and combination in the people, there was reason enough to believe their impious hands would be lifted up against his own person, and (which he much more apprehended) against the person of his royal consort; and lastly, that (besides the difficulty of getting thither, except he would have gone alone) he had no ground to be very confident of his own army: I say, whoever sadly contemplates this will find cause to confess the part which the King had to act was not only harder than any prince, but than any private gentleman had been incumbent to; and that it is much easier, upon the accidents and occurrences which have since happened, to determine what was not to have been done, than at that time to have foreseen by what means to have freed himself from the labyrinth in which he was involved.

All things being thus transacted, to conclude the fate of this great person, he was on the twelfth day of May brought from the Tower of London (where he had been a prisoner near six months) to the scaffold on Tower Hill; where, with a composed, undaunted courage, he told the people he was come thither to satisfy them with his head; but that he much feared the reformation which was begun in blood would not prove so fortunate to the kingdom as they expected and he wished: and after great expressions of his devotion to the Church of England, and the Protestant religion established by law and professed in that Church, of his loyalty to the King, and affection to the peace and welfare of the kingdom, with marvelous tranquillity of mind he delivered his head to the block, where it was severed from his body at a blow: many of the standers by, who had not been over-charitable to him in his life, being much affected with the courage and Christianity of his death.

Thus fell the greatest subject in power, and little inferior to any in fortune, that was at that time in either of the three kingdoms; who could well remember the time when he led those people who then pursued him to his grave. He was a man of great parts and extraordinary endowments of nature, not unadorned with some addition of art and learning, though that again was more improved and illustrated by the other; for he had a readiness of conception, and sharpness of expression, which made his learning thought more than in truth it was. His first inclinations and addresses to the Court were only to establish his greatness in the country; where he apprehended some acts of power from the old Lord Savill, who had been his rival always there, and of late had strengthened himself by being made a Privy Councillor and officer at Court: but his first attempts were so prosperous, that he contented not himself with being secure from his power in the country, but rested not till he had bereaved him of all power and place in Court, and so sent him down, a most abject, disconsolate old man, to his country, where he was to have the superintendency over him too, by getting himself at that time made Lord President of the North. These successes, applied to a nature too elate and arrogant of itself, and a quicker progress into the greatest employments and trust, made him more transported with disdain of other men, and more contemning the forms of business, than happily he would have been if he had met with some interruptions in the beginning, and had passed in a more leisurely gradation to the office of a statesman.

He was, no doubt, of great observation, and a piercing judgment, both into things and persons; but his too good skill in persons made him judge the worse of things; for it was his misfortune to be of a time wherein very few wise men were equally employed with him, and scarce any (but the Lord Coventry, whose trust was more confined) whose faculties and abilities were equal to his, so that upon the matter he wholly relied upon himself, and, discerning many defects in most men, he too much neglected what they said or did. Of all his passions his pride was most predominant, which a moderate exercise of ill fortune might have corrected and reformed; and which was by the hand of heaven strangely punished, by bringing his destruction upon him by two things that he most despised, the people and Sir Harry Vane. In a word, the epitaph which Plutarch records that Silla wrote for himself, may not be unfitly applied to him, "that no man did ever pass him, either in doing good to his friends, or in doing mischief to his enemies"; for his acts of both kinds were most exemplar and notorious.

BOOK IV

[THE IMPEACHMENT AND ARREST OF THE FIVE MEMBERS]

IN THE afternoon of a day when the two Houses sat, Herbert, the King's Attorney, informed the House of Peers that he had somewhat to say to them from the King; and thereupon, having a paper in his hand, he said, that the King commanded him to accuse the Lord Kimbolton, a member of that House, and five gentlemen, who were all members of the House of Commons, of high treason; and that His Majesty had himself delivered him in writing several articles upon which he accused them; and thereupon he read in a paper these ensuing articles, by which the Lord Mandevill, Denzil Holles, Sir Arthur Hazlerigg, Mr. Pym, Mr. Hampden, and Mr. Strode, stood accused of high treason, for conspiring against the King and the Parliament.

Articles of high treason, and other misdemeanors, against the Lord Kimbolton, Mr. Pym, John Hampden, Denzil Holles, Sir Arthur Hazlerigg and William Strode, members of the House of Commons.

1. That they have traitorously endeavored to subvert the fundamental laws and government of this kingdom; and deprive

the King of his regal power; and to place on his subjects an arbitrary and tyrannical power.

2. That they have endeavored by many foul aspersions upon His Majesty and his government to alienate the affections of his people, and to make His Majesty odious to them.

3. That they have endeavored to draw His Majesty's late army to disobedience to His Majesty's command, and to side with them in their traitorous design.

4. That they have traitorously invited and encouraged a foreign power to invade His Majesty's kingdom of England.

5. That they have traitorously endeavored to subvert the very rights and beings of Parliament.

6. That, for the completing of their traitorous designs, they have endeavored, as far as in them lay, by force and terror to compel the Parliament to join with them in their traitorous designs, and to that end have actually raised and countenanced tumults against the King and Parliament.

7. That they have traitorously conspired to levy, and actually have levied, war against the King.

The House of Peers was somewhat appalled at this alarum, but took time to consider of it till the next day, that they might see how their masters the Commons would behave themselves; the Lord Kimbolton being present in the House, and making great professions of his innocence, and no lord being so hardy [as] to press for his commitment on the behalf of the King.

At the same time, a sergeant-at-arms demanded to be heard at the House of Commons from the King, and, being sent for to the bar, demanded the persons of the five members to be delivered to him in His Majesty's name, His Majesty having accused them of high treason. But the Commons were not so much surprised with the accident; for besides that they quickly knew what had passed with the Lords, some servants of the King's, by special warrant, had visited the lodgings of some of the accused members, and sealed up their studies and trunks; upon information whereof, before the sergeant came to the House, or public notice was taken of the accusation, an order was made by the Commons: "That if any person whatsoever should come to the lodgings of any member of that House, and there offer to seal the doors, trunks, or papers of such members, or to seize upon their persons, that then such member should require

the aid of the next constable, to keep such persons in safe custody
till the House should give further order: that if any person whatsoever should offer to arrest or detain any member of that House,
without first acquainting that House therewith and receiving further order from thence, that it should be lawful for such member
to stand upon his guard, and make resistance, and [for] any person
to assist him, according to the protestation taken to defend the
privileges of Parliament." And so, when the sergeant had delivered his message, he was no more called in; but a message sent
to the King, "that the members should be forthcoming as soon
as a legal charge should be preferred against them"; and so the
House adjourned till the next day, every one of the accused
persons taking a copy of that order, which was made for their
security.

The next day in the afternoon, the King, attended only by
his own guard, and some few gentlemen who put themselves
into their company in the way, came to the House of Commons;
and commanding all his attendants to wait at the door, and to
give offence to no man, himself, with his nephew, the Prince
Elector, went into the House, to the great amazement of all:
and the Speaker leaving the chair, the King went into it, and
told the House, "He was sorry for that occasion of coming to
them; that yesterday he had sent his sergeant-at-arms to apprehend some that by his command were accused of high treason;
whereunto he expected obedience, but instead thereof he had
received a message. He declared to them, that no King of
England had been ever, or should be, more careful to maintain
their privileges than he would be; but that in cases of treason no
man had privilege; and therefore he came to see if any of those
persons whom he had accused were there; for he was resolved
to have them, wheresoever he should find them." And looking
then about, and asking the Speaker whether they were in the
House, and he making no answer, he said, "he perceived the
birds were all flown, but expected they should be sent to him
as soon as they returned thither"; and assured them in the word
of a King that he never intended any force, but would proceed
against them in a fair and legal way; and so returned to Whitehall; the accused persons, upon information and intelligence
what His Majesty intended to do, how secretly soever it was

carried at Court, having withdrawn from the House about half an hour before the King came thither.

The House, in great disorder, as soon as the King was gone adjourned till the next day in the afternoon; the Lords being in so great apprehension upon notice of the King's being at the House of Commons, that the Earl of Essex expressed a tender sense he had of the inconveniences which were like to ensue those divisions; and moved, "that the House of Peers, as a work very proper for them, would interpose between the King and his people, and mediate to His Majesty on the behalf of the persons accused"; for which he was reprehended by his friends, and afterwards laughed at himself, when he found how much a stronger defence they had than the best mediation could prove on their behalf.

How secretly soever this affair was carried, it was evident that the coming of the King to the House was discovered, by the members withdrawing themselves, and by a composedness which appeared in the countenances of many who used to be disturbed at less surprising occurrences; and though the purpose of accusing the members was only consulted between the King and the Lord Digby, yet it was generally believed that the King's purpose of going to the House was communicated to William Murry of the bedchamber, with whom the Lord Digby had great friendship, and that it was betrayed by him. And that Lord who had promised the King to move the House for the commitment of the Lord Kimbolton, as soon as the Attorney-General should have accused him (which if he had done would probably have raised a very hot dispute in the House, where many would have joined with him), never spake the least word; but, on the contrary, seemed the most surprised and perplexed with the Attorney's impeachment; and sitting at that time next to the Lord Mandevill, with whom he pretended to live with much friendship, he whispered him in the ear with some commotion (as he had a rare talent in dissimulation), "that the King was very mischievously advised, and that it should go very hard but he would know whence that counsel proceeded; in order to which, and to prevent further mischief, he would go immediately to His Majesty"; and so went out of the House; whereas he was the only person who gave the counsel, named the persons, and particularly named the Lord Mandevill (against whom less could be said than against many others, and who was more generally beloved), and undertook to prove that he bade the rabble, when they were about the Parliament House, that they should go to Whitehall.

And when he found the ill success of the impeachment in both Houses, and how unsatisfied all were with the proceeding, he advised the King the next morning to go to the Guildhall, and to inform the mayor and aldermen of the grounds of his proceeding; which will be mentioned anon. And that people might not believe that there was any dejection of mind or sorrow for what was done, the same night the same counsel caused a proclamation to be prepared for the stopping the ports, that the accused persons might not escape out of the kingdom, and to forbid all persons to receive and harbor them: when it was well known, that they were all together in a house in the city, without any fear of their security. And all this was done without the least communication with anybody but the Lord Digby, who advised it, and, it is very true, was so willing to take the utmost hazard upon himself, that he did offer the King, when he knew in what house they were together, with a select company of gentlemen, who would accompany him, whereof Sir Thomas Lunsford was one, to seize upon them, and bring them away alive or leave them dead in the place: but the King liked not such enterprises.

That night the persons accused removed themselves into their stronghold, the city: not that they durst not venture themselves at their old lodgings, for no man would have presumed to trouble them, but that the city might see that they relied upon that place for a sanctuary of their privileges against violence and oppression; and so might put on an early concernment for them. And they were not disappointed; for, in spite of all the lord mayor could do to compose their distempers (who, like a very wise and stout magistrate, bestirred himself), the city was that whole night in arms; some people, designed to that purpose, running from one gate to another, and crying out that the Cavaliers were coming to fire the city; and some saying that the King himself was in the head of them.

The next morning the King, being informed of much that had passed that night, according to the advice he had received, sent to the lord mayor to call a Common Council immediately; and about ten of the clock, himself, attended only by three or four lords, went to the Guildhall; and in the room where the people were assembled, told them "he was very sorry to hear of the apprehensions they had entertained of danger; that he was come to them to show how much he relied upon their affections for his security and guard, having brought no other with him; that he had accused certain men of high treason, against whom he would proceed in a legal way; and therefore he presumed they would not shelter them in the city." And using many other very gracious expressions of his value of them, and telling one of the sheriffs (who was of the two thought less inclined to his service) that he would dine with him, he departed, without that applause and cheerfulness which he might have expected from the extraordinary grace he vouchsafed to them, and, in his passage through the city, the rude people flocking together, and crying out, "Privilege of Parliament, privilege of Parliament," some of them pressing very near his own coach, and amongst the rest one calling out with a very loud voice, "To your tents, O Israel." However the King, though much mortified, continued his resolution, taking little notice of the distempers; and, having dined at the sheriff's, returned in the afternoon to Whitehall; and published the next day a proclamation for the apprehension of all those whom he accused of high treason, forbidding any person to harbor them; the articles of their charge being likewise printed and dispersed.

BOOK VII

[CHARACTER OF HAMPDEN]

[MR. HAMPDEN] was a gentleman of a good family in Buckinghamshire, and born to a fair fortune, and of a most civil and affable deportment. In his entrance into the world he indulged to himself all the license in sports and exercises and company which was used by men of the most jolly conversation; afterwards he retired to a more reserved and melancholic society, yet preserving his own natural cheerfulness and vivacity, and above all a flowing courtesy to all men. Though they who conversed nearly with him, found him growing into a dislike of the ecclesiastical government of the Church, yet most believed it rather a dislike of some churchmen, and of some introducements of theirs which he apprehended might disquiet the public peace. He was rather of reputation in his own country, than of public discourse or fame in the kingdom before the business of ship-money; but then he grew the argument of all tongues, every man inquiring who and what he was, that durst at his own charge support the liberty and property of the kingdom, and rescue his country from being made a prey to the Court. His carriage throughout that agitation was with that rare temper and modesty, that they who watched him narrowly to find some advantage against his person, to make him less resolute in his cause, were compelled to give him a just testimony; and the judgment that was given against him infinitely more advanced him than the service for which it was given. When this Parliament began (being returned knight of the shire for the county where he lived), the eyes of all men were fixed on him as their *patriæ pater*, and the pilot that must steer their vessel through the tempests and rocks which threatened it. And I am persuaded his power and interest at that time was greater to do good or hurt than any man's in the kingdom, or than any man of his rank hath had in any time: for his reputation of honesty was universal, and his affections seemed so publicly guided that no corrupt or private ends could bias them.

He was of that rare affability and temper in debate, and of that seeming humility and submission of judgment, as if he brought no opinions with him, but a desire of information and instruction; yet he had so subtle a way of interrogating, and, under the notion of doubts, insinuating his objections, that he left his opinions with those from whom he pretended to learn and receive them. And even with them who were able to preserve themselves from his infusions, and discerned those opinions to be fixed in him with which they could not comply, he always left the character of an ingenious and conscientious person. He was indeed a very wise man, and of great parts, and possessed with the most absolute spirit of popularity, that is, the most absolute faculties to govern the people, of any man I ever knew. For the first year of the Parliament, he seemed rather to moderate and soften the violent and distempered humors than to inflame them. But wise and dispassioned men plainly discerned that that moderation proceeded from prudence, and observation that the season was not ripe, [rather] than that he approved of the moderation; and that he begat many opinions and motions, the education whereof he committed to other men, so far disguising his own designs, that he seemed seldom to wish more than was concluded; and in many gross conclusions, which would hereafter contribute to designs not yet set on foot, when he found them sufficiently backed by majority of voices, he would withdraw himself before the question, that he might seem not to consent to so much visible unreasonableness; which produced as great a doubt in some, as it did approbation in others, of his integrity. What combination soever had been originally with the Scots for the invasion of England, and what farther was entered into afterwards in favor of them, and to advance any alteration in Parliament, no man doubts was at least with the privity of this gentleman.

After he was amongst those members accused by the King of high treason, he was much altered, his nature and carriage seeming much fiercer than it did before. And without question, when he first drew his sword he threw away the scabbard; for he passionately opposed the overture made by the King for a treaty from Nottingham, and, as eminently, any expedients that might have produced an accommodation in this that was at Oxford; and was principally relied on to prevent any infusions which might be made into the Earl of Essex towards peace, or to render them ineffectual if they were made; and was indeed much more relied on by that party than the general himself. In the first entrance into the troubles, he undertook the command of a regiment of foot, and performed the duty of a colonel on all occasions most punctually. He was very temperate in diet, and a supreme governor over all his passions and affections, and had thereby a great power over other men's. He was of an industry and vigilance not to be tired out, or wearied by the most laborious, and of parts not to be imposed upon by the most subtle or sharp; and of a personal courage equal to his best parts; so that he was an enemy not to be wished wherever he might have been made a friend, and as much to be apprehended where he was so, as any man could deserve to be. And therefore his death was no less congratulated on the one party than it was condoled on the other. In a word, what was said of Cinna might well be applied to him: *Erat illi consilium ad facinus aptum, consilio autem neque lingua neque manus deerat;* "he had a head to contrive, and a tongue to persuade, and a hand to execute, any mischief." His death therefore seemed to be a great deliverance to the nation.[1]

[CHARACTER OF LORD FALKLAND]

BUT I must here take leave a little longer to discontinue this narration; and if the celebrating the memory of eminent and extraordinary persons, and transmitting their great virtues for the imitation of posterity, be one of the principal ends and duties of history, it will not be thought impertinent in this place to remember a loss which no time will suffer to be forgotten, and no success or good fortune could repair. In this unhappy battle was slain the Lord Viscount Falkland, a person of such prodigious parts of learning and knowledge, of that inimitable sweetness and delight in conversation, of so flowing and obliging a humanity and goodness to mankind, and of that primitive simplicity and integrity of life, that if there were no other brand upon this odious and accursed civil war than that single loss, it must be most infamous and execrable to all posterity.

Turpe mori, post te, solo non posse dolore.[2]

Before this Parliament his condition of life was so happy that it was hardly capable of improvement. Before he came to twenty years of age, he was master of a noble fortune, which descended to him by the gift of a grandfather, without passing through his father or mother, who were then both alive and not well enough contented to find themselves passed by in the descent. His education for some years had been in Ireland, where his father was lord deputy; so that, when he returned into England, to the possession of his fortune, he was unentangled with any acquaintance or friends, which usually grow up by the custom of conversation, and therefore was to make a pure election of his company; which he chose by other rules than were prescribed to the young nobility of that time. And it cannot be denied, though he admitted some few to his friendship for the agree-

---

[1] This last sentence was written later than the rest of the character. (D. Nichol Smith, *Characters of the Seventeenth Century*, p. 286.)

[2] It is shameful if I cannot die of grief alone, when you are dead.

ableness of their natures, and their undoubted affection to him, that his familiarity and friendship for the most part was with men of the most eminent and sublime parts, and of untouched reputation in point of integrity; and such men had a title to his bosom.

He was a great cherisher of wit, and fancy, and good parts in any man; and, if he found them clouded with poverty or want, a most liberal and bountiful patron towards them, even above his fortune; of which in those administrations he was such a dispenser, as, if he had been trusted with it to such uses, and if there had been the least of vice in his expense, he might have been thought too prodigal. He was constant and pertinacious in whatsoever he resolved to do, and not to be wearied by any pains that were necessary to that end, and therefore having once resolved not to see London (which he loved above all places) till he had perfectly learned the Greek tongue, he went to his own house in the country, and pursued it with that indefatigable industry that it will not be believed in how short a time he was master of it, and accurately read all the Greek historians.

In this time, his house being within ten miles of Oxford, he contracted familiarity and friendship with the most polite and accurate men of that university; who found such an immenseness of wit, and such a solidity of judgment in him, so infinite a fancy bound in by a most logical ratiocination, such a vast knowledge, that he was not ignorant in anything, yet such an excessive humility, as if he had known nothing, that they frequently resorted, and dwelt with him, as in a college situated in a purer air; so that his house was a university bound in a lesser volume, whither they came not so much for repose as study; and to examine and refine those grosser propositions which laziness and consent made current in vulgar conversation.

Many attempts were made upon him by the instigation of his mother (who was a lady of another persuasion in religion, and of a most masculine understanding, allayed with the passion and infirmities of her own sex) to pervert him in his piety to the Church of England and to reconcile him to that of Rome, which they prosecuted with the more confidence, because he declined no opportunity or occasion of conference with those of that religion, whether priests or laics; having diligently studied the controversies, and exactly read all, or the choicest of the Greek and Latin fathers, and having a memory so stupendous, that he remembered on all occasions whatsoever he read. And he was so great an enemy to that passion and uncharitableness which he saw produced by difference of opinion in matters of religion, that in all those disputations with priests and others of the Roman Church, he affected to manifest all possible civility to their persons, and estimation of their parts; which made them retain still some hope of his reduction, even when they had given over offering farther reasons to him to that purpose. But this charity towards them was much lessened, and any correspondence with them quite declined, when by sinister arts they had corrupted his two younger brothers, being both children, and stolen them from his house and transported them beyond seas, and perverted his sisters; upon which occasion he writ two large discourses against the principal positions of that religion, with that sharpness of style, and full weight of reason, that the Church is deprived of great jewels in the concealment of them, and that they are not published to the world.

He was superior to all those passions and affections which attend vulgar minds, and was guilty of no other ambition than of knowledge, and to be reputed a lover of all good men; and that made him too much a contemner of those arts which must be indulged in the transaction of human affairs. In the last short Parliament, he was a burgess in the House of Commons; and, from the debates, which were then managed with all imaginable gravity and sobriety, he contracted such a reverence to parliaments, that he thought it really impossible they could ever produce mischief or inconvenience to the kingdom, or that the kingdom could be tolerably happy in the intermission of them. And from the unhappy and unseasonable dissolution of that convention, he harbored, it may be, some jealousy and prejudice of the Court, towards which he was not before immoderately inclined; his father having wasted a full fortune there, in those offices and employments by which other men use to obtain a greater. He was chosen again this Parliament to serve in the same place, and, in the beginning of it, declared himself very sharply and severely against those exorbitances which had been most grievous to the state; for he was so rigid an observer of established laws and rules that he could not endure the least breach or deviation from them, and thought no mischief so intolerable as the presumption of ministers of state to break positive rules for reasons of state, or judges to transgress known laws, upon the title of conveniency or necessity, which made him so severe against the Earl of Strafford and the Lord Finch, contrary to his natural gentleness and temper; insomuch as they who did not know his composition to be as free from revenge as it was from pride, thought that the sharpness to the former might proceed from the memory of some unkindnesses, not without a mixture of injustice, from him towards his father. But without doubt he was free from those temptations, and was only misled by the authority of those who, he believed, understood the laws perfectly, of which himself was utterly ignorant; and if the assumption, which was scarce controverted, had been true, that an endeavor to overthrow the fundamental laws of the kingdom had been treason, a strict understanding might make reasonable conclusions, to satisfy his own judgment, from the exorbitant parts of their several charges.

The great opinion he had of the uprightness and integrity of those persons who appeared most active, especially of Mr. Hampden, kept him longer from suspecting any design against the peace of the kingdom; and though he differed from them commonly in conclusions, he believed long their purposes were honest. When he grew better informed what was law, and discerned in them a desire to control that law by a vote of one or both Houses, no man more opposed those attempts, and gave the adverse party more trouble by reason and argumentation, insomuch as he was, by degrees, looked upon as an advocate for the Court, to which he contributed so little, that he declined those addresses, and even those invitations, which he was obliged almost by civility to entertain. And he was so jealous of the least imagination that he should incline to preferment, that he affected even a morosity to the Court, and to the courtiers; and left nothing undone which might prevent and divert the King's or Queen's favor towards him, but the deserving it. For when the King sent for him once or twice to speak with him, and to give him thanks for his excellent comportment in those councils, which His Majesty graciously termed "doing him service," his answers were more negligent and less satisfactory, than might be expected; as if he cared only that his actions should be just, not that they should be acceptable, and that His Majesty should think that

they proceeded only from the impulsion of conscience, without
any sympathy in his affections; which, from a stoical and sullen
nature, might not have been misinterpreted, yet, from a person
of so perfect a habit of generous and obsequious compliance with
all good men, might very well have been interpreted by the King
as more than an ordinary averseness to his service; so that he
took more pains, and more forced his nature to actions unagree-
able and unpleasant to it, that he might not be thought to incline
to the Court, than any man hath done to procure an office there.
And if anything but not doing his duty could have kept him
from receiving a testimony of the King's grace and trust at that
time, he had not been called to his council; not that he was in
truth averse to the Court or from receiving public employment;
for he had a great devotion to the King's person, and had before
used some small endeavor to be recommended to him for a
foreign negotiation, and had once a desire to be sent ambassador
into France; but he abhorred an imagination or doubt should
sink into the thoughts of any man that, in the discharge of his
trust and duty in Parliament, he had any bias to the Court, or
that the King himself should apprehend that he looked for a reward for being honest.

For this reason, when he heard it first whispered that the
King had a purpose to make him a councillor, for which there
was in the beginning no other ground but because he was known
sufficient (*haud semper errat fama, aliquando et eligit*),[1] he resolved to decline it, and at last suffered himself only to be over-
ruled by the advice and persuasions of his friends to submit
to it. Afterwards, when he found that the King intended to
make him his secretary of state, he was positive to refuse it; declaring to his friends that he was most unfit for it, and that he
must either do that which would be great disquiet to his own
nature or leave that undone which was most necessary to be
done by one that was honored with that place, for that the most
just and honest men did every day that which he could not give
himself leave to do. And indeed he was so exact and strict an
observer of justice and truth, *ad amussim*,[2] that he believed those
necessary condescensions and applications to the weakness of

---

[1]Rumor does not always err; sometimes it even chooses rightly.

[2]By the carpenter's rule (precisely).

other men, and those arts and insinuations which are necessary for discoveries and prevention of ill, would be in him a declension from the rule which he acknowledged fit and absolutely necessary to be practised in those employments; and was, in truth, so precise in the practic principles he prescribed to himself (to all others he was as indulgent), as if he had lived *in republica Platonis, non in fæce Romuli.*[1]

Two reasons prevailed with him to receive the seals, and but for those he had resolutely avoided them: the first, the consideration that it might bring some blemish upon the King's affairs, and that men would have believed that he had refused so great an honor and trust, because he must have been with it obliged to do somewhat else not justifiable. And this he made matter of conscience, since he knew the King made choice of him before other men especially because he thought him more honest than other men. The other was, lest he might be thought to avoid it out of fear to do an ungracious thing to the House of Commons, who were sorely troubled at the displacing Sir Harry Vane, whom they looked upon as removed for having done them those offices they stood in need of; and the disdain of so popular an incumbrance wrought upon him next to the other. For as he had a full appetite of fame by just and generous actions, so he had an equal contempt of it by any servile expedients; and he so much the more consented to and approved the justice upon Sir Harry Vane, in his own private judgment, by how much he surpassed most men in the religious observation of a trust, the violation whereof he would not admit of any excuse for.

For these reasons he submitted to the King's command, and became his secretary, with as humble and devout an acknowledgment of the greatness of the obligation as could be expressed, and as true a sense of it in his heart. Yet two things he could never bring himself to whilst he continued in that office, that was, to his death; for which he was contented to be reproached, as for omissions in a most necessary part of his place: the one, employing of spies, or giving any countenance or entertainment to them; I do not mean such emissaries as with danger would venture to view the enemy's camp, and bring intelligence of their number or quartering, or such generals as such an observation

---

[1] In Plato's ideal state, not here in degenerate Rome.

can comprehend, but those, who by communication of guilt, or dissimulation of manners, wound themselves into such trusts and secrets as enabled them to make discoveries for the benefit of the state; the other, the liberty of opening letters, upon a suspicion that they might contain matter of dangerous consequence. For the first, he would say, such instruments must be void of all ingenuity, and common honesty, before they could be of use, and afterwards they could never be fit to be credited; and that no single preservation could be worth so general a wound and corruption of human society as the cherishing such persons would carry with it. The last, he thought such a violation of the law of nature, that no qualification by office could justify a single person in the trespass; and though he was convinced by the necessity and iniquity of the time that those advantages of information were not to be declined, and were necessarily to be practised, he found means to shift it from himself, when he confessed he needed excuse and pardon for the omission; so unwilling he was to resign anything in his nature to an obligation in his office. In all other particulars he filled his place plentifully, being sufficiently versed in languages to understand any that is used in business, and to make himself again understood. To speak of his integrity and his high disdain of any bait that might seem to look towards corruption, *in tanto viro, injuria virtutum fuerit.*[1]

Some sharp expressions he used against the Archbishop of Canterbury, and his concurring in the first bill to take away the votes of bishops in the House of Peers, gave occasion to some to believe, and opportunity to others to conclude and publish, that he was no friend to the Church, and the established government of it, and troubled his very friends much, who were more confident of the contrary than prepared to answer the allegations.

The truth is, he had unhappily contracted some prejudice to the Archbishop; and having only known him enough to observe his passion, when it may be multiplicity of business or other indisposition had possessed him, did wish him less entangled and engaged in the business of the Court or State; though, I speak it knowingly, he had a singular estimation and reverence

---

[1] In the case of so great a man, it would be an insult to his character.

of his great learning and confessed integrity, and really thought his letting himself to those expressions which implied a dis-esteem of him, or at least an acknowledgment of his infirmities, would enable him to shelter him from part of the storm he saw raised for his destruction, which he abominated with his soul.

The giving his consent to the first bill for the displacing the bishops did proceed from two grounds; the first, his not under-standing the original of their right and suffrage there; the other, an opinion that the combination against the whole government of the Church by bishops was so violent and furious, that a less composition than the dispensing with their intermeddling in secular affairs would not preserve the order. And he was persuaded to this by the profession of many persons of honor, who declared they did desire the one, and would then not press the other; which in that particular misled many men. But when his observation and experience made him discern more of their intentions, than he before suspected, with great frankness he opposed the second bill that was preferred for that purpose; and had, without scruple, the order itself in perfect reverence, and thought too great encouragement could not possibly be given to learning, nor too great rewards to learned men; and was never in the least degree swayed or moved by the objections which were made against that government, holding them most ridiculous, or affected to the other which those men fancied to themselves.

He had a courage of the most clear and keen temper, and so far from fear that he was not without appetite of danger; and therefore upon any occasion of action he always engaged his person in those troops, which he thought by the forwardness of the commanders, to be most like to be farthest engaged; and in all such encounters he had about him a strange cheerfulness and companiableness, without at all affecting the execution that was then principally to be attended, in which he took no delight, but took pains to prevent it, where it was not, by resistance, neces-sary; insomuch that at Edgehill, when the enemy was routed, he was like to have incurred great peril by interposing to save those who had thrown away their arms, and against whom it may be others were more fierce for their having thrown them away; insomuch as a man might think he came into the field only out of curiosity to see the face of danger, and charity to prevent the shedding of blood. Yet in his natural inclination he acknowledged he was addicted to the profession of a soldier; and shortly after he came to his fortune, and before he came to age, he went into the Low Countries with a resolution of procuring command, and to give himself up to it, from which he was converted by the complete inactivity of that summer; and so he returned into England, and shortly after entered upon that vehement course of study we mentioned before, till the first alarum from the north; and then again he made ready for the field, and though he received some repulse in the command of a troop of horse, of which he had a promise, he went a volunteer with the Earl of Essex.

From the entrance into this unnatural war, his natural cheerfulness and vivacity grew clouded, and a kind of sadness and dejection of spirit stole upon him, which he had never been used to; yet being one of those who believed that one battle would end all differences, and that there would be so great a victory on one side, that the other would be compelled to submit to any conditions from the victor (which supposition and conclusion, generally sunk into the minds of most men, prevented the looking after many advantages which might then have been laid hold of), he resisted those indispositions, *et in luctu bellum inter remedia erat*.[1]   But after the King's return from Brentford, and the furious resolution of the two Houses not to admit any treaty for peace, those indispositions, which had before touched him, grew into a perfect habit of uncheerfulness; and he, who had been so exactly unreserved and affable to all men that his face and countenance was always present and vacant to his company, and held any cloudiness and less pleasantness of the visage a kind of rudeness or incivility, became on a sudden less communicable, and thence very sad, pale, and exceedingly affected with the spleen.   In his clothes and habit, which he had intended before always with more neatness and industry and expense than is usual to so great a mind, he was not now only incurious, but too negligent; and in his reception of suitors, and the necessary or casual addresses to his place, so quick and sharp and severe, that there wanted not some men (who were

---

[1]And in his sorrow found some comfort in fighting.

strangers to his nature and disposition), who believed him proud and imperious, from which no mortal man was ever more free. The truth is, that as he was of a most incomparable gentleness, application, and even demissness and submission to good and worthy and entire men, so he was naturally (which could not but be more evident in his place, which objected him to another conversation and intermixture than his own election had done), *adversus malos injucundus*,[1] and was so ill a dissembler of his dislike and disinclination to ill men that it was not possible for such not to discern it. There was once in the House of Commons such a declared acceptation of the good service an eminent member had done to them, and, as they said, to the whole kingdom, that it was moved, he being present, that the Speaker might, in the name of the whole House, give him thanks, and then, that every member might, as a testimony of his particular acknowledgment, stir or move his hat towards him; the which (though not ordered) when very many did, the Lord Falkland (who believed the service itself not to be of that moment, and that an honorable and generous person could not have stooped to it for any recompense), instead of moving his hat stretched both his arms out and clasped his hands together upon the crown of his hat, and held it close down to his head; that all men might see how odious that flattery was to him, and the very approbation of the person, though at that time most popular.

When there was any overture or hope of peace, he would be more erect and vigorous, and exceedingly solicitous to press anything which he thought might promote it; and sitting amongst his friends, often, after a deep silence and frequent sighs, would, with a shrill and sad accent, ingeminate the word *Peace, Peace*; and would passionately profess, that the very agony of the war, and the view of the calamities and desolation the kingdom did and must endure, took his sleep from him, and would shortly break his heart. This made some think, or pretend to think, that he was so much enamored on peace, that he would have been glad the King should have bought it at any price, which was a most unreasonable calumny. As if a man, that was himself the most punctual and precise in every circumstance that might reflect upon conscience or honor, could have wished the King to

---

[1] Unpleasant toward the unworthy.

have committed a trespass against either. And yet this senseless scandal made some impression upon him, or at least he used it for an excuse of the daringness of his spirit; for at the leaguer before Gloucester, when his friends passionately reprehended him for exposing his person unnecessarily to danger (as he delighted to visit the trenches and nearest approaches, and to discover what the enemy did), as being so much beside the duty of his place, that it might be understood against it, he would say merrily, that his office could not take away the privileges of his age, and that a secretary in war might be present at the greatest secret of danger; but withal alleged seriously that it concerned him to be more active in enterprises of hazard than other men, that all might see that his impatiency for peace proceeded not from pusillanimity, or fear to adventure his own person.

In the morning, before the battle, as always upon action, he was very cheerful, and put himself into the first rank of the Lord Byron's regiment, who was then advancing upon the enemy, who had lined the hedges on both sides with musketeers; from whence he was shot with a musket on the lower part of the belly, and in the instant falling from his horse, his body was not found till the next morning; till when there was some hope he might have been a prisoner; though his nearest friends, who knew his temper, received small comfort from that imagination. Thus fell that incomparable young man, in the four and thirtieth year of his age, having so much despatched the business of life that the oldest rarely attain to that immense knowledge, and the youngest enter not into the world with more innocence; and whosoever leads such a life, need not care upon how short warning it be taken from him.

BIOGRAPHY

IZAAK WALTON (1593–1683)

Izaak Walton was born within a few months of the death of Marlowe and died five years before the birth of Pope, but his long life—he retired from business during the Civil War—contained few events, apart from the acquisition of friends and new tricks in angling. A peace-loving old man—one feels that he must have been born middle-aged, but with the innocence of youth—he had unshakeable reverence for Church and Crown. As a critic remarks, he "greatly loved the society of the clergy: he connected himself with Episcopal families, and he had a natural taste for a bishop." His *Life of Dr. John Donne*, prefixed to a collection of Donne's Sermons, first appeared in 1640; the *Life of Sir Henry Wotton* was issued in 1651, and the other three *Lives*—of Hooker, George Herbert, and Sanderson—came out at later intervals. Though Walton was not a "man of letters," his fresh, fragrant prose was no accident; he was a careful artist in words. His short biographies are inaccurate in detail and deficient in perspective, but their virtues of style and temper are obvious. Here, for instance, he does not dwell on the life of "Jack Donne," preferring "the noble pleasure of praising."

THE LIFE OF DR. JOHN DONNE[1]
(1640; *revised later*)

MASTER JOHN DONNE was born in London, in the year 1573, of good and virtuous parents: and, though his own learning and other multiplied merits may justly appear sufficient to dignify both himself and his posterity, yet the reader may be pleased to know that his father was masculinely and lineally descended from a very ancient family in Wales, where many of his name now live, that deserve and have great reputation in that country.

By his mother he was descended of the family of the famous and learned Sir Thomas More, sometime Lord Chancellor of

---

[1]Abridged.

England: as also, from that worthy and laborious Judge Rastell, who left posterity the vast statutes of the law of this nation most exactly abridged.

He had his first breeding in his father's house, where a private tutor had the care of him, until the tenth year of his age; and, in his eleventh year, was sent to the University of Oxford, having at that time a good command both of the French and Latin tongue. This, and some other of his remarkable abilities, made one then give this censure of him: that this age had brought forth another Picus Mirandula, of whom story says that he was rather born than made wise by study.

There he remained for some years in Hart Hall, having, for the advancement of his studies, tutors of several sciences to attend and instruct him, till time made him capable, and his learning expressed in public exercises declared him worthy to receive his first degree in the schools, which he forbore by advice from his friends, who, being for their religion of the Romish persuasion, were conscionably averse to some parts of the oath that is always tendered at those times, and not to be refused by those that expect the titulary honor of their studies.

About the fourteenth year of his age he was transplanted from Oxford to Cambridge, where, that he might receive nourishment from both soils, he stayed till his seventeenth year; all which time he was a most laborious student, often changing his studies, but endeavoring to take no degree, for the reasons formerly mentioned.

About the seventeenth year of his age he was removed to London, and then admitted into Lincoln's Inn, with an intent to study the law, where he gave great testimonies of his wit, his learning, and of his improvement in that profession; which never served him for other use than an ornament and self-satisfaction.

His father died before his admission into this society; and, being a merchant, left him his portion in money. (It was £3,000). His mother, and those to whose care he was committed, were watchful to improve his knowledge, and to that end appointed him tutors both in the mathematics, and in all the other liberal sciences, to attend him. But with these arts they were advised to instil into him particular principles of the Romish Church; of which those tutors professed, though secretly, themselves to be members.

They had almost obliged him to their faith; having for their advantage, besides many opportunities, the example of his dear and pious parents, which was a most powerful persuasion, and did work much upon him, as he professeth in his preface to his *Pseudo-Martyr*, a book of which the reader shall have some account in what follows.

He was now entered into the eighteenth year of his age; and at that time had betrothed himself to no religion that might give him any other denomination than a Christian. And reason and piety had both persuaded him that there could be no such sin as schism, if an adherence to some visible church were not necessary.

About the nineteenth year of his age, he, being then unresolved what religion to adhere to, and considering how much it concerned his soul to choose the most orthodox, did therefore—though his youth and health promised him a long life—to rectify all scruples that might concern that, presently lay aside all study of the law, and of all other sciences that might give him a denomination; and begun seriously to survey and consider the body of divinity, as it was then controverted betwixt the Reformed and the Roman Church. And, as God's blessed Spirit did then awaken him to the search, and in that industry did never forsake him—they be his own words[1]—so he calls the same Holy Spirit to witness this protestation; that in that disquisition and search he proceeded with humility and diffidence in himself, and by that which he took to be the safest way, namely, frequent prayers, and an indifferent affection to both parties; and, indeed, truth had too much light about her to be hid from so sharp an inquirer; and he had too much ingenuity not to acknowledge he had found her.

Being to undertake this search, he believed the Cardinal Bellarmine to be the best defender of the Roman cause, and therefore betook himself to the examination of his reasons. The cause was weighty, and wilful delays had been inexcusable both towards God and his own conscience: he therefore proceeded in this search with all moderate haste, and about the twentieth year of his age did show the then Dean of Gloucester—whose name my memory hath now lost—all the Cardinal's

---

[1] In his preface to *Pseudo-Martyr*.

works marked with many weighty observations under his own hand; which works were bequeathed by him, at his death, as a legacy to a most dear friend.

About a year following he resolved to travel: and the Earl of Essex going first the Cales, and after the Island voyages, the first *anno* 1596, the second 1597, he took the advantage of those opportunities, waited upon his lordship, and was an eye-witness of those happy and unhappy employments.

But he returned not back into England till he had stayed some years, first in Italy and then in Spain, where he made many useful observations of those countries, their laws and manner of government, and returned perfect in their languages.

The time that he spent in Spain was, at his first going into Italy, designed for traveling to the Holy Land, and for viewing Jerusalem and the sepulchre of our Savior. But at his being in the furthest parts of Italy, the disappointment of company, or of a safe convoy, or the uncertainty of returns of money into those remote parts, denied him that happiness, which he did often occasionally mention with a deploration.

Not long after his return into England, that exemplary pattern of gravity and wisdom, the Lord Ellesmere, then Keeper of the Great Seal, the Lord Chancellor of England, taking notice of his learning, languages, and other abilities, and much affecting his person and behavior, took him to be his chief secretary; supposing and intending it to be an introduction to some more weighty employment in the state; for which, his lordship did often protest, he thought him very fit.

Nor did his lordship, in this time of Master Donne's attendance upon him, account him to be so much his servant as to forget he was his friend; and, to testify it, did always use him with much courtesy, appointing him a place at his own table, to which he esteemed his company and discourse to be a great ornament.

He continued that employment for the space of five years, being daily useful, and not mercenary to his friends. During which time he—I dare not say unhappily—fell into such a liking, as—with her approbation—increased into a love, with a young gentlewoman that lived in that family, who was niece to the Lady Ellesmere, and daughter to Sir George More, then Chancellor of the Garter and Lieutenant of the Tower.

Sir George had some intimation of it, and, knowing prevention to be a great part of wisdom, did therefore remove her with much haste from that to his own house at Lothesley, in the county of Surrey; but too late, by reason of some faithful promises which were so interchangeably passed, as never to be violated by either party.

These promises were only known to themselves; and the friends of both parties used much diligence, and many arguments, to kill or cool their affections to each other; but in vain, for love is a flattering mischief, that hath denied aged and wise men a foresight of those evils that too often prove to be the children of that blind father; a passion that carries us to commit errors with as much ease as whirlwinds remove feathers, and begets in us an unwearied industry to the attainment of what we desire. And such an industry did, notwithstanding much watchfulness against it, bring them secretly together—I forbear to tell the manner how—and at last to a marriage too, without the allowance of those friends whose approbation always was, and ever will be necessary, to make even a virtuous love become lawful.

And that the knowledge of their marriage might not fall, like an unexpected tempest, on those that were unwilling to have it so; and that pre-apprehensions might make it the less enormous when it was known, it was purposely whispered into the ears of many that it was so, yet by none that could affirm it. But, to put a period to the jealousies of Sir George—doubt often begetting more restless thoughts than the certain knowledge of what we fear—the news was, in favor to Mr. Donne, and with his allowance, made known to Sir George, by his honorable friend and neighbor Henry, Earl of Northumberland; but it was to Sir George so immeasurably unwelcome, and so transported him that, as though his passion of anger and inconsideration might exceed theirs of love and error, he presently engaged his sister, the Lady Ellesmere, to join with him to procure her lord to discharge Mr. Donne of the place he held under his lordship. This request was followed with violence; and though Sir George were remembered that errors might be overpunished, and desired therefore to forbear till second considerations might clear some scruples, yet he became restless until his suit was granted and the punishment executed. And though the Lord Chancellor did not,

at Mr. Donne's dismission, give him such a commendation as
the great Emperor Charles the Fifth did of his Secretary Eraso,
when he presented him to his son and successor, Philip the
Second, saying, "That in his Eraso, he gave to him a greater
gift than all his estate, and all the kingdoms which he then re-
signed to him;" yet the Lord Chancellor said, "He parted with
a friend, and such a secretary as was fitter to serve a king than
a subject."

Immediately after his dismission from his service, he sent
a sad letter to his wife to acquaint her with it; and after the sub-
scription of his name, writ,

John Donne, Anne Donne, Un-done,

and God knows it proved too true. For this bitter physic of
Mr. Donne's dismission was not enough to purge out all Sir
George's choler, for he was not satisfied till Mr. Donne and his
sometime com-pupil in Cambridge that married him, namely,
Samuel Brooke (who was after Doctor in Divinity and Master
of Trinity College) and his brother Mr. Christopher Brooke,
sometime Mr. Donne's chamber-fellow in Lincoln's Inn, who
gave Mr. Donne his wife, and witnessed the marriage, were all
committed to three several prisons.

Mr. Donne was first enlarged, who neither gave rest to his
body or brain, nor to any friend in whom he might hope to have
an interest, until he had procured an enlargement for his two
imprisoned friends.

He was now at liberty, but his days were still cloudy; and,
being past these troubles, others did still multiply upon him;
for his wife was—to her extreme sorrow—detained from him;
and though, with Jacob, he endured not a hard service for her,
yet he lost a good one, and was forced to make good his title,
and to get possession of her by a long and restless suit in law,
which proved troublesome and sadly chargeable to him, whose
youth, and travel, and needless bounty, had brought his estate
into a narrow compass.

It is observed, and most truly, that silence and submission
are charming qualities, and work most upon passionate men;
and it proved so with Sir George; for these, and a general report
of Mr. Donne's merits, together with his winning behavior—

which, when it would entice, had a strange kind of elegant irresistible art—these, and time, had so dispassionated Sir George, that, as the world had approved his daughter's choice, so he also could not but see a more than ordinary merit in his new son; and this at last melted him into so much remorse—for love and anger are so like agues as to have hot and cold fits; and love in parents, though it may be quenched, yet is easily rekindled, and expires not till death denies mankind a natural heat—that he labored his son's restoration to his place; using to that end both his own and his sister's power to her lord; but with no success, for his answer was, "That though he was unfeignedly sorry for what he had done, yet it was inconsistent with his place and credit, to discharge and readmit servants at the request of passionate petitioners."

Sir George's endeavor for Mr. Donne's readmission was by all means to be kept secret—for men do more naturally reluct for errors than submit to put on those blemishes that attend their visible acknowledgment. But, however, it was not long before Sir George appeared to be so far reconciled as to wish their happiness, and not to deny them his paternal blessing, but yet refused to contribute any means that might conduce to their livelihood.

Mr. Donne's estate was the greatest part spent in many and chargeable travels, books, and dear-bought experience: he out of all employment that might yield a support for himself and wife, who had been curiously and plentifully educated; both their natures generous, and accustomed to confer, and not to receive, courtesies; these and other considerations, but chiefly that his wife was to bear a part in his sufferings, surrounded him with many sad thoughts, and some apparent apprehensions of want.

But his sorrows were lessened and his wants prevented by the seasonable courtesy of their noble kinsman, Sir Francis Wolly, of Pirford in Surrey, who entreated them to a cohabitation with him; where they remained with much freedom to themselves, and equal content to him, for some years; and as their charge increased—she had yearly a child—so did his love and bounty. . . .

At the hearing of this [Dr. Morton's appeal to him to enter the ministry], Mr. Donne's faint breath and perplexed countenance gave a visible testimony of an inward conflict; but he performed his promise, and departed without returning an answer till the third day, and then his answer was to this effect:

"My most worthy and most dear friend, since I saw you I have been faithful to my promise, and have also meditated much of your great kindness, which hath been such as would exceed even my gratitude; but that it cannot do; and more I cannot return you; and I do that with an heart full of humility and thanks, though I may not accept of your offer: but, sir, my refusal is not for that I think myself too good for that calling, for which kings, if they think so, are not good enough; nor for that my education and learning, though not eminent, may not, being assisted with God's grace and humility, render me in some measure fit for it: but I dare make so dear a friend as you are my confessor. Some irregularities of my life have been so visible to some men, that though I have, I thank God, made my peace with him by penitential resolutions against them, and by the assistance of his grace banished them my affections; yet this, which God knows to be so, is not so visible to man as to free me from their censures, and it may be that sacred calling from a dishonor. And besides, whereas it is determined by the best of casuists that God's glory should be the first end, and a maintenance the second motive to embrace that calling, and though each man may propose to himself both together, yet the first may not be put last without a violation of conscience, which he that searches the heart will judge. And truly my present condition is such that if I ask my own conscience whether it be reconcilable to that rule, it is at this time so perplexed about it, that I can neither give myself nor you an answer. . . ."

. . . Mr. Donne and his wife continued with Sir Francis Wolly till his death: a little before which time Sir Francis was so happy as to make a perfect reconciliation between Sir George and his forsaken son and daughter: Sir George conditioning by bond to pay to Mr. Donne £800 at a certain day, as a portion with his wife, or £20 quarterly for their maintenance, as the interest for it, till the said portion was paid.

Most of those years that he lived with Sir Francis he studied the Civil and Canon Laws; in which he acquired such a perfection, as was judged to hold proportion with many who had made that study the employment of their whole life.

Sir Francis being dead, and that happy family dissolved, Mr. Donne took for himself a house in Mitcham, near to Croydon in Surrey, a place noted for good air and choice company: there his wife and children remained; and for himself he took lodgings in London, near to Whitehall, whither his friends and occasions drew him very often, and where he was as often visited by many of the nobility and others of this nation, who used him in their counsels of greatest consideration, and with some rewards for his better subsistence. . . .

Thus he did bemoan himself; and thus in other letters:

"—For we hardly discover a sin when it is but an omission of some good, and no accusing act: with this or the former I have often suspected myself to be overtaken; which is, with an over-earnest desire of the next life: and, though I know it is not merely a weariness of this, because I had the same desire when I went with the tide, and enjoyed fairer hopes than I now do; yet I doubt worldly troubles have increased it; 'tis now spring, and all the pleasures of it displease me; every other tree blossoms, and I wither; I grow older, and not better; my strength diminisheth, and my load grows heavier; and yet I would fain be or do something, but that I cannot tell what is no wonder in this time of my sadness; for to choose is to do, but to be no part of any body is as to be nothing: and so I am, and shall so judge myself, unless I could be so incorporated into a part of the world as by business to contribute some sustentation to the whole. This I made account; I began early, when I understood the study of our laws; but was diverted by leaving that, and embracing the worst voluptuousness, an hydroptic immoderate desire of human learning and languages: beautiful ornaments indeed to men of great fortunes, but mine was grown so low as to need an occupation; which I thought I entered well into, when I subjected myself to such a service as I thought might exercise my poor abilities: and there I stumbled, and fell too; and now I am become so little, or such a nothing, that I am not a subject good enough for one of my own letters. . . . You would pity me now if you saw me write, for my pain hath drawn my head so much awry, and holds it so, that my eye cannot follow my pen. I therefore receive you into my prayers with mine own weary soul, and commend myself to yours. . . ."

By this you have seen a part of the picture of his narrow fortune, and the perplexities of his generous mind: and thus it continued with him for about two years, all which time his family remained constantly at Mitcham; and to which place he often retired himself, and destined some days to a constant study of some points of controversy betwixt the English and Roman Church, and especially those of supremacy and allegiance: and to that place and such studies he could willingly have wedded himself during his life; but the earnest persuasion of friends became at last to be so powerful as to cause the removal of himself and family to London, where Sir Robert Drury, a gentleman of a very noble estate, and a more liberal mind, assigned him and his wife an useful apartment in his own large house in Drury Lane, and not only rent-free, but was also a cherisher of his studies, and such a friend as sympathized with him and his in all their joy and sorrows.

At this time of Mr. Donne's and his wife's living in Sir Robert's house, the Lord Hay was by King James sent upon a glorious embassy to the then French King, Henry the Fourth; and Sir Robert put on a sudden resolution to accompany him to the French Court, and to be present at his audience there. And Sir Robert put on as sudden a resolution to solicit Mr. Donne to be his companion in that journey. And this desire was suddenly made known to his wife, who was then with child, and otherways under so dangerous a habit of body as to her health, that she professed an unwillingness to allow him any absence from her, saying, "Her divining soul boded her some ill in his absence"; and therefore desired him not to leave her. This made Mr. Donne lay aside all thoughts of the journey, and really to resolve against it. But Sir Robert became restless in his persuasions for it, and Mr. Donne was so generous as to think he had sold his liberty when he received so many charitable kindnesses from him, and told his wife so; who did therefore, with an unwilling willingness, give a faint consent to the journey, which was proposed to be but for two months; for about that time they determined their return. Within a few days after this resolve, the Ambassador, Sir Robert, and Mr. Donne, left London; and were the twelfth day got all safe to Paris. Two days after their arrival there, Mr. Donne was left alone in that room in which Sir Robert and he and some other friends had dined together. To this place Sir Robert returned within half an hour;

and as he left, so he found, Mr. Donne alone; but in such an ecstasy, and so altered as to his looks, as amazed Sir Robert to behold him; insomuch that he earnestly desired Mr. Donne to declare what had befallen him in the short time of his absence. To which Mr. Donne was not able to make a present answer; but, after a long and perplexed pause, did at last say, "I have seen a dreadful vision since I saw you: I have seen my dear wife pass twice by me through this room, with her hair hanging about her shoulders, and a dead child in her arms: this I have seen since I saw you." To which Sir Robert replied, "Sure, sir, you have slept since I saw you; and this is the result of some melancholy dream, which I desire you to forget, for you are now awake." To which Mr. Donne's reply was: "I cannot be surer that I now live than that I have not slept since I saw you: and am as sure that at her second appearing she stopped and looked me in the face, and vanished." Rest and sleep had not altered Mr. Donne's opinion the next day: for he then affirmed this vision with a more deliberate, and so confirmed a confidence, that he inclined Sir Robert to a faint belief that the vision was true. It is truly said that desire and doubt have no rest, and it proved so with Sir Robert; for he immediately sent a servant to Drury House, with a charge to hasten back and bring him word whether Mrs. Donne were alive, and, if alive, in what condition she was as to her health. The twelfth day the messenger returned with this account:—that he found and left Mrs. Donne very sad and sick in her bed; and that, after a long and dangerous labor, she had been delivered of a dead child. And, upon examination, the abortion proved to be the same day, and about the very hour that Mr. Donne affirmed he saw her pass by him in his chamber. . .

I return from my account of the vision to tell the reader that both before Mr. Donne's going into France, at his being there, and after his return, many of the nobility and others that were powerful at Court, were watchful and solicitous to the King for some secular employment for him. The King had formerly both known and put a value upon his company, and had also given him some hopes of a state employment; being always much pleased when Mr. Donne attended him, especially at his meals, where there were usually many deep discourses of general learning and very often friendly disputes or debates of religion be-

twixt His Majesty and those divines whose places required their
attendance on him at those times: particularly the Dean of the
Chapel, who then was Bishop Montague—the publisher of the
learned and eloquent works of His Majesty—and the most reverend Doctor Andrewes, the late learned Bishop of Winchester,
who was then the King's Almoner.

About this time there grew many disputes that concerned the
oath of supremacy and allegiance, in which the King had appeared, and engaged himself by his public writings now extant:
and His Majesty discoursing with Mr. Donne, concerning many
of the reasons which are usually urged against the taking of
those oaths, apprehended such a validity and clearness in his
stating the questions, and his answers to them, that His Majesty
commanded him to bestow some time in drawing the arguments
into a method, and then to write his answers to them; and, having done that, not to send, but be his own messenger, and bring
them to him. To this he presently and diligently applied himself, and within six weeks brought them to him under his own
handwriting, as they be now printed; the book bearing the name
of *Pseudo-Martyr*, printed *anno* 1610.

When the King had read and considered that book, he persuaded Mr. Donne to enter into the ministry; to which, at that
time, he was, and appeared, very unwilling, apprehending it—
such was his mistaken modesty—to be too weighty for his
abilities. . . .

Such strifes as these St. Austin had, when St. Ambrose
endeavored his conversion to Christianity; with which he confesseth he acquainted his friend Alipius. Our learned author—
a man fit to write after no mean copy—did the like. And declaring his intentions to his dear friend Dr. King, then
Bishop of London, a man famous in his generation, and no
stranger to Mr. Donne's abilities—for he had been chaplain to
the Lord Chancellor, at the time of Mr. Donne's being his lordship's secretary—that reverend man did receive the news with
much gladness; and, after some expressions of joy, and a persuasion to be constant in his pious purpose, he proceeded with all
convenient speed to ordain him first deacon, and then priest
not long after.

Now the English Church had gained a second St. Austin, for
I think none was so like him before his conversion, none so like

St. Ambrose after it: and if his youth had the infirmities of the one, his age had the excellencies of the other; the learning and holiness of both.

And now all his studies, which had been occasionally diffused, were all concentered in divinity. Now he had a new calling, new thoughts, and a new employment for his wit and eloquence. Now, all his earthly affections were changed into divine love, and all the faculties of his own soul were engaged in the conversion of others, in preaching the glad tidings of remission to repenting sinners, and peace to each troubled soul. . . .

Presently after he entered into his holy profession, the King sent for him, and made him his chaplain in ordinary, and promised to take a particular care for his preferment.

And, though his long familiarity with scholars and persons of greatest quality was such as might have given some men boldness enough to have preached to any eminent auditory, yet his modesty in this employment was such that he could not be persuaded to it, but went usually accompanied with some one friend to preach privately in some village not far from London, his first sermon being preached at Paddington. This he did, till His Majesty sent and appointed him a day to preach to him at Whitehall; and, though much were expected from him, both by His Majesty and others, yet he was so happy—which few are— as to satisfy and exceed their expectations: preaching the Word so, as showed his own heart was possessed with those very thoughts and joys that he labored to distil into others: a preacher in earnest; weeping sometimes for his auditory, sometimes with them; always preaching to himself like an angel from a cloud, but in none; carrying some, as St. Paul was, to heaven in holy raptures, and enticing others by a sacred art and courtship to amend their lives: here picturing a vice so as to make it ugly to those that practised it; and a virtue so as to make it beloved, even by those that loved it not; and all this with a most particular grace and an unexpressible addition of comeliness. . . .

Immediately after his return from Cambridge his wife died, leaving him a man of a narrow, unsettled estate, and—having buried five—the careful father of seven children then living, to whom he gave a voluntary assurance never to bring them under the subjection of a step-mother; which promise he kept most faithfully, burying with his tears all his earthly joys in his most dear and deserving wife's grave, and betook himself to a most retired and solitary life.

In this retiredness, which was often from the sight of his dearest friends, he became crucified to the world, and all those vanities, those imaginary pleasures, that are daily acted on that restless stage, and they were as perfectly crucified to him. . . .

His first motion from his house was to preach where his beloved wife lay buried (in St. Clement's Church, near Temple Bar, London), and his text was a part of the Prophet Jeremy's *Lamentation:* "Lo, I am the man that have seen affliction. . . ."

In this time of sadness he was importuned by the grave Benchers of Lincoln's Inn, who were once the companions and friends of his youth, to accept of their lecture, which, by reason of Dr. Gataker's removal from thence, was then void; of which he accepted, being most glad to renew his intermitted friendship with those whom he so much loved, and where he had been a Saul,—though not to persecute Christianity, or to deride it, yet in his irregular youth to neglect the visible practice of it,— there to become a Paul, and preach salvation to his beloved brethren. . . .

About a year after his return out of Germany, Dr. Carey was made Bishop of Exeter, and by his removal the deanery of St. Paul's being vacant, the King sent to Dr. Donne, and appointed him to attend him at dinner the next day. When His Majesty was sat down, before he had eat any meat, he said after his pleasant manner, "Dr. Donne, I have invited you to dinner; and, though you sit not down with me, yet I will carve to you of a dish that I know you love well; for, knowing you love London, I do therefore make you Dean of St. Paul's; and, when I have dined, then do you take your beloved dish home to your study, say grace there to yourself, and much good may it do you."

Immediately after he came to his deanery, he employed workmen to repair and beautify the chapel; suffering, as holy David once vowed, "his eyes and temples to take no rest till he had first beautified the house of God."

The next quarter following, when his father-in-law, Sir George More,—whom time had made a lover and admirer of him—came to pay to him the conditioned sum of twenty pounds, he refused to receive it; and said (as good Jacob did, when he heard his beloved son Joseph was alive, "It is enough"), "You have been kind to me and mine: I know your present condition is such as not to abound, and I hope mine is or will be such as not to need it: I will therefore receive no more from you upon that contract"; and in testimony of it freely gave him up his bond.

Immediately after his admission into his deanery the vicarage of St. Dunstan in the West, London, fell to him by the death of Dr. White, the advowson of it having been given to him long before by his honorable friend Richard Earl of Dorset, then the patron, and confirmed by his brother, the late deceased Edward, both of them men of much honor.

By these, and another ecclesiastical endowment which fell to him about the same time, given to him formerly by the Earl of Kent, he was enabled to become charitable to the poor, and kind to his friends, and to make such provision for his children, that they were not left scandalous as relating to their or his profession and quality.

The next Parliament, which was within that present year, he was chosen Prolocutor to the Convocation, and about that time was appointed by His Majesty, his most gracious master, to preach very many occasional sermons, as at St. Paul's Cross, and other places. All which employments he performed to the admiration of the representative body of the whole clergy of this nation. . . .

He was made dean in the fiftieth year of his age, and in his fifty-fourth year a dangerous sickness seized him, which inclined him to a consumption; but God, as Job thankfully acknowledged, preserved his spirit, and kept his intellectuals as clear and perfect as when that sickness first seized his body; but it continued long, and threatened him with death, which he dreaded not. . . .

Within a few days his distempers abated; and as his strength increased, so did his thankfulness to Almighty God, testified in his most excellent book of *Devotions*, which he published at his recovery; in which the reader may see the most secret thoughts that then possessed his soul, paraphrased and made public: a book that may not unfitly be called a sacred picture of spiritual ecstasies, occasioned and appliable to the emergencies of that sickness; which book, being a composition of meditations, disquisitions, and prayers, he writ on his sick-bed; herein imitating the holy patriarchs, who were wont to build their altars in that place where they had received their blessings.

This sickness brought him so near to the gates of death, and he saw the grave so ready to devour him, that he would often say his recovery was supernatural: but that God that then restored his health continued it to him till the fifty-ninth year of his life: and then, in August, 1630, being with his eldest daughter, Mrs. Harvey, at Abury Hatch, in Essex, he there fell into a fever, which, with the help of his constant infirmity—vapors from the spleen—hastened him into so visible a consumption that his beholders might say, as St. Paul of himself, "He dies daily"; and he might say with Job, "My welfare passeth away as a cloud, the days of my affliction have taken hold of me, and weary nights are appointed for me". . .

The recreations of his youth were poetry, in which he was so happy as if nature and all her varieties had been made only to exercise his sharp wit and high fancy; and in those pieces which were facetiously composed and carelessly scattered—most of them being written before the twentieth year of his age—it may appear by his choice metaphors that both nature and all the arts joined to assist him with their utmost skill.

It is a truth, that in his penitential years, viewing some of those pieces that had been loosely—God knows, too loosely—scattered in his youth, he wished they had been abortive, or so short-lived that his own eyes had witnessed their funerals; but, though he was no friend to them, he was not so fallen out with heavenly poetry, as to forsake that; no, not in his declining age; witnessed then by many divine sonnets, and other high, holy, and harmonious composures. Yea, even on his former sick-bed he wrote this heavenly hymn, expressing the great joy that then possessed his soul, in the assurance of God's favor to him when he composed it:—

AN HYMN

TO GOD THE FATHER

Wilt thou forgive that sin where I begun,
   Which was my sin, though it were done before?
Wilt thou forgive that sin through which I run,
   And do run still, though still I do deplore?
When thou hast done, thou hast not done,
             For I have more.

Wilt thou forgive that sin, which I have won
    Others to sin, and made my sin their door?
Wilt thou forgive that sin which I did shun
    A year or two:—but wallow'd in a score?
When thou hast done, thou has not done,
                        For I have more.

I have a sin of fear, that when I've spun
    My last thread, I shall perish on the shore;
But swear by thyself, that at my death thy Son
    Shall shine as he shines now, and heretofore;
And having done that, thou hast done,
                        I fear no more.

I have the rather mentioned this hymn, for that he caused it
to be set to a most grave and solemn tune, and to be often sung
to the organ by the choristers of St. Paul's Church, in his own
hearing; especially at the evening service, and at his return from
his customary devotions in that place, did occasionally say to a
friend, "The words of this hymn have restored to me the same
thoughts of joy that possessed my soul in my sickness, when I
composed it. And, O the power of church-music! that harmony
added to this hymn has raised the affections of my heart, and
quickened my graces of zeal and gratitude; and I observe that I
always return from paying this public duty of prayer and praise
to God, with an unexpressible tranquillity of mind, and a willingness to leave the world." . . .

The latter part of his life may be said to be a continued study;
for as he usually preached once a week, if not oftener, so after
his sermon he never gave his eyes rest till he had chosen out a
new text, and that night cast his sermon into a form, and his text
into divisions; and the next day betook himself to consult the
Fathers, and so commit his meditations to his memory, which
was excellent. But upon Saturday he usually gave himself and
his mind a rest from the weary burthen of his week's meditations,
and usually spent that day in visitation of friends, or some other
diversions of his thoughts; and would say, "that he gave both his
body and mind that refreshment, that he might be enabled to
do the work of the day following, not faintly, but with courage
and cheerfulness."

Nor was his age only so industrious, but in the most unsettled
days of his youth, his bed was not able to detain him beyond the

hour of four in a morning; and it was no common business that drew him out of his chamber till past ten; all which time was employed in study, though he took great liberty after it. And if this seem strange, it may gain a belief by the visible fruits of his labors, some of which remain as testimonies of what is here written: for he left the resultance of 1400 authors, most of them abridged and analyzed with his own hand: he left also six score of his sermons, all written with his own hand, also an exact and laborious treatise concerning self-murder, called *Biathanatos;* wherein all the laws violated by that act are diligently surveyed, and judiciously censured: a treatise written in his younger days, which alone might declare him then not only perfect in the Civil and Canon Law, but in many other such studies and arguments, as enter not into the consideration of many that labor to be thought great clerks, and pretend to know all things. . . .

Before that month ended, he was appointed to preach upon his old constant day, the first Friday in Lent: he had notice of it, and had in his sickness so prepared for that employment, that as he had long thirsted for it, so he resolved his weakness should not hinder his journey; he came therefore to London some few days before his appointed day of preaching. At his coming thither, many of his friends—who with sorrow saw his sickness had left him but so much flesh as did only cover his bones— doubted his strength to perform that task, and did therefore dissuade him from undertaking it, assuring him, however, it was like to shorten his life; but he passionately denied their requests, saying "he would not doubt that that God, who in so many weaknesses had assisted him with an unexpected strength, would now withdraw it in his last employment; professing an holy ambition to perform that sacred work." And when, to the amazement of some beholders, he appeared in the pulpit, many of them thought he presented himself not to preach mortification by a living voice, but mortality by a decayed body, and a dying face. And doubtless many did secretly ask that question in Ezekiel, "Do these bones live? or, can that soul organize that tongue, to speak so long time as the sand in that glass will move towards its centre, and measure out an hour of this dying man's unspent life? Doubtless it cannot." And yet, after some faint pauses in his zealous prayer, his strong desires enabled his weak body to discharge his memory of his preconceived meditations, which were of dying, the text being, "To God the Lord belong the issues from death." Many that then saw his tears, and heard his faint and hollow voice, professing they thought the text prophetically chosen, and that Dr. Donne had preached his own funeral sermon.

Being full of joy that God had enabled him to perform this desired duty, he hastened to his house; out of which he never moved, till, like St. Stephen, "he was carried by devout men to his grave."

The next day after his sermon, his strength being much wasted, and his spirits so spent as indisposed him to business or to talk, a friend that had often been a witness of his free and facetious discourse asked him, "Why are you sad?" To whom he replied with a countenance so full of cheerful gravity as gave testimony of an inward tranquillity of mind, and of a soul willing to take a farewell of this world, and said:—

"I am not sad, but most of the night past I have entertained myself with many thoughts of several friends that have left me here, and are gone to that place from which they shall not return; and that within a few days I also shall go hence, and be no more seen. And my preparation for this change is become my nightly meditation upon my bed, which my infirmities have now made restless to me. But at this present time, I was in a serious contemplation of the providence and goodness of God to me; to me, who am less than the least of his mercies: and looking back upon my life past, I now plainly see it was his hand that prevented me from all temporal employment; and that it was his will I should never settle nor thrive till I entered into the ministry; in which I have now lived almost twenty years—I hope to his glory,—and by which, I most humbly thank him, I have been enabled to requite most of those friends which showed me kindness when my fortune was very low, as God knows it was: and—as it hath occasioned the expression of my gratitude—I thank God most of them have stood in need of my requital. I have lived to be useful and comfortable to my good father-in-law, Sir George More, whose patience God hath been pleased to exercise with many temporal crosses; I have maintained my own mother, whom it hath pleased God, after a plentiful fortune in her younger days, to bring to great decay in her very old age. I have quieted the consciences of many that have groaned under the burden of a wounded spirit, whose prayers I hope are available for me. I cannot plead innocency of life, especially of my youth; but I am to be judged by a merciful God, who is not willing to see what I have done amiss. And though of myself I have nothing to present to him but sins and misery, yet I know he looks not upon me now as I am of myself, but as I am in my Savior, and hath given me, even at this present time, some testimonies by his Holy Spirit, that I am of the number of his elect: I am therefore full of inexpressible joy, and shall die in peace." . . .

A monument being resolved upon, Dr. Donne sent for a carver to make for him in wood the figure of an urn, giving him directions for the compass and height of it; and to bring with it a board of the just height of his body. "These being got, then without delay a choice painter was got to be in readiness to draw his picture, which was taken as followeth.—Several charcoal fires being first made in his large study, he brought with him into that place his winding-sheet in his hand, and having put off all his clothes, had this sheet put on him, and so tied with knots at his head and feet, and his hands so placed as dead bodies are usually fitted, to be shrouded and put into their coffin, or grave. Upon this urn he thus stood, with his eyes shut, and with so much of the sheet turned aside as might show his lean, pale, and death-like face, which was purposely turned towards the east, from whence he expected the second coming of his and our Savior Jesus." In this posture he was drawn at his just height; and when the picture was fully finished, he caused it to be set by his bedside, where it continued and became his hourly object till his death, and was then given to his dearest friend and executor Dr. Henry King, then chief Residentiary of St. Paul's, who caused him to be thus carved in one entire piece of white marble, as it now stands in that church. . . .

Upon Monday, after the drawing this picture, he took his last leave of his beloved study; and, being sensible of his hourly decay, retired himself to his bed-chamber; and that week sent at several times for many of his most considerable friends, with whom he took a solemn and deliberate farewell, commending to their considerations some sentences useful for the regulation of their lives; and then dismissed them, as good Jacob did his sons, with a spiritual benediction. The Sunday following, he appointed his servants, that if there were any business yet undone, that concerned him or themselves, it should be prepared against Saturday next; for after that day he would not mix his thoughts with any thing that concerned this world; nor ever did; but, as Job, so he "waited for the appointed day of his dissolution."

And now he was so happy as to have nothing to do but to die, to do which he stood in need of no longer time; for he had studied it long, and to so happy a perfection, that in a former sickness he called God to witness[1], "He was that minute ready to deliver his soul into his hands, if that minute God would determine his dissolution." In that sickness he begged of God the constancy to be preserved in that estate for ever; and his patient expectation to have his immortal soul disrobed from her garment of mortality makes me confident that he now had a modest assurance that his prayers were then heard, and his petition granted. He lay fifteen days earnestly expecting his hourly change; and in the last hour of his last day, as his body melted away, and vapored into spirit, his soul having, I verily believe, some revelation of the beatifical vision, he said, "I were miserable if I might not die;" and after those words, closed many periods of his faint breath by saying often, "Thy kingdom come, thy will be done." His speech, which had long been his ready and faithful servant, left him not till the last minute of his life, and then forsook him, not to serve another master—for who speaks like him—but died before him; for that it was then become useless to him, that now conversed with God on earth as angels are said to do in heaven, only by thoughts and looks. Being speechless, and seeing heaven by that illumination by which he saw it, he did, as St. Stephen, "look steadfastly into it, till he saw the Son of Man standing at the right hand of God his Father"; and being satisfied with this blessed sight, as his soul ascended, and his last breath departed from him, he closed his own eyes, and then disposed his hands and body into such a posture, as required not the least alteration by those that came to shroud him.

Thus variable, thus virtuous was the life; thus excellent, thus exemplary was the death of this memorable man.

---

[1]In his book of *Devotions* written then.

He was buried in that place of St. Paul's Church, which he had appointed for that use some years before his death; and by which he passed daily to pay his public devotions to Almighty God—who was then served twice a day by a public form of prayer and praises in that place; but he was not buried privately, though he desired it; for, beside an unnumbered number of others, many persons of nobility, and of eminence for learning, who did love and honor him in his life, did show it at his death, by a voluntary and sad attendance of his body to the grave, where nothing was so remarkable as a public sorrow. . . .

He was of stature moderately tall, of a straight and equally proportioned body, to which all his words and actions gave an unexpressible addition of comeliness.

The melancholy and pleasant humor were in him so contempered that each gave advantage to the other, and made his company one of the delights of mankind.

His fancy was unimitably high, equalled only by his great wit, both being made useful by a commanding judgment.

His aspect was cheerful, and such as gave a silent testimony of a clear knowing soul, and of a conscience at peace with itself.

His melting eye showed that he had a soft heart, full of noble compassion; of too brave a soul to offer injuries, and too much a Christian not to pardon them in others.

He did much contemplate—especially after he entered into his sacred calling—the mercies of Almighty God, the immortality of the soul, and the joys of heaven: and would often say in a kind of sacred ecstasy—"Blessed be God that he is God, only and divinely like himself."

He was by nature highly passionate, but more apt to reluct at the excesses of it. A great lover of the offices of humanity, and of so merciful a spirit that he never beheld the miseries of mankind without pity and relief.

He was earnest and unwearied in the search of knowledge, with which his vigorous soul is now satisfied, and employed in a continual praise of that God that first breathed it into his active body, that body which once was a temple of the Holy Ghost, and is now become a small quantity of Christian dust:—

But I shall see it re-animated.

THOMAS FULLER (1608–1661)

One "character" from this book has been reproduced above (p. 110), and two short biographies from the same work are given here. Paracelsus and Mr. Perkins have no special affinity, but Fuller is a born essayist and *raconteur* and nothing human is alien to him. His easy manner and lambent wit have always distressed the literal-minded—those whom Lamb would put in the Caledonian category—but many of his sayings are condensed essays. What could be more admirably critical than this, about the harshness of Scaliger's poems—"he rather snorted than slept on Parnassus," or the famous judgment on Sternhold and Hopkins, that they had drunk more of Jordan than of Helicon? Or more pleasing than that tribute to an invalid saint—"God, who denied her legs, gave her wings"? Or more quietly beautiful than this—"Mr. John Dod, who, in the midst of troublesome times, quietly withdrew himself to heaven"? And Fuller's works are strewn with these casual things. There were many noisier and more pretentious men than Fuller, but few wiser, and none more robustly charming.

THE HOLY AND PROFANE STATE (1642)

THE LIFE OF PARACELSUS

Philip Theophrastus Bombastus of Hoenhaim, or Paracelsus, born as he saith himself in the wilderness of Helvetia, *anno* 1493, of the noble and ancient family of the Hoenhaims. But Thomas Erastus, making strict enquiry after his pedigree, found none of his name or kindred in that place. Yet it is fit so great a chemist should make himself to be of noble extraction: and let us believe him to be of high descent, as perchance born on some mountain in Switzerland.

As for his education, he himself boasts that he lived in most universities of Europe; surely rather as a traveler than a student, and a vagrant than a traveler. Yea, some will not allow him so much, and one who hath exactly measured the length of his life, though crowding his pretended travels very close, finds not room enough for them. But 'tis too ridiculous what a scholar of his relates, that he lived ten years in Arabia to get learning, and conversed in Greece with the Athenian philosophers. Whereas in that age Arabia the Happy was accursed with barbarism, and Athens grown a stranger to herself; both which places being then subjected to the Turks, the very ruins of all learning were ruined there. Thus we see how he better knew to act his part than to lay his scene, and had not chronology enough to tell the clock of time, when and where to place his lies to make them like truth.

The first five and twenty years of his age he lived very civilly; being thirty years old he came to Basle, just at the alteration of religion, when many papists were expelled the University, and places rather wanted professors, than professors places. Here by the favor of Oecolampadius he was admitted to read physic, and for two years behaved himself fairly, till this accident caused his departure. A rich canon of Basle, being sick, promised Paracelsus an hundred florins to recover him, which, being restored to his health, he denied to pay. Paracelsus sues him, is cast in his suit, the magistrate adjudging him only an ordinary fee, because the cure was done presently with a few pills. The physician, enraged hereat, talked treason against the state in all his discourses, till the nimbleness of his tongue forced the nimbleness of his feet, and he was fain to fly into Alsatia. Here keeping company with the gentry of the country, he gave himself over to all licentiousness. His body was the sea wherein the tide of drunkenness was ever ebbing and flowing; for by putting his finger in his throat he used to spew out his drink and drunkenness together, and from that instant date himself sober to return to his cups again. Every month he had a new suit, not for pride but necessity; his apparel serving both for wearing and bedding: and having given his clothes many vomits, he gave them to the poor. Being Codrus over night, he would be Crœsus in the morning, flush of money as if he carried the invisible Indies in his pocket. Some suspected the devil was his pursebearer, and that he carried a spirit in the pommel of his sword, his constant companion, whilst others maintain that by the heat of the furnace he could ripen any metal into gold.

All the diet he prescribed his patients was this, to eat what, and how often, they thought fitting themselves, and yet he did most strange cures. Like the quicksilver he so much dealt with he would never be fixed in one place, or live anywhere longer than a twelvemonth: for some observe that by that time the maladies reverted again, which he formerly cured. He gave so strong physic as summoned nature with all her force to expel the present disease, but the remnant dregs thereof, afterwards reinforcing themselves, did assault nature, tired out with the violence of her former task, and easily subdued it.

His scholars brag that the fragments of his learning would feast all the philosophers in the world, boasting that the gout, the disgrace of physic, was the honor of Paracelsus, who by curing it removed that scandal from his profession: whereas others say he had little learning, and less Latin. When any asked him the name of an herb he knew not, he would tell them there was no use thereof in physic; and yet this man would undertake not only to cure men, but to cure the art of curing men, and reform physic itself.

As for his religion, it would as well pose himself as others to tell what it was. He boasted that shortly he would order Luther and the Pope, as well as he had done Galen and Hippocrates. He was never seen to pray, and seldom came to church. He was not only skilled in natural magic (the utmost bounds whereof border on the suburbs of hell), but is charged to converse constantly with familiars. Guilty he was of all vices but wantonness; and I find an honest man his compurgator, that he was not given to women; perchance he drank himself into wantonness and past it, quenching the fire of his lust by piling fuel too hard and fast upon it.

Boasting that he could make a man immortal, he himself died at forty-seven years in the city of Salzburg. His scholars say he was poisoned through the envy (that dark shadow ever waiting on a shining merit) and malice of his adversaries. However, his body should have been so fenced with antidotes that the battery of no poison might make a breach therein; except we impute it more to his neglect than want of skill, and that rather his own security than his enemies' malice brought him to his grave. But it may be he was willing to die, counting a twelvemonth's time enough to stay in one place, and forty-seven years long enough to live in one world. We may more admire that so beastly a drunkard lived so long, than that so skilful a man died so soon.   In a word, he boasted of more than he could do, did more cures seemingly than really, more cures really than lawfully; of more parts than learning, of more fame than parts; a better physician than a man, and a better chirurgeon than physician.

THE LIFE OF MR. PERKINS

WILLIAM PERKINS, born at Marston nigh Coventry in Warwickshire, was afterwards brought up in Christ College in Cambridge, where he so well profited in his studies that he got the grounds of all liberal arts, and in the 24. of Queen Elizabeth was chosen Fellow of that College, the same year wherein Doctor Andrew Willet (one of admirable industry), and Doctor Richard Clark (whose learned sermons commend him to posterity), were elected into the same society.

There goeth an uncontrolled tradition that Perkins, when a young scholar, was a great studier of magic, occasioned perchance by his skill in mathematics.   For ignorant people count all circles above their own sphere to be conjuring, and presently cry out those things are done by black art for which their dim eyes can see no color in reason.   And in such cases, when they cannot fly up to heaven to make it a miracle, they fetch it from hell to make it magic, though it may lawfully be done by natural causes.   True it is he was very wild in his youth, till God (the best chemic, who can fix quicksilver itself) graciously reclaimed him.

After his entrance into the ministry, the first beam he sent forth shined to those *which sat in darkness and the shadow of death*, I mean the prisoners in the castle of Cambridge, people (as generally in such places) living in England out of Christendom, wanting the means of their salvation, bound in their bodies, but too loose in their lives, yea, often branded in their flesh, and seared in their consciences.   Perkins prevailed so far with their jailer, that the prisoners were brought (fettered) to the shire-house hard by, where he preached unto them every Lord's day. Thus was the prison his parish, his own charity his patron presenting him unto it, and his work was all his wages.   Many an Onesimus here he begat, and, as the instrument, freed the prisoners from the captivity of sin.   When this began to be known, some of good quality of the neighboring parishes became his auditors, and counted it their feast to feed out of the prisoners' basket. Hence afterwards he became preacher of S. Andrew's parish in Cambridge, where he continued to the day of his death.

His sermons were not so plain but that the piously learned did admire them, nor so learned but that the plain did understand them. What was said of Socrates, that he first humbled the towering speculations of philosophers into practice and morality, so our Perkins brought the schools into the pulpit, and, unshelling their controversies out of their hard school-terms, made thereof plain and wholesome meat for his people. For he had a capacious head with angles winding and roomy enough to lodge all controversial intricacies; and, had not preaching diverted him from that way, he had no doubt attained to eminency therein. An excellent chirurgeon he was at jointing of a broken soul, and at stating of a doubtful conscience. And sure in case-divinity Protestants are defective. For (save that a smith or two of late have built them forges, and set up shop), we go down to our enemies to sharpen all our instruments, and are beholden to them for offensive and defensive weapons in cases of conscience.

He would pronounce the word *Damn* with such an emphasis as left a doleful echo in his auditors' ears a good while after. And when catechist of Christ College, in expounding the Commandments, applied them so home, able almost to make his hearers' hearts fall down, and hairs to stand upright. But in his older age he altered his voice, and remitted much of his former rigidness, often professing that to preach mercy was the proper office of the ministers of the gospel.

Some object that his doctrine, referring all to an absolute decree, hamstrings all industry, and cuts off the sinews of men's endeavors towards salvation. For, ascribing all to the wind of God's spirit (which bloweth where it listeth), he leaveth nothing to the oars of man's diligence, either to help or hinder to the attaining of happiness, but rather opens a wide door to licentious security. Were this the hardest objection against Perkins his doctrine, his own life was a sufficient answer thereunto, so pious, so spotless, that malice was afraid to bite at his credit, into which she knew her teeth could not enter.

He had a rare felicity in speedy reading of books, and as it were but turning them over would give an exact account of all considerables therein. So that, as it were, riding post through an author, he took strict notice of all passages, as if he had dwelt on them particularly; perusing books so speedily, one would think he read nothing; so accurately, one would think he read all.

He was of a cheerful nature and pleasant disposition: indeed to mere strangers he was reserved and close, suffering them to knock a good while before he would open himself unto them; but on the least acquaintance he was merry and very familiar.

Besides his assiduity in preaching he wrote many books, extant at this day. And pity it was, that he set not forth more of them himself; for though some of his orphan works lighted on good guardians, yet all were not so happy; and indeed no nurse for a child to the own mother.

He died in the 44. year of his age of a violent fit of the stone. It hath been reported that he died in the conflict of a troubled conscience; which admit were so, had been no wonder. For God sometimes seemingly leaves his saints when they leave the world, plunging them on their death-beds in deep temptations, and casting their souls down to hell, to rebound the higher to heaven. Besides, the devil is most busy on the last day of his term; and a tenant to be outed cares not what mischief he doth. But here was no such matter. Indeed he always cried out *Mercy, Mercy:* which some standers by misinterpreted for despair, as if he felt not God's favor, because he called for it: whereas mercy is a grace which they hold the fastest, that most catch after it. 'Tis true that many on less reason have expressed more confidence of their future happiness, and have delivered themselves in larger speeches concerning the same. But who could expect a long oration from him, where every word was accented with pain in so sharp a disease?

His funerals were solemnly and sumptuously performed of the sole charges of Christ College, which challenged, as she gave him his breeding, to pay for his burial; the university and town lovingly contending which should express more sorrow thereat. Doctor Montague, afterwards Bishop of Winchester, preached his funeral sermon, and excellently discharged the place, taking for his text, *Moses my servant is dead.*

He was of a ruddy complexion, very fat and corpulent, lame of his right hand; and yet this Ehud with a lefthanded pen did stab the Romish cause, and as one saith,

> *Dextera quantumvis fuerat tibi manca, docendi*
> *Pollebas mira dexteritate tamen.*

Though nature thee of thy right hand bereft,
Right well thou writest with thy hand that's left.

He was born the first, and died the last year of Queen Elizabeth, so that his life streamed in equal length with her reign, and they both had their fountains and falls together.

I must not forget how his books after his death were translated into most modern Christian languages. For though he excellently improved his talent in the English tongue, yet foreigners thought it but wrapped up in a napkin, whilst folded in an unknown language. Wherefore some translated the main body of his works into French, Dutch, and Italian; and his books speak more tongues, than the maker ever understood. His *Reformed Catholic* was done into Spanish, and no Spaniard ever since durst take up that gauntlet of defiance our champion cast down: yea, their Inquisition rather chose to answer it with tortures than arguments.

LORD HERBERT OF CHERBURY (1583-1648)

If one were to lapse into the easy vice of affixing labels one might call Lord Herbert the last Elizabethan. Arrogant toward equals, he risks his life to save his servant; philosopher and bragging duellist, author of a highly sceptical book, he awaits on his knees a sign from heaven to sanction its publication; half man, half child, with the vitality and the passions of both, Herbert belongs in many ways to the age of Raleigh and Essex. That hot temper, a family failing over which even his brother the poet was a little complacent, Lord Herbert "sublimated" into an extravagant conception of his knightly obligations, which he managed to reconcile with the no less extravagant conception of himself as a lover of peace. In fact, he was "like one of those fellows that when he enters the confines of a tavern claps me his sword upon the table and says, 'God send me no need of thee!' and by the operation of the second cup draws him on the drawer, when, indeed, there is no need." Yet he is a figure in the history of philosophy and deism. His *Autobiography* (which stops in 1624) was written about 1643, and first published by Horace Walpole in 1764.[1]

AUTOBIOGRAPHY

HAVING thus passed over all human literature, it will be fit to say something of moral virtues and theological learning. As for the first, since the Christians and the heathens are in a manner agreed concerning the definitions of virtues, it would not be inconvenient to begin with those definitions which Aristotle in his Morals hath given, as being confirmed for the most part by the Platonics, Stoics, and other philosophers, and in general by the Christian Church, as well as all nations in the world whatsoever; they being doctrines imprinted in the soul in its first original, and containing the principal and first notices

---

[1]The following extracts are taken by permission from *The Autobiography of Edward, Lord Herbert*, published and copyright by George Routledge & Sons, London, and E. P. Dutton & Co., Inc., New York.

by which man may attain his happiness here or hereafter; there being no man that is given to vice that doth not find much opposition both in his own conscience, and in the religion and law as taught elsewhere; and this I dare say, that a virtuous man may not only go securely through all the religions, but all the laws in the world, and, whatsoever obstructions he meet, obtain both an inward peace and outward welcome among all with whom he shall negotiate or converse; this virtue, therefore, I shall recommend to my posterity as the greatest perfection he can attain unto in this life, and the pledge of eternal happiness hereafter; there being none that can justly hope of an union with the supreme God, that doth not come as near to him in this life in virtue and goodness as he can; so that if human frailty do interrupt this union, by committing faults that make him incapable of his everlasting happiness, it will be fit, by a serious repentance, to expiate and emaculate those faults, and for the rest, trust to the mercy of God his Creator, Redeemer, and Preserver, who, being our Father, and knowing well in what a weak condition through infirmities we are, will, I doubt not, commiserate those transgressions we commit when they are done without desire to offend his divine majesty, and together rectify our understanding through his grace; since we commonly sin through no other cause but that we mistook a true good for that which was only apparent, and so were deceived, by making an undue election in the objects proposed to us; wherein, though it will be fit for every man to confess that he hath offended an infinite majesty and power, yet, as upon better consideration, he finds he did not mean infinitely to offend, there will be just reason to believe that God will not inflict an infinite punishment upon him if he be truly penitent, so that his justice may be satisfied, if not with man's repentance, yet at least with some temporal punishment here or hereafter, such as may be proportionable to the offence; though I cannot deny but when man would infinitely offend God in a despiteful and contemptuous way, it will be but just that he suffer an infinite punishment: but as I hope none are so wicked as to sin purposedly and with an high hand against the eternal majesty of God; so when they shall commit any sins out of frailty, I shall believe, either, that unless they be finally impenitent, and (as they say, sold ingeniously over to sin), God's mercy will accept of their endeavors to return into a right way, and so make their peace with him by all those good means that are possible. Having thus recommended the learning of moral philosophy and practice of virtue as the most necessary knowledge and useful exercise of man's life, I shall observe that even in the employing of our virtues discretion is required; for every virtue is not promiscuously to be used, but such only as is proper for the present occasion. Therefore, though a wary and discreet wisdom be most useful where no imminent danger appears, yet, where an enemy draweth his sword against you, you shall have most use of fortitude, prevention being too late when the danger is so pressing. On the other side, there is no occasion to use your fortitude against wrongs done by women or children, or ignorant persons, that I may say nothing of those that are much your superiors, who are magistrates, etc., since you might by a discreet wisdom have declined the injury, or when it were too late to do so, you may with more equal mind support that which is done, either by authority in the one, or frailty in the other. And certainly to such kind of persons forgiveness will be proper; in which kind I am confident no man of my time hath exceeded me; for though, whensoever my honor hath been engaged, no man hath ever been more forward to hazard his life, yet where with my honor I could forgive, I never used revenge, as leaving it always to God, who, the less I punish mine enemies, will inflict so much the more punishment on them; and to this forgiveness of others three considerations have especially invited me.

1. That he that cannot forgive others breaks the bridge over which he must pass himself, for every man hath need to be forgiven.

2. That when a man wants or comes short of an entire and accomplished virtue, our defects may be supplied this way, since the forgiving of evil deeds in others amounteth to no less than virtue in us; that therefore it may be not unaptly called the payment of our debts with another man's money.

3. That it is the most necessary and proper work of every man; for, though when I do not a just thing, or a charitable or a wise, another man may do it for me, yet no man can forgive my enemy but myself. And these have been the chief motives for which I have ever been inclined to forgiveness; whereof, though I have rarely found other effect than that my servants,

tenants, and neighbors have thereupon more frequently offended me, yet at least I have had within me an inward peace and comfort thereby; since I can truly say nothing ever gave my mind more ease than when I had forgiven my enemies, which freed me from many cares and perturbations, which otherwise would have molested me.

. . . .

About the year of our Lord 1600 I came to London, shortly after which the attempt of the Earl of Essex, related in our history, followed; which I had rather were seen in the writers of that argument than here. Not long after this curiosity, rather than ambition, brought me to court; and as it was the manner of those times for all men to kneel down before the great Queen Elizabeth, who then reigned, I was likewise upon my knees in the presence-chamber, when she passed by to the chapel at Whitehall. As soon as she saw me she stopped, and, swearing her usual oath, demanded, "Who is this?" Everybody there present looked upon me, but no man knew me, until Sir James Croft, a pensioner, finding the Queen stayed, returned back and told who I was, and that I had married Sir William Herbert of St. Julian's daughter. The Queen hereupon looked attentively upon me, and, swearing again her ordinary oath, said it is pity he was married so young, and thereupon gave her hand to kiss twice, both times gently clapping me on the cheek. I remember little more of myself but that, from that time until King James's coming to the crown, I had a son which died shortly afterwards, and that I attended my studies seriously; the more I learnt out of my books adding still a desire to know more.

King James being now acknowledged King, and coming towards London, I thought fit to meet His Majesty at Burleigh, near Stamford. Shortly after I was made Knight of the Bath, with the usual ceremonies belonging to that ancient order. I could tell how much my person was commended by the lords and ladies that came to see the solemnity then used; but I shall flatter myself too much if I believed it.

I must not forget yet the ancient custom, being that some principal person was to put on the right spur of those the King had appointed to receive that dignity. The Earl of Shrewsbury, seeing my esquire there with my spur in his hand, voluntarily came to me, and said, "Cousin, I believe you will be a good knight, and therefore I will put on your spur"; whereupon, after my most humble thanks for so great a favor, I held up my leg against the wall, and he put on my spur.

There is another custom likewise, that the knights the first day wear the gown of some religious order, and the night following to be bathed; after which they take an oath never to sit in place where injustice should be done, but they shall right it to the uttermost of their power; and particularly ladies and gentlewomen that shall be wronged in their honor, if they demand assistance, and many other points, not unlike the romances of knight errantry.

．　．　．　．　．　．　．　．

Passing two or three days here ["at the castle of Merlou, being about twenty-four miles from Paris"], it happened one evening that a daughter of the Duchess, of about ten or eleven years of age, going one evening from the castle to walk in the meadows, myself, with divers French gentlemen, attended her and some gentlewomen that were with her. This young lady wearing a knot of ribbon on her head, a French chevalier took it suddenly, and fastened it to his hatband. The young lady, offended herewith, demands her ribbon, but he refusing to restore it, the young lady, addressing herself to me, said, "Monsieur, I pray get my ribbon from that gentleman." Hereupon, going towards him, I courteously, with my hat in my hand, desired him to do me the honor that I may deliver the lady her ribbon or bouquet again; but he roughly answering me, "Do you think I will give it you, when I have refused it to her?" I replied, "Nay then, sir, I will make you restore it by force"; whereupon also, putting on my hat and reaching at his, he to save himself ran away, and, after a long course in the meadow, finding that I had almost overtook him, he turned short, and running to the young lady, was about to put the ribbon on her hand, when I, seizing upon his arm, said to the young lady, "It was I that gave it." "Pardon me," quoth she, "it is he that gives it me." I said then, "Madam, I will not contradict you; but if he dare say that I did not constrain him to give it, I will fight with him." The French gentleman answered nothing thereunto for the present, and so conducted the young lady again to the castle. The next day I desired Mr. Aurelian Townsend to tell the French cavalier that either he must confess that I constrained him to restore the ribbon, or fight with me; but the gentleman seeing him, unwilling to accept of this challenge, went out from the place, whereupon, I following him, some of the gentlemen that belonged to the Constable taking notice hereof, acquainted him therewith, who sending for the French cavalier, checked him well for his sauciness in taking the ribbon away from his grandchild, and afterwards bid him depart his house; and this was all that I ever heard of the gentleman, with whom I proceeded in that manner because I thought myself obliged thereunto by the oath taken when I was made Knight of the Bath, as I formerly related upon this occasion.

I must remember also that three other times I engaged myself to challenge men to fight with me who I conceived had injured ladies and gentlewomen. . . .

These passages, though different in time, I have related here together, both for the similitude of argument, and that it may appear how strictly I held myself to my oath of knighthood; since for the rest I can truly say that, though I have lived in the armies and courts of the greatest princes in Christendom, yet I never had quarrel with man for my own sake; so that, although in mine own nature I was ever choleric and hasty, yet I never without occasion quarreled with anybody, and as little did anybody attempt to give me offence, as having as clear a reputation for my courage as whosoever of my time. For my friends often I have hazarded myself; but never yet drew my sword for my own sake singly, as hating ever the doing of injury, contenting myself only to resent them when they were offered me. After this digression I shall return to my history.

. . . .

I can say little more memorable concerning myself from the year 1611, when I was hurt, until the year of our Lord 1614, than that I passed my time sometimes in the Court, where (I protest before God) I had more favors than I desired, and sometimes in the country, without any memorable accident; but only that it happened one time going from St. Julian's to

Abergavenny, in the way to Montgomery Castle, Richard
Griffiths, a servant of mine, being come near a bridge over Usk,
not far from the town, thought fit to water his horse, but the
river being deep and strong in that place where he entered it,
he was carried down the stream. My servants that were before
me seeing this, cried aloud Dick Griffiths was drowning, which I
no sooner heard but I put spurs to my horse, and coming up to
the place, where I saw him as high as his middle in water, leapt
into the river a little below him, and swimming up to him, bore
him up with one of my hands, and brought him unto the middle
of the river, where (through God's great providence), was a bank
of sand. Coming hither, not without some difficulty, we rested
ourselves, and advised whether it were better to return back
unto the side from whence we came, or to go on forwards; but
Dick Griffiths saying we were sure to swim if we returned back,
and that perchance the river might be shallow the other way, I
followed his counsel, and putting my horse below him, bore him
up in the manner I did formerly, and swimming through the river
brought him safe to the other side. The horse I rode upon I
remember cost me £40, and was the same horse which Sir John
Ayres hurt under me, and did swim excellently well, carrying
me and his back above water, whereas that little nag upon which
Richard Griffiths rid swam so low that he must needs have
drowned if I had not supported him.

.   .   .   .

From Venice, after some stay, I went to Florence, where I met
the Earl of Oxford and Sir Benjamin Rudyerd. Having seen
the rarities of this place likewise, and particularly that rare
chapel made for the house of Medici, beautified on all the inside
with a coarser kind of precious stone, as also that nail which was
at one end iron and the other gold, made so by virtue of a tincture into which it was put, I went to Siena, and from thence, a
little before the Christmas holidays, to Rome. I was no sooner
alighted at my inn, but I went straight to the English College,
where demanding for the regent or master thereof, a grave person not long after appeared at the door, to whom I spake in this
manner: "Sir, I need not tell you my country when you hear
my language; I come not here to study controversies, but to see
the antiquities of the place; if without scandal to the religion in

which I was born and bred up, I may take this liberty, I should be glad to spend some convenient time here; if not, my horse is yet unsaddled, and myself willing to go out of town." The answer returned by him to me was that he never heard anybody before me profess himself of any other religion than what was used in Rome; for his part, he approved much my freedom, as collecting thereby I was a person of honor; for the rest, that he could give me no warrant for my stay there, howbeit that experience did teach that those men who gave no affronts to the Roman Catholic religion received none; whereupon also he demanded my name. I telling him I was called Sir Edward Herbert, he replied that he had heard men oftentimes speak of me both for learning and courage, and presently invited me to dinner; I told him that I took his courteous offer as an argument of his affection; that I desired him to excuse me if I did not accept it; the uttermost liberty I had (as the times then were in England) being already taken in coming to that city only, lest they should think me a factious person; I thought fit to tell him that I conceived the points agreed upon on both sides are greater bonds of amity betwixt us than that the points disagreed on could break them; that for my part I loved everybody that was of a pious and virtuous life, and thought the errors on what side soever were more worthy pity than hate; and having declared myself thus far, I took my leave of him courteously, and spent about a month's time in seeing the antiquities of that place, which first found means to establish so great an empire over the persons of men, and afterwards over their consciences, the articles of confession and absolving sinners being a greater *arcanum imperii*[1] for governing the world than all the arts invented by statists formerly were.

.   .   .   .

The Queen, though she seemed very willing to hear me, yet handled the business so that Père Séguerend was together informed who had made this complaint against him, whereupon also he was so distempered that by one Monsieur Gaellac, a Provençal, his own countryman, he sent me this message; that he knew well who had accused him to Her Majesty, and that

---

[1]Secret of power.

he was sensible thereof; that he wished me to be assured that wheresoever I was in the world he would hinder my fortune. The answer I returned by Monsieur Gaellac was that nothing in all France but a friar or a woman durst have sent me such a message.

Shortly after this, coming again to the Queen-mother, I told her that what I said concerning Père Séguerend was spoken with a good intention, and that my words were now discovered to him in that manner that he sent me a very affronting message, adding, after a merry fashion, these words, that I thought Séguerend so malicious that his malice was beyond the malice of women: the Queen, being a little startled hereat, said, *A moy femme, et parler ainsi?*—"To me a woman, and say so?" I replied gently, *Je parle a vôtre majesté comme reyne, et non pas comme femme*—"I speak to Your Majesty as a queen, and not as a woman," and so took my leave of her. What Père Séguerend did afterwards, in way of performing his threat, I know not; but sure I am, that had I been ambitious of worldly greatness, I might have often remembered his words, though, as I ever loved my book and a private life, more than any busy preferments, I did frustrate and render vain his greatest power to hurt me.

My book, *De veritate prout distinguitur a revelatione verisimili, possibili, et a falso*, having been begun by me in England, and formed there in all its principal parts, was about this time finished; all the spare hours which I could get from my visits and negotiations being employed to perfect this work, which was no sooner done but that I communicated it to Hugo Grotius, that great scholar, who, having escaped his prison in the Low Countries, came into France, and was much welcomed by me and Monsieur Tielenus also, one of the greatest scholars of his time, who, after they had perused it, and given it more commendations than is fit for me to repeat, exhorted me earnestly to print and publish it; howbeit, as the frame of my whole book was so different from anything which had been written heretofore, I found I must either renounce the authority of all that had written formerly concerning the method of finding out truth, and consequently insist upon my own way, or hazard myself to a general censure concerning the whole argument of my book; I must confess it did not a little animate me that the two great persons above mentioned did so highly value it, yet as I knew it would meet with much opposition, I did consider whether it was not better for me a while to suppress it. Being thus doubtful in my chamber, one fair day in the summer, my casement being opened towards the south, the sun shining clear, I took my book, *De veritate*, in my hand, and, kneeling on my knees, devoutly said these words:—

"O thou eternal God, author of the light which now shines upon me, and giver of all inward illuminations, I do beseech thee, of thy infinite goodness, to pardon a greater request than a sinner ought to make; I am not satisfied enough whether I shall publish this book, *De veritate;* if it be for thy glory, I beseech thee give me some sign from heaven; if not, I shall suppress it."

I had no sooner spoken these words but a loud though yet gentle noise came from the heavens, for it was like nothing on earth, which did so comfort and cheer me that I took my petition as granted, and that I had the sign I demanded, whereupon also I resolved to print my book. This, how strange soever it may seem, I protest before the eternal God is true, neither am I any way superstitiously deceived herein, since I did not only clearly hear the noise, but in the serenest sky that ever I saw, being without all cloud, did to my thinking see the place from whence it came.

And now I sent my book to be printed in Paris, at my own cost and charges, without suffering it to be divulged to others than to such as I thought might be worthy readers of it; though afterwards reprinting it in England, I not only dispersed it among the prime scholars of Europe, but was sent to not only from the nearest but furthest parts of Christendom, to desire the sight of my book, for which they promised anything I should desire by way of return; but hereof more amply in its place.

PHILOSOPHY AND SCIENCE

FRANCIS BACON (1561-1626)

Although Bacon had a greatly exaggerated opinion of both the novelty and the efficacy of his scientific program, he was one of those men who in their way are no less important than practical investigators, who gather up, digest, and philosophize the aspirations and intellectual achievements of whole epochs. It is doubtless true that the course of science would have been the same if Bacon had never lived, but our understanding of its progress would have been infinitely poorer if Bacon had not been a powerful focal lens. *The Advancement of Learning* is, therefore, quite apart from Bacon's undisputed mastery of prose, one of the great books. The extracts from Book I represent Bacon's analysis and condemnation of the mediaeval tradition—from the tentacles of which his own mind was not as free as he thought it was. The extracts from Book II—as we indicated above—illuminate Bacon's method and aims in the writing of his *Essays*.

As we have said already, the importance of science is sufficient reason for including extracts from the modern English version of the *Novum Organum*. The trenchant and majestic aphorisms which pronounce sentence of death on the old science and outline the methods of the new have the quietly exultant finality of a special revelation—even though Bacon's dream of card-indexing nature was a most unscientific dream. And his power of philosophic generalization is nowhere better displayed than in the analysis of the Idols of the Tribe, Cave, Market-place, and Theatre; we have them still, with new names.

ADVANCEMENT OF LEARNING (1605)

BOOK I

[VANITIES IN STUDIES]

Now I proceed to those errors and vanities which have intervened amongst the studies themselves of the learned, which is that which is principal and proper to the present argument; wherein my purpose is not to make a justification of the errors, but by a censure and separation of the errors to make a justification of that which is good and sound, and to deliver that from the aspersion of the other. For we see that it is the manner of men to scandalize and deprave that which retaineth the state and virtue, by taking advantage upon that which is corrupt and degenerate: as the heathens in the primitive Church used to blemish and taint the Christians with the faults and corruptions of heretics. But nevertheless I have no meaning at this time to make any exact animadversion of the errors and impediments in matters of learning, which are more secret and remote from vulgar opinion, but only to speak unto such as do fall under or near unto a popular observation.

There be therefore chiefly three vanities in studies, whereby learning hath been most traduced. For those things we do esteem vain, which are either false or frivolous, those which either have no truth or no use: and those persons we esteem vain, which are either credulous or curious; and curiosity is either in matter or words: so that in reason as well as in experience there fall out to be these three distempers (as I may term them) of learning: the first, fantastical learning; the second, contentious learning; and the last, delicate learning; vain imaginations, vain altercations, and vain affectations; and with the last I will begin. Martin Luther, conducted (no doubt) by an higher providence, but in discourse of reason, finding what a province he had undertaken against the bishop of Rome and the degenerate traditions of the Church, and finding his own solitude, being no ways aided by the opinions of his own time, was enforced to awake all antiquity, and to call former times to his succors to make a party against the present time: so that the ancient authors, both in divinity and in humanity, which had long time slept in libraries, began generally to be read and revolved. This by consequence did draw on a necessity of a more exquisite travail in the languages original, wherein those authors did write, for the better understanding of those authors, and the better advantage of pressing and applying their words. And thereof grew again a delight in their manner of style and phrase, and an admiration of that kind of writing; which was much furthered and precipitated by the enmity and opposition that the propounders of those primitive but seeming new opinions had against the schoolmen; who were generally of the contrary part, and whose writings were altogether in a different style and form; taking liberty to coin and frame new terms of art to express their own sense, and to avoid circuit of speech, without regard to the pureness, pleasantness, and (as I may call it) lawfulness of the phrase or word. And again, because the great labor then was with the people (of whom the Pharisees were wont to say, *Execrabilis ista turba, quæ non novit legem*),[1] for the winning and persuading of them, there grew of necessity in chief price and request eloquence and variety of discourse, as the fittest and forciblest access into the capacity of the vulgar sort: so that these four causes concurring, the admiration of ancient authors, the hate of the schoolmen, the exact study of languages, and the efficacy of preaching, did bring in an affectionate study of eloquence and *copia* of speech, which then began to flourish. This grew speedily to an excess; for men began to hunt more after words than matter; more after the choiceness of the phrase, and the round and clean composition of the sentence, and the sweet falling of the clauses, and the varying and illustration of their works with tropes and figures, than after the weight of matter, worth of subject, soundness of argument, life of invention, or depth of judgment. Then grew the flowing and watery vein of Osorius, the Portugal bishop, to be in price. Then did Sturmius spend such infinite and curious pains upon Cicero the Orator, and Hermogenes the Rhetorician, besides his own books of Periods and Imitation, and the like. Then did Car of Cambridge and Ascham with their lectures and writings almost deify Cicero and Demosthenes, and allure all young men that were studious unto that delicate and polished kind of learning. Then did Erasmus take occasion to make the scoffing echo, *Decem annos consumpsi in legendo Cicerone*[2]; and the echo answered in Greek 'Ότε, *Asine*.[3] Then grew the learning of the schoolmen to be utterly despised as barbarous. In sum, the whole inclination and bent of those times was rather towards *copia* than weight.

Here therefore is the first distemper of learning, when men study words and not matter; whereof, though I have represented an example of late times, yet it hath been and will be *secundum*

---

[1] That wretched crowd that knoweth not the law.
[2] I have spent ten years in reading Cicero.
[3] You ass.

majus et minus[1] in all time. And how is it possible but this should have an operation to discredit learning, even with vulgar capacities, when they see learned men's works like the first letter of a patent, or limned book; which though it hath large flourishes, yet it is but a letter? It seems to me that Pygmalion's frenzy is a good emblem or portraiture of this vanity: for words are but the images of matter; and except they have life of reason and invention, to fall in love with them is all one as to fall in love with a picture.

But yet notwithstanding it is a thing not hastily to be condemned, to clothe and adorn the obscurity even of philosophy itself with sensible and plausible elocution. For hereof we have great examples in Xenophon, Cicero, Seneca, Plutarch, and of Plato also in some degree; and hereof likewise there is great use: for surely, to the severe inquisition of truth and the deep progress into philosophy, it is some hindrance; because it is too early satisfactory to the mind of man, and quencheth the desire of further search, before we come to a just period. But then if a man be to have any use of such knowledge in civil occasions, of conference, counsel, persuasion, discourse, or the like, then shall he find it prepared to his hands in those authors which write in that manner. But the excess of this is so justly contemptible, that as Hercules, when he saw the image of Adonis, Venus' minion, in a temple, said in disdain, *Nil sacri es*;[2] so there is none of Hercules' followers in learning, that is, the more severe and laborious sort of inquirers into truth, but will despise those delicacies and affectations, as indeed capable of no divineness. And thus much of the first disease or distemper of learning.

The second which followeth is in nature worse than the former: for as substance of matter is better than beauty of words, so contrariwise vain matter is worse than vain words: wherein it seemeth the reprehension of Saint Paul was not only proper for those times, but prophetical for the times following; and not only respective to divinity, but extensive to all knowledge: *Devita profanas vocum novitates, et oppositiones falsi nominis scientiæ.*[3] For he assigneth two marks and badges of suspected and falsified science: the one, the novelty and strangeness of

[1] In a greater or less degree.
[2] You are no god.
[3] Shun profane novelties of terms and oppositions of science falsely so called.

terms; the other, the strictness of positions, which of necessity doth induce oppositions, and so questions and altercations. Surely, like as many substances in nature which are solid do putrefy and corrupt into worms; so it is the property of good and sound knowledge to putrefy and dissolve into a number of subtle, idle, unwholesome, and (as I may term them) vermiculate questions, which have indeed a kind of quickness and life of spirit, but no soundness of matter or goodness of quality. This kind of degenerate learning did chiefly reign amongst the school-men: who having sharp and strong wits, and abundance of leisure, and small variety of reading, but their wits being shut up in the cells of a few authors (chiefly Aristotle their dictator) as their persons were shut up in the cells of monasteries and colleges, and knowing little history, either of nature or time, did out of no great quantity of matter and infinite agitation of wit spin out unto us those laborious webs of learning which are extant in their books. For the wit and mind of man, if it work upon matter, which is the contemplation of the creatures of God, worketh according to the stuff and is limited thereby; but if it work upon itself, as the spider worketh his web, then it is endless, and brings forth indeed cobwebs of learning, admirable for the fineness of thread and work, but of no substance or profit.

This same unprofitable subtlety or curiosity is of two sorts; either in the subject itself that they handle, when it is a fruitless speculation or controversy (whereof there are no small number both in divinity and philosophy), or in the manner or method of handling of a knowledge, which amongst them was this; upon every particular position or assertion to frame objections, and to those objections, solutions; which solutions were for the most part not confutations, but distinctions: whereas indeed the strength of all sciences is, as the strength of the old man's faggot, in the bond. For the harmony of a science, supporting each part the other, is and ought to be the true and brief confutation and suppression of all the smaller sort of objections. But, on the other side, if you take out every axiom, as the sticks of the faggot, one by one, you may quarrel with them and bend them and break them at your pleasure: so that as was said of Seneca, *Verborum minutiis rerum frangit pondera*,[1] so a man may truly

---

[1] By his verbal subtleties he breaks up the weight of the matter.

say of the schoolmen, *Quæstionum minutiis scientiarum frangunt soliditatem.*[1] For were it not better for a man in a fair room to set up one great light, or branching candlestick of lights, than to go about with a small watch candle into every corner? And such is their method, that rests not so much upon evidence of truth proved by arguments, authorities, similitudes, examples, as upon particular confutations and solutions of every scruple, cavillation, and objection; breeding for the most part one question as fast as it solveth another; even as in the former resemblance, when you carry the light into one corner, you darken the rest; so that the fable and fiction of Scylla seemeth to be a lively image of this kind of philosophy or knowledge; which was transformed into a comely virgin for the upper parts; but then *candida succinctam latrantibus inguina monstris:*[2] so the generalities of the schoolmen are for a while good and proportionable; but then when you descend into their distinctions and decisions, instead of a fruitful womb for the use and benefit of man's life, they end in monstrous altercations and barking questions. So as it is not possible but this quality of knowledge must fall under popular contempt, the people being apt to contemn truth upon occasion of controversies and altercations and to think they are all out of their way which never meet; and when they see such digladiation about subtleties, and matter of no use or moment, they easily fall upon that judgment of Dionysius of Syracusa, *Verba ista sunt senum otiosorum.*[3]

Notwithstanding, certain it is that if those schoolmen to their great thirst of truth and unwearied travail of wit had joined variety and universality of reading and contemplation, they had proved excellent lights, to the great advancement of all learning and knowledge; but as they are, they are great undertakers indeed, and fierce with dark keeping; but as in the inquiry of the divine truth, their pride inclined to leave the oracle of God's word, and to vanish in the mixture of their own inventions; so in the inquisition of nature, they ever left the oracle of God's works, and adored the deceiving and deformed images which the unequal mirror of their own minds, or a few received authors or

---

[1] By minute questions they break up the solidity of sciences.
[2] With barking monsters about her fair hips.
[3] Those are the words of idle old men.

principles, did represent unto them. And thus much for the second disease of learning.

For the third vice or disease of learning, which concerneth deceit or untruth, it is of all the rest the foulest; as that which doth destroy the essential form of knowledge, which is nothing but a representation of truth: for the truth of being and the truth of knowing are one, differing no more than the direct beam and the beam reflected. This vice therefore brancheth itself into two sorts; delight in deceiving and aptness to be deceived; imposture and credulity; which, although they appear to be of a diverse nature, the one seeming to proceed of cunning and the other of simplicity, yet certainly they do for the most part concur: for, as the verse noteth,

Percontatorem fugito, nam garrulus idem est,

an inquisitive man is a prattler; so upon the like reason a credulous man is a deceiver: as we see it in fame, that he that will easily believe rumors, will as easily augment rumors and add somewhat to them of his own; which Tacitus wisely noteth, when he saith, *Fingunt simul creduntque*[1]: so great an affinity hath fiction and belief.

This facility of credit and accepting or admitting things weakly authorized or warranted, is of two kinds according to the subject: for it is either a belief of history, or, as the lawyers speak, matter of fact; or else of matter of art and opinion. As to the former, we see the experience and inconvenience of this error in ecclesiastical history; which hath too easily received and registered reports and narrations of miracles wrought by martyrs, hermits, or monks of the desert, and other holy men, and their relics, shrines, chapels, and images: which though they had a passage for a time by the ignorance of the people, the superstitious simplicity of some, and the politic toleration of others, holding them but as divine poesies; yet after a period of time, when the mist began to clear up, they grew to be esteemed but as old wives' fables, impostures of the clergy, illusions of spirits, and badges of Antichrist, to the great scandal and detriment of religion.

---

[1]They invent and at the same time believe.

So in natural history, we see there hath not been that choice and judgment used as ought to have been; as may appear in the writings of Plinius, Cardanus, Albertus, and divers of the Arabians, being fraught with much fabulous matter, a great part not only untried, but notoriously untrue, to the great derogation of the credit of natural philosophy with the grave and sober kind of wits: wherein the wisdom and integrity of Aristotle is worthy to be observed; that, having made so diligent and exquisite a history of living creatures, hath mingled it sparingly with any vain or feigned matter: and yet on the other side hath cast all prodigious narrations, which he thought worthy the recording, into one book: excellently discerning that matter of manifest truth, such whereupon observation and rule was to be built, was not to be mingled or weakened with matter of doubtful credit; and yet again, that rarities and reports that seem uncredible are not to be suppressed or denied to the memory of men.

And as for the facility of credit which is yielded to arts and opinions, it is likewise of two kinds; either when too much belief is attributed to the arts themselves, or to certain authors in any art. The sciences themselves, which have had better intelligence and confederacy with the imagination of man than with his reason, are three in number: astrology, natural magic, and alchemy: of which sciences, nevertheless, the ends or pretences are noble. For astrology pretendeth to discover that correspondence or concatenation which is between the superior globe and the inferior: natural magic pretendeth to call and reduce natural philosophy from variety of speculations to the magnitude of works: and alchemy pretendeth to make separation of all the unlike parts of bodies which in mixtures of nature are incorporate. But the derivations and prosecutions to these ends, both in the theories and in the practices, are full of error and vanity; which the great professors themselves have sought to veil over and conceal by enigmatical writings, and referring themselves to auricular traditions and such other devices, to save the credit of impostures. And yet surely to alchemy this right is due, that it may be compared to the husbandman whereof Aesop makes the fable; that, when he died, told his sons that he had left unto them gold buried under ground in his vineyard; and they digged over all the ground, and gold they found none; but by reason of their stirring and digging the mould about the roots of their vines, they had a great vintage the year following: so assuredly the search and stir to make gold hath brought to light a great number of good and fruitful inventions and experiments, as well for the disclosing of nature as for the use of man's life.

And as for the overmuch credit that hath been given unto authors in sciences, in making them dictators, that their words should stand, and not consuls to give advice; the damage is infinite that sciences have received thereby, as the principal cause that hath kept them low at a stay without growth or advancement. For hence it hath come, that in arts mechanical the first deviser comes shortest, and time addeth and perfecteth; but in sciences the first author goeth furthest, and time leeseth and corrupteth. So we see, artillery, sailing, printing, and the like, were grossly managed at the first, and by time accommodated and refined; but contrariwise, the philosophies and sciences of Aristotle, Plato, Democritus, Hippocrates, Euclides, Archimedes, of most vigor at the first and by time degenerate and imbased; whereof the reason is no other, but that in the former many wits and industries have contributed in one; and in the latter many wits and industries have been spent about the wit of some one, whom many times they have rather depraved than illustrated. For as water will not ascend higher than the level of the first springhead from whence it descendeth, so knowledge derived from Aristotle, and exempted from liberty of examination, will not rise again higher than the knowledge of Aristotle. And therefore although the position be good, *Oportet discentem credere*,[1] yet it must be coupled with this, *Oportet edoctum judicare;*[2] for disciples do owe unto masters only a temporary belief and a suspension of their own judgment till they be fully instructed, and not an absolute resignation or perpetual captivity: and therefore, to conclude this point, I will say no more, but so let great authors have their due, as time, which is the author of authors, be not deprived of his due, which is, further and further to discover truth. Thus have I gone over these three diseases of learning; besides the which there are some other

[1]While learning we should believe.
[2]When we have learned we should judge.

rather peccant humors than formed diseases, which nevertheless are not so secret and intrinsic but that they fall under a popular observation and traducement, and therefore are not to be passed over.

The first of these is the extreme affecting of two extremities: the one antiquity, the other novelty; wherein it seemeth the children of time do take after the nature and malice of the father. For as he devoureth his children, so one of them seeketh to devour and suppress the other; while antiquity envieth there should be new additions, and novelty cannot be content to add but it must deface: surely the advice of the prophet is the true direction in this matter, *State super vias antiquas, et videte quænam sit via recta et bona et ambulate in ea.*[1] Antiquity deserveth that reverence, that men should make a stand thereupon and discover what is the best way; but when the discovery is well taken, then to make progression. And to speak truly, *Antiquitas sæculi juventus mundi.*[2] These times are the ancient times, when the world is ancient, and not those which we account ancient *ordine retrogrado*, by a computation backward from ourselves.

Another error induced by the former is a distrust that anything should be now to be found out, which the world should have missed and passed over so long time; as if the same objection were to be made to time, that Lucian maketh to Jupiter and other the heathen gods; of which he wondereth that they begot so many children in old time, and begot none in his time; and asketh whether they were become septuagenary, or whether the law *Papia*, made against old men's marriages, had restrained them. So it seemeth men doubt lest time is become past children and generation; wherein contrariwise we see commonly the levity and unconstancy of men's judgments, which till a matter be done, wonder that it can be done; and as soon as it is done, wonder again that it was no sooner done: as we see in the expedition of Alexander into Asia, which at first was prejudged as a vast and impossible enterprise; and yet afterwards it pleaseth Livy to make no more of it than this, *Nil aliud quam*

---

[1] Stand upon the old paths and see which is the straight and good road, and walk in it.

[2] Antiquity was the youth of the world.

bene ausus vana contemnere.[1] And the same happened to Columbus in the western navigation. But in intellectual matters it is much more common; as may be seen in most of the propositions of Euclid; which till they be demonstrate, they seem strange to our assent; but being demonstrate, our mind accepteth of them by a kind of relation (as the lawyers speak) as if we had known them before.

Another error, that hath also some affinity with the former, is a conceit that of former opinions or sects after variety and examination the best hath still prevailed and suppressed the rest; so as if a man should begin the labor of a new search, he were but like to light upon somewhat formerly rejected, and by rejection brought into oblivion: as if the multitude, or the wisest for the multitude's sake, were not ready to give passage rather to that which is popular and superficial, than to that which is substantial and profound; for the truth is, that time seemeth to be of the nature of a river or stream, which carrieth down to us that which is light and blown up, and sinketh and drowneth that which is weighty and solid.

Another error, of a diverse nature from all the former, is the over-early and peremptory reduction of knowledge into arts and methods; from which time commonly sciences receive small or no augmentation. But as young men, when they knit and shape perfectly, do seldom grow to a further stature; so knowledge, while it is in aphorisms and observations, it is in growth, but when it once is comprehended in exact methods, it may perchance be further polished and illustrate and accommodated for use and practice; but it increaseth no more in bulk and substance.

Another error which doth succeed that which we last mentioned is, that after the distribution of particular arts and sciences, men have abandoned universality, or *philosophia prima:* which cannot but cease and stop all progression. For no perfect discovery can be made upon a flat or a level: neither is it possible to discover the more remote and deeper parts of any science, if you stand but upon the level of the same science, and ascend not to a higher science.

Another error hath proceeded from too great a reverence,

---

[1]He was simply bold enough to scorn idle fears.

and a kind of adoration of the mind and understanding of man; by means whereof, men have withdrawn themselves too much from the contemplation of nature, and the observations of experience, and have tumbled up and down in their own reason and conceits. Upon these intellectualists, which are notwithstanding commonly taken for the most sublime and divine philosophers, Heraclitus gave a just censure, saying, "Men sought truth in their own little worlds, and not in the great and common world"; for they disdain to spell, and so by degrees to read in the volume of God's works: and contrariwise by continual meditation and agitation of wit do urge and as it were invocate their own spirits to divine and give oracles unto them, whereby they are deservedly deluded.

Another error that hath some connexion with this latter is, that men have used to infect their meditations, opinions, and doctrines, with some conceits which they have most admired, or some sciences which they have most applied; and given all things else a tincture according to them, utterly untrue and unproper. So hath Plato intermingled his philosophy with theology, and Aristotle with logic; and the second school of Plato, Proclus and the rest, with the mathematics. For these were the arts which had a kind of primogeniture with them severally. So have the alchemists made a philosophy out of a few experiments of the furnace; and Gilbertus our countryman hath made a philosophy out of the observations of a loadstone. So Cicero, when, reciting the several opinions of the nature of the soul, he found a musician that held the soul was but a harmony, saith pleasantly, *Hic ab arte sua non recessit*,[1] etc. But of these conceits Aristotle speaketh seriously and wisely when he saith, *Qui respiciunt ad pauca de facili pronunciant*.[2]

Another error is an impatience of doubt, and haste to assertion without due and mature suspension of judgment. For the two ways of contemplation are not unlike the two ways of action commonly spoken of by the ancients: the one plain and smooth in the beginning, and in the end impassable; the other rough and troublesome in the entrance, but after a while fair and even:

---

[1] This man is true to his art.

[2] Those who look at only a few things are ready with opinions.

so it is in contemplation; if a man will begin with certainties, he shall end in doubts; but if he will be content to begin with doubts, he shall end in certainties.

Another error is in the manner of the tradition and delivery of knowledge, which is for the most part magistral and peremptory, and not ingenuous and faithful; in a sort as may be soonest believed, and not easiliest examined. It is true that in compendious treatises for practice that form is not to be disallowed: but in the true handling of knowledge, men ought not to fall either on the one side into the vein of Velleius the Epicurean, *Nil tam metuens, quam ne dubitare aliqua de re videretur;*[1] nor on the other side into Socrates his ironical doubting of all things; but to propound things sincerely with more or less asseveration, as they stand in a man's own judgment proved more or less.

Other errors there are in the scope that men propound to themselves, whereunto they bend their endeavors; for whereas the more constant and devote kind of professors of any science ought to propound to themselves to make some additions to their science, they convert their labors to aspire to certain second prizes: as to be a profound interpreter or commenter, to be a sharp champion or defender, to be a methodical compounder or abridger, and so the patrimony of knowledge cometh to be sometimes improved, but seldom augmented.

But the greatest error of all the rest is the mistaking or misplacing of the last or furthest end of knowledge. For men have entered into a desire of learning and knowledge, sometimes upon a natural curiosity and inquisitive appetite; sometimes to entertain their minds with variety and delight; sometimes for ornament and reputation; and sometimes to enable them to victory of wit and contradiction; and most times for lucre and profession; and seldom sincerely to give a true account of their gift of reason, to the benefit and use of men: as if there were sought in knowledge a couch whereupon to rest a searching and restless spirit; or a tarasse for a wandering and variable mind to walk up and down with a fair prospect; or a tower of state for a proud mind to raise itself upon; or a fort or commanding ground for strife and contention; or a shop for profit or sale; and not a

---

[1] Fearing nothing so much as that he might seem to be in doubt about anything.

rich storehouse for the glory of the Creator and the relief of man's estate. But this is that which will indeed dignify and exalt knowledge, if contemplation and action may be more nearly and straitly conjoined and united together than they have been; a conjunction like unto that of the two highest planets, Saturn, the planet of rest and contemplation, and Jupiter, the planet of civil society and action. Howbeit, I do not mean, when I speak of use and action, that end before-mentioned of the applying of knowledge to lucre and profession; for I am not ignorant how much that diverteth and interrupteth the prosecution and advancement of knowledge, like unto the golden ball thrown before Atalanta, which while she goeth aside and stoopeth to take up, the race is hindered,

Declinat cursus, aurumque volubile tollit.[1]

Neither is my meaning, as was spoken of Socrates, to call philosophy down from heaven to converse upon the earth; that is, to leave natural philosophy aside, and to apply knowledge only to manners and policy. But as both heaven and earth do conspire and contribute to the use and benefit of man; so the end ought to be, from both philosophies to separate and reject vain speculations, and whatsoever is empty and void, and to preserve and augment whatsoever is solid and fruitful: that knowledge may not be as a courtesan, for pleasure and vanity only, or as a bondwoman, to acquire and gain to her master's use; but as a spouse, for generation, fruit, and comfort.

Thus have I described and opened, as by a kind of dissection, those peccant humors (the principal of them) which have not only given impediment to the proficience of learning, but have given also occasion to the traducement thereof: wherein if I have been too plain, it must be remembered, *fidelia vulnera amantis, sed dolosa oscula malignantis*.[2] This I think I have gained, that I ought to be the better believed in that which I shall say pertaining to commendation; because I have proceeded so freely in that which concerneth censure. And yet I have no purpose to enter into a laudative of learning, or to make a hymn to the Muses (though I am of opinion that it is long since their rites

---

[1] She swerves from the course to pick up the rolling gold.

[2] Faithful are the wounds of a friend, but the kisses of an enemy are deceitful.

were duly celebrated), but my intent is, without varnish or amplification justly to weigh the dignity of knowledge in the balance with other things, and to take the true value thereof by testimonies and arguments divine and human. . . .

BOOK II

[THE APHORISTIC METHOD]

ANOTHER diversity of method, whereof the consequence is great, is the delivery of knowledge in aphorisms, or in methods; wherein we may observe that it hath been too much taken into custom, out of a few axioms or observations upon any subject, to make a solemn and formal art, filling it with some discourses, and illustrating it with examples, and digesting it into a sensible method. But the writing in aphorisms hath many excellent virtues, whereto the writing in method doth not approach.

For first, it trieth the writer, whether he be superficial or solid: for aphorisms, except they should be ridiculous, cannot be made but of the pith and heart of sciences; for discourse of illustration is cut off; recitals of examples are cut off; discourse of connexion and order is cut off; descriptions of practice are cut off.   So there remaineth nothing to fill the aphorisms but some good quantity of observation: and therefore no man can suffice, nor in reason will attempt, to write aphorisms, but he that is sound and grounded.   But in methods,

> *Tantum series juncturaque pollet,*
> *Tantum de medio sumptis accedit honoris,*[1]

as a man shall make a great show of an art, which, if it were disjointed, would come to little.   Secondly, methods are more fit to win consent or belief, but less fit to point to action; for they carry a kind of demonstration in orb or circle, one part illuminating another, and therefore satisfy.   But particulars being dispersed do best agree with dispersed directions.   And lastly, aphorisms, representing a knowledge broken, do invite men to inquire further; whereas methods, carrying the show of a total, do secure men, as if they were at furthest. . . .

---

[1]Order and arrangement are worth a great deal, they add luster to the cheap and familiar.

[POINTS OF NATURE AND FORTUNE IN THE CULTURE AND
CURE OF THE MIND OF MAN]

First therefore in this, as in all things which are practical, we ought to cast up our account, what is in our power, and what not; for the one may be dealt with by way of alteration, but the other by way of application only. The husbandman cannot command, neither the nature of the earth, nor the seasons of the weather; no more can the physician the constitution of the patient, nor the variety of accidents. So in the culture and cure of the mind of man, two things are without our command; points of nature, and points of fortune. For to the basis of the one, and the conditions of the other, our work is limited and tied. In these things therefore it is left unto us to proceed by application:

Vincenda est omnis fortuna ferendo:[1]

and so likewise,

Vincenda est omnis Natura ferendo.[2]

But when that we speak of suffering, we do not speak of a dull and neglected suffering, but of a wise and industrious suffering, which draweth and contriveth use and advantage out of that which seemeth adverse and contrary; which is that properly which we call accommodating or applying. Now the wisdom of application resteth principally in the exact and distinct knowledge of the precedent state or disposition, unto which we do apply: for we cannot fit a garment, except we first take measure of the body.

So then the first article of this knowledge is, to set down sound and true distributions and descriptions of the several characters and tempers of men's natures and dispositions; specially having regard to those differences which are most radical in being the fountains and causes of the rest, or most frequent in concurrence or commixture; wherein it is not the handling of a few of them in passage, the better to describe the mediocrities of virtues, that can satisfy this intention. For if it deserve

---

[1]All fortune may be conquered by suffering.

[2]All nature may be conquered by suffering.

to be considered, that there are minds which are proportioned to great matters, and others to small (which Aristotle handleth or ought to have handled by the name of magnanimity), doth it not deserve as well to be considered, that there are minds proportioned to intend many matters, and others to few? So that some can divide themselves: others can perchance do exactly well, but it must be but in few things at once: and so there cometh to be a narrowness of mind, as well as a pusillanimity. And again, that some minds are proportioned to that which may be dispatched at once, or within a short return of time; others to that which begins afar off, and is to be won with length of pursuit:

Jam tum tenditque fovetque.[1]

So that there may be fitly said to be a longanimity, which is commonly also ascribed to God as a magnanimity. So further deserved it to be considered by Aristotle, "That there is a disposition in conversation (supposing it in things which do in no sort touch or concern a man's self) to soothe and please; and a disposition contrary to contradict and cross": and deserveth it not much better to be considered, "That there is a disposition, not in conversation or talk, but in matter of more serious nature (and supposing it still in things merely indifferent), to take pleasure in the good of another: and a disposition contrariwise, to take distaste at the good of another?" which is that properly which we call good nature or ill nature, benignity or malignity: and therefore I cannot sufficiently marvel that this part of knowledge, touching the several characters of natures and dispositions, should be omitted both in morality and policy; considering it is of so great ministry and suppeditation to them both. A man shall find in the traditions of astrology some pretty and apt divisions of men's natures, according to the predominances of the planets; lovers of quiet, lovers of action, lovers of victory, lovers of honor, lovers of pleasure, lovers of arts, lovers of change, and so forth. A man shall find in the wisest sort of these relations which the Italians make touching conclaves, the natures of the several cardinals handsomely and lively painted forth. A man shall meet with in every day's conference the denominations of sensitive, dry, formal, real, humorous, certain,

---

[1] Even so early he nurses and attends to his plan.

huomo di prima impressione, huomo di ultima impressione,[1] and the like: and yet nevertheless this kind of observations wandereth in words, but is not fixed in inquiry. For the distinctions are found (many of them), but we conclude no precepts upon them: wherein our fault is the greater; because both history, poesy, and daily experience are as goodly fields where these observations grow; whereof we make a few posies to hold in our hands, but no man bringeth them to the confectionary, that receipts mought be made of them for use of life.

Of much like kind are those impressions of nature, which are imposed upon the mind by the sex, by the age, by the region, by health and sickness, by beauty and deformity, and the like, which are inherent and not extern; and again, those which are caused by extern fortune; as sovereignty, nobility, obscure birth, riches, want, magistracy, privateness, prosperity, adversity, constant fortune, variable fortune, rising *per saltum, per gradus,*[2] and the like. And therefore we see that Plautus maketh it a wonder to see an old man beneficent, *benignitas hujus ut adolescentuli est.*[3] Saint Paul concludeth that severity of discipline was to be used to the Cretans, *increpa eos dure,*[4] upon the disposition of their country, *Cretenses semper mendaces, malae bestiæ, ventres pigri.*[5] Sallust noteth that it is usual with kings to desire contradictories: *Sed plerumque regiæ voluntates, ut vehementes sunt, sic mobiles, sæpeque ipsæ sibi adversæ.*[6] Tacitus observeth how rarely raising of the fortune mendeth the disposition: *solus Vespasianus mutatus in melius.*[7] Pindarus maketh an observation, that great and sudden fortune for the most part defeateth men *qui magnam felicitatem concoquere non possunt.*[8] So the Psalm showeth it is more easy to keep a measure in the enjoying of fortune, than in the increase of fortune: *Divitiæ si*

---

[1]Men of the first impression, men of the last impression.

[2]By leaps, by degrees.

[3]As generous as if he were a young man.

[4]Rebuke them severely.

[5]The Cretans are always liars, evil beasts, sluggish bellies.

[6]But as a rule the wishes of monarchs are no less changeable than strong, and often contradictory.

[7]Vespasian was the only emperor who changed for the better.

[8]Who cannot digest great fortune.

affluant, nolite cor apponere.[1] These observations and the like I deny not but are touched a little by Aristotle as in passage in his Rhetorics, and are handled in some scattered discourses: but they were never incorporate into moral philosophy, to which they do essentially appertain; as the knowledge of the diversity of grounds and moulds doth to agriculture, and the knowledge of the diversity of complexions and constitutions doth to the physician; except we mean to follow the indiscretion of empirics, which minister the same medicines to all patients.

Another article of this knowledge is the inquiry touching the affections; for as in medicining of the body, it is in order first to know the divers complexions and constitutions; secondly, the diseases; and lastly, the cures: so in medicining of the mind, after knowledge of the divers characters of men's natures, it followeth in order to know the diseases and infirmities of the mind, which are no other than the perturbations and distempers of the affections. For as the ancient politiques in popular estates were wont to compare the people to the sea, and the orators to the winds; because as the sea would of itself be calm and quiet, if the winds did not move and trouble it; so the people would be peaceable and tractable, if the seditious orators did not set them in working and agitation: so it may be fitly said, that the mind in the nature thereof would be temperate and stayed, if the affections, as winds, did not put it into tumult and perturbation. And here again I find strange, as before, that Aristotle should have written divers volumes of *Ethics*, and never handled the affections, which is the principal subject thereof; and yet in his *Rhetorics*, where they are considered but collaterally and in a second degree (as they may be moved by speech), he findeth place for them, and handleth them well for the quantity; but where their true place is, he pretermitteth them. For it is not his disputations about pleasure and pain that can satisfy this inquiry, no more than he that should generally handle the nature of light can be said to handle the nature of colors; for pleasure and pain are to the particular affections, as light is to particular colors. Better travails, I suppose, had the Stoics taken in this argument, as far as I can gather by that which we have at second hand. But yet it is like it was after

---

[1] If riches increase, set not your heart upon them.

their manner, rather in subtlety of definitions (which in a subject of this nature are but curiosities), than in active and ample descriptions and observations. So likewise I find some particular writings of an elegant nature, touching some of the affections; as of anger, of comfort upon adverse accidents, of tenderness of countenance, and other. But the poets and writers of histories are the best doctors of this knowledge; where we may find painted forth with great life, how affections are kindled and incited; and how pacified and refrained; and how again contained from act and further degree; how they disclose themselves; how they work; how they vary; how they gather and fortify; how they are enwrapped one within another; and how they do fight and encounter one with another; and other the like particularities. Amongst the which this last is of special use in moral and civil matters; how, I say, to set affection against affection, and to master one by another; even as we use to hunt beast with beast, and fly bird with bird, which otherwise percase we could not so easily recover; upon which foundation is erected that excellent use of *præmium* and *poena*, whereby civil states consist: employing the predominant affections of fear and hope, for the suppressing and bridling the rest. For as in the government of states it is sometimes necessary to bridle one faction with another, so it is in the government within.

Now come we to those points which are within our own command, and have force and operation upon the mind, to affect the will and appetite, and to alter manners: wherein they ought to have handled custom, exercise, habit, education, example, imitation, emulation, company, friends, praise, reproof, exhortation, fame, laws, books, studies: these as they have determinate use in moralities, from these the mind suffereth; and of these are such receipts and regiments compounded and described, as may serve to recover or preserve the health and good estate of the mind, as far as pertaineth to human medicine: of which number we will insist upon some one or two, an example of the rest, because it were too long to prosecute all; and therefore we do resume custom and habit to speak of.

The opinion of Aristotle seemeth to me a negligent opinion, that of those things which consist by nature, nothing can be changed by custom; using for example, that if a stone be thrown ten thousand times up, it will not learn to ascend; and that by often seeing or hearing, we do not learn to see or hear the better. For though this principle be true in things wherein nature is peremptory (the reason whereof we cannot now stand to discuss), yet it is otherwise in things wherein nature admitteth a latitude. For he mought see that a strait glove will come more easily on with use; and that a wand will by use bend otherwise than it grew; and that by use of the voice we speak louder and stronger; and that by use of enduring heat or cold, we endure it the better, and the like: which latter sort have a nearer resemblance unto that subject of manners he handleth, than those instances which he allegeth. But allowing his conclusion, that virtues and vices consist in habit, he ought so much the more to have taught the manner of superinducing that habit: for there be many precepts of the wise ordering the exercises of the mind, as there is of ordering the exercises of the body; whereof we will recite a few.

The first shall be, that we beware we take not at the first, either too high a strain, or too weak: for if too high, in a diffident nature you discourage, in a confident nature you breed an opinion of facility, and so a sloth; and in all natures you breed a further expectation than can hold out, and so an insatisfaction in the end: if too weak, of the other side, you may not look to perform and overcome any great task. . . .

NOVUM ORGANUM (1620)[1]

BOOK I

[SCIENCE OLD AND NEW]

I

MAN, being the servant and interpreter of Nature, can do and understand so much and so much only as he has observed in fact or in thought of the course of nature: beyond this he neither knows anything nor can do anything.

II

Neither the naked hand nor the understanding left to itself can effect much. It is by instruments and helps that the work

---

[1]Translated by Ellis and Spedding.

is done, which are as much wanted for the understanding as for the hand. And as the instruments of the hand either give motion or guide it, so the instruments of the mind supply either suggestions for the understanding or cautions.

III

Human knowledge and human power meet in one; for where the cause is not known the effect cannot be produced. Nature to be commanded must be obeyed; and that which in contemplation is as the cause is in operation as the rule.

VI

It would be an unsound fancy and self-contradictory to expect that things which have never yet been done can be done except by means which have never yet been tried.

VIII

Moreover the works already known are due to chance and experiment rather than to sciences; for the sciences we now possess are merely systems for the nice ordering and setting forth of things already invented; not methods of invention or directions for new works.

XIV

The syllogism consists of propositions, propositions consist of words, words are symbols of notions. Therefore if the notions themselves (which is the root of the matter) are confused and over-hastily abstracted from the facts, there can be no firmness in the superstructure. Our only hope therefore lies in a true induction.

XVIII

The discoveries which have hitherto been made in the sciences are such as lie close to vulgar notions, scarcely beneath the surface. In order to penetrate into the inner and further recesses of nature, it is necessary that both notions and axioms be derived from things by a more sure and guarded way; and that a method of intellectual operation be introduced altogether better and more certain.

XIX

There are and can be only two ways of searching into and discovering truth. The one flies from the senses and particulars to the most general axioms, and from these principles, the truth of which it takes for settled and immovable, proceeds to judgment and to the discovery of middle axioms. And this way is now in fashion. The other derives axioms from the senses and particulars, rising by a gradual and unbroken ascent, so that it arrives at the most general axioms last of all. This is the true way, but as yet untried.

XXII

Both ways set out from the senses and particulars, and rest in the highest generalities; but the difference between them is infinite. For the one just glances at experiment and particulars in passing, the other dwells duly and orderly among them. The one, again, begins at once by establishing certain abstract and useless generalities, the other rises by gradual steps to that which is prior and better known in the order of nature.

XXIII

There is a great difference between the Idols of the human mind and the Ideas of the divine. That is to say, between certain empty dogmas, and the true signatures and marks set upon the works of creation as they are found in nature.

XXIV

It cannot be that axioms established by argumentation should avail for the discovery of new works; since the subtlety of nature is greater many times over than the subtlety of argument. But axioms duly and orderly formed from particulars easily discover the way to new particulars, and thus render sciences active.

XXXI

It is idle to expect any great advancement in science from the superinducing and engrafting of new things upon old. We must begin anew from the very foundations, unless we would revolve for ever in a circle with mean and contemptible progress.

XXXII

The honor of the ancient authors, and indeed of all, remains untouched; since the comparison I challenge is not of wits or faculties, but of ways and methods, and the part I take upon myself is not that of a judge, but of a guide.

XXXIII

This must be plainly avowed: no judgment can be rightly formed either of my method or of the discoveries to which it leads, by means of anticipations (that is to say, of the reasoning which is now in use); since I cannot be called on to abide by the sentence of a tribunal which is itself on its trial.

XXXVI

One method of delivery alone remains to us; which is simply this: we must lead men to the particulars themselves, and their series and order; while men on their side must force themselves for a while to lay their notions by and begin to familiarize themselves with facts.

XXXVII

The doctrine of those who have denied that certainty could be attained at all, has some agreement with my way of proceeding at the first setting out; but they end in being infinitely separated and opposed. For the holders of that doctrine assert simply that nothing can be known; I also assert that not much can be known in nature by the way which is now in use. But then they go on to destroy the authority of the senses and understanding; whereas I proceed to devise and supply helps for the same.

[IDOLS]

XXXVIII

THE Idols and false notions which are now in possession of the human understanding, and have taken deep root therein, not only so beset men's minds that truth can hardly find entrance, but even after entrance obtained, they will again in the very instauration of the sciences meet and trouble us, unless men being forewarned of the danger fortify themselves as far as may be against their assaults.

XXXIX

There are four classes of Idols which beset men's minds. To these for distinction's sake I have assigned names—calling the first class *Idols of the Tribe*; the second, *Idols of the Cave*; the third, *Idols of the Market-place*; the fourth, *Idols of the Theatre*.

XL

The formation of ideas and axioms by true induction is no doubt the proper remedy to be applied for the keeping off and clearing away of idols. To point them out, however, is of great use; for the doctrine of Idols is to the Interpretation of Nature what the doctrine of the refutation of Sophisms is to common Logic.

XLI

The Idols of the Tribe have their foundation in human nature itself, and in the tribe or race of men. For it is a false assertion that the sense of man is the measure of things. On the contrary, all perceptions as well of the sense as of the mind are according to the measure of the individual and not according to the measure of the universe. And the human understanding is like a false mirror, which, receiving rays irregularly, distorts and discolors the nature of things by mingling its own nature with it.

XLII

The Idols of the Cave are the Idols of the individual man. For every one (besides the errors common to human nature in general) has a cave or den of his own, which refracts and discolors the light of nature; owing either to his own proper and peculiar nature; or to his education and conversation with others; or to the reading of books, and the authority of those whom he esteems and admires; or to the differences of impressions, accordingly as they take place in a mind preoccupied and predisposed or in a mind indifferent and settled; or the like. So that the spirit of man (according as it is meted out to different individuals) is in fact a thing variable and full of perturbation, and governed as it were by chance. Whence it was well observed by Heraclitus that men look for sciences in their own lesser worlds, and not in the greater or common world.

XLIII

There are also Idols formed by the intercourse and association of men with each other, which I call Idols of the Market-place, on account of the commerce and consort of men there. For it is by discourse that men associate; and words are imposed according to the apprehension of the vulgar. And therefore the ill and unfit choice of words wonderfully obstructs the understanding. Nor do the definitions or explanations wherewith in some things learned men are wont to guard and defend themselves, by any means set the matter right. But words plainly force and overrule the understanding, and throw all into confusion and lead men away into numberless empty controversies and idle fancies.

XLIV

Lastly, there are Idols which have immigrated into men's minds from the various dogmas of philosophies, and also from wrong laws of demonstration. These I call Idols of the Theatre; because in my judgment all the received systems are but so many stage-plays, representing worlds of their own creation after an unreal and scenic fashion. Nor is it only of the systems now in vogue, or only of the ancient sects and philosophies, that I speak; for many more plays of the same kind may yet be composed and in like artificial manner set forth; seeing that errors the most widely different have nevertheless causes for the most part alike. Neither again do I mean this only of entire systems, but also of many principles and axioms in science, which by tradition, credulity, and negligence have come to be received.

But of these several kinds of Idols I must speak more largely and exactly, that the understanding may be duly cautioned.

XLV

The human understanding is of its own nature prone to suppose the existence of more order and regularity in the world than it finds. And though there be many things in nature which are singular and unmatched, yet it devises for them parallels and conjugates and relatives which do not exist. Hence the fiction that all celestial bodies move in perfect circles; spirals and dragons being (except in name) utterly rejected. Hence too the element of fire with its orb is brought in, to make up the square with the other three which the sense perceives. Hence also the ratio of density of the so-called elements is arbitrarily fixed at ten to one. And so on of other dreams. And these fancies affect not dogmas only, but simple notions also.

XLVI

The human understanding when it has once adopted an opinion (either as being the received opinion or as being agreeable to itself) draws all things else to support and agree with it. And though there be a greater number and weight of instances to be found on the other side, yet these it either neglects and despises, or else by some distinction sets aside and rejects; in order that by this great and pernicious pre-determination the authority of its former conclusions may remain inviolate. And therefore it was a good answer that was made by one who when they showed him hanging in a temple a picture of those who had paid their vows as having escaped shipwreck, and would have him say whether he did not now acknowledge the power of the gods—"Ay," asked he again, "but where are they painted that were drowned after their vows?" And such is the way of all superstition, whether in astrology, dreams, omens, divine judgments, or the like; wherein men having a delight in such vanities, mark the events where they are fulfilled, but where they fail, though this happen much oftener, neglect and pass them by. But with far more subtlety does this mischief insinuate itself into philosophy and the sciences; in which the first conclusion colors and brings into conformity with itself all that come after, though far sounder and better. Besides, independently of that delight and vanity which I have described, it is the peculiar and perpetual error of the human intellect to be more moved and excited by affirmatives than by negatives; whereas it ought properly to hold itself indifferently disposed towards both alike. Indeed in the establishment of any true axiom, the negative instance is the more forcible of the two.

XLVII

The human understanding is moved by those things most which strike and enter the mind simultaneously and suddenly, and so fill the imagination; and then it feigns and supposes all other things to be somehow, though it cannot see how, similar to those few things by which it is surrounded. But for that going to and fro to remote and heterogeneous instances, by which axioms are tried as in the fire, the intellect is altogether slow and unfit, unless it be forced thereto by severe laws and overruling authority.

XLVIII

The human understanding is unquiet; it cannot stop or rest, and still presses onward, but in vain. Therefore it is that we cannot conceive of any end or limit to the world; but always as of necessity it occurs to us that there is something beyond. Neither again can it be conceived how eternity has flowed down to the present day; for that distinction which is commonly received of infinity in time past and in time to come can by no means hold; for it would thence follow that one infinity is greater than another, and that infinity is wasting away and tending to become finite. The like subtlety arises touching the infinite divisibility of lines, from the same inability of thought to stop. But this inability interferes more mischievously in the discovery of causes: for although the most general principles in nature ought to be held merely positive, as they are discovered, and cannot with truth be referred to a cause; nevertheless the human understanding being unable to rest still seeks something prior in the order of nature. And then it is that in struggling towards that which is further off it falls back upon that which is more nigh at hand; namely, on final causes: which have relation clearly to the nature of man rather than to the nature of the universe, and from this source have strangely defiled philosophy. But he is no less an unskilled and shallow philosopher who seeks causes of that which is most general, than he who in things subordinate and subaltern omits to do so.

XLIX

The human understanding is no dry light, but receives an infusion from the will and affections; whence proceed sciences which may be called "sciences as one would." For what a man had rather were true he more readily believes. Therefore he rejects difficult things from impatience of research; sober things, because they narrow hope; the deeper things of nature, from superstition; the light of experience, from arrogance and pride, lest his mind should seem to be occupied with things mean and transitory; things not commonly believed, out of deference to the opinion of the vulgar. Numberless in short are the ways, and sometimes imperceptible, in which the affections color and infect the understanding.

L

But by far the greatest hindrance and aberration of the human understanding proceeds from the dullness, incompetency, and deceptions of the senses; in that things which strike the sense outweigh things which do not immediately strike it, though they be more important. Hence it is that speculation commonly ceases where sight ceases; insomuch that of things invisible there is little or no observation. Hence all the working of the spirits inclosed in tangible bodies lies hid and unobserved of men. So also all the more subtle changes of form in the parts of coarser substances (which they commonly call alteration, though it is in truth local motion through exceedingly small spaces) is in like manner unobserved. And yet unless these two things just mentioned be searched out and brought to light, nothing great can be achieved in nature, as far as the production of works is concerned. So again the essential nature of our common air, and of all bodies less dense than air (which are very many), is almost unknown. For the sense by itself is a thing infirm and erring; neither can instruments for enlarging or sharpening the senses do much; but all the truer kind of interpretation of nature is effected by instances and experiments fit and apposite; wherein the sense decides touching the experiment only, and the experiment touching the point in nature and the thing itself.

LI

The human understanding is of its own nature prone to abstractions and gives a substance and reality to things which are fleeting. But to resolve nature into abstractions is less to our purpose than to dissect her into parts; as did the school of Democritus, which went further into nature than the rest. Matter rather than forms should be the object of our attention, its configurations and changes of configuration, and simple action, and law of action or motion; for forms are figments of the human mind, unless you will call those laws of action forms.

LII

Such then are the idols which I call *Idols of the Tribe*; and which take their rise either from the homogeneity of the substance of the human spirit, or from its preoccupation, or from its narrowness, or from its restless motion, or from an infusion of the affections, or from the incompetency of the senses, or from the mode of impression.

LIII

The *Idols of the Cave* take their rise in the peculiar constitution, mental or bodily, of each individual; and also in education, habit, and accident. Of this kind there is a great number and variety; but I will instance those the pointing out of which contains the most important caution, and which have most effect in disturbing the clearness of the understanding.

LIV

Men become attached to certain particular sciences and speculations, either because they fancy themselves the authors and inventors thereof, or because they have bestowed the greatest pains upon them and become most habituated to them. But men of this kind, if they betake themselves to philosophy and contemplations of a general character, distort and color them in obedience to their former fancies; a thing especially to be noticed in Aristotle, who made his natural philosophy a mere bondservant to his logic, thereby rendering it contentious and well nigh useless. The race of chemists again out of a few experiments of the furnace have built up a fantastic philosophy, framed with reference to a few things; and Gilbert also, after he had employed himself most laboriously in the study and observation of the loadstone, proceeded at once to construct an entire system in accordance with his favorite subject.

LV

There is one principal and as it were radical distinction between different minds, in respect of philosophy and the sciences, which is this: that some minds are stronger and apter to mark the differences of things, others to mark their resemblances. The steady and acute mind can fix its contemplations and dwell and fasten on the subtlest distinctions: the lofty and discursive mind recognizes and puts together the finest and most general resemblances. Both kinds however easily err in excess, by catching the one at gradations the other at shadows.

LVI

There are found some minds given to an extreme admiration of antiquity, others to an extreme love and appetite for novelty; but few so duly tempered that they can hold the mean, neither carping at what has been well laid down by the ancients, nor despising what is well introduced by the moderns. This however turns to the great injury of the sciences and philosophy; since these affectations of antiquity and novelty are the humors of partisans rather than judgments; and truth is to be sought for not in the felicity of any age, which is an unstable thing, but in the light of nature and experience, which is eternal. These factions therefore must be abjured, and care must be taken that the intellect be not hurried by them into assent.

LVII

Contemplations of nature and of bodies in their simple form break up and distract the understanding, while contemplations of nature and bodies in their composition and configuration overpower and dissolve the understanding: a distinction well seen in the school of Leucippus and Democritus as compared with the other philosophies. For that school is so busied with the particles that it hardly attends to the structure; while the others are so lost in admiration of the structure that they do not penetrate to the simplicity of nature. These kinds of contemplation should therefore be alternated and taken by turns; that so the understanding may be rendered at once penetrating and comprehensive, and the inconveniences above mentioned, with the idols which proceed from them, may be avoided.

LVIII

Let such then be our provision and contemplative prudence for keeping off and dislodging the *Idols of the Cave*, which grow for the most part either out of the predominance of a favorite subject, or out of an excessive tendency to compare or to distinguish, or out of partiality for particular ages, or out of the largeness or minuteness of the objects contemplated. And generally let every student of nature take this as a rule,—that whatever his mind seizes and dwells upon with peculiar satisfaction is to be held in suspicion, and that so much the more care is to be taken in dealing with such questions to keep the understanding even and clear.

LIX

But the *Idols of the Market-place* are the most troublesome of all: idols which have crept into the understanding through the alliances of words and names. For men believe that their reason governs words; but it is also true that words react on the understanding; and this it is that has rendered philosophy, and the sciences sophistical and inactive. Now words, being commonly framed and applied according to the capacity of the vulgar, follow those lines of division which are most obvious to the vulgar understanding. And whenever an understanding of greater acuteness or a more diligent observation would alter those lines to suit the true divisions of nature, words stand in the way and resist the change. Whence it comes to pass that the high and formal discussions of learned men end oftentimes in disputes about words and names; with which (according to the use and wisdom of the mathematicians) it would be more prudent to begin, and so by means of definitions reduce them to order. Yet even definitions cannot cure this evil in dealing with natural and material things; since the definitions themselves consist of words, and those words beget others: so that it is necessary to recur to individual instances, and those in due series and order; as I shall say presently when I come to the method and scheme for the formation of notions and axioms.

LX

The Idols imposed by words on the understanding are of two kinds. They are either names of things which do not exist (for as there are things left unnamed through lack of observation, so likewise are there names which result from fantastic suppositions and to which nothing in reality corresponds), or they are names of things which exist, but yet confused and ill-defined, and hastily and irregularly derived from realities. Of the former kind are Fortune, the Prime Mover, Planetary Orbits,

Element of Fire, and like fictions which owe their origin to false and idle theories. And this class of idols is more easily expelled, because to get rid of them it is only necessary that all theories should be steadily rejected and dismissed as obsolete.

But the other class, which springs out of a faulty and unskilful abstraction, is intricate and deeply rooted. Let us take for example such a word as *humid*; and see how far the several things which the word is used to signify agree with each other; and we shall find the word *humid* to be nothing else than a mark loosely and confusedly applied to denote a variety of actions which will not bear to be reduced to any constant meaning. For it both signifies that which easily spreads itself round any other body; and that which in itself is indeterminate and cannot solidize; and that which readily yields in every direction; and that which easily divides and scatters itself; and that which easily unites and collects itself; and that which readily flows and is put in motion; and that which readily clings to another body and wets it; and that which is easily reduced to a liquid, or being solid easily melts. Accordingly when you come to apply the word,—if you take it in one sense, flame is humid; if in another, air is not humid; if in another, fine dust is humid; if in another, glass is humid. So that it is easy to see that the notion is taken by abstraction only from water and common and ordinary liquids, without any due verification.

There are however in words certain degrees of distortion and error. One of the least faulty kinds is that of names of substances, especially of lowest species and well-deduced (for the notion of *chalk* and of *mud* is good, of *earth* bad); a more faulty kind is that of actions, as *to generate, to corrupt, to alter*; the most faulty is of qualities (except such as are the immediate objects of the sense) as *heavy, light, rare, dense*, and the like. Yet in all these cases some notions are of necessity a little better than others, in proportion to the greater variety of subjects that fall within the range of the human sense.

LXI

But the *Idols of the Theatre* are not innate, nor do they steal into the understanding secretly, but are plainly impressed and received into the mind from the play-books of philosophical systems and the perverted rules of demonstration. To attempt refutations in this case would be merely inconsistent with what I have already said: for since we agree neither upon principles nor upon demonstrations there is no place for argument. And this is so far well, inasmuch as it leaves the honor of the ancients untouched. For they are no wise disparaged—the question between them and me being only as to the way. For as the saying is, the lame man who keeps the right road outstrips the runner who takes a wrong one. Nay it is obvious that when a man runs the wrong way, the more active and swift he is the further he will go astray.

But the course I propose for the discovery of sciences is such as leaves but little to the acuteness and strength of wits, but places all wits and understandings nearly on a level. For as in the drawing of a straight line or perfect circle, much depends on the steadiness and practice of the hand, if it be done by aim of hand only, but if with the aid of rule or compass, little or nothing; so is it exactly with my plan. But though particular confutations would be of no avail, yet touching the sects and general divisions of such systems I must say something; something also touching the external signs which show that they are unsound; and finally something touching the causes of such great infelicity and of such lasting and general agreement in error; that so the access to truth may be made less difficult, and the human understanding may the more willingly submit to its purgation and dismiss its Idols.

LXII

Idols of the Theatre, or of Systems, are many, and there can be and perhaps will be yet many more. For were it not that now for many ages men's minds have been busied with religion and theology; and were it not that civil governments, especially monarchies, have been averse to such novelties, even in matters speculative; so that men labor therein to the peril and harming of their fortunes,—not only unrewarded, but exposed also to contempt and envy; doubtless there would have arisen ·many other philosophical sects like to those which in great variety flourished once among the Greeks. For as on the phenomena of the heavens many hypotheses may be constructed, so likewise (and more also) many various dogmas may be set up and established on the phenomena of philosophy. And in the plays of this philosophical theatre you may observe the same thing which is found in the theatre of the poets, that stories invented for the stage are more compact and elegant, and more as one would wish them to be, than true stories out of history.

In general however there is taken for the material of philosophy either a great deal out of a few things, or a very little out of many things; so that on both sides philosophy is based on too narrow a foundation of experiment and natural history, and decides on the authority of too few cases. For the rational school of philosophers snatches from experience a variety of common instances, neither duly ascertained nor diligently examined and weighed, and leaves all the rest to meditation and agitation of wit.

There is also another class of philosophers, who having bestowed much diligent and careful labor on a few experiments, have thence made bold to educe and construct systems; wresting all other facts in a strange fashion to conformity therewith.

And there is yet a third class, consisting of those who out of faith and veneration mix their philosophy with theology and traditions; among whom the vanity of some has gone so far aside as to seek the origin of sciences among spirits and genii. So that this parent stock of errors—this false philosophy—is of three kinds; the sophistical, the empirical, and the superstitious.

LXIII

The most conspicuous example of the first class was Aristotle, who corrupted natural philosophy by his logic: fashioning the world out of categories; assigning to the human soul, the noblest of substances, a genus from words of the second intention; doing the business of density and rarity (which is to make bodies of greater or less dimensions, that is, occupy greater or less spaces), by the frigid distinction of act and power; asserting that single bodies have each a single and proper motion, and that if they participate in any other, then this results from an external cause; and imposing countless other arbitrary restrictions on the nature of things; being always more solicitous to provide an answer to the question and affirm something positive in words, than about the inner truth of things; a failing best shown when his philosophy is compared with other systems of note among the Greeks.

For the Homœomera of Anaxagoras; the Atoms of Leucippus and Democritus; the Heaven and Earth of Parmenides; the Strife and Friendship of Empedocles; Heraclitus's doctrine how bodies are resolved into the indifferent nature of fire, and remoulded into solids; have all of them some taste of the natural philosopher—some savor of the nature of things, and experience, and bodies; whereas in the physics of Aristotle you hear hardly anything but the words of logic; which in his metaphysics also, under a more imposing name, and more forsooth as a realist than a nominalist, he has handled over again. Nor let any weight be given to the fact, that in his books on animals and his problems, and other of his treatises, there is frequent dealing with experiments. For he had come to his conclusion before; he did not consult experience, as he should have done, in order to the framing of his decisions and axioms; but having first determined the question according to his will, he then resorts to experience, and bending her into conformity with his placets leads her about like a captive in a procession; so that even on this count he is more guilty than his modern followers, the schoolmen, who have abandoned experience altogether.

LXVIII

So much concerning the several classes of Idols, and their equipage: all of which must be renounced and put away with a fixed and solemn determination, and the understanding thoroughly freed and cleansed; the entrance into the kingdom of man, founded on the sciences, being not much other than the entrance into the kingdom of heaven, whereinto none may enter except as a little child.

[AIMS OF THE NEW SCIENCE]

CXIV

LASTLY, even if the breath of hope which blows on us from that New Continent were fainter than it is and harder to perceive; yet the trial (if we would not bear a spirit altogether abject) must by all means be made. For there is no comparison between that which we may lose by not trying and by not succeeding; since by not trying we throw away the chance of an immense good; by not succeeding we only incur the loss of a little human labor. But as it is, it appears to me from what has been said, and also from what has been left unsaid, that there is hope enough and to spare, not only to make a bold man try, but also to make a sober-minded and wise man believe.

CXV

Concerning the grounds then for putting away despair, which has been one of the most powerful causes of delay and hindrance to the progress of knowledge, I have now spoken. And this also concludes what I had to say touching the *signs* and *causes* of the errors, sluggishness, and ignorance which have prevailed; especially since the more subtle causes, which do not fall under popular judgment and observation, must be referred to what has been said on the Idols of the human mind.

And here likewise should close that part of my Instauration which is devoted to pulling down; which part is performed by three refutations; first, by the refutation of the *natural human reason*, left to itself; secondly, by the refutation of the *demonstrations*; and thirdly, by the refutation of the *theories*, or the received systems of philosophy and doctrine. And the refutation of these has been such, as alone it could be: that is to say, by signs and the evidence of causes since no other kind of confutation was open to me, differing as I do from others; both on first principles and on rules of demonstration.

It is time therefore to proceed to the art itself and rule of interpreting nature; still however there remains something to be premised. For whereas in this first book of aphorisms I proposed to prepare men's minds as well for understanding as for receiving what is to follow; now that I have purged and swept and leveled the floor of the mind, it remains that I place the mind in a good position and as it were in a favorable aspect towards what I have to lay before it. For in a new matter, it is not only the strong preoccupation of some old opinion that tends to create a prejudice, but also a false preconception or prefiguration of the new thing which is presented. I will endeavor therefore to impart sound and true opinions as to the things I propose, although they are to serve only for the time, and by way of interest (so to speak), till the thing itself, which is the principal, be fully known.

CXVI

First, then, I must request men not to suppose that after the fashion of ancient Greeks, and of certain moderns, as Telesius, Patricius, Severinus, I wish to found a new sect in philosophy. For this is not what I am about; nor do I think that it matters much to the fortunes of men what abstract notions one may entertain concerning nature and the principles of things; and no doubt many old theories of this kind can be revived and many new ones introduced; just as many theories of the heavens may be supposed, which agree well enough with the phenomena and yet differ with each other.

But for my part I do not trouble myself with any such speculative, and withal unprofitable matters. My purpose, on the contrary, is to try whether I cannot in very fact lay more firmly the foundations, and extend more widely the limits, of the power and greatness of man. And although on some special subjects and in an incomplete form I am in possession of results which I take to be far more true and more certain and withal more fruitful than those now received, (and these I have collected into the fifth part of my Instauration,) yet I have no entire or universal theory to propound. For it does not seem that the time is come for such an attempt. Neither can I hope to live to complete the sixth part of the Instauration (which is destined for the philosophy discovered by the legitimate interpretation of nature), but hold it enough if in the intermediate business I bear myself soberly and profitably, sowing in the meantime for future ages the seeds of a purer truth, and performing my part towards the commencement of the great undertaking.

CXXIV

Again, it will be thought, no doubt, that the goal and mark of knowledge which I myself set up (the very point which I object to in others) is not the true or the best; for that the contemplation of truth is a thing worthier and loftier than all utility and magnitude of works; and that this long and anxious dwelling with experience and matter and the fluctuations of individual things, drags down the mind to earth or rather sinks it to a very Tartarus of turmoil and confusion; removing and withdrawing it from the serene tranquillity of abstract wisdom, a condition

far more heavenly. Now to this I readily assent; and indeed
this which they point at as so much to be preferred, is the very
thing of all others which I am about. For I am building in
the human understanding a true model of the world, such as it
is in fact, not such as a man's own reason would have it to be; a
thing which cannot be done without a very diligent dissection
and anatomy of the world. But I say that those foolish and
apish images of worlds which the fancies of men have created in
philosophical systems, must be utterly scattered to the winds.
Be it known then how vast a difference there is (as I said above)
between the Idols of the human mind and the Ideas of the divine.
The former are nothing more than arbitrary abstractions; the
latter are the Creator's own stamp upon creation, impressed
and defined in matter by true and exquisite lines. Truth therefore and utility are here the very same things; and works themselves are of greater value as pledges of truth than as contributing to the comforts of life.

NEW ATLANTIS

(1622–4; *pub.* 1627)

(SALOMON'S HOUSE)

. . . And as we were thus in conference, there came one
that seemed to be a messenger, in a rich huke, that spake with
the Jew; whereupon he turned to me, and said, "You will
pardon me, for I am commanded away in haste." The next
morning he came to me again, joyful as it seemed, and said,
"There is word come to the Governor of the city, that one of
the fathers of Salomon's House will be here this day seven-
night; we have seen none of them this dozen years. His coming
is in state; but the cause of his coming is secret. I will provide
you and your fellows of a good standing to see his entry." I
thanked him, and told him I was most glad of the news.

The day being come he made his entry. He was a man of
middle stature and age, comely of person, and had an aspect as
if he pitied men. He was clothed in a robe of fine black cloth,
with wide sleeves, and a cape: his under garment was of excellent
white linen down to the foot, girt with a girdle of the same; and

a sindon or tippet of the same about his neck. He had gloves that were curious, and set with stone; and shoes of peach-colored velvet. His neck was bare to the shoulders. His hat was like a helmet, or Spanish montera; and his locks curled below it decently: they were of color brown. His beard was cut round and of the same color with his hair, somewhat lighter. He was carried in a rich chariot, without wheels, litter-wise, with two horses at either end, richly trapped in blue velvet embroidered; and two footmen on each side in the like attire. The chariot was all of cedar, gilt, and adorned with crystal; save that the fore-end had panels of sapphires, set in borders of gold, and the hinder-end the like of emeralds of the Peru color. There was also a sun of gold, radiant, upon the top, in the midst; and on the top before, a small cherub of gold, with wings displayed. The chariot was covered with cloth of gold tissued upon blue. He had before him fifty attendants, young men all, in white satin loose coats to the mid-leg; and stockings of white silk, and shoes of blue velvet; and hats of blue velvet, with fine plumes of divers colors, set round like hat-bands. Next before the chariot went two men, bare-headed, in linen garments down to the foot, girt, and shoes of blue velvet, who carried the one a crosier, the other a pastoral staff like a sheep-hook: neither of them of metal, but the crosier of balm-wood, the pastoral staff of cedar. Horsemen he had none, neither before nor behind his chariot: as it seemeth, to avoid all tumult and trouble. Behind his chariot went all the officers and principals of the companies of the city. He sat alone, upon cushions, of a kind of excellent plush, blue; and under his foot curious carpets of silk of divers colors, like the Persian, but far finer. He held up his bare hand, as he went, as blessing the people, but in silence. The street was wonderfully well kept; so that there was never any army had their men stand in better battle-array than the people stood. The windows likewise were not crowded, but every one stood in them, as if they had been placed.

When the show was passed, the Jew said to me, "I shall not be able to attend you as I would, in regard of some charge the city hath laid upon me for the entertaining of this great person." Three days after the Jew came to me again, and said, "Ye are happy men; for the father of Salomon's House taketh knowledge of your being here, and commanded me to tell you, that he will

admit all your company to his presence, and have private conference with one of you, that ye shall choose; and for this hath
appointed the next day after to-morrow.   And because he mean-
eth to give you his blessing, he hath appointed it in the fore,
noon."

We came at our day and hour, and I was chosen by my fellows
for the private access.   We found him in a fair chamber, richly
hanged, and carpeted under foot, without any degrees to the
state.   He was set upon a low throne richly adorned, and a rich
cloth of state over his head, of blue satin embroidered.   He was
alone, save that he had two pages of honor, on either hand one,
finely attired in white.   His under garments were the like that
we saw him wear in the chariot; but instead of his gown, he had
on him a mantle with a cape, of the same fine black, fastened
about him.   When we came in, as we were taught, we bowed
low at our first entrance; and when we were come near his chair,
he stood up, holding forth his hand ungloved, and in posture of
blessing; and we every one of us stooped down, and kissed the
hem of his tippet.   That done, the rest departed, and I remained.   Then he warned the pages forth of the room, and
caused me to sit down beside him, and spake to me thus in the
Spanish tongue:

"God bless thee, my son; I will give thee the greatest jewel
I have.   For I will impart unto thee, for the love of God and
men, a relation of the true state of Salomon's House.   Son, to
make you know the true state of Salomon's House, I will keep
this order.   First, I will set forth unto you the end of our foundation.   Secondly, the preparations and instruments we have
for our works.   Thirdly, the several employments and functions
whereto our fellows are assigned.   And fourthly, the ordinances
and rites which we observe.

"The end of our foundation is the knowledge of causes, and
secret motions of things; and the enlarging of the bounds
of human empire, to the effecting of all things possible.

"The preparations and instruments are these.   We have large
and deep caves of several depths: the deepest are sunk six hundred fathom; and some of them are digged and made under great
hills and mountains; so that if you reckon together the depth of
the hill, and the depth of the cave, they are, some of them, above
three miles deep.   For we find that the depth of a hill, and the

depth of a cave from the flat, is the same thing; both remote alike from the sun and heaven's beams, and from the open air. These caves we call the lower region, and we use them for all coagulations, indurations, refrigerations, and conservations of bodies. We use them likewise for the imitation of natural mines, and the producing also of new artificial metals, by compositions and materials which we use, and lay there for many years. We use them also sometimes (which may seem strange) for curing of some diseases, and for prolongation of life, in some hermits that choose to live there, well accommodated of all things necessary, and indeed live very long; by whom also we learn many things.

"We have burials in several earths, where we put divers cements, as the Chinese do their porcelain. But we have them in greater variety, and some of them more fine. We also have great variety of composts and soils, for the making of the earth fruitful.

"We have high towers, the highest about half a mile in height, and some of them likewise set upon high mountains, so that the vantage of the hill, with the tower, is in the highest of them three miles at least. And these places we call the upper region, accounting the air between the high places and the low as a middle region. We use these towers, according to their several heights and situations, for insolation, refrigeration, conservation, and for the view of divers meteors—as winds, rain, snow, hail; and some of the fiery meteors also. And upon them, in some places, are dwellings of hermits, whom we visit sometimes, and instruct what to observe.

"We have great lakes, both salt and fresh, whereof we have use for the fish and fowl. We use them also for burials of some natural bodies, for we find a difference in things buried in earth, or in air below the earth, and things buried in water. We have also pools, of which some do strain fresh water out of salt, and others by art do turn fresh water into salt. We have also some rocks in the midst of the sea, and some bays upon the shore for some works, wherein is required the air and vapor of the sea. We have likewise violent streams and cataracts, which serve us for many motions; and likewise engines for multiplying and enforcing of winds to set also on going divers motions.

"We have also a number of artificial wells and fountains,

made in imitation of the natural sources and baths, as tincted upon vitriol, sulphur, steel, brass, lead, nitre, and other minerals; and again, we have little wells for infusions of many things, where the waters take the virtue quicker and better than in vessels or basins. And amongst them we have a water, which we call Water of Paradise, being by that we do to it made very sovereign for health and prolongation of life.

"We have also great and spacious houses, where we imitate and demonstrate meteors—as snow, hail, rain, some artificial rains of bodies, and not of water, thunders, lightnings; also generations of bodies in air—as frogs, flies, and divers others.

"We have also certain chambers, which we call chambers of health, where we qualify the air as we think good and proper for the cure of divers diseases, and preservation of health.

"We have also fair and large baths, of several mixtures, for the cure of diseases, and the restoring of man's body from arefaction; and others for the confirming of it in strength of sinews, vital parts, and the very juice and substance of the body.

"We have also large and various orchards and gardens, wherein we do not so much respect beauty as variety of ground and soil, proper for divers trees and herbs, and some very spacious, where trees and berries are set, whereof we make divers kinds of drinks, besides the vineyards. In these we practise likewise all conclusions of grafting and inoculating, as well of wild-trees as fruit-trees, which produceth many effects. And we make by art, in the same orchards and gardens, trees and flowers, to come earlier or later than their seasons, and to come up and bear more speedily than by their natural course they do. We make them also by art greater much than their nature; and their fruit greater and sweeter, and of differing taste, smell, color, and figure, from their nature. And many of them we so order as they become of medicinal use.

"We have also means to make divers plants rise by mixtures of earths without seeds, and likewise to make divers new plants, differing from the vulgar, and to make one tree or plant turn into another.

"We have also parks, and enclosures of all sorts, of beasts and birds; which we use not only for view or rareness, but likewise for dissections and trials, that thereby we may take light what may be wrought upon the body of man. Wherein we find many strange effects: as continuing life in them, though divers parts, which you account vital, be perished and taken forth; resuscitating of some that seem dead in appearance, and the like. We try also all poisons, and other medicines upon them, as well of chirurgery as physic. By art likewise we make them greater or taller than their kind is, and contrariwise dwarf them and stay their growth; we make them more fruitful and bearing than their kind is, and contrariwise barren and not generative. Also we make them differ in color, shape, activity, many ways. We find means to make commixtures and copulations of divers kinds, which have produced many new kinds, and them not barren, as the general opinion is. We make a number of kinds, of serpents, worms, flies, fishes, of putrefaction, whereof some are advanced (in effect) to be perfect creatures, like beasts or birds, and have sexes, and do propagate. Neither do we this by chance, but we know beforehand of what matter and commixture, what kind of those creatures will arise.

"We have also particular pools where we make trials upon fishes, as we have said before of beasts and birds.

"We have also places for breed and generation of those kinds of worms and flies which are of special use; such as are with you your silkworms and bees.

"I will not hold you long with recounting of our brew-houses, bake-houses, and kitchens, where are made divers drinks, breads, and meats, rare and of special effects. Wines we have of grapes, and drinks of other juice, of fruits, of grains, and of roots, and of mixtures with honey, sugar, manna, and fruits dried and decocted; also of the tears or woundings of trees, and of the pulp of canes. And these drinks are of several ages, some to the age or last of forty years. We have drinks also brewed with several herbs, and roots and spices; yea, with several fleshes and white-meats; whereof some of the drinks are such as they are in effect meat and drink both, so that divers, especially in age, do desire to live with them with little or no meat or bread. And above all we strive to have drinks of extreme thin parts, to insinuate into the body, and yet without all biting, sharpness, or fretting; insomuch as some of them, put upon the back of your hand, will with a little stay pass through to the palm, and taste yet mild to the mouth. We have also waters, which we ripen in that fashion as they become nourishing, so that they are indeed excellent drink, and many will use no other. Breads we have of several grains, roots, and kernels; yea, and some of flesh, and fish, dried; with divers kinds of leavenings and seasonings; so that some do extremely move appetites, some do nourish so, as divers do live of them, without any other meat, who live very long. So for meats, we have some of them so beaten, and made tender, and mortified, yet without all corrupting, as a weak heat of the stomach will turn them into good chylus, as well as a strong heat would meat otherwise prepared. We have some meats also, and breads, and drinks, which taken by men, enable them to fast long after; and some other, that used make the very flesh of men's bodies sensibly more hard and tough, and their strength far greater than otherwise it would be.

"We have dispensatories or shops of medicines; wherein you may easily think, if we have such variety of plants, and living creatures, more than you have in Europe (for we know what you have), the simples, drugs and ingredients of medicines, must likewise be in so much the greater variety. We have them likewise of divers ages, and long fermentations. And for their preparations, we have not only all manner of exquisite distillations and separations, and especially by gentle heats, and percolations through divers strainers, yea, and substances; but also exact forms of composition, whereby they incorporate almost as they were natural simples.

"We have also divers mechanical arts, which you have not; and stuffs made by them, as papers, linen, silks, tissues, dainty works of feathers of wonderful luster, excellent dyes, and many others: and shops likewise, as well for such as are not brought into vulgar use amongst us, as for those that are. For you must know, that of the things before recited, many of them are grown into use throughout the kingdom, but yet, if they did flow from our invention, we have of them also for patterns and principals.

"We have also furnaces of great diversities, and that keep great diversity of heats: fierce and quick, strong and constant, soft and mild; blown, quiet, dry, moist, and the like. But above all we have heats, in imitation of the sun's and heavenly bodies' heats, that pass divers inequalities, and (as it were) orbs, progresses, and returns, whereby we produce admirable effects. Besides, we have heats of dungs, and of bellies and maws of living creatures and of their bloods and bodies, and of hays and herbs laid up moist, of lime unquenched, and such like. Instruments also which generate heat only by motion. And farther, places for strong insolations; and again, places under the earth, which by nature or art yield heat. These divers heats we use as the nature of the operation which we intend requireth.

"We have also perspective houses, where we make demonstrations of all lights and radiations, and of all colors; and out of things uncolored and transparent, we can represent unto you all several colors, not in rainbows (as it is in gems and prisms), but of themselves single. We represent also all multiplications of light, which we carry to great distance, and make so sharp, as to discern small points and lines. Also all colorations of light; all delusions and deceits of the sight, in figures, magnitudes, motions, colors; all demonstrations of shadows. We find also divers means yet unknown to you, of producing of light originally from divers bodies. We procure means of seeing objects afar off, as in the heaven and remote places; and represent things near as afar off, and things afar off as near; making feigned distances. We have also helps for the sight, far above spectacles and glasses in use. We have also glasses and means to see small and minute bodies, perfectly and distinctly; as the shapes and colors of small flies and worms, grains, and flaws in gems which cannot otherwise be seen, observations in urine and blood not otherwise to be seen. We make artificial rainbows, halos, and circles about light. We represent also all manner of reflections, refractions, and multiplications of visual beams of objects.

"We have also precious stones of all kinds, many of them of great beauty and to you unknown; crystals likewise, and glasses of divers kinds; and amongst them some of metals vitrificated, and other materials, besides those of which you make glass. Also a number of fossils and imperfect minerals, which you have not. Likewise loadstones of prodigious virtue: and other rare stones, both natural and artificial.

"We have also sound-houses, where we practise and demonstrate all sounds and their generation. We have harmonies which you have not, of quarter-sounds and lesser slides of sounds. Divers instruments of music likewise to you unknown, some sweeter than any you have; together with bells and rings that are dainty and sweet. We represent small sounds as great and deep; likewise great sounds, extenuate and sharp; we make divers tremblings and warblings of sounds, which in their original are entire. We represent and imitate all articulate sounds and letters, and the voices and notes of beasts and birds. We have certain helps, which set to the ear do further the hearing greatly. We have also divers strange and artificial echoes, reflecting the voice many times, and as it were tossing it; and some that give back the voice louder than it came, some shriller and some deeper; yea, some rendering the voice, differing in the letters or articulate sound from that they receive. We have also means to convey sounds in trunks and pipes, in strange lines and distances.

"We have also perfume-houses, wherewith we join also practices of taste. We multiply smells, which may seem strange: we imitate smells, making all smells to breathe out of other mixtures than those that give them. We make divers imitations of taste likewise, so that they will deceive any man's taste. And in this house we contain also a confiture-house, where we make all sweetmeats, dry and moist, and divers pleasant wines, milks, broths, and sallets, far in greater variety than you have.

"We have also engine-houses, where are prepared engines and instruments for all sorts of motions. There we imitate and practise to make swifter motions than any you have, either out of your muskets or any engine that you have; and to make them and multiply them more easily and with small force, by wheels and other means, and to make them stronger and more violent than yours are, exceeding your greatest cannons and basilisks. We represent also ordnance and instruments of war and engines of all kinds; and likewise new mixtures and compositions of gunpowder, wild-fires burning in water and unquenchable; also fire-works of all variety, both for pleasure and use. We imitate also flights of birds; we have some degrees of flying in the air. We have ships and boats for going under water and brooking of seas, also swimming-girdles and supporters. We have divers curious clocks, and other like motions of return, and some perpetual motions. We imitate also motions of living creatures by images of men, beasts, birds, fishes and serpents; we have also a great number of other various motions, strange for equality, fineness, and subtlety.

"We have also a mathematical house, where are represented all instruments, as well of geometry as astronomy, exquisitely made.

"We have also houses of deceits of the senses, where we represent all manner of feats of juggling, false apparitions, impostures and illusions, and their fallacies. And surely you will easily believe that we, that have so many things truly natural which induce admiration, could in a world of particulars deceive the senses if we would disguise those things, and labor to make them seem more miraculous. But we do hate all impostures and lies, insomuch as we have severely forbidden it to all our fellows, under pain of ignominy and fines, that they do not show any natural work or thing adorned or swelling, but only pure as it is, and without all affectation of strangeness.

"These are, my son, the riches of Salomon's House.

"For the several employments and offices of our fellows, we have twelve that sail into foreign countries under the names of other nations (for our own we conceal), who bring us the books and abstracts, and patterns of experiments of all other parts. These we call Merchants of Light.

"We have three that collect the experiments which are in all books. These we call Depredators.

"We have three that collect the experiments of all mechanical arts, and also of liberal sciences, and also of practices which are not brought into arts. These we call Mystery-men.

"We have three that try new experiments, such as themselves think good. These we call Pioneers or Miners.

"We have three that draw the experiments of the former four into titles and tables, to give the better light for the drawing of observations and axioms out of them. These we call Compilers.

"We have three that bend themselves, looking into the experiments of their fellows, and cast about how to draw out of them things of use and practice for man's life and knowledge, as well for works as for plain demonstration of causes, means of natural divinations, and the easy and clear discovery of the virtues and parts of bodies. These we call Dowry-men or Benefactors.

"Then after divers meetings and consults of our whole number, to consider of the former labors and collections, we have three that take care out of them to direct new experiments, of a higher light, more penetrating into Nature than the former. These we call Lamps.

"We have three others that do execute the experiments so directed, and report them. These we call Inoculators.

"Lastly, we have three that raise the former discoveries by experiments into greater observations, axioms, and aphorisms. These we call Interpreters of Nature.

"We have also, as you must think, novices and apprentices, that the succession of the former employed men do not fail; besides a great number of servants and attendants, men and women. And this we do also: we have consultations, which of the inventions and experiences which we have discovered shall be published, and which not: and take all an oath of secrecy for the concealing of those which we think fit to keep secret: though some of those we do reveal sometimes to the State, and some not.

"For our ordinances and rites, we have two very long and fair galleries: in one of these we place patterns and samples of all manner of the more rare and excellent inventions: in the other we place the statuas of all principal inventors. There we have the statua of your Columbus, that discovered the West Indies: also the inventor of ships: your monk that was the inventor of ordnance and of gunpowder: the inventor of music: the inventor of letters: the inventor of printing: the inventor of observations of astronomy: the inventor of works in metal: the inventor of glass: the inventor of silk of the worm: the inventor of wine: the inventor of corn and bread: the inventor of sugars: and all these by more certain tradition than you have. Then we have divers inventors of our own, of excellent works, which since you have not seen, it were too long to make descriptions of them; and besides, in the right understanding of those descriptions you might easily err. For upon every invention of value we erect a statua to the inventor, and give him a liberal and honorable reward. These statuas are some of brass, some of marble and touchstone, some of cedar and other special woods gilt and adorned; some of iron, some of silver, some of gold.

"We have certain hymns and services, which we say daily, of laud and thanks to God for his marvelous works. And forms of prayer, imploring his aid and blessing for the illumination of our labors, and the turning of them into good and holy uses.

"Lastly, we have circuits or visits, of divers principal cities of the kingdom; where, as it cometh to pass, we do publish such new profitable inventions as we think good. And we do also declare natural divinations of diseases, plagues, swarms of hurtful creatures, scarcity, tempests, earthquakes, great inundations, comets, temperature of the year, and divers other things; and we give counsel thereupon, what the people shall do for the prevention and remedy of them."

And when he had said this he stood up; and I, as I had been taught, kneeled down; and he laid his right hand upon my head, and said, "God bless thee, my son, and God bless this relation which I have made. I give thee leave to publish it, for the good of other nations; for we here are in God's bosom, a land unknown." And so he left me; having assigned a value of about two thousand ducats for a bounty to me and my fellows. For they give great largesses, where they come, upon all occasions.

The rest was not perfected

ROBERT BURTON (1577–1640)

Burton lived forty-seven years in Oxford, forty of those years in one college, Christ Church; his first period of university life was spent at Brasenose. It is a fitting background for the author of the most learned book in English literature. *The Anatomy of Melancholy* (1621 *et seq.*), revived by the Romantic generation as a storehouse of oddities, was a scientific medical or psycho-pathological treatise which, for all its vast scope and infinite detail, steers a straight course from beginning to end. But the book was also a monument of literature because, in a sceptical, disillusioned, and melancholy age, it was a profound inquiry into the outer and inner world of man and man's life, and because it was written by one of the sanest of men in the raciest of prose. It is nothing less than a *comédie humaine* with a tragic reading of life in the background. Burton's manner, his variety of incidental themes, his pell-mell quotations—so happily different from modern psychological writings—should not blind one to his scientific method and his sensitive exploration of the darker places of the soul.

ANATOMY OF MELANCHOLY (1621 *et seq.*)

DEMOCRITUS JUNIOR TO THE READER

GENTLE READER, I presume thou wilt be very inquisitive to know what antic or personate actor this is that so insolently intrudes upon this common theatre to the world's view, arrogating another man's name, whence he is, why he doth it, and what he hath to say. Although, as he said, *Primum si noluero, non respondebo, quis coacturus est?* I am a free man born, and may choose whether I will tell; who can compel me?—if I be urged, I will as readily reply as that Egyptian in Plutarch, when a curious fellow would needs know what he had in his basket, *Quum vides velatam, quid inquiris in rem absconditam?* It was therefore covered, because he should not know what was in it. Seek not after that which is hid; if the contents please thee, and be for thy use, suppose the man in the moon, or whom thou wilt, to be the author; I would not willingly be known. Yet in some sort to give thee satisfaction, which is more than I need, I will show a reason, both of this usurped name, title, and subject. And first of the name of Democritus; lest any man by reason of it should be deceived, expecting a pasquil, a satire, some ridiculous treatise (as I myself should have done), some prodigious tenent, or paradox of the earth's motion, of infinite worlds, *in infinito vacuo, ex fortuita atomorum collisione*, in an infinite waste, so caused by an accidental collision of motes in the sun, all which Democritus held, Epicurus and their master Leucippus of old maintained, and are lately revived by Copernicus, Brunus, and some others. Besides it hath been always an ordinary custom, as Gellius observes, for later writers and impostors to broach many absurd and insolent fictions, under the name of so noble a philosopher as Democritus, to get themselves credit, and by that means the more to be respected, as artificers usually do, *novo qui marmori ascribunt Praxitelen suo.*[1] 'Tis not so with me.

> *Non hic Centauros, non Gorgonas Harpyasque*
> *Invenies, hominem pagina nostra sapit.*

> No Centaurs here, or Gorgons look to find,
> My subject is of man, and human kind.

Thou thyself art the subject of my discourse.

> *Quicquid agunt homines, votum, timor, ira, voluptas,*
> *Gaudia, discursus, nostri farrago libelli.*

> Whate'er men do, vows, fears, in ire, in sport,
> Joys, wanderings, are the sum of my report.

My intent is no otherwise to use his name than Mercurius Gallobelgicus, Mercurius Britannicus, use the name of Mercury, Democritus Christianus, etc. Although there be some other circumstances for which I have masked myself under this visard and some peculiar respects which I cannot so well express until I have set down a brief character of this our Democritus, what he was, with an epitome of his life. Democritus, as he is described by Hippocrates, and Laertius, was a little wearish old man, very

---

[1]Who put Praxiteles' name on their new marble statue.

melancholy by nature, averse from company in his latter days, and much given to solitariness, a famous philosopher in his age, *cœvus* with Socrates, wholly addicted to his studies at the last and to a private life, writ many excellent works, a great divine, according to the divinity of those times, an expert physician, a politician, an excellent mathematician, as *Diacosmus* and the rest of his works do witness. He was much delighted with the studies of husbandry, saith Columella, and often I find him cited by Constantinus and others treating of that subject. He knew the natures, differences of all beasts, plants, fishes, birds; and, as some say, could understand the tunes and voices of them. In a word, he was *omnifariam doctus*, a general scholar, a great student; and to the intent he might better contemplate, I find it related by some that he put out his eyes and was in his old age voluntarily blind, yet saw more than all Greece besides, and writ of every subject, *Nihil in toto opificio naturæ de quo non scripsit*. A man of an excellent wit, profound conceit; and to attain knowledge the better in his younger years, he traveled to Egypt and Athens, to confer with learned men, admired of some, despised of others. After a wandering life, he settled at Abdera, a town in Thrace, and was sent for thither to be their law-maker, recorder or town clerk as some will; or as others, he was there bred and born. Howsoever it was, there he lived at last in a garden in the suburbs, wholly betaking himself to his studies and a private life, saving that sometimes he would walk down to the haven, and laugh heartily at such variety of ridiculous objects which there he saw. Such a one was Democritus.

But in the meantime, how doth this concern me, or upon what reference do I usurp his habit? I confess indeed that to compare myself unto him for aught I have yet said were both impudency and arrogancy; I do not presume to make any parallel, *Antistat mihi millibus trecentis, parvus sum, nullus sum, altum nec spiro, nec spero.*[1] Yet thus much I will say of myself, and that I hope without all suspicion of pride or self-conceit, I have lived a silent, sedentary, solitary, private life, *mihi et musis*[2] in the University as long almost as Xenocrates in Athens, *ad senectam fere,*[3] to

---

[1] He excels me in infinite respects, I am a poor creature, a nobody, I have no lofty aims or hopes.

[2] To myself and the Muses.

[3] Almost to old age.

learn wisdom as he did, penned up most part in my study. For I have been brought up a student in the most flourishing College of Europe, *augustissimo collegio*, and can brag with Jovius, almost, *in ea luce domicilii Vaticani, totius orbis celeberrimi, per 37 annos multa opportunaque didici*,[1] for 30 years I have continued (having the use of as good libraries as ever he had) a scholar, and would be therefore loth, either by living as a drone, to be an unprofitable or unworthy a member of so learned and noble a society, or to write that which should be any way dishonorable to such a royal and ample foundation. Something I have done, though by my profession a divine, yet *turbine raptus ingenii*, as he said, out of a running wit, an unconstant, unsettled mind, I had a great desire (not able to attain to a superficial skill in any) to have some smattering in all, to be *aliquis in omnibus, nullus in singulis*,[2] which Plato commends, out of him Lipsius approves and furthers, as fit to be imprinted in all curious wits, not be a slave of one science, or dwell altogether in one subject as most do, but to rove abroad, *centum puer artium*,[3] to have an oar in everyman's boat, to taste of every dish, and sip of every cup, which saith Montaigne was well performed by Aristotle and his learned countryman Adrian Turnebus. This roving humor (though not with like success) I have ever had, and like a ranging spaniel, that barks at every bird he sees, leaving his game, I have followed all, saving that which I should, and may justly complain, and truly, *qui ubique est, nusquam est*,[4] which Gesner did in modesty, that I have read many books, but to little purpose, for want of good method, I have confusedly tumbled over divers authors in our libraries, with small profit for want of art, order, memory, judgment. I never traveled but in map or card, in which my unconfined thoughts have freely expatiated, as having ever been especially delighted with the study of cosmography. Saturn was the lord of my geniture, culminating, etc., and Mars principal *significator* of manners, in partile conjunction with mine ascendant; both fortunate in their houses, etc. I am not poor, I am not rich; *nihil est, nihil deest*,

---

[1]In that light of the Vatican, the greatest library in the world, during thirty-seven years my studies bore manifold fruit.

[2]Someone in everything, no authority in anything.

[3]A youth of a hundred arts.

[4]One who is everywhere is nowhere.

I have little, I want nothing: all my treasure is in Minerva's
tower. Greater preferment as I could never get, so am I not in
debt for it, I have a competency (*Laus Deo*) from my noble and
munificent patrons, though I live still a collegiate student, as
Democritus in his garden, and lead a monastic life, *ipse mihi
theatrum*,[1] sequestered from those tumults and troubles of the
world, *et tanquam in specula positus*,[2] (as he said) in some high
place above you all, like *Stoicus sapiens, omnia sæcula, præterita
presentiaque videns, uno velut intuitu*;[3] I hear and see what is
done abroad, how others run, ride, turmoil, and macerate themselves in court and country, far from those wrangling lawsuits,
aulæ vanitatem, fori ambitionem, ridere mecum soleo;[4] I laugh at
all, only secure lest my suit go amiss, my ships perish, corn and
cattle miscarry, trade decay. I have no wife nor children good
or bad to provide for. A mere spectator of other men's fortunes
and adventures, and how they act their parts, which methinks
are diversely presented unto me as from a common theatre or
scene. I hear new news every day, and those ordinary rumors
of war, plagues, fires, inundations, thefts, murders, massacres,
meteors, comets, spectrums, prodigies, apparitions, of towns
taken, cities besieged in France, Germany, Turkey, Persia,
Poland, etc., daily musters and preparations, and such like, which
these tempestuous times afford, battles fought, so many men
slain, monomachies, shipwrecks, piracies, and sea-fights, peace,
leagues, stratagems, and fresh alarms. A vast confusion of
vows, wishes, actions, edicts, petitions, lawsuits, pleas, laws,
proclamations, complaints, grievances are daily brought to our
ears. New books every day, pamphlets, currantoes, stories,
whole catalogues of volumes of all sorts, new paradoxes, opinions,
schisms, heresies, controversies in philosophy, religion, etc.
Now come tidings of weddings, maskings, mummeries, entertainments, jubilees, embassies, tilts and tournaments, trophies,
triumphs, revels, sports, plays: then again, as in a new shifted
scene, treasons, cheating tricks, robberies, enormous villainies
in all kinds, funerals, burials, deaths of princes, new discoveries,

---

[1] A theatre to myself.

[2] As if placed among mirrors.

[3] The wise Stoic, seeing all ages, past and present, as if at a glance.

[4] I am wont to laugh to myself at the vanity of the court and the ambition of
the forum.

expeditions; now comical, then tragical matters. To-day we hear of new lords and officers created, to-morrow of some great men deposed, and then again of fresh honors conferred; one is let loose, another imprisoned; one purchaseth, another breaketh; he thrives, his neighbor turns bankrupt; now plenty, then again dearth and famine; one runs, another rides, wrangles, laughs, weeps, etc. Thus I daily hear, and such like, both private and public news. Amidst the gallantry and misery of the world; jollity, pride, perplexities and cares, simplicity and villainy; subtlety, knavery, candor and integrity, mutually mixed and offering themselves, I rub on *privus privatus*;[1] as I have still lived, so I now continue, *statu quo prius*,[2] left to a solitary life and mine own domestic discontents: saving that sometimes, *ne quid mentiar*,[3] as Diogenes went into the city, and Democritus to the haven, to see fashions, I did for my recreation now and then walk abroad, look into the world, and could not choose but make some little observation, *non tam sagax observator ac simplex recitator*,[4] not as they did to scoff or laugh at all, but with a mixed passion.

Bilem, sæpe jocum vestri movere tumultus.[5]

I did sometimes laugh and scoff with Lucian, and satirically tax with Menippus, lament with Heraclitus; sometimes again I was *petulanti splene cachinno*,[6] and then again, *urere bilis jecur*,[7] I was much moved to see that abuse which I could not amend. In which passion howsoever I may sympathize with him or them, 'tis for no such respect I shroud myself under his name, but either in an unknown habit to assume a little more liberty and freedom of speech, or if you will needs know, for that reason and only respect, which Hippocrates relates at large in his Epistle to Damagetus, wherein he doth express how coming to visit him one day, he found Democritus in his garden at Abdera, in the

---

[1] In a strictly private life.
[2] In the same condition as before.
[3] Not to tell a lie.
[4] Not so much a wise observer as a simple narrator.
[5] Your passions have often stirred me to anger or mirth.
[6] A laugher with saucy spleen.
[7] My liver burned with anger.

suburbs, under a shady bower, with a book on his knees, busy at his study, sometimes writing, sometimes walking. The subject of his book was melancholy and madness; about him lay the carcasses of many several beasts newly by him cut up and anatomized, not that he did contemn God's creatures, as he told Hippocrates, but to find out the seat of this *atra bilis*, or melancholy, whence it proceeds, and how it was engendered in men's bodies, to the intent he might better cure it in himself, [and] by his writings and observations teach others how to prevent and avoid it. Which good intent of his Hippocrates highly commended: Democritus Junior is therefore bold to imitate, and because he left it unperfect, and it is now lost, *quasi succenturiator Democriti*,[1] to revive again, prosecute and finish, in this treatise. You have had a reason of the name. If the title and inscription offend your gravity, were it a sufficient justification to accuse others I could produce many sober treatises, even sermons themselves, which in their fronts carry more fantastical names. Howsoever it is a kind of policy in these days to prefix a fantastical title to a book which is to be sold. For as larks come down to a day-net, many vain readers will tarry and stand gazing like silly passengers at an antic picture in a painter's shop, that will not look at a judicious piece. And indeed, as Scaliger observes, nothing more invites a reader than an argument unlooked for, unthought of, and sells better than a scurrile pamphlet, *tum maxime cum novitas excitat palatum*.[2] Many men, saith Gellius, are very conceited in their inscriptions, and able (as Pliny quotes out of Seneca) to make him loiter by the way that went in haste to fetch a midwife for his daughter, now ready to lie down. For my part I have honorable precedents for this which I have done: I will cite one for all, Anthony Zara, *Pap. Episc.* his Anatomy of Wit, in four sections, members, subsections, etc., to be read in our libraries.

If any man except against the matter or manner of treating of this my subject, and will demand a reason of it, I can allege more than one. I writ of melancholy by being busy to avoid melancholy. There is no greater cause of melancholy than idleness, no better cure than business, as Rhasis holds: and howbeit

---

[1]As a substitute for Democritus.

[2]Most of all when novelty tickles the palate.

stultus labor est ineptiarum, to be busied in toys is to small purpose, yet hear that divine Seneca, better *aliud agere quam nihil,* better do to no end than nothing. I writ therefore, and busied myself in this playing labor, *otiosaque diligentia ut vitarem torporem feriandi,*[1] with Vectius in Macrobius, *atque otium in utile verterem negotium.*[2]

——*Simul et jucunda et idonea dicere vitæ,*
Lectorem delectando simul atque monendo.[3]

To this end I writ, like them, saith Lucian, that recite to trees, and declaim to pillars, for want of auditors: as Paulus Ægineta ingeniously confesseth, not that anything was unknown or omitted, but to exercise myself, which course if some took, I think it would be good for their bodies, and much better for their souls; or peradventure as others do, for fame, to show myself, (*Scire tuum nihil est, nisi te scire hoc sciat alter.*[4]) I might be of Thucydides' opinion, to know a thing and not to express it is all one as if he knew it not. When I first took this task in hand, *et quod ait ille, impellente genio negotium suscepi,*[5] this I aimed at, *vel ut lenirem animum scribendo,* to ease my mind by writing, for I had *gravidum cor, fœdum caput,* a kind of imposthume in my head, which I was very desirous to be unladen of, and could imagine no fitter evacuation than this. Besides I might not well refrain, for *ubi dolor, ibi digitus,* one must needs scratch where it itches. I was not a little offended with this malady, shall I say my Mistress Melancholy, my Egeria, or my *Malus Genius?*[6] And for that cause, as he that is stung with a scorpion, I would expel *clavum clavo,* comfort one sorrow with another, idleness with idleness, *ut ex vipera theriacum,*[7] make an antidote out of that which was the prime cause of my disease. Or as he did of whom Felix Plater speaks, that thought he had some of Aristophanes' frogs in his belly, still crying *Brececcex, coax, coax,*

---

[1] To avoid, with idle labor, the torpor of idleness.

[2] And turn my leisure to fruitful use.

[3] At once to say things pleasant and profitable, to give the reader both pleasure and counsel.

[4] Your knowledge is nothing unless another know that you know.

[5] And, as he says, urged by my genius I undertook the task.

[6] Evil genius.

[7] From the snake make an antidote against snake-poison.

oop, *oop*, and for that cause studied physic seven years and traveled over most part of Europe to ease himself. To do myself good I turned over such physicians as our libraries would afford, or my private friends impart, and have taken this pains. And why not? Cardan professeth he writ his book *De Consolatione* after his son's death to comfort himself; so did Tully write of the same subject with like intent after his daughter's departure, if it be his at least, or some impostor's put out in his name, which Lipsius probably suspects. Concerning myself, I can peradventure affirm with Marius in Sallust, that which others hear or read of, I felt and practised myself; they get their knowledge by books, I mine by melancholizing. *Experto crede Roberto.*[1] Something I can speak out of experience, *ærumnabilis experientia me docuit*,[2] and with her in the poet, *Haud ignara mali miseris succurrere disco:* I would help others out of a fellow-feeling, and as that virtuous lady did of old, being a leper herself, bestow all her portion to build an hospital for lepers, I will spend my time and knowledge, which are my greatest fortunes, for the common good of all. . . .

I have laboriously collected this cento out of divers writers, and that *sine injuria;* I have wronged no authors, but given every man his own, which Hierome so much commends in Nepotian; he stole not whole verses, pages, tracts, as some do nowadays, concealing their authors' names, but still said, this was Cyprian's, that Lactantius', that Hilarius', so said Minucius Felix, so Victorinus, thus far Arnobius. I cite and quote mine authors (which howsoever some illiterate scribblers account pedantical, as a cloak of ignorance, and opposite to their affected fine style, I must and will use) *sumpsi, non surripui*,[4] and what Varro *De Re Rust.* speaks of bees, *minime maleficæ [quod] nullius opus vellicantes faciunt deterius*,[5] I can say of myself, whom have I injured? The matter is theirs most part and yet mine, *apparet unde sumptum sit* (which Seneca approves) *aliud tamen quam unde sumptum sit apparet;*[6] which nature doth with the aliment

---

[1]Believe Robert, who has experience.
[2]Painful experience has taught me.
[3]Not ignorant of evil, I have learned to succor the wretched.
[4]I have borrowed, not stolen.
[5]They are not evil-doers, because, when they extract honey, they do no injury.
[6]Its original is clear, yet it is clearly something different from its original.

of our bodies incorporate, digest, assimilate, I do *concoquere quod hausi*, dispose of what I take. I make them pay tribute to set out this my *macaronicon;* the method only is mine own, I must usurp that of Wecker *e Ter.*, *nihil dictum quod non dictum prius, methodus sola artificem ostendit*, we can say nothing but what hath been said, the composition and method is ours only, and shows a scholar. Oribasius, Aëtius, Avicenna have all out of Galen, but to their own method, *diverso stilo, non diversa fide.*[1] Our poets steal from Homer; he spews, saith Ælian, they lick it up. Divines use Austin's words *verbatim* still, and our story-dressers do as much; he that comes last is commonly best,

——*donec quid grandius ætas*
Postera sorsque ferat melior.[2]

Though there were many giants of old in physic and philosophy, yet I say with Didacus Stella, a dwarf standing on the shoulders of a giant may see farther than a giant himself; I may likely add, alter, and see farther than my predecessors. And it is no greater prejudice for me to indite after others than for Ælianus Montaltus, that famous physician, to write *de morbis capitis*[3] after Jason Pratensis, Heurnius, Hildesheim, etc., many horses to run in a race, one logician, one rhetorician, after another. Oppose then what thou wilt.

Allatres licet usque nos et usque,
Et gannitibus improbis lacessas,[4]

I solve it thus. And for those other faults of barbarism, Doric dialect, extemporanean style, tautologies, apish imitation, a rhapsody of rags gathered together from several dung-hills, excrements of authors, toys and fopperies confusedly tumbled out, without art, invention, judgment, wit, learning, harsh, raw, rude, fantastical, absurd, insolent, indiscreet, ill-composed, indigested, vain, scurrile, idle, dull and dry, I confess all ('tis partly affected); thou canst not think worse of me than I do of myself. 'Tis not worth the reading, I yield it; I desire thee not to lose time

---

[1] A different style, not a different faith.
[2] Until a later age and happier lot produce something greater.
[3] On diseases of the head.
[4] You may bark and attack me with vicious snarls if you like.

in perusing so vain a subject; I should be peradventure loth myself to read him or thee so writing; 'tis not *operæ pretium*.[1] All I
say is this, that I have precedents for it, which Isocrates calls
perfugium iis qui peccant,[2] others as absurd, vain, idle, illiterate,
etc. *Nonnulli alii idem fecerunt*, others have done as much, it
may be more, and perhaps thou thyself, *Novimus et qui te, etc.*,[3]
we have all our faults; *scimus et hanc veniam, etc.*[4], thou censurest
me, so have I done others, and may do thee, *Cædimus, inque
vicem, etc.*[5], 'tis *lex talionis*,[6] *quid pro quo*.[7] Go now, censure,
criticize, scoff and rail.

> *Nasutus sis usque licet, sis denique nasus:*
> *Non potes in nugas dicere plura meas,*
> *Ipse ego quam dixi, etc.*

Wert thou all scoffs and flouts, a very Momus:
Than we ourselves thou canst not say worse of us.

. . . .

I am therefore in this point a professed disciple of Apollonius, a
scholar of Socrates; I neglect phrases, and labor wholly to inform
my reader's understanding, not to please his ear; 'tis not my
study or intent to compose neatly, which an orator requires, but
to express myself readily and plainly as it happens. So that as
a river runs, sometimes precipitate and swift, then dull and slow;
now direct, then *per ambages*,[8] now deep, then shallow; now
muddy, then clear; now broad, then narrow; doth my style flow:
now serious, then light; now comical, then satirical; now more
elaborate, then remiss, as the present subject required, or as at
that time I was affected. And if thou vouchsafe to read this
treatise, it shall seem no otherwise to thee than the way to an
ordinary traveler, sometimes fair, sometimes foul; here cham-

---

[1]Worth the trouble.
[2]A refuge for sinners.
[3]We know who sported with you . . .
[4]We know, and this excuse [we appeal to and allow].
[5]We strike, and in turn [expose ourselves].
[6]Law of reprisals.
[7]Tit for tat.
[8]Winding about.

paign, there inclosed; barren in one place, better soil in another: by woods, groves, hills, dales, plains, etc. I shall lead thee *per ardua montium, et lubrica vallium, et roscida cespitum, et glebosa camporum*,[1] through variety of objects, that which thou shalt like and surely dislike. . . .

If any physician in the meantime shall infer, *Ne sutor ultra crepidam*,[2] and find himself grieved that I have intruded into his profession, I will tell him in brief I do not otherwise by them than they do by us. If it be for their advantage, I know many of their sect which have taken orders in hope of a benefice, 'tis a common transition, and why not a melancholy divine, that can get nothing but by simony, profess physic? Drusianus an Italian (Crusianus, but corruptly, Trithemius calls him) because he was not fortunate in his practice, forsook his profession, and writ afterwards in divinity. Marcilius Ficinus was *semel et simul*,[3] a priest and a physician at once, and T. Linacre in his old age took orders. The Jesuits profess both at this time, divers of them *permissu superiorum*,[4] chirurgeons, panders, bawds, and midwives, etc. Many poor country vicars, for want of other means, are driven to their shifts; to turn mountebanks, quacksalvers, empirics, and if our greedy patrons hold us to such hard conditions as commonly they do, they will make most of us work at some trade, as Paul did, at last turn taskers, malsters, costermongers, graziers, sell ale as some have done, or worse. Howsoever, in undertaking this task, I hope I shall commit no great error or *indecorum*, if all be considered aright; I can vindicate myself with Georgius Brunnius, and Hieronymus Henninges, those two learned divines, who (to borrow a line or two of mine elder brother) drawn by a natural love, the one of pictures and maps, prospectives and chorographical delights, writ that ample *Theatre of Cities*; the other to the study of genealogies, penned *Theatrum Genealogicum*. Or else I can excuse my studies with Lessius the Jesuit in like case. It is a disease of the soul on which I am to treat, and as much appertaining to a divine as to a physician; and who knows not what an agreement

---

[1] Over steep mountains, slippery valleys, and moist turf and clodded fields.
[2] The cobbler should stick to his last.
[3] At one and the same time.
[4] By the permission of their superiors.

there is betwixt these two professions? A good divine either is or ought to be a good physician, a spiritual physician at least, as our Savior calls himself, and was indeed, *Mat.* 4.23; *Luke* 5.18; *Luke* 7.21. They differ but in object, the one of the body, the other of the soul, and use divers medicines to cure: one amends *animam per corpus*[1] the other *corpus per animam*,[2] as our Regius Professor of Physic well informed us in a learned lecture of his not long since. One helps the vices and passions of the soul, anger, lust, desperation, pride, presumption, etc., by applying the spiritual physic; as the other uses proper remedies in bodily diseases. Now this being a common infirmity of body and soul, and such a one that hath as much need of a spiritual as corporal cure, I could not find a fitter task to busy myself about, a more apposite theme, so necessary, so commodious, and generally concerning all sorts of men, that should so equally participate of both, and require a whole physician. A divine in this compound mixed malady can do little alone, a physician in some kinds of melancholy much less; both make an absolute cure.

Alterius sic altera poscit opem.[3]

. . . .

To conclude, this being granted, that all the world is melancholy, or mad, dotes, and every member of it, I have ended my task, and sufficiently illustrated that which I took upon me to demonstrate at first. At this present I have no more to say. *His sanam mentem Democritus*,[4] I can but wish myself and them a good physician, and all of us a better mind.

And although, for the above-named reasons, I had a just cause to undertake this subject, to point at these particular species of dotage, that so men might acknowledge their imperfections, and seek to reform what is amiss; yet I have a more serious intent at this time; and to omit all impertinent digressions, to say no more of such as are improperly melancholy, or metaphorically mad, lightly mad, or in disposition, as stupid, angry, drunken, silly, sottish, sullen, proud, vain-glorious, ridiculous, beastly, peevish,

[1]The soul through the body.
[2]The body through the soul.
[3]So each needs the help of the other.
[4]Democritus Junior wishes them a sound mind.

obstinate, impudent, extravagant, dry, doting, dull, desperate, harebrain, etc., mad, frantic, foolish, heteroclites, which no new hospital can hold, no physic help: my purpose and endeavor is, in the following discourse, to anatomize this humor of melancholy, through all his parts and species, as it is an habit, or an ordinary disease, and that philosophically, medicinally, to show the causes, symptoms, and several cures of it, that it may be the better avoided; moved thereunto for the generality of it, and to do good, it being a disease so frequent, as Mercurialis observes, in these our days; so often happening, saith Laurentius, in our miserable times, as few there are that feel not the smart of it. Of the same mind is Ælian Montaltus, Melancthon, and others; Julius Cæsar Claudinus calls it the fountain of all other diseases, and so common in this crazed age of ours, that scarce one of a thousand is free from it: and that splenetic hypochondriacal wind especially, which proceeds from the spleen and short ribs. Being then it is a disease so grievous, so common, I know not wherein to do a more general service, and spend my time better, than to prescribe means how to prevent and cure so universal a malady, an epidemical disease, that so often, so much, crucifies the body and mind. . . .

PROGNOSTICS OF MELANCHOLY

PART. I, SECT. IV, MEM. I.

. . . In such sort doth the torture and extremity of his misery torment him, that he can take no pleasure in his life, but is in a manner enforced to offer violence unto himself, to be freed from his present insufferable pains. So some (saith Fracastorius) in fury, but most in despair, sorrow, fear, and out of the anguish and vexation of their souls, offer violence to themselves: for their life is unhappy and miserable. They can take no rest in the night, nor sleep, or, if they do slumber, fearful dreams astonish them. In the day time they are affrighted still by some terrible object, and torn in pieces with suspicion, fear, sorrow, discontents, cares, shame, anguish, etc., as so many wild horses, that they cannot be quiet an hour, a minute of time, but even against their wills they are intent, and still thinking of it, they cannot forget it, it grinds their souls day and night, they are perpetually tormented, a burden to themselves, as Job was, they can neither eat, drink or sleep. *Psal.* 107, 18; their soul abhorreth all meat, and they are brought to death's door, being bound in misery and iron: they curse their stars with Job, and day of their birth, and wish for death: for, as Pineda and most interpreters hold, Job was even melancholy to despair, and almost madness itself; they murmur many times against the world, friends, allies, all mankind, even against God himself in the bitterness of their passion, *vivere nolunt, mori nesciunt,* live they will not, die they cannot. And in the midst of these squalid, ugly, and such irksome days, they seek at last, finding no comfort, no remedy, in this wretched life, to be eased of all by death. *Omnia appetunt bonum,* all creatures seek the best, and for their good as they hope, *sub specie,* in show at least, *vel quia mori pulchrum putant* (saith Hippocrates) *vel quia putant inde se majoribus malis liberari,*[1] to be freed as they wish. Though many times, as Æsop's fishes, they leap from the frying-pan into the fire itself, yet they hope to be eased by this means; and therefore, saith Felix Platerus, after many tedious days, at last, either by drowning, hanging, or some such fearful end, they precipitate or make away themselves: many lamentable examples are daily seen amongst us: *alius ante [amicæ] fores laqueo pependit,* (as Seneca notes), *alius se præcipitavit a tecto, ne dominum stomachantem [diutius] audiret, alius, ne reduceretur a fuga, ferrum redegit in viscera,*[2] so many causes there are—*His amor exitio est, furor his*[3] —love, grief, anger, madness, and shame, etc. 'Tis a common calamity, a fatal end to this disease, they are condemned to a violent death by a jury of physicians, furiously disposed, carried headlong by their tyrannizing wills, enforced by miseries, and there remains no more to such persons, if that heavenly Physician, by his assisting grace and mercy alone, do not prevent, (for no human persuasion or art can help), but to be their own butchers, and execute themselves. Socrates his *cicuta,*[4] Lucretia's dagger, Timon's halter, are yet to be had; Cato's knife and Nero's

[1] Either because they think it fine to die, or because they think thus to be freed from greater evils.

[2] One hanged himself before his mistress' door; another cast himself from the roof, that he might no longer hear his master's angry words; another, to avoid being brought back after flight, plunged a dagger into his vitals.

[3] Some love destroys, some madness.

[4] Hemlock.

sword are left behind them, as so many fatal engines, bequeathed to posterity, and will be used to the world's end by such distressed souls: so intolerable, unsufferable, grievous, and violent, is their pain, so unspeakable, and continuate. One day of grief is an hundred years, as Cardan observes: 'tis *carnificina hominum*, *angor animi*, as well saith Aretæus, a plague of the soul, the cramp and convulsion of the soul, an epitome of hell; and if there be an hell upon earth, it is to be found in a melancholy man's heart.

> For that deep torture may be call'd an hell,
> When more is felt than one hath power to tell.

Yea, that which scoffing Lucian said of the gout in jest, I may truly affirm of melancholy in earnest.

> *O triste nomen! O Diis odibile!*
> *Melancholia lacrimosa, Cocyti filia!*
> *Tu Tartari specubus opacis edita*
> *Erinnys, utero quam Megæra suo tulit,*
> *Et ab uberibus aluit, cuique parvulæ*
> *Amarulentum in os lac Alecto dedit.*
> *Omnes abominabilem te dæmones*
> *Produxere in lucem exitio mortalium.*
> Et paulo post.[1]

> *Non Jupiter fert tale telum fulminis,*
> *Non ulla sic procella sævit æquoris,*
> *Non impetuosi tanta vis est turbinis.*
> *An asperos sustineo morsus Cerberi?*
> *Num virus Echidnæ membra mea depascitur?*
> *Aut tunica sanie tincta Nessi sanguinis?*
> *Illacrimabile et immedicabile malum hoc.*

> O sad and odious name! a name so fell,
> Is this of melancholy, brat of hell,
> There born in hellish darkness doth it dwell.
> The Furies brought it up, Megæra's teat,
> Alecto gave it bitter milk to eat.
> And all conspired a bane to mortal men,
> To bring this devil out of that black den.

---

[1] And a little further on.

Jupiter's thunderbolt, nor storm at sea,
Nor whirlwind, doth our hearts so much dismay.
What? am I bit by that fierce Cerberus?
Or stung by serpent so pestiferous?
Or put on shirt that's dipt in Nessus' blood?
My pain's past cure; physic can do no good.

No torture of body like unto it! *Siculi non invenere tyranni majus tormentum,*[1] no strappadoes, hot irons, Phalaris' bulls,

Nec ira deum tantum, nec tela, nec hostis,
Quantum sola noces animis illapsa.

Jove's wrath nor Devil's can
Do so much harm to th' soul of man.

All fears, griefs, suspicions, discontents, imbonities, insuavities, are swallowed up and drowned in this Euripus, this Irish Sea, this ocean of misery, as so many small brooks; 'tis *coagulum omnium ærumnarum*[2]: which Ammianus applied to his distressed Palladius. I say of our melancholy man, he is the cream of human adversity, the quintessence, and upshot; all other diseases whatsoever are but flea-bitings to melancholy in extent: 'tis the pith of them all,

Hospitium est calamitatis. Quid verbis opus est?
Quamcunque malam rem quæris, illic reperies:

What need more words? 'tis calamity's inn.
Where seek for any mischief, 'tis within;

and a melancholy man is that true Prometheus, which is bound to Caucasus; the true Tityus, whose bowels are still by a vulture devoured (as poets feign), for so doth Lilius Geraldus interpret it, of anxieties, and those griping cares, and so ought it to be understood. In all other maladies we seek for help; if a leg or an arm ache, through any distemperature or wound, or that we have an ordinary disease, above all things whatsoever we desire help and health, a present recovery, if by any means possible it may be procured: we will freely part with all our other fortunes,

---

[1] Sicilian tyrants invented no worse torture.
[2] A collection of all woes.

substance, endure any misery, drink bitter potions, swallow those distasteful pills, suffer our joints to be seared, to be cut off, any thing for future health; so sweet, so dear, so precious above all other things in this world is life: 'tis that we chiefly desire, long and happy days, *multos da, Jupiter, annos!* increase of years all men wish; but to a melancholy man nothing so tedious, nothing so odious; that which they so carefully seek to preserve he abhors, he alone. So intolerable are his pains, some make a question *graviores morbi corporis an animi*, whether the diseases of the body or mind be more grievous, but there is no comparison, no doubt to be made of it, *multo enim sævior longeque est atrocior animi quam corporis cruciatus*, (Lem. *l.* 1. *c.* 12.), the diseases of the mind are far more grievous.—*Totum hic pro vulnere corpus*, body and soul is misaffected here, but the soul especially. So Cardan testifies, *De rerum var. lib.* 8. 40: Maximus Tyrius, a Platonist, and Plutarch have made just volumes to prove it. *Dies adimit ægritudinem hominibus*,[1] in other diseases there is some hope likely, but these unhappy men are born to misery, past all hope of recovery, incurably sick; the longer they live the worse they are, and death alone must ease them.

HEROICAL LOVE CAUSING MELANCHOLY

PART. III, SECT. II, MEM. I, SUBS. I

PHILOSTRATUS, in his fourth book *De Vita Apollonii*, hath a memorable instance in this kind, which I may not omit, of one Menippus Lycius, a young man 25 years of age, that, going betwixt Cenchreæ and Corinth, met such a phantasm in the habit of a fair gentlewoman, which, taking him by the hand, carried him home to her house in the suburbs of Corinth, and told him she was a Phœnician by birth, and if he would tarry with her he should hear her sing and play, and drink such wine as never any drank, and no man should molest him; but she being fair and lovely would live and die with him, that was fair and lovely to behold. The young man, a philosopher, otherwise staid and discreet, able to moderate his passions, though not this of love, tarried with her a while to his great content, and at last married her, to whose wedding, among other guests, came

---

[1] Time takes away sorrows from men.

Apollonius, who by some probable conjectures found her out to be a serpent, a *Lamia*, and that all her furniture was like Tantalus' gold described by Homer, no substance, but mere illusions. When she saw herself descried, she wept, and desired Apollonius to be silent, but he would not be moved, and thereupon she, plate, house, and all that was in it, vanished in an instant: many thousands took notice of this fact, for it was done in the midst of Greece.

PROGNOSTICS OF LOVE-MELANCHOLY

PART. III, SECT. II, MEM. IV, SUBS. I

WHAT fires, torments, cares, jealousies, suspicions, fears, griefs, anxieties, accompany such as are in love, I have sufficiently said: the next question is, what will be the event of such miseries, what they foretell. Some are of opinion that this love cannot be cured, *nullis amor est medicabilis herbis*, it accompanies them to the last.

Idem amor exitio est pecori pecorisque magistro,[1]

and is so continuate that by no persuasion almost it may be relieved. Bid me not love, said Euryalus, bid the mountains come down into the plains, bid the rivers run back to their fountains; I can as soon leave to love as the sun leave his course.

Et prius æquoribus pisces, et montibus umbræ,
Et volucres deerunt silvis, et murmura ventis,
Quam mihi discedent formosæ Amaryllidis ignes.

First seas shall want their fish, the mountains shade,
Woods singing birds, the wind's murmur shall fade,
Than my fair Amaryllis' love allay'd.

Bid me not love, bid a deaf man hear, a blind man see, a dumb speak, lame run, counsel can do no good, a sick man cannot relish, no physic can ease me.

Non prosunt domino quæ prosunt omnibus artes,[2]

---

[1] Love destroys alike both sheep and shepherd.

[2] Those arts which help all men help not their master.

as Apollo confessed, and Jupiter himself could not be cured.

Omnes humanos curat medicina dolores,
Solus amor morbi non habet artificem.

Physic can soon cure every disease,
Excepting love, that can it not appease.

But whether love may be cured or no, and by what means, shall be explained in his place; in the meantime, if it take his course and be not otherwise eased or amended, it breaks out often into outrageous and prodigious events. *Amor et Liber violenti dii sunt,* as Tatius observes, *et eo usque animum incendunt, ut pudoris oblivisci cogant,* Love and Bacchus are so violent gods, so furiously rage in our minds, that they make us forget all honesty, shame, and common civility. For such men ordinarily as are thoroughly possessed with this humor, become *insensati et insani,* for it is *amor insanus,* as the poet calls it, beside themselves, and as I have proved, no better than beasts, irrational, stupid, headstrong, void of fear of God or men; they frequently forswear themselves, spend, steal, commit incests, rapes, adulteries, murders, depopulate towns, cities, countries, to satisfy their lust.

A devil 'tis, and mischief such doth work,
As never yet did pagan, Jew, or Turk.

The wars of Troy may be a sufficient witness; and as Appian, *Hist. lib. 5,* saith of Antony and Cleopatra, their love brought themselves and all Egypt into extreme and miserable calamities, the end of her is as bitter as wormwood, and as sharp as a two-edged sword. *Prov.* v 4, 5: Her feet go down to death, her steps lead on to hell. She is more bitter than death (*Eccles.* vii. 26.) and the sinner shall be taken by her.

Qui in amore præcipitavit, pejus perit quam si saxo saliat.

He that runs headlong from the top of a rock is not in so bad a case as he that falls into the gulf of love. For hence, saith Platina, comes repentance, dotage, they lose themselves, their wits, and make shipwreck of their fortunes altogether: madness, to make away themselves and others, violent death. *Prog-*

nosticatio est talis, saith Gordonius, *si non succurratur iis, aut in maniam cadunt, aut moriuntur*, the prognostication is, they will either run mad or die. For if this passion continue, saith Ælian Montaltus, it makes the blood hot, thick, and black; and if the inflammation get into the brain, with continual meditation and waking, it so dries it up that madness follows, or else they make away themselves.

> *O Corydon, Corydon, quæ te dementia cepit?*[1]

Now, as Arnoldus adds, it will speedily work these effects if it be not presently helped; they will pine away, run mad, and die upon a sudden; *facile incidant in maniam*, saith Valescus, quickly mad, *nisi succurratur*, if good order be not taken,

> *Eheu triste jugum quisquis amoris habet,*
> *Is prius ac norit se periisse perit.*

> Oh heavy yoke of love, which whoso bears,
> Is quite undone, and that at unawares.

So she confessed of herself in the poet,

> ——*Insaniam priusquam quis sentiat,*
> *Vix pili intervallo a furore absum.*

> I shall be mad before it be perceived,
> A hair-breadth off scarce am I, now distracted.

As mad as Orlando for his Angelica, or Hercules for his Hylas,

> *At ille ruebat quo pedes ducebant, furibundus,*
> *Nam illi sævus Deus intus jecur laniabat.*

> He went he car'd not whither, mad he was,
> The cruel god so tortur'd him, alas!

At the sight of Hero I cannot tell how many ran mad,

> *Alius vulnus celans insanit pulchritudine puellæ.*

> And whilst he doth conceal his grief,
> Madness comes on him like a thief.

---

[1] O Corydon, Corydon, what madness has seized you?

Go to Bedlam for examples. It is so well known in every village how many have either died for love or voluntarily made away themselves that I need not much labor to prove it; *Nec modus aut requies nisi mors reperitur amoris:* death is the common catastrophe to such persons.

> *Mori mihi contingat, non enim alia*
> *Liberatio ab ærumnis fuerit ullo pacto istis.*

> Would I were dead! for nought, God knows,
> But death can rid me of these woes.

As soon as Euryalus departed from Siena, Lucretia, his paramour, never looked up, no jests could exhilarate her sad mind, no joys comfort her wounded and distressed soul, but a little after she fell sick and died. But this is a gentle end, a natural death; such persons commonly make away themselves.

> ——*proprioque in sanguine lætus,*
> *Indignantem animam vacuas effudit in auras.*[1]

So did Dido,

> *Sed moriamur! ait, Sic, sic juvat ire sub umbras;*[2]

Pyramus and Thisbe, Medea, Coresus and Callirhoe, Theagenes the philosopher, and many myriads besides, and so will ever do,

> ——*et mihi fortis*
> *Est manus, est et amor, dabit hic in vulnera vires.*[3]

> Who ever heard a story of more woe,
> Than that of Juliet and her Romeo?

Read Parthenium *In Eroticis*, and Plutarch's *amatorias narrationes*, or love-stories, all tending almost to this purpose. Valleriola, *lib. 2. observ.* 7, hath a lamentable narration of a merchant his patient, that raving through impatience of love, had he not been watched, would every while have offered vio-

---

[1] Happy in his own blood, he poured his angry soul into the empty air.
[2] "But let me die," she said, "thus, thus, it is a joy to go down to the shades."
[3] My hand is strong, strong too is love, and will give strength for wounds.

lence to himself. Amatus Lusitanus, *cent. 3. car. 56*, hath such another story, and Felix Plater, *Med. obser. lib.* 1., a third of a young gentleman that studied physic, and for the love of a doctor's daughter, having no hope to compass his desire, poisoned himself. *Anno* 1615, a barber in Frankfort, because his wench was betrothed to another, cut his own throat. At Neuburg the same year a young man, because he could not get her parents' consent, killed his sweetheart, and afterwards himself, desiring this of the magistrate, as he gave up the ghost, that they might be buried in one grave,

Quodque rogis superest una requiescat in urna,[1]

which Gismunda besought of Tancredus her father, that she might be in like sort buried with Guiscardus her lover, that so their bodies might lie together in the grave, as their souls wander about *campos lugentes*[2] in the Elysian fields,

————*quos durus amor crudeli tabe peredit,*[3]

in a myrtle grove

————*et myrtea circum*
Silva tegit: curæ non ipsa in morte relinquunt.[4]

You have not yet heard the worst; they do not offer violence to themselves in this rage of lust, but unto others, their nearest and dearest friends. Catiline killed his only son, *misitque ad orci pallida, lethi obnubila, obsita tenebris loca,*[5] for the love of Aurelia Orestilla, *quod ejus nuptias vivo filio recusaret.*[6] Laodice, the sister of Mithridates, poisoned her husband to give content to a base fellow whom she loved. Alexander to please Thais, a concubine of his, set Persepolis on fire. Nereus' wife, a widow and lady of Athens, for the love of a Venetian gentleman, betrayed the

---

[1]And that what remains from the pyre may lie in one urn.

[2]The fields of mourning.

[3]Whom cruel love destroyed with its wasting power.

[4]And a myrtle grove shelters them; even in death care does not leave them.

[5]Sent him to the shades of Orcus, the darkness of death, the region environed with gloom.

[3]Because she would not marry him while his son lived.

city; and he for her sake murthered his wife, the daughter of a noble man in Venice. Constantine Despota made away Catherine his wife, turned his son Michael and his other children out of doors, for the love of a base scrivener's daughter in Thessalonica, with whose beauty he was enamored. Leucophrye betrayed the city where she dwelt, for her sweetheart's sake, that was in the enemy's camp. Pisidice, the Governor's daughter of Methymna, for the love of Achilles, betrayed the whole island to him, her father's enemy. Diognetus did as much, in the city where he dwelt, for the love of Polycrite, Medea for the love of Jason; she taught him how to tame the fire-breathing, brass-feeted bulls, and kill the mighty dragon that kept the golden fleece; and tore her little brother Absyrtus in pieces, that her father Aeëtes might have something to detain him, while she ran away with her beloved Jason, etc. Such acts and scenes hath this tragicomedy of love.

RELIGIOUS MELANCHOLY

PART. III, SECT. IV, MEM. I, SUBS. I.

THAT there is such a distinct species of love-melancholy no man hath ever yet doubted; but whether this subdivision of Religious Melancholy be warrantable, it may be controverted.

> *Pergite Pierides, medio nec calle vagantem*
> *Linquite me, qua nulla pedum vestigia ducunt,*
> *Nulla rotæ currus testantur signa priores.*[1]

I have no pattern to follow, as in some of the rest, no man to imitate. No physician hath as yet distinctly written of it as of the other; all acknowledge it a most notable symptom, some a cause, but few a species or kind. Aretæus, Alexander, Rhasis, Avicenna, and most of our late writers, as Gordonius, Fuchsius, Plater, Bruel, Montaltus, etc., repeat it as a symptom. Some seem to be inspired of the Holy Ghost, some take upon them to be prophets, some are addicted to new opinions, some foretell strange things, *de statu mundi et Antichristi,*[2] saith Gordonius.

---

[1]Proceed, Muses, nor leave me wandering in the middle of the way, where no footprints lead, no chariot wheels have left any marks.

[2]Concerning the state of the world and Antichrist.

Some will prophesy of the end of the world to a day almost, and the fall of the Antichrist, as they have been addicted or brought up; for so melancholy works with them, as Laurentius holds. If they have been precisely given, all their meditations tend that way, and in conclusion produce strange effects; the humor imprints symptoms according to their several inclinations and conditions, which makes Guianerius and Felix Plater put too much devotion, blind zeal, fear of eternal punishment, and that last judgment, for a cause of those enthusiastics and desperate persons; but some do not obscurely make a distinct species of it, dividing love-melancholy into that whose object is women; and into the other, whose object is God. Plato, in *Convivio*, makes mention of two distinct furies; and amongst our Neoterics, Hercules de Saxonia, *lib. 1. pract. med. cap. 16. cap. de Melanch.*, doth expressly treat of it in a distinct species. Love-melancholy (saith he) is twofold, the first is that (to which peradventure some will not vouchsafe this name or species of melancholy) affection of those which put God for their object, and are altogether about prayer, fasting, etc., the other about women. Peter Forestus in his *Observations* delivereth as much in the same words: and Felix Platerus, *De mentis alienat. cap. 3. frequentissima est ejus species, in qua curanda sæpissime multum fui impeditus*[1]; 'tis a frequent disease; and they have a ground of what they say, forth of Aretæus and Plato. Aretæus, an old author, in his third book, *cap.* 6, doth so divide love-melancholy, and derives this second from the first, which comes by inspiration or otherwise. Plato in his *Phædrus* hath these words: Apollo's priests at Delphi, and at Dodona, in their fury do many pretty feats, and benefit the Greeks, but never in their right wits. He makes them all mad, as well he might; and he that shall but consider that superstition of old, those prodigious effects of it (as in its place I will show the several furies of our *Fatidici Dii*, Pythonissas, Sibyls, enthusiasts, pseudoprophets, heretics and schismatics in these our latter ages) shall instantly confess, that all the world again cannot afford so much matter of madness, so many stupend symptoms as superstition, heresy, schism hath brought out: that this species alone may be parallel'd to all the former, hath a greater latitude, and more miracu-

---

[1] It is the commonest kind, and in treating it I have most often had trouble.

lous effects; that it more besots and infatuates men than any other above named whatsoever, doth more harm, works more disquietness to mankind, and hath more crucified the souls of mortal men (such hath been the devil's craft) than wars, plagues, sicknesses, dearth, famine, and all the rest.

Give me but a little leave, and I will set before your eyes in brief a stupend, vast, infinite ocean of incredible madness and folly: a sea full of shelves and rocks, sands, gulfs, Euripuses, and contrary tides, full of fearful monsters, uncouth shapes, roaring waves, tempests, and siren calms, halcyonian seas, unspeakable misery, such comedies and tragedies, such absurd and ridiculous, feral and lamentable fits, that I know not whether they are more to be pitied or derided, or may be believed, but that we daily see the same still practised in our days, fresh examples, *nova novitia*, fresh objects of misery and madness in this kind, that are still represented unto us, abroad, at home, in the midst of us, in our bosoms. . . .

CAUSES OF DESPAIR

PART. III, SECT. IV, MEM. II, SUBS. III

THE principal agent and procurer of this mischief is the devil; those whom God forsakes, the devil, by his permission, lays hold on. Sometimes he persecutes them with that worm of conscience, as he did Judas, Saul, and others. The poets call it Nemesis, but it is indeed God's just judgment, *sero sed serio*, he strikes home at last, and setteth upon them as a thief in the night, 1 *Thes*. [v.] 2. This temporary passion made David cry out: Lord, rebuke me not in thine anger, neither chasten me in thine heavy displeasure; for thine arrows have lit upon me, etc. There is nothing sound in my flesh, because of thine anger. Again, I roar for the very grief of my heart; and *Psal*. 22, My God, my God, why hast thou forsaken me, and art so far from my health, and the words of my crying? I am like to water poured out, my bones are out of joint, mine heart is like wax, that is molten in the midst of my bowels. So *Psal*. 88. 15. and 16. *vers*. and *Psal*. 102. I am in misery, at the point of death, from my youth I suffer thy terrors, doubting for my life; thine indignations have gone over me, and thy fear hath cut me off. Job doth often complain in this kind; and those

God doth not assist, the devil is ready to try and torment, still seeking whom he may devour. If he find them merry, saith Gregory, he tempts them forthwith to some dissolute act; if pensive and sad, to a desperate end. *Aut suadendo blanditur aut minando terret,* sometimes by fair means, sometimes again by foul, as he perceives men severally inclined. His ordinary engine by which he produceth this effect is the melancholy humor itself, which is *balneum Diaboli,* the devil's bath; and as in Saul, those evil spirits get in, as it were, and take possession of us. Black choler is a shoeing-horn, a bait to allure them, insomuch that many writers make melancholy an ordinary cause and a symptom of despair, for that such men are most apt by reason of their ill-disposed temper to distrust, fear, grieve, mistake, and amplify whatsoever they preposterously conceive or falsely apprehend. *Conscientia scrupulosa nascitur ex vitio naturali, complexione melancholica* (saith Navarrus *cap.* 27. *num.* 282. *Tom.* 2. *cas. conscien.*) The body works upon the mind, by obfuscating the spirits and corrupted instruments, which Perkins illustrates by simile of an artificer that hath a bad tool; his skill is good, ability correspondent; by reason of ill tools his work must needs be lame and unperfect. But melancholy and despair, though often, do not always concur; there is much difference; melancholy fears without a cause, this upon great occasion; melancholy is caused by fear and grief, but this torment procures them all extremity of bitterness; much melancholy is without affliction of conscience, as Bright and Perkins illustrate by four reasons; and yet melancholy alone again may be sometimes a sufficient cause of this terror of conscience. Felix Plater so found it in his observations, *e melancholicis alii damnatos se putant, Deo curæ non esse, nec prædestinatos, etc.* They think they are not predestinate, God hath forsaken them; and yet otherwise very zealous and religious; and 'tis common to be seen, melancholy for fear of God's judgment and hell fire, drives men to desperation; fear and sorrow, if they be immoderate, end often with it. Intolerable pain and anguish, long sickness, captivity, misery, loss of goods, loss of friends, and those lesser griefs do sometimes effect it, or such dismal accidents. *Si non statim relevantur,* saith Marcennus, *dubitant an sit Deus,* if they be not eased forthwith, they doubt whether there be any God, they rave, curse, and are desperately mad, because good men are oppressed, wicked men flourish, they have not as they think to their desert, and through impatience of calamities are so misaffected. Democritus put out his eyes, *ne malorum civium prosperos videret successus,* because he could not abide to see wicked men prosper, and was therefore ready to make away himself, as A. Gellius writes of him. Felix Plater hath a memorable example in this kind, of a painter's wife in Basle, that was melancholy for her son's death, and for melancholy became desperate; she thought God would not pardon her sins, and for four months still raved that she was in hell fire, already damned. When the humor is stirred up, every small object aggravates and incenseth it, as the parties are addicted. The same author hath an example of a merchant-man that for the loss of a little wheat, which he had over-long kept, was troubled in conscience for that he had not sold it sooner or given it to the poor, yet a good scholar and a great divine; no persuasion would serve to the contrary, but that for this fact he was damned; in other matters very judicious and discreet. Solitariness, much fasting, divine meditations, and contemplations of God's judgments, most part accompany this melancholy, and are main causes, as Navarrus holds; to converse with such kind of persons so troubled is sufficient occasion of trouble to some men. *Nonnulli ob longas inedias, studia et meditationes cœlestes de rebus sacris et religione, semper agitant[ur], etc.* Many (saith P. Forestus) through long fasting, serious meditations of heavenly things, fall into such fits; and, as Lemnius adds, *lib.* 4. *cap.* 21, if they be solitary given, superstitious, precise, or very devout: seldom shall you find a merchant, a soldier, an innkeeper, a bawd, an host, an usurer so troubled in mind; they have cheverel consciences that will stretch, they are seldom moved in this kind or molested: young men and middle age are more wild, and less apprehensive; but old folks, most part, such as are timorous and religiously given. Pet. Forestus, *observat. lib.* 10. *cap.* 12 *de morbis cerebri,* hath a fearful example of a minister, that through precise fasting in Lent and overmuch meditation, contracted this mischief, and in the end became desperate, thought he saw devils in his chamber, and that he could not be saved; he smelled nothing, as he said, but fire and brimstone, was already in hell, and would ask them still if they did not smell as much. I told him he was melancholy, but he laughed me to scorn, and replied that he saw devils, talked with them in good earnest, would spit in my face, and ask me if I did not smell brimstone, but at last he was by him cured. Such another story I find in Plater, *observat. lib.* 1. A poor fellow had done some foul offence, and for fourteen days would eat no meat, in the end became desperate, the divines about him could not ease him, but so he died. Continual meditation of God's judgments troubles many. *Multi ob timorem futuri judicii,* saith Guatinerius, *cap. 5. tract.* 15, *et suspicionem desperabundi sunt:* David himself complains that God's judgments terrified his soul, *Psal.* 119. part. 15, vers. 8, My flesh trembleth for fear of thee, and I am afraid of thy judgments. *Quoties diem illum cogito* (saith Hierome) *toto corpore contremisco,* I tremble as often as I think of it. The terrible meditation of hell-fire and eternal punishment much torments a sinful silly soul. What's a thousand years to eternity? *Ubi mæror, ubi fletus, ubi dolor sempiternus; mors sine morte, finis sine fine;*[1] a finger burnt by chance we may not endure, the pain is so grievous, we may not abide an hour, a night is intolerable; and what shall this unspeakable fire then be that burns for ever, innumerable infinite millions of years, *in omne ævum, in æternum!* O eternity!

Æternitas est illa vox,
Vox illa fulminatrix,
Tonitruis minacior,
Fragoribusque cœli,
Æternitas est illa vox,
—meta carens et ortu, etc.
Tormenta nulla territant,
Quæ finiuntur annis;
Æternitas, æternitas
Versat coquitque pectus.
Auget hæc pœnas in dies,
Centuplicatque flammas, etc.[2]

---

[1]Where grief and lamentation and sorrow is eternal, death without death, end without end.

[2]Eternity is that word, that terrible word, more threatening than the thunder and lightning of heaven; eternity is that word, without end or beginning.... No torments dismay which are ended in time; eternity, eternity, shakes and burns the heart. This increases the punishment from day to day, multiplies the flames. . . .

This meditation terrifies these poor distressed souls, especially if their bodies be predisposed by melancholy, they religiously given, and have tender consciences; every small object affrights them, the very inconsiderate reading of Scripture itself, and misinterpretation of some places of it, as: Many are called, few are chosen. Not every one that saith Lord. Fear not, little flock. He that stands, let him take heed lest he fall. Work out your salvation with fear and trembling. That night two shall be in a bed, one received, the other left. Strait is the way that leads to heaven, and few there are that enter therein. The parable of the seed and of the sower; some fell on barren ground, some was choked. Whom he hath predestinated, he hath chosen. He will have mercy on whom he will have mercy. *Non est volentis nec currentis, sed miserentis Dei.*[1] These and the like places terrify the souls of many; election, predestination, reprobation, preposterously conceived, offend divers, with a deal of foolish presumption, curiosity, needless speculation, contemplation, solicitude, wherein they trouble and puzzle themselves about those questions of grace, free-will, perseverance, God's secrets; they will know more than is revealed by God in his word, human capacity, or ignorance can apprehend, and too importunate inquiry after that which is revealed; mysteries, ceremonies, observation of Sabbaths, laws, duties, etc., with many such which the casuists discuss, and schoolmen broach, which divers mistake, misconstrue, misapply to themselves, to their own undoing, and so fall into this gulf. They doubt of their election, how they shall know it, by what signs. And so far forth, saith Luther, with such nice points, torture and crucify themselves, that they are almost mad, and all they get by it is this, they lay open a gap to the devil by desperation to carry them to hell. But the greatest harm of all proceeds from those thundering ministers, a most frequent cause they are of this malady: and do more harm in the church (saith Erasmus) than they that flatter; great danger on both sides, the one lulls them asleep in carnal security, the other drives them to despair. . . .

---

[1] So then it is not of him that willeth, nor of him that runneth, but of God that showeth mercy.

CURE OF DESPAIR

PART. III, SECT. IV, MEM. II, SUBS. VI

But to my former task. The last main torture and trouble of a distressed mind is, not so much this doubt of election, and that the promises of grace are smothered and extinct in them, nay quite blotted out, as they suppose, but withal God's heavy wrath, a most intolerable pain and grief of heart seizeth on them: to their thinking they are already damned, they suffer the pains of hell, and more than possibly can be expressed, they smell brimstone, talk familiarly with devils, hear and see chimeras, prodigious, uncouth shapes, bears, owls, antics, black dogs, fiends, hideous outcries, fearful noises, shrieks, lamentable complaints; they are possessed, and through impatience they roar and howl, curse, blaspheme, deny God, call his power in question, abjure religion, and are still ready to offer violence unto themselves, by hanging, drowning, etc. Never any miserable wretch from the beginning of the world was in such a woeful case. To such persons I oppose God's mercy and his justice, *judicia Dei occulta, non injusta:* his secret counsel, and just judgment, by which he spares some, and sore afflicts others again in this life: his judgment is to be adored, trembled at, not to be searched or inquired after by mortal men: he hath reasons reserved to himself, which our frailty cannot apprehend. He may punish all, if he will, and that justly for sin; in that he doth it in some, is to make a way for his mercy that they repent and be saved, to heal them, to try them, exercise their patience, and make them call upon him, to confess their sins, and pray unto him, as David did, *Psal.* 119.137, Righteous art thou, O Lord, and just are thy judgments. As the poor publican, *Luke*, 18. 13, Lord have mercy upon me a miserable sinner. To put confidence, and have an assured hope in him, as Job had, 13. 15, Though he kill me, I will trust in him: *Ure, seca, occide, O Domine,* (saith Austin) *modo serves animam,* kill, cut in pieces, burn my body (O Lord) to save my soul. A small sickness, one lash of affliction, a little misery, many times, will more humiliate a man, sooner convert, bring him home to know himself, than all those paraenetical discourses, the whole theory of philosophy, law, physic and divinity, or a world of instances and examples. So that this, which they take to be such an insupportable plague, is an evident sign of God's mercy and justice, of his love and goodness: *periissent nisi periissent*, had they not thus been undone, they had finally been undone. Many a carnal man is lulled asleep in perverse security, foolish presumption, is stupefied in his sins, and hath no feeling at all of them: I have sinned (he saith) and what evil shall come unto me? *Eccles.* 5. 4. and tush, how shall God know it? And so in a reprobate sense goes down to hell. . . .

Last of all: if the party affected shall certainly know this malady to have proceeded from too much fasting, meditation, precise life, contemplation of God's judgments (for the devil deceives many by such means) in that other extreme he circumvents melancholy itself, reading some books, treatises, hearing rigid preachers, etc. If he shall perceive that it hath begun first from some great loss, grievous accident, disaster, seeing others in like case, or any such terrible object, let him speedily remove the cause, which to the cure of this disease Navarrus so much commends, *avertat cogitationem a re scrupulosa*,[1] by all apposite means, art, and industry, let him *laxare animum*, by all honest recreations, refresh and recreate his distressed soul; let him direct his thoughts, by himself and other of his friends. Let him read no more such tracts or subjects, hear no more such fearful tones, avoid such companies, and by all means open himself, submit himself to the advice of good physicians and divines, which is *contraventio scrupulorum*,[2] as he calls it, hear them speak to whom the Lord hath given the tongue of the learned, to be able to minister a word to him that is weary, whose words are as flagons of wine. Let him not be obstinate, headstrong, peevish, wilful, self-conceited (as in this malady they are) but give ear to good advice, be ruled and persuaded; and no doubt but such good counsel may prove as prosperous to his soul, as the angel was to Peter, that opened the iron gates, loosed his bands, brought him out of prison, and delivered him from bodily thraldom; they may ease his afflicted mind, relieve his wounded soul, and take him out of the jaws of hell itself. I can say no more, or give better advice to such as are any way

---

[1] Let him turn his thoughts away from the painful subject.
[2] A relief from anxiety.

distressed in this kind, than what I have given and said. Only take this for a corollary and conclusion, as thou tenderest thine own welfare in this, and all other melancholy, thy good health of body and mind, observe this short precept, give not way to solitariness and idleness. *Be not solitary, be not idle.*

SPERATE MISERI,
CAVETE FELICES.[1]

Vis a dubio liberari? Vis quod incertum est evadere? Age pœnitentiam dum sanus es; sic agens dico tibi quod securus es, quod pœnitentiam egisti eo tempore quo peccare potuisti. Austin.[2]

FINIS

[1] Ye wretched ones, hope; ye happy ones, fear.

[2] Do you wish to be freed from doubt? Do you wish to escape from uncertainty? Be penitent while you are well; so, I tell you, you are safe, because you have been penitent when you could have sinned.

SIR THOMAS BROWNE (1605–1682)

After receiving degrees from Oxford in 1626 and 1629 Browne enjoyed a prolonged sojourn on the continent, studying at the great medical schools of Montpellier, Padua, and Leyden. A few years after his return to England he settled in Norwich, the town with which his name is forever linked. There he lived quietly and happily in the practice of his profession, supervising the nurture of his sons with more than paternal solicitude, exploring strange problems of science and antiquarianism, and clothing his meditations on life and death in the most sumptuous and rhythmic language of an age supreme in ornate prose. He lived to welcome the Restoration, and in 1671 he was knighted during a royal visit to Norwich—the uniquely generous Lord Mayor effacing himself in favor of the town's most illustrious citizen.

Browne's chief writings were the *Religio Medici*, 1643; *Pseudodoxia Epidemica*, or *Vulgar Errors*, 1646; *Urn Burial* and *The Garden of Cyrus*, 1658; *Letter to a Friend* and *Christian Morals*, posthumously printed in 1690 and 1716. *Vulgar Errors*, judged by the standards of its time, is much less fantastic than it seems, but, even so, Browne's bizarre whimsies and mediæval habit of mind are constantly obstructing his sober scientific aspirations. We see him speculating *in vacuo* about the badger, yet taking the trouble to inspect a whale. The book is a treasury of humor, conscious and unconscious—witness the "with some few others" in the account of Oppianus.

Selections from other works are given under "Religion and Religious Philosophy"—though all of Browne is religious in spirit.

PSEUDODOXIA EPIDEMICA (1646)

THE FIRST BOOK

CHAPTER III

OF THE SECOND CAUSE OF POPULAR ERRORS, THE ERRONEOUS DISPOSITION OF THE PEOPLE

Having thus declared the fallible nature of man even from his first production, we have beheld the general cause of error.

288

But as for popular errors, they are more nearly founded upon an erroneous inclination of the people, as being the most deceptable part of mankind and ready with open arms to receive the encroachments of error. Which condition of theirs, although deducible from many grounds, yet shall we evidence it but from a few, and such as most nearly and undeniably declare their natures.

How unequal discerners of truth they are, and openly exposed unto error, will first appear from their unqualified intellectuals, unable to umpire the difficulty of its dissensions. For error, to speak largely, is a false judgment of things, or, an assent unto falsity. Now whether the object whereunto they deliver up their assent be true or false, they are incompetent judges.

For the assured truth of things is derived from the principles of knowledge, and causes which determine their verities. Whereof their uncultivated understandings, scarce holding any theory, they are but bad discerners of verity; and in the numerous track of error but casually do hit the point and unity of truth.

Their understanding is so feeble in the discernment of falsities, and averting the errors of reason, that it submitteth unto the fallacies of sense, and is unable to rectify the error of its sensations. Thus the greater part of mankind, having but one eye of sense and reason, conceive the earth far bigger than the sun, the fixed stars lesser than the moon, their figures plane, and their spaces from earth equidistant. For thus their sense informeth them, and herein their reason cannot rectify them, and therefore hopelessly continuing in mistakes, they live and die in their absurdities; passing their days in perverted apprehensions, and conceptions of the world derogatory unto God and the wisdom of the creation. . . .

CHAPTER V

OF CREDULITY AND SUPINITY

A THIRD cause of common errors is the credulity of men, that is, an easy assent to what is obtruded, or a believing at first ear what is delivered by others. This is a weakness in the understanding, without examination assenting unto things which from their natures and causes do carry no persuasion; whereby men often swallow falsities for truths, dubiosities for certainties, feasibilities for possibilities, and things impossible as possibilities themselves. Which, though the weakness of the intellect and most discoverable in vulgar heads, yet hath it sometime fallen upon wiser brains and great advancers of truth. . . .

The fourth is a supinity, or neglect of inquiry, even of matters whereof we doubt, rather believing than going to see; or doubting with ease and *gratis* than believing with difficulty or purchase. Whereby, either from a temperamental inactivity we are unready to put in execution the suggestions or dictates of reason, or by a content and acquiescence in every species of truth we embrace the shadow thereof, or so much as may palliate its just and substantial acquirements. Had our forefathers sat down in these resolutions, or had their curiosities been sedentary, who pursued the knowledge of things through all the corners of nature, the face of truth had been obscure unto us, whose luster in some part their industries have revealed. . . .

CHAPTER VI

OF ADHERENCE UNTO ANTIQUITY

But the mortalest enemy unto knowledge, and that which hath done the greatest execution upon truth, hath been a peremptory adhesion unto authority, and more especially the establishing of our belief upon the dictates of antiquity. For (as every capacity may observe) most men of ages present so superstitiously do look on ages past, that the authorities of the one exceed the reasons of the other: whose persons indeed being far removed from our times, their works, which seldom with us pass uncontrolled, either by contemporaries or immediate successors, are now become out of the distance of envies; and the farther removed from present times, are conceived to approach the nearer unto truth itself. Now hereby methinks we manifestly delude ourselves, and widely walk out of the track of truth.

For first, men hereby impose a thraldom on their times, which the ingenuity of no age should endure, or indeed the presumption of any did ever yet enjoin. Thus Hippocrates about 2000 years ago conceived it no injustice either to examine or refute the doctrines of his predecessors; Galen the like, and

Aristotle the most of any. Yet did not any of these conceive themselves infallible, or set down their dictates as verities irrefragable, but when they deliver their own inventions, or reject other men's opinions, they proceed with judgment and ingenuity, establishing their assertions not only with great solidity, but submitting them also unto the correction of future discovery.

Secondly, men that adore times past consider not that those times were once present; that is, as our own are at this instant, and we ourselves unto those to come as they unto us at present; as we rely on them, even so will those on us, and magnify us hereafter who at present condemn ourselves. Which very absurdity is daily committed amongst us, even in the esteem and censure of our own times. . . .

Thirdly, the testimonies of antiquity and such as pass oraculously amongst us were not, if we consider them, always so exact as to examine the doctrine they delivered. For some, and those the acutest of them, have left unto us many things of falsity, controllable not only by critical and collective reason, but common and country observation.

Hereof there want not many examples in Aristotle, through all his Book of Animals. . . .

CHAPTER VIII

A BRIEF ENUMERATION OF AUTHORS

. . . . 5 PLINIUS SECUNDUS of Verona, a man of great eloquence and industry indefatigable, as may appear by his writings, especially those now extant, and which are never like to perish but even with learning itself, that is, his *Natural History*. He was the greatest collector or rhapsodist of the Latins, and, as Suetonius observeth, he collected this piece out of two thousand Latin and Greek authors. Now what is very strange, there is scarce a popular error passant in our days which is not either directly expressed or deductively contained in this work; which, being in the hands of most men, hath proved a powerful occasion of their propagation. Wherein notwithstanding the credulity of the reader is more condemnable than the curiosity of the author, for commonly he nameth the authors from whom he received those accounts, and writes but as he reads, as in his preface to Vespasian he acknowledgeth. . . .

9. . . . We might perhaps let pass Oppianus, that famous Cilician poet. There are extant of his in Greek four books of Cynegetics or Venation, five of Halieutics or Piscation, commented and published by Ritterhusius; wherein describing beasts of venery and fishes, he hath indeed but sparingly inserted the vulgar conceptions thereof. So that, abating the annual mutation of sexes in the hyena, the single sex of the rhinoceros, the antipathy between two drums of a lamb and a wolf's skin, the informity of cubs, the venation of centaurs, the copulation of the murena and the viper, with some few others, he may be read with great delight and profit. It is not without some wonder his elegant lines are so neglected. . . .

THE THIRD BOOK

Of divers popular and received tenets concerning animals, which, examined, prove either false or dubious.

CHAPTER I

OF THE ELEPHANT

The first shall be of the elephant, whereof there generally passeth an opinion it hath no joints; and this absurdity is seconded with another, that being unable to lie down it sleepeth against a tree; which the hunters observing, do saw it almost asunder, whereon the beast relying, by the fall of the tree falls also down itself, and is able to rise no more. Which conceit is not the daughter of later times, but an old and gray-headed error, even in the days of Aristotle, as he delivereth in his book *De Incessu Animalium*, and stands successively related by several other authors, by Diodorus Siculus, Strabo, Ambrose, Cassiodore, Solinus, and many more. Now herein methinks men much forget themselves, not well considering the absurdity of such assertions.

For first, they affirm it hath no joints, and yet concede it walks and moves about; whereby they conceive there may be a progression or advancement made in motion without inflexion of parts. Now all progression or animals' locomotion being (as Aristotle teacheth) performed *tractu et pulsu*, that is, by drawing on or impelling forward some part which was before in station or at quiet, where there are no joints or flexures neither can there be these actions. And this is true not only in quadrupeds, volatiles, and fishes, which have distinct and prominent organs of motion, legs, wings, and fins, but in such also as perform their progression by the trunk, as serpents, worms, and leeches. Whereof though some want bones and all extended articulations, yet have they arthritical analogies, and by the motion of fibrous and musculous parts are able to make progression. Which to conceive in bodies inflexible, and without all protrusion of parts, were to expect a race from Hercules his pillars, or hope to behold the effects of Orpheus his harp, when trees found joints and danced after his music.

Again, while men conceive they never lie down, and enjoy not the position of rest ordained unto all pedestrious animals, hereby they imagine (what reason cannot conceive) that an animal of the vastest dimension and longest duration should live in a continual motion, without that alternity and vicissitude of rest whereby all others continue; and yet must thus much come to pass if we opinion they lie not down and enjoy no decumbence at all. For station is properly no rest, but one kind of motion, relating unto that which physicians (from Galen) do name extensive or tonical, that is, an extension of the muscles and organs of motion maintaining the body at length or in its proper figure. . . .

Moreover men herein do strangely forget the obvious relations of history, affirming they have no joints, whereas they daily read of several actions which are not performable without them. They forget what is delivered by Xiphilinus, and also by Suetonius in the lives of Nero and Galba, that elephants have been instructed to walk on ropes in public shows before the people. Which is not easily performed by man, and requireth not only a broad foot but a pliable flexure of joints and commandible disposure of all parts of progression. They pass by that memorable place in Curtius, concerning the elephant of King Porus, *Indus qui elephantem regebat, descendere eum ratus, more solito procumbere jussit in genua, cæteri quoque (ita enim instituti erant*) *demisere corpora in terram.*[1] They remember not the expression of Osorius, when he speaks of the elephant presented to Leo the Tenth, *Pontificem ter genibus flexis, et demisso corporis habitu venerabundus salutavit.*[2] But above all, they call not to mind that memorable show of Germanicus, wherein twelve elephants danced unto the sound of music, and after laid them down in the tricliniums, or places of festival recumbency. . . .

CHAPTER V

OF THE BADGER

THAT a brock or badger hath the legs on one side shorter than of the other, though an opinion perhaps not very ancient, is yet very general, received not only by theorists and unexperienced believers but assented unto by most who have the opportunity to behold and hunt them daily. Which notwithstanding upon inquiry I find repugnant unto the three determinators of truth, authority, sense, and reason. For first, Albertus Magnus speaks dubiously, confessing he could not confirm the verity hereof; but Aldrovandus plainly affirmeth there can be no such inequality observed. And for my own part, upon indifferent inquiry, I cannot discover this difference, although the regardable side be defined, and the brevity by most imputed unto the left.

Again, it seems no easy affront unto reason, and generally repugnant unto the course of nature, for if we survey the total set of animals, we may in their legs, or organs of progression, observe an equality of length and parity of numeration; that is, not any to have an odd leg, or the supporters and movers of one side not exactly answered by the other. Although the hinder may be unequal unto the fore and middle legs, as in frogs, locusts, and grasshoppers, or both unto the middle, as in some beetles and spiders, as is determined by Aristotle, *De Incessu Animalium.* Perfect and viviparous quadrupeds, so standing in

---

[1]The Indian who guided the elephant, thinking that Porus was getting down, ordered the beast to sink to his knees in the usual way; the other elephants also, such was their training, lowered their bodies to the ground.

[2]Three times, with knees bent and body bowed down, he saluted the pontiff with reverence.

their position of proneness that the opposite joints of neighbor-legs consist in the same plane; and a line descending from their navel intersects at right angles the axis of the earth. It happeneth often I confess that a lobster hath the chely or great claw of one side longer than the other; but this is not properly their leg, but a part of apprehension, and whereby they hold or seize upon their prey; for the legs and proper parts of progression are inverted backward, and stand in a position opposite unto these.

Lastly, the monstrosity is ill contrived, and with some disadvantage, the shortness being affixed unto the legs of one side, which might have been more tolerably placed upon the thwart or diagonial movers. For the progression of quadrupeds being performed *per diametrum*, that is, the cross legs moving or resting together, so that two are always in motion, and two in station at the same time, the brevity had been more tolerable in the cross legs. For then the motion and station had been performed by equal legs; whereas herein they are both performed by unequal organs, and the imperfection becomes discoverable at every hand.

CHAPTER XXVI

OF SPERMACETI AND THE SPERMACETI WHALE

. . . THAT it [spermaceti] proceedeth from a whale, beside the relation of Clusius and other learned observers, was indubitably determined not many years since by a spermaceti whale cast on our coast of Norfolk. Which, to lead on further inquiry, we cannot omit to inform. It contained no less than sixty foot in length, the head somewhat peculiar, with a large prominency over the mouth; teeth only in the lower jaw, received into fleshly sockets in the upper. The weight of the largest about two pound; no gristly substances in the mouth, commonly called whale-bones; only two short fins seated forwardly on the back; the eyes but small, the pizzle large and prominent. A lesser whale of this kind above twenty years ago was cast upon the same shore. . . .

Had the abominable scent permitted, enquiry had been made into that strange composure of the head and hillock of flesh about it: since the workmen affirmed they met with spermaceti before they came to the bone, and the head yet preserved seems to confirm the same. The sphincters inserving unto the fistula or spout might have been examined, since they are so notably contrived in other cetaceous animals; as also the larynx or throttle, whether answerable unto that of dolphins and porpoises in the strange composure and figure which it maketh. What figure the stomach maintained in this animal of one jaw of teeth, since in porpoises, which abound in both, the ventricle is trebly divided, and since in that formerly taken nothing was found but weeds and a loligo. . . .

CHAPTER XXVII

. . . SUNDRY TENENTS CONCERNING OTHER ANIMALS . . .

AND first from great antiquity, and before the melody of sirens, the musical note of swans hath been commended, and that they sing most sweetly before their death. For thus we read in Plato that from the opinion of metempsychosis, or transmigration of the souls of men into the bodies of beasts most suitable unto their human condition, after his death Orpheus the musician became a swan. Thus was it the bird of Apollo, the god of music, by the Greeks; and an hieroglyphic of music among the Egyptians, from whom the Greeks derived the conception; hath been the affirmation of many Latins, and hath not wanted asserters almost from every nation. . . .

When therefore we consider the dissension of authors, the falsity of relations, the indisposition of the organs, and the immusical note of all we ever beheld or heard of; if generally taken and comprehending all swans, or of all places, we cannot assent thereto. Surely he that is bit with a tarantula shall never be cured by this music; and with the same hopes we expect to hear the harmony of the spheres.

THE FIFTH BOOK

CHAPTER XXII

. . . QUESTIONABLE CUSTOMS, OPINIONS . . .

. . . WE SHALL not, I hope, disparage the resurrection of our Redeemer, if we say the sun doth not dance on Easter day. And though we would willingly assent unto any sympathetical exultation, yet cannot conceive therein any more than a tropical expression. Whether any such motion there were in that day wherein Christ arised, Scripture hath not revealed, which hath been punctual in other records concerning solary miracles; and the Areopagite, that was amazed at the eclipse, took no notice of this. And if metaphorical expressions go so far, we may be bold to affirm not only that one sun danced, but two arose that day; that light appeared at his nativity, and darkness at his death, and yet a light at both; for even that darkness was a light unto the Gentiles, illuminated by that obscurity. That 'twas the first time the sun set above the horizon; that although there were darkness above the earth, there was light beneath it, nor dare we say that hell was dark if he were in it.

PUBLIC AFFAIRS AND POLITICS

JOHN MILTON (1608–1674)

The main facts of Milton's life need not be recorded here; the auto-biographical extract given below mentions some outward events and, what is more important, reveals, in his own high manner, the spirit in which he approached both poetry and public affairs. It is common to regret the twenty years which Milton gave to controversy, but it is a question if the poetry would be what it is if it had not come from a man who, with an epic in his mind, could sacrifice it to obey the call of civic duty. Besides, *Areopagitica* (1644) is at least a partial compensation. Though only one of many protests against the rigors of intolerance, and though it failed of its immediate object, it dwarfs all others, except Taylor's *Liberty of Prophesying* (see p. 366). If the puritan sometimes gets the better of the humanist, it is not so in this plea for individual freedom, the central theme of Milton's life and work, which unifies his writings on religion, ethics, divorce, politics, education. His plea is not, of course, for the empty liberty of doing as one likes, but, with the Renaissance humanist's confidence in the essential goodness of man and his capacity for self-direction, he seeks freedom for the will to operate. Imbibing that doctrine of freedom from ancient fountains, he knows that the first requisite in education is strenuous discipline, and his letter on Education is the last great utterance in a series of humanistic treatises which had begun two centuries and a half before. Of such discipline freedom is the logical end and crown.

THE REASON OF CHURCH GOVERNMENT (1641)

How happy were it for this frail, and as it may be truly called, mortal life of man, since all earthly things, which have the name of good and convenient in our daily use, are withal so cumbersome and full of trouble, if knowledge, yet which is the best and lightsomest possession of the mind, were, as the common saying is, no burden; and that what it wanted of being a load to any part of the body, it did not with a heavy advantage overlay upon the spirit! For not to speak of that knowledge that rests in the contemplation of natural causes and dimensions, which must needs be a lower wisdom, as the object is low, certain it is that he who hath obtained in more than the scantest measure to know anything distinctly of God, and of his true worship; and what is infallibly good and happy in the state of man's life, what in itself evil and miserable, though vulgarly not so esteemed; he that hath obtained to know this, the only high valuable wisdom indeed, remembering also that God, even to a strictness, requires the improvement of these his entrusted gifts, cannot but sustain a sorer burden of mind, and more pressing, than any supportable toil or weight which the body can labor under, how and in what manner he shall dispose and employ those sums of knowledge and illumination, which God hath sent him into this world to trade with.

And that which aggravates the burden more, is, that, having received amongst his allotted parcels certain precious truths, of such an orient luster as no diamond can equal, which nevertheless he has in charge to put off at any cheap rate, yea, for nothing to them that will; the great merchants of this world, fearing that this course would soon discover and disgrace the false glitter of their deceitful wares, wherewith they abuse the people, like poor Indians with beads and glasses, practise by all means how they may suppress the venting of such rarities, and such a cheapness as would undo them, and turn their trash upon their hands. Therefore, by gratifying the corrupt desires of men in fleshly doctrines, they stir them up to persecute with hatred and contempt all those that seek to bear themselves uprightly in this their spiritual factory: which they foreseeing, though they cannot but testify of truth, and the excellency of that heavenly traffic which they bring, against what opposition or danger soever, yet needs must it sit heavily upon their spirits, that being, in God's prime intention and their own, selected heralds of peace and dispensers of treasure inestimable, without price, to them that have no pence, they find in the discharge of their commission, that they are made the greatest variance and offence, a very sword and fire both in house and city over the whole earth.

This is that which the sad prophet Jeremiah laments: "Woe is me, my mother, that thou hast borne me a man of strife and contention!" And although divine inspiration must certainly have been sweet to those ancient prophets, yet the irksomeness of that truth which they brought was so unpleasant to them, that everywhere they call it a burden. Yea, that mysterious book of Revelation, which the great evangelist was bid to eat, as it had been some eye-brightening electuary of knowledge and foresight, though it were sweet in his mouth and in the learning, it was bitter in his belly, bitter in the denouncing. Nor was this hid from the wise poet Sophocles, who in that place of his tragedy where Tiresias is called to resolve King Œdipus in a matter which he knew would be grievous, brings him in bemoaning his lot, that he knew more than other men. For surely to every good and peaceable man, it must in nature needs be a hateful thing to be the displeaser and molester of thousands; much better would it like him doubtless to be the messenger of gladness and contentment, which is his chief intended business, to all mankind, but that they resist and oppose their own true happiness.

But when God commands to take the trumpet, and blow a dolorous or a jarring blast, it lies not in man's will what he shall say, or what he shall conceal. If he shall think to be silent as Jeremiah did, because of the reproach and derision he met with daily, "and all his familiar friends watched for his halting," to be revenged on him for speaking the truth, he would be forced to confess as he confessed: "His word was in my heart as a burning fire shut up in my bones; I was weary with forbearing, and could not stay." Which might teach these times not suddenly to condemn all things that are sharply spoken or vehemently written, as proceeding out of stomach, virulence, and ill-nature; but to consider rather that, if the prelates have leave to say the worst that can be said, and do the worst that can be done, while they strive to keep to themselves, to their great pleasure and commodity, those things which they ought to render up, no man can be justly offended with him that shall endeavor to impart and bestow, without any gain to himself, those sharp but saving words which would be a terror and a torment in him to keep back.

For me, I have determined to lay up as the best treasure and solace of a good old age, if God vouchsafe it me, the honest liberty of free speech from my youth, where I shall think it available in so dear a concernment as the Church's good. For if I be, either by disposition or what other cause, too inquisitive, or suspicious of myself and mine own doings, who can help it? But this I foresee, that should the Church be brought under heavy oppression, and God have given me ability the while to reason against that man that should be the author of so foul a deed; or should she, by blessing from above on the industry and courage of faithful men, change this her distracted estate into better days, without the least furtherance or contribution of those few talents which God at that present had lent me; I foresee what stories I should hear within myself, all my life after, of discourage and reproach.

"Timorous and ungrateful, the Church of God is now again at the foot of her insulting enemies, and thou bewailest. What matters it for thee, or thy bewailing? When time was, thou couldst not find a syllable of all that thou hadst read, or studied, to utter in her behalf. Yet ease and leisure was given thee for thy retired thoughts, out of the sweat of other men. Thou hadst the diligence, the parts, the language of a man, if a vain subject were to be adorned or beautified; but when the cause of God and his Church was to be pleaded, for which purpose that tongue was given thee which thou hast, God listened if he could hear thy voice among his zealous servants, but thou wert dumb as a beast; from henceforward be that which thine own brutish silence hath made thee."

Or else I should have heard on the other ear: "Slothful, and ever to be set light by, the Church hath now overcome her late distresses after the unwearied labors of many her true servants that stood up in her defence; thou also wouldst take upon thee to share amongst them of their joy: but wherefore thou? Where canst thou show any word or deed of thine which might have hastened her peace? Whatever thou dost now talk, or write, or look, is the alms of other men's active prudence and zeal. Dare not now to say or do anything better than thy former sloth and infancy; or if thou darest, thou dost impudently to make a thrifty purchase of boldness to thyself out of the painful merits of other men; what before was thy sin is now thy duty to be, abject and worthless."

These, and such like lessons as these, I know would have been my matins duly, and my evensong. But now by this little

diligence, mark what a privilege I have gained, with good men
and saints to claim my right of lamenting the tribulations of
the Church, if she should suffer, when others, that have ventured
nothing for her sake, have not the honor to be admitted mourners. But if she lift up her drooping head and prosper, among
those that have something more than wished her welfare, I
have my charter and freehold of rejoicing to me and my heirs.
Concerning therefore this wayward subject against prelaty, the
touching whereof is so distasteful and disquietous to a number
of men, as by what hath been said I may deserve of charitable
readers to be credited, that neither envy nor gall hath entered me
upon this controversy, but the enforcement of conscience only,
and a preventive fear lest the omitting of this duty should be
against me, when I would store up to myself the good provision
of peaceful hours: so, lest it be still imputed to me, as I have
found it hath been, that some self-pleasing humor of vain-glory
hath incited me to contest with men of high estimation, now
while green years are upon my head; from this needless surmisal
I shall hope to dissuade the intelligent and equal auditor, if I
can but say successfully that which in this exigent behoves
me; although I would be heard only, if it might be, by the elegant
and learned reader, to whom principally for a while I shall beg
leave I may address myself.

To him it will be no new thing, though I tell him that if I
hunted after praise, by the ostentation of wit and learning, I
should not write thus out of mine own season, when I have
neither yet completed to my mind the full circle of my private
studies, although I complain not of any insufficiency to the
matter in hand; or were I ready to my wishes, it were a folly to
commit anything elaborately composed to the careless and interrupted listening of these tumultuous times. Next, if I were
wise only to my own ends, I would certainly take such a subject
as of itself might catch applause, whereas this hath all the
disadvantages on the contrary; and such a subject as the pub-
lishing whereof might be delayed at pleasure, and time enough
to pencil it over with all the curious touches of art, even to the
perfection of a faultless picture; whenas in this argument the
not deferring is of great moment to the good speeding, that, if
solidity have leisure to do her office, art cannot have much.
Lastly, I should not choose this manner of writing, wherein

knowing myself inferior to myself, led by the genial power of nature to another task, I have the use, as I may account, but of my left hand.

And though I shall be foolish in saying more to this purpose, yet, since it will be such a folly as wisest men going about to commit, have only confessed and so committed, I may trust with more reason, because with more folly, to have courteous pardon. For although a poet, soaring in the high region of his fancies, with his garland and singing robes about him, might, without apology, speak more of himself than I mean to do, yet for me sitting here below in the cool element of prose, a mortal thing among many readers of no empyreal conceit, to venture and divulge unusual things of myself, I shall petition to the gentler sort, it may not be envy to me.

I must say, therefore, that after I had from my first years, by the ceaseless diligence and care of my father (whom God recompense!), been exercised to the tongues and some sciences, as my age would suffer, by sundry masters and teachers, both at home and at the schools, it was found that whether aught was imposed me by them that had the overlooking, or betaken to of mine own choice in English, or other tongue, prosing or versing, but chiefly this latter, the style, by certain vital signs it had, was likely to live. But much latelier in the private academies of Italy, whither I was favored to resort, perceiving that some trifles which I had in memory, composed at under twenty or thereabout (for the manner is, that everyone must give some proof of his wit and reading there), met with acceptance above what was looked for; and other things, which I had shifted in scarcity of books and conveniences to patch up amongst them, were received with written encomiums, which the Italian is not forward to bestow on men of this side the Alps; I began thus far to assent both to them and divers of my friends here at home, and not less to an inward prompting which now grew daily upon me, that by labor and intent study (which I take to be my portion in this life), joined with the strong propensity of nature, I might perhaps leave something so written to aftertimes, as they should not willingly let it die.

These thoughts at once possessed me, and these other; that if I were certain to write as men buy leases, for three lives and downward, there ought no regard be sooner had than to God's glory, by the honor and instruction of my country. For which cause, and not only for that I knew it would be hard to arrive at the second rank among the Latins, I applied myself to that resolution, which Ariosto followed against the persuasions of Bembo, to fix all the industry and art I could unite to the adorning of my native tongue; not to make verbal curiosities the end (that were a toilsome vanity), but to be an interpreter and relater of the best and sagest things among mine own citizens throughout this island in the mother dialect. That, what the greatest and choicest wits of Athens, Rome, or modern Italy, and those Hebrews of old did for their country, I, in my proportion, with this over and above of being a Christian, might do for mine; not caring to be once named abroad, though perhaps I could attain to that, but content with these British islands as my world; whose fortune hath hitherto been that, if the Athenians, as some say, made their small deeds great and renowned by their eloquent writers, England hath had her noble achievements made small by the unskilful handling of monks and mechanics.

Time serves not now, and perhaps I might seem too profuse, to give any certain account of what the mind at home, in the spacious circuits of her musing, hath liberty to propose to herself, though of highest hope and hardest attempting; whether that epic form whereof the two poems of Homer, and those other two of Virgil and Tasso, are a diffuse, and the book of Job a brief model: or whether the rules of Aristotle herein are strictly to be kept, or nature to be followed, which in them that know art, and use judgment, is no transgression, but an enriching of art; and lastly, what king or knight, before the conquest, might be chosen in whom to lay the pattern of a Christian hero. And as Tasso gave to a prince of Italy his choice whether he would command him to write of Godfrey's expedition against the infidels, or Belisarius against the Goths, or Charlemain against the Lombards; if to the instinct of nature and the emboldening of art aught may be trusted, and that there be nothing adverse in our climate, or the fate of this age, it haply would be no rashness, from an equal diligence and inclination, to present the like offer in our own ancient stories; or whether those dramatic constitutions, wherein Sophocles and Euripides reign, shall be found more doctrinal and exemplary to a nation.

The Scripture also affords us a divine pastoral drama in the Song of Salomon, consisting of two persons, and a double chorus, as Origen rightly judges. And the Apocalypse of St. John is the majestic image of a high and stately tragedy, shutting up and intermingling her solemn scenes and acts with a sevenfold chorus of hallelujahs and harping symphonies: and this my opinion the grave authority of Paræus, commenting that book, is sufficient to confirm. Or if occasion shall lead, to imitate those magnific odes and hymns, wherein Pindarus and Callimachus are in most things worthy, some others in their frame judicious, in their matter most an end faulty. But those frequent songs throughout the law and prophets beyond all these, not in their divine argument alone, but in the very critical art of composition, may be easily made appear over all the kinds of lyric poesy to be incomparable.

These abilities, wheresoever they be found, are the inspired gift of God, rarely bestowed, but yet to some (though most abuse) in every nation; and are of power, beside the office of a pulpit, to inbreed and cherish in a great people the seeds of virtue and public civility, to allay the perturbations of the mind, and set the affections in right tune; to celebrate in glorious and lofty hymns the throne and equipage of God's almightiness, and what he works, and what he suffers to be wrought with high providence in his Church; to sing victorious agonies of martyrs and saints, the deeds and triumphs of just and pious nations, doing valiantly through faith against the enemies of Christ; to deplore the general relapses of kingdoms and states from justice and God's true worship.

Lastly, whatsoever in religion is holy and sublime, in virtue amiable or grave, whatsoever hath passion or admiration in all the changes of that which is called fortune from without, or the wily subtleties and refluxes of man's thoughts from within; all these things with a solid and treatable smoothness to paint out and describe. Teaching over the whole book of sanctity and virtue, through all the instances of example, with such delight to those especially of soft and delicious temper, who will not so much as look upon truth herself, unless they see her elegantly dressed; that whereas the paths of honesty and good life appear now rugged and difficult, though they be indeed easy and pleasant, they will then appear to all men both easy and pleasant, though they were rugged and difficult indeed. And what a benefit this would be to our youth and gentry, may be soon guessed by what we know of the corruption and bane which they suck in daily from the writings and interludes of libidinous and ignorant poetasters; who, having scarce ever heard of that which is the main consistence of a true poem, the choice of such persons as they ought to introduce, and what is moral and decent to each one, do for the most part lay up vicious principles in sweet pills to be swallowed down, and make the taste of virtuous documents harsh and sour.

But because the spirit of man cannot demean itself lively in this body, without some recreating intermission of labor and serious things, it were happy for the commonwealth, if our magistrates, as in those famous governments of old, would take into their care, not only the deciding of our contentious law-cases and brawls, but the managing of our public sports and festival pastimes; that they might be, not such as were authorized a while since, the provocations of drunkenness and lust, but such as may inure and harden our bodies by martial exercises to all warlike skill and performance; and may civilize, adorn, and make discreet our minds by the learned and affable meeting of frequent academies, and the procurement of wise and artful recitations, sweetened with eloquent and graceful enticements to the love and practice of justice, temperance, and fortitude, instructing and bettering the nation at all opportunities, that the call of wisdom and virtue may be heard everywhere, as Salomon saith: "She crieth without, she uttereth her voice in the streets, in the top of high places, in the chief concourse, and in the openings of the gates." Whether this may not be, not only in pulpits, but after another persuasive method, at set and solemn paneguries, in theatres, porches, or what other place or way may win most upon the people to receive at once both recreation and instruction, let them in authority consult.

The thing which I had to say, and those intentions which have lived within me ever since I could conceive myself anything worth to my country, I return to crave excuse that urgent reason hath plucked from me, by an abortive and foredated discovery. And the accomplishment of them lies not but in a power above man's to promise; but that none hath by more studious ways endeavored, and with more unwearied spirit that none shall, that I dare almost aver of myself, as far as life and free leisure will extend; and that the land had once en-franchised herself from this impertinent yoke of prelaty, under whose inquisitorious and tyrannical duncery no free and splendid wit can flourish.

Neither do I think it shame to covenant with any knowing reader, that for some few years yet I may go on trust with him toward the payment of what I am now indebted, as being a work not to be raised from the heat of youth, or the vapors of wine; like that which flows at waste from the pen of some vulgar amorist, or the trencher fury of a rhyming parasite; nor to be obtained by the invocation of dame memory and her siren daughters; but by devout prayer to that eternal Spirit who can enrich with all utterance and knowledge, and sends out his seraphim, with the hallowed fire of his altar, to touch and purify the lips of whom he pleases: to this must be added industrious and select reading, steady observation, insight into all seemly and generous arts and affairs; till which in some measure be compassed, at mine own peril and cost I refuse not to sustain this expectation from as many as are not loth to hazard so much credulity upon the best pledges that I can give them.

Although it nothing content me to have disclosed thus much beforehand, but that I trust hereby to make it manifest with what small willingness I endure to interrupt the pursuit of no less hopes than these, and leave a calm and pleasing solitariness, fed with cheerful and confident thoughts, to embark in a troubled sea of noises and hoarse disputes, put from beholding the bright countenance of truth in the quiet and still air of delightful studies, to come into the dim reflection of hollow antiquities sold by the seeming bulk, and there be fain to club quotations with men whose learning and belief lies in marginal stuffings; who, when they have, like good sumpters, laid ye down their horse-loads of citations and fathers at your door with a rhap-sody of who and who were bishops here or there, ye may take off their pack-saddles, their day's work is done, and episcopacy, as they think, stoutly vindicated. Let any gentle apprehension that can distinguish learned pains from unlearned drudgery, imagine what pleasure or profoundness can be in this, or what honor to deal against such adversaries.

But were it the meanest under-service, if God by his secretary conscience enjoin it, it were sad for me if I should draw back; for me especially, now when all men offer their aid to help ease and lighten the difficult labors of the Church, to whose service, by the intentions of my parents and friends, I was destined of a child, and in mine own resolutions: till coming to some maturity of years, and perceiving what tyranny had invaded the Church, that he who would take orders must subscribe slave, and take an oath withal, which unless he took with a conscience that would retch, he must either straight perjure, or split his faith; I thought it better to prefer a blameless silence before the sacred office of speaking, bought and begun with servitude and forswearing. Howsoever, thus church-outed by the prelates, hence may appear the right I have to meddle in these matters, as before the necessity and constraint appeared.

OF EDUCATION

LETTER TO MR. HARTLIB (1644)

Master Hartlib,

I am long since persuaded that to say or do aught worth memory and imitation, no purpose or respect should sooner move us than simply the love of God and of mankind. Nevertheless, to write now the reforming of education, though it be one of the greatest and noblest designs that can be thought on, and for the want whereof this nation perishes, I had not yet at this time been induced but by your earnest entreaties and serious conjurements; as having my mind for the present half diverted in the pursuance of some other assertions, the knowledge and the use of which cannot but be a great furtherance both to the enlargement of truth and honest living with much more peace.

Nor should the laws of any private friendship have prevailed with me to divide thus or transpose my former thoughts; but that I see those aims, those actions which have won you with me the esteem of a person sent hither by some good providence from a far country to be the occasion and the incitement of great good to this island. And (as I hear) you have obtained the same repute with men of most approved wisdom and some of highest authority among us; not to mention the learned correspondence which you hold in foreign parts, and the extraordinary pains and diligence which you have used in this matter both here and beyond the seas, either by the definite will of God so ruling, or the peculiar sway of nature, which also is God's working.

Neither can I think that, so reputed and so valued as you are, you would, to the forefeit of your own discerning ability, impose upon me an unfit and over-ponderous argument; but that the satisfaction, which you profess to have received from those incidental discourses which we have wandered into, hath pressed and almost constrained you into a persuasion, that what you require from me in this point I neither ought nor can in conscience defer beyond this time, both of so much need at once, and so much opportunity to try what God hath determined.

I will not resist, therefore, whatever it is either of divine or human obligement that you lay upon me; but will forthwith set down in writing, as you request me, that voluntary idea, which hath long in silence presented itself to me, of a better education, in extent and comprehension far more large, and yet of time far shorter and of attainment far more certain, than hath been yet in practice. Brief I shall endeavor to be; for that which I have to say assuredly this nation hath extreme need should be done sooner than spoken. To tell you, therefore, what I have benefited herein among old renowned authors I shall spare; and to search what many modern Januas and Didactics more than ever I shall read have projected, my inclination leads me not. But if you can accept of these few observations which have flowered off, and are, as it were, the burnishing of many contemplative years altogether spent in the search of religious and civil knowledge, and such as pleased you so well in the relating, I here give you them to dispose of.

The end, then, of learning is to repair the ruins of our first parents by regaining to know God aright, and out of that knowledge to love him, to imitate him, to be like him, as we may the nearest, by possessing our souls of true virtue, which, being united to the heavenly grace of faith, makes up the highest perfection. But because our understanding cannot in this body found itself but on sensible things, nor arrive so clearly to the knowledge of God and things invisible as by orderly conning over the visible and inferior creature, the same method is necessarily to be followed in all discreet teaching.

And seeing every nation affords not experience and tradition enough for all kind of learning, therefore we are chiefly taught the languages of those people who have at any time been most industrious after wisdom; so that language is but the instrument conveying to us things useful to be known. And though a linguist should pride himself to have all the tongues that Babel cleft the world into, yet if he have not studied the solid things in them as well as the words and lexicons, he were nothing so much to be esteemed a learned man as any yeoman or tradesman competently wise in his mother dialect only.

Hence appear the many mistakes which have made learning generally so unpleasing and so unsuccessful. First, we do amiss to spend seven or eight years merely in scraping together so much miserable Latin and Greek as might be learned otherwise easily and delightfully in one year. And that which casts our proficiency therein so much behind is our time lost in too oft idle vacancies given both to schools and universities; partly in a preposterous exaction, forcing the empty wits of children to compose themes, verses, and orations, which are the acts of ripest judgment, and the final work of a head filled, by long reading and observing, with elegant maxims and copious invention.

These are not matters to be wrung from poor striplings, like blood out of the nose, or the plucking of untimely fruit; besides the ill habit which they get of wretched barbarizing against the Latin and Greek idiom, with their untutored Anglicisms, odious to be read, yet not to be avoided without a well-continued and judicious conversing among pure authors, digested, which they scarce taste. Whereas, if after some preparatory grounds of speech by their certain forms got into memory they were led to the praxis thereof in some chosen short book lessoned thoroughly to them, they might then forthwith proceed to learn the substance of good things and arts in due order, which would bring the whole language quickly into their power. This I take to be the most rational and most profitable way of learning languages, and whereby we may best hope to give account to God of our youth spent herein.

And for the usual method of teaching arts, I deem it to be an old error of universities, not yet well recovered from the scholastic grossness of barbarous ages, that, instead of beginning with arts most easy (and those be such as are most obvious to the sense), they present their young unmatriculated novices at first coming with the most intellective abstractions of logic and metaphysics; so that they, having but newly left those grammatic flats and shallows where they stuck unreasonably to learn a few words with lamentable construction, and now on the sudden transported under another climate, to be tossed and turmoiled with their unballasted wits in fathomless and unquiet deeps of controversy, do, for the most part, grow into hatred and contempt of learning, mocked and deluded all this while with ragged notions and babblements, while they expected worthy and delightful knowledge; till poverty or youthful years call them importunately their several ways, and hasten them, with the sway of friends, either to an ambitious and mercenary, or ignorantly zealous divinity: some allured to the trade of law, grounding their purposes not on the prudent and heavenly contemplation of justice and equity, which was never taught them, but on the promising and pleasing thoughts of litigious terms, fat contentions, and flowing fees. Others betake them to state affairs with souls so unprincipled in virtue and true generous breeding, that flattery, and court-shifts, and tyrannous aphorisms appear to them the highest points of wisdom, instilling their barren hearts with a conscientious slavery, if, as I rather think, it be not feigned. Others, lastly, of a more delicious and airy spirit, retire themselves, knowing no better, to the enjoyments of ease and luxury, living out their days in feast and jollity; which, indeed, is the wisest and safest course of all these, unless they were with more integrity undertaken. And these are the errors, and these are the fruits of mis-spending our prime youth at the schools and universities, as we do, either in learning mere words, or such things chiefly as were better unlearned.

I shall detain you no longer in the demonstration of what we should not do, but straight conduct ye to a hillside, where I will point ye out the right path of a virtuous and noble education; laborious indeed at the first ascent, but else so smooth, so green, so full of goodly prospect and melodious sounds on every side, that the harp of Orpheus was not more charming. I doubt not but ye shall have more ado to drive our dullest and laziest youth, our stocks and stubs, from the infinite desire

of such a happy nurture, than we have now to haul and drag
our choicest and hopefullest wits to that asinine feast of sow-
thistles and brambles which is commonly set before them as
all the food and entertainment of their tenderest and most
docible age. I call, therefore, a complete and generous education, that which fits a man to perform justly, skilfully, and mag-
nanimously all the offices, both private and public, of peace and
war. And how all this may be done between twelve and one-
and-twenty, less time than is now bestowed in pure trifling at
grammar and sophistry, is to be thus ordered.

First, to find out a spacious house and ground about it fit
for an academy, and big enough to lodge a hundred and fifty
persons, whereof twenty or thereabout may be attendants, all
under the government of one who shall be thought of desert
sufficient, and ability either to do all, or wisely to direct and
oversee it done. This place should be at once both school and
university, not needing a remove to any other house of scholarship, except it be some peculiar college of law or physic, where
they mean to be practitioners; but as for those general studies
which take up all our time from Lilly to the commencing, as
they term it, Master of Art, it should be absolute. After this
pattern, as many edifices may be converted to this use as shall
be needful in every city throughout this land, which would tend
much to the increase of learning and civility everywhere. This
number, less or more, thus collected, to the convenience of a
foot-company or interchangeably two troops of cavalry, should
divide their day's work into three parts as it lies orderly—their
studies, their exercise, and their diet.

For their studies: first, they should begin with the chief and
necessary rules of some good grammar, either that now used,
or any better; and while this is doing, their speech is to be
fashioned to a distinct and clear pronunciation, as near as may
be to the Italian, especially in the vowels. For we Englishmen,
being far northerly, do not open our mouths in the cold air
wide enough to grace a southern tongue, but are observed by
all other nations to speak exceeding close and inward; so that
to smatter Latin with an English mouth is as ill a hearing as law
French.

Next, to make them expert in the usefullest points of grammar, and withal to season them and win them early to the love of

virtue and true labor, ere any flattering seducement or vain principle seize them wandering, some easy and delightful book of education would be read to them, whereof the Greeks have store, as Cebes, Plutarch, and other Socratic discourses; but in Latin we have none of classic authority extant, except the two or three first books of Quintilian and some select pieces else-where.

But here the main skill and groundwork will be to temper them such lectures and explanations upon every opportunity, as may lead and draw them in willing obedience, inflamed with the study of learning and the admiration of virtue, stirred up with high hopes of living to be brave men and worthy patriots, dear to God and famous to all ages: that they may despise and scorn all their childish and ill-taught qualities, to delight in manly and liberal exercises; which he who hath the art and proper eloquence to catch them with, what with mild and effectual persuasions, and what with the intimation of some fear, if need be, but chiefly by his own example, might in a short space gain them to an incredible diligence and courage, infusing into their young breasts such an ingenuous and noble ardor as would not fail to make many of them renowned and matchless men.

At the same time, some other hour of the day might be taught them the rules of arithmetic, and, soon after, the elements of geometry, even playing, as the old manner was. After evening repast till bed-time their thoughts would be best taken up in the easy grounds of religion and the story of Scripture.

The next step would be to the authors of agriculture, Cato, Varro, and Columella, for the matter is most easy; and if the language be difficult, so much the better; it is not a difficulty above their years. And here will be an occasion of inciting and enabling them hereafter to improve the tillage of their country, to recover the bad soil, and to remedy the waste that is made of good; for this was one of Hercules' praises.

Ere half these authors be read (which will soon be with plying hard and daily) they cannot choose but be masters of any ordinary prose: so that it will be then seasonable for them to learn in any modern author the use of the globes and all the maps, first with the old names and then with the new; or they might be then capable to read any compendious method of natural philosophy; and, at the same time, might be entering into the Greek tongue, after the same manner as was before prescribed in the Latin; whereby the difficulties of grammar being soon overcome, all the historical physiology of Aristotle and Theophrastus are open before them and, as I may say, under contribution. The like access will be to Vitruvius, to Seneca's *Natural Questions*, to Mela, Celsus, Pliny, or Solinus. And having thus passed the principles of arithmetic, geometry, astronomy, and geography, with a general compact of physics, they may descend in mathematics to the instrumental science of trigonometry, and from thence to fortification, architecture, enginery, or navigation. And in natural philosophy they may proceed leisurely from the history of meteors, minerals, plants, and living creatures, as far as anatomy.

Then also in course might be read to them out of some not tedious writer the institution of physic; that they may know the tempers, the humors, the seasons, and how to manage a crudity; which he who can wisely and timely do is not only a great physician to himself and to his friends, but also may at some time or other save an army by this frugal and expenseless means only, and not let the healthy and stout bodies of young men rot away under him for want of this discipline, which is a great pity, and no less a shame to the commander.

To set forward all these proceedings in nature and mathematics, what hinders but that they may procure, as oft as shall be needful, the helpful experiences of hunters, fowlers, fishermen, shepherds, gardeners, apothecaries; and in other sciences, architects, engineers, mariners, anatomists, who, doubtless, would be ready, some for reward and some to favor such a hopeful seminary. And this will give them such a real tincture of natural knowledge as they shall never forget, but daily augment with delight. Then also those poets which are now counted most hard will be both facile and pleasant, Orpheus, Hesiod, Theocritus, Aratus, Nicander, Oppian, Dionysius; and, in Latin, Lucretius, Manilius, and the rural part of Virgil.

By this time years and good general precepts will have furnished them more distinctly with that act of reason which in ethics is called proairesis, that they may with some judgment contemplate upon moral good and evil. Then will be required a special reinforcement of constant and sound indoctrinating to set them right and firm, instructing them more amply in the knowledge of virtue and the hatred of vice, while their young and pliant affections are led through all the moral works of Plato, Xenophon, Cicero, Plutarch, Laertius, and those Locrian remnants; but still to be reduced in their nightward studies, wherewith they close the day's work, under the determinate sentence of David or Salomon, or the evangels and apostolic Scriptures.

Being perfect in the knowledge of personal duty, they may then begin the study of economics.   And either now or before this they may have easily learned at any odd hour the Italian tongue.   And soon after, but with wariness and good antidote, it would be wholesome enough to let them taste some choice comedies, Greek, Latin, or Italian; those tragedies also that treat of household matters, as *Trachiniæ, Alcestis*, and the like.

The next remove must be to the study of politics; to know the beginning, end, and reasons of political societies, that they may not, in a dangerous fit of the commonwealth, be such poor, shaken, uncertain reeds, of such a tottering conscience as many of our great counsellors have lately shown themselves, but steadfast pillars of the state.   After this they are to dive into the grounds of law and legal justice, delivered first and with best warrant by Moses, and, as far as human prudence can be trusted, in those extolled remains of Grecian law-givers, Lycurgus, Solon, Zaleucus, Charondas; and thence to all the Roman edicts and tables, with their Justinian; and so down to the Saxon and common laws of England and the statutes.

Sundays also and every evening may now be understandingly spent in the highest matters of theology and church history, ancient and modern: and ere this time the Hebrew tongue at a set hour might have been gained, that the Scriptures may be now read in their own original; whereto it would be no impossibility to add the Chaldee and the Syrian dialect.

When all these employments are well conquered, then will the choice histories, heroic poems, and Attic tragedies of stateliest and most regal argument, with all the famous political orations, offer themselves; which, if they were not only read, but some of them got by memory, and solemnly pronounced with right accent and grace, as might be taught, would endue them even with the spirit and vigor of Demosthenes or Cicero, Euripides or Sophocles.

And now, lastly, will be the time to read with them those organic arts which enable men to discourse and write perspicuously, elegantly, and according to the fitted style of lofty, mean or lowly. Logic, therefore, so much as is useful, is to be referred to this due place, with all her well-couched heads and topics, until it be time to open her contracted palm into a graceful and ornate rhetoric taught out of the rule of Plato, Aristotle, Phalereus, Cicero, Hermogenes, Longinus.

To which poetry would be made subsequent, or, indeed, rather precedent, as being less subtle and fine, but more simple, sensuous, and passionate; I mean not here the prosody of a verse which they could not but have hit on before among the rudiments of grammar, but that sublime art which in Aristotle's *Poetics*, in Horace, and the Italian commentaries of Castelvetro, Tasso, Mazzoni, and others, teaches what the laws are of a true epic poem, what of a dramatic, what of a lyric, what decorum is, which is the grand masterpiece to observe. This would make them soon perceive what despicable creatures our common rhymers and play-writers be; and show them what religious, what glorious and magnificent use might be made of poetry, both in divine and human things.

From hence, and not till now, will be the right season of forming them to be able writers and composers in every excellent matter, when they shall be thus fraught with an universal insight into things: or whether they be to speak in parliament or council, honor and attention would be waiting on their lips. There would then also appear in pulpits other visages, other gestures, and stuff otherwise wrought than what we now sit under, oft-times to as great a trial of our patience as any other that they preach to us.

These are the studies wherein our noble and our gentle youth ought to bestow their time in a disciplinary way from twelve to one-and-twenty, unless they rely more upon their ancestors dead than upon themselves living. In which methodical course it is so supposed they must proceed by the steady pace of learning onward, as at convenient times for memory's sake to retire back into the middle ward, and sometimes into the rear, of what they have been taught, until they have confirmed and solidly united the whole body of their perfected knowledge, like the last embattling of a Roman legion. Now will be worth the seeing what exercises and recreations may best agree and become those studies.

The course of study hitherto briefly described is, what I can guess by reading, likest to those ancient and famous schools of Pythagoras, Plato, Isocrates, Aristotle, and such others, out of which were bred such a number of renowned philosophers, orators, historians, poets, and princes all over Greece, Italy, and Asia, besides the flourishing studies of Cyrene and Alexandria. But herein it shall exceed them, and supply a defect as great as that which Plato noted in the commonwealth of Sparta. Whereas that city trained up their youth most for war, and these in their academies and Lyceum all for the gown, this institution of breeding which I here delineate shall be equally good both for peace and war. Therefore, about an hour and a half ere they eat at noon should be allowed them for exercise, and due rest afterwards; but the time for this may be enlarged at pleasure, according as their rising in the morning shall be early. The exercise which I commend first is the exact use of their weapon, to guard, and to strike safely with edge or point. This will keep them healthy, nimble, strong, and well in breath; is also the likeliest means to make them grow large and tall, and to inspire them with a gallant and fearless courage; which, being tempered with seasonable lectures and precepts to them of true fortitude and patience, will turn into a native and heroic valor, and make them hate the cowardice of doing wrong. They must be also practised in all the locks and gripes of wrestling, wherein Englishmen were wont to excel, as need may often be in fight to tug, to grapple, and to close. And this, perhaps, will be enough wherein to prove and heat their single strength.

The interim of unsweating themselves regularly, and convenient rest before meat, may both with profit and delight be taken up in recreating and composing their travailed spirits with the solemn and divine harmonies of music heard or learned; either whilst the skilful organist plies his grave and fancied descant in lofty fugues, or the whole symphony with artful and unimaginable touches adorn and grace the well-studied chords of some choice composer; sometimes the lute or soft organ-stop,

waiting on elegant voices either to religious, martial, or civil
ditties; which, if wise men and prophets be not extremely out,
have a great power over dispositions and manners, to smooth
and make them gentle from rustic harshness and distempered
passions. The like also would not be inexpedient after meat,
to assist and cherish nature in her first concoction, and send their
minds back to study in good tune and satisfaction.

Where having followed it close under vigilant eyes until about
two hours before supper, they are, by a sudden alarum or watch-
word, to be called out to their military motions, under sky or
covert, according to the season, as was the Roman wont; first
on foot, then, as their age permits, on horseback, to all the art of
cavalry; that having in sport, but with much exactness and daily
muster, served out the rudiments of their soldiership in all the
skill of embattling, marching, encamping, fortifying, besieging,
and battering, with all the helps of ancient and modern stratagems, tactics, and warlike maxims, they may, as it were out of
a long war, come forth renowned and perfect commanders in the
service of their country.

They would not then, if they were trusted with fair and
hopeful armies, suffer them for want of just and wise discipline
to shed away from about them like sick feathers, though they
be never so oft supplied; they would not suffer their empty and
unrecruitable colonels of twenty men in a company to quaff
out or convey into secret hoards the wages of a delusive list and a
miserable remnant; yet in the meanwhile to be overmastered
with a score or two of drunkards, the only soldiery left about
them, or else to comply with all rapines and violences. No,
certainly, if they knew aught of that knowledge that belongs
to good men or good governors, they would not suffer these
things.

But to return to our own institute. Besides these constant
exercises at home, there is another opportunity of gaining
experience to be won from pleasure itself abroad: in those
vernal seasons of the year, when the air is calm and pleasant, it
were an injury and sullenness against nature not to go out and
see her riches and partake in her rejoicing with heaven and
earth. I should not, therefore, be a persuader to them of studying much then, after two or three years that they have well laid
their grounds, but to ride out in companies with prudent and

staid guides to all the quarters of the land, learning and observing all places of strength, all commodities of building and of soil, for towns and tillage, harbors, and ports for trade. Sometimes taking sea as far as to our navy, to learn there also what they can in the practical knowledge of sailing and of sea-fight.

These ways would try all their peculiar gifts of nature, and if there were any secret excellence among them, would fetch it out and give it fair opportunity to advance itself by, which could not but mightily redound to the good of this nation, and bring into fashion again those old admired virtues and excellencies, with far more advantage now in this purity of Christian knowledge.

Nor shall we then need the monsieurs of Paris to take our hopeful youth into their slight and prodigal custodies, and send them over back again transformed into mimics, apes, and kickshaws. But if they desire to see other countries at three or four and twenty years of age, not to learn principles, but to enlarge experience and make wise observation, they will by that time be such as shall deserve the regard and honor of all men where they pass, and the society and friendship of those in all places who are best and most eminent. And perhaps then other nations will be glad to visit us for their breeding, or else to imitate us in their own country.

Now, lastly, for their diet there cannot be much to say, save only that it would be best in the same house; for much time else would be lost abroad, and many ill habits got; and that it should be plain, healthful, and moderate, I suppose is out of controversy.

Thus, Mr. Hartlib, you have a general view in writing, as your desire was, of that which at several times I had discoursed with you concerning the best and noblest way of education; not beginning, as some have done, from the cradle, which yet might be worth many considerations, if brevity had not been my scope. Many other circumstances also I could have mentioned; but this, to such as have the worth in them to make trial, for light and direction may be enough. Only I believe that this is not a bow for every man to shoot in that counts himself a teacher, but will require sinews almost equal to those which Homer gave Ulysses. Yet I am withal persuaded that it may prove much more easy in the assay than it now seems at dis-

tance, and much more illustrious: howbeit not more difficult
than I imagine; and that imagination presents me with nothing
but very happy and very possible according to best wishes, if
God have so decreed, and this age have spirit and capacity
enough to apprehend.

AREOPAGITICA

A SPEECH FOR THE LIBERTY OF UNLICENSED PRINTING, TO THE PARLIAMENT OF ENGLAND (1644)

THEY, who to states and governors of the Commonwealth
direct their speech, High Court of Parliament, or, wanting such
access in a private condition, write that which they foresee may
advance the public good; I suppose them, as at the beginning of
no mean endeavor, not a little altered and moved inwardly
in their minds: some with doubt of what will be the success,
others with fear of what will be the censure; some with hope,
others with confidence of what they have to speak. And me
perhaps each of these dispositions, as the subject was whereon
I entered, may have at other times variously affected; and likely
might in these foremost expressions now also disclose which of
them swayed most, but that the very attempt of this address
thus made, and the thought of whom it hath recourse to, hath
got the power within me to a passion, far more welcome than
incidental to a preface.

Which though I stay not to confess ere any ask, I shall be
blameless, if it be no other than the joy and gratulation which
it brings to all who wish and promote their country's liberty;
whereof this whole discourse proposed will be a certain testimony, if not a trophy. For this is not the liberty which we can
hope, that no grievance ever should arise in the Commonwealth
—that let no man in this world expect; but when complaints
are freely heard, deeply considered and speedily reformed, then
is the utmost bound of civil liberty attained that wise men look
for. To which if I now manifest by the very sound of this which
I shall utter, that we are already in good part arrived, and yet
from such a steep disadvantage of tyranny and superstition
grounded into our principles as was beyond the manhood of
a Roman recovery, it will be attributed first, as is most due,

to the strong assistance of God our deliverer, next to your faithful guidance and undaunted wisdom, Lords and Commons of England. Neither is it in God's esteem the diminution of his glory, when honorable things are spoken of good men and worthy magistrates; which if I now first should begin to do, after so fair a progress of your laudable deeds, and such a long obligement upon the whole realm to your indefatigable virtues, I might be justly reckoned among the tardiest, and the unwillingest of them that praise ye.

Nevertheless there being three principal things, without which all praising is but courtship and flattery: first, when that only is praised which is solidly worth praise: next, when greatest likelihoods are brought that such things are truly and really in those persons to whom they are ascribed: the other, when he who praises, by showing that such his actual persuasion is of whom he writes, can demonstrate that he flatters not; the former two of these I have heretofore endeavored, rescuing the employment from him who went about to impair your merits with a trivial and malignant encomium; the latter as belonging chiefly to mine own acquittal, that whom I so extolled I did not flatter, hath been reserved opportunely to this occasion.

For he who freely magnifies what hath been nobly done, and fears not to declare as freely what might be done better, gives ye the best covenant of his fidelity; and that his loyalest affection and his hope waits on your proceedings. His highest praising is not flattery, and his plainest advice is a kind of praising. For though I should affirm and hold by argument, that it would fare better with truth, with learning and the Commonwealth, if one of your published Orders, which I should name, were called in; yet at the same time it could not but much redound to the luster of your mild and equal government, whenas private persons are hereby animated to think ye better pleased with public advice, than other statists have been delighted heretofore with public flattery. And men will then see what difference there is between the magnanimity of a triennial Parliament, and that jealous haughtiness of prelates and cabin counsellors that usurped of late, whenas they shall observe ye in the midst of your victories and successes more gently brooking written exceptions against a voted Order than other Courts, which had produced nothing worth memory but the weak ostentation of wealth, would have endured the least signified dislike at any sudden proclamation.

If I should thus far presume upon the meek demeanor of your civil and gentle greatness, Lords and Commons, as what your published Order hath directly said, that to gainsay, I might defend myself with ease, if any should accuse me of being new or insolent, did they but know how much better I find ye esteem it to imitate the old and elegant humanity of Greece, than the barbaric pride of a Hunnish and Norwegian stateliness. And out of those ages, to whose polite wisdom and letters we owe that we are not yet Goths and Jutlanders, I could name him who from his private house wrote that discourse to the Parliament of Athens, that persuades them to change the form of democraty which was then established. Such honor was done in those days to men who professed the study of wisdom and eloquence, not only in their own country, but in other lands, that cities and signiories heard them gladly, and with great respect, if they had aught in public to admonish the state. Thus did Dion Prusæus, a stranger and a private orator, counsel the Rhodians against a former edict; and I abound with other like examples, which to set here would be superfluous.

But if from the industry of a life wholly dedicated to studious labors, and those natural endowments haply not the worse for two and fifty degrees of northern latitude, so much must be derogated, as to count me not equal to any of those who had this privilege, I would obtain to be thought not so inferior, as yourselves are superior to the most of them who received their counsel: and how far you excel them, be assured, Lords and Commons, there can no greater testimony appear, than when your prudent spirit acknowledges and obeys the voice of reason from what quarter soever it be heard speaking; and renders ye as willing to repeal any Act of your own setting forth, as any set forth by your predecessors.

If ye be thus resolved, as it were injury to think ye were not, I know not what should withhold me from presenting ye with a fit instance wherein to show both that love of truth which ye eminently profess, and that uprightness of your judgment which is not wont to be partial to yourselves; by judging over again that Order which ye have ordained to regulate printing:—that no book, pamphlet, or paper shall be henceforth printed, unless the same be first approved and licensed by such, or at least one of such, as shall be thereto appointed. For that part which preserves justly every man's copy to himself, or provides for the poor, I touch not, only wish they be not made pretences to abuse and persecute honest and painful men, who offend not in either of these particulars. But that other clause of licensing books, which we thought had died with his brother quadragesimal and matrimonial when the prelates expired, I shall now attend with such a homily, as shall lay before ye, first the inventors of it to be those whom ye will be loth to own; next what is to be thought in general of reading, whatever sort the books be; and that this Order avails nothing to the suppressing of scandalous, seditious, and libellous books, which were mainly intended to be suppressed. Last, that it will be primely to the discouragement of all learning, and the stop of truth, not only by disexercising and blunting our abilities in what we know already, but by hindering and cropping the discovery that might be yet further made both in religious and civil wisdom.

I deny not, but that it is of greatest concernment in the Church and Commonwealth, to have a vigilant eye how books demean themselves as well as men; and thereafter to confine, imprison, and do sharpest justice on them as malefactors. For books are not absolutely dead things, but do contain a potency of life in them to be as active as that soul was whose progeny they are; nay, they do preserve as in a vial the purest efficacy and extraction of that living intellect that bred them. I know they are as lively, and as vigorously productive, as those fabulous dragon's teeth; and being sown up and down, may chance to spring up armed men. And yet, on the other hand, unless wariness be used, as good almost kill a man as kill a good book. Who kills a man kills a reasonable creature, God's image; but he who destroys a good book, kills reason itself, kills the image of God, as it were in the eye. Many a man lives a burden to the earth; but a good book is the precious life-blood of a master spirit, embalmed and treasured up on purpose to a life beyond life. 'Tis true, no age can restore a life, whereof perhaps there is no great loss; and revolutions of ages do not oft recover the loss of a rejected truth, for the want of which whole nations fare the worse.

We should be wary therefore what persecution we raise

against the living labors of public men, how we spill that
seasoned life of man preserved and stored up in books; since
we see a kind of homicide may be thus committed, sometimes
a martyrdom, and if it extend to the whole impression, a kind
of massacre; whereof the execution ends not in the slaying
of an elemental life, but strikes at that ethereal and fifth essence, the breath of reason itself, slays an immortality rather
than a life. But lest I should be condemned of introducing
license, while I oppose licensing, I refuse not the pains to be
so much historical, as will serve to show what hath been done
by ancient and famous commonwealths against this disorder,
till the very time that this project of licensing crept out of the
Inquisition, was catched up by our prelates, and hath caught
some of our presbyters.

In Athens, where books and wits were ever busier than in
any other part of Greece, I find but only two sorts of writings
which the magistrate cared to take notice of; those either
blasphemous and atheistical, or libellous. Thus the books of
Protagoras were by the judges of Areopagus commanded to
be burnt, and himself banished the territory for a discourse
begun with his confessing not to know "whether there were
gods, or whether not." And against defaming, it was agreed
that none should be traduced by name, as was the manner of
Vetus Comœdia, whereby we may guess how they censured
libelling. And this course was quick enough, as Cicero writes,
to quell both the desperate wits of other atheists, and the open
way of defaming, as the event showed. Of other sects and opinions, though tending to voluptuousness, and the denying of
Divine Providence, they took no heed.

Therefore we do not read that either Epicurus, or that
libertine school of Cyrene, or what the Cynic impudence uttered,
was ever questioned by the laws. Neither is it recorded that the
writings of those old comedians were suppressed, though the
acting of them were forbid; and that Plato commended the reading of Aristophanes, the loosest of them all, to his royal scholar
Dionysius, is commonly known, and may be excused, if holy
Chrysostom, as is reported, nightly studied so much the same
author and had the art to cleanse a scurrilous vehemence into
the style of a rousing sermon.

That other leading city of Greece, Lacedæmon, considering

that Lycurgus their lawgiver was so addicted to elegant learning, as to have been the first that brought out of Ionia the scattered works of Homer, and sent the poet Thales from Crete to prepare and mollify the Spartan surliness with his smooth songs and odes, the better to plant among them law and civility, it is to be wondered how museless and unbookish they were, minding naught but the feats of war. There needed no licensing of books among them, for they disliked all but their own laconic apothegms, and took a slight occasion to chase Archilochus out of their city, perhaps for composing in a higher strain than their own soldierly ballads and roundels could reach to. Or if it were for his broad verses, they were not therein so cautious but they were as dissolute in their promiscuous conversing; whence Euripides affirms in *Andromache*, that their women were all unchaste. Thus much may give us light after what sort of books were prohibited among the Greeks.

The Romans also, for many ages trained up only to a military roughness resembling most the Lacedæmonian guise, knew of learning little but what their twelve Tables, and the Pontific College with their augurs and flamens taught them in religion and law, so unacquainted with other learning, that when Carneades and Critolaus, with the Stoic Diogenes coming ambassadors to Rome, took thereby occasion to give the city a taste of their philosophy, they were suspected for seducers by no less a man than Cato the Censor, who moved it in the Senate to dismiss them speedily, and to banish all such Attic babblers out of Italy. But Scipio and others of the noblest senators withstood him and his old Sabine austerity; honored and admired the men; and the censor himself at last, in his old age, fell to the study of that whereof before he was so scrupulous. And yet at the same time, Nævius and Plautus, the first Latin comedians, had filled the city with all the borrowed scenes of Menander and Philemon. Then began to be considered there also what was to be done to libellous books and authors; for Nævius was quickly cast into prison for his unbridled pen, and released by the tribunes upon his recantation; we read also that libels were burnt, and the makers punished by Augustus. The like severity, no doubt, was used, if aught were impiously written against their esteemed gods. Except in these two points, how the world went in books, the magistrate kept no reckoning.

And therefore Lucretius without impeachment versifies his Epicurism to Memmius, and had the honor to be set forth the second time by Cicero, so great a father of the commonwealth; although himself disputes against that opinion in his own writings. Nor was the satirical sharpness or naked plainness of Lucilius, or Catullus, or Flaccus, by any order prohibited. And for matters of state, the story of Titus Livius, though it extolled that part which Pompey held, was not therefore suppressed by Octavius Cæsar of the other faction. But that Naso was by him banished in his old age, for the wanton poems of his youth, was but a mere covert of state over some secret cause: and besides, the books were neither banished nor called in. From hence we shall meet with little else but tyranny in the Roman empire, that we may not marvel, if not so often bad as good books were silenced. I shall therefore deem to have been large enough, in producing what among the ancients was punishable to write; save only which, all other arguments were free to treat on.

By this time the emperors were become Christians, whose discipline in this point I do not find to have been more severe than what was formerly in practice. The books of those whom they took to be grand heretics were examined, refuted, and condemned in the general Councils; and not till then were prohibited, or burnt, by authority of the emperor. As for the writings of heathen authors, unless they were plain invectives against Christianity, as those of Porphyrius and Proclus, they met with no interdict that can be cited, till about the year 400, in a Carthaginian Council, wherein bishops themselves were forbid to read the books of Gentiles, but heresies they might read: while others long before them, on the contrary, scrupled more the books of heretics than of Gentiles. And that the primitive Councils and bishops were wont only to declare what books were not commendable, passing no further, but leaving it to each one's conscience to read or to lay by, till after the year 800, is observed already by Padre Paolo, the great unmasker of the Trentine Council.

After which time the Popes of Rome, engrossing what they pleased of political rule into their own hands, extended their dominion over men's eyes, as they had before over their judgments, burning and prohibiting to be read what they fancied not; yet sparing in their censures, and the books not many which they so dealt with: till Martin V, by his bull, not only prohibited, but was the first that excommunicated the reading of heretical books; for about that time Wickliffe and Huss, growing terrible, were they who first drove the Papal Court to a stricter policy of prohibiting.   Which course Leo X and his successors followed, until the Council of Trent and the Spanish Inquisition engendering together brought forth, or perfected, those Catalogues and expurging Indexes, that rake through the entrails of many an old good author, with a violation worse than any could be offered to his tomb.   Nor did they stay in matters heretical, but any subject that was not to their palate, they either condemned in a Prohibition, or had it straight into the new purgatory of an Index.

To fill up the measure of encroachment, their last invention was to ordain that no book, pamphlet, or paper should be printed (as if St. Peter had bequeathed them the keys of the press also out of paradise) unless it were approved and licensed under the hands of two or three glutton friars.   For example:

Let the Chancellor Cini be pleased to see if in this present work be contained aught that may withstand the printing.
                              Vincent Rabbatta, Vicar of Florence.

I have seen this present work, and find nothing athwart the Catholic faith and good manners: in witness whereof I have given, etc.
                              Nicolo Cini, Chancellor of Florence.

Attending the precedent relation, it is allowed that this present work of Davanzati may be printed.
                              Vincent Rabbatta, etc.

It may be printed, July 15.
          Friar Simon Mompei d'Amelia, Chancellor of the holy office in Florence.

Sure they have a conceit, if he of the bottomless pit had not long since broke prison, that this quadruple exorcism would bar him down.   I fear their next design will be to get into their custody the licensing of that which they say Claudius intended,

but went not through with.   Vouchsafe to see another of their
forms, the Roman stamp:

> Imprimatur, If it seem good to the reverend master of the holy
> palace.
>
>   Belcastro, Vicegerent.
>
> Imprimatur, Friar Nicolo Rodolphi, Master of the holy palace.

Sometimes five Imprimaturs are seen together dialogue-wise
in the piazza of one title-page, complimenting and ducking each
to other with their shaven reverences, whether the author, who
stands by in perplexity at the foot of his epistle, shall to the
press or to the sponge.   These are the pretty responsories, these
are the dear antiphonies, that so bewitched of late our prelates
and their chaplains with the goodly echo they made; and be-
sotted us to the gay imitation of a lordly Imprimatur, one from
Lambeth House, another from the west end of Paul's; so apishly
Romanizing, that the word of command still was set down
in Latin; as if the learned grammatical pen that wrote it would
cast no ink without Latin; or perhaps, as they thought, because
no vulgar tongue was worthy to express the pure conceit of an
Imprimatur; but rather, as I hope, for that our English, the
language of men ever famous and foremost in the achievements
of liberty, will not easily find servile letters enow to spell such a
dictatory presumption English.

And thus ye have the inventors and the original of book-
licensing ripped up and drawn as lineally as any pedigree.   We
have it not, that can be heard of, from any ancient state, or
polity or church; nor by any statute left us by our ancestors
elder or later; nor from the modern custom of any reformed city
or church abroad; but from the most Anti-christian Council
and the most tyrannous Inquisition that ever inquired.   Till
then books were ever as freely admitted into the world as any
other birth; the issue of the brain was no more stifled than the
issue of the womb: no envious Juno sat cross-legged over the
nativity of any man's intellectual offspring; but if it proved a
monster, who denies, but that it was justly burnt, or sunk into
the sea?   But that a book, in worse condition than a peccant
soul, should be to stand before a jury ere it be born to the world,
and undergo yet in darkness the judgment of Radamanth and

his colleagues, ere it can pass the ferry backward into light, was never heard before, till that mysterious iniquity, provoked and troubled at the first entrance of Reformation, sought out new limbos and new hells wherein they might include our books also within the number of their damned. And this was the rare morsel so officiously snatched up, and so ill-favoredly imitated by our inquisiturient bishops, and the attendant minorites their chaplains. That ye like not now these most certain authors of this licensing order, and that all sinister intention was far distant from your thoughts, when ye were importuned the passing it, all men who know the integrity of your actions, and how ye honor truth, will clear ye readily.

But some will say, What though the inventors were bad, the thing for all that may be good? It may so; yet if that thing be no such deep invention, but obvious, and easy for any man to light on, and yet best and wisest commonwealths through all ages and occasions have forborne to use it, and falsest seducers and oppressors of men were the first who took it up, and to no other purpose but to obstruct and hinder the first approach of Reformation; I am of those who believe it will be a harder alchemy than Lullius ever knew, to sublimate any good use out of such an invention. Yet this only is what I request to gain from this reason, that it may be held a dangerous and suspicious fruit, as certainly it deserves, for the tree that bore it, until I can dissect one by one the properties it has. But I have first to finish, as was propounded, what is to be thought in general of reading books, whatever sort they be, and whether be more the benefit or the harm that thence proceeds?

Not to insist upon the examples of Moses, Daniel, and Paul, who were skilful in all the learning of the Egyptians, Chaldeans, and Greeks, which could not probably be without reading their books of all sorts; in Paul especially, who thought it no defilement to insert into Holy Scripture the sentences of three Greek poets, and one of them a tragedian; the question was notwithstanding sometimes controverted among the primitive doctors, but with great odds on that side which affirmed it both lawful and profitable; as was then evidently perceived, when Julian the Apostate, and subtlest enemy to our faith, made a decree forbidding Christians the study of heathen learning; for, said he, they wound us with our own weapons, and with our own arts and sciences they overcome us. And indeed the Christians were put so to their shifts by this crafty means, and so much in danger to decline into all ignorance, that the two Apollinarii were fain, as a man may say, to coin all the seven liberal sciences out of the Bible, reducing it into divers forms of orations, poems, dialogues, even to the calculating of a new Christian grammar. But, saith the historian Socrates, the providence of God provided better than the industry of Apollinarius and his son, by taking away that illiterate law with the life of him who devised it.   So great an injury they then held it to be deprived of Hellenic learning; and thought it a persecution more undermining, and secretly decaying the Church, than the open cruelty of Decius or Diocletian.

And perhaps it was the same politic drift that the devil whipped St. Jerome in a Lenten dream, for reading Cicero; or else it was a phantasm bred by the fever which had then seized him. For had an angel been his discipliner, unless it were for dwelling too much upon Ciceronianisms, and had chastised the reading, not the vanity, it had been plainly partial; first to correct him for grave Cicero, and not for scurrile Plautus, whom he confesses to have been reading not long before; next to correct him only, and let so many more ancient Fathers wax old in those pleasant and florid studies without the lash of such a tutoring apparition; insomuch that Basil teaches how some good use may be made of *Margites*, a sportful poem, not now extant, writ by Homer; and why not then of *Morgante*, an Italian romance much to the same purpose?

But if it be agreed we shall be tried by visions, there is a vision recorded by Eusebius, far ancienter than this tale of Jerome to the nun Eustochium, and, besides, has nothing of a fever in it.   Dionysius Alexandrinus was about the year 240 a person of great name in the Church for piety and learning, who had wont to avail himself much against heretics by being conversant in their books; until a certain presbyter laid it scrupulously to his conscience, how he durst venture himself among those defiling volumes.   The worthy man, loth to give offence, fell into a new debate with himself what was to be thought; when suddenly a vision sent from God (it is his own epistle that so avers it) confirmed him in these words: "Read any books whatever come to thy hands, for thou art sufficient both to judge aright, and to examine each matter." To this revelation he assented the sooner, as he confesses, because it was answerable to that of the Apostle to the Thessalonians, Prove all things, hold fast that which is good. And he might have added another remarkable saying of the same author: To the pure, all things are pure; not only meats and drinks, but all kind of knowledge whether of good or evil; the knowledge cannot defile, nor consequently the books, if the will and conscience be not defiled.

For books are as meats and viands are; some of good, some of evil substance; and yet God, in that unapocryphal vision, said without exception, "Rise, Peter, kill and eat," leaving the choice to each man's discretion. Wholesome meats to a vitiated stomach differ little or nothing from unwholesome; and best books to a naughty mind are not unappliable to occasions of evil. Bad meats will scarce breed good nourishment in the healthiest concoction; but herein the difference is of bad books, that they to a discreet and judicious reader serve in many respects to discover, to confute, to forewarn, and to illustrate. Whereof what better witness can ye expect I should produce, than one of your own now sitting in Parliament, the chief of learned men reputed in this land, Mr. Selden; whose volume of natural and national laws proves, not only by great authorities brought together, but by exquisite reasons and theorems almost mathematically demonstrative, that all opinions, yea errors, known, read, and collated, are of main service and assistance toward the speedy attainment of what is truest. I conceive, therefore, that when God did enlarge the universal diet of man's body, saving ever the rules of temperance, he then also, as before, left arbitrary the dieting and repasting of our minds; as wherein every mature man might have to exercise his own leading capacity.

How great a virtue is temperance, how much of moment through the whole life of man! Yet God commits the managing so great a trust, without particular law or prescription, wholly to the demeanor of every grown man. And therefore when he himself tabled the Jews from heaven, that omer, which was every man's daily portion of manna, is computed to have been more than might have well sufficed the heartiest feeder thrice as many meals. For those actions which enter into a man, rather than issue out of him, and therefore defile not, God uses not to captivate under a perpetual childhood of prescription, but trusts him with the gift of reason to be his own chooser; there were but little work left for preaching, if law and compulsion should grow so fast upon those things which heretofore were governed only by exhortation. Salomon informs us that much reading is a weariness to the flesh; but neither he nor other inspired author tells us that such or such reading is unlawful: yet certainly had God thought good to limit us herein, it had been much more expedient to have told us what was unlawful than what was wearisome. As for the burning of those Ephesian books by St. Paul's converts, 'tis replied the books were magic, the Syriac so renders them. It was a private act, a voluntary act, and leaves us to a voluntary imitation: the men in remorse burnt those books which were their own; the magistrate by this example is not appointed; these men practised the books, another might perhaps have read them in some sort usefully.

Good and evil we know in the field of this world grow up together almost inseparably; and the knowledge of good is so involved and interwoven with the knowledge of evil, and in so many cunning resemblances hardly to be discerned, that those confused seeds which were imposed on Psyche as an incessant labor to cull out, and sort asunder, were not more intermixed. It was from out the rind of one apple tasted, that the knowledge of good and evil, as two twins cleaving together, leaped forth into the world. And perhaps this is that doom which Adam fell into of knowing good and evil, that is to say of knowing good by evil. As therefore the state of man now is, what wisdom can there be to choose, what continence to forbear without the knowledge of evil? He that can apprehend and consider vice with all her baits and seeming pleasures, and yet abstain, and yet distinguish, and yet prefer that which is truly better, he is the true wayfaring Christian.

I cannot praise a fugitive and cloistered virtue, unexercised and unbreathed, that never sallies out and sees her adversary, but slinks out of the race, where that immortal garland is to be run for, not without dust and heat. Assuredly we bring not innocence into the world, we bring impurity much rather; that which purifies us is trial, and trial is by what is contrary. That virtue therefore which is but a youngling in the contemplation of evil, and knows not the utmost that vice promises to her followers, and rejects it, is but a blank virtue, not a pure; her whiteness is but an excremental whiteness. Which was the reason why our sage and serious poet Spenser, whom I dare be known to think a better teacher than Scotus or Aquinas, describing true temperance under the person of Guyon, brings him in with his palmer through the cave of Mammon, and the bower of earthly bliss, that he might see and know, and yet abstain. Since therefore the knowledge and survey of vice is in this world so necessary to the constituting of human virtue, and the scanning of error to the confirmation of truth, how can we more safely, and with less danger, scout into the regions of sin and falsity than by reading all manner of tractates and hearing all manner of reason? And this is the benefit which may be had of books promiscuously read.

But of the harm that may result hence three kinds are usually reckoned. First, is feared the infection that may spread; but then all human learning and controversy in religious points must remove out of the world, yea the Bible itself; for that oft-times relates blasphemy not nicely, it describes the carnal sense of wicked men not unelegantly, it brings in holiest men passionately murmuring against Providence through all the arguments of Epicurus: in other great disputes it answers dubiously and darkly to the common reader. And ask a Talmudist what ails the modesty of his marginal Keri, that Moses and all the prophets cannot persuade him to pronounce the textual Chetiv. For these causes we all know the Bible itself put by the papist into the first rank of prohibited books. The ancientest Fathers must be next removed, as Clement of Alexandria, and that Eusebian book of evangelic preparation, transmitting our ears through a hoard of heathenish obscenities to receive the Gospel. Who finds not that Irenæus, Epiphanius, Jerome, and others discover more heresies than they well confute, and that oft for heresy which is the truer opinion?

Nor boots it to say for these, and all the heathen writers of greatest infection, if it must be thought so, with whom is bound up the life of human learning, that they writ in an unknown tongue, so long as we are sure those languages are known as well to the worst of men, who are both most able, and most diligent to instil the poison they suck, first into the courts of princes, acquainting them with the choicest delights and criticisms of sin. As perhaps did that Petronius whom Nero called his

Arbiter, the master of his revels; and the notorious ribald of Arezzo, dreaded and yet dear to the Italian courtiers. I name not him for posterity's sake, whom Harry the 8. named in merriment his vicar of hell. By which compendious way all the contagion that foreign books can infuse will find a passage to the people far easier and shorter than an Indian voyage, though it could be sailed either by the north of Cataio eastward, or of Canada westward, while our Spanish licensing gags the English press never so severely.

But on the other side that infection which is from books of controversy in religion is more doubtful and dangerous to the learned than to the ignorant; and yet those books must be permitted untouched by the licenser. It will be hard to instance where any ignorant man hath been ever seduced by papistical book in English, unless it were commended and expounded to him by some of that clergy: and indeed all such tractates, whether false or true, are as the prophecy of Isaiah was to the eunuch, not to be understood without a guide. But of our priests and doctors how many have been corrupted by studying the comments of Jesuits and Sorbonists, and how fast they could transfuse that corruption into the people, our experience is both late and sad. It is not forgot, since the acute and distinct Arminius was perverted merely by the perusing of a nameless discourse written at Delft, which at first he took in hand to confute.

Seeing, therefore, that those books, and those in great abundance, which are likeliest to taint both life and doctrine, cannot be suppressed without the fall of learning and of all ability in disputation, and that these books of either sort are most and soonest catching to the learned, from whom to the common people whatever is heretical or dissolute may quickly be conveyed, and that evil manners are as perfectly learnt without books a thousand other ways which cannot be stopped, and evil doctrine not with books can propagate, except a teacher guide, which he might also do without writing, and so beyond prohibiting, I am not able to unfold, how this cautelous enterprise of licensing can be exempted from the number of vain and impossible attempts. And he who were pleasantly disposed could not well avoid to liken it to the exploit of that gallant man who thought to pound up the crows by shutting his park gate.

Besides another inconvenience, if learned men be the first receivers out of books and dispreaders both of vice and error, how shall the licensers themselves be confided in, unless we can confer upon them, or they assume to themselves above all others in the land, the grace of infallibility and uncorruptedness? And again, if it be true that a wise man, like a good refiner, can gather gold out of the drossiest volume, and that a fool will be a fool with the best book, yea or without book; there is no reason that we should deprive a wise man of any advantage to his wisdom, while we seek to restrain from a fool, that which being restrained will be no hindrance to his folly. For if there should be so much exactness always used to keep that from him which is unfit for his reading, we should in the judgment of Aristotle not only, but of Salomon and of our Savior, not vouchsafe him good precepts, and by consequence not willingly admit him to good books; as being certain that a wise man will make better use of an idle pamphlet, than a fool will do of sacred Scripture.

'Tis next alleged we must not expose ourselves to temptations without necessity, and next to that, not employ our time in vain things. To both these objections one answer will serve, out of the grounds already laid, that to all men such books are not temptations, nor vanities, but useful drugs and materials wherewith to temper and compose effective and strong medicines, which man's life cannot want. The rest, as children and childish men, who have not the art to qualify and prepare these working minerals, well may be exhorted to forbear, but hindered forcibly they cannot be by all the licensing that sainted Inquisition could ever yet contrive. Which is what I promised to deliver next, that this order of licensing conduces nothing to the end for which it was framed; and hath almost prevented me by being clear already while thus much hath been explaining. See the ingenuity of truth, who, when she gets a free and willing hand, opens herself faster than the pace of method and discourse can overtake her.

It was the task which I began with, to show that no nation, or well-instituted state, if they valued books at all, did ever use this way of licensing; and it might be answered, that this is a piece of prudence lately discovered. To which I return, that as it was a thing slight and obvious to think on, so if it has been difficult to find out, there wanted not among them long since who suggested such a course; which they not following, leave us a pattern of their judgment that it was not the not knowing, but the not approving, which was the cause of their not using it.

Plato, a man of high authority, indeed, but least of all for his commonwealth, in the book of his Laws, which no city ever yet received, fed his fancy with making many edicts to his airy burgomasters, which they who otherwise admire him wish had been rather buried and excused in the genial cups of an Academic night-sitting. By which laws he seems to tolerate no kind of learning but by unalterable decree, consisting most of practical traditions, to the attainment whereof a library of smaller bulk than his own dialogues would be abundant. And there also enacts that no poet should so much as read to any private man what he had written, until the judges and law-keepers had seen it, and allowed it. But that Plato meant this law peculiarly to that commonwealth which he had imagined, and to no other, is evident. Why was he not else a lawgiver to himself, but a transgressor, and to be expelled by his own magistrates; both for the wanton epigrams and dialogues which he made, and his perpetual reading of Sophron Mimus and Aristophanes, books of grossest infamy, and also for commending the latter of them, though he were the malicious libeller of his chief friends, to be read by the tyrant Dionysius, who had little need of such trash to spend his time on? But that he knew this licensing of poems had reference and dependence to many other provisos there set down in his fancied republic, which in this world could have no place: and so neither he himself, nor any magistrate, or city ever imitated that course, which, taken apart from those other collateral injunctions, must needs be vain and fruitless. For if they fell upon one kind of strictness, unless their care were equal to regulate all other things of like aptness to corrupt the mind, that single endeavor they knew would be but a fond labor; to shut and fortify one gate against corruption, and be necessitated to leave others round about wide open.

If we think to regulate printing, thereby to rectify manners, we must regulate all recreations and pastimes, all that is delightful to man. No music must be heard, no song be set or sung, but what is grave and Doric. There must be licensing dancers, that no gesture, motion, or deportment be taught our youth but what by their allowance shall be thought honest; for such Plato was provided of; it will ask more than the work of twenty licensers to examine all the lutes, the violins, and the guitars in every house; they must not be suffered to prattle as they do, but must be licensed what they may say. And who shall silence all the airs and madrigals that whisper softness in chambers? The windows also, and the balconies must be thought on; there are shrewd books, with dangerous frontispieces, set to sale; who shall prohibit them, shall twenty licensers? The villages also must have their visitors to inquire what lectures the bagpipe and the rebeck reads even to the ballatry and the gamut of every municipal fiddler, for these are the countryman's *Arcadias*, and his Monte Mayors.

Next, what more national corruption, for which England hears ill abroad, than household gluttony: who shall be the rectors of our daily rioting? And what shall be done to inhibit the multitudes that frequent those houses where drunkenness is sold and harbored? Our garments also should be referred to the licensing of some more sober workmasters to see them cut into a less wanton garb. Who shall regulate all the mixed conversation of our youth, male and female together, as is the fashion of this country? Who shall still appoint what shall be discoursed, what presumed, and no further? Lastly, who shall forbid and separate all idle resort, all evil company? These things will be, and must be; but how they shall be least hurtful, how least enticing, herein consists the grave and governing wisdom of a state.

To sequester out of the world into Atlantic and Utopian polities which never can be drawn into use, will not mend our condition; but to ordain wisely as in this world of evil, in the midst whereof God hath placed us unavoidably. Nor is it Plato's licensing of books will do this, which necessarily pulls along with it so many other kinds of licensing, as will make us all both ridiculous and weary, and yet frustrate; but those unwritten, or at least unconstraining, laws of virtuous education, religious and civil nurture, which Plato there mentions as the bonds and ligaments of the commonwealth, the pillars and the sustainers of every written statute; these they be which will bear chief sway in such matters as these, when all licensing will be easily eluded. Impunity and remissness, for certain, are the bane of a commonwealth; but here the great art lies, to discern in what the law is to bid restraint and punishment, and in what things persuasion only is to work.

If every action, which is good or evil in man at ripe years, were to be under pittance and prescription and compulsion, what were virtue but a name, what praise could be then due to well-doing, what gramercy to be sober, just, or continent? Many there be that complain of Divine Providence for suffering Adam to transgress; foolish tongues! When God gave him reason, he gave him freedom to choose, for reason is but choosing; he had been else a mere artificial Adam, such an Adam as he is in the motions. We ourselves esteem not of that obedience, or love, or gift, which is of force: God therefore left him free, set before him a provoking object, ever almost in his eyes; herein consisted his merit, herein the right of his reward, the praise of his abstinence. Wherefore did he create passions within us, pleasures round about us, but that these rightly tempered are the very ingredients of virtue?

They are not skilful considerers of human things, who imagine to remove sin by removing the matter of sin; for, besides that it is a huge heap increasing under the very act of diminishing, though some part of it may for a time be withdrawn from some persons, it cannot from all, in such a universal thing as books are; and when this is done, yet the sin remains entire. Though ye take from a covetous man all his treasure, he has yet one jewel left, ye cannot bereave him of his covetousness. Banish all objects of lust, shut up all youth into the severest discipline that can be exercised in any hermitage, ye cannot make them chaste, that came not thither so: such great care and wisdom is required to the right managing of this point. Suppose we could expel sin by this means; look how much we thus expel of sin, so much we expel of virtue: for the matter of them both is the same; remove that, and ye remove them both alike.

This justifies the high providence of God, who, though he commands us temperance, justice, continence, yet pours out before us, even to a profuseness, all desirable things, and gives us minds that can wander beyond all limit and satiety. Why should we then affect a rigor contrary to the manner of God and of nature, by abridging or scanting those means, which books freely permitted are, both to the trial of virtue and the exercise of truth? It would be better done, to learn that the law must needs be frivolous, which goes to restrain things, uncertainly and yet equally working to good and to evil. And were I the chooser, a dram of well-doing should be preferred before many times as much the forcible hindrance of evil-doing. For God sure esteems the growth and completing of one virtuous person more than the restraint of ten vicious.

And albeit whatever thing we hear or see, sitting, walking, traveling, or conversing, may be fitly called our book, and is of the same effect that writings are, yet grant the thing to be prohibited were only books, it appears that this order hitherto is far insufficient to the end which it intends. Do we not see, not once or oftener, but weekly, that continued court-libel against the Parliament and city, printed, as the wet sheets can witness, and dispersed among us, for all that licensing can do? Yet this is the prime service a man would think, wherein this Order should give proof of itself. If it were executed, you'll say. But certain, if execution be remiss or blindfold now, and in this particular, what will it be hereafter and in other books? If then the Order shall not be vain and frustrate, behold a new labor, Lords and Commons, ye must repeal and proscribe all scandalous and unlicensed books already printed and divulged; after ye have drawn them up into a list, that all may know which are condemned, and which not; and ordain that no foreign books be delivered out of custody, till they have been read over. This office will require the whole time of not a few overseers, and those no vulgar men. There be also books which are partly useful and excellent, partly culpable and pernicious; this work will ask as many more officials, to make expurgations and expunctions, that the commonwealth of learning be not damnified. In fine, when the multitude of books increase upon their hands, ye must be fain to catalogue all those printers who are found frequently offending, and forbid the importation of their whole suspected typography. In a word, that this your Order may be exact and not deficient, ye must reform it perfectly according to the model of Trent and Seville, which I know ye abhor to do.

Yet though ye should condescend to this, which God forbid, the Order still would be but fruitless and defective to that end whereto ye meant it. If to prevent sects and schisms, who is so unread or so uncatechised in story, that hath not heard of many sects refusing books as a hindrance, and preserving their doctrine unmixed for many ages, only by unwritten traditions? The Christian faith, for that was once a schism, is not unknown to have spread all over Asia, ere any Gospel or Epistle was seen in writing. If the amendment of manners be aimed at, look into Italy and Spain, whether those places be one scruple the better, the honester, the wiser, the chaster, since all the inquisitional rigor that hath been executed upon books.

Another reason, whereby to make it plain that this Order will miss the end it seeks, consider by the quality which ought to be in every licenser. It cannot be denied but that he who is made judge to sit upon the birth or death of books, whether they may be wafted into this world or not, had need to be a man above the common measure, both studious, learned, and judicious; there may be else no mean mistakes in the censure of what is passable or not; which is also no mean injury. If he be of such worth as behoves him, there cannot be a more tedious and unpleasing journey-work, a greater loss of time levied upon his head, than to be made the perpetual reader of unchosen books and pamphlets, oft-times huge volumes. There is no book that is acceptable unless at certain seasons; but to be enjoined the reading of that at all times, and in a hand scarce legible, whereof three pages would not down at any time in the fairest print, is an imposition which I cannot believe how he that values time and his own studies, or is but of a sensible nostril, should be able to endure. In this one thing I crave leave of the present licensers to be pardoned for so thinking; who doubtless took this office up, looking on it through their obedience to the Parliament, whose command perhaps made all things seem easy and unlaborious to them; but that this short trial hath wearied them out already, their own expressions and excuses to them who make so many journeys to solicit their license are testimony enough. Seeing therefore those who now possess the employment by all evident signs wish themselves well rid of it; and that no man of worth, none that is not a plain unthrift of his own hours is ever likely to succeed them, except he mean to put himself to the salary of a press corrector; we may easily foresee what kind of licensers we are to expect hereafter, either ignorant, imperious, and remiss, or basely pecuniary. This is what I had to show, wherein this Order cannot conduce to that end whereof it bears the intention.

I lastly proceed from the no good it can do, to the manifest hurt it causes, in being first the greatest discouragement and affront that can be offered to learning, and to learned men.

It was the complaint and lamentation of prelates, upon every least breath of a motion to remove pluralities, and distribute more equally Church revenues, that then all learning would be for ever dashed and discouraged. But as for that opinion, I never found cause to think that the tenth part of learning stood or fell with the clergy: nor could I ever but hold it for a sordid and unworthy speech of any churchman who had a competency left him. If therefore ye be loth to dishearten utterly and discontent, not the mercenary crew of false pretenders to learning, but the free and ingenuous sort of such as evidently were born to study, and love learning for itself, not for lucre or any other end but the service of God and of truth, and perhaps that lasting fame and perpetuity of praise which God and good men have consented shall be the reward of those whose published labors advance the good of mankind, then know that, so far to distrust the judgment and the honesty of one who hath but a common repute in learning, and never yet offended, as not to count him fit to print his mind without a tutor and examiner, lest he should drop a schism, or something of corruption, is the greatest displeasure and indignity to a free and knowing spirit that can be put upon him.

What advantage is it to be a man over it is to be a boy at school, if we have only escaped the ferula to come under the fescue of an Imprimatur, if serious and elaborate writings, as if they were no more than the theme of a grammar-lad under his pedagogue, must not be uttered without the cursory eyes of a temporizing and extemporizing licenser? He who is not trusted with his own actions, his drift not being known to be evil, and standing to the hazard of law and penalty, has no great argument to think himself reputed in the commonwealth, wherein he was born, for other than a fool or a foreigner. When a man writes to the world, he summons up all his reason and deliberation to assist him; he searches, meditates, is industrious, and likely consults and confers with his judicious friends; after all which done he takes himself to be informed in what he writes, as well as any that writ before him. If, in this the most consummate act of his fidelity and ripeness, no years, no industry, no former proof of his abilities can bring him to that state of maturity, as not to be still mistrusted and suspected, unless he carry all his considerate diligence, all his midnight watchings and expense of Palladian oil, to the hasty view of an unleisured licenser, perhaps much his younger, perhaps far his inferior in judgment, perhaps one who never knew the labor of bookwriting, and if he be not repulsed or slighted, must appear in print like a puny with his guardian, and his censor's hand on the back of his title to be his bail and surety that he is no idiot or seducer, it cannot be but a dishonor and derogation to the author, to the book, to the privilege and dignity of learning.

And what if the author shall be one so copious of fancy, as to have many things well worth the adding come into his mind after licensing, while the book is yet under the press, which not seldom happens to the best and diligentest writers; and that perhaps a dozen times in one book? The printer dares not go beyond his licensed copy; so often then must the author trudge to his leave-giver, that those his new insertions may be viewed; and many a jaunt will be made, ere that licenser, for it must be the same man, can either be found, or found at leisure; meanwhile either the press must stand still, which is no small damage, or the author lose his accuratest thoughts, and send the book forth worse than he had made it, which to a diligent writer is the greatest melancholy and vexation that can befall.

And how can a man teach with authority, which is the life of teaching, how can he be a doctor in his book as he ought to be, or else had better be silent, whenas all he teaches, all he delivers, is but under the tuition, under the correction of his patriarchal licenser to blot or alter what precisely accords not with the hidebound humor which he calls his judgment? When every acute reader, upon the first sight of a pedantic license, will be ready with these like words to ding the book a quoit's distance from him: I hate a pupil teacher, I endure not an instructor that comes to me under the wardship of an overseeing fist. I know nothing of the licenser, but that I have his own hand here for his arrogance; who shall warrant me his judgment? The state, sir, replies the stationer, but has a quick return: The state shall be my governors, but not my critics; they may be mistaken in the choice of a licenser, as easily as this licenser may be mistaken in an author; this is some common stuff; and he might add from Sir Francis Bacon, that such authorized books are but the language of the times. For though a licenser should happen to be judicious more than ordinary, which will be a great jeopardy of the next succession, yet his very office and his commission enjoins him to let pass nothing but what is vulgarly received already.

Nay, which is more lamentable, if the work of any deceased author, though never so famous in his lifetime and even to this day, come to their hands for license to be printed, or reprinted, if there be found in his book one sentence of a venturous edge, uttered in the height of zeal and who knows whether it might not be the dictate of a divine spirit, yet not suiting with every low decrepit humor of their own, though it were Knox himself, the reformer of a kingdom, that spake it, they will not pardon him their dash: the sense of that great man shall to all posterity be lost, for the fearfulness of the presumptuous rashness of a perfunctory licenser. And to what an author this violence hath been lately done, and in what book of greatest consequence to be faithfully published, I could now instance, but shall forbear till a more convenient season.

Yet if these things be not resented seriously and timely by them who have the remedy in their power, but that such iron moulds as these shall have authority to gnaw out the choicest periods of exquisitest books, and to commit such a treacherous fraud against the orphan remainders of worthiest men after death, the more sorrow will belong to that hapless race of men, whose misfortune it is to have understanding. Henceforth let no man care to learn, or care to be more than worldly wise; for certainly in higher matters to be ignorant and slothful, to be a common steadfast dunce, will be the only pleasant life, and only in request.

And as it is a particular disesteem of every knowing person alive, and most injurious to the written labors and monuments of the dead, so to me it seems an undervaluing and vilifying of the whole nation. I cannot set so light by all the invention, the art, the wit, the grave and solid judgment which is in England, so that it can be comprehended in any twenty capacities how good soever, much less that it should not pass except their superintendence be over it, except it be sifted and strained with their strainers, that it should be uncurrent without their manual stamp. Truth and understanding are not such wares as to be monopolized and traded in by tickets and statutes and standards. We must not think to make a staple commodity of all the knowledge in the land, to mark and license it like our broadcloth and our woolpacks. What is it but a servitude like that imposed by the Philistines, not to be allowed the sharpening of our own axes and coulters, but we must repair from all quarters to twenty licensing forges? Had anyone written and divulged erroneous things and scandalous to honest life, misusing and forfeiting the esteem had of his reason among men, if after conviction this only censure were adjudged him, that he should never henceforth write but what were first examined by an appointed officer whose hand should be annexed to pass his credit for him that now he might be safely read; it could not be apprehended less than a disgraceful punishment. Whence to include the whole nation, and those that never yet thus offended, under such a diffident and suspectful prohibition, may plainly be understood what a disparagement it is. So much the more, whenas debtors and delinquents may walk abroad without a keeper, but unoffensive books must not stir forth without a visible jailer in their title.

Nor is it to the common people less than a reproach; for if we be so jealous over them, as that we dare not trust them with an English pamphlet, what do we but censure them for a giddy, vicious, and ungrounded people; in such a sick and weak state of faith and discretion, as to be able to take nothing down but through the pipe of a licenser? That this is care or love of them, we cannot pretend, whenas, in those popish places where the laity are most hated and despised, the same strictness is used over them. Wisdom we cannot call it, because it stops but one breach of license, nor that neither: whenas those corruptions which it seeks to prevent, break in faster at other doors which cannot be shut.

And in conclusion it reflects to the disrepute of our ministers also, of whose labors we should hope better, and of the proficiency which their flock reaps by them, than that after all this light of the Gospel which is, and is to be, and all this continual preaching, they should be still frequented with such an unprincipled, unedified and laic rabble, as that the whiff of every new pamphlet should stagger them out of their catechism, and Christian walking. This may have much reason to discourage the ministers when such a low conceit is had of all their exhortations, and the benefiting of their hearers, as that they are not thought fit to be turned loose to three sheets of paper without a licenser; that all the sermons, all the lectures preached, printed, vented in such numbers, and such volumes, as have now well-nigh made all other books unsaleable, should not be armor enough against one single enchiridion, without the castle St. Angelo of an Imprimatur.

And lest some should persuade ye, Lords and Commons, that these arguments of learned men's discouragement at this your Order are mere flourishes, and not real, I could recount what I have seen and heard in other countries, where this kind of inquisition tyrannizes; when I have sat among their learned men, for that honor I had, and been counted happy to be born in such a place of philosophic freedom, as they supposed England was, while themselves did nothing but bemoan the servile condition into which learning amongst them was brought; that this was it which had damped the glory of Italian wits; that nothing had been there written now these many years but flattery and fustian. There it was that I found and visited the famous Galileo, grown old, a prisoner to the Inquisition, for thinking in astronomy otherwise than the Franciscan and Dominican licensers thought.

And though I knew that England then was groaning loudest under the prelatical yoke, nevertheless I took it as a pledge of future happiness, that other nations were so persuaded of her liberty. Yet was it beyond my hope that those worthies were then breathing in her air, who should be her leaders to such a deliverance, as shall never be forgotten by any revolution of time that this world hath to finish. When that was once begun, it was as little in my fear that, what words of complaint I heard among learned men of other parts uttered against the Inquisition, the same I should hear by as learned men at home uttered in time of Parliament against an order of licensing; and that so generally that, when I had disclosed myself a companion of their discontent, I might say, if without envy, that he whom an honest quæstorship had endeared to the Sicilians was not more

by them importuned against Verres, than the favorable opinion
which I had among many who honor ye, and are known and
respected by ye, loaded me with entreaties and persuasions,
that I would not despair to lay together that which just reason
should bring into my mind, toward the removal of an undeserved
thraldom upon learning. That this is not therefore the disburden-
ing of a particular fancy, but the common grievance of all those
who had prepared their minds and studies above the vulgar pitch
to advance truth in others, and from others to entertain it, thus
much may satisfy.

And in their name I shall for neither friend nor foe conceal
what the general murmur is; that if it come to inquisitioning
again and licensing, and that we are so timorous of ourselves,
and so suspicious of all men, as to fear each book and the shaking
of every leaf, before we know what the contents are; if some who
but of late were little better than silenced from preaching shall
come now to silence us from reading, except what they please,
it cannot be guessed what is intended by some but a second
tyranny over learning: and will soon put it out of controversy
that bishops and presbyters are the same to us, both name and
thing. That those evils of prelaty, which before from five or six
and twenty sees were distributively charged upon the whole
people, will now light wholly upon learning, is not obscure to
us: whenas now the pastor of a small unlearned parish on the
sudden shall be exalted archbishop over a large diocese of books,
and yet not remove, but keep his other cure too, a mystical
pluralist. He who but of late cried down the sole ordination
of every novice Bachelor of Art, and denied sole jurisdiction
over the simplest parishioner, shall now at home in his private
chair assume both these over worthiest and excellentest books
and ablest authors that write them.

This is not, ye Covenants and Protestations that we have
made! this is not to put down prelaty; this is but to chop an
episcopacy; this but to translate the Palace Metropolitan
from one kind of dominion into another; this is but an old
canonical sleight of commuting our penance. To startle thus
betimes at a mere unlicensed pamphlet will after a while be
afraid of every conventicle, and a while after will make a
conventicle of every Christian meeting. But I am certain that
a state governed by the rules of justice and fortitude, or a church

built and founded upon the rock of faith and true knowledge, cannot be so pusillanimous. While things are yet not constituted in religion, that freedom of writing should be restrained by a discipline imitated from the prelates and learnt by them from the Inquisition, to shut us up all again into the breast of a licenser, must needs give cause of doubt and discouragement to all learned and religious men.

Who cannot but discern the fineness of this politic drift, and who are the contrivers; that while bishops were to be baited down, then all presses might be open; it was the people's birthright and privilege in time of Parliament, it was the breaking forth of light? But now, the bishops abrogated and voided out the Church, as if our Reformation sought no more but to make room for others into their seats under another name, the episcopal arts begin to bud again, the cruse of truth must run no more oil, liberty of printing must be enthralled again under a prelatical commission of twenty, the privilege of the people nullified, and, which is worse, the freedom of learning must groan again, and to her old fetters: all this the Parliament yet sitting. Although their own late arguments and defences against the prelates might remember them that this obstructing violence meets for the most part with an event utterly opposite to the end which it drives at: instead of suppressing sects and schisms, it raises them and invests them with a reputation. "The punishing of wits enhances their authority," saith the Viscount St. Albans; "and a forbidden writing is thought to be a certain spark of truth that flies up in the faces of them who seek to tread it out." This Order, therefore, may prove a nursing-mother to sects, but I shall easily show how it will be a stepdame to truth: and first by disenabling us to the maintenance of what is known already.

Well knows he who uses to consider, that our faith and knowledge thrives by exercise, as well as our limbs and complexion. Truth is compared in Scripture to a streaming fountain; if her waters flow not in a perpetual progression, they sicken into a muddy pool of conformity and tradition. A man may be a heretic in the truth; and if he believe things only because his pastor says so, or the Assembly so determines, without knowing other reason, though his belief be true, yet the very truth he holds becomes his heresy.

There is not any burden that some would gladlier post off to another than the charge and care of their religion. There be—who knows not that there be?—of protestants and professors who live and die in as arrant an implicit faith as any lay papist of Loretto. A wealthy man, addicted to his pleasure and to his profits, finds religion to be a traffic so entangled, and of so many piddling accounts, that of all mysteries he cannot skill to keep a stock going upon that trade. What should he do? Fain he would have the name to be religious, fain he would bear up with his neighbors in that. What does he therefore, but resolve to give over toiling, and to find himself out some factor, to whose care and credit he may commit the whole managing of his religious affairs? some divine of note and estimation that must be. To him he adheres, resigns the whole warehouse of his religion, with all the locks and keys, into his custody; and indeed makes the very person of that man his religion; esteems his associating with him a sufficient evidence and commendatory of his own piety. So that a man may say his religion is now no more within himself, but is become a dividual movable, and goes and comes near him, according as that good man frequents the house. He entertains him, gives him gifts, feasts him, lodges him; his religion comes home at night, prays, is liberally supped, and sumptuously laid to sleep, rises, is saluted, and after the malmsey, or some well-spiced brewage, and better breakfasted than he whose morning appetite would have gladly fed on green figs between Bethany and Jerusalem, his religion walks abroad at eight, and leaves his kind entertainer in the shop trading all day without his religion.

Another sort there be who, when they hear that all things shall be ordered, all things regulated and settled, nothing written but what passes through the custom-house of certain publicans that have the tonnaging and poundaging of all free-spoken truth, will straight give themselves up into your hands, make 'em and cut 'em out what religion ye please: there be delights, there be recreations and jolly pastimes that will fetch the day about from sun to sun, and rock the tedious year as in a delightful dream. What need they torture their heads with that which others have taken so strictly and so unalterably into their own purveying? These are the fruits which a dull ease and cessation of our knowledge will bring forth among the people. How goodly and how to be wished were such an obedient unanimity as this, what a fine conformity would it starch us all into! Doubtless a staunch and solid piece of framework, as any January could freeze together.

Nor much better will be the consequence even among the clergy themselves. It is no new thing never heard of before, for a parochial minister, who has his reward and is at his Hercules' pillars in a warm benefice, to be easily inclinable, if he have nothing else that may rouse up his studies, to finish his circuit in an English concordance and a topic folio, the gatherings and savings of a sober graduateship, a harmony and a catena; treading the constant round of certain common doctrinal heads, attended with the uses, motives, marks, and means, out of which, as out of an alphabet, or sol-fa, by forming and transforming, joining and disjoining variously, a little bookcraft, and two hours' meditation, might furnish him unspeakably to the performance of more than a weekly charge of sermoning: not to reckon up the infinite helps of interlinearies, breviaries, synopses, and other loitering gear. But as for the multitude of sermons ready printed and piled up, on every text that is not difficult, our London trading St. Thomas in his vestry, and add to boot St. Martin and St. Hugh, have not within their hallowed limits more vendible ware of all sorts ready made: so that penury he never need fear of pulpit provision, having where so plenteously to refresh his magazine. But if his rear and flanks be not impaled, if his back door be not secured by the rigid licenser, but that a bold book may now and then issue forth and give the assault to some of his old collections in their trenches, it will concern him then to keep waking, to stand in watch, to set good guards and sentinels about his received opinions, to walk the round and counter-round with his fellow inspectors, fearing lest any of his flock be seduced, who also then would be better instructed, better exercised and disciplined. And God send that the fear of this diligence, which must then be used, do not make us affect the laziness of a licensing church.

For if we be sure we are in the right, and do not hold the truth guiltily, which becomes not, if we ourselves condemn not our own weak and frivolous teaching, and the people for an untaught and irreligious gadding rout, what can be more fair than when a man judicious, learned, and of a conscience, for aught we know, as good as theirs that taught us what we know, shall not privily from house to house, which is more dangerous, but openly by writing publish to the world what his opinion is, what his reasons, and wherefore that which is now thought cannot be sound? Christ urged it as wherewith to justify himself, that he preached in public; yet writing is more public than preaching; and more easy to refutation, if need be, there being so many whose business and profession merely it is to be the champions of truth; which if they neglect, what can be imputed but their sloth, or unability?

Thus much we are hindered and disinured by this course of licensing, toward the true knowledge of what we seem to know. For how much it hurts and hinders the licensers themselves in the calling of their ministry, more than any secular employment, if they will discharge that office as they ought, so that of necessity they must neglect either the one duty or the other, I insist not, because it is a particular, but leave it to their own conscience, how they will decide it there.

There is yet behind of what I purposed to lay open, the incredible loss and detriment that this plot of licensing puts us to; more than if some enemy at sea should stop up all our havens and ports and creeks, it hinders and retards the importation of our richest merchandise, truth; nay, it was first established and put in practice by antichristian malice and mystery on set purpose to extinguish, if it were possible, the light of Reformation, and to settle falsehood; little differing from that policy wherewith the Turk upholds his Alcoran, by the prohibition of printing. 'Tis not denied, but gladly confessed, we are to send our thanks and vows to Heaven louder than most of nations, for that great measure of truth which we enjoy, especially in those main points between us and the Pope, with his appurtenances the prelates: but he who thinks we are to pitch our tent here, and have attained the utmost prospect of reformation that the mortal glass wherein we contemplate can show us, till we come to beatific vision, that man by this very opinion declares that he is yet far short of truth.

Truth indeed came once into the world with her Divine Master, and was a perfect shape most glorious to look on: but when he ascended, and his Apostles after him were laid asleep, then straight arose a wicked race of deceivers, who, as that story goes of the Egyptian Typhon with his conspirators, how they dealt with the good Osiris, took the virgin Truth, hewed her lovely form into a thousand pieces, and scattered them to the four winds. From that time ever since, the sad friends of Truth, such as durst appear, imitating the careful search that Isis made for the mangled body of Osiris, went up and down gathering up limb by limb, still as they could find them. We have not yet found them all, Lords and Commons, nor ever shall do, till her Master's second coming; he shall bring together every joint and member, and shall mould them into an immortal feature of loveliness and perfection. Suffer not these licensing prohibitions to stand at every place of opportunity, forbidding and disturbing them that continue seeking, that continue to do our obsequies to the torn body of our martyred saint.

We boast our light; but if we look not wisely on the sun itself, it smites us into darkness. Who can discern those planets that are oft combust, and those stars of brightest magnitude that rise and set with the sun, until the opposite motion of their orbs bring them to such a place in the firmament, where they may be seen evening or morning? The light which we have gained was given us, not to be ever staring on, but by it to discover onward things more remote from our knowledge. It is not the unfrocking of a priest, the unmitring of a bishop, and the removing him from off the presbyterian shoulders, that will make us a happy nation. No, if other things as great in the Church, and in the rule of life both economical and polit-ical, be not looked into and reformed, we have looked so long upon the blaze that Zuinglius and Calvin hath beaconed up to us, that we are stark blind. There be who perpetually com-plain of schisms and sects, and make it such a calamity that any man dissents from their maxims. 'Tis their own pride and ignorance which causes the disturbing, who neither will hear with meekness, nor can convince; yet all must be suppressed which is not found in their syntagma. They are the troublers, they are the dividers of unity, who neglect and permit not others to unite those dissevered pieces which are yet wanting to the body of Truth. To be still searching what we know not by what we know, still closing up truth to truth as we find it (for all her body is homogeneal and proportional), this is the golden rule in theology as well as in arithmetic, and makes up the best harmony in a church; not the forced and outward union of cold and neutral, and inwardly divided minds.

Lords and Commons of England, consider what nation it is whereof ye are, and whereof ye are the governors: a nation not slow and dull, but of a quick, ingenious and piercing spirit, acute to invent, subtle and sinewy to discourse, not beneath the reach of any point, the highest that human capacity can soar to.   Therefore the studies of learning in her deepest sciences have been so ancient and so eminent among us, that writers of good antiquity and ablest judgment have been persuaded that even the school of Pythagoras and the Persian wisdom took beginning from the old philosophy of this island.   And that wise and civil Roman, Julius Agricola, who governed once here for Cæsar, preferred the natural wits of Britain before the labored studies of the French.   Nor is it for nothing that the grave and frugal Transylvanian sends out yearly from as far as the mountainous borders of Russia, and beyond the Hercynian wilderness, not their youth, but their staid men, to learn our language and our theologic arts.

Yet that which is above all this, the favor and the love of Heaven, we have great argument to think in a peculiar manner propitious and propending towards us.   Why else was this nation chosen before any other, that out of her, as out of Sion, should be proclaimed and sounded forth the first tidings and trumpet of Reformation to all Europe?   And had it not been the obstinate perverseness of our prelates against the divine and admirable spirit of Wickliffe, to suppress him as a schismatic and innovator, perhaps neither the Bohemian Huss and Jerome, no nor the name of Luther or of Calvin, had been ever known: the glory of reforming all our neighbors had been completely ours. But now, as our obdurate clergy have with violence demeaned the matter, we are become hitherto the latest and backwardest scholars, of whom God offered to have made us the teachers. Now once again by all concurrence of signs, and by the general instinct of holy and devout men, as they daily and solemnly express their thoughts, God is decreeing to begin some new and great period in his Church, even to the reforming of Reformation itself: what does he then but reveal himself to his servants, and as his manner is, first to his Englishmen?   I say, as his manner is, first to us, though we mark not the method of his counsels, and are unworthy.

Behold now this vast city: a city of refuge, the mansion house of liberty, encompassed and surrounded with his protection; the shop of war hath not there more anvils and hammers waking, to fashion out the plates and instruments of armed justice in defence of beleaguered truth, than there be pens and heads there, sitting by their studious lamps, musing, searching, revolving new notions and ideas wherewith to present, as with their homage and their fealty, the approaching Reformation: others as fast reading, trying all things, assenting to the force of reason and convincement. What could a man require more from a nation so pliant and so prone to seek after knowledge? What wants there to such a towardly and pregnant soil, but wise and faithful laborers, to make a knowing people, a nation of prophets, of sages, and of worthies? We reckon more than five months yet to harvest; there need not be five weeks; had we but eyes to lift up, the fields are white already.

Where there is much desire to learn, there of necessity will be much arguing, much writing, many opinions; for opinion in good men is but knowledge in the making. Under these fantastic terrors of sect and schism, we wrong the earnest and zealous thirst after knowledge and understanding which God hath stirred up in this city. What some lament of, we rather should rejoice at, should rather praise this pious forwardness among men, to reassume the ill-deputed care of their religion into their own hands again. A little generous prudence, a little forbearance of one another, and some grain of charity might win all these diligences to join, and unite in one general and brotherly search after truth; could we but forego this prelatical tradition of crowding free consciences and Christian liberties into canons and precepts of men. I doubt not, if some great and worthy stranger should come among us, wise to discern the mould and temper of a people, and how to govern it, observing the high hopes and aims, the diligent alacrity of our extended thoughts and reasonings in the pursuance of truth and freedom, but that he would cry out as Pyrrhus did, admiring the Roman docility and courage: If such were my Epirots, I would not despair the greatest design that could be attempted, to make a church or kingdom happy.

Yet these are the men cried out against for schismatics and sectaries; as if, while the temple of the Lord was building, some cutting, some squaring the marble, others hewing the cedars, there should be a sort of irrational men who could not consider there must be many schisms and many dissections made in the quarry and in the timber, ere the house of God can be built. And when every stone is laid artfully together, it cannot be united into a continuity, it can but be contiguous in this world; neither can every piece of the building be of one form; nay rather the perfection consists in this, that, out of many moderate varieties and brotherly dissimilitudes that are not vastly disproportional, arises the goodly and the graceful symmetry that commends the whole pile and structure.

Let us therefore be more considerate builders, more wise in spiritual architecture, when great reformation is expected. For now the time seems come, wherein Moses the great prophet may sit in heaven rejoicing to see that memorable and glorious wish of his fulfilled, when not only our seventy elders, but all the Lord's people, are become prophets. No marvel then though some men, and some good men too perhaps, but young in goodness, as Joshua then was, envy them. They fret, and out of their own weakness are in agony, lest these divisions and subdivisions will undo us. The adversary again applauds, and waits the hour: When they have branched themselves out, saith he, small enough into parties and partitions, then will be our time. Fool! he sees not the firm root, out of which we all grow, though into branches: nor will beware until he see our small divided maniples cutting through at every angle of his ill-united and unwieldy brigade. And that we are to hope better of all these supposed sects and schisms, and that we shall not need that solicitude, honest perhaps though over-timorous of them that vex in this behalf, but shall laugh in the end at those malicious applauders of our differences, I have these reasons to persuade me.

First, when a city shall be as it were besieged and blocked about, her navigable river infested, inroads and incursions round, defiance and battle oft rumored to be marching up even to her walls and suburb trenches, that then the people, or the greater part, more than at other times, wholly taken up with the study of highest and most important matters to be reformed, should be disputing, reasoning, reading, inventing, discoursing, even to a rarity and admiration, things not before discoursed or written of, argues first a singular goodwill, contentedness and confidence in your prudent foresight and safe government, Lords and Commons; and from thence derives itself to a gallant bravery and well-grounded contempt of their enemies, as if there were no small number of as great spirits among us, as his was, who when Rome was nigh besieged by Hannibal, being in the city, bought that piece of ground at no cheap rate, whereon Hannibal himself encamped his own regiment.

Next, it is a lively and cheerful presage of our happy success and victory. For as in a body, when the blood is fresh, the spirits pure and vigorous, not only to vital but to rational faculties, and those in the acutest and the pertest operations of wit and subtlety, it argues in what good plight and constitution the body is, so when the cheerfulness of the people is so sprightly up, as that it has not only wherewith to guard well its own freedom and safety, but to spare, and to bestow upon the solidest and sublimest points of controversy and new invention, it betokens us not degenerated, nor drooping to a fatal decay, but casting off the old and wrinkled skin of corruption to outlive these pangs and wax young again, entering the glorious ways of truth and prosperous virtue, destined to become great and honorable in these latter ages. Methinks I see in my mind a noble and puissant nation rousing herself like a strong man after sleep, and shaking her invincible locks. Methinks I see her as an eagle mewing her mighty youth, and kindling her undazzled eyes at the full mid-day beam; purging and unscaling her long-abused sight at the fountain itself of heavenly radiance; while the whole noise of timorous and flocking birds, with those also that love the twilight, flutter about, amazed at what she means, and in their envious gabble would prognosticate a year of sects and schisms.

What should ye do then, should ye suppress all this flowery crop of knowledge and new light sprung up and yet springing daily in this city? Should ye set an oligarchy of twenty engrossers over it, to bring a famine upon our minds again, when we shall know nothing but what is measured to us by their bushel? Believe it, Lords and Commons, they who counsel ye to such a suppressing do as good as bid ye suppress yourselves; and I will soon show how. If it be desired to know the immediate cause of all this free writing and free speaking, there cannot be assigned a truer than your own mild and free and humane government. It is the liberty, Lords and Commons, which your own valorous and happy counsels have purchased us, liberty which is the nurse of all great wits; this is that which hath rarefied and enlightened our spirits like the influence of heaven; this is that which hath enfranchised, enlarged and lifted up our apprehensions degrees above themselves.

Ye cannot make us now less capable, less knowing, less eagerly pursuing of the truth, unless ye first make yourselves, that made us so, less the lovers, less the founders of our true liberty. We can grow ignorant again, brutish, formal and slavish, as ye found us; but you then must first become that which ye cannot be, oppressive, arbitrary and tyrannous, as they were from whom ye have freed us. That our hearts are now more capacious, our thoughts more erected to the search and expectation of greatest and exactest things, is the issue of your own virtue propagated in us; ye cannot suppress that, unless ye reinforce an abrogated and merciless law, that fathers may despatch at will their own children. And who shall then stick closest to ye, and excite others? Not he who takes up arms for coat and conduct, and his four nobles of Danegelt. Although I dispraise not the defence of just immunities, yet love my peace better, if that were all. Give me the liberty to know, to utter, and to argue freely according to conscience, above all liberties.

What would be best advised, then, if it be found so hurtful and so unequal to suppress opinions for the newness or the unsuitableness to a customary acceptance, will not be my task to say. I only shall repeat what I have learned from one of your own honorable number, a right noble and pious lord, who, had he not sacrificed his life and fortunes to the Church and Commonwealth, we had not now missed and bewailed a worthy and undoubted patron of this argument. Ye know him, I am sure; yet I for honor's sake, and may it be eternal to him, shall name him, the Lord Brook. He, writing of episcopacy and by the way treating of sects and schisms, left ye his vote, or rather now the last words of his dying charge, which I know will ever be of dear and honored regard with ye, so full of meekness and breathing charity, that next to his last testament, who bequeathed love and peace to his disciples, I cannot call to mind where I have read or heard words more mild and peaceful. He there exhorts us to hear with patience and humility those, however they be miscalled, that desire to live purely, in such a use of God's ordinances, as the best guidance of their conscience gives them, and to tolerate them, though in some disconformity to ourselves. The book itself will tell us more at large, being published to the world, and dedicated to the Parliament by him who, both for his life and for his death, deserves that what advice he left be not laid by without perusal.

And now the time in special is, by privilege to write and speak what may help to the further discussing of matters in agitation. The temple of Janus with his two controversial faces might now not unsignificantly be set open. And though all the winds of doctrine were let loose to play upon the earth, so truth be in the field, we do injuriously, by licensing and prohibiting, to misdoubt her strength. Let her and falsehood grapple; who ever knew truth put to the worse, in a free and open encounter? Her confuting is the best and surest suppressing. He who hears what praying there is for light and clearer knowledge to be sent down among us, would think of other matters to be constituted beyond the discipline of Geneva, framed and fabricked already to our hands. Yet when the new light which we beg for shines in upon us, there be who envy and oppose, if it come not first in at their casements. What a collusion is this, whenas we are exhorted by the wise man to use diligence, to seek for wisdom as for hidden treasures early and late, that another order shall enjoin us to know nothing but by statute? When a man hath been laboring the hardest labor in the deep mines of knowledge, hath furnished out his findings in all their equipage, drawn forth his reasons as it were a battle ranged, scattered and defeated all objections in his way, calls out his adversary into the plain, offers him the advantage of wind and sun, if he please, only that he may try the matter by dint of argument, for his opponents then to skulk, to lay ambushments, to keep a narrow bridge of licensing where the challenger should pass, though it be valor enough in soldiership, is but weakness and cowardice in the wars of truth.

For who knows not that truth is strong, next to the Almighty? She needs no policies, nor stratagems, nor licensings to make her victorious; those are the shifts and the defences that error uses against her power. Give her but room, and do not bind her when she sleeps, for then she speaks not true, as the old Proteus did, who spake oracles only when he was caught and bound, but then rather she turns herself into all shapes, except her own, and perhaps tunes her voice according to the time, as Micaiah did before Ahab, until she be adjured into her own likeness. Yet is it not impossible that she may have more shapes than one. What else is all that rank of things indifferent, wherein truth may be on this side or on the other, without being unlike herself? What but a vain shadow else is the abolition of those ordinances, that hand-writing nailed to the cross? What great purchase is this Christian liberty which Paul so often boasts of? His doctrine is, that he who eats or eats not, regards a day or regards it not, may do either to the Lord. How many other things might be tolerated in peace, and left to conscience, had we but charity, and were it not the chief stronghold of our hypocrisy to be ever judging one another?

I fear yet this iron yoke of outward conformity hath left a slavish print upon our necks; the ghost of a linen decency yet haunts us. We stumble and are impatient at the least dividing of one visible congregation from another, though it be not in fundamentals; and through our forwardness to suppress, and our backwardness to recover any enthralled piece of truth out of the gripe of custom, we care not to keep truth separated from truth which is the fiercest rent and disunion of all. We do not see that, while we still affect by all means a rigid external formality, we may as soon fall again into a gross conforming stupidity, a stark and dead congealment of wood and hay and stubble, forced and frozen together, which is more to the sudden degenerating of a Church than many subdichotomies of petty schisms.

Not that I can think well of every light separation, or that all in a Church is to be expected gold and silver and precious stones: it is not possible for man to sever the wheat from the tares, the good fish from the other fry; that must be the angels' ministry at the end of mortal things. Yet if all cannot be of one mind—as who looks they should be?—this doubtless is more wholesome, more prudent, and more Christian that many be tolerated, rather than all compelled. I mean not tolerated popery, and open superstition, which, as it extirpates all religions and civil supremacies, so itself should be extirpate, provided first that all charitable and compassionate means be used to win and regain the weak and the misled: that also which is impious or evil absolutely either against faith or manners no law can possibly permit, that intends not to unlaw itself: but those neighboring differences, or rather indifferences, are what I speak of, whether in some point of doctrine or of discipline, which, though they may be many, yet need not interrupt the unity of spirit, if we could but find among us the bond of peace.

In the meanwhile if anyone would write, and bring his helpful hand to the slow-moving Reformation which we labor under, if truth have spoken to him before others, or but seemed at least to speak, who hath so bejesuited us that we should trouble that man with asking license to do so worthy a deed? And not consider this, that if it come to prohibiting, there is not aught more likely to be prohibited than truth itself; whose first appearance to our eyes, bleared and dimmed with prejudice and custom, is more unsightly and unplausible than many errors, even as the person is of many a great man slight and contemptible to see to? And what do they tell us vainly of new opinions, when this very opinion of theirs, that none must be heard, but whom they like, is the worst and newest opinion of all others; and is the chief cause why sects and schisms do so much abound, and true knowledge is kept at distance from us; besides yet a greater danger which is in it?

For when God shakes a kingdom with strong and healthful commotions to a general reforming, 'tis not untrue that many sectaries and false teachers are then busiest in seducing; but yet more true it is, that God then raises to his own work men of rare abilities, and more than common industry, not only to look back and revise what hath been taught heretofore, but to gain further and go on some new enlightened steps in the discovery of truth. For such is the order of God's enlightening his Church, to dispense and deal out by degrees his beam, so as our earthly eyes may best sustain it.

Neither is God appointed and confined, where and out of what place these his chosen shall be first heard to speak; for he sees not as man sees, chooses not as man chooses, lest we should devote ourselves again to set places, and assemblies, and outward callings of men; planting our faith one while in the old Convocation house, and another while in the Chapel at Westminster; when all the faith and religion that shall be there canonized is not sufficient without plain convincement, and the charity of patient instruction to supple the least bruise of conscience, to edify the meanest Christian, who desires to walk in the spirit, and not in the letter of human trust, for all the number of voices that can be there made; no, though Harry the 7. himself there, with all his liege tombs about him, should lend them voices from the dead, to swell their number.

And if the men be erroneous who appear to be the leading schismatics, what withholds us but our sloth, our self-will, and distrust in the right cause, that we do not give them gentle meeting and gentle dismissions, that we debate not and examine the matter thoroughly with liberal and frequent audience; if not for their sakes, yet for our own? Seeing no man who hath tasted learning, but will confess the many ways of profiting by those who, not contented with stale receipts, are able to manage and set forth new positions to the world. And were they but as the dust and cinders of our feet, so long as in that notion they may yet serve to polish and brighten the armory of truth, even for that respect they were not utterly to be cast away. But if they be of those whom God hath fitted for the special use of these times with eminent and ample gifts, and those perhaps neither among the priests nor among the Pharisees, and we in the haste of a precipitant zeal shall make no distinction, but resolve to stop their mouths, because we fear they come with new and dangerous opinions, as we commonly forejudge them ere we understand them, no less than woe to us, while, thinking thus to defend the Gospel, we are found the persecutors.

There have been not a few since the beginning of this Parliament, both of the presbytery and others, who by their unlicensed books, to the contempt of an Imprimatur, first broke that triple ice clung about our hearts, and taught the people to see day: I hope that none of those were the persuaders to renew upon us this bondage which they themselves have wrought so much good by contemning. But if neither the check that Moses gave to young Joshua, nor the countermand which our Savior gave to young John, who was so ready to prohibit those whom he thought unlicensed, be not enough to admonish our elders how unacceptable to God their testy mood of prohibiting is, if neither their own remembrance what evil hath abounded in the Church by this let of licensing, and what good they themselves have begun by transgressing it, be not enough, but that they will persuade and execute the most Dominican part of the Inquisition over us, and are already with one foot in the stirrup so active at suppressing, it would be no unequal distribution in the first place to suppress the suppressors themselves: whom the change of their condition hath puffed up, more than their late experience of harder times hath made wise.

And as for regulating the press, let no man think to have the honor of advising ye better than yourselves have done in that Order published next before this, "that no book be printed, unless the printer's and the author's name, or at least the printer's, be registered." Those which otherwise come forth, if they be found mischievous and libellous, the fire and the executioner will be the timeliest and the most effectual remedy that man's prevention can use. For this authentic Spanish policy of licensing books, if I have said aught, will prove the most unlicensed book itself within a short while; and was the immediate image of a Star Chamber decree to that purpose made in those very times when that Court did the rest of those her pious works, for which she is now fallen from the stars with Lucifer. Whereby ye may guess what kind of state prudence, what love of the people, what care of religion or good manners there was at the contriving, although with singular hypocrisy it pretended to bind books to their good behavior. And how it got the upper hand of your precedent Order so well constituted before, if we may believe those men whose profession gives them cause to inquire most, it may be doubted there was in it the fraud of some old patentees and monopolizers in the trade of bookselling; who under pretence of the poor in their Company not to be defrauded, and the just retaining of each man his several copy, which God forbid should be gainsaid, brought divers glosing colors to the House, which were indeed but colors, and serving to no end except it be to exercise a superiority over their neighbors; men who do not therefore labor in an honest profession to which learning is indebted, that they should be made other men's vassals. Another end is thought was aimed at by some of them in procuring by petition this

Order, that, having power in their hands, malignant books might the easier scape abroad, as the event shows.

But of these sophisms and elenchs of merchandise I skill not. This I know, that errors in a good government and in a bad are equally almost incident; for what magistrate may not be misinformed, and much the sooner, if liberty of printing be reduced into the power of a few? But to redress willingly and speedily what hath been erred, and in highest authority to esteem a plain advertisement more than others have done a sumptuous bribe, is a virtue (honored Lords and Commons) answerable to your highest actions, and whereof none can participate but greatest and wisest men.

JEREMY TAYLOR (1613–1667)

After a quiet and studious youth Jeremy Taylor, at the age of twenty-one, suddenly became known to a larger world than Cambridge. Acting as substitute for a friend, Taylor preached from the pulpit Donne had left three years before, and the beauty of his person, manner, and discourse enchanted his hearers. Henceforth his progress was supervised by the watchful eye of Archbishop Laud. An ardent royalist, and chaplain to Charles I during the Civil War, Taylor suffered in consequence; but he enjoyed some years of happy retirement with his patrons, Lord and Lady Carbery, at Golden Grove in Wales, where he preached many of his finest sermons. A time of trouble and poverty followed, partly alleviated by the help and friendship of Evelyn, the diarist. At the Restoration, Taylor received an Irish bishopric, but friction with his diocese, which was mainly presbyterian, clouded his last years.

The Liberty of Prophesying was a landmark in Taylor's development, for in it he broke through the shell of Laudian principles in which he had dwelt, and appeared—influenced by such latitudinarians as Chillingworth—as a champion of tolerance and charity. The book was a landmark also in the development of freedom of conscience at a time when the struggle for such freedom was too commonly understood to mean the right of a dominant sect to enslave others. Naturally the style is not that of Taylor's sermons and devotional works, but it has its own restrained emotion.

THE LIBERTY OF PROPHESYING (1647)

EPISTLE DEDICATORY

. . . For I had no books of my own here, nor any in the voisinage. . . . I had this only advantage besides, that I have chosen a subject in which, if my own reason does not abuse me, I needed no other books or aids than what a man carries with him on horseback, I mean the common principles of Christianity, and those ἀξιώματα which men use in the transactions of the ordinary occurrences of civil society: and upon the strength of them, and some other collateral assistances, I have run through it *utcunque;* and the sum of the following discourses is nothing but the sense of these words of Scripture, that since "we know in part, and prophesy in part, and that now we see through a glass darkly," we would not despise or contemn persons not so knowing as ourselves, but "him that is weak in the faith we should receive, but not to doubtful disputations"; therefore, certainly to charity, and not to vexations, not to those which are the idle effects of impertinent wranglings. And provided they keep close to the foundation, which is faith and obedience, let them build upon this foundation matter more or less precious, yet if the foundation be entire, they shall be saved with or without loss. And since we profess ourselves servants of so meek a Master, and disciples of so charitable an institute, "Let us walk worthy of the vocation wherewith we are called, with all lowliness and meekness, with long-suffering, forbearing one another in love"; for this is the best endeavoring to keep the unity of the Spirit, when it is fast tied in the bond of peace. And although it be a duty of Christianity that "we all speak the same thing, that there be no divisions among us, but that we be perfectly joined together in the same mind and in the same judgment," yet this unity is to be estimated according to the unity of faith, in things necessary, in matters of creed, and articles fundamental: for as for other things, it is more to be wished than to be hoped for. There are some "doubtful disputations," and in such "the scribe, the wise, the disputer of this world," are, most commonly, very far from certainty, and, many times, from truth. There are diversity of persuasions in matters adiaphorous, as meats, and drinks, and holy days, etc., and both parties, the affirmative and the negative, affirm and deny with innocence enough; for the observer, and he that observes not, intend both to God; and God is our common Master, we are all fellow-servants, and not the judge of each other in matters of conscience or doubtful disputation; and every man that "hath faith, must have it to himself before God," but no man must, in such matters, either "judge his brother or set him at naught"; but "let us follow after the things which make for peace, and things wherewith one may edify another." And the way to do that is not by knowledge, but by charity, for "knowledge puffeth up, but charity edifieth." And since there is not in "every man the same knowledge, but the consciences of some are weak"; as "my liberty must not be judged of another man's weak conscience," so must not I please myself so much in my right opinion but I must also take order that his "weak conscience be not offended or despised"; for no man must "seek his own, but every man another's wealth." And although we must contend earnestly for the faith, yet, "above all things, we must put on charity, which is the bond of perfectness." And, therefore, this contention must be with arms fit for the Christian warfare, "the sword of the Spirit, and the shield of faith, and preparation of the Gospel of peace, instead of shoes, and a helmet of salvation." But not with other arms; for a churchman must not be πληκτικὸς, "a striker"; for "the weapons of our warfare are not carnal, but spiritual," and the persons that use them ought to be "gentle, and easy to be entreated"; and we "must give an account of our faith to them that ask us, with meekness and humility, for so is the will of God, that with well-doing ye may put to silence the ignorance of foolish men." These, and thousands more to the same purpose, are the doctrines of Christianity, whose sense and intendment I have prosecuted in the following discourse, being very much displeased that so many opinions and new doctrines are commenced among us; but more troubled that every man that hath an opinion thinks his own and other men's salvation is concerned in its maintenance; but most of all, that men should be persecuted and afflicted for disagreeing in such opinions, which they cannot, with sufficient grounds, obtrude upon others necessarily, because they cannot propound them infallibly, and because they have no warrant from Scripture so to do. For if I shall tie other men to believe my opinion, because I think I have a place of Scripture which seems to warrant it to my understanding, why may not he serve up another dish to me in the same dress, and exact the same task of me to believe the contradictory? And then, since all the heretics in the world have offered to prove their articles by the same means by which true believers propound theirs, it is necessary that some separation either of doctrine or of persons be clearly made, and that all pretences may not be admitted, nor any just allegations be rejected; and yet, that in some other questions, whether they be truly or falsely pretended, if not evidently or demonstratively, there may be considerations had to the persons of men, and to the laws of charity, more than to the triumphing in any opinion or doctrine not simply necessary. Now because some doctrines are clearly not necessary, and some are absolutely necessary, why may not the first separation be made upon this difference, and articles necessary be only urged as necessary, and the rest left to men indifferently, as they were by the Scripture indeterminately? And it were well if men would as much consider themselves as the doctrines, and think that they may as well be deceived by their own weakness as persuaded by the arguments of a doctrine which other men, as wise, call inevident. For it is a hard case that we should think all Papists and Anabaptists and sacramentaries to be fools and wicked persons; certainly among all these sects there are very many wise men and good men, as well as erring. And although some zeals are so hot, and their eyes so inflamed with their ardors, that they do not think their adversaries look like other men; yet certainly we find by the results of their discourses and the transactions of their affairs of civil society, that they are men that speak and make syllogisms, and use reason, and read Scripture; and although they do no more understand all of it than we do, yet they endeavor to understand as much as concerns them, even all that they can, even all that concerns repentance from dead works, and faith in our Lord Jesus Christ. And, therefore, methinks this also should be another consideration distinguishing the persons: for, if the persons be Christians in their lives, and Christians in their profession, if they acknowledge the eternal Son of God for their Master and their Lord, and live in all relations as becomes persons making such professions, why then should I hate such persons whom God loves, and who love God, who are partakers of Christ, and Christ hath a title to them, who dwell in Christ and Christ in them, because their understandings have not been brought up like mine, have not had the same masters, they have not met with the same books, nor the same company, or have not the same interest, or are not so wise, or else are wiser; that is, for some reason or other, which I neither do understand nor ought to blame,—have not the same opinions that I have, and do not determine their school-questions to the sense of my sect or interest? . . .

And, first, I answer that whatsoever is against the foundation of faith, or contrary to good life and the laws of obedience, or destructive to human society and the public and just interests of bodies politic, is out of the limits of my question, and does not pretend to compliance or toleration: so that I allow no indifferency nor any countenance to those religions whose principles destroy government, nor to those religions (if there be any such) that teach ill life; nor do I think that anything will now excuse from belief of a fundamental article except stupidity or sottishness, and natural inability. This alone is sufficient answer to this vanity, but I have much more to say.

Secondly, the intendment of my discourse is that permissions should be in questions speculative, indeterminable, curious, and unnecessary; and that men would not make more necessities than God made, which indeed are not many. The fault I find, and seek to remedy, is that men are so dogmatical and resolute in their opinions, and impatient of others disagreeing, in those things wherein is no sufficient means of union and determination; but that men should let opinions and problems keep their own forms, and not be obtruded as axioms, nor questions in the vast collection of the system of divinity be adopted into the family of faith. And, I think, I have reason to desire this.

Thirdly, it is hard to say that he who would not have men put to death, or punished corporally, for such things for which no human authority is sufficient, either for cognizance or determination, or competent for infliction, that he persuades to an indifferency when he refers to another judicatory which is competent, sufficient, infallible, just, and highly severe. No man or company of men can judge or punish our thoughts or secret purposes, whilst they so remain. And yet it will be unequal to say that he who owns this doctrine, preaches it lawful for men to think or purpose what they will. And so it is in matters of doubtful disputation, such as are the distinguishing articles of most of the sects of Christendom; so it is in matters intellectual which are not cognizable by a secular power: in matters spiritual, which are to be discerned by spiritual authority, which cannot make corporal inflictions; and in questions indeterminate, which are doubtfully propounded, or obscurely, and, therefore, may be *in utramque partem* disputed or believed. For God alone must be judge of these matters, who alone is master of our souls, and hath a dominion over human understanding; and he that says this does not say that indifferency is persuaded, because God alone is judge of erring persons.

Fourthly, no part of this discourse teaches or encourages variety of sects and contradiction in opinions, but supposes them already in being: and, therefore, since there are, and ever were, and ever will be, variety of opinions, because there is variety of human understandings and uncertainty in things, no man should be too forward in determining all questions, nor so forward in prescribing to others, nor invade that liberty which God hath left to us entire, by propounding many things obscurely, and by exempting our souls and understandings from all power externally compulsory. So that the restraint is laid upon men's tyranny, but no license given to men's opinions; they are not considered in any of the conclusions, but in the premises only, as an argument to exhort to charity. So that if I persuade a license of discrediting anything which God hath commanded us to believe, and allow a liberty where God hath not allowed it, let it be shown, and let the objection press as hard as it can: but to say that men are too forward in condemning, where God hath declared no sentence, nor prescribed any rule, is to dissuade from tyranny, not to encourage licentiousness; is to take away a license of judging, not to give a license of dogmatizing what every one please, or as may best serve his turn. And for the other part of the objection:

Fifthly, this discourse is so far from giving leave to men to profess anything, though they believe the contrary, that it takes order that no man shall be put to it: for I earnestly contend that another man's opinion shall be no rule to mine, and that my opinion shall be no snare and prejudice to myself; that men use one another so charitably and so gently that no error or violence tempt men to hypocrisy; this very thing being one of the arguments I use to persuade permissions, lest compulsion introduce hypocrisy, and make sincerity troublesome and unsafe.

Sixthly, if men would not call all opinions by the name of religion, and superstructures by the name of fundamental articles, and all fancies by the glorious appellative of faith, this objection would have no pretence or footing: so that it is the disease of the men, not any cause that is ministered by such precepts of charity, that makes them perpetually clamorous. And it would be hard to say that such physicians are incurious of their patients, and neglectful of their health, who speak against the unreasonableness of such empirics, that would cut off a man's head if they see but a wart upon his cheek or a dimple upon his chin, or any lines in his face to distinguish him from another man: the case is altogether the same, and we may as well decree a wart to be mortal, as a various opinion *in re alioqui non necessaria*[1] to be capital and damnable.

For I consider that there are but few doctrines of Christianity that were ordered to be preached to all the world, to every single person, and made a necessary article of his explicit belief.   Other doctrines, which are all of them not simply necessary, are either such as are not clearly revealed, or such as are. If they be clearly revealed, and that I know so too, or may, but for my own fault,—I am not to be excused: but for this I am to be left to God's judgment, unless my fault be externally such as to be cognizable and punishable in human judicatory. But, then, if it be not so revealed but that wise men and good men differ in their opinions, it is a clear case it is not *inter dogmata necessaria simpliciter;* and then it is certain I may, therefore, safely disbelieve it, because I may be safely ignorant of it.   For if I may, with innocence, be ignorant, then to know it or believe it is not simply obligatory: ignorance is absolutely inconsistent with such an obligation because it is destructive and a plain negative to its performance; and if I do my honest endeavor to understand it, and yet do not attain it, it is certain that it is not obligatory to me so much as by accident; for no obligation can press the person of a man if it be impossible; no man is bound to do more than his best, no man is bound to have an excellent understanding, or to be infallible, or to be wiser than he can; for these are things that are not in his choice, and therefore not a matter of law, nor subject to reward or punishment. . . .

And yet, such is the iniquity of men, that they suck in opinions as wild asses do the wind, without distinguishing the wholesome from the corrupted air, and then live upon it at a venture; and when all their confidence is built upon zeal and mistake, yet, therefore, because they are zealous and mistaken, they are impatient of contradiction. . . .

---

[1]In a matter otherwise not essential.

If I tell him ["an honest citizen whose employment and parts will not enable him to judge the disputes and arguings of great clerks"] that he must live a good life, and believe the creed, and not trouble himself with their disputes, or interest himself in sects and factions, I speak reason; because no law of God ties him to believe more than what is of essential necessity, and whatsoever he shall come to know to be revealed by God. Now if he believes his creed, he believes all that is necessary to all, or of itself; and if he does his moral endeavor beside, he can do no more toward finding out all the rest, and then he is secured. But then, if this will secure him, why do men press further and pretend every opinion as necessary, and that in so high a degree that if they all said true, or any two indeed of them, in five hundred sects which are in the world (and for aught I know there may be five thousand), it is five hundred to one but that every man is damned; for every sect damns all but itself, and that is damned of four hundred and ninety-nine, and it is excellent fortune then if that escape. And there is the same reason in every one of them, that is, it is extreme unreasonableness, in all of them, to pronounce damnation against such persons, against whom clearly and dogmatically Holy Scripture hath not. *In odiosis, quod minimum est sequimur; in favoribus, quod est maximum*,[1] saith the law; and therefore we should say anything, or make any excuse that is in any degree reasonable, rather than condemn all the world to hell, especially if we consider these two things,—that we ourselves are apt to be deceived, as any are; and that they who are deceived, when they used their moral industry that they might not be deceived, if they perish for this, they perish for what they could not help.

. . . .

SECTION IV

. . . The sum is this: since Holy Scripture is the repository of divine truths, and the great rule of faith, to which all sects of Christians do appeal for probation of their several opinions; and since all agree in the articles of the creed as things

---

[1] We should make as little as possible of unfavorable things, as much as possible of favorable.

clearly and plainly set down, and as containing all that which is
of simple and prime necessity; and since, on the other side, there
are in Scripture many other mysteries and matters of question
upon which there is a veil; since there are so many copies with
infinite varieties of reading; since a various interpunction, a
parenthesis, a letter, an accent, may much alter the sense;
since some places have divers literal senses, many have spiritual,
mystical, and allegorical meanings; since there are so many
tropes, metonymies, ironies, hyperboles, proprieties and impro-
prieties of language, whose understanding depends upon such
circumstances that it is almost impossible to know its proper
interpretation, now that the knowledge of such circumstances
and particular stories is irrevocably lost; since there are some
mysteries which, at the best advantage of expression, are not
easy to be apprehended, and whose explication, by reason of our
imperfections, must needs be dark, sometimes weak, sometimes
unintelligible; and, lastly, since those ordinary means of expounding Scripture, as searching the originals, conference of
places, parity of reason, and analogy of faith, are all dubious,
uncertain, and very fallible,—he that is the wisest, and by consequence the likeliest to expound truest in all probability of reason, will be very far from confidence; because every one of these,
and many more, are like so many degrees of improbability and
uncertainty, all depressing our certainty of finding out truth
in such mysteries, and amidst so many difficulties. And therefore a wise man that considers this would not willingly be prescribed to by others; and therefore, if he be also a just man,
he will not impose upon others; for it is best every man should
be left in that liberty from which no man can justly take him,
unless he could secure him from error: so that here also there
is a necessity to conserve the liberty of prophesying and interpreting Scripture; a necessity derived from the consideration
of the difficulty of Scripture in questions controverted, and the
uncertainty of any internal medium of interpretation.

SECTION XIII

. . . .

EIGHTHLY: force in matters of opinion can do no good, but
is very apt to do hurt; for no man can change his opinion when

he will, or be satisfied in his reason that his opinion is false because discountenanced. If a man could change his opinion when he lists he might cure many inconveniences of his life: all his fears and his sorrows would soon disband if he would but alter his opinion whereby he is persuaded that such an accident that afflicts him is an evil, and such an object formidable: let him but believe himself impregnable, or that he receives a benefit when he is plundered, disgraced, imprisoned, condemned, and afflicted, neither his steps need to be disturbed, nor his quietness discomposed. But if a man cannot change his opinion when he lists, nor ever does heartily or resolutely but when he cannot do otherwise, then to use force may make him a hypocrite, but never to be a right believer; and so, instead of erecting a trophy to God and true religion, we build a monument for the devil. . . .

THOMAS HOBBES (1588–1679)

The main events of Hobbes's long life were intellectual, though he was a somewhat migratory person. After graduation from Oxford he spent many years as tutor to various noble pupils, and his duties included continental tours which made him acquainted with thinkers abroad, and helped to emancipate him from the scholastic tradition. To this result acquaintance with Bacon doubtless contributed also, though Hobbes's own philosophic instrument was quite the opposite of Baconian induction. He was also a friend of William Harvey. Somewhat exaggerating possible dangers to himself, Hobbes became one of the English refugees in Paris, but returned before the Restoration. The main lines of his political philosophy had been laid down before the Civil War. Although born earlier than many of the men represented in this book, Hobbes is the most forward-looking mind among them; the effect of his thought, in psychology, politics, religion, indeed the whole range of philosophy, must be studied in the period beyond our limits. Even his plain, strong style—"the life of man solitary, poor, nasty, brutish, and short"—belongs to the next age.

LEVIATHAN (1651)

PART I: OF MAN

CHAPTER XIII

OF THE NATURAL CONDITION OF MANKIND AS CONCERNING THEIR FELICITY AND MISERY

NATURE hath made men so equal in the faculties of body and mind as that, though there be found one man sometimes manifestly stronger in body or of quicker mind than another, yet when all is reckoned together the difference between man and man is not so considerable as that one man can thereupon claim to himself any benefit to which another may not pretend as well as he. For, as to the strength of body, the weakest has

strength enough to kill the strongest, either by secret machina-
tion or by confederacy with others that are in the same danger
with himself.

And, as to the faculties of the mind, setting aside the arts
grounded upon words and especially that skill of proceeding
upon general and infallible rules called science, which very
few have and but in few things, as being not a native faculty
born with us, nor attained, as prudence, while we look after
somewhat else, I find yet a greater equality amongst men than
that of strength. For prudence is but experience, which equal
time equally bestows on all men in those things they equally
apply themselves unto. That which may perhaps make such
equality incredible is but a vain conceit of one's own wisdom,
which almost all men think they have in a greater degree than
the vulgar, that is, than all men but themselves, and a few others
whom by fame or for concurring with themselves they approve.
For such is the nature of men that, howsoever they may acknowledge many others to be more witty or more eloquent or more
learned, yet they will hardly believe there be many so wise as
themselves, for they see their own wit at hand and other men's
at a distance. But this proveth rather that men are in that
point equal than unequal. For there is not ordinarily a greater
sign of the equal distribution of anything than that every man
is contented with his share.

From this equality of ability ariseth equality of hope in the
attaining of our ends. And therefore, if any two men desire
the same thing which nevertheless they cannot both enjoy,
they become enemies; and, in the way to their end, which is
principally their own conservation and sometimes their delecta-
tion only, endeavor to destroy or subdue one another. And
from hence it comes to pass that, where an invader hath no
more to fear than another man's single power, if one plant, sow,
build, or possess, a convenient seat, other may probably be expected to come prepared with forces united to dispossess and
deprive him not only of the fruit of his labor but also of his
life or liberty. And the invader again is in the like danger of
another.

And from this diffidence of one another there is no way for
any man to secure himself so reasonable as anticipation, that is,
by force or wiles to master the persons of all men he can so long

till he see no other power great enough to endanger him; and this is no more than his own conservation requireth and is generally allowed. Also, because there be some that, taking pleasure in contemplating their own power in the acts of conquest, which they pursue farther than their security requires, if others, that otherwise would be glad to be at ease within modest bounds, should not by invasion increase their power, they would not be able long time, by standing only on their defence, to subsist. And by consequence, such augmentation of dominion over men being necessary to a man's conservation, it ought to be allowed him.

Again, men have no pleasure, but on the contrary a great deal of grief, in keeping company where there is no power able to overawe them all. For every man looketh that his companion should value him at the same rate he sets upon himself, and, upon all signs of contempt or undervaluing, naturally endeavors as far as he dares (which amongst them that have no common power to keep them in quiet, is far enough to make them destroy each other) to extort a greater value from his contemners by damage, and from others by the example.

So that in the nature of man we find three principal causes of quarrel. First, competition; secondly, diffidence; thirdly, glory.

The first maketh man invade for gain; the second, for safety; and the third, for reputation. The first use violence, to make themselves masters of other men's persons, wives, children, and cattle; the second, to defend them; the third, for trifles, as a word, a smile, a different opinion, and any other sign of undervalue, either direct in their persons or by reflection in their kindred, their friends, their nation, their profession, or their name.

Hereby it is manifest that, during the time men live without a common power to keep them all in awe, they are in that condition which is called war, and such a war as is of every man against every man. For "war" consisteth not in battle only or the act of fighting, but in a tract of time wherein the will to contend by battle is sufficiently known, and therefore the notion of "time" is to be considered in the nature of war, as it is in the nature of weather. For as the nature of foul weather lieth not in a shower or two of rain but in an inclination thereto of many days together, so the nature of war consisteth not in actual fighting but in the known disposition thereto, during all the time there is no assurance to the contrary. All other time is "peace."

Whatsoever therefore is consequent to a time of war, where every man is enemy to every man, the same is consequent to the time wherein men live without other security than what their own strength and their own invention shall furnish them withal. In such condition there is no place for industry, because the fruit thereof is uncertain, and consequently no culture of the earth, no navigations nor use of the commodities that may be imported by sea, no commodious building, no instruments of moving and removing such things as require much force, no knowledge of the face of the earth; no account of time, no arts, no letters, no society, and, which is worst of all, continual fear and danger of violent death, and the life of man solitary, poor, nasty, brutish, and short.

It may seem strange to some man that has not well weighed these things that Nature should thus dissociate and render men apt to invade and destroy one another; and he may therefore, not trusting to this inference made from the passions, desire perhaps to have the same confirmed by experience. Let him therefore consider with himself, when taking a journey, he arms himself and seeks to go well accompanied; when going to sleep, he locks his doors; when even in his house, he locks his chests; and this when he knows there be laws and public officers armed to revenge all injuries shall be done him; what opinion he has of his fellow-subjects, when he rides armed; of his fellow-citizens, when he locks his doors; and of his children and servants, when he locks his chests. Does he not there as much accuse mankind by his actions as I do by my words? But neither of us accuse man's nature in it. The desires and other passions of man are in themselves no sin. No more are the actions that proceed from those passions, till they know a law that forbids them; which, till laws be made, they cannot know, nor can any law be made till they have agreed upon the persons that shall make it.

It may peradventure be thought there was never such a time nor condition of war as this; and I believe it was never generally so over all the world, but there are many places where they live so now. For the savage people in many places of America, except the government of small families the concord whereof dependeth on natural lust, have no government at all, and live at this day in that brutish manner as I said before. Howsoever, it may be perceived what manner of life there would be where there were no common power to fear, by the manner of life which men that have formerly lived under a peaceful government use to degenerate into in a civil war.

But, though there had never been any time wherein particular men were in a condition of war one against another, yet in all times kings and persons of sovereign authority, because of their independency, are in continual jealousies and in the state and posture of gladiators, having their weapons pointing, and their eyes fixed on one another, that is, their forts, garrisons, and guns, upon the frontiers of their kingdoms, and continual spies upon their neighbors: which is a posture of war. But because they uphold thereby the industry of their subjects, there does not follow from it that misery which accompanies the liberty of particular men.

To this war of every man against every man this also is consequent, that nothing can be unjust. The notions of right and wrong, justice and injustice, have there no place. Where there is no common power, there is no law; where no law, no injustice. Force and fraud are in war the two cardinal virtues. Justice and injustice are none of the faculties neither of the body nor mind. If they were, they might be in a man that were alone in the world, as well as his senses and passions. They are qualities that relate to men in society, not in solitude. It is consequent also to the same condition that there be no propriety, no dominion, no "mine" and "thine" distinct, but only that to be every man's that he can get, and for so long as he can keep it. And thus much for the ill condition which man by mere Nature is actually placed in, though with a possibility to come out of it, consisting partly in the passions, partly in his reason.

The passions that incline men to peace are fear of death, desire of such things as are necessary to commodious living, and a hope by their industry to obtain them. And reason suggesteth convenient articles of peace, upon which men may be drawn to agreement. These articles are they which otherwise are called the Laws of Nature, whereof I shall speak more particularly in the two following chapters.

CHAPTER XIV

OF THE FIRST AND SECOND NATURAL LAWS, AND OF CONTRACTS

THE "right of Nature," which writers commonly call *jus naturale*, is the liberty each man hath to use his own power as he will himself for the preservation of his own nature, that is to say, of his own life; and consequently of doing anything which in his own judgment and reason he shall conceive to be the aptest means thereunto.

By "liberty" is understood, according to the proper signification of the word, the absence of external impediments; which impediments may oft take away part of a man's power to do what he would, but cannot hinder him from using the power left him according as his judgment and reason shall dictate to him.

A "law of Nature," *lex naturalis*, is a precept or general rule found out by reason by which a man is forbidden to do that which is destructive of his life or taketh away the means of preserving the same, and to omit that by which he thinketh it may be best preserved. For, though they that speak of this subject use to confound *jus* and *lex*, "right" and "law," yet they ought to be distinguished; because "right" consisteth in liberty to do or to forbear, whereas "law" determineth and bindeth to one of them; so that law and right differ as much as obligation and liberty; which in one and the same matter are inconsistent.

And because the condition of man, as hath been declared in the precedent chapter, is a condition of war of every one against every one, in which case every one is governed by his own reason, and there is nothing he can make use of that may not be a help unto him in preserving his life against his enemies, it followeth that in such a condition every man has a right to everything, even to one another's body. And therefore, as long as this natural right of every man to everything endureth, there can be no security to any man, how strong or wise soever he be, of living out the time which Nature ordinarily alloweth men to live. And consequently it is a precept or general rule of reason "that every man ought to endeavor peace as far as he has hope of obtaining it, and, when he cannot obtain it, that he may seek and use all helps and advantages of war." The first branch of which rule containeth the first and fundamental law of Nature, which is, "to seek peace, and follow it." The second, the sum of the right of Nature, which is, "by all means we can, to defend ourselves."

From this fundamental law of Nature, by which men are commanded to endeavor peace, is derived this second law, "that a man may be willing, when others are so too, as far-forth as for peace and defence of himself he shall think it necessary, to lay down this right to all things, and be contented with so much liberty against other men as he would allow other men against himself." For as long as every man holdeth this right of doing anything he liketh, so long are all men in the condition of war. But if other men will not lay down their right as well as he, then there is no reason for any one to divest himself of his; for that were to expose himself to prey, which no man is bound to, rather than to dispose himself to peace. This is that law of the Gospel: "whatsoever you require that others should do to you, that do ye to them." And that law of all men, *quod tibi fieri non vis, alteri ne feceris.*[1]

To "lay down" a man's "right" to anything is to "divest" himself of the "liberty" of hindering another of the benefit of his own right to the same. For he that renounceth or passeth away his right giveth not to any other man a right which he had not before, because there is nothing to which every man had not right by Nature: but only standeth out of his way that he may enjoy his own original right without hindrance from him, not without hindrance from another. So that the effect which redoundeth to one man, by another man's defect of right, is but so much diminution of impediments to the use of his own right original.

Right is laid aside either by simply renouncing it, or by transferring it to another. By "simply renouncing" when he cares not to whom the benefit thereof redoundeth. By "transferring," when he intendeth the benefit thereof to some certain person or persons. And when a man hath in either manner abandoned or granted away his right, then is he said to be "obliged" or "bound"

---

[1] What you do not wish to be done to you, do not do to another.

not to hinder those to whom such right is granted or abandoned from the benefit of it; and that he "ought," and it is his "duty," not to make void that voluntary act of his own; and that such hindrance is "injustice" and "injury" as being *sine jure*, the right being before renounced or transferred. So that "injury" or "injustice," in the controversies of the world, is somewhat like to that which in the disputations of scholars is called "absurdity." For, as it is there called an absurdity to contradict what one maintained in the beginning, so in the world it is called injustice and injury voluntarily to undo that which from the beginning he had voluntarily done. The way by which a man either simply renounceth or transferreth his right is a declaration or signification, by some voluntary and sufficient sign or signs, that he doth so renounce or transfer, or hath so renounced or transferred, the same, to him that accepteth it. And these signs are either words only or actions only, or, as it happeneth most often, both words and actions. And the same are the "bonds" by which men are bound and obliged: bonds that have their strength not from their own nature, for nothing is more easily broken than a man's word, but from fear of some evil consequence upon the rupture.

Whensoever a man transferreth his right or renounceth it, it is either in consideration of some right reciprocally transferred to himself, or for some other good he hopeth for thereby. For it is a voluntary act; and of the voluntary acts of every man the object is some "good to himself." And therefore there be some rights which no man can be understood by any words or other signs to have abandoned or transferred. As first a man cannot lay down the right of resisting them that assault him by force to take away his life, because he cannot be understood to aim thereby at any good to himself. The same may be said of wounds, and chains, and imprisonment, both because there is no benefit consequent to such patience, as there is to the patience of suffering another to be wounded or imprisoned, as also because a man cannot tell when he seeth men proceed against him by violence whether they intend his death or not. And lastly the motive and end for which this renouncing and transferring of right is introduced is nothing else but the security of a man's person in his life and in the means of so preserving life as not to be weary of it. And therefore, if a man by words or other signs seem to despoil himself of the end for which those signs were intended, he is not to be understood as if he meant it or that it was his will, but that he was ignorant of how such words and actions were to be interpreted.

The mutual transferring of right is that which men call "contract."

There is difference between transferring of right to the thing and transferring or tradition, that is the delivery of the thing itself. For the thing may be delivered together with the translation of the right, as in buying and selling with ready money, or exchange of goods or lands; and it may be delivered some time after.

Again, one of the contractors may deliver the thing contracted for on his part, and leave the other to perform his part at some determinate time after, and in the meantime be trusted; and then the contract on his part is called "pact," or "covenant"; or both parts may contract now to perform hereafter; in which cases he that is to perform in time to come, being trusted, his performance is called "keeping of promise," or faith, and the failing of performance, if it be voluntary, "violation of faith."

When the transferring of right is not mutual, but one of the parties transferreth in hope to gain thereby friendship or service from another or from his friends, or in hope to gain the reputation of charity or magnanimity, or to deliver his mind from the pain of compassion, or in hope of reward in heaven, this is not contract but "gift," "free gift," "grace," which words signify one and the same thing.

Signs of contract are either "express" or "by inference." Express are words spoken with understanding of what they signify, and such words are either of the time "present" or "past," as "I give," "I grant," "I have given," "I have granted," "I will that this be yours"; or of the future, as "I will give," "I will grant," which words of the future are called "promise."

Signs by inference are sometimes the consequence of words, sometimes the consequence of silence, sometimes the consequence of actions, sometimes the consequence of forbearing an action; and generally a sign by inference of any contract is whatsoever sufficiently argues the will of the contractor.

Words alone, if they be of the time to come and contain a bare promise, are an insufficient sign of a free gift, and therefore not obligatory. For if they be of the time to come, as "to-morrow I will give," they are a sign I have not given yet, and consequently that my right is not transferred, but remaineth till I transfer it by some other act. But if the words be of the time present or past, as "I have given," or "do give to be de-livered to-morrow," then is my to-morrow's right given away to-day, and that by the virtue of the words, though there were no other argument of my will. And there is a great difference in the signification of these words *volo hoc tuum esse cras* and *cras dabo*, that is, between "I will that this be thine to-morrow" and "I will give it thee to-morrow," for the word "I will," in the former manner of speech, signifies an act of the will present, but in the latter it signifies a promise of an act of the will to come; and therefore the former words, being of the present, transfer a future right; the latter, that be of the future, transfer nothing. But if there be other signs of the will to transfer a right besides words, then, though the gift be free, yet may the right be understood to pass by words of the future; as, if a man propound a prize to him that comes first to the end of a race, the gift is free; and, though the words be of the future, yet the right passeth; for if he would not have his words so be understood he should not have let them run.

In contracts the right passeth not only where the words are of the time present or past, but also where they are of the future; because all contract is mutual translation or change of right, and therefore he that promiseth only because he hath already received the benefit for which he promiseth is to be understood as if he intended the right should pass, for, unless he had been content to have his words so understood, the other would not have performed his part first. And for that cause, in buying and selling and other acts of contract, a promise is equivalent to a covenant, and therefore obligatory.

He that performeth first in the case of a contract is said to "merit" that which he is to receive by the performance of the other, and he hath it as "due." Also when a prize is pro-pounded to many which is to be given to him only that winneth, or money is thrown amongst many to be enjoyed by them that catch it, though this be a free gift, yet so to win or so to catch is to "merit," and to have it as "due." For the right is trans-ferred in the propounding of the prize and in throwing down the money, though it be not determined to whom but by the event of the contention. But there is between these two sorts of merit this difference, that in contract I merit by virtue of my own power and the contractor's need, but in this case of free gift I am enabled to merit only by the benignity of the giver: in contract I merit at the contractor's hand that he should part with his right; in this case of gift I merit not that the giver should part with his right, but that, when he has parted with it, it should be mine rather than another's. And this I think to be the meaning of that distinction of the schools between *meritum congrui* and *meritum condigni*. For God Almighty, having promised paradise to those men hoodwinked with carnal desires that can walk through this world according to the precepts and limits prescribed by him, they say he that shall so walk shall merit paradise *ex congruo*. But because no man can demand a right to it by his own righteousness or any other power in himself, but by the free grace of God only, they say, no man can merit paradise *ex condigno*. This, I say, I think is the meaning of that distinction; but, because disputers do not agree upon the signification of their own terms of art longer than it serves their turn, I will not affirm anything of their meaning: only this I say—when a gift is given indefinitely as a prize to be contended for, he that winneth meriteth, and may claim the prize as due.

If a covenant be made wherein neither of the parties perform presently but trust one another, in the condition of mere nature, which is a condition of war of every man against every man, upon any reasonable suspicion, it is void; but, if there be a common power set over them both with right and force sufficient to compel performance, it is not void. For he that performeth first has no assurance the other will perform after, because the bonds of words are too weak to bridle men's ambition, avarice, anger, and other passions, without the fear of some coercive power, which in the condition of mere nature, where all men are equal and judges of the justness of their own fears, cannot possibly be supposed. And therefore he which performeth first does but betray himself to his enemy, contrary to the right he can never abandon, of defending his life and means of living.

But in a civil estate, where there is a power set up to constrain those that would otherwise violate their faith, that fear is no more reasonable, and for that cause he which by the covenant is to perform first is obliged so to do.

The cause of fear, which maketh such a covenant invalid, must be always something arising from the covenant made, as some new fact or other sign of the will not to perform; else it cannot make the covenant void. For that which could not hinder a man from promising ought not to be admitted as a hindrance of performing.

He that transferreth any right transferreth the means of enjoying it as far as lieth in his power. As he that selleth land is understood to transfer the herbage and whatsoever grows upon it; nor can he that sells a mill turn away the stream that drives it. And they that give to a man the right of government in sovereignty are understood to give him the right of levying money to maintain soldiers, and of appointing magistrates for the administration of justice.

To make covenants with brute beasts is impossible, because not understanding our speech, they understand not nor accept of any translation of right; nor can translate any right to another; and without mutual acceptation, there is no covenant.

To make covenant with God is impossible, but by mediation of such as God speaketh to, either by revelation supernatural or by his lieutenants that govern under him and in his name; for otherwise we know not whether our covenants be accepted or not. And therefore they that vow anything contrary to any law of Nature vow in vain, as being a thing unjust to pay such vow. And, if it be a thing commanded by the law of Nature, it is not the vow but the law that binds them.

The matter or subject of a covenant is always something that falleth under deliberation, for to covenant is an act of the will, that is to say an act, and the last act of deliberation, and is therefore always understood to be something to come, and which is judged possible for him that covenanteth to perform.

And therefore to promise that which is known to be impossible is no covenant. But, if that prove impossible afterwards which before was thought possible, the covenant is valid and bindeth, though not to the thing itself, yet to the value, or, if that also be impossible, to the unfeigned endeavor of performing as much as is possible, for to more no man can be obliged.

Men are freed of their covenants two ways: by performing

or by being forgiven. For performance is the natural end of obligation, and forgiveness the restitution of liberty, as being a retransferring of that right in which the obligation consisteth.

Covenants entered into by fear, in the condition of mere nature, are obligatory. For example, if I covenant to pay a ransom or service for my life to an enemy, I am bound by it, for it is a contract wherein one receiveth the benefit of life; the other is to receive money or service for it; and consequently where no other law, as in the condition of mere nature, forbiddeth the performance, the covenant is valid. Therefore prisoners of war, if trusted with the payment of their ransom, are obliged to pay it; and, if a weaker prince make a disadvantageous peace with a stronger, for fear, he is bound to keep it, unless, as hath been said before, there ariseth some new and just cause of fear to renew the war. And even in commonwealths, if I be forced to redeem myself from a thief by promising him money, I am bound to pay it, till the civil law discharge me. For whatsoever I may lawfully do without obligation, the same I may lawfully covenant to do through fear, and what I lawfully covenant I cannot lawfully break.

A former covenant makes void a later. For a man that hath passed away his right to one man to-day hath it not to pass to-morrow to another, and therefore the later promise passeth no right, but is null.

A covenant not to defend myself from force by force is always void. For, as I have showed before, no man can transfer or lay down his right to save himself from death, wounds, and imprisonment, the avoiding whereof is the only end of laying down any right; and therefore the promise of not resisting force in no covenant transferreth any right, nor is obliging. For, though a man may covenant thus, "unless I do so or so, kill me," he cannot covenant thus, "unless I do so or so, I will not resist you when you come to kill me." For man by nature chooseth the lesser evil, which is danger of death in resisting, rather than the greater, which is certain and present death in not resisting. And this is granted to be true by all men, in that they lead criminals to execution and prison with armed men, notwithstanding that such criminals have consented to the law by which they are condemned.

A covenant to accuse oneself, without assurance of pardon, is likewise invalid. For in the condition of nature, where every man is judge, there is no place for accusation; and in the civil state the accusation is followed with punishment, which, being force, a man is not obliged not to resist. The same is also true of the accusation of those by whose condemnation a man falls into misery, as of a father, wife, or benefactor. For the testimony of such an accuser, if it be not willingly given, is presumed to be corrupted by nature, and therefore not to be received; and where a man's testimony is not to be credited he is not bound to give it. Also accusations upon torture are not to be reputed as testimonies. For torture is to be used but as means of conjecture and light, in the further examination and search of truth; and what is in that case confessed tendeth to the ease of him that is tortured, not to the informing of the torturers, and therefore ought not to have the credit of a sufficient testimony, for, whether he delivers himself by true or false accusation, he does it by the right of preserving his own life.

The force of words being, as I have formerly noted, too weak to hold men to the performance of their covenants, there are in man's nature but two imaginable helps to strengthen it. And those are either a fear of the consequence of breaking their word, or a glory or pride in appearing not to need to break it. This latter is a generosity too rarely found to be presumed on, especially in the pursuers of wealth, command, or sensual pleasure, which are the greatest part of mankind. The passion to be reckoned upon is fear, whereof there be two very general objects: one, the power of spirits invisible, the other the power of those men they shall therein offend. Of these two, though the former be the greater power, yet the fear of the latter is commonly the greater fear. The fear of the former is in every man his own religion, which hath place in the nature of man before civil society. The latter hath not so, at least not place enough to keep men to their promises; because in the condition of mere nature the inequality of power is not discerned but by the event of battle. So that before the time of civil society, or in the interruption thereof by war, there is nothing can strengthen a covenant of peace agreed on against the temptations of avarice, ambition, lust, or other strong desire, but the fear of that invisible power which they every one worship as God and fear as a revenger of their perfidy. All therefore that can be done between two men not subject to civil power is to put one another to swear by the God he feareth, which "swearing," or "oath," is "a form of speech, added to a promise; by which he that promiseth signifieth that, unless he perform, he renounceth the mercy of his God or calleth to him for vengeance on himself." Such was the heathen form, "Let Jupiter kill me else, as I kill this beast." So is our form, "I shall do thus, and thus, so help me God." And this, with the rites and ceremonies which every one useth in his own religion, that the fear of breaking faith might be the greater.

By this it appears that an oath taken according to any other form or rite than his that sweareth is in vain, and no oath; and that there is no swearing by anything which the swearer thinks not God. For though men have sometimes used to swear by their kings, for fear or flattery, yet they would have it thereby understood they attributed to them divine honor. And that swearing unnecessarily by God is but profaning of his name; and swearing by other things, as men do in common discourse, is not swearing but an impious custom, gotten by too much vehemence of talking.

It appears also that the oath adds nothing to the obligation. For a covenant, if lawful, binds in the sight of God without the oath as much as with it: if unlawful, bindeth not at all, though it be confirmed with an oath.

PART II: OF COMMONWEALTH

CHAPTER XVII

OF THE CAUSES, GENERATION, AND DEFINITION OF A COMMONWEALTH

THE final cause, end, or design, of men, who naturally love liberty and dominion over others, in the introduction of that restraint upon themselves in which we see them live in commonwealths, is the foresight of their own preservation and of a more contented life thereby; that is to say, of getting themselves out from that miserable condition of war which is necessarily consequent, as hath been shown to the natural passions of men, when there is no visible power to keep them in awe, and tie them by fear of punishment to the performance of their covenants and observation of those laws of Nature set down in the fourteenth and fifteenth chapters.

For the laws of Nature, as "justice," "equity," "modesty," "mercy" and, in sum, "doing to others as we would be done to," of themselves, without the terror of some power to cause them to be observed, are contrary to our natural passions, that carry us to partiality, pride, revenge, and the like. And covenants, without the sword, are but words, and of no strength to secure a man at all. Therefore, notwithstanding the laws of Nature, which every one hath then kept when he has the will to keep them, when he can do it safely, if there be no power erected or not great enough for our security, every man will, and may lawfully, rely on his own strength and art for caution against all other men. And in all places where men have lived by small families, to rob and spoil one another has been a trade, and so far from being reputed against the law of Nature, that the greater spoils they gained, the greater was their honor; and men observed no other laws therein but the laws of honor, that is, to abstain from cruelty, leaving to men their lives and instruments of husbandry. And as small families did then, so now do cities and kingdoms, which are but greater families, for their own security enlarge their dominions, upon all pretences of danger and fear of invasion or assistance that may be given to invaders, endeavor as much as they can to subdue or weaken their neighbors by open force and secret arts, for want of other caution, justly; and are remembered for it in after ages with honor.

Nor is it the joining together of a small number of men that gives them this security, because, in small numbers, small additions on the one side or the other make the advantage of strength so great as is sufficient to carry the victory, and therefore gives encouragement to an invasion. The multitude sufficient to confide in for our security is not determined by any certain number, but by comparison with the enemy we fear; and is then sufficient when the odds of the enemy is not of so visible and conspicuous moment to determine the event of war as to move him to attempt.

And be there never so great a multitude, yet, if their actions be directed according to their particular judgments and particular appetites, they can expect thereby no defence nor protection, neither against a common enemy nor against the injuries of one another. For, being distracted in opinions concerning the best use and application of their strength, they do not help, but hinder, one another, and reduce their strength by mutual opposition to nothing; whereby they are easily not only subdued by a very few that agree together, but also, when there is no common enemy, they make war upon each other for their particular interests. For, if we could suppose a great multitude of men to consent in the observation of justice and other laws of Nature, without a common power to keep them all in awe, we might as well suppose all mankind to do the same; and then there neither would be nor need to be any civil government or commonwealth at all, because there would be peace without subjection.

Nor is it enough for the security which men desire should last all the time of their life that they be governed and directed by one judgment for a limited time, as in one battle or one war. For, though they obtain a victory by their unanimous endeavor against a foreign enemy, yet afterwards, when either they have no common enemy or he that by one part is held for an enemy is by another part held for a friend, they must needs by the difference of their interests dissolve and fall again into a war amongst themselves.

It is true that certain living creatures, as bees and ants, live sociably one with another, which are therefore by Aristotle numbered amongst political creatures, and yet have no other direction than their particular judgments and appetites; nor speech, whereby one of them can signify to another what he thinks expedient for the common benefit; and therefore some man may perhaps desire to know why mankind cannot do the same. To which I answer:

First, that men are continually in competition for honor and dignity, which these creatures are not; and consequently amongst men there ariseth on that ground envy and hatred, and finally war; but amongst these not so.

Secondly, that amongst these creatures the common good differeth not from the private; and, being by nature inclined to their private, they procure thereby the common benefit. But man, whose joy consisteth in comparing himself with other men, can relish nothing but what is eminent.

Thirdly, that these creatures, having not, as man, the use of reason, do not see nor think they see any fault in the administration of their common business, whereas amongst men there are very many that think themselves wiser and abler to govern the public better than the rest; and these strive to reform and innovate one this way, another that way, and thereby bring it into distraction and civil war.

Fourthly, that these creatures, though they have some use of voice in making known to one another their desires and other affections, yet they want that art of words by which some men can represent to others that which is good in the likeness of evil, and evil in the likeness of good, and augment or diminish the apparent greatness of good and evil; discontenting men, and troubling their peace at their pleasure.

Fifthly, irrational creatures cannot distinguish between "injury" and "damage"; and therefore, as long as they be at ease, they are not offended with their fellows; whereas man is then most troublesome when he is most at ease; for then it is that he loves to show his wisdom and control the actions of them that govern the commonwealth.

Lastly, the agreement of these creatures is natural; that of men is by covenant only, which is artificial: and therefore it is no wonder if there be somewhat else required besides covenant to make their agreement constant and lasting; which is a common power to keep them in awe and to direct their actions to the common benefit.

The only way to erect such a common power as may be able to defend them from the invasion of foreigners and the injuries of one another, and thereby to secure them in such sort as that by their own industry and by the fruits of the earth they may nourish themselves and live contentedly, is to confer all their power and strength upon one man, or upon one assembly of men, that may reduce all their wills by plurality of voices unto one will; which is as much as to say, to appoint one man or assembly of men to bear their person; and every one to own and acknowledge himself to be author of whatsoever he that so beareth their person shall act, or cause to be acted, in those things which concern the common peace and safety; and therein to submit their will, every one to his will, and their judgments to his judgment. This is more than consent or concord: it is a real unity of them all, in one and the same person, made by covenant of every man with every man, in such manner as if every man should say to every man, "I authorize and give up my right of governing myself to this man, or to this assembly of men, on this condition, that thou give up thy right to him and authorize all his actions in like manner." This done, the multitude so united in one person is called a "commonwealth," in Latin *civitas*. This is the generation of that great "leviathan," or, rather, to speak more reverently, of that "mortal god," to which we owe, under the "immortal God," our peace and defence. For by this authority, given him by every particular man in the commonwealth, he hath the use of so much power and strength conferred on him that by terror thereof he is enabled to form the wills of them all, to peace at home and mutual aid against their enemies abroad. And in him consisteth the essence of the commonwealth; which, to define it, is "one person, of whose acts a great multitude by mutual covenants one with another have made themselves every one the author, to the end he may use the strength and means of them all as he shall think expedient, for their peace and common defence."

And he that carrieth this person is called "sovereign," and said to have "sovereign power"; and every one besides his "subject."

The attaining to this sovereign power is by two ways. One by natural force, as when a man maketh his children to submit themselves and their children to his government, as being able to destroy them if they refuse; or by war subdueth his enemies to his will, giving them their lives on that condition. The other is when men agree amongst themselves to submit to some man, or assembly of men, voluntarily, on confidence to be protected by him against all others. This latter may be called a political commonwealth, or commonwealth by "institution"; and the former, a commonwealth by "acquisition." And first I shall speak of a commonwealth by institution.

CHAPTER XVIII

OF THE RIGHTS OF SOVEREIGNS BY INSTITUTION

A "COMMONWEALTH" is said to be "instituted" when a "multitude" of men do agree and "covenant, every one with every one" that to whatsoever "man," or "assembly of men," shall be given by the major part the "right " to "present" the person of them all, that is to say, to be their "representative"; every one, as well he that "voted for it" as he that "voted against it," shall "authorize" all the actions and judgments of that man, or assembly of men, in the same manner as if they were his own, to the end to live peaceably amongst themselves and be protected against other men.

From this institution of a commonwealth are derived all the "rights" and "faculties" of him, or them, on whom sovereign power is conferred by the consent of the people assembled.

First, because they covenant, it is to be understood they are not obliged by former covenant to anything repugnant hereunto. And consequently they that have already instituted a commonwealth, being thereby bound by covenant to own the actions and judgments of one, cannot lawfully make a new covenant amongst themselves to be obedient to any other in any case whatsoever without his permission. And, therefore, they that are subjects to a monarch cannot without his leave cast off monarchy and return to the confusion of a disunited multitude, nor transfer their person from him that beareth it to another man, or other assembly of men; for they are bound, every man to every man, to own and be reputed author of all that he that already is their sovereign shall do and judge fit to be done; so that, any one man dissenting, all the rest should break their covenant made to that man, which is injustice, and they have also every man given the sovereignty to him that beareth their person, and, therefore, if they depose him, they take from him that which is his own, and so again it is injustice. Besides, if he that attempteth to depose his sovereign be killed or punished by him for such attempt, he is author of his own punishment, as being by the institution author of all his sovereign shall do; and, because it is injustice for a man to do anything for which he may be punished by his own authority, he is also upon that title unjust. And whereas some men have pretended for their disobedience to their sovereign a new covenant, made not with men but with God, this also is unjust; for there is no covenant with God but by mediation of somebody that representeth God's person; which none doth but God's lieutenant, who hath the sovereignty under God. But this pretence of covenant with God is so evident a lie, even in the pretenders' own consciences, that it is not only an act of an unjust, but also of a vile and unmanly, disposition.

Secondly, because the right of bearing the person of them all is given to him they make sovereign, by covenant only of one to another and not of him to any of them, there can happen no breach of covenant on the part of the sovereign; and consequently none of his subjects, by any pretence of forfeiture, can be freed from his subjection. That he which is made sovereign maketh no covenant with his subjects beforehand is manifest, because either he must make it with the whole multitude as one party to the covenant, or he must make a several covenant with every man. With the whole as one party, it is impossible, because as yet they are not one person; and, if he make so many several covenants as there be men, those covenants after he hath the sovereignty are void, because what act soever can be pretended by any one of them for breach thereof is the act both of himself and of all the rest, because done in the person and by the right of every one of them in particular. Besides, if any one or more of them pretend a breach of the covenant made by the sovereign at his institution, and others or any other of his subjects, or himself alone, pretend there was no such breach, there is in this case no judge to decide the controversy: it returns therefore to the sword again, and every man recovereth the right of protecting himself by his own strength, contrary to the design they had in the institution. It is therefore in vain to grant sovereignty by way of precedent covenant. The opinion that any monarch receiveth his power by covenant, that is to say on condition, proceedeth from want of understanding this easy truth, that covenants, being but words and breath, have no force to oblige, contain, constrain, or protect any man but what it has from the public sword; that is from the untied hands of that man, or assembly of men, that hath the sovereignty, and whose actions are avouched by them all, and performed by the strength of them all, in him united. But when an assembly of men is made sovereign, then no man imagineth any such covenant to have passed in the institution; for no man is so dull as to say, for example, the people of Rome made a covenant with the Romans to hold the sovereignty on such or such conditions, which not performed, the Romans might lawfully depose the Roman people. That men see not the reason to be alike in a monarchy and in a popular government proceedeth from the ambition of some that are kinder to the government of an assembly, whereof they may hope to participate, than of monarchy, which they despair to enjoy.

Thirdly, because the major part hath by consenting voices declared a sovereign, he that dissenteth must now consent with the rest; that is, be contented to avow all the actions he shall do, or else justly be destroyed by the rest. For, if he voluntarily entered into the congregation of them that were assembled, he sufficiently declared thereby his will, and therefore tacitly covenanteth to stand to what the major part should ordain; and therefore, if he refuse to stand thereto or make protestation against any of their decrees, he does contrary to his covenant, and therefore unjustly. And whether he be of the congregation or not, and whether his consent be asked or not, he must either submit to their decrees, or be left in the condition of war he was in before; wherein he might without injustice be destroyed by any man whatsoever.

Fourthly, because every subject is by this institution author of all the actions and judgments of the sovereign instituted, it follows that, whatsoever he doth, it can be no injury to any of his subjects, nor ought he to be by any of them accused of injustice. For he that doth anything by authority from another doth therein no injury to him by whose authority he acteth; but by this institution of a commonwealth every particular man is author of all the sovereign doth, and consequently he that complaineth of injury from his sovereign complaineth of that whereof he himself is author, and therefore ought not to accuse any man but himself, no, nor himself of injury, because to do injury to one's self is impossible. It is true that they that have sovereign power may commit iniquity, but not injustice or injury in the proper signification.

Fifthly, and consequently to that which was said last, no man that hath sovereign power can justly be put to death or otherwise in any manner by his subjects punished. For, seeing every subject is author of the actions of his sovereign, he punisheth another for the actions committed by himself.

And, because the end of this institution is the peace and defence of them all, and whosoever has right to the end has right to the means, it belongeth of right to whatsoever man or assembly that hath the sovereignty to be judge both of the means of peace and defence, and also of the hindrances and disturbances of the same, and to do whatsoever he shall think necessary to be done, both beforehand, for the preserving of peace and security by prevention of discord at home and hostility from abroad; and, when peace and security are lost, for the recovery of the same. And, therefore,

Sixthly, it is annexed to the sovereignty to be judge of what opinions and doctrines are averse and what conducing to peace; and, consequently, on what occasions, how far, and what men are to be trusted withal, in speaking to multitudes of people, and who shall examine the doctrines of all books before they be published. For the actions of men proceed from their opinions, and in the well-governing of opinions consisteth the well-governing of men's actions in order to their peace and concord. And, though in matter of doctrine nothing ought to be regarded but the truth, yet this is not repugnant to regulating of the same by peace. For doctrine repugnant to peace can be no more true than peace and concord can be against the law of Nature. It is true that in a commonwealth, where by the negligence or unskilfulness of governors and teachers, false doctrines are by time generally received, the contrary truths may be generally offensive. Yet the most sudden and rough bustling in of a new truth that can be does never break the peace, but only sometimes awake the war. For those men that are so remissly governed that they dare take up arms to defend or introduce an opinion are still in war; and their condition not peace, but only a cessation of arms for fear of one another; and they live, as it were, in the precincts of battle continually. It belongeth therefore to him that hath the sovereign power to be a judge, or constitute all judges of opinions and doctrines, as a thing necessary to peace, thereby to prevent discord and civil war.

Seventhly, is annexed to the sovereignty the whole power of prescribing the rules whereby every man may know what goods he may enjoy, and what actions he may do, without being molested by any of his fellow-subjects; and this is it men call "propriety." For before constitution of sovereign power, as hath already been shown, all men had right to all things, which necessarily causeth war; and therefore this propriety, being necessary to peace and depending on sovereign power, is the act of that power in order to the public peace. These rules of propriety, or *meum* and *tuum*, and of "good," "evil," "lawful," and "unlawful," in the actions of subjects, are the civil laws, that is to say the laws of each commonwealth in particular; though the name of civil law be now restrained to the ancient civil laws of the city of Rome, which, being the head of a great part of the world, her laws at that time were in these parts the civil law.

Eighthly, is annexed to the sovereignty the right of judicature; that is to say of hearing and deciding all controversies which may arise concerning law, either civil or natural, or concerning fact. For without the decision of controversies there is no protection of one subject against the injuries of another, the laws concerning *meum* and *tuum* are in vain, and to every man remaineth, from the natural and necessary appetite of his own conservation, the right of protecting himself by his private strength, which is the condition of war and contrary to the end for which every commonwealth is instituted.

Ninthly, is annexed to the sovereignty the right of making war and peace with other nations and commonwealths; that is to say, of judging when it is for the public good, and how great forces are to be assembled, armed, and paid for that end; and to levy money upon the subjects to defray the expenses thereof. For the power by which the people are to be defended consisteth in their armies, and the strength of an army in the union of their strength under one command, which command the sovereign instituted therefore hath; because the command of the "militia," without other institution, maketh him that hath it sovereign. And therefore whosoever is made general of an army, he that hath the sovereign power is always generalissimo.

Tenthly, is annexed to the sovereignty the choosing of all counsellors, ministers, magistrates, and officers, both in peace and war. For, seeing the sovereign is charged with the end, which is the common peace and defence, he is understood to have power to use such means as he shall think most fit for his discharge.

Eleventhly, to the sovereign is committed the power of rewarding with riches or honor, and of punishing with corporal or pecuniary punishment or with ignominy, every subject according to the law he hath formerly made; or, if there be no law made, according as he shall judge most to conduce to the encouraging of men to serve the commonwealth or deterring of them from doing disservice to the same.

Lastly, considering what values men are naturally apt to set upon themselves, what respect they look for from others, and how little they value other men—from whence continually arise amongst them emulation, quarrels, factions, and at last war, to the destroying of one another and diminution of their strength against a common enemy—it is necessary that there be laws of honor, and a public rate of the worth of such men as have deserved, or are able to deserve, well of the commonwealth; and that there be force in the hands of some or other to put those laws in execution. But it hath already been shown that not only the whole "militia" or forces of the commonwealth, but also the judicature of all controversies, is annexed to the sovereignty. To the sovereign therefore it belongeth also to give titles of honor, and to appoint what order of place and dignity each man shall hold, and what signs of respect, in public or private meetings, they shall give to one another.

These are the rights which make the essence of sovereignty, and which are the marks whereby a man may discern in what man, or assembly of men, the sovereign power is placed and resideth. For these are incommunicable and inseparable. The power to coin money, to dispose of the estate and persons of infant heirs, to have pre-emption in markets, and all other statute prerogatives, may be transferred by the sovereign, and yet the power to protect his subjects be retained. But if he transfer the "militia," he retains the judicature in vain, for want of execution of the laws; or, if he grant away the power of raising money, the "militia" is in vain; or, if he give away the government of doctrines, men will be frighted into rebellion with the fear of spirits. And so, if we consider any one of the said rights, we shall presently see that the holding of all the rest will produce no effect in the conservation of peace and justice, the end for which all commonwealths are instituted. And this division is it whereof it is said: "a kingdom divided in itself cannot stand"; for, unless this division precede, division into opposite armies can never happen. If there had not first been an opinion received of the greatest part of England that these powers were divided between the King and the Lords and the House of

Commons, the people had never been divided and fallen into this civil war, first between those that disagreed in politics, and after between the dissenters about the liberty of religion; which have so instructed men in this point of sovereign right that there be few now in England that do not see that these rights are inseparable, and will be so generally acknowledged at the next return of peace; and so continue till their miseries are forgotten and no longer, except the vulgar be better taught than they have hitherto been.

And, because they are essential and inseparable rights, it follows necessarily that, in whatsoever words any of them seem to be granted away, yet, if the sovereign power itself be not in direct terms renounced and the name of sovereign no more given by the grantees to him that grants them, the grant is void; for when he has granted all he can, if we grant back the sovereignty, all is restored as inseparably annexed thereunto.

This great authority being indivisible and inseparably annexed to the sovereignty, there is little ground for the opinion of them that say of sovereign kings, though they be *singulis majores*, of greater power than every one of their subjects, yet they be *universis minores*, of less power than them all together. For, if by "all together" they mean not the collective body as one person, then "all together" and "every one" signify the same, and the speech is absurd. But, if by "all together" they understand them as one person, which person the sovereign bears, then the power of all together is the same with the sovereign's power, and so again the speech is absurd—which absurdity they see well enough when the sovereignty is in an assembly of the people, but in a monarch they see it not; and yet the power of sovereignty is the same in whomsoever it be placed.

And as the power, so also the honor, of the sovereign, ought to be greater than that of any or all the subjects. For in the sovereignty is the fountain of honor. The dignities of lord, earl, duke, and prince, are his creatures. As in the presence of the master the servants are equal and without any honor at all, so are the subjects in the presence of the sovereign. And, though they shine, some more, some less, when they are out of his sight, yet in his presence they shine no more than the stars in presence of the sun.

But a man may here object that the condition of subjects is

very miserable, as being obnoxious to the lusts and other irregular passions of him or them that have so unlimited a power in their hands.   And commonly they that live under a monarch think it the fault of monarchy, and they that live under the government of democracy or other sovereign assembly attribute all the inconvenience to that form of commonwealth; whereas the power in all forms, if they be perfect enough to protect them, is the same; not considering that the estate of man can never be without some incommodity or other, and that the greatest that in any form of government can possibly happen to the people in general is scarce sensible, in respect of the miseries and horrible calamities that accompany a civil war, or that dissolute condition of masterless men without subjection to laws, and a coercive power to tie their hands from rapine and revenge; nor considering that the greatest pressure of sovereign governors proceedeth not from any delight or profit they can expect in the damage or weaking of their subjects, in whose vigor consisteth their own strength and glory, but in the restiveness of themselves that, unwillingly contributing to their own defence, make it necessary for their governors to draw from them what they can in time of peace that they may have means on any emergent occasion or sudden need to resist or take advantage on their enemies. For all men are by nature provided of notable multiplying glasses, that is, their passions and self-love, through which every little payment appeareth a great grievance, but are destitute of those prospective glasses, namely, moral and civil science, to see afar off the miseries that hang over them and cannot without such payments be avoided.

CHAPTER XXI

OF THE LIBERTY OF SUBJECTS

LIBERTY, or "freedom," signifieth, properly, the absence of opposition—by opposition, I mean external impediments of motion; and may be applied no less to irrational and inanimate creatures than to rational. For whatsoever is so tied or environed as it cannot move but within a certain space, which space is determined by the opposition of some external body, we say it hath not liberty to go further.   And so of all living creatures whilst they are imprisoned or restrained with walls or chains;

and of the water whilst it is kept in by banks or vessels, that otherwise would spread itself into a larger space, we use to say they are not at liberty to move in such manner as without those external impediments they would. But, when the impediment of motion is in the constitution of the thing itself, we use not to say it wants the liberty, but the power, to move, as when a stone lieth still, or a man is fastened to his bed by sickness.

And, according to this proper and generally received meaning of the word, a "freeman is he that in those things which by his strength and wit he is able to do is not hindered to do what he has a will to." But, when the words "free" and "liberty" are applied to anything but "bodies," they are abused; for that which is not subject to motion is not subject to impediment; and, therefore, when it is said, for example, the way is free, no liberty of the way is signified, but of those that walk in it without stop. And when we say a gift is free, there is not meant any liberty of the gift, but of the giver, that was not bound by any law or covenant to give it. So, when we "speak freely," it is not the liberty of voice or pronunciation, but of the man, whom no law hath obliged to speak otherwise than he did. Lastly, from the use of the word "free-will" no liberty can be inferred of the will, desire, or inclination, but the liberty of the man, which consisteth in this, that he finds no stop in doing what he has the will, desire, or inclination, to do.

Fear and liberty are consistent; as when a man throweth his goods into the sea for "fear" the ship should sink, he doth it nevertheless very willingly, and may refuse to do it if he will: it is therefore the action of one that was "free"; so a man sometimes pays his debt, only for "fear" of imprisonment, which, because nobody hindered him from detaining, was the action of a man at "liberty." And, generally, all actions which men do in commonwealths for "fear" of the law are actions which the doers had "liberty" to omit.

"Liberty" and "necessity" are consistent, as in the water that hath not only "liberty" but a "necessity" of descending by the channel; so likewise in the actions which men voluntarily do, which, because they proceed from their will, proceed from "liberty," and yet—because every act of man's will, and every desire and inclination, proceedeth from some cause, and that from another cause, in a continual chain whose first link is in the hand of God, the first of all causes—proceed from "necessity." So that, to him that could see the connection of those causes, the "necessity" of all men's voluntary actions would appear manifest. And therefore God, that seeth and disposeth all things, seeth also that the "liberty" of man in doing what he will is accompanied with the "necessity" of doing that which God will, and no more nor less. For, though men may do many things which God does not command, nor is therefore author of them, yet they can have no passion nor appetite to anything of which appetite God's will is not the cause. And did not his will assure the "necessity" of man's will, and consequently of all that on man's will dependeth, the "liberty" of men would be a contradiction and impediment to the omnipotence and "liberty" of God. And this shall suffice, as to the matter in hand, of that natural "liberty" which only is properly called "liberty."

But as men, for the attaining of peace and conservation of themselves thereby, have made an artificial man which we call a commonwealth, so also have they made artificial chains, called "civil laws," which they themselves by mutual covenants have fastened at one end to the lips of that man, or assembly, to whom they have given the sovereign power, and at the other end to their own ears. These bonds, in their own nature but weak, may nevertheless be made to hold by the danger, though not by the difficulty, of breaking them.

In relation to these bonds only it is that I am to speak now of the "liberty" of "subjects." For, seeing there is no commonwealth in the world wherein there be rules enough set down for the regulating of all the actions and words of men, as being a thing impossible, it followeth necessarily that, in all kinds of actions by the laws pretermitted, men have the liberty of doing what their own reasons shall suggest for the most profitable to themselves. For, if we take liberty in the proper sense for corporal liberty—that is to say, freedom from chains and prison—it were very absurd for men to clamor as they do for the liberty they so manifestly enjoy. Again, if we take liberty for an exemption from laws, it is no less absurd for men to demand as they do that liberty by which all other men may be masters of their lives. And yet, as absurd as it is, this it is they demand, not knowing that the laws are of no power to protect them, without a sword in the hands of a man or men to cause those laws to be put in execution. The liberty of a subject lieth therefore only in those things which in regulating their actions the sovereign hath pretermitted, such as is the liberty to buy and sell and otherwise contract with one another, to choose their own abode, their own diet, their own trade of life, and institute their children as they themselves think fit, and the like.

Nevertheless we are not to understand that by such liberty the sovereign power of life and death is either abolished or limited. For it has been already shown that nothing the sovereign representative can do to a subject, on what pretence soever, can properly be called injustice or injury, because every subject is author of every act the sovereign doth; so that he never wanteth right to anything, otherwise than as he himself is the subject of God, and bound thereby to observe the laws of Nature. And therefore it may, and doth, often happen in commonwealths that a subject may be put to death by the command of the sovereign power; and yet neither do the other wrong; as when Jephtha caused his daughter to be sacrificed; in which, and the like cases, he that so dieth had liberty to do the action for which he is nevertheless without injury put to death. And the same holdeth also in a sovereign prince that putteth to death an innocent subject. For, though the action be against the law of Nature as being contrary to equity, as was the killing of Uriah by David, yet it was not an injury to Uriah, but to God. Not to Uriah, because the right to do what he pleased was given him by Uriah himself; and yet to God, because David was God's subject, and prohibited all iniquity by the law of Nature; which distinction David himself, when he repented the fact, evidently confirmed, saying: "To Thee only have I sinned." In the same manner the people of Athens, when they banished the most potent of their commonwealth for ten years, thought they committed no injustice; and yet they never questioned what crime he had done, but what hurt he would do: nay, they commanded the banishment of they knew not whom; and every citizen bringing his oyster shell into the market-place written with the name of him he desired should be banished, without actually accusing him, sometimes banished an Aristides, for his reputation of justice, and sometimes a scurrilous jester, as

Hyperbolus, to make a jest of it. And yet a man cannot say the sovereign people of Athens wanted right to banish them, or an Athenian the liberty to jest or to be just.

The liberty whereof there is so frequent and honorable mention in the histories and philosophy of the ancient Greeks and Romans, and in the writings and discourse of those that from them have received all their learning in the politics, is not the liberty of particular men, but the liberty of the commonwealth; which is the same with that which every man then should have, if there were no civil laws nor commonwealth at all. And the effects of it also be the same. For as amongst masterless men there is perpetual war of every man against his neighbor; no inheritance to transmit to the son, nor to expect from the father; no propriety of goods, or lands; no security, but a full and absolute liberty in every particular man: so in states and commonwealths not dependent on one another every commonwealth, not every man, has an absolute liberty to do what it shall judge, that is to say, what that man, or assembly that representeth it, shall judge, most conducing to their benefit. But withal they live in the condition of a perpetual war, and upon the confines of battle, with their frontiers armed and cannons planted against their neighbors round about. The Athenians and Romans were free, that is, free commonwealths; not that any particular men had the liberty to resist their own representative, but that their representative had the liberty to resist or invade other people. There is written on the turrets of the city of Lucca, in great characters, at this day, the word "Libertas"; yet no man can thence infer that a particular man has more liberty or immunity from the service of the commonwealth there than in Constantinople. Whether a commonwealth be monarchical or popular the freedom is still the same.

But it is an easy thing for men to be deceived by the specious name of liberty; and, for want of judgment to distinguish, mistake that for their private inheritance and birthright which is the right of the public only. And, when the same error is confirmed by the authority of men in reputation for their writings on this subject, it is no wonder if it produce sedition, and change of government. In these western parts of the world we are made to receive our opinions concerning the institution and rights of commonwealths, from Aristotle, Cicero, and other men, Greeks and Romans, that, living under popular states, derived those rights not from the principles of Nature, but transcribed them into their books out of the practice of their own commonwealths, which were popular; as the grammarians describe the rules of language out of the practice of the time, or the rules of poetry out of the poems of Homer and Vergil. And, because the Athenians were taught, to keep them from desire of changing their government, that they were free men, and all that lived under monarchy were slaves, therefore Aristotle put it down in his *Politics* (lib. 6, cap. ii): "In democracy 'liberty' is to be supposed; for it is commonly held that no man is 'free' in any other government." And as Aristotle, so Cicero and other writers have grounded their civil doctrine on the opinions of the Romans, who were taught to hate monarchy, at first, by them that having deposed their sovereign shared amongst them the sovereignty of Rome, and afterwards by their successors. And by reading of these Greek and Latin authors men from their childhood have gotten a habit, under a false show of liberty, of favoring tumults, and of licentious controlling the actions of their sovereigns, and again of controlling those controllers; with the effusion of so much blood as I think I may truly say there was never anything so dearly bought as these western parts have bought the learning of the Greek and Latin tongues.

To come now to the particulars of the true liberty of a subject, that is to say, what are the things which, though commanded by the sovereign, he may nevertheless without injustice refuse to do; we are to consider what rights we pass away, when we make a commonwealth; or, which is all one, what liberty we deny ourselves by owning all the actions, without exception, of the man or assembly we make our sovereign. For in the act of our "submission" consisteth both our "obligation" and our "liberty," which must therefore be inferred by arguments taken from thence, there being no obligation on any man which ariseth not from some act of his own; for all men equally are by Nature free. And, because such arguments must either be drawn from the express words "I authorize all his actions" or from the intention of him that submitteth himself to his power, which intention is to be understood by the end for which he so submitteth, the obligation and liberty of the subject is to be derived either from those words or other equivalent, or else from the end of the institution of sovereignty, namely, the peace of the subjects within themselves and their defence against a common enemy.

First, therefore, seeing sovereignty by institution is by covenant of every one, to every one, and sovereignty by acquisition by covenants of the vanquished to the victor or child to the parent, it is manifest that every subject has liberty in all those things the right whereof cannot by covenant be transferred. I have shown before in the 14th chapter that covenants not to defend a man's own body are void. Therefore:

If the sovereign command a man, though justly condemned, to kill, wound, or maim himself, or not to resist those that assault him, or to abstain from the use of food, air, medicine, or any other thing without which he cannot live, yet hath that man the liberty to disobey.

If a man be interrogated by the sovereign or his authority concerning a crime done by himself, he is not bound, without assurance of pardon, to confess it; because no man, as I have shown in the same chapter, can be obliged by covenant to accuse himself.

Again, the consent of a subject to sovereign power is contained in these words, "I authorize, or take upon me , all his actions," in which there is no restriction at all of his own former natural liberty; for by allowing him to "kill me" I am not bound to kill myself when he commands me. It is one thing to say "kill me, or my fellow, if you please," another thing to say "I will kill myself, or my fellow." It followeth therefore, that:

No man is bound by the words themselves either to kill himself or any other man; and, consequently, that the obligation a man may sometimes have, upon the command of the sovereign to execute any dangerous or dishonorable office, dependeth not on the words of our submission, but on the intention, which is to be understood by the end thereof. When therefore our refusal to obey frustrates the end for which the sovereignty was ordained, then there is no liberty to refuse: otherwise there is.

Upon this ground a man that is commanded as a soldier to fight against the enemy, though his sovereign have right enough to punish his refusal with death, may nevertheless in many cases refuse, without injustice; as when he substituteth a sufficient soldier in his place, for in this case he deserteth not the service of the commonwealth. And there is allowance to be made for natural timorousness; not only to women, of whom no such dangerous duty is expected, but also to men of feminine courage. When armies fight, there is on one side, or both, a running away; yet when they do it not out of treachery, but fear, they are not esteemed to do it unjustly, but dishonorably. For the same reason, to avoid battle is not injustice, but cowardice. But he that enrolleth himself a soldier or taketh impressed money taketh away the excuse of a timorous nature; and is obliged not only to go to the battle but also not to run from it without his captain's leave. And when the defence of the commonwealth requireth at once the help of all that are able to bear arms, every one is obliged, because otherwise the institution of the commonwealth, which they have not the purpose or courage to preserve, was in vain.

To resist the sword of the commonwealth in defence of another man, guilty or innocent, no man hath liberty; because such liberty takes away from the sovereign the means of protecting us, and is therefore destructive of the very essence of government. But in case a great many men together have already resisted the sovereign power unjustly, or committed some capital crime for which every one of them expecteth death, whether have they not the liberty then to join together, and assist and defend one another? Certainly they have; for they but defend their lives, which the guilty man may as well do as the innocent. There was indeed injustice in the first breach of their duty; their bearing of arms subsequent to it, though it be to maintain what they have done, is no new unjust act. And, if it be only to defend their persons, it is not unjust at all. But the offer of pardon taketh from them to whom it is offered the plea of self-defence, and maketh their perseverance in assisting or defending the rest unlawful.

As for other liberty, they depend on the silence of the law. In cases where the sovereign hath prescribed no rule, there the subject hath the liberty to do or forbear, according to his own discretion. And therefore such liberty is in some places more, and in some less; and in some times more, in other times less, according as they that have the sovereignty shall think most inconvenient. As for example, there was a time when in England a man might enter into his own land, and dispossess such as wrongfully possessed it, by force. But in aftertimes that liberty of forcible entry was taken away by a statute made by the king in parliament. And in some places of the world men have the liberty of many wives; in other places such liberty is not allowed.

If a subject have a controversy with his sovereign, of debt or of right of possession of lands or goods, or concerning any service required at his hands, or concerning any penalty, corporal or pecuniary, grounded on a precedent law, he hath the same liberty to sue for his right as if it were against a subject, and before such judges as are appointed by the sovereign. For, seeing the sovereign demandeth by force of a former law, and not by virtue of his power, he declareth thereby that he requireth no more than shall appear to be due by that law. The suit therefore is not contrary to the will of the sovereign; and consequently the subject hath the liberty to demand the hearing of his cause, and sentence, according to that law. But, if he demand or take anything by pretence of his power, there lieth in that case no action of law; for all that is done by him in virtue of his power is done by the authority of every subject, and consequently he that brings an action against the sovereign brings it against himself.

If a monarch or sovereign assembly grant a liberty to all or any of his subjects, which grant standing, he is disabled to provide for their safety, the grant is void, unless he directly renounce or transfer the sovereignty to another. For in that he might openly, if it had been his will, and in plain terms, have renounced or transferred it, and did not; it is to be understood it was not his will, but that the grant proceeded from ignorance of the repugnancy between such a liberty and the sovereign power, and therefore the sovereignty is still retained; and consequently all those powers which are necessary to the exercising thereof, such as are the power of war and peace, of judicature, of appointing officers and counsellors, of levying money, and the rest named in the 18th chapter.

The obligation of subjects to the sovereign is understood to last as long, and no longer, than the power lasteth by which he is able to protect them. For the right men have by nature to protect themselves, when none else can protect them, can by no covenant be relinquished. The sovereignty is the soul of the commonwealth, which once departed from the body, the members do no more receive their motion from it. The end of obedience is protection, which, wheresoever a man seeth it, either in his own or in another's sword, nature applieth his obedience to it, and his endeavor to maintain it. And though sovereignty, in the intention of them that make it, be immortal, yet is it in its own nature not only subject to violent death by foreign war, but also, through the ignorance and passions of men, it hath in it, from the very institution, many seeds of a natural mortality by intestine discord.

If a subject be taken prisoner in war, or his person or his means of life be within the guards of the enemy, and hath his life and corporal liberty given him on condition he be subject to the victor, he hath liberty to accept the condition; and, having accepted it, is the subject of him that took him, because he had no other way to preserve himself. The case is the same if he be detained on the same terms in a foreign country. But if a man be held in prison or bonds, or is not trusted with the liberty of his body, he cannot be understood to be bound by covenant to subjection; and therefore may, if he can, make his escape by any means whatsoever.

If a monarch shall relinquish the sovereignty, both for himself and his heirs, his subjects return to the absolute liberty of nature; because, though nature may declare who are his sons and who are the nearest of his kin, yet it dependeth on his own will, as hath been said in the precedent chapter, who shall be his heir. If therefore he will have no heir, there is no sovereignty nor subjection. The case is the same if he die without known kindred, and without declaration of his heir. For then there can no heir be known, and consequently no subjection be due.

If the sovereign banish his subject, during the banishment he is not subject. But he that is sent on a message, or hath leave to travel, is still subject; but it is by contract between sovereigns, not by virtue of the covenant of subjection. For whosoever entereth into another's dominion is subject to all the laws thereof, unless he have a privilege by the amity of the sovereigns or by special license.

If a monarch subdued by war render himself subject to the victor, his subjects are delivered from their former obligation, and become obliged to the victor. But, if he be held prisoner or have not the liberty of his own body, he is not understood to have given away the right of sovereignty; and therefore his subjects are obliged to yield obedience to the magistrates formerly placed, governing not in their own name, but in his. For, his right remaining, the question is only of the administration; that is to say, of the magistrates and officers, which, if he have not means to name, he is supposed to approve those which he himself had formerly appointed.

RELIGION AND RELIGIOUS PHILOSOPHY

THOMAS DEKKER (?1570–1641?)

Not a great deal is known of the life of Dekker, except that, like
Dr. Johnson's luckless acquaintance, "he lived in London and hung
loose upon society." And like so many dwellers in Grub Street, Dekker
had his period in jail. But the difficulties of existence do not seem to
have embittered the essential sweetness of his temper, or dried up the
poetry in him. Though versatility was the note of the age, one might
not expect a Bohemian dramatist and journalist to write a book of
prayers. The *Four Birds*, however, along with Dekker's own tenderness of feeling, achieves something of the tone and movement of the
liturgy and the Bible.

FOUR BIRDS OF NOAH'S ARK (1609)

A PRAYER FOR A CHILD BEFORE HE GOETH TO HIS STUDY
OR TO SCHOOL

O GOD, that art the fountain of all wisdom, and founder of all
learning, breathe into my soul the spirit of understanding, that
in my childhood I may learn, and (as I grow farther into years)
may practise, the study only of thee and of thy laws. Feed me,
O Lord, as babes are fed, with the milk of thy holy word, that I
may grow strong in setting forth thy praises. Make me, O
Jesus thou Son of God, one of those of whom thou speakest
thus, *Suffer little children to come unto me, and forbid them not.*
And as thou hast promised that thy wonders should be sounded
forth by the tongues of infants and sucking babes, so pour into
my lips the waters of the well of life, that whatsoever I learn
may be to proclaim thy glory. Polish thou my mind, O God,
that it may shine bright in goodness, and that I may not defile
or deface this weak temple of my body by corrupted manners or
lewd speeches; but so season my tongue that all the lessons which
I take forth may seem to be read to me in thine own school.
Be thou my schoolmaster to instruct me, so shall I repeat the

rules of true wisdom; keep thou me in fear of the rod of thy displeasure, so shall I be sure to have my name set in the book of life. Make me obedient to my parents, dutiful to my teachers, loving to my school-fellows, humble to my superiors, full of reverence to old men, proud towards no man, and that I may win the love of all men. Bless me, O Lord, this day; guide my feet, direct my mind, sanctify my studies, govern all my actions, preserve my body in health, my soul from uncleanness. Grant this, O my God, for thy Son's sake, Jesus Christ; or if it be thy pleasure to cut me off before night, and that this flower of my youth shall fade in all the beauty of it, yet make me, O my gracious Shepherd, for one of thy lambs, to whom thou wilt say, *Come you blessed*, and clothe me in a white robe of righteousness, that I may be one of those singers who shall cry to thee *Allelluia*. Amen.

A PRAYER FOR A PRENTICE GOING TO HIS LABOR

O THE builder of this world, whose workmanship is to be seen excellent even in the frames of the least and basest creatures which thou hast set together, cast a gracious eye upon me, and lend me thy directing hand that the labors which this day I am to undertake may prosper. Let me not, O God, go about my business with eye-service; but sithence thou hast ordained that, like poor Joseph, I must enter into the state of a servant, so humble my mind that I may perform with a cheerful willingness whatsoever my master commands me, and that all his commandments may be agreeable to the serving of thee. Bestow upon me thy grace that I may deal uprightly with all men, and that I may show myself to him who is set over me, a ruler, as I another day would desire to have others behave themselves to me. Take away from him, that is, my master, all thoughts of cruelty, that like the children of Israel under the subjection of Pharaoh's servants I may not be set to a task above my strength; or if I be, stretch thou out my sinews, O God, that I may with unwearied limbs accomplish it. Fill my veins with blood, that I may go through the hardest labors, sithence it is a law set down by thyself that I must earn my bread with the sweat of my own brows. Give me courage to begin, patience to go forward, and ability to finish them. Cleanse my heart, O thou that art the fountain of purity, from all falsehood, from all swearing, from all abuse of thy sacred name, from all foul, loose, and unreverend languages. Let my thoughts when I am alone be of thee; let my mirth in company be to sing Psalms, and the arguments of my talk only touching the works of thy hand. Take sloth from my fingers, and drowsiness from the lids of mine eye; whether I rise early or lie down late so gladly let me do it as if my prenticeship were to be consumed in thy service. The glass of my years shall thereby run out in pleasure, and I in the end shall be made free of that city of thine, the heavenly Jerusalem; into whose fellowship I beseech thee to enfranchise and enroll me, and that after I have faithfully labored six days of my life here upon earth, I may upon the seventh rest in thy everlasting Sabbath. Amen.

A PRAYER FOR A PRISONER

MY FEET, O my Savior, are in the snares of the hunter, and like a beast in the wilderness have my enemies pursued me; I am now entangled in the chains of captivity, yet, O my God, bestow thou upon me the freedom of my soul, soften thou the flinty hearts of those men that have cast me into this house of mourning and heaviness; and as thou didst to Daniel in the lions' den, defend and keep me from the jaws of misery that are stretched wide open to swallow me up alive. It is for my sin that I am thus round beset with poverty, shame, and dishonor. Receive thou therefore these sacrifices of my contrition, and turn not away thine ear when my prayers are flying towards thee. The sighs of a sinner repenting is a sweet breath in thy nostrils, his tears are precious, and like those tears that washed the feet of Christ. Accept therefore this offering from the altar of an humble, contrite, and wounded heart.

Put into my bosom good and charitable thoughts, that I may pray for them that persecute and trouble me, and that I may undergo and pass over all their oppressions and bearings of me down with a settled, constant, and suffering spirit. Let this imprisonment, O Lord, be always unto me a book wherein I may read, first the knowledge of thee, which hitherto I have not studied, and secondly the knowledge of myself. Let it be a glass wherein I may see all the blemishes of my youth, as riots, whoredoms, drunkenness, pride, and such like foul and ulcerous spots that have disfigured my soul. Change, O merciful God, if it be thy will, my wants into plenty, my thraldom into liberty, my mourning into gladness, for thy Son Jesus Christ his sake, who was a prisoner upon the cross only to set all mankind free. Work pity, O my Savior, in the breasts of my adversaries, that I may sing with the prophet: *Blessed is he that considereth the poor and needy; the Lord shall deliver him in the time of trouble.* But if it be thy will and pleasure that I must groan under this trouble and affliction, arm me, O God, with a constant patience to bear all.   Amen.

A PRAYER FOR MEN THAT WORK IN DANGEROUS WORKS, AS COALPITS, MINES, ETC.

Out of my bed, the image of my grave, hast thou raised me, O Lord, thy angels sat upon mine eyelids like sentinels to guard me all the while I lay asleep; O suffer thou the same watchmen to protect me now I am awake.   I need thy help always (for what is man without thee?), but so near the house of danger must I this day dwell that on my knees I entreat thee to keep side by side with me in my goings.   Save my body, O Lord, for death is (at every turning about) at my elbow.   Save my soul, whatsoever falls upon my body.   Which divine part of me, that it may come into thy heavenly treasure-house, inspire me with that wisdom which descendeth from above.   Purify my thoughts and let them with spotless wings be continually flying about thy throne.   Purge my heart, that it may come before thee like a bridegroom, full of chaste love.   Refine my soul, that, like silver seven times tried in the fire, it may bear the bright figure of salvation.   In vain doth the builder lay his foundation, unless thy hand be at the setting up.   Set therefore thy hand to this work of mine, encourage me to undertake it, embolden me to go forward, and enable me to finish it.   Amen.

A PRAYER FOR THE TWO UNIVERSITIES

O thou insearchable depth of all wisdom, open thou the fountains of knowledge, and let the streams of it equally run to the two famous nurseries of learning, the two universities of this land, Oxford and Cambridge, that from the breasts of those two, as it were from the tender nipples of mothers, the youth and gentry of this land may suck the milk both of divine and human science. Graft thou, O Lord, upon those two great trees infinite numbers of plants, that in good time may yield much fruit to thy Church, and profit to the weal public. And seeing that these two stars of learning are to give comfort, or to fill with darkness this our whole kingdom, bestow upon them, O Lord, such beams of heavenly light that even foreign countries, as well as our own, may be glorified in their splendor. Direct all the studies of those that live upon the food of the soul there, which is wisdom, to a holy end. Make them to love as brethren and to live as Christians; suffer not vainglory to engender pride amongst them, nor fantasticness of wit to drown them in ridiculous and apish folly. But so mould both their minds and bodies that they may enter into those sanctified temples as thy children, and come from thence as servants of thy ministry. Amen.

A PRAYER TO STAY THE PESTILENCE

CALL home, O Lord, thy messengers whom thou hast sent forth with full vials of thy wrath to pour upon thy people, O stay the invader's arm, who shooteth darts of pestilence so thickly amongst us, that in heaps we descend into the merciless grave. Death is but thy servant, and can execute none but those whom thou condemnest, yet he hath (and still doth) played the cruel tyrant, for the living whom he spareth are not able to bury carcases so fast as he destroyeth them. Check him therefore, O God, and charge him no more to spoil these temples made by thine own hands. O God of heaven, we have broken thy laws, we confess so much; we repent that we have angered so good and gracious a Father. O Son of God, we have crucified thee again and again in our sins, we confess so much; we repent that we have abused so excellent an author of our redemption; yet have mercy upon us. O Father, speak in our behalf, O thou blessed Son, plead for our pardon, be thou our mediator, reconcile us to the king of heaven and earth, against whom we have committed treason. And whatsoever becomes of our bodies, or how soon soever they must turn into earth, yet have mercy on our souls, save them, O Savior, challenge them for thine own, and lay them up in the treasure-house of heaven, because they are the jewels bought with the price of thy precious blood. Amen.

A PRAYER FOR THE EVENING

THUS, O God, am I nearer to old age than I was in the morning, but, I fear, not nearer to goodness, for he that strives to do best comes short of his duty.   The night now stealeth upon me, like a thief; O defend me from the horror of it.   When I am to lie down in my bed let me imagine I am to lie in my winding sheet, and suffer me not to close mine eyes till my soul and I have reckoned and made even for all the offences which not only this day, but all the former minutes of my life, I have committed against thy divine majesty.   Pardon them, O Lord, forgive me my sins, which are more infinite than the stars, and more heavy than if mountains lay upon my bosom; but thy mercy, and the merits of my Redeemer, do I trust in.   In his name do I sue for a pardon.   Suffer, O Lord, no unclean thoughts this night to pollute my body and soul, but keep my cogitations chaste, and let my dreams be like those of innocents and sucking babes.   Grant, O Lord, that the sun may not go down upon my wrath; but if any man this day hath done me wrong, that I may freely and heartily forgive him, as I desire at thy hands to be forgiven.   Whether I sleep or wake, give thy angels charge over me, that at what hour soever thou callest me, I may like a faithful soldier be found ready to encounter death, and to follow the Lamb wheresoever he goeth.   Amen.

WILLIAM DRUMMOND (1585–1649)

Drummond studied at the University of Edinburgh and abroad, and after the death of his father settled down, on his estate of Hawthornden, to a life of reading and writing. He had literary friends in England, such as Drayton and Ben Jonson, the latter of whom visited him in 1618–19. The impact of the tremendous Ben upon a poetic recluse of somewhat low vitality—which is recorded in Drummond's *Conversations*—must have been parallel to the arrival of Heracles at the house of Admetus. When Drummond composed his chief prose work his natural melancholy had been deepened by severe illness and by the loss, some years before, of the woman he loved. *A Cypress Grove* is the first elaborate prose poem on death in a period rich in such meditations, and is no less ornate than its more famous successors. Drummond would not be himself if he did not echo others, such as Montaigne, but he is no less himself in his exalted strain of Christianized Neo-Platonism.

A CYPRESS GROVE (1623)

. . . If thou dost complain that there shall be a time in the which thou shalt not be, why dost thou not too grieve that there was a time in the which thou wast not, and so that thou art not as old as that enlifening planet of time? For not to have been a thousand years before this moment is as much to be deplored as not to be a thousand after it, the effect of them both being one: that will be after us which long, long ere we were was. Our children's children have that same reason to murmur that they were not young men in our days, which we now, to complain that we shall not be old in theirs. The violets have their time, though they empurple not the winter, and the roses keep their season, though they discover not their beauty in the spring.

Empires, states, kingdoms, have, by the doom of the Supreme Providence, their fatal periods; great cities lie sadly buried in their dust; arts and sciences have not only their eclipses, but their wanings and deaths; the ghastly wonders of the world, raised by the ambition of ages, are overthrown and trampled; some lights above, deserving to be entitled stars, are loosed and never more seen of us; the excellent fabric of this universe itself shall one day suffer ruin, or a change like a ruin; and poor earthlings thus to be handled complain!

But is this life so great a good that the loss of it should be so dear unto man? If it be, the meanest creatures of nature thus be happy, for they live no less than he. If it be so great a felicity, how is it esteemed of man himself at so small a rate, that for so poor gains, nay, one disgraceful word, he will not stand to lose it? What excellency is there in it, for the which he should desire it perpetual, and repine to be at rest, and return to his old Grandmother Dust? Of what moment are the labors and actions of it, that the interruption and leaving-off of them should be to him so distasteful, and with such grudging lamentations received?

Is not the entering into life weakness? the continuing sorrow? In the one he is exposed to all the injuries of the elements, and like a condemned trespasser (as if it were a fault to come to light), no sooner born than fast manacled and bound: in the other he is restlessly, like a ball, tossed in the tennis-court of this world; when he is in the brightest meridian of his glory there needeth nothing to destroy him but to let him fall his own height; a reflex of the sun, a blast of wind, nay, the glance of an eye is sufficient to undo him. How can that be any great matter, of which so small instruments and slender actions are masters?

His body is but a mass of discording humors, composed and elemented by the conspiring influences of superior lights, which, though agreeing for a trace of time, yet can never be made uniform and kept in a just proportion. To what sickness is it subject unto, beyond those of the other sensitive creatures! No part of it being which is not particularly infected and afflicted by some one; nay, every part with many, yea, so many that the masters of that art can scarce number or name them. So that the life of divers of the meanest creatures of nature hath with great reason by the most wise been preferred to the natural life of man; and we should rather wonder how so fragile a matter should so long endure, than how so soon dissolve and decay.

Are the actions of the most part of men much differing from the exercise of the spider, that pitcheth toils and is tapist, to prey on the smaller creatures, and for the weaving of a scornful web eviscerateth itself many days; which when with much industry finished, a little puff of wind carrieth away both the work and the worker? Or are they not like the plays of children, or (to hold them at their highest rate) as is a May game, a masque, or, what is more earnest, some study at chess? Every day we rise and lie down, apparel our bodies and disapparel them, make them sepulchres of dead creatures, weary them and refresh them: which is a circle of idle travails and labors, like Penelope's task, unprofitably renewed. Some time we are in a chase after a fading beauty; now we seek to enlarge our bounds, increase our treasure, living poorly, to purchase what we must leave to those we shall never see, or, haply, to a fool or a prodigal heir. Raised with the wind of ambition, we court that idle name of honor, not considering how they mounted aloft in the highest ascendant of earthly glory are but tortured ghosts, wandering with golden fetters in glistering prisons, having fear and danger their unseparable executioners, in the midst of multitudes rather guarded than regarded. They whom opaque imaginations, and inward thoughtfulness, have made weary of the world's eye, though they have withdrawn themselves from the course of vulgar affairs, by vain contemplations, curious searches, think their life away, are more disquieted, and live worse than others, their wit being too sharp to give them a true taste of present in felicities and to aggravate their woes; while they of a more shallow and blunt conceit have want of knowledge and ignorance of themselves, for a remedy and antidote against all the grievances and encumbrances of life.

What chameleon, what Euripe, what rainbow, what moon doth change so oft as man? He seemeth not the same person in one and the same day; what pleaseth him in the morning is in the evening distasteful unto him. Young, he scorneth his childish conceits, and wading deeper in years (for years are a sea, into which he wadeth until he drown) he esteemeth his youth unconstancy, rashness, folly; old, he beginneth to pity himself, plaining, because he is changed, that the world is changed, like those in a ship, which, when they launch from the shore, are brought to think the shore doth fly from them. He hath no sooner acquired what he did desire, but he beginneth to enter into new cares, and desire what he shall never be able to acquire. When he seemeth freed of evil in his own estate, he grudgeth and vexeth himself at the happiness and fortunes of others. He is pressed with care for what is present, with grief for what is past, with fear for what is to come, nay, for what will never come; and as in the eye one tear draweth another after it, so maketh he one sorrow follow upon a former, and every day lay up stuff of grief for the next.

The air, the sea, the fire, the beasts be cruel executioners of man; yet beasts, fire, sea, and air, are pitiful to man in comparison of man, for more men are destroyed by men, than by them all. What scorns, wrongs, contumelies, imprisonments, torments, poisons, receiveth man of man! What engines and new works of death are daily found out by man against man! What laws to thrall his liberty, fantasies and bugbears to infatuate and inveigle his reason! Amongst the beasts is there any that hath so servile a lot in another's behalf as man? Yet neither is content, nor he who reigneth, nor he who serveth.

The half of our life is spent in sleep; which hath such a resemblance to death, that often it separates the soul from the body, and teacheth it a sort of being above it, making it soar beyond the sphere of sensual delights, and attain to knowledge unto which, while the body did awake, it dared scarce aspire. And who would not, rather than remain chained in this loathsome galley of the world, sleep ever (that is, die), having all things at one stay, be free from those vexations, disasters, contempts, indignities, and many many anguishes, unto which this life is envassaled and made thrall? And, well looked unto, our greatest contentment and happiness here seemeth rather to consist in an absence of misery, than in the enjoying of any great good.

What have the dearest favorites of the world, created to the patterns of the fairest ideas of mortality, to glory in? Is it greatness? Who can be great on so small a round as is this earth, and bounded with so short a course of time? How like is that to castles or imaginary cities raised in the skies by chance-meeting clouds; or to giants modeled, for a sport, of snow, which at the hotter looks of the sun melt away, and lie drowned in their own moisture! Such an impetuous vicissitude touzeth the estate of this world. Is it knowledge? But we have not yet attained to a perfect understanding of the smallest flower, and why the grass should rather be green than red. The

element of fire is quite put out, the air is but water rarefied, the earth is found to move, and is no more the center
of the universe, is turned into a magnet; stars are not
fixed, but swim in the ethereal spaces, comets are mounted
above the planets. Some affirm there is another world of
men and sensitive creatures, with cities and palaces, in the
moon: the sun is lost, for it is but a light made of the conjunction
of many shining bodies together, a cleft in the lower heavens,
through which the rays of the highest diffuse themselves;
is observed to have spots. Thus sciences, by the diverse motions
of this globe of the brain of man, are become opinions, nay,
errors, and leave the imagination in a thousand labyrinths.
What is all we know, compared with what we know not? We
have not yet agreed about the chief good and felicity. It is
perhaps artificial cunning. How many curiosities be framed by
the least creatures of nature (who like a wise painter showeth in
a small portrait more ingine than in a great) unto which the
industry of the most curious artisans doth not attain! Is it
riches? What are they, but the idols of fools, the casting out of
friends, snares of liberty, bands to such as have them, possessing
rather than possessed, metals which nature hath hid (foreseeing
the great harms they should occasion), and the only opinion of
man hath brought in estimation? They are like to thorns,
which laid on an open hand are easily blown away, and wound
the closing and hard-gripping. Prodigals mis-spend them,
wretches mis-keep them: when we have gathered the greatest
abundance, we ourselves can enjoy no more of them than so
much as belongs to one man. They take not away want, but
occasion it: what great and rich men do by others, the meaner
and more contented sort do by themselves. Will some talk of our
pleasures? It is not, though in the fables, told out of purpose,
that Pleasure, being called up to heaven, to disburthen herself
and become more light, did here leave her apparel, which Sorrow
(then naked, forsaken, and wandering) finding, did afterwards
attire herself with. And if we would say the truth of most of
our joys, we must confess them to be but disguised sorrows: remorse ever ensueth them, and (being the heirs of displeasure)
seldom do they appear, except sadness and some wakening grief
hath really preceded and forewent them. Will some ladies
vaunt of their beauty? That is but skin-thick, of two senses

only known, short even of marble statues and pictures; not the same to all eyes, dangerous to the beholder, and hurtful to the possessor; an enemy to chastity, a frame made to delight others more than those which have it, a superficial varnish hiding bones and the brains, things fearful to be looked upon: growth in years doth blast it, or sickness or sorrow preventing them. Our strength, matched with that of the unreasonable creatures, is but weakness. All we can set our eyes upon in these intricate mazes of life is but alchemy, vain perspective, and deceiving shadows, appearing far otherwise afar off, than when enjoyed and looked upon at a near distance. O! who, if before he had a being he could have knowledge of the manifold miseries of it, would enter this woeful hospital of the world, and accept of life upon such hard conditions?

If death be good, why should it be feared, and if it be the work of nature, how should it not be good? For nature is an ordinance, disposition, and rule which God hath established in creating this universe, as is the law of a king which cannot err. For how should the maker of that ordinance err, sith in him there is no impotency and weakness, by the which he might bring forth what is unperfect, no perverseness of will, of which might proceed any vicious action, no ignorance, by the which he might go wrong in working; being most powerful, most good, most wise, nay, all-wise, all-good, all-powerful? He is the first orderer, and marshalleth every other order; the highest essence, giving essence to all other things; of all causes the cause. He worketh powerfully, bounteously, wisely, and maketh nature (his artificial organ) do the same. How is not death of nature, sith what is naturally generate is subject to corruption, and sith such an harmony, which is life, arising of the mixture of the four elements which are the ingredients of our bodies, cannot ever endure; the contrarieties of their qualities, as a consuming rust in the baser metals, being an inward cause of a necessary dissolution? O of frail and instable things the constant, firm, and eternal order! For even in their changes they keep ever universal, ancient, and uncorruptible laws.

Again how can death be evil, sith it is the thaw of all these vanities which the frost of life bindeth together? If there be a satiety in life, then must there not be a sweetness in death? Man were an intolerable thing, were he not mortal; the earth were not ample enough to contain her offspring, if none died. In two or three ages, without death, what an unpleasant and lamentable spectacle were the most flourishing cities! For, what should there be to be seen in them, save bodies languishing and courbing again unto the earth, pale disfigured faces, skeletons instead of men? And what to be heard, but the exclamations of the young, complaints of the old, with the pitiful cries of sick and pining persons? There is almost no infirmity worse than age.

If there be any evil in death, it would appear to be that pain and torment which we apprehend to arise from the breaking of those strait bands which keep the soul and body together; which, sith not without great struggling and motion, seemeth to prove itself vehement and most extreme. The senses are the only cause of pain, but before the last trances of death they are so brought under, that they have no, or very little, strength; and their strength lessening, the strength of pain too must be lessened. How should we doubt but the weakness of sense lesseneth pain, sith we know that weakened and maimed parts which receive not nourishment, are a great deal less sensible than the other parts of the body; and see that old, strengthless, decrepit persons leave this world almost without pain, as in a sleep? If bodies of the most sound and wholesome constitution be those which most vehemently feel pain, it must then follow that they of a distempered and crazy constitution have least feeling of pain; and by this reason, all weak and sick bodies should not much feel pain; for if they were not distempered and evil complexioned, they would not be sick. That the sight, hearing, taste, smelling, leave us without pain, and unawares, we are undoubtedly assured; and why should we not think the same of the feeling? That by which we are capable of feeling, is the vital spirits animated by the brain, which, in a man in perfect health, by veins and arteries are spread and extended through the whole body, and hence it is that the whole body is capable of pain; but in dying bodies we see that by pauses and degrees those parts which are furthest removed from the heart become cold, and being deprived of natural heat, all the pain which they feel, is that they do feel no pain. Now, even as, ere the sick be aware, the vital spirits have withdrawn themselves from the whole extension of the body, to succor the heart (like distressed citizens

which, finding their walls battered down, fly to the defence of
their citadel), so do they abandon the heart without any sensible touch; as the flame, the oil failing, leaveth the wick, or as
the light the air which it doth invest. As to those shrinking
motions and convulsions of sinews and members, which appear
to witness great pain, let one represent to himself the strings
of an high-tuned lute, which, breaking, retire to their natural
windings, or a piece of ice, that without any outward violence
cracketh at a thaw: no otherwise do the sinews of the body,
finding themselves slack and unbended from the brain, and
their wonted labors and motions cease, struggle, and seem to stir
themselves, but without either pain or sense. Swooning is a
true portrait of death, or rather it is the same, being a cessation
from all action, motion, and function of sense and life; but in
swooning there is no pain, but a silent rest, and so deep and sound
a sleep, that the natural is nothing in comparison of it. What
great pain then can there be in death, which is but a continued
swooning, a sweet ignorance of cares, and a never again returning
to the works and dolorous felicity of life? The wise and all-
provident Creator hath made death by many signs of pain appear terrible, to the effect, that if man, for relief of miseries and
present evils, should have unto it recourse, it being (apparently)
a worser, he should rather constantly endure what he knoweth,
than have refuge unto that which he feareth and knoweth not.
The terrors of death seem the guardians of life.

Now although death were an extreme pain, sith it comes in an
instant, what can it be? Why should we fear it, for, while we
are, it cometh not, and it being come, we are no more? Nay,
though it were most painful, long continuing, and terrible-ugly,
why should we fear it, sith fear is a foolish passion but where
it may preserve? But it cannot preserve us from death; yea,
rather fear maketh us to meet with that which we would shun,
and banishing the comforts of present contentments, bringeth
death more near unto us. That is ever terrible which is unknown; so do little children fear to go in the dark, and their
fear is increased with tales. . . .

. . . But, my soul, what aileth thee, to be thus backward
and astonished at the remembrance of death, sith it doth not
reach thee more than darkness doth those far-shining lamps
above? Rouse thyself for shame; why shouldst thou fear to be

without a body, sith thy Maker, and the spiritual and super-
celestial inhabitants have no bodies? Hast thou ever seen any
prisoner, who, when the jail gates were broken up, and he en-
franchised and set loose, would rather plain and sit still on his
fetters than seek his freedom? Or any mariner, who, in the
midst of storms arriving near the shore, would launch forth
again unto the main, rather than strike sail and joyfully enter
the leas of a safe harbor? If thou rightly know thyself, thou
hast but small cause of anguish; for, if there be any resemblance
of that which is infinite in what is finite (which yet by an infinite
imperfection is from it distant), if thou be not an image, thou
art a shadow of that unsearchable Trinity, in thy three essential
powers, Understanding, Will, Memory; which, though three,
are in thee but one, and abiding one, are distinctly three. But
in nothing more comest thou near that sovereign Good than by
thy perpetuity, which who strive to improve, by that same do it
prove: like those that by arguing themselves to be without all
reason, by the very arguing show how they have some. For,
how can what is wholly mortal more think upon, consider, or
know that which is immortal, than the eye can know sounds,
or the ear discern of colors? If none had eyes, who would ever
dispute of light or shadow? And if all were deaf, who would
descant of music? To thee nothing in this visible world is comparable: thou art so wonderful a beauty, and so beautiful a
wonder, that if but once thou couldst be gazed upon by bodily
eyes, every heart would be inflamed with thy love, and ravished
from all servile baseness and earthly desires. Thy being depends not on matter; hence by thine understanding dost thou
dive into the being of every other thing; and therein art so
pregnant, that nothing by place, similitude, subject, time, is so
conjoined, which thou canst not separate; as what neither is,
nor any ways can exist, thou canst feign and give an abstract
being unto. Thou seemest a world in thyself, containing heaven,
stars, seas, earth, floods, mountains, forests, and all that lives:
yet rests thou not satiate with what is in thyself, nor with all in
the wide universe (because thou knowest their defects), until
thou raise thyself to the contemplation of that first illuminating
Intelligence, far above time, and even reaching eternity itself,
into which thou art transformed; for, by receiving, thou, beyond all other things, art made that which thou receivest. The

more thou knowest the more apt thou art to know, not being amated with any object that excelleth in predominance, as sense by objects sensible. Thy will is uncompellable, resisting force, daunting necessity, despising danger, triumphing over affliction, unmoved by pity, and not constrained by all the toils and disasters of life. What the Arts-master of this universe is in governing this universe, thou art in the body; and as he is wholly in every part of it, so art thou wholly in every part of the body: like unto a mirror, every small parcel of which apart doth represent and do the same, what the whole did entire and together. By thee man is that Hymen of eternal and mortal things, that chain, together binding unbodied and bodily substances, without which the goodly fabric of this world were unperfect. Thou hast not thy beginning from the fecundity, power, nor action of the elemental qualities, being an immediate masterpiece of that great Maker. Hence hast thou the forms and figures of all things imprinted in thee from thy first original. Thou only at once art capable of contraries; of the three parts of time thou makest but one; thou knowest thyself so separate, absolute, and diverse an essence from thy body, that thou disposest of it as it pleaseth thee, for in thee there is no passion so weak which mastereth not the fear of leaving it. Thou shouldst be so far from repining at this separation, that it should be the chief of thy desires; sith it is the passage and means to attain thy perfection and happiness. Thou art here, but as in an infected and leprous inn, plunged in a flood of humors, oppressed with cares, suppressed with ignorance, defiled and distained with vice, retrograde in the course of virtue; small things seem here great unto thee, and great things small, folly appeareth wisdom and wisdom folly. Freed of thy fleshly care, thou shalt rightly discern the beauty of thyself and have perfect fruition of that all-sufficient and all-sufficing happiness, which is God himself: to whom thou owest thy being, to him thou owest thy well-being; he and happiness are the same. For, if God had not happiness, he were not God, because happiness is the highest and greatest good: if then God have happiness, it cannot be a thing differing from him, for, if there were anything in him differing from him, he should be an essence composed and not simple. More, what is differing in anything, is either an accident or a part of itself: in God happiness cannot be an accident, because he is not subject to any accidents; if it were a part of him (since the part is before the whole) we should be forced to grant that something was before God. Bedded and bathed in these earthly ordures, thou canst not come near this sovereign Good, nor have any glimpse of the far-off dawning of his unaccessible brightness, no, not so much as the eyes of the birds of the night have of the sun. Think, then, by death that thy shell is broken, and thou then but even hatched; that thou art a pearl, raised from thy mother, to be enchased in gold, and that the deathday of thy body is thy birthday to eternity. . . .

JOHN DONNE (1571-2-1631)

Descended from the prominent Roman Catholic families of Mores and Heywoods, John Donne had, as he says, his "first breeding and conversation with men of a suppressed and afflicted religion, accustomed to the despite of death, and hungry of an imagin'd martyrdom," and the fact must never be forgotten. From the beginning he strove to satisfy what he calls "that worst voluptuousness, which is an hydroptic, immoderate desire of human learning and languages." After several years at each of the universities he went to London to study law—and life—but his intellectual passions ranged far beyond the law. The events of his life need not be summarized here, since they are told in Walton's *Life*, which, necessarily abridged, appears elsewhere in this volume. While Walton glides over the career of wild "Jack Donne" and devotes himself to the great preacher, there were volcanic depths even in the preacher which Walton's untroubled soul could not fathom. There was no real break in Donne's spiritual progress. The celebrant of naturalistic love found an earthly anchorage in Anne More, and, when he was ordained in 1615, a heavenly one. His life in religion, like his approach to it, was no less intellectual than emotional,—but one cannot separate faculties which in him were fused with passionate intensity. Beautiful and even moving as are the writings of Jeremy Taylor, they have not that bitter cry of agonized repentance, sometimes of fear, which gives to Donne his strange power, and which cannot but recall St. Paul and St. Augustine.

Donne's prose is uneven, and, while one great sermon is reproduced entire, there is no need of excuse for giving a number of extracts from the prose poetry which is constantly gushing out of theological deserts. Only thus can various facets of his mind be shown—witness, for example, the ardor with which he follows the newest developments in science, and recollect the attitude of Bacon, the professed scientist; and for Donne in his mystic "watch-tower," scientific discovery leads not so much to the alleviation of man's estate as to the revelation of God. But that unevenness of Donne's prose may be taken as a sign of a certain lack of inner discipline—which his poetry, great as it is, likewise reveals. A kindred symptom is the fact that his culture was mainly mediæval and modern, not classical.

SERMON XXVII

PREACHED TO THE LORDS, UPON EASTER DAY, AT THE
COMMUNION, 1619
(THE KING BEING THEN DANGEROUSLY SICK AT NEW-
MARKET)

Death and life are in the power of the tongue, says Solomon, in
another sense; and in this sense too, if my tongue, suggested by
my heart, and by my heart rooted in faith, can say *Non moriar,
non moriar;*[1] if I can say (and my conscience do not tell me that
I belie mine own state), if I can say that the blood of my Savior
runs in my veins, that the breath of his Spirit quickens all my
purposes, that all my deaths have their resurrection, all my sins
their remorses, all my rebellions their reconciliations, I will
hearken no more after this question, as it is intended *de morte
naturali,* of a natural death; I know I must die that death, what
care I? Nor *de morte spirituali,* the death of sin, I know I do,
and shall die so; why despair I? But I will find out another
death, *mortem raptus,* a death of rapture, and of ecstasy, that
death which St. Paul died more than once, the death which St.
Gregory speaks of, *Divina contemplatio quoddam sepulchrum
animæ,* the contemplation of God and heaven is a kind of burial
and sepulchre and rest of the soul; and in this death of rapture
and ecstasy, in this death of the contemplation of my interest in
my Savior, I shall find myself, and all my sins, interred and entombed in his wounds, and like a lily in Paradise, out of red earth,
I shall see my soul rise out of his blade, in a candor, and in an
innocence, contracted there, acceptable in the sight of his Father.

SERMON LXXVI

PREACHED TO THE EARL OF CARLISLE AND HIS COMPANY,
AT SION [PROBABLY AFTER 1622].[2]

THAT God should let my soul fall out of his hand into a bottomless pit, and roll an unremovable stone upon it, and leave
it to that which it finds there (and it shall find that there which

---

[1] I shall not die.
[2] E. M. Spearing, *Mod. Lang. Review,* 8:479.

it never imagined till it came thither), and never think more of
that soul, never have more to do with it; that of that providence
of God, that studies the life of every weed and worm and ant and
spider and toad and viper, there should never, never, any beam
flow out upon me; that that God who looked upon me when I
was nothing, and called me when I was not as though I had been,
out of the womb and depth of darkness, will not look upon me
now, when, though a miserable, and a banished, and a damned
creature, yet I am his creature still, and contribute something
to his glory, even in my damnation; that that God, who hath often looked upon me in my foulest uncleanness, and when I had
shut out the eye of the day, the sun, and the eye of the night,
the taper, and the eyes of all the world, with curtains and windows and doors, did yet see me, and see me in mercy, by making
me see that he saw me, and sometimes brought me to a present
remorse, and (for that time) to a forbearing of that sin, should so
turn himself from me to his glorious saints and angels, as that no
saint nor angel, nor Christ Jesus himself, should ever pray
him to look towards me, never remember him that such a soul
there is; that that God, who hath so often said to my soul,
"*Quare morieris?* Why wilt thou die?" and so often sworn to
my soul, "*Vivit Dominus*, as the Lord liveth, I would not have
thee die, but live," will neither let me die, nor let me live, but die
an everlasting life, and live an everlasting death; that that God,
who, when he could not get into me by standing, and knocking,
by his ordinary means of entering, by his word, his mercies, hath
applied his judgments, and hath shaked the house, this body,
with agues and palsies, and set this house on fire with fevers and
calentures, and frightened the master of the house, my soul, with
horrors and heavy apprehensions, and so made an entrance into
me; that that God should frustrate all his own purposes and
practices upon me, and leave me, and cast me away, as though
I had cost him nothing, that this God at last should let this soul
go away, as a smoke, as a vapor, as a bubble, and that then
this soul cannot be a smoke, a vapor, nor a bubble, but must lie
in darkness as long as the Lord of light is light itself, and never
spark of that light reach to my soul; what Tophet is not paradise,
what brimstone is not amber, what gnashing is not a comfort,
what gnawing of the worm is not a tickling, what torment is not
a marriage-bed to this damnation, to be secluded eternally,

eternally, eternally, from the sight of God? Especially to us, for as the perpetual loss of that is most heavy, with which we have been best acquainted, and to which we have been most accustomed; so shall this damnation, which consists in the loss of the sight and presence of God, be heavier to us than others, because God hath so graciously, and so evidently, and so diversely, appeared to us, in his pillar of fire, in the light of prosperity, and in the pillar of the cloud, in hiding himself for a while from us: we that have seen him in all the parts of this commission, in his word, in his sacraments, and in good example, and not believed, shall be further removed from his sight, in the next world, than they to whom he never appeared in this. But *vincenti et credenti*, to him that believes aright, and overcomes all tentations to a wrong belief, God shall give the accomplishment of fullness, and fullness of joy, and joy rooted in glory, and glory established in eternity, and this eternity is God; to him that believes and overcomes, God shall give himself in an everlasting presence and fruition. Amen.

SERMON II

PREACHED IN THE EVENING OF CHRISTMAS DAY, 1624

If I should declare what God hath done (done occasionally) for my soul, where he instructed me for fear of falling, where he raised me when I was fallen, perchance you would rather fix your thoughts upon my illness, and wonder at that, than at God's goodness, and glorify him in that; rather wonder at my sins than at his mercies, rather consider how ill a man I was than how good a God he is. If I should inquire upon what occasion God elected me and writ my name in the book of life, I should sooner be afraid that it were not so than find a reason why it should be so. God made sun and moon to distinguish seasons, and day and night, and we cannot have the fruits of the earth but in their seasons; but God hath made no decree to distinguish the seasons of his mercies; in paradise the fruits were ripe the first minute, and in heaven it is always autumn, his mercies are ever in their maturity. We ask[1] our daily bread, and God never says you should have come yesterday, he never says you must

---

[1] L. P. Smith (*Donne's Sermons*, p. 139), though not Alford, reads *panem quotidianum*.

again to-morrow, but *to-day if you will hear his voice*, to-day he will hear you. If some king of the earth have so large an extent of dominion in north and south as that he hath winter and summer together in his dominions, so large an extent east and west as that he hath day and night together in his dominions, much more hath God mercy and judgment together; he brought light out of darkness, not out of a lesser light; he can bring thy summer out of winter, though thou have no spring; though in the ways of fortune, or understanding, or conscience, thou have been benighted till now, wintered and frozen, clouded and eclipsed, damped and benumbed, smothered and stupefied till now, now God comes to thee, not as in the dawning of the day, not as in the bud of the spring, but as the sun at noon, to illustrate all shadows, as the sheaves in harvest, to fill all penuries; all occasions invite his mercies, and all times are his seasons.

SERMON LXVI

PREACHED AT ST. PAUL'S, JANUARY 29, 1625

PSAL. 63. 7.   *Because thou hast been my help, therefore in the shadow of thy wings will I rejoice.*

THE Psalms are the manna of the Church. As manna tasted to every man like that that he liked best, so do the Psalms minister instruction and satisfaction to every man in every emergency and occasion. David was not only a clear prophet of Christ himself, but a prophet of every particular Christian; he foretells what I, what any, shall do, and suffer, and say. And as the whole book of Psalms is *oleum effusum* (as the spouse speaks of the name of Christ), an ointment poured out upon all sorts of sores, a cerecloth that supples all bruises, a balm that searches all wounds; so are there some certain Psalms that are imperial Psalms, that command over all affections, and spread themselves over all occasions, catholic, universal Psalms, that apply themselves to all necessities. This is one of those; for of those constitutions which are called apostolical, one is that the Church should meet every day to sing this Psalm. And accordingly St. Chrysostom testifies that it was decreed and ordained by the primitive Fathers that no day should pass without the public singing of this Psalm. Under both these obligations (those ancient constitutions, called the Apostles', and those ancient decrees made by the primitive Fathers), belongs to me, who have my part in the service of God's Church, the especial meditation and recommendation of this Psalm.   And under a third obligation, too, that it is one of those five Psalms the daily rehearsing whereof is enjoined to me by the constitutions of this Church, as five other are to every other person of our body.   As the whole book is manna, so these five Psalms are my gomer, which I am to fill and empty every day of this manna.

Now as the spirit and soul of the whole book of Psalms is contracted into this Psalm, so is the spirit and soul of this whole Psalm contracted into this verse.   The key of the Psalm (as St. Hierome calls the titles of the Psalms) tells us that David uttered this Psalm *when he was in the wilderness of Judah;* there we see the present occasion that moved him; and we see what was passed between God and him before, in the first clause of our text (*Because thou hast been my help*), and then we see what was to come, by the rest (*therefore in the shadow of thy wings will I rejoice*).   So that we have here the whole compass of time, past, present, and future; and these three parts of time shall be at this time the three parts of this exercise; first, what David's distress put him upon for the present, and that lies in the context; secondly, how David built his assurance upon that which was past (*Because thou hast been my help*); and thirdly, what he established to himself for the future (*therefore in the shadow of thy wings will I rejoice*).   First, his distress in the wilderness, his present estate carried him upon the memory of that which God had done for him before, and the remembrance of that carried him upon that of which he assured himself after.   Fix upon God anywhere, and you shall find him a circle; he is with you now, when you fix upon him; he was with you before, for he brought you to this fixation; and he will be with you hereafter for *he is yesterday, and to-day, and the same for ever.*

For David's present condition, who was now in a banishment, in a persecution in the wilderness of Judah (which is our first part), we shall only insist upon that (which is indeed spread over all the Psalm to the text, and ratified in the text), that in all those temporal calamities David was only sensible of his spiritual loss; it grieved him not that he was kept from Saul's court, but that he was kept from God's Church.   For when he says, by way of lamentation, *that he was in a dry and thirsty land, where no water was,* he expresses what penury, what barrenness, what drought and what thirst he meant: *to see thy power, and thy glory, so as I have seen thee in the sanctuary.* For there, *my soul shall be satisfied as with marrow, and with fatness,* and there, *my mouth shall praise thee with joyful lips.* And in some few considerations conducing to this, that spiritual losses are incomparably heavier than temporal, and that therefore the restitution to our spiritual happiness, or the continuation of it, is rather to be made the subject of our prayers to God in all pressures and distresses, than of temporal, we shall determine that first part. And for the particular branches of both the other parts (the remembering of God's benefits past, and the building of an assurance for the future upon that remembrance), it may be fitter to open them to you, anon when we come to handle them, than now. Proceed we now to our first part, the comparing of temporal and spiritual afflictions.

In the way of this comparison falls first the consideration of the universality of afflictions in general, and the inevitableness thereof. It is a blessed metaphor that the Holy Ghost hath put into the mouth of the Apostle, *pondus gloriæ,* that our *afflictions* are but *light,* because there is an *exceeding* and an *eternal weight of glory* attending them. If it were not for that exceeding weight of glory, no other weight in this world could turn the scale, or weigh down those infinite weights of afflictions that oppress us here. There is not only *pestis valde gravis (the pestilence grows heavy upon the land),* but there is *musca valde gravis,* God calls in but the fly to vex Egypt, and even the fly is a heavy burden unto them. It is not only Job that complains, *that he was a burden to himself,* but even Absalom's hair was a burden to him till it was polled. It is not only Jeremy that complains, *Aggravavit compedes,* that God had made their fetters and their chains heavy to them, but the workmen in harvest complain that God had made a fair day heavy unto them (*We have borne the heat and the burden of the day*). *Sand is heavy,* says Solomon; and how many suffer so? Under a sand-hill of crosses, daily, hourly afflictions, that are heavy by their number, if not by their single weight? And *a stone is heavy* (says he in the same place), and how many suffer so? How many, without any former preparatory cross, or comminatory, or commonitory cross, even in the midst of prosperity and security, fall under some one stone, some grindstone, some millstone, some one insupportable cross that ruins them? But then (says Solomon there), *a fool's anger is heavier than both;* and how many children, and servants, and wives, suffer under the anger, and morosity, and peevishness, and jealousy of foolish masters, and parents, and husbands, though they must not say so? David and Solomon have cried out, that all this world is *vanity* and *levity;* and (God knows) all is weight, and burden, and heaviness, and oppression; and if there were not a weight of future glory to counterpoise it, we should all sink into nothing.

I ask not Mary Magdalen whether lightness were not a burden (for sin is certainly, sensibly, a burden), but I ask Susanna whether even chaste beauty were not a burden to her; and I ask Joseph whether personal comeliness were not a burden to him. I ask not Dives, who perished in the next world, the question; but I ask them who are made examples of Solomon's rule, of that *sore evil* (as he calls it), *riches kept to the owners thereof for their hurt,* whether riches be not a burden.

All our life is a continual burden, yet we must not groan; a continual squeezing, yet we must not pant; and as in the tenderness of our childhood we suffer, and yet are whipped if we cry, so we are complained of if we complain, and made delinquents if we call the times ill. And that which adds weight to weight, and multiplies the sadness of this consideration, is this, that still the best men have had most laid upon them. As soon as I hear God say that he hath found *an upright man, that fears God, and eschews evil,* in the next lines I find a commission to Satan to bring in Sabeans and Chaldeans upon his cattle and servants, and fire and tempest upon his children, and loathsome diseases upon himself. As soon as I hear God say that he hath found *a man according to his own heart,* I see his sons ravish his daughters, and then murder one another, and then rebel against the father, and put him into straits for his life. As soon as I hear God testify of Christ at his baptism, *This is my beloved Son in whom I am well pleased,* I find that Son of his *led up by the Spirit, to be tempted of the devil.* And after I hear God ratify the same testimony again, at his transfiguration (*This is my beloved Son, in whom I am well pleased*), I find that beloved Son of his deserted, abandoned, and given over to scribes, and Pharisees, and publicans, and Herodians, and priests, and soldiers, and people, and judges, and witnesses, and executioners, and he that was called the beloved Son of God, and made partaker of the glory of heaven, in this world, in his transfiguration is made now the sewer of all the corruption, of all the sins of this world, as no Son of God, but a mere man, as no man, but a contemptible worm. As though the greatest weakness in this world were man, and the greatest fault in man were to be good, man is more miserable than other creatures, and good men more miserable than any other men.

But then there is *pondus gloriæ, an exceeding weight of eternal glory*, and that turns the scale; for as it makes all worldly prosperity as dung, so it makes all worldly adversity as feathers. And so it had need; for in the scale against it there are not only put temporal afflictions but spiritual too; and to these two kinds we may accommodate those words, *He that falls upon this stone* (upon temporal afflictions) may be bruised, broken, *but he upon whom that stone falls* (spiritual afflictions) *is in danger to be ground to powder*. And then, the great and yet ordinary danger is that these spiritual afflictions grow out of temporal; murmuring, and diffidence in God, and obduration, out of worldly calamities; and so against nature, the fruit is greater and heavier than the tree, spiritual heavier than temporal afflictions.

They who write of natural story propose that plant for the greatest wonder in nature, which, being no firmer than a bulrush or a reed, produces and bears for the fruit thereof no other but an entire and very hard stone. That temporal affliction should produce spiritual stoniness and obduration is unnatural, yet ordinary. Therefore doth God propose it as one of those greatest blessings, which he multiplies upon his people, *I will take away your stony hearts, and give you hearts of flesh;* an*, Lord, let me have a fleshly heart in any sense, rather than a stony heart. We find mention amongst the observers of rarities in nature of hairy hearts, hearts of men, that have been overgrown with hair; but of petrified hearts, hearts of men grown into stone, we read not; for this petrifaction of the heart, this stupefaction of a man, is the last blow of God's hand upon the heart of man in this world. Those great afflictions which are poured out of the vials of the seven angels upon the world are still accompanied with that heavy effect, that that affliction hardened them. *They were scorched with heats and plagues* by the fourth angel, and it follows *they blasphemed the name of God, and repented not, to give him glory.* Darkness was induced upon them by the fifth angel, and it follows, *they blasphemed the God of heaven, and repented not of their deeds.* And from the seventh angel there fell hailstones of the weight of talents (perchance four pound weight) upon men; and yet these men had so much life left as to *blaspheme God,* out of that respect which alone should have brought them to glorify God, *because the plague thereof was exceeding great.* And when a great plague brings them to blaspheme, how great shall that second plague be that comes upon them for blaspheming?

Let me wither and wear out mine age in a discomfortable, in an unwholesome, in a penurious prison, and so pay my debts with my bones, and recompense the wastefulness of my youth with the beggary of mine age; let me wither in a spital under sharp, and foul, and infamous diseases, and so recompense the wantonness of my youth with that loathsomeness in mine age; yet, if God withdraw not his spiritual blessings, his grace, his patience, if I can call my suffering his doing, my passion his action, all this that is temporal is but a caterpillar got into one corner of my garden, but a mildew fallen upon one acre of my corn; the body of all, the substance of all is safe, as long as the soul is safe. But when I shall trust to that which we call a good spirit, and God shall deject, and impoverish, and evacuate that spirit, when I shall rely upon a moral constancy, and God shall shake, and enfeeble, and enervate, destroy and demolish that constancy; when I shall think to refresh myself in the serenity and sweet air of a good conscience, and God shall call up the damps and vapors of hell itself, and spread a cloud of diffidence, and an impenetrable crust of desperation upon my conscience; when health shall fly from me, and I shall lay hold upon riches to succor me and comfort me in my sickness, and riches shall fly from me, and I shall snatch after favor and good opinion to comfort me in my poverty; when even this good opinion shall leave me, and calumnies and misinformations shall prevail against me; when I shall need peace, because there is none but thou, O Lord, that should stand for me, and then shall find that all the wounds that I have come from thy hand, all the arrows that stick in me from thy quiver; when I shall see that because I have given myself to my corrupt nature thou hast changed thine; and because I am all evil towards thee, therefore thou hast given over being good towards me; when it comes to this height, that the fever is not in the humors, but in the spirits, that mine enemy is not an imaginary enemy, fortune, nor a transitory enemy, malice in great persons, but a real, and an irresistible, and an inexorable, and an everlasting enemy, the Lord of Hosts himself, the Almighty God himself, the Almighty God himself only knows the weight of this affliction, and except he put in that *pondus gloriæ*, that exceeding weight of an eternal glory, with his own hand into the other scale, we are weighed down, we are swallowed up, irreparably, irrevocably, irrecoverably, irremediably.

This is the fearful depth, this is spiritual misery, to be thus fallen from God. But was this David's case? Was he fallen thus far into a diffidence in God? No. But the danger, the precipice, the slippery sliding into that bottomless depth, is to be excluded from the means of coming to God, or staying with God; and this is that that David laments here, that by being banished, and driven into the wilderness of Judah, he had not access to the sanctuary of the Lord, to sacrifice his part in the praise, and to receive his part in the prayers of the congregation; for angels pass not to ends but by ways and means, nor men to the glory of the triumphant Church but by participation of the communion of the militant. To this note David sets his harp in many, many Psalms: sometimes, that God had suffered his enemies to possess his tabernacle (*He forsook the tabernacle of Shiloh, he delivered his strength into captivity, and his glory into the enemies' hands*), but most commonly he complains that God disabled him from coming to the sanctuary. In which one thing he had summed up all his desires, all his prayers. (*One thing have I desired of the Lord, that will I look after; that I may dwell in the house of the Lord all the days of my life, to behold the beauty of the Lord, and to inquire in his temple*); his vehement desire of this he expresses again (*my soul thirsteth for God, for the living God; when shall I come and appear before God?*). He expresses a holy jealousy, a religious envy, even to the sparrows and swallows, (yea, *the sparrow hath found a house, and the swallow a nest for herself, and where she may lay her young, even thine altars, O Lord of Hosts, my King and my God).* Thou art my King and my God, and yet excludest me from that which thou affordest to sparrows, *and are not we of more value than many sparrows?*

And as though David felt some false ease, some half-tentation, some whispering that way, that God is *in the wilderness of Judah*, in every place, as well as in his *sanctuary*, there is in the original in that place a pathetical, a vehement, a broken expressing expressed, *O thine altars;* it is true (says David) thou art here in the wilderness, and I may see thee here, and serve thee here, but, *O thine altars, O Lord of Hosts, my King and my God*. When David could not come in person to that place, yet he bent towards the temple, (*In thy fear will I worship towards thy holy temple*). Which was also Daniel's devotion; when he prayed, *his chamber windows were open towards Jerusalem;* and so is Hezekiah's turning to the wall to weep, and to pray in his sick-bed, understood to be to that purpose, to conform and compose himself towards the temple. In the place consecrated for that use God by Moses fixes the service, and fixes the reward; and towards that place (when they could not come to it) doth Solomon direct their devotion in the consecration of the temple, (*when they are in the wars, when they are in captivity, and pray towards this house, do thou hear them*). For as in private prayer, when (according to Christ's command) we are shut in our chamber, there is exercised *modestia fidei*, the modesty and bashfulness of our faith, not pressing upon God in his house: so in the public prayers of the congregation there is exercised the fervor and holy courage of our faith, for *agmine facto obsidemus Deum*, it is a mustering of our forces and a besieging of God. Therefore does David so much magnify their blessedness that are in this house of God (*Blessed are they that dwell in thy house, for they will be still praising thee*.) Those that look towards it may praise thee sometimes, but those men who dwell in the Church, and whose whole service lies in the Church, have certainly an advantage of all other men (who are necessarily withdrawn by worldly businesses) in making themselves acceptable to Almighty God, if they do their duties, and observe their Church-services aright.

Man being therefore thus subject naturally to manifold

calamities, and spiritual calamities being incomparably heavier than temporal, and the greatest danger of falling into such spiritual calamities being in our absence from God's Church, where only the outward means of happiness are ministered unto us, certainly there is much tenderness and deliberation to be used before the Church doors be shut against any man. If I would not direct a prayer to God to excommunicate any man from the triumphant Church (which were to damn him), I would not oil the key, I would not make the way too slippery for excommunications in the militant Church; for that is to endanger him. I know how distasteful a sin to God contumacy, and contempt, and disobedience to order and authority is; and I know (and all men that choose not ignorance may know) that our excommunications (though calumniators impute them to small things because, many times, the first complaint is of some small matter) never issue but upon contumacies, contempts, disobediences to the Church. But they are real contumacies, not interpretative, apparent contumacies, not presumptive, that excommunicate a man in heaven; and much circumspection is required, and (I am far from doubting it) exercised, in those cases upon earth; for, though every excommunication upon earth be not sealed in heaven, though it damn not the man, yet it dams up that man's way by shutting him out of that Church through which he must go to the other; which being so great a danger, let every man take heed of excommunicating himself. The impersuasible recusant does so; the negligent libertine does so; the fantastic separatist does so; the half-present man, he whose body is here, and mind away, does so; and he whose body is but half here, his limbs are here upon a cushion, but his eyes, his ears, are not here, does so: all these are self-excommunicators, and keep themselves from hence. Only he enjoys that blessing, the want whereof David deplores, that is here entirely, and is glad he is here, and glad to find this kind of service here that he does, and wishes no other.

And so we have done with our first part, David's aspect, his present condition, and his danger of falling into spiritual miseries, because his persecution and banishment amounted to an excommunication, to an excluding of him from the service of God in the Church. And we pass, in our order proposed at first,

to the second, his retrospect, the consideration what God had
done for him before, *because thou hast been my help*.

Through this second part we shall pass by these three steps.
First, that it behoves us, in all our purposes and actions to propose to ourselves a copy to write by, a pattern to work by, a
rule or an example to proceed by: because it hath been thus
heretofore, says David, I will resolve upon this course for the
future.   And secondly, that the copy, the pattern, the precedent
which we are to propose to ourselves is the observation of God's
former ways and proceedings upon us; because God hath already
gone this way, this way I will await his going still.   And then,
thirdly and lastly, in this second part, the way that God had
formerly gone with David, which was that he had been his help
(*because thou hast been my help*.)

First then, from the meanest artificer through the wisest
philosopher to God himself, all that is well done, or wisely
undertaken, is undertaken and done according to preconceptions, fore-imaginations, designs, and patterns proposed to
ourselves beforehand.   A carpenter builds not a house but that
he first sets up a frame in his own mind what kind of house
he will build.   The little great philosopher Epictetus would
undertake no action but he would first propose to himself what
Socrates or Plato, what a wise man would do in that case, and
according to that he would proceed.   Of God himself it is safely
resolved in the school that he never did anything in any part of
time of which he had not an eternal preconception, an eternal
Idea, in himself before.   Of which Ideas, that is, preconceptions,
pre-determinations in God, St. Augustine pronounces *Tanta
vis in ideis constituitur;* there is so much truth and so much
power in these Ideas, as that without acknowledging them no
man can acknowledge God, for he does not allow God counsel,
and wisdom, and deliberation in his actions, but sets God on
work before he have thought what he will do.   And therefore
he and others of the Fathers read that place (which we read
otherwise), *Quod factum est, in ipso vita erat;* that is, in all their
expositions, whatsoever is made, in time, was alive in God before
it was made, that is, in that eternal Idea and pattern which was
in him.   So also do divers of those Fathers read those words to
the Hebrews (which we read, *The things that are seen, are not*

made of things that do appear), *Ex invisibilibus visibilia facta sunt,* *things formerly invisible were made visible;* that is, we see them not till now, till they are made, but they had an invisible being in that Idea, in that pre-notion, in that purpose of God before, for ever before. Of all things in heaven and earth but of himself, God had an Idea, a pattern in himself, before he made it.

And therefore let him be our pattern for that, to work after patterns; to propose to ourselves rules and examples for all our actions; and the more the more immediately, the more directly, our actions concern the service of God. If I ask God by what Idea he made me, God produces his *Faciamus hominem ad* *imaginem nostram,* that there was a concurrence of the whole Trinity to make me in Adam, according to that image which they were, and according to that Idea which they had predetermined. If I pretend to serve God, and he ask me for my Idea, how I mean to serve him, shall I be able to produce none? If he ask me an Idea of my religion and my opinions, shall I not be able to say, it is that which thy word and thy Catholic Church hath imprinted in me? If he ask me an Idea of my prayers, shall I not be able to say, it is that which my particular necessities, that which the form prescribed by thy Son, that which the care and piety of the Church, in conceiving fit prayers, hath imprinted in me? If he ask me an Idea of my sermons, shall I not be able to say, it is that which the analogy of faith, the edification of the congregation, the zeal of thy work, the meditations of my heart have imprinted in me? But if I come to pray or to preach without this kind of Idea, if I come to extemporal prayer and extemporal preaching, I shall come to an extemporal faith and extemporal religion; and then I must look for an extemporal heaven, a heaven to be made for me; for to that heaven which belongs to the Catholic Church I shall never come, except I go by the way of the Catholic Church, by former Ideas, former examples, former patterns, to believe according to ancient beliefs, to pray according to ancient forms, to preach according to former meditations. God does nothing, man does nothing well, without these Ideas, these retrospects, this recourse to preconceptions, pre-deliberations.

Something then I must propose to myself to be the rule and the reason of my present and future actions, which was our first branch in this second part; and then the second is, that I can propose nothing more availably than the contemplation of the history of God's former proceeding with me; which is David's way here, because this was God's way before, I will look for God in this way still. That language in which God spake to man, the Hebrew, hath no present tense; they form not their verbs as our western languages do, in the present, *I hear*, or *I see*, or *I read*, but they begin at that which is past, *I have seen* and *heard*, and *read*. God carries us in his language, in his speaking, upon that which is past, upon that which he hath done already; I cannot have better security for present, nor future, than God's former mercies exhibited to me. *Quis non gaudeat*, says St. Augustine, who does not triumph with joy, when he considers what God hath done? *Quis non et ea, quæ nondum venerunt, ventura sperat, propter illa, quæ jam tanta impleta sunt?* Who can doubt of the performance of all, that sees the greatest part of a prophecy performed? If I have found that true that God hath said of the person of Antichrist, why should I doubt of that which he says of the ruin of Antichrist? *Credamus modicum quod restat*, says the same Father, it is much that we have seen done, and it is but little that God hath reserved to our faith, to believe that it shall be done.

There is no state, no Church, no man, that hath not this tie upon God, that hath not God in these bands, that God by having done much for them already hath bound himself to do more. Men proceed in their former ways, sometimes, lest they should confess an error and acknowledge that they had been in a wrong way. God is obnoxious to no error, and therefore he does still as he did before. Every one of you can say now to God, Lord, thou broughtest me hither, therefore enable me to hear; Lord, thou doest that, therefore make me understand; and that, therefore let me believe; and that too, therefore strengthen me to the practice; and all that, therefore continue me to a perseverance. Carry it up to the first sense and apprehension that ever thou hadst of God's working upon thee, either in thyself, when thou camest first to the use of reason, or in others in thy behalf, in thy baptism, yet when thou thinkest thou art at the first, God had done something for thee before all that; before that, he had elected thee, in that election which St. Augustine speaks of, *Habet electos, quos creaturus est eligendos*, God hath elected certain men, whom he intends to create, that he may elect them; that is, that he may declare his election upon them.   God had thee, before he made thee; he loved thee first, and then created thee, that, thou loving him, he might continue his love to thee.   The surest way, and the nearest way to lay hold upon God, is the consideration of that which he had done already.   So David does; and that which he takes knowledge of, in particular, in God's former proceedings towards him, is, because God had been his help, which is our last branch in this part, *because thou hast been my help*.

From this one word, that God hath been my *help*, I make account that we have both these notions; first, that God hath not left me to myself, he hath come to my succor, he hath helped me; and then, that God hath not left out myself; he hath been my help, but he hath left something for me to do with him, and by his help.   My security for the future, in this consideration of that which is past, lies not only in this, that God hath delivered me, but in this also, that he hath delivered me by way of a help, and help always presumes an endeavor and co-operation in him that is helped.   God did not elect me as a helper, nor create me, nor redeem me, nor convert me, by way of helping me; for he alone did all, and he had no use at all of me.   God infuses his first grace, the first way, merely as a giver, entirely, all himself; but his subsequent graces, as a helper; therefore we call them auxiliant graces, helping graces; and we always receive them when we endeavor to make use of his former grace.   *Lord, I believe* (says the man in the Gospel to Christ), *Help mine unbelief*.   If there had not been unbelief, weakness, unperfectness in that faith, there had needed no help; but if there had not been a belief, a faith, it had not been capable of help and assistance, but it must have been an entire act, without any concurrence on the man's part.

So that if I have truly the testimony of a rectified conscience that God hath helped me, it is in both respects; first, that he hath never forsaken me, and then, that he hath never suffered me to forsake myself; he hath blessed me with that grace that I trust in no help but his, and with this grace too, that I cannot look for his help except I help myself also.   God did not help heaven and earth to proceed out of nothing in the creation, for they had no possibility of any disposition towards it; for they had no being: but God did help the earth to produce grass and herbs; for, for that, God had infused a seminal disposition into the earth, which, for all that, it could not have perfected without his farther help. As in the making of woman, there is the very word of our text, *gnazar*, God made him a *helper*, one that was to do much for him, but not without him. So that then, if I will make God's former working upon me an argument of his future gracious purposes, as I must acknowledge that God hath done much for me, so I must find that I have done what I could, by the benefit of that grace with him; for God promises to be but a helper. *Lord open thou my lips*, says David; that is God's work entirely; and then, *My mouth, my mouth shall show forth thy praise;* there enters David into the work with God. And then, says God to him, *Dilata os tuum*, *Open thy mouth* (it is now made *thy mouth*, and therefore do thou open it), *and I will fill it;* all inchoations and consummations, beginnings and perfectings, are of God, of God alone; but in the way there is a concurrence on our part (by a successive continuation of God's grace), in which God proceeds as a helper; and I put him to more than that if I do nothing. But if I pray for his help, and apprehend and husband his graces well, when they come, then he is truly, properly, my helper; and upon that security, that testimony of a rectified conscience, I can proceed to David's confidence for the future, *Because thou hast been my help, therefore in the shadow of thy wings will I rejoice;* which is our third and last general part.

In this last part, which is (after David's aspect, and consideration of his present condition, which was, in the effect, an exclusion from God's temple, and his retrospect, his consideration of God's former mercies to him, that he had been his help), his prospect, his confidence for the future, we shall stay a little upon these two steps; first, that that which he promises himself is not an immunity from all powerful enemies, nor a sword of revenge upon those enemies; it is not that he shall have no adversary, nor that that adversary shall be able to do him no harm, but that he should have a refreshing, a respiration, *in velamento alarum*, under the shadow of God's wings. And then (in the second place), that this way which God shall be pleased to take, this manner, this measure of refreshing, which God shall vouchsafe to afford (though it amount not to a full deliverance), must produce a joy, a rejoicing in us; we must not only not decline to a murmuring, that we have no more, no, nor rest upon a patience for that which remains, but we must ascend to a holy joy, as if all were done and accomplished, *in the shadow of thy wings will I rejoice.*

First then, lest any man in his dejection of spirit, or of fortune, should stray into a jealousy or suspicion of God's power to deliver him, as God hath spangled the firmament with stars, so hath he his Scriptures with names, and metaphors, and denotations of power. Sometimes he shines out in the name of a sword, and of a target, and of a wall, and of a tower, and of a rock, and of a hill; and sometimes in that glorious and manifold constellation of all together, *Dominus exercituum, the Lord of Hosts.* God, as God, is never represented to us with defensive arms; he needs them not. When the poets present their great heroes and their worthies they always insist upon their arms, they spend much of their invention upon the description of their arms; both because the greatest valor and strength needs arms, (Goliah himself was armed), and because to expose one's self to danger unarmed is not valor, but rashness. But God is invulnerable in himself, and is never represented armed; you find no shirts of mail, no helmets, no cuirasses in God's armory. In that one place of Isaiah, where it may seem to be otherwise, where God is said *to have put on righteousness as a breastplate, and a helmet of salvation upon his head;* in that prophecy God is Christ, and is therefore in that place, called *the Redeemer.* Christ needed defensive arms, God does not. God's word does; his Scriptures do; and therefore St. Hierome hath armed them, and set before every book his *prologum galeatum,* that prologue that arms and defends every book from calumny. But though God need not, nor receive not defensive arms for himself, yet God is to us a helmet, a breastplate, a strong tower, a rock, everything that may give us assurance and defence; and as often as he will he can refresh that proclamation, *Nolite tangere Christos meos,* our enemies shall not so much as touch us.

But here, by occasion of his metaphor in this text, (*sub umbra alarum, in the shadow of thy wings*), we do not so much consider an absolute immunity that we shall not be touched, as a refreshing and consolation when we are touched, though we be pinched and wounded. The names of God which are most frequent in the Scriptures are these three, *Elohim*, and *Adonai*, and *Jehovah;* and to assure us of his power to deliver us, two of these three are names of power. *Elohim* is *Deus fortis*, the mighty, the powerful God: and (which deserves a particular consideration) *Elohim* is a plural name; it is not *Deus fortis*, but *Dii fortes*, powerful gods. God is all kind of gods; all kinds, which either idolaters and Gentiles can imagine, (as riches, or justice, or wisdom, or valor, or such) and all kinds which God himself hath called gods, (as princes, and magistrates, and prelates, and all that assist and help one another), God is *Elohim*, all these gods, and all these in their height and best of their power; for *Elohim* is *Dii fortes*, gods in the plural, and those plural gods in their exaltation.

The second name of God is a name of power too, *Adonai*. For *Adonai* is *Dominus*, the Lord, such a lord as is lord and proprietary of all his creatures, and all creatures are his creatures; and then, *Dominium est potestas tum utendi, tum abutendi*, says the law; to be absolute lord of anything gives that lord a power to do what he will with that thing. God, as he is *Adonai, The Lord*, may give and take, quicken and kill, build and throw down, where and whom he will. So then two of God's three names are names of absolute power, to imprint and re-imprint an assurance in us that he can absolutely deliver us and fully revenge us, if he will. But then his third name, and that name which he chooses to himself, and in the signification of which name he employs Moses for the relief of his people under Pharaoh, that name Jehovah, is not a name of power, but only of essence, of being, of subsistence, and yet in the virtue of that name God relieved his people. And if, in my afflictions, God vouchsafe to visit me in that name, to preserve me in my being, in my subsistence in him, that I be not shaked out of him, disinherited in him, excommunicate from him, divested of him, annihilated towards him, let him, at his good pleasure, reserve his *Elohim* and his *Adonai*, the exercises and declarations of his mighty power, to those great public causes that more concern his glory than anything that can befall me; but if he impart his *Jehovah*, enlarge himself so far towards me, as that I may live, and move, and have my being in him, though I be not instantly delivered, nor mine enemies absolutely destroyed, yet this is as much as I should promise myself, this is as much as the Holy

Ghost intends in this metaphor, *sub umbra alarum, under the shadow of thy wings*, that is, a refreshing, a respiration, a conservation, a consolation in all afflictions that are inflicted upon me.

Yet is not this metaphor of *wings* without a denotation of power. As no act of God's, though it seem to imply but spiritual comfort, is without a denotation of power, (for it is the power of God that comforts me: to overcome that sadness of soul, and that dejection of spirit, which the adversary by temporal afflictions would induce upon me, is an act of his power), so this metaphor, *the shadow of his wings*, (which in this place expresses no more than consolation and refreshing in misery, and not a powerful deliverance out of it), is so often in the Scriptures made a denotation of power too, as that we can doubt of no act of power if we have this shadow of his wings. For in this metaphor of *wings* doth the Holy Ghost express the maritime power, the power of some nations at sea, in navies, (*Woe to the land shadowing with wings*); that is, that hovers over the world, and intimidates it with her sails and ships. In this metaphor doth God remember his people of his powerful deliverance of them, (*You have seen what I did unto the Egyptians, and how I bare you on eagles' wings, and brought you to myself*). In this metaphor doth God threaten his and their enemies, what he can do, (*The noise of the wings of his cherubims are as the noise of great waters, and of an army*). So also, what he will do, (*He shall spread his wings over Bozrah, and at that day shall the hearts of the mighty men of Edom be as the heart of a woman in her pangs*). So that, if I have the shadow of his wings, I have the earnest of the power of them too; if I have refreshing and respiration from them, I am able to say (as those three confessors did to Nebuchadnezzar), *My God is able to deliver me*, I am sure he hath power; *And my God will deliver me*, when it conduces to his glory, I know he will; *But, if he do not, be it known unto thee, O King, we will not serve thy gods*; be it known unto thee, O Satan, how long soever God defer my deliverance, I will not seek false comforts, the miserable comforts of this world. I will not, for I need not; for I can subsist under this shadow of these wings, though I have no more.

The mercy-seat itself was covered with the cherubim's wings; and who would have more than mercy, and a mercy-seat; that is, established, resident mercy, permanent and perpetual mercy; present and familiar mercy; a mercy-seat? Our Savior Christ intends as much as would have served their turn, if they had laid hold upon it, when he says, *that he would have gathered Jerusalem as a hen gathers her chickens under her wings.* And though the other prophets do (as ye have heard) mingle the signification of power and actual deliverance in this metaphor of wings, yet our prophet, whom we have now in especial consideration, David, never doth so; but in every place where he uses this metaphor of wings (which are in five or six several Psalms) still he rests and determines in that sense which is his meaning here; that though God do not actually deliver us, nor actually destroy our enemies, yet if he refresh us in the shadow of his wings, if he maintain our subsistence (which is a religious constancy) in him, this should not only establish our patience (for that is but half the work), but it should also produce a joy, and rise to an exultation, which is our last circumstance, *therefore in the shadow of thy wings, I will rejoice.*

I would always raise your hearts, and dilate your hearts, to a holy joy, to a joy in the Holy Ghost. There may be a just fear that men do not grieve enough for their sins; but there may be a just jealousy, and suspicion too, that they may fall into inordinate grief and diffidence of God's mercy; and God hath reserved us to such times, as, being the later times, give us even the dregs and lees of misery to drink. For God hath not only let loose into the world a new spiritual disease; which is an equality and an indifferency, which religion our children, or our servants, or our companions, profess; (I would not keep company with a man that thought me a knave or a traitor; with him that thought I loved not my prince, or were a faithless man, not to be believed, I would not associate myself; and yet I will make him my bosom companion that thinks I do not love God, that thinks I cannot be saved), but God hath accompanied and complicated almost all our bodily diseases of these times with an extraordinary sadness, a predominant melancholy, a faintness of heart, a cheerlessness, a joylessness of spirit, and therefore I return often to this endeavor of raising your hearts, dilating your hearts with a holy joy, joy in the Holy Ghost, for *under the shadow of his wings,* you may, you should *rejoice.*

If you look upon this world in a map, you find two hemispheres, two half-worlds. If you crush heaven into a map, you may find two hemispheres too, two half-heavens; half will be joy, and half will be glory; for in these two, the joy of heaven, and the glory of heaven, is all heaven represented unto us. And as of those two hemispheres of the world, the first hath been known long before, but the other (that of America, which is the richer in treasure), God reserved for later discoveries; so though he reserve that hemisphere of heaven, which is the glory thereof, to the resurrection, yet the other hemisphere, the joy of heaven, God opens to our discovery, and delivers for our habitation even whilst we dwell in this world. As God hath cast upon the unrepentant sinner two deaths, a temporal and a spiritual death, so hath he breathed into us two lives; for so as the word for death is doubled, *Morte morieris, Thou shalt die the death*, so is the word for life expressed in the plural, *Chaiim, vitarum, God breathed into his nostrils the breath of lives*, of divers lives. Though our natural life were no life, but rather a continual dying, yet we have two lives besides that, an eternal life reserved for heaven, but yet a heavenly life too, a spiritual life, even in this world; and as God doth thus inflict two deaths, and infuse two lives, so doth he also pass two judgments upon man, or rather repeats the same judgment twice. For that which Christ shall say to thy soul then at the last judgment, *Enter into thy Master's joy*, he says to thy conscience now, *Enter into thy Master's joy*. The everlastingness of the joy is the blessedness of the next life, but the entering, the inchoation, is afforded here. For that which Christ shall say then to us, *Venite benedicti, Come ye blessed*, are words intended to persons that are coming, that are upon the way, though not at home; here in this world he bids us *Come*, there in the next, he shall bid us *Welcome*. The angels of heaven have joy in thy conversion, and canst thou be without that joy in thyself? If thou desire revenge upon thine enemies, as they are God's enemies, that God would be pleased to remove and root out all such as oppose him, that affection appertains to glory; let that alone till thou come to the hemisphere of glory; there join with those martyrs under the altar, *Usquequo Domine*, how long, O Lord, dost thou defer judgment? and thou shalt have thine answer there for that. Whilst thou art here, here join with David and the other saints of God in that holy increpation of a dangerous sadness, *Why art thou cast down, O my soul? why art thou dis-*

quieted in me? That soul that is dissected and anatomized to God in a sincere confession, washed in the tears of true contrition, embalmed in the blood of reconciliation, the blood of Christ Jesus, can assign no reason, can give no just answer to that interrogatory, *Why art thou cast down, O my soul? why art thou disquieted in me?* No man is so little as that he can be lost under these wings, no man so great as that they cannot reach to him; *Semper ille major est, quantumcumque creverimus,* to what temporal, to what spiritual greatness soever we grow, still pray we him to shadow us under his wings; for the poor need those wings against oppression, and the rich against envy. The Holy Ghost, who is a dove, shadowed the whole world under his wings; *incubabat aquis,* he hovered over the waters, he sat upon the waters, and he hatched all that was produced, and all that was produced so was good. Be thou a mother where the Holy Ghost would be a father; conceive by him; and be content that he produce joy in thy heart here. First think that as a man must have some land, or else he cannot be in wardship, so a man must have some of the love of God, or else he could not fall under God's correction; God would not give him his physic, God would not study his cure, if he cared not for him. And then think also, that if God afford thee the shadow of his wings, that is, consolation, respiration, refreshing, though not a present and plenary deliverance in thy afflictions, not to thank God is a murmuring, and not to rejoice in God's ways is an unthankfulness. Howling is the noise of hell, singing the voice of heaven; sadness the damp of hell, rejoicing the serenity of heaven. And he that hath not this joy here lacks one of the best pieces of his evidence for the joys of heaven; and hath neglected or refused that earnest by which God uses to bind his bargain, that true joy in this world shall flow into the joy of heaven as a river flows into the sea; this joy shall not be put out in death, and a new joy kindled in me in heaven; but as my soul, as soon as it is out of my body, is in heaven, and does not stay for the possession of heaven, nor for the fruition of the sight of God, till it be ascended through air, and fire, and moon, and sun, and planets, and firmament, to that place which we conceive to be heaven, but without the thousandth part of a minute's stop, as soon as it issues is in a glorious light, which is heaven, (for all the way to heaven is heaven; and as those angels which came from heaven hither, bring heaven with them, and are in heaven here, so that soul that goes to heaven, meets heaven here; and as those angels do not divest heaven by coming, so these souls invest heaven in their going). As my soul shall not go towards heaven, but go by heaven to heaven, to the heaven of heavens, so the true joy of a good soul in this world is the very joy of heaven; and we go thither, not that being without joy we might have joy infused into us, but that as Christ says, *our joy might be full*, perfected, sealed with an everlastingness; for as he promises, *that no man shall take our joy from us*, so neither shall death itself take it away, nor so much as interrupt it, or discontinue it, but as in the face of death, when he lays hold upon me, and in the face of the devil, when he attempts me, I shall see the face of God (for everything shall be a glass, to reflect God upon me), so in the agonies of death, in the anguish of that dissolution, in the sorrows of that valediction, in the irreversibleness of that transmigration, I shall have a joy which shall no more evaporate than my soul shall evaporate, a joy that shall pass up, and put on a more glorious garment above, and be joy superinvested in glory. Amen.

SERMON LXXIII

PREACHED TO THE KING IN MY ORDINARY WAITING AT WHITEHALL, 18th APRIL, 1626

AND then a third beam of this consolation is that in this house of his Father's, thus by him made ours, there are mansions; in which word the consolation is not placed (I do not say that there is not truth in it), but the consolation is not placed in this, that some of these mansions are below, some above stairs, some better seated, better lighted, better vaulted, better fretted, better furnished than others; but only in this, that they are mansions; which word, in the original and Latin and our language, signifies a remaining, and denotes the perpetuity, the everlastingness, of that state. A state but of one day, because no night shall overtake or determine it, but such a day as is not of a thousand years, which is the longest measure in the Scriptures, but of a thousand millions of millions of generations: *Qui nec præceditur hesterno, nec excluditur crastino*, a day that hath no *pridie* nor *postridie*, yesterday doth not usher it in, nor to-morrow shall not drive it out. Methusalem, with all his hundreds of years, was but a mushroom of a night's growth to this day, and all the four monarchies, with all their thousands of years, and all the powerful kings, and all the beautiful queens of this world, were but as a bed of flowers, some gathered at six, some at seven, some at eight, all in one morning, in respect of this day.   In all the two thousand years of nature, before the law given by Moses, and the two thousand years of law, before the Gospel given by Christ, and the two thousand of grace, which are running now (of which last hour we have heard three quarters strike, more than fifteen hundred of this last two thousand spent), in all this six thousand, and in all those which God may be pleased to add, *in domo patris*, in this house of his Father's, there was never heard quarter clock to strike, never seen minute glass to turn.

SERMON LXXX

PREACHED AT THE FUNERALS OF SIR WILLIAM COKAYNE, KNT., ALDERMAN OF LONDON, DECEMBER 12, 1626

IN ENTERING upon the first branch of our first part, that in spiritual things nothing is perfect, we may well afford a kind of spiritual nature to knowledge; and how imperfect is all our knowledge! What one thing do we know perfectly? Whether we consider arts or sciences, the servant knows but according to the proportion of his master's knowledge in that art, and the scholar knows but according to the proportion of his master's knowledge in that science; young men mend not their sight by using old men's spectacles; and yet we look upon nature but with Aristotle's spectacles, and upon the body of man but with Galen's, and upon the frame of the world but with Ptolemy's spectacles.   Almost all knowledge is rather like a child that is embalmed to make mummy than that is nursed to make a man; rather conserved in the stature of the first age than grown to be greater; and if there be any addition to knowledge, it is rather a new knowledge than a greater knowledge; rather a singularity in a desire of proposing something that was not known at all before, than an improving, an advancing, a multiplying, of former inceptions; and by that means, no knowledge comes to be perfect.   One philosopher thinks he has dived to the bottom when he says he knows nothing but this, that he knows nothing; and yet another thinks that he hath expressed more knowledge than he in saying that he knows not so much as that, that he knows nothing. St. Paul found that to be all knowledge, to know Christ; and Mahomet thinks himself wise therefore because he knows not, acknowledges not Christ, as St. Paul does.

.   .   .   .

But when we consider with a religious seriousness the manifold weaknesses of the strongest devotions in time of prayer, it is a sad consideration. I throw myself down in my chamber, and I call in and invite God and his angels thither, and when they are there I neglect God and his angels for the noise of a fly, for the rattling of a coach, for the whining of a door; I talk on, in the same posture of praying, eyes lifted up, knees bowed down, as though I prayed to God; and if God or his angels should ask me when I thought last of God in that prayer, I cannot tell; sometimes I find that I had forgot what I was about, but when I began to forget it I cannot tell. A memory of yesterday's pleasures, a fear of to-morrow's dangers, a straw under my knee, a noise in mine ear, a light in mine eye, an anything, a nothing, a fancy, a chimera in my brain, troubles me in my prayer. So certainly is there nothing, nothing in spiritual things, perfect in this world.

.   .   .   .

I need not call in new philosophy, that denies a settledness, an acquiescence, in the very body of the earth, but makes the earth to move in that place where we thought the sun had moved; I need not that help, that the earth itself is in motion, to prove this, that nothing upon earth is permanent; the assertion will stand of itself till some man assign me some instance, something that a man may rely upon and find permanent. Consider the greatest bodies upon earth, the monarchies, objects which, one would think, destiny might stand and stare at, but not shake; consider the smallest bodies upon earth, the hairs of our head, objects which, one would think, destiny would not observe, or could not discern; and yet destiny (to speak to a natural man), and God (to speak to a Christian), is no more troubled to make a monarchy ruinous than to make a hair gray. Nay, nothing needs be done to either by God or destiny; a monarchy will ruin, as a hair will grow gray, of itself. In the elements themselves, of which all sub-elementary things are composed, there is no acquiescence, but a vicissitudinary transmutation into one another; air condensed becomes water, a more solid body, and air rarefied becomes fire, a body more disputable and inapparent. It is so in the conditions of men, too; a merchant condensed, kneaded, and packed up in a great estate, becomes a lord; and a merchant rarefied, blown up by a perfidious factor or by a riotous son, evaporates into air, into nothing, and is not seen. And if there were anything permanent and durable in this world, yet we get nothing by it, because howsoever that might last in itself, yet we could not last to enjoy it; if our goods were not amongst movables, yet we ourselves are; if they could stay with us, yet we cannot stay with them. . . .

SIR THOMAS BROWNE (1605–1682)

The authorized edition of *Religio Medici* (1643) states that it was composed "about seven years past," that is, when the writer was thirty. It is a private confession or rather declaration of faith, the effort of a young scientist who has been immersed in the currents of continental scepticism and materialism to find secure footing, to harmonize the discoveries of his intellect and his soul. He finds salvation through his mystical temperament rather than his nimble and curious mind, though he regards this latter as a highly critical instrument. It is almost sacrilege to make excerpts from Browne, but anthologists are helpless—as the reader is not.

RELIGIO MEDICI (1643)

THE FIRST PART

FOR my religion, though there be several circumstances that might persuade the world I have none at all, as the general scandal of my profession, the natural course of my studies, the indifference of my behavior and discourse in matters of religion, neither violently defending one, nor with that common ardor and contention opposing another; yet, in despite hereof, I dare without usurpation assume the honorable style of a Christian. Not that I merely owe this title to the font, my education, or the clime wherein I was born, as being bred up either to confirm those principles my parents instilled into my unwary understanding, or by a general consent proceed in the religion of my country; but having in my riper years and confirmed judgment seen and examined all, I find myself obliged by the principles of grace, and the law of mine own reason, to embrace no other name but this. Neither doth herein my zeal so far make me forget the general charity I owe unto humanity, as rather to hate than pity Turks, infidels, and (what is worse) Jews; rather contenting myself to enjoy that happy style, than maligning those who refuse so glorious a title.

But, because the name of a Christian is become too general to express our faith, there being a geography of religions as well as lands, and every clime distinguished not only by their laws and limits, but circumscribed by their doctrines and rules of faith; to be particular, I am of that reformed new-cast religion, wherein I dislike nothing but the name; of the same belief our Savior taught, the Apostles disseminated, the Fathers authorized, and the Martyrs confirmed; but by the sinister ends of princes, the ambition and avarice of prelates, and the fatal corruption of times, so decayed, impaired, and fallen from its native beauty, that it required the careful and charitable hands of these times to restore it to its primitive integrity. Now the accidental occasion whereupon, the slender means whereby, the low and abject condition of the person by whom so good a work was set on foot, which in our adversaries beget contempt and scorn, fills me with wonder, and is the very same objection the insolent pagans first cast at Christ and his disciples.

Yet have I not so shaken hands with those desperate resolutions, who had rather venture at large their decayed bottom, than bring her in to be new trimm'd in the dock; who had rather promiscuously retain all, than abridge any, and obstinately be what they are, than what they have been, as to stand in diameter and sword's point with them. We have reformed from them, not against them; for, omitting those improperations and terms of scurrility betwixt us, which only difference our affections, and not our cause, there is between us one common name and appellation, one faith and necessary body of principles common to us both; and therefore I am not scrupulous to converse and live with them, to enter their churches in defect of ours, and either pray with them, or for them. I could never perceive any rational consequence from those many texts which prohibit the children of Israel to pollute themselves with the temples of the heathens; we being all Christians, and not divided by such detested impieties as might profane our prayers, or the place wherein we make them; or that a resolved conscience may not adore her Creator anywhere, especially in places devoted to his service; where, if their devotions offend him, mine may please him; if theirs profane it, mine may hallow it. Holy-water and crucifix (dangerous to the common people) deceive not my judgment, nor abuse my devotion at all. I am, I confess, naturally inclined to that which misguided zeal terms superstition. My common conversation I do acknowledge austere, my behavior full of rigor, sometimes not without morosity; yet at my devotion I love to use the civility of my knee, my hat, and hand, with all those outward and sensible motions which may express or promote my invisible devotion. I should violate my own arm rather than a church; nor willingly deface the name of saint or martyr. At the sight of a cross or crucifix I can dispense with my hat, but scarce with the thought or memory of my Savior. I cannot laugh at, but rather pity, the fruitless journeys of pilgrims, or contemn the miserable condition of friars; for, though misplaced in circumstances, there is something in it of devotion. I could never hear the Ave-Mary bell without an elevation; or think it a sufficient warrant, because they erred in one circumstance, for me to err in all, that is, in silence and dumb contempt. Whilst, therefore, they directed their devotions to her, I offered mine to God, and rectified the errors of their prayers by rightly ordering mine own. At a solemn procession I have wept abundantly, while my consorts, blind with opposition and prejudice, have fallen into an excess of scorn and laughter. There are, questionless, both in Greek, Roman, and African churches, solemnities and ceremonies, whereof the wiser zeals do make a Christian use, and stand condemned by us, not as evil in themselves, but as allurements and baits of superstition to those vulgar heads that look asquint on the face of truth, and those unstable judgments that cannot consist in the narrow point and center of virtue without a reel or stagger to the circumference.

As there were many reformers, so likewise many reformations; every country proceeding in a particular way and method, according as their national interest, together with their constitution and clime, inclined them; some angrily, and with extremity; others calmly, and with mediocrity, not rending, but easily dividing the community, and leaving an honest possibility of a reconciliation; which though peaceable spirits do desire, and may conceive that revolution of time and the mercies of God may effect, yet that judgment that shall consider the present antipathies between the two extremes, their contrarieties in condition, affection, and opinion, may with the same hopes expect an union in the poles of heaven.

But, to difference myself nearer, and draw into a lesser circle, there is no church whose every part so squares unto my conscience; whose articles, constitutions, and customs seem so consonant unto reason, and as it were framed to my particular devotion, as this whereof I hold my belief, the Church of England; to whose faith I am a sworn subject, and therefore in a double obligation subscribe unto her articles, and endeavor to observe her constitutions. Whatsoever is beyond, as points indifferent, I observe according to the rules of my private reason, or the humor and fashion of my devotion; neither believing this, because Luther affirmed it, or disproving that, because Calvin hath disavouched it. I condemn not all things in the Council of Trent, nor approve all in the Synod of Dort. In brief, where the Scripture is silent, the Church is my text; where that speaks, 'tis but my comment: where there is a joint silence of both, I borrow not the rules of my religion from Rome or Geneva, but the dictates of my own reason. It is an unjust scandal of our adversaries, and a gross error in ourselves, to compute the nativity of our religion from Henry the Eighth, who, though he rejected the Pope, refus'd not the faith of Rome, and effected no more than what his own predecessors desired and assayed in ages past, and was conceived the state of Venice would have attempted in our days. It is as uncharitable a point in us to fall upon those popular scurrilities and opprobrious scoffs of the Bishop of Rome, to whom, as a temporal prince, we owe the duty of good language. I confess there is cause of passion between us: by his sentence I stand excommunicated; *heretic* is the best language he affords me; yet can no ear witness I ever returned him the name of *Antichrist, Man of Sin,* or *Whore of Babylon.* It is the method of charity to suffer without reaction: those usual satires and invectives of the pulpit may perchance produce a good effect on the vulgar, whose ears are opener to rhetoric than logic; yet do they in no wise confirm the faith of wiser believers, who know that a good cause needs not to be patron'd by passion, but can sustain itself upon a temperate dispute.

I could never divide myself from any man upon the difference of an opinion, or be angry with his judgment for not agreeing with me in that from which perhaps within a few days I should dissent myself. I have no genius to disputes in religion, and have often thought it wisdom to decline them, especially upon a disadvantage, or when the cause of truth might suffer in the weakness of my patronage. Where we desire to be informed, 'tis good to contest with men above ourselves; but to confirm and establish our opinions, 'tis best to argue with judgments below our own, that the frequent spoils and victories over their reasons may settle in ourselves an esteem and confirmed opinion of our own. Every man is not a proper champion for truth, nor fit to take up the gauntlet in the cause of verity. Many, from the ignorance of these maxims, and an inconsiderate zeal unto truth, have too rashly charged the troops of error, and remain as trophies unto the enemies of truth. A man may be in as just possession of truth as of a city, and yet be forced to surrender; 'tis therefore far better to enjoy her with peace, than to hazard her on a battle. If, therefore, there rise any doubts in my way, I do forget them, or at least defer them till my better settled judgment and more manly reason be able to resolve them; for I perceive every man's own reason is his best Œdipus, and will, upon a reasonable truce, find a way to loose those bonds wherewith the subtleties of error have enchained our more flexible and tender judgments. In philosophy, where truth seems double-fac'd, there is no man more paradoxical than myself: but in divinity I love to keep the road; and, though not in an implicit, yet an humble faith, follow the great wheel of the Church, by which I move, not reserving any proper poles or motion from the epicycle of my own brain. By this means I leave no gap for heresies, schisms, or errors, of which at present I hope I shall not injure truth to say I have no taint or tincture. I must confess my greener studies have been polluted with two or three; not any begotten in the latter centuries, but old and obsolete, such as could never have been revived, but by such extravagant and irregular heads as mine: for indeed heresies perish not with their authors, but, like the river Arethusa, though they lose their currents in one place, they rise up again in another. One General Council is not able to extirpate one single heresy: it may be cancell'd for the present; but revolution of time, and the like aspects from heaven, will restore it, when it will flourish till it be condemned again. For as though there were a metempsychosis, and the soul of one man passed into another, opinions do find, after certain revolutions, men and minds like those that first begat them.   To see ourselves again, we need not look for Plato's year: every man is not only himself; there hath been many Diogenes, and as many Timons, though but few of that name: men are liv'd over again, the world is now as it was in ages past; there was none then, but there hath been some one since that parallels him, and is, as it were, his revived self.

Now the first of mine was that of the Arabians, that the souls of men perished with their bodies, but should yet be raised again at the last day.   Not that I did absolutely conceive a mortality of the soul; but if that were, which faith, not philosophy, hath yet thoroughly disproved, and that both entered the grave together, yet I held the same conceit thereof that we all do of the body, that it should rise again.   Surely it is but the merits of our unworthy natures, if we sleep in darkness until the last alarum.   A serious reflex upon my own unworthiness did make me backward from challenging this prerogative of my soul: so that I might enjoy my Savior at the last, I could with patience be nothing almost unto eternity.

The second was that of Origen, that God would not persist in his vengeance for ever, but after a definite time of his wrath, he would release the damned souls from torture.   Which error I fell into upon a serious contemplation of the great attribute of God, his mercy; and did a little cherish it in myself, because I found therein no malice, and a ready weight to sway me from the other extreme of despair, whereunto melancholy and contemplative natures are too easily disposed.

A third there is, which I did never positively maintain or practise, but have often wished it had been consonant to truth, and not offensive to my religion, and that is, the prayer for the dead; whereunto I was inclin'd from some charitable inducements, whereby I could scarce contain my prayers for a friend at the ringing of a bell, or behold his corpse without an orison for his soul.   'Twas a good way, methought, to be remembered by posterity, and far more noble than an history.

These opinions I never maintained with pertinacy, or endeavored to inveigle any man's belief unto mine, nor so much as ever revealed or disputed them with my dearest friends; by which means I neither propagated them in others, nor confirmed them in myself; but suffering them to flame upon their own substance, without addition of new fuel, they went out insensibly of themselves. Therefore these opinions, though condemned by lawful Councils, were not heresies in me, but bare errors, and single lapses of my understanding, without a joint depravity of my will. Those have not only depraved understandings, but diseased affections, which cannot enjoy a singularity without an heresy, or be the author of an opinion without they be of a sect also. This was the villainy of the first schism of Lucifer, who was not content to err alone, but drew into his faction many legions of spirits; and upon this experience he tempted only Eve, as well understanding the communicable nature of sin, and that to deceive but one was tacitly and upon consequence to delude them both.

That heresies should arise, we have the prophecy of Christ; but that old ones should be abolished, we hold no prediction. That there must be heresies, is true, not only in our Church, but also in any other: even in doctrines heretical, there will be super-heresies; and Arians not only divided from their Church, but also among themselves. For heads that are disposed unto schism and complexionally propense to innovation, are naturally indisposed for a community, nor will be ever confined unto the order or economy of one body; and, therefore, when they separate from others, they knit but loosely among themselves; nor contented with a general breach or dichotomy with their church do subdivide and mince themselves almost into atoms. 'Tis true, that men of singular parts and humors have not been free from singular opinions and conceits in all ages; retaining something, not only beside the opinion of his own church or any other, but also any particular author; which, notwithstanding, a sober judgment may do without offence or heresy; for there is yet, after all the decrees of Councils and the niceties of the schools, many things untouch'd, unimagin'd, wherein the liberty of an honest reason may play and expatiate with security, and far without the circle of an heresy.

As for those wingy mysteries in divinity, and airy subtleties in religion, which have unhing'd the brains of better heads, they never stretched the *pia mater* of mine. Methinks there be not impossibilities enough in religion for an active faith; the deepest mysteries ours contains have not only been illustrated, but maintained, by syllogism and the rule of reason. I love to lose myself in a mystery, to pursue my reason to an *O altitudo!* 'Tis my solitary recreation to pose my apprehension with those involved enigmas and riddles of the Trinity, with incarnation, and resurrection. I can answer all the objections of Satan and my rebellious reason with that odd resolution I learned of Tertullian, *Certum est, quia impossibile est.*[1] I desire to exercise my faith in the difficultest point; for to credit ordinary and visible objects is not faith, but persuasion. Some believe the better for seeing Christ's sepulchre; and, when they have seen the Red Sea, doubt not of the miracle. Now, contrarily, I bless myself and am thankful that I lived not in the days of miracles, that I never saw Christ nor his disciples. I would not have been one of those Israelites that pass'd the Red Sea, nor one of Christ's patients on whom he wrought his wonders; then had my faith been thrust upon me, nor should I enjoy that greater blessing pronounced to all that believe and saw not. 'Tis an easy and necessary belief, to credit what our eye and sense hath examined. I believe he was dead, and buried, and rose again; and desire to see him in his glory, rather than to contemplate him in his cenotaph or sepulchre. Nor is this much to believe; as we have reason, we owe this faith unto history; they only had the advantage of a bold and noble faith, who lived before his coming, who upon obscure prophecies and mystical types could raise a belief, and expect apparent impossibilities.

'Tis true, there is an edge in all firm belief, and with an easy metaphor we may say, the sword of faith; but in these obscurities I rather use it in the adjunct the Apostle gives it, a buckler; under which I conceive a wary combatant may lie invulnerable. Since I was of understanding to know we knew nothing, my reason hath been more pliable to the will of faith; I am now content to understand a mystery without a rigid definition, in an easy and Platonic description. That allegorical description of Hermes pleaseth me beyond all the metaphysical definitions of divines. Where I cannot satisfy my reason, I love to humor my fancy: I had as lief you tell me that *anima est angelus hominis, est corpus Dei,* as *Entelechia;—Lux est umbra Dei,* as *actus*

---

[1] It is certain, because impossible.

perspicui.[1] Where there is an obscurity too deep for our reason,
'tis good to sit down with a description, periphrasis, or adum-
bration; for by acquainting our reason how unable it is to display the visible and obvious effects of nature, it becomes more
humble and submissive unto the subtleties of faith; and thus I
teach my haggard and unreclaimed reason to stoop unto the
lure of faith. I believe there was already a tree whose fruit our
unhappy parents tasted, though, in the same chapter when God
forbids it, 'tis positively said, the plants of the field were not
yet grown, *for* God *had not caus'd it to rain upon the earth.* I
believe that the serpent, (if we shall literally understand it),
from his proper form and figure, made his motion on his belly
before the curse. I find the trial of the pucellage and virginity
of women, which God ordained the Jews, is very fallible.
Experience and history informs me, that not only many particular women, but likewise whole nations, have escaped the curse
of childbirth, which God seems to pronounce upon the whole
sex. Yet do I believe that all this is true, which indeed my
reason would persuade me to be false; and this I think is no
vulgar part of faith, to believe a thing not only above but contrary to reason, and against the arguments of our proper senses.
  In my solitary and retired imagination

> (*neque enim cum porticus aut me*
> *Lectulus accepit, desum mihi,*)[2]

I remember I am not alone, and therefore forget not to contemplate him and his attributes who is ever with me, especially
those two mighty ones, his wisdom and eternity. With the
one I recreate, with the other I confound, my understanding; for
who can speak of eternity without a solecism, or think thereof
without an ecstasy? Time we may comprehend; 'tis but five
days elder than ourselves, and hath the same horoscope with the
world; but to retire so far back as to apprehend a beginning, to
give such an infinite start forwards as to conceive an end, in an
essence that we affirm hath neither the one nor the other, it puts

---

[1] A brief paraphrase may serve here better than translation: "I had as lief
you tell me that the soul is an intelligence that moves man, is the body of
God, as that it is the actual being, that which naturally makes the body move;
that light is the shadow of God, as that it is energy of illumination."

[2] For neither when I am in the colonnade nor in bed do I fail myself.

my reason to St. Paul's sanctuary. My philosophy dares not say the angels can do it. God hath not made a creature that can comprehend him; 'tis a privilege of his own nature. *I am that I am*, was his own definition unto Moses; and 'twas a short one, to confound mortality, that durst question God, or ask him what he was. Indeed, he only is; all others have and shall be. But in eternity there is no distinction of tenses; and therefore that terrible term *predestination*, which hath troubled so many weak heads to conceive, and the wisest to explain, is in respect to God no prescious determination of our estates to come, but a definitive blast of his will already fulfilled, and at the instant that he first decreed it; for to his eternity, which is indivisible and all together, the last trump is already sounded, the reprobates in the flame, and the blessed in Abraham's bosom. St. Peter speaks modestly, when he saith, *a thousand years to* God *are but as one day*; for, to speak like a philosopher, those continued instances of time which flow into a thousand years, make not to him one moment: what to us is to come, to his eternity is present, his whole duration being but one permanent point, without succession, parts, flux, or division.

There is no attribute that adds more difficulty to the mystery of the Trinity, where, though in a relative way of Father and Son, we must deny a priority. I wonder how Aristotle could conceive the world eternal, or how he could make good two eternities. His similitude of a triangle comprehended in a square doth somewhat illustrate the trinity of our souls, and that the triple unity of God; for there is in us not three, but a trinity of souls; because there is in us, if not three distinct souls, yet differing faculties, that can and do subsist apart in different subjects, and yet in us are so united as to make but one soul and substance. If one soul were so perfect as to inform three distinct bodies, that were a petty trinity: conceive the distinct number of three, not divided nor separated by the intellect, but actually comprehended in its unity, and that is a perfect trinity. I have often admired the mystical way of Pythagoras, and the secret magic of numbers. *Beware of philosophy* is a precept not to be received in too large a sense; for in this mass of nature there is a set of things that carry in their front, though not in capital letters, yet in stenography and short characters, something of divinity, which to wiser reasons serve as luminaries in the abyss of knowledge, and to judicious beliefs as scales and roundles to mount the pinnacles and highest pieces of divinity. The severe schools shall never laugh me out of the philosophy of Hermes, that this visible world is but a picture of the invisible, wherein, as in a portrait, things are not truly, but in equivocal shapes, and as they counterfeit some more real substance in that invisible fabric.

That other attribute wherewith I recreate my devotion, is his wisdom, in which I am happy; and for the contemplation of this only, do not repent me that I was bred in the way of study: the advantage I have of the vulgar, with the content and happiness I conceive therein, is an ample recompense for all my endeavors, in what part of knowledge soever. Wisdom is his most beauteous attribute; no man can attain unto it, yet Solomon pleased God when he desired it. He is wise, because he knows all things; and he knoweth all things, because he made them all: but his greatest knowledge is in comprehending that he made not, that is, himself. And this is also the greatest knowledge in man. For this do I honor my own profession, and embrace the counsel even of the devil himself: had he read such a lecture in paradise as he did at Delphos, we had better known ourselves, nor had we stood in fear to know him. I know he is wise in all, wonderful in what we conceive, but far more in what we comprehend not; for we behold him but asquint, upon reflex or shadow; our understanding is dimmer than Moses' eye; we are ignorant of the back-parts or lower side of his divinity; therefore to pry into the maze of his counsels is not only folly in man, but presumption even in angels. Like us, they are his servants, not his senators; he holds no counsel, but that mystical one of the Trinity, wherein, though there be three persons, there is but one mind that decrees without contradiction. Nor needs he any: his actions are not begot with deliberation, his wisdom naturally knows what's best; his intellect stands ready fraught with the superlative and purest ideas of goodness; consultation and election, which are two motions in us, make but one in him, his actions springing from his power at the first touch of his will. These are contemplations metaphysical: my humble speculations have another method, and are content to trace and discover those expressions he hath left in his creatures, and the obvious effects of nature. There is no danger to profound these mysteries, no *sanctum sanctorum* in philosophy. The world was made to be inhabited by beasts, but studied and contemplated by man: 'tis the debt of our reason we owe unto God, and the homage we pay for not being beasts. Without this, the world is still as though it had not been, or as it was before the sixth day, when as yet there was not a creature that could conceive or say there was a world. The wisdom of God receives small honor from those vulgar heads that rudely stare about, and with a gross rusticity admire his works: those highly magnify him, whose judicious inquiry into his acts, and deliberate research into his creatures, return the duty of a devout and learned admiration. Therefore,

> Search while thou wilt, and let thy reason go,
> To ransom truth, even to th' abyss below;
> Rally the scattered causes; and that line,
> Which nature twists, be able to untwine.
> It is thy Maker's will, for unto none
> But unto reason can he e'er be known.
> The devils do know thee, but those damn'd meteors
> Build not thy glory, but confound thy creatures.
> Teach my endeavors so thy works to read,
> That learning them in thee, I may proceed.
> Give thou my reason that instructive flight,
> Whose weary wings may on thy hands still light.
> Teach me to soar aloft, yet ever so
> When near the sun, to stoop again below.
> Thus shall my humble feathers safely hover,
> And, though near earth, more than the heavens discover.
> And then at last, when homeward I shall drive,
> Rich with the spoils of nature, to my hive,
> There will I sit like that industrious fly,
> Buzzing thy praises, which shall never die,
> Till death abrupts them, and succeeding glory
> Bid me go on in a more lasting story.

And this is almost all wherein an humble creature may endeavor to requite and some way to retribute unto his Creator: for if *not he that saith, "Lord, Lord," but he that doth the will of his Father, shall be saved;* certainly our wills must be our performances, and our intents make out our actions; otherwise our pious labors shall find anxiety in our graves, and our best endeavors not hope, but fear, a resurrection.

There is but one first cause, and four second causes of all things. Some are without efficient, as God; others without matter, as angels; some without form, as the first matter: but every essence, created or uncreated, hath its final cause, and some positive end both of its essence and operation. This is the cause I grope after in the works of nature; on this hangs the providence of God. To raise so beauteous a structure as the world and the creatures thereof, was but his art; but their sundry and divided operations, with their predestinated ends, are from the treasure of his wisdom. In the causes, nature, and affections of the eclipses of the sun and moon, there is most excellent speculation; but to profound farther, and to contemplate a reason why his providence hath so disposed and ordered their motions in that vast circle as to conjoin and obscure each other, is a sweeter piece of reason, and a diviner point of philosophy. Therefore sometimes, and in some things, there appears to me as much divinity in Galen his books *De Usu Partium*, as in Suarez' metaphysics. Had Aristotle been as curious in the inquiry of this cause as he was of the other, he had not left behind him an imperfect piece of philosophy, but an absolute tract of divinity.

Natura nihil agit frustra,[1] is the only indisputed axiom in philosophy. There are no grotesques in nature; not anything framed to fill up empty cantons, and unnecessary spaces. In the most imperfect creatures, and such as were not preserved in the ark, but, having their seeds and principles in the womb of nature, are everywhere, where the power of the sun is, in these is the wisdom of his hand discovered. Out of this rank Solomon chose the object of his admiration. Indeed, what reason may not go to school to the wisdom of bees, ants, and spiders? What wise hand teacheth them to do what reason cannot teach us? Ruder heads stand amazed at those prodigious pieces of nature, whales, elephants, dromedaries and camels; these, I confess, are the Colossus and majestic pieces of her hand: but in these narrow engines there is more curious mathematics; and

---

[1]Nature does nothing in vain.

the civility of these little citizens more neatly sets forth the wisdom of their Maker. Who admires not Regio-Montanus his fly beyond his eagle, or wonders not more at the operation of two souls in those little bodies, than but one in the trunk of a cedar? I could never content my contemplation with those general pieces of wonder, the flux and reflux of the sea, the increase of Nile, the conversion of the needle to the north; and have studied to match and parallel those in the more obvious and neglected pieces of nature, which without further travel I can do in the cosmography of myself. We carry with us the wonders we seek without us: there is all Africa and her prodigies in us; we are that bold and adventurous piece of nature, which he that studies wisely learns in a compendium what others labor at in a divided piece and endless volume.

Thus there are two books from whence I collect my divinity; besides that written one of God, another of his servant nature, that universal and public manuscript, that lies expans'd unto the eyes of all: those that never saw him in the one, have discover'd him in the other. This was the scripture and theology of the heathens: the natural motion of the sun made them more admire him than its supernatural station did the children of Israel; the ordinary effects of nature wrought more admiration in them than in the other all his miracles. Surely the heathens knew better how to join and read these mystical letters than we Christians, who cast a more careless eye on these common hieroglyphics, and disdain to suck divinity from the flowers of nature. Nor do I so forget God as to adore the name of nature; which I define not, with the schools, to be the principle of motion and rest, but that straight and regular line, that settled and constant course the wisdom of God hath ordained the actions of his creatures, according to their several kinds. To make a revolution every day is the nature of the sun, because of that necessary course which God hath ordained it, from which it cannot swerve but by a faculty from that voice which first did give it motion. Now this course of nature God seldom alters or perverts, but, like an excellent artist, hath so contrived his work, that with the self same instrument, without a new creation, he may effect his obscurest designs. Thus he sweeteneth the water with a wood, preserveth the creatures in the ark, which the blast of his mouth might have as easily created; for God is like a skilful geometrician, who, when more easily and with one stroke of his compass he might describe or divide a right line, had yet rather do this in a circle or longer way, according to the constituted and fore-laid principles of his art. Yet this rule of his he doth sometimes pervert, to acquaint the world with his prerogative, lest the arrogancy of our reason should question his power, and conclude he could not. And thus I call the effects of nature the works of God, whose hand and instrument she only is; and therefore to ascribe his actions unto her, is to devolve the honor of the principal agent upon the instrument; which if with reason we may do, then let our hammers rise up and boast they have built our houses, and our pens receive the honor of our writings. I hold there is a general beauty in the works of God, and therefore no deformity in any kind or species of creature whatsoever. I cannot tell by what logic we call a toad, a bear, or an elephant ugly; they being created in those outward shapes and figures which best express the actions of their inward forms, and having past that general visitation of God, who saw that all that he had made was good, that is, conformable to his will, which abhors deformity, and is the rule of order and beauty. There is no deformity but in monstrosity; wherein, notwithstanding, there is a kind of beauty; nature so ingeniously contriving the irregular parts, as they become sometimes more remarkable than the principal fabric. To speak yet more narrowly, there was never anything ugly or mis-shapen, but the chaos; wherein, notwithstanding, to speak strictly, there was no deformity, because no form; nor was it yet impregnate by the voice of God. Now nature is not at variance with art, nor art with nature, they being both servants of his providence. Art is the perfection of nature. Were the world now as it was the sixth day, there were yet a chaos. Nature hath made one world, and art another. In brief, all things are artificial; for nature is the art of God.

.   .   .   .

That miracles are ceased, I can neither prove, nor absolutely deny, much less define the time and period of their cessation. That they survived Christ, is manifest upon the record of Scripture; that they outlived the Apostles also, and were revived at the conversion of nations many years after, we cannot deny, if we shall not question those writers whose testimonies we do not controvert in points that make for our own opinions. Therefore that may have some truth in it that is reported by the Jesuits of their miracles in the Indies; I could wish it were true, or had any other testimony than their own pens. They may easily believe those miracles abroad, who daily conceive a greater at home, the transmutation of those visible elements into the body and blood of our Savior. For the conversion of water into wine, which he wrought in Cana, or, what the devil would have had him done in the wilderness, of stones into bread, compared to this, will scarce deserve the name of a miracle: though indeed, to speak properly, there is not one miracle greater than another, they being the extraordinary effects of the hand of God, to which all things are of an equal facility; and to create the world, as easy as one single creature. For this is also a miracle, not only to produce effects against or above nature, but before nature; and to create nature, as great a miracle as to contradict or transcend her. We do too narrowly define the power of God, restraining it to our capacities. I hold that God can do all things; how he should work contradictions, I do not understand, yet dare not therefore deny. I cannot see why the angel of God should question Esdras to recall the time past, if it were beyond his own power; or that God should pose mortality in that which he was not able to perform himself. I will not say God cannot, but he will not, perform many things, which we plainly affirm he cannot. This I am sure, is the mannerliest proposition, wherein, notwithstanding, I hold no paradox; for, strictly, his power is the same with his will, and they both, with all the rest, do make but one God.

Therefore that miracles have been, I do believe; that they may yet be wrought by the living, I do not deny; but have no confidence in those which are fathered on the dead. And this hath ever made me suspect the efficacy of relics, to examine the bones, question the habits and appurtenances of saints, and even of Christ himself. I cannot conceive why the cross that Helena found, and whereon Christ himself died, should have power to restore others unto life. I excuse not Constantine from a fall off his horse, or a mischief from his enemies, upon the wearing those nails on his bridle, which our Savior bore upon the cross in his hands.   I compute among your *piæ fraudes*,[1] nor many degrees before consecrated swords and roses, that which Baldwin, King of Jerusalem, returned the Genovese for their cost and pains in his war, to wit, the ashes of John the Baptist. Those that hold the sanctity of their souls doth leave behind a tincture and sacred faculty on their bodies, speak naturally of miracles, and do not salve the doubt.   Now one reason I tender so little devotion unto relics, is, I think, the slender and doubtful respect I have always held unto antiquities.   For that indeed which I admire, is far before antiquity, that is, eternity; and that is, God himself; who, though he be styled *the Ancient of Days*, cannot receive the adjunct of antiquity; who was before the world, and shall be after it, yet is not older than it; for in his years there is no climacter; his duration is eternity, and far more venerable than antiquity.

But above all things I wonder how the curiosity of wiser heads could pass that great and indisputable miracle, the cessation of oracles; and in what swoon their reasons lay, to content themselves and sit down with such a far-fetch'd and ridiculous reason as Plutarch allegeth for it.   The Jews, that can believe the supernatural solstice of the sun in the days of Joshua, have yet the impudence to deny the eclipse which every pagan confessed, at his death: but for this, it is evident beyond all contradiction, the devil himself confessed it.   Certainly it is not a warrantable curiosity, to examine the verity of Scripture by the concordance of human history, or seek to confirm the chronicle of Hester or Daniel, by the authority of Megasthenes or Herodotus.   I confess, I have had an unhappy curiosity this way, till I laughed myself out of it with a piece of Justin, where he delivers that the children of Israel for being scabbed were banished out of Egypt.   And truly since I have understood the occurrences of the world, and know in what counterfeit shapes and deceitful vizards times present represent on the stage things past, I do believe them little more than things to come.   Some have been of my opinion, and endeavored to write the history of their own lives; wherein Moses hath outgone them all, and left not only the story of his life, but as some will have it, of his death also.

It is a riddle to me, how this story of oracles hath not worm'd

---

[1]Pious frauds.

out of the world that doubtful conceit of spirits and witches; how so many learned heads should so far forget their metaphysics, and destroy the ladder and scale of creatures, as to question the existence of spirits. For my part, I have ever believed and do now know, that there are witches:[1] they that doubt of these, do not only deny them, but spirits; and are obliquely and upon consequence a sort not of infidels, but atheists. Those that to confute their incredulity desire to see apparitions, shall questionless never behold any, nor have the power to be so much as witches; the devil hath them already in a heresy as capital as witchcraft; and to appear to them, were but to convert them. Of all the delusions wherewith he deceives mortality, there is not any that puzzleth me more than the legerdemain of changelings. I do not credit those transformations of reasonable creatures into beasts, or that the devil hath a power to transpeciate a man into a horse, who tempted Christ (as a trial of his divinity) to convert but stones into bread. I could believe that spirits use with man the act of carnality, and that in both sexes; I conceive they may assume, steal, or contrive a body, wherein there may be action enough to content decrepit lust, or passion to satisfy more active veneries; yet, in both, without a possibility of generation: and therefore that opinion that Antichrist should be born of the tribe of Dan by conjunction with the devil, is ridiculous, and a conceit fitter for a Rabbin than a Christian. I hold that the devil doth really possess some men, the spirit of melancholy others, the spirit of delusion others; that, as the devil is concealed and denied by some, so God and good angels are pretended by others, whereof the late defection of the Maid of Germany hath left a pregnant example.

Again, I believe that all that use sorceries, incantations, and spells, are not witches, or, as we term them, magicians. I conceive there is a traditional magic, not learned immediately from the devil, but at second hand from his scholars, who, having once the secret betrayed, are able, and do empirically practise without his advice, they both proceeding upon the principles of nature; where actives, aptly conjoined to disposed passives, will under any master produce their effects. Thus I

---

[1]The reader may be referred to Howell's opinion of witches (p. 598), and Howell was not wont to lose himself in an *O altitudo.*

think at first a great part of philosophy was witchcraft; which, being afterward derived to one another, proved but philosophy, and was indeed no more but the honest effects of nature: what, invented by us, is philosophy, learned from him, is magic. We do surely owe the discovery of many secrets to the discovery of good and bad angels. I could never pass that sentence of Paracelsus without an asterisk or annotation; *Ascendens constellatum multa revelat quærentibus magnalia naturæ*, (i.e. *opera Dei*.)[1] I do think that many mysteries ascribed to our own inventions have been the courteous revelations of spirits; for those noble essences in heaven bear a friendly regard unto their fellow natures on earth; and therefore believe that those many prodigies and ominous prognostics, which fore-run the ruins of states, princes, and private persons, are the charitable premonitions of good angels, which more careless inquiries term but the effects of chance and nature.

Now, besides these particular and divided spirits, there may be (for aught I know) an universal and common spirit to the whole world. It was the opinion of Plato, and it is yet of the Hermetical philosophers. If there be a common nature that unites and ties the scattered and divided individuals into one species, why may there not be one that unites them all? However, I am sure there is a common spirit that plays within us, yet makes no part of us; and that is, the spirit of God, the fire and scintillation of that noble and mighty essence, which is the life and radical heat of spirits, and those essences that know not the virtue of the sun; a fire quite contrary to the fire of hell. This is that gentle heat that brooded on the waters, and in six days hatched the world; this is that irradiation that dispels the mists of hell, the clouds of horror, fear, sorrow, despair; and preserves the region of the mind in serenity. Whosoever feels not the warm gale and gentle ventilation of this spirit, though I feel his pulse, I dare not say he lives: for truly, without this, to me there is no heat under the tropic; nor any light, though I dwelt in the body of the sun.

> As, when the laboring sun hath wrought his track
> Up to the top of lofty Cancer's back,

[1] The stars rising into view reveal much to those who are searching the great things of nature (that is, the works of God).

The icy ocean cracks, the frozen pole
Thaws with the heat of the celestial coal;
So, when thy absent beams begin t' impart
Again a solstice on my frozen heart,
My winter's ov'r, my drooping spirits sing,
And every part revives into a spring.
But if thy quickening beams a while decline,
And with their light bless not this orb of mine,
A chilly frost surpriseth every member,
And in the midst of June I feel December.
O how this earthly temper doth debase
The noble soul, in this her humble place;
Whose wingy nature ever doth aspire
To reach that place whence first it took its fire.
These flames I feel, which in my heart do dwell,
Are not thy beams, but take their fire from hell:
O quench them all, and let thy light divine
Be as the sun to this poor orb of mine;
And to thy sacred spirit convert those fires,
Whose earthly fumes choke my devout aspires.

Therefore for spirits, I am so far from denying their existence, that I could easily believe, that not only whole countries, but particular persons, have their tutelary and guardian angels. It is not a new opinion of the Church of Rome, but an old one of Pythagoras and Plato; there is no heresy in it; and if not manifestly defin'd in Scripture, yet is it an opinion of a good and wholesome use in the course and actions of a man's life, and would serve as an hypothesis to salve many doubts, whereof common philosophy affordeth no solution. Now, if you demand my opinion and metaphysics of their natures, I confess them very shallow; most of them in a negative way, like that of God; or in a comparative, between ourselves and fellow-creatures; for there is in this universe a stair, or manifest scale of creatures, rising not disorderly, or in confusion, but with a comely method and proportion. Between creatures of mere existence and things of life, there is a large disproportion of nature; between plants, and animals or creatures of sense, a wider difference; between them and man, a far greater: and if the proportion hold on, between man and angels there should be yet a greater. We do not comprehend their natures, who retain the first definition of Porphyry, and distinguish them from ourselves by immortality; for before his fall, 'tis thought, man also was immortal; yet must we needs affirm that he had a different essence from the angels. Having therefore no certain knowledge of their natures, 'tis no bad method of the schools, whatsoever perfection we find obscurely in ourselves, in a more complete and absolute way to ascribe unto them. I believe they have an extemporary knowledge, and upon the first motion of their reason do what we cannot without study or deliberation; that they know things by their forms, and define by specifical difference what we describe by accidents and properties; and therefore probabilities to us may be demonstrations unto them: that they have knowledge not only of the specifical, but numerical forms of individuals, and understand by what reserved difference each single hypostasis (besides the relation to its species,) becomes its numerical self: that, as the soul hath a power to move the body it informs, so there's a faculty to move any, though inform none: ours upon restraint of time, place, and distance; but that invisible hand that conveyed Habakkuk to the lion's den, or Philip to Azotus, infringeth this rule, and hath a secret conveyance, wherewith mortality is not acquainted. If they have that intuitive knowledge, whereby as in reflection they behold the thoughts of one another, I cannot peremptorily deny but they know a great part of ours. They that, to refute the invocation of saints, have denied that they have any knowledge of our affairs below, have proceeded too far, and must pardon my opinion till I can thoroughly answer that piece of Scripture, *At the conversion of a sinner the angels in heaven rejoice.* I cannot, with those in that great Father, securely interpret the work of the first day, *Fiat lux*, to the creation of angels; though I confess, there is not any creature that hath so near a glimpse of their nature as light in the sun and elements. We style it a bare accident; but, where it subsists alone, 'tis a spiritual substance, and may be an angel: in brief, conceive light invisible, and that is a spirit.

These are certainly the magisterial and masterpieces of the Creator, the flower, or (as we may say) the best part of nothing; actually existing, what we are but in hopes and probability. We are only that amphibious piece between a corporal and spiritual essence, that middle form that links those two together, and makes good the method of God and nature, that jumps not from extremes, but unites the incompatible distances by some middle and participating natures. That we are the breath and similitude of God, it is indisputable, and upon record of Holy Scripture; but to call ourselves a microcosm, or little world, I thought it only a pleasant trope of rhetoric, till my near judgment and second thoughts told me there was a real truth therein. For first we are a rude mass, and in the rank of creatures which only are, and have a dull kind of being, not yet privileged with life, or preferred to sense or reason; next we live the life of plants, the life of animals, the life of men, and at last the life of spirits, running on in one mysterious nature those five kinds of existences, which comprehend the creatures, not only of the world, but of the universe. Thus is man that great and true *amphibium*, whose nature is disposed to live, not only like other creatures in divers elements, but in divided and distinguished worlds: for though there be but one to sense, there are two to reason, the one visible, the other invisible; whereof Moses seems to have left description, and of the other so obscurely, that some parts thereof are yet in controversy. And truly, for the first chapters of *Genesis*, I must confess a great deal of obscurity; though divines have to the power of human reason endeavored to make all go in a literal meaning, yet those allegorical interpretations are also probable, and perhaps the mystical method of Moses bred up in the hieroglyphical schools of the Egyptians.

Now for that immaterial world, methinks we need not wander so far as beyond the first movable; for even in this material fabric the spirits walk as freely exempt from the affection of time, place, and motion, as beyond the extremest circumference. Do but extract from the corpulency of bodies, or resolve things beyond their first matter, and you discover the habitation of angels, which if I call the ubiquitary and omnipresent essence of God, I hope I shall not offend divinity: for before the creation of the world God was really all things. For the angels he created no new world, or determinate mansion, and therefore they are everywhere where is his essence, and do live at a distance even in himself. That God made all things for man, is in some sense true, yet not so far as to subordinate the creation of those purer creatures unto ours, though as ministering spirits they do, and are willing to fulfil the will of God in these lower and sublunary affairs of man. God made all things for himself, and it is impossible he should make them for any other end than his own glory; it is all he can receive, and all that is without himself. For, honor being an external adjunct, and in the honorer rather than in the person honored, it was necessary to make a creature, from whom he might receive this homage; and that is, in the other world, angels, in this, man; which when we neglect, we forget the very end of our creation, and may justly provoke God, not only to repent that he hath made the world, but that he hath sworn he would not destroy it. That there is but one world, is a conclusion of faith: Aristotle with all his philosophy hath not been able to prove it, and as weakly that the world was eternal. That dispute much troubled the pen of the ancient philosophers, but Moses decided that question, and all is salved with the new term of a creation, that is, a production of something out of nothing. And what is that? Whatsoever is opposite to something; or more exactly, that which is truly contrary unto God: for he only is, all others have an existence with dependency, and are something but by a distinction. And herein is divinity conformant unto philosophy, and generation not only founded on contrarieties, but also creation; God, being all things, is contrary unto nothing, out of which were made all things, and so nothing became something, and omneity informed nullity into an essence.

The whole creation is a mystery, and particularly that of man. At the blast of his mouth were the rest of the creatures made, and at his bare word they started out of nothing: but in the frame of man (as the text describes it) he played the sensible operator, and seemed not so much to create, as make him. When he had separated the materials of other creatures, there consequently resulted a form and soul; but, having raised the walls of man, he was driven to a second and harder creation of a substance like himself, an incorruptible and immortal soul. For these two affections we have the philosophy and opinion of the heathens, the flat affirmative of Plato, and not a negative from Aristotle. There is another scruple cast in by divinity concerning its production, much disputed in the German auditories, and with that indifferency and equality of arguments, as leave the controversy undetermined. I am not of Paracelsus' mind, that boldly delivers a receipt to make a man without

conjunction; yet cannot but wonder at the multitude of heads
that do deny traduction, having no other argument to confirm
their belief than that rhetorical sentence and *antimetathesis* of
Augustine, *Creando infunditur, infundendo creatur*.[1] Either
opinion will consist well enough with religion: yet I should rather
incline to this, did not one objection haunt me, not wrung from
speculations and subtleties, but from common sense and observation; not picked from the leaves of any author, but bred amongst
the weeds and tares of mine own brain; and this is a conclusion
from the equivocal and monstrous productions in the copulation of man with beast: for if the soul of man be not transmitted
and transfused in the seed of the parents, why are not those
productions merely beasts, but have also an impression and
tincture of reason in as high a measure as it can evidence itself
in those improper organs? Nor, truly, can I peremptorily
deny that the soul, in this her sublunary estate, is wholly and in
all acceptions inorganical; but that for the performance of her
ordinary actions there is required not only a symmetry and
proper disposition of organs, but a crasis and temper correspondent to its operations; yet is not this mass of flesh and visible
structure the instrument and proper corpse of the soul, but
rather of sense, and that the hand of reason. In our study of
anatomy there is a mass of mysterious philosophy, and such as
reduced the very heathens to divinity; yet, amongst all those
rare discoveries and curious pieces I find in the fabric of man, I
do not so much content myself, as in that I find not, there is no
organ or instrument for the rational soul; for in the brain, which
we term the seat of reason, there is not anything of moment
more than I can discover in the crany of a beast: and this is a
sensible and no inconsiderable argument of the inorganity of
the soul, at least in that sense we usually so receive it. Thus
we are men, and we know not how: there is something in us
that can be without us, and will be after us; though it is strange
that it hath no history what it was before us, nor cannot tell
how it entered in us.

Now, for these walls of flesh, wherein the soul doth seem to be
immured before the resurrection, it is nothing but an elemental
composition, and a fabric that must fall to ashes. *All flesh is*

---

[1] The soul is infused at creation, and in infusion is created.

grass, is not only metaphorically, but literally, true; for all those creatures we behold are but the herbs of the field, digested into flesh in them, or more remotely carnified in ourselves. Nay further, we are what we all abhor, *Anthropophagi* and cannibals, devourers not only of men, but of ourselves; and that not in an allegory, but a positive truth; for all this mass of flesh which we behold, came in at our mouths; this frame we look upon, hath been upon our trenchers; in brief, we have devour'd ourselves. I cannot believe the wisdom of Pythagoras did ever positively, and in a literal sense, affirm his metempsychosis, or impossible transmigration of the souls of men into beasts. Of all metamorphoses or transmigrations, I believe only one, that is of Lot's wife; for that of Nebuchodonosor proceeded not so far; in all others I conceive there is no further verity than is contained in their implicit sense and morality. I believe that the whole frame of a beast doth perish, and is left in the same state after death as before it was materialed unto life: that the souls of men know neither contrary nor corruption; that they subsist beyond the body, and outlive death by the privilege of their proper natures, and without a miracle; that the souls of the faithful, as they leave earth, take possession of heaven: that those apparitions and ghosts of departed persons are not the wandering souls of men, but the unquiet walks of devils, prompting and suggesting us unto mischief, blood, and villainy; instilling and stealing into our hearts that the blessed spirits are not at rest in their graves, but wander solicitous of the affairs of the world. But that those phantasms appear often, and do frequent cemeteries, charnel-houses, and churches, it is because those are the dormitories of the dead, where the devil, like an insolent champion, beholds with pride the spoils and trophies of his victory over Adam.

This is that dismal conquest we all deplore, that makes us so often cry, *O Adam, quid fecisti?*[1] I thank God I have not those strait ligaments, or narrow obligations to the world, as to dote on life, or be convulsed and tremble at the name of death. Not that I am insensible of the dread and horror thereof; or by raking into the bowels of the deceased, continual sight of anatomies, skeletons, or cadaverous relics, like vespilloes, or grave-makers,

---

[1] O thou Adam, what hast thou done?

I am become stupid, or have forgot the apprehension of mortality; but that, marshalling all the horrors, and contemplating the extremities thereof, I find not anything therein able to daunt the courage of a man, much less a well-resolved Christian; and therefore am not angry at the error of our first parents, or unwilling to bear a part of this common fate, and like the best of them to die, that is, to cease to breathe, to take a farewell of the elements, to be a kind of nothing for a moment, to be within one instant of a spirit. When I take a full view and circle of myself without this reasonable moderator, and equal piece of justice, death, I do conceive myself the miserablest person extant. Were there not another life that I hope for, all the vanities of this world should not entreat a moment's breath from me: could the devil work my belief to imagine I could never die, I would not outlive that very thought. I have so abject a conceit of this common way of existence, this retaining to the sun and elements, I cannot think this is to be a man, or to live according to the dignity of humanity. In expectation of a better, I can with patience embrace this life, yet in my best meditations do often defy death; I honor any man that contemns it, nor can I highly love any that is afraid of it: this makes me naturally love a soldier, and honor those tattered and contemptible regiments that will die at the command of a sergeant. For a pagan there may be some motives to be in love with life; but for a Christian to be amazed at death, I see not how he can escape this dilemma, that he is too sensible of this life, or hopeless of the life to come.

Some divines count Adam thirty years old at his creation, because they suppose him created in the perfect age and stature of man. And surely we are all out of the computation of our age, and every man is some months elder than he bethinks him; for we live, move, have a being, and are subject to the actions of the elements, and the malice of diseases, in that other world, the truest microcosm, the womb of our mother. For besides that general and common existence we are conceived to hold in our chaos, and whilst we sleep within the bosom of our causes, we enjoy a being and life in three distinct worlds, wherein we receive most manifest graduations. In that obscure world and womb of our mother, our time is short, computed by the moon, yet longer than the days of many creatures that behold the sun;

ourselves being not yet without life, sense, and reason; though for the manifestation of its actions, it awaits the opportunity of objects, and seems to live there but in its root and soul ·of vegetation. Entering afterwards upon the scene of the world, we arise up and become another creature, performing the reasonable actions of man, and obscurely manifesting that part of divinity in us; but not in complement and perfection, till we have once more cast our secondine, that is, this slough of flesh, and are delivered into the last world, that is, that ineffable place of Paul, that proper *ubi* of spirits.   The smattering I have of the philosopher's stone (which is something more than the perfect exaltation of gold) hath taught me a great deal of divinity, and instructed my belief, how that immortal spirit and incorruptible substance of my soul may lie obscure, and sleep a while within this house of flesh.   Those strange and mystical transmigrations that I have observed in silkworms, turned my philosophy into divinity.   There is in these works of nature, which seem to puzzle reason, something divine, and hath more in it than the eye of a common spectator doth discover.

I am naturally bashful; nor hath conversation, age, or travel, been able to effront or enharden me; yet I have one part of modesty which I have seldom discovered in another, that is, (to speak truly) I am not so much afraid of death, as ashamed thereof.   'Tis the very disgrace and ignominy of our natures, that in a moment can so disfigure us, that our nearest friends, wife and children, stand afraid and start at us. The birds and beasts of the field, that before in a natural fear obeyed us, forgetting all allegiance, begin to prey upon us.   This very conceit hath in a tempest disposed and left me willing to be swallowed up in the abyss of waters, wherein I had perished unseen, unpitied, without wondering eyes, tears of pity, lectures of mortality, and none had said,

Quantum mutatus ab illo ![1]

Not that I am ashamed of the anatomy of my parts, or can accuse nature for playing the bungler in any part of me, or my own vicious life for contracting any shameful disease upon me,

---

[1]How greatly changed from what he was!

whereby I might not call myself as wholesome a morsel for the worms as any.

Some, upon the courage of a fruitful issue, wherein, as in the truest chronicle, they seem to outlive themselves, can with greater patience away with death.   This conceit and counterfeit subsisting in our progenies seems to me a mere fallacy, unworthy the desires of a man that can but conceive a thought of the next world; who, in a nobler ambition, should desire to live in his substance in heaven, rather than his name and shadow in the earth.   And therefore at my death I mean to take a total adieu of the world, not caring for a monument, history, or epitaph, not so much as the bare memory of my name to be found anywhere but in the universal register of God.   I am not yet so cynical as to approve the testament of Diogenes; nor do I altogether allow that *rodomontado* of Lucan,

> ——*Cælo tegitur, qui non habet urnam.*

> He that unburied lies wants not his hearse,
> For unto him a tomb's the universe——

but commend in my calmer judgment those ingenuous intentions that desire to sleep by the urns of their fathers, and strive to go the neatest way unto corruption.   I do not envy the temper of crows and daws, nor the numerous and weary days of our fathers before the Flood.   If there be any truth in astrology, I may outlive a jubilee: as yet I have not seen one revolution of Saturn, nor hath my pulse beat thirty years; and yet, excepting one, have seen the ashes and left under ground all the kings of Europe; have been contemporary to three emperors, four Grand Signiors, and as many Popes.   Methinks I have outlived myself, and begin to be weary of the sun; I have shaken hands with delight; in my warm blood and canicular days, I perceive I do anticipate the vices of age; the world to me is but a dream or mock-show, and we all therein but pantaloons and antics, to my severer contemplations.

.   .   .   .

The number of those who pretend unto salvation, and those infinite swarms who think to pass through the eye of this needle, have much amazed me. That name and compellation of *little flock*, doth not comfort, but deject, my devotion; especially, when I reflect upon mine own unworthiness, wherein, according to my humble apprehensions, I am below them all. I believe there shall never be an anarchy in heaven; but, as there are hierarchies amongst the angels, so shall there be degrees of priority amongst the saints. Yet it is (I protest) beyond my ambition to aspire unto the first ranks; my desires only are, and I shall be happy therein, to be but the last man, and bring up the rear in heaven.

Again, I am confident and fully persuaded, yet dare not take my oath, of my salvation. I am as it were sure, and do believe without all doubt, that there is such a city as Constantinople; yet for me to take my oath thereon were a kind of perjury, because I hold no infallible warrant from my own sense to confirm me in the certainty thereof. And truly, though many pretend an absolute certainty of their salvation, yet, when an humble soul shall contemplate her own unworthiness, she shall meet with many doubts, and suddenly find how little we stand in need of the precept of St. Paul, *Work out your salvation with fear and trembling.* That which is the cause of my election, I hold to be the cause of my salvation, which was the mercy and *beneplacit* of God, before I was, or the foundation of the world. *Before Abraham was, I am,* is the saying of Christ; yet is it true in some sense, if I say it of myself; for I was not only before myself, but Adam, that is, in the idea of God, and the decree of that synod held from all eternity. And in this sense, I say, the world was before the creation, and at an end before it had a beginning; and thus was I dead before I was alive: though my grave be England, my dying place was paradise: and Eve miscarried of me before she conceiv'd of Cain.

Insolent zeals, that do decry good works and rely only upon faith, take not away merit: for, depending upon the efficacy of their faith, they enforce the condition of God, and in a more sophistical way do seem to challenge heaven. It was decreed by God, that only those that lapped in the water like dogs should have the honor to destroy the Midianites; yet could none of those justly challenge, or imagine he deserved, that honor thereupon. I do not deny but that true faith, and such as God requires, is not only a mark or token, but also a means, of our salvation; but where to find this, is as obscure to me as my last end. And if our Savior could object unto his own disciples and favorites a faith, that, to the quantity of a grain of mustardseed, is able to remove mountains; surely, that which we boast of, is not anything, or at the most, but a remove from nothing. This is the tenor of my belief; wherein though there be many things singular, and to the humor of my irregular self, yet, if they square not with maturer judgments, I disclaim them, and do no further father them, than the learned and best judgments shall authorize them.

THE SECOND PART

Now for that other virtue of charity, without which faith is a mere notion, and of no existence, I have ever endeavored to nourish the merciful disposition and humane inclination I borrowed from my parents, and regulate it to the written and prescribed laws of charity. And if I hold the true anatomy of myself, I am delineated and naturally framed to such a piece of virtue; for I am of a constitution so general, that it consorts and sympathizeth with all things. I have no antipathy, or rather idiosyncrasy, in diet, humor, air, anything. I wonder not at the French for their dishes of frogs, snails and toadstools, nor at the Jews for locusts and grasshoppers; but being amongst them, make them my common viands, and I find they agree with my stomach as well as theirs. I could digest a salad gathered in a churchyard, as well as in a garden. I cannot start at the presence of a serpent, scorpion, lizard, or salamander: at the sight of a toad or viper, I find in me no desire to take up a stone to destroy them. I feel not in myself those common antipathies that I can discover in others: those national repugnances do not touch me, nor do I behold with prejudice the French, Italian, Spaniard, or Dutch: but where I find their actions in balance with my countrymen's, I honor, love, and embrace them in the same degree. I was born in the eighth climate, but seem for to be framed and constellated unto all. I am no plant that will not prosper out of a garden. All places, all airs, make unto me one country; I am in England everywhere, and under any meridian. I have been shipwrecked, yet am not enemy with the sea or winds; I can study, play, or sleep in a tempest. In brief, I am averse from nothing: my conscience would give me the lie if I should say I absolutely detest or hate any essence but the devil; or so at least abhor anything, but that we might come to composition. If there be any among those common objects of hatred I do contemn and laugh at, it is that great enemy of reason, virtue, and religion, the multitude: that numerous piece of monstrosity, which, taken asunder, seem men, and the reasonable creatures of God; but, confused together, make but one great beast, and a monstrosity more prodigious than hydra. It is no breach of charity to call these fools; it is the style all holy writers have afforded them, set down by Solomon in canonical Scripture, and a point of our faith to believe so. Neither in the name of multitude do I only include the base and minor sort of people; there is a rabble even amongst the gentry, a sort of plebeian heads, whose fancy moves with the same wheel as these; men in the same level with mechanics, though their fortunes do somewhat gild their infirmities, and their purses compound for their follies. But as, in casting account, three or four men together come short in account of one man placed by himself below them; so neither are a troop of these ignorant *doradoes* of that true esteem and value, as many a forlorn person, whose condition doth place him below their feet. Let us speak like politicians: there is a nobility without heraldry, a natural dignity, whereby one man is ranked with another, another filed before him, according to the quality of his desert, and pre-eminence of his good parts. Though the corruption of these times and the bias of present practice wheel another way, thus it was in the first and primitive commonwealths, and is yet in the integrity and cradle of well-order'd polities, till corruption getteth ground; ruder desires laboring after that which wiser considerations contemn, everyone having a liberty to amass and heap up riches, and they a license or faculty to do or purchase any thing.

. . . .

There is, I think, no man that apprehends his own miseries less than myself, and no man that so nearly apprehends another's. I could lose an arm without a tear, and with few groans, methinks, be quartered into pieces; yet can I weep most seriously at a play, and receive with true passion the counterfeit grief of those known and professed impostures. It is a barbarous part of inhumanity to add unto any afflicted party's misery, or endeavor to multiply in any man a passion whose single nature is already above his patience. This was the greatest affliction of Job, and those oblique expostulations of his friends a deeper injury than the downright blows of the devil. It is not the tears of our own eyes only, but of our friends also, that do exhaust the current of our sorrows; which, falling into many streams, runs more peaceably, and is contented with a narrower channel. It is an act within the power of charity, to translate a passion out of one breast into another, and to divide a sorrow almost out of itself; for an affliction, like a dimension, may be so divided, as, if not indivisible, at least to become insensible. Now with my friend I desire not to share or participate, but to engross, his sorrows; that, by making them mine own, I may more easily discuss them; for in mine own reason, and within myself, I can command that which I cannot entreat without myself, and within the circle of another. I have often thought those noble pairs and examples of friendship not so truly histories of what had been, as fictions of what should be; but I now perceive nothing in them but possibilities, nor anything in the heroic examples of Damon and Pythias, Achilles and Patroclus, which methinks upon some grounds I could not perform within the narrow compass of myself. That a man should lay down his life for his friend, seems strange to vulgar affections, and such as confine themselves within that worldly principle, *Charity begins at home*. For mine own part I could never remember the relations that I held unto myself, nor the respect that I owe unto my own nature, in the cause of God, my country, and my friends. Next to these three, I do embrace myself. I confess I do not observe that order that the schools ordain our affections, to love our parents, wives, children, and then our friends; for, excepting the injunctions of religion, I do not find in myself such a necessary and indissoluble sympathy to all those of my blood. I hope I do not break the fifth commandment, if I conceive I may love my friend before the nearest of my blood, even those to whom I owe the principles of life. I never yet cast a true affection on a woman; but I have loved my friend as I do virtue, my soul, my God. From hence methinks I do conceive how God loves man, what happiness there is in the love of God. Omitting all other, there are three most mystical unions: two natures in one person; three persons in one nature; one soul in two bodies; for though indeed they be really divided, yet are they so united, as they seem but one, and make rather a duality than two distinct souls.

There are wonders in true affection: it is a body of enigmas, mysteries, and riddles; wherein two so become one, as they both become two. I love my friend before myself, and yet methinks I do not love him enough: some few months hence my multiplied affection will make me believe I have not loved him at all. When I am from him, I am dead till I be with him; when I am with him, I am not satisfied, but would still be nearer him. United souls are not satisfied with embraces, but desire to be truly each other; which being impossible, their desires are infinite, and must proceed without a possibility of satisfaction. Another misery there is in affection, that whom we truly love like our own selves, we forget their looks, nor can our memory retain the idea of their faces; and it is no wonder, for they are ourselves, and our affection makes their looks our own. This noble affection falls not on vulgar and common constitutions, but on such as are mark'd for virtue: he that can love his friend with this noble ardor, will in a competent degree affect all. Now, if we can bring our affections to look beyond the body, and cast an eye upon the soul, we have found out the true object, not only of friendship, but charity; and the greatest happiness that we can bequeath the soul, is that wherein we all do place our last felicity, salvation; which though it be not in our power to bestow, it is in our charity and pious invocations to desire, if not procure and further. I cannot contentedly frame a prayer for myself in particular, without a catalogue for my friends; nor request a happiness, wherein my sociable disposition doth not desire the fellowship of my neighbor. I never hear the toll of a passing bell, though in my mirth, without my prayers and best wishes for the departing spirit; I cannot go to cure the body of my patient, but I forget my profession, and call unto God for his soul; I cannot see one say his prayers, but, instead of imitating him, I fall into a supplication for him, who perhaps is no more to me than a common nature: and if God hath vouchsafed an ear to my supplications, there are surely many happy that never saw me, and enjoy the blessing of mine unknown devotions. To pray for enemies, that is, for their salvation, is no harsh precept, but the practice of our daily and ordinary devotions. I cannot believe the story of the Italian: our bad wishes and uncharitable desires proceed no further than this life; it is the devil, and the uncharitable votes of hell, that desire our misery in the world to come.

To do no injury, nor take none, was a principle, which to my former years and impatient affections seemed to contain enough of morality; but my more settled years and Christian constitution have fallen upon severer resolutions. I can hold there is no such thing as injury; that, if there be, there is no such injury as revenge, and no such revenge as the contempt of an injury; that to hate another, is to malign himself; that the truest way to love another, is to despise ourselves. I were unjust unto mine own conscience, if I should say I am at variance with anything like myself. I find there are many pieces in this one fabric of man; this frame is raised upon a mass of antipathies. I am one methinks, but as the world; wherein notwithstanding there are a swarm of distinct essences, and in them another world of contrarieties; we carry private and domestic enemies within, public and more hostile adversaries without. The devil, that did but buffet St. Paul, plays methinks at sharp with me. Let me be nothing, if within the compass of myself I do not find the battle of Lepanto, passion against reason, reason against faith, faith against the devil, and my conscience against all. There is another man within me, that's angry with me, rebukes, commands, and dastards me. I have no conscience of marble to resist the hammer of more heavy offences; nor yet so soft and waxen, as to take the impression of each single peccadillo or scape of infirmity. I am of a strange belief, that it is as easy to be forgiven some sins, as to commit some others. For my original sin, I hold it to be washed away in my baptism: for my actual transgressions, I compute and reckon with God but from my last repentance, sacrament, or general absolution; and therefore am not terrified with the sins or madness of my youth. I thank the goodness of God, I have no sins that want a name; I am not singular in offences; my transgressions are epidemical, and from the common breath of our corruption. For there are certain tempers of body, which, matched with an humorous depravity of mind, do hatch and produce vitiosities, whose newness and monstrosity of nature admits no name: this was the temper of that lecher that fell in love with a statua, and the constitution of Nero in his spintrian recreations. For the heavens are not only fruitful in new and unheard-of stars, the earth in plants and animals, but men's minds also in villainy and vices. Now the dullness of my reason, and the vulgarity of my disposition, never prompted my invention, nor solicited my affection unto any of those; yet even those common and quotidian infirmities that so necessarily attend me, and do seem to be my very nature, have so dejected me, so broken the estimation that I should have otherwise of myself, that I repute myself the most abjectest piece of mortality. Divines prescribe a fit of sorrow to repentance: there goes indignation, anger, sorrow, hatred, into mine; passions of a contrary nature, which neither seem to suit with this action, nor my proper constitution. It is no breach of charity to ourselves, to be at variance with our vices, nor to abhor that part of us which is an enemy to the ground of charity, our God; wherein we do but imitate our great selves, the world, whose divided antipathies and contrary faces do yet carry a charitable regard unto the whole, by their particular discords preserving the common harmony, and keeping in fetters those powers, whose rebellions, once masters, might be the ruin of all.

I thank God, amongst those millions of vices I do inherit and hold from Adam, I have escaped one, and that a mortal enemy to charity, the first and father-sin, not only of man, but of the devil, pride: a vice whose name is comprehended in a monosyllable, but in its nature not circumscribed with a world. I have escaped it in a condition that can hardly avoid it. Those petty acquisitions and reputed perfections that advance and elevate the conceits of other men, add no feathers unto mine. I have seen a grammarian tower and plume himself over a single line in Horace, and show more pride in the construction of one ode, than the author in the composure of the whole book. For my own part, besides the jargon and patois of several provinces, I understand no less than six languages; yet I protest I have no higher conceit of myself, than had our fathers before the confusion of Babel, when there was but one language in the world, and none to boast himself either linguist or critic. I have not only seen several countries, beheld the nature of their climes, the chorography of their provinces, topography of their cities, but understood their several laws, customs, and policies; yet cannot all this persuade the dullness of my spirit unto such an opinion of myself, as I behold in nimbler and conceited heads, that never looked a degree beyond their nests. I know the names, and somewhat more, of all the constellations in my horizon; yet I have seen a prating mariner, that could only name the pointers and the north star, out-talk me, and conceit himself a whole sphere above me. I know most of the plants of my country, and of those about me; yet methinks I do not know so many as when I did but know a hundred, and had scarcely ever simpled further than Cheapside. For, indeed, heads of capacity, and such as are not full with a handful or easy measure of knowledge, think they know nothing till they know all; which being impossible, they fall upon the opinion of Socrates, and only know they know not anything. I cannot think that Homer pin'd away upon the riddle of the fishermen; or that Aristotle, who understood the uncertainty of knowledge, and confessed so often the reason of man too weak for the works of nature, did ever drown himself upon the flux and reflux of Euripus. We do but learn to-day what our better advanced judgments will unteach to-morrow; and Aristotle doth but instruct us, as Plato did him; that is, to confute himself. I have run through all sorts, yet find no rest in any: though our first studies and junior endeavors may style us Peripatetics, Stoics, or Academics; yet I perceive the wisest heads prove, at last, almost all sceptics, and stand like Janus in the field of knowledge. I have therefore one common and authentic philosophy I learned in the schools, whereby I discourse and satisfy the reason of other men; another more reserved, and drawn from experience, whereby I content mine own. Solomon, that complained of ignorance in the height of knowledge, hath not only humbled my conceits, but discouraged my endeavors. There is yet another conceit that hath sometimes made me shut my books, which tells me it is a vanity to waste our days in the blind pursuit of knowledge; it is but attending a little longer, and we shall enjoy that by instinct and infusion, which we endeavor at here by labor and inquisition. It is better to sit down in a modest ignorance, and rest contented with the natural blessing of our own reasons, than buy the uncertain knowledge of this life with sweat and vexation, which death gives every fool *gratis*, and is an accessary of our glorification.

I was never yet once, and commend their resolutions who never marry twice: not that I disallow of second marriage; as neither, in all cases, of polygamy, which, considering some times, and the unequal number of both sexes, may be also necessary. The whole world was made for man, but the twelfth part of man for woman: man is the whole world, and the breath of God; woman the rib and crooked piece of man. I could be content that we might procreate like trees, without conjunction, or that there were any way to perpetuate the world without this trivial and vulgar way of coition: it is the foolishest act a wise man commits in all his life; nor is there any thing that will more deject his cool'd imagination, when he shall consider what an odd and unworthy piece of folly he hath committed. I speak not in prejudice, nor am averse from that sweet sex, but naturally amorous of all that is beautiful. I can look a whole day with delight upon a handsome picture, though it be but of an horse. It is my temper, and I like it the better, to affect all harmony; and sure there is music even in the beauty, and the silent note which Cupid strikes, far sweeter than the sound of an instrument. For there is a music wherever there is a harmony, order, or proportion: and thus far we may maintain the music of the spheres; for those well-ordered motions, and regular paces, though they give no sound unto the ear, yet to the understanding they strike a note most full of harmony. Whosoever is harmonically composed delights in harmony; which makes me much distrust the symmetry of those heads which declaim against all church-music. For myself, not only from my obedience, but my particular genius, I do embrace it: for even that vulgar and tavern-music, which makes one man merry, another mad, strikes in me a deep fit of devotion, and a profound contemplation of the First Composer. There is something in it of divinity more than the ear discovers: it is an hieroglyphical and shadowed lesson of the whole world, and creatures of God; such a melody to the ear, as the whole world, well understood, would afford the understanding. In brief, it is a sensible fit of that harmony which intellectually sounds in the ears of

God. I will not say, with Plato, the soul is an harmony, but harmonical, and hath its nearest sympathy unto music; thus some, whose temper of body agrees and humors the constitution of their souls, are born poets, though indeed all are naturally inclined unto rhythm. This made Tacitus, in the very first line of his story, fall upon a verse; and Cicero, the worst of poets, but declaiming for a poet, falls in the very first sentence upon a perfect hexameter. I feel not in me those sordid and unchristian desires of my profession; I do not secretly implore and wish for plagues, rejoice at famines, revolve ephemerides and almanacs in expectation of malignant aspects, fatal conjunctions, and eclipses. I rejoice not at unwholesome springs, nor unseasonable winters: my prayer goes with the husbandman's; I desire everything in its proper season, that neither men nor the times be put out of temper. Let me be sick myself, if sometimes the malady of my patient be not a disease unto me. I desire rather to cure his infirmities than my own necessities. Where I do him no good, methinks it is scarce honest gain; though I confess 'tis but the worthy salary of our well-intended endeavors. I am not only ashamed, but heartily sorry, that, besides death, there are diseases incurable: yet not for my own sake, or that they be beyond my art, but for the general cause and sake of humanity, whose common cause I apprehend as mine own. And to speak more generally, those three noble professions which all civil commonwealths do honor, are raised upon the fall of Adam, and are not any way exempt from their infirmities; there are not only diseases incurable in physic, but cases indissolvable in laws, vices incorrigible in divinity. If General Councils may err, I do not see why particular courts should be infallible: their perfectest rules are raised upon the erroneous reasons of man, and the laws of one do but condemn the rules of another; as Aristotle oft-times the opinions of his predecessors, because, though agreeable to reason, yet were not consonant to his own rules, and the logic of his proper principles. Again, to speak nothing of the sin against the Holy Ghost, whose cure not only, but whose nature is unknown, I can cure the gout or stone in some, sooner than divinity, pride or avarice in others. I can cure vices by physic when they remain incurable by divinity, and shall obey my pills when they contemn their precepts. I boast nothing, but plainly say, we all labor

against our own cure; for death is the cure of all diseases.   There
is no *catholicon* or universal remedy I know, but this; which,
though nauseous to queasy stomachs, yet to prepared appetites is
nectar, and a pleasant potion of immortality.

For my conversation, it is like the sun's, with all men, and
with a friendly aspect to good and bad.   Methinks there is no
man bad, and the worst, best; that is, while they are kept
within the circle of those qualities wherein they are good: there
is no man's mind of such discordant and jarring a temper, to
which a tunable disposition may not strike a harmony.   *Magnæ
virtutes, nec minora vitia;*[1] it is the posy of the best natures, and
may be inverted on the worst; there are in the most depraved
and venomous dispositions, certain pieces that remain untouched, which by an *antiperistasis* become more excellent, or
by the excellency of their antipathies are able to preserve themselves from the contagion of their enemy vices, and persist entire beyond the general corruption.   For it is also thus in nature:
the greatest balsams do lie enveloped in the bodies of most
powerful corrosives.   I say, moreover, and I ground upon experience, that poisons contain within themselves their own
antidote, and that which preserves them from the venom of
themselves, without which they were not deleterious to others
only, but to themselves also.   But it is the corruption that I
fear within me, not the contagion of commerce without me.   'Tis
that unruly regiment within me, that will destroy me; 'tis I that
do infect myself; the man without a navel yet lives in me; I
feel that original canker corrode and devour me; and therefore
Defienda me Dios de mi, "Lord deliver me from myself," is a
part of my litany, and the first voice of my retired imaginations.
There is no man alone, because every man is a microcosm, and
carries the whole world about him.   *Nunquam minus solus
quam cum solus,*[2] though it be the apothegm of a wise man, is
yet true in the mouth of a fool.   Indeed, though in a wilderness,
a man is never alone, not only because he is with himself and his
own thoughts, but because he is with the devil, who ever consorts
with our solitude, and is that unruly rebel that musters up
those disordered motions which accompany our sequestered

---

[1]Great virtues, vices no less.
[2]Never less alone than when alone.

imaginations. And to speak more narrowly, there is no such thing as solitude, nor anything that can be said to be alone and by itself, but God, who is his own circle, and can subsist by himself; all others, besides their dissimilary and heterogeneous parts, which in a manner multiply their natures, cannot subsist without the concourse of God, and the society of that hand which doth uphold their natures. In brief, there can be nothing truly alone and by itself, which is not truly one; and such is only God: all others do transcend an unity, and so by consequence are many.

Now for my life, it is a miracle of thirty years, which to relate, were not a history, but a piece of poetry, and would sound to common ears like a fable. For the world, I count it not an inn, but an hospital; and a place not to live, but to die in. The world that I regard is myself; it is the microcosm of my own frame that I cast mine eye on; for the other, I use it but like my globe, and turn it round sometimes for my recreation. Men that look upon my outside, perusing only my condition and fortunes, do err in my altitude; for I am above Atlas his shoulders. The earth is a point not only in respect of the heavens above us, but of that heavenly and celestial part within us; that mass of flesh that circumscribes me, limits not my mind: that surface that tells the heavens it hath an end, cannot persuade me I have any: I take my circle to be above three hundred and sixty; though the number of the ark do measure my body, it comprehendeth not my mind: whilst I study to find how I am a microcosm, or little world, I find myself something more than the great. There is surely a piece of divinity in us, something that was before the elements, and owes no homage unto the sun. Nature tells me I am the image of God, as well as Scripture: he that understands not thus much, hath not his introduction or first lesson, and is yet to begin the alphabet of man. Let me not injure the felicity of others, if I say I am as happy as any: *Ruat cælum, fiat voluntas tua,*[1] salveth all; so that whatsoever happens, it is but what our daily prayers desire. In brief, I am content; and what should Providence add more? Surely this is it we call happiness, and this do I enjoy; with this I am happy in a dream, and as content to enjoy a happiness in a fancy, as others in a

---

[1] Though the heavens fall, let thy will be done.

more apparent truth and realty. There is surely a nearer apprehension of anything that delights us in our dreams, than in our waked senses: without this I were unhappy; for my awaked judgment discontents me, ever whispering unto me, that I am from my friend; but my friendly dreams in the night requite me, and make me think I am within his arms. I thank God for my happy dreams, as I do for my good rest; for there is a satisfaction in them unto reasonable desires, and such as can be content with a fit of happiness: and surely it is not a melancholy conceit to think we are all asleep in this world, and that the conceits of this life are as mere dreams to those of the next; as the phantasms of the night, to the conceits of the day. There is an equal delusion in both, and the one doth but seem to be the emblem or picture of the other: we are somewhat more than ourselves in our sleeps, and the slumber of the body seems to be but the waking of the soul. It is the ligation of sense, but the liberty of reason; and our waking conceptions do not match the fancies of our sleeps. At my nativity my ascendant was the watery sign of Scorpius; I was born in the planetary hour of Saturn, and I think I have a piece of that leaden planet in me. I am no way facetious, nor disposed for the mirth and galliardize of company; yet in one dream I can compose a whole comedy, behold the action, apprehend the jests, and laugh myself awake at the conceits thereof. Were my memory as faithful as my reason is then fruitful, I would never study but in my dreams; and this time also would I choose for my devotions: but our grosser memories have then so little hold of our abstracted understandings, that they forget the story, and can only relate to our awaked souls a confused and broken tale of that that hath passed. Aristotle, who hath written a singular tract *Of Sleep*, hath not, methinks, thoroughly defined it; nor yet Galen, though he seem to have corrected it; for those *noctambuloes* and night-walkers, though in their sleep, do yet enjoy the action of their senses. We must therefore say that there is something in us that is not in the jurisdiction of Morpheus; and that those abstracted and ecstatic souls do walk about in their own corpse, as spirits with the bodies they assume, wherein they seem to hear, see, and feel, though indeed the organs are destitute of sense, and their natures of those faculties that should inform them. Thus it is observed, that men sometimes, upon the hour of their departure, do speak and reason above themselves; for then the soul, beginning to be freed from the ligaments of the body, begins to reason like herself, and to discourse in a strain above mortality.

We term sleep a death; and yet it is waking that kills us, and destroys those spirits that are the house of life. 'Tis indeed a part of life that best expresseth death; for every man truly lives, so long as he acts his nature, or some way makes good the faculties of himself. Themistocles, therefore, that slew his soldier in his sleep, was a merciful executioner: 'tis a kind of punishment the mildness of no laws hath invented: I wonder the fancy of Lucan and Seneca did not discover it. It is that death by which we may be literally said to die daily; a death which Adam died before his mortality; a death whereby we live a middle and moderating point between life and death: in fine, so like death, I dare not trust it without my prayers, and an half adieu unto the world, and take my farewell in a colloquy with God.

> The night is come, like to the day,
> Depart not thou, great God, away.
> Let not my sins, black as the night,
> Eclipse the luster of thy light:
> Keep still in my horizon; for to me
> The sun makes not the day, but thee.
> Thou, whose nature cannot sleep,
> On my temples sentry keep;
> Guard me 'gainst those watchful foes,
> Whose eyes are open while mine close.
> Let no dreams my head infest,
> But such as Jacob's temples blest.
> While I do rest, my soul advance;
> Make my sleep a holy trance;
> That I may, my rest being wrought,
> Awake into some holy thought;
> And with as active vigor run
> My course, as doth the nimble sun.
> Sleep is a death; O make me try,
> By sleeping, what it is to die;
> And as gently lay my head
> On my grave, as now my bed.
> Howe'er I rest, great God, let me
> Awake again at last with thee;
> And thus assur'd, behold I lie
> Securely, or to awake or die.

These are my drowsy days; in vain
I do now wake to sleep again:
O come that hour, when I shall never
Sleep again, but wake for ever.

This is the dormitive I take to bedward; I need no other lau-
danum than this to make me sleep; after which I close mine eyes
in security, content to take my leave of the sun, and sleep unto
the resurrection.

The method I should use in distributive justice, I often observe in commutative; and keep a geometrical proportion in
both, whereby becoming equable to others, I become unjust to
myself, and supererogate in that common principle, *Do unto
others as thou wouldst be done unto thyself.* I was not born unto
riches, neither is it, I think, my star to be wealthy; or, if it were,
the freedom of my mind, and frankness of my disposition, were
able to contradict and cross my fates: for to me, avarice seems
not so much a vice, as a deplorable piece of madness; to conceive
ourselves urinals, or be persuaded that we are dead, is not so
ridiculous, nor so many degrees beyond the power of hellebore,
as this. The opinions of theory, and positions of men, are not
so void of reason as their practised conclusions. Some have held
that snow is black, that the earth moves, that the soul is air, fire,
water; but all this is philosophy, and there is no delirium, if we
do but speculate the folly and indisputable dotage of avarice to
that subterraneous idol and god of the earth. I do confess I
am an atheist; I cannot persuade myself to honor that the world
adores; whatsoever virtue its prepared substance may have within
my body, it hath no influence nor operation without. I would
not entertain a base design, or an action that should call me
villain, for the Indies; and for this only do I love and honor my
own soul, and have methinks two arms too few to embrace myself. Aristotle is too severe, that will not allow us to be truly
liberal without wealth, and the bountiful hand of fortune. If
this be true, I must confess I am charitable only in my liberal
intentions, and bountiful well-wishes; but if the example of the
mite be not only an act of wonder, but an example of the noblest
charity, surely poor men may also build hospitals, and the rich
alone have not erected cathedrals. I have a private method
which others observe not; I take the opportunity of myself to

do good; I borrow occasion of charity from mine own necessities, and supply the wants of others, when I am in most need myself: for it is an honest stratagem to take advantage of ourselves, and so to husband the acts of virtue, that, where they are defective in one circumstance, they may repay their want and multiply their goodness in another. I have not Peru in my desires, but a competence, and ability to perform those good works to which he hath inclined my nature. He is rich, who hath enough to be charitable; and it is hard to be so poor, that a noble mind may not find a way to this piece of goodness. *He that giveth to the poor, lendeth to the Lord*: there is more rhetoric in that one sentence, than in a library of sermons; and indeed, if those sentences were understood by the reader, with the same emphasis as they are delivered by the author, we needed not those volumes of instructions, but might be honest by an epitome. Upon this motive only I cannot behold a beggar without relieving his necessities with my purse, or his soul with my prayers; these scenical and accidental differences between us cannot make me forget that common and untouched part of us both: there is under these centoes and miserable outsides, these mutilate and semi-bodies, a soul of the same alloy with our own, whose genealogy is God as well as ours, and in as fair a way to salvation as ourselves. Statists that labor to contrive a commonwealth without poverty, take away the object of charity, not understanding only the commonwealth of a Christian, but forgetting the prophecy of Christ.

Now, there is another part of charity, which is the basis and pillar of this, and that is the love of God, for whom we love our neighbor; for this I think charity, to love God for himself, and our neighbor for God. All that is truly amiable is God, or as it were a divided piece of him, that retains a reflex or shadow of himself. Nor is it strange that we should place affection on that which is invisible: all that we truly love is thus; what we adore under affection of our senses, deserves not the honor of so pure a title. Thus we adore virtue, though to the eyes of sense she be invisible: thus that part of our noble friends that we love, is not that part that we embrace, but that insensible part that our arms cannot embrace. God, being all goodness, can love nothing but himself; he loves us but for that part which is as it were himself, and the traduction of his Holy Spirit. Let us call to assize the loves of our parents, the affection of our wives and children, and they are all dumb shows and dreams, without reality, truth, or constancy. For first there is a strong bond of affection between us and our parents; yet how easily dissolved! We betake ourselves to a woman, forget our mother in a wife, and the womb that bare us, in that that shall bear our image. This woman blessing us with children, our affection leaves the level it held before, and sinks from our bed unto our issue and picture of posterity, where affection holds no steady mansion. They, growing up in years, desire our ends; or applying themselves to a woman, take a lawful way to love another better than ourselves. Thus I perceive a man may be buried alive, and behold his grave in his own issue.

I conclude therefore, and say, there is no happiness under (or, as Copernicus will have it, above) the sun nor any *crambe* in that repeated verity and burthen of all the wisdom of Solomon, *All is vanity and vexation of spirit*. There is no felicity in that the world adores. Aristotle, whilst he labors to refute the Ideas of Plato, falls upon one himself; for his *summum bonum* is a chimera, and there is no such thing as his felicity. That wherein God himself is happy, the holy angels are happy, in whose defect the devils are unhappy, that dare I call happiness: whatsoever conduceth unto this, may with an easy metaphor deserve that name; whatsoever else the world terms happiness, is to me a story out of Pliny, tale of Boccace or Malizspini, an apparition, or neat delusion, wherein there is no more of happiness than the name. Bless me in this life with but peace of my conscience, command of my affections, the love of thyself and my dearest friends, and I shall be happy enough to pity Cæsar. These are, O Lord, the humble desires of my most reasonable ambition, and all I dare call happiness on earth; wherein I set no rule or limit to thy hand or providence. Dispose of me according to the wisdom of thy pleasure: thy will be done, though in my own undoing.

HYDRIOTAPHIA: URN BURIAL (1658)

Starting from the discovery of some buried urns "in a field of old Walsingham, not many months past," Browne produced what is ostensibly an antiquarian piece on modes of burial, but is really—as when in the fifth chapter all the stops of his great organ are opened—the most gorgeous descant in English on the timeless theme *vanitas vanitatum*. No one has understood more sensitively than Browne the secret of that mixture of Saxon and Latin of which the liturgy first realized the beauty, and his purple is the richer and stronger for its threads of homespun—"Grave-stones tell truth scarce forty years."

CHAPTER V

Now since these dead bones have already outlasted the living ones of Methuselah, and in a yard under ground, and thin walls of clay, outworn all the strong and specious buildings above it; and quietly rested under the drums and tramplings of three conquests; what prince can promise such diuturnity unto his relics, or might not gladly say,

Sic ego componi versus in ossa velim?[1]

Time which antiquates antiquities, and hath an art to make dust of all things, hath yet spared these minor monuments.

In vain we hope to be known by open and visible conservatories, when to be unknown was the means of their continuation, and obscurity their protection: if they died by violent hands, and were thrust into their urns, these bones become considerable, and some old philosophers would honor them, whose souls they conceived most pure, which were thus snatched from their bodies; and to retain a stronger propension unto them: whereas they weariedly left a languishing corpse, and with faint desires of reunion. If they fell by long and aged decay, yet wrapt up in the bundle of time, they fall into indistinction, and make but one blot with infants. If we begin to die when we live, and long life be but a prolongation of death, our life is a sad composition;

---

[1]Thus, when I am turned to bones, I should wish to be laid to rest.

we live with death, and die not in a moment. How many pulses
made up the life of Methuselah, were work for Archimedes: common counters sum up the life of Moses his man. Our days
become considerable, like petty sums, by minute accumulations;
where numerous fractions make up but small round numbers;
and our days of a span long make not one little finger.

If the nearness of our last necessity brought a nearer conformity unto it, there were a happiness in hoary hairs, and no calamity
in half-senses. But the long habit of living indisposeth us for
dying; when avarice makes us the sport of death; when even
David grew politicly cruel; and Solomon could hardly be
said to be the wisest of men. But many are too early old, and
before the date of age. Adversity stretcheth our days, misery
makes Alcmena's nights, and time hath no wings unto it.
But the most tedious being is that which can unwish itself, content to be nothing, or never to have been, which was beyond the
malcontent of Job, who cursed not the day of his life, but his
nativity: content to have so far been, as to have a title to future
being; although he had lived here but in an hidden state of life,
and as it were an abortion.

What songs the sirens sang, or what name Achilles assumed
when he hid himself among women, though puzzling questions,
are not beyond all conjecture. What time the persons of these
ossuaries entered the famous nations of the dead, and slept with
princes and counsellors, might admit a wide solution. But who
were the proprietaries of these bones, or what bodies these ashes
made up, were a question above antiquarism; not to be resolved
by man, nor easily perhaps by spirits, except we consult the provincial guardians, or tutelary observators. Had they made as
good provision for their names, as they have done for their relics,
they had not so grossly erred in the art of perpetuation. But to
subsist in bones, and be but pyramidally extant, is a fallacy in
duration. Vain ashes, which in the oblivion of names, persons,
times, and sexes, have found unto themselves a fruitless continuation, and only arise unto late posterity, as emblems of
mortal vanities; antidotes against pride, vain-glory, and madding
vices. Pagan vain-glories which thought the world might last
forever, had encouragement for ambition, and, finding no
Atropos unto the immortality of their names, were never damped
with the necessity of oblivion. Even old ambitions had the

advantage of ours, in the attempts of their vain-glories, who acting early, and before the probable meridian of time, have by this time found great accomplishment of their designs, whereby the ancient heroes have already outlasted their monuments, and mechanical preservations. But in this latter scene of time, we cannot expect such mummies unto our memories, when ambition may fear the prophecy of Elias, and Charles the Fifth can never hope to live within two Methuselahs of Hector.

And therefore restless inquietude for the diuturnity of our memories unto present considerations, seems a vanity almost out of date, and superannuated piece of folly. We cannot hope to live so long in our names, as some have done in their persons; one face of Janus holds no proportion to the other. 'Tis too late to be ambitious. The great mutations of the world are acted, or time may be too short for our designs. To extend our memories by monuments, whose death we daily pray for, and whose duration we cannot hope, without injury to our expectations, in the advent of the last day, were a contradiction to our beliefs. We whose generations are ordained in this setting part of time, are providentially taken off from such imaginations; and being necessitated to eye the remaining particle of futurity, are naturally constituted unto thoughts of the next world, and cannot excusably decline the consideration of that duration, which maketh pyramids pillars of snow, and all that's past a moment.

Circles and right lines limit and close all bodies, and the mortal right-lined circle must conclude and shut up all. There is no antidote against the opium of time, which temporally considereth all things; our fathers find their graves in our short memories, and sadly tell us how we may be buried in our survivors. Gravestones tell truth scarce forty years. Generations pass while some trees stand, and old families last not three oaks. To be read by bare inscriptions like many in Gruter, to hope for eternity by enigmatical epithets or first letters of our names, to be studied by antiquaries, who we were, and have new names given us like many of the mummies, are cold consolations unto the students of perpetuity, even by everlasting languages.

To be content that times to come should only know there was such a man, not caring whether they knew more of him, was a frigid ambition in Cardan; disparaging his horoscopal in-

clination and judgment of himself. Who cares to subsist like
Hippocrates' patients, or Achilles' horses in Homer, under
naked nominations, without deserts and noble acts, which are
the balsam of our memories, the *entelechia* and soul of our sub-
sistences? To be nameless in worthy deeds exceeds an infamous
history. The Canaanitish woman lives more happily without
a name, than Herodias with one. And who had not rather have
been the good thief, than Pilate?

But the iniquity of oblivion blindly scattereth her poppy,
and deals with the memory of men without distinction to merit
of perpetuity. Who can but pity the founder of the pyramids?
Herostratus lives that burnt the temple of Diana, he is almost
lost that built it; time hath spared the epitaph of Adrian's
horse, confounded that of himself. In vain we compute our
felicities by the advantage of our good names, since bad have
equal durations; and Thersites is like to live as long as Agamemnon. Who knows whether the best of men be known? Or
whether there be not more remarkable persons forgot, than any
that stand remembered in the known account of time? Without
the favor of the everlasting register, the first man had been as
unknown as the last, and Methuselah's long life had been his
only chronicle.

Oblivion is not to be hired: the greater part must be content
to be as though they had not been, to be found in the register
of God, not in the record of man. Twenty-seven names make
up the first story,[1] and the recorded names ever since contain not one living century. The number of the dead long exceedeth all that shall live. The night of time far surpasseth
the day, and who knows when was the equinox? Every hour
adds unto that current arithmetic which scarce stands one moment. And since death must be the Lucina of life, and even
pagans could doubt whether thus to live, were to die; since our
longest sun sets at right descensions, and makes but winter
arches, and therefore it cannot be long before we lie down in
darkness, and have our light in ashes; since the brother of death
daily haunts us with dying *mementos*, and time that grows old
itself, bids us hope no long duration: diuturnity is a dream and
folly of expectation.

---

[1] Before the flood.

Darkness and light divide the course of time, and oblivion shares with memory a great part even of our living beings; we slightly remember our felicities, and the smartest strokes of affliction leave but short smart upon us. Sense endureth no extremities, and sorrows destroy us or themselves. To weep into stones are fables. Afflictions induce callosities, miseries are slippery, or fall like snow upon us, which notwithstanding is no unhappy stupidity. To be ignorant of evils to come, and forgetful of evils past, is merciful provision in nature, whereby we digest the mixture of our few and evil days, and, our delivered senses not relapsing into cutting remembrances, our sorrows are not kept raw by the edge of repetitions. A great part of antiquity contented their hopes of subsistency with a transmigration of their souls: a good way to continue their memories, while having the advantage of plural successions, they could not but act something remarkable in such variety of beings, and enjoying the fame of their passed selves, make accumulation of glory unto their last durations. Others, rather than be lost in the uncomfortable night of nothing, were content to recede into the common being, and make one particle of the public soul of all things, which was no more than to return into their unknown and divine original again. Egyptian ingenuity was more unsatisfied, contriving their bodies in sweet consistencies, to attend the return of their souls. But all was vanity, feeding the wind, and folly. The Egyptian mummies, which Cambyses or time hath spared, avarice now consumeth. Mummy is become merchandise, Mizraim cures wounds, and Pharaoh is sold for balsams.

In vain do individuals hope for immortality, or any patent from oblivion, in preservations below the moon: men have been deceived even in their flatteries above the sun, and studied conceits to perpetuate their names in heaven. The various cosmography of that part hath already varied the names of contrived constellations; Nimrod is lost in Orion, and Osiris in the dog-star. While we look for incorruption in the heavens, we find they are but like the earth; durable in their main bodies, alterable in their parts: whereof beside comets and new stars, perspectives begin to tell tales. And the spots that wander about the sun, with Phaeton's favor, would make clear conviction.

There is nothing strictly immortal, but immortality; whatever hath no beginning may be confident of no end (all others have a dependent being, and within the reach of destruction); which is the peculiar of that necessary essence that cannot destroy itself; and the highest strain of omnipotency, to be so powerfully constituted as not to suffer even from the power of itself. But the sufficiency of Christian immortality frustrates all earthly glory, and the quality of either state after death makes a folly of posthumous memory. God who can only destroy our souls, and hath assured our resurrection, either of our bodies or names hath directly promised no duration. Wherein there is so much of chance that the boldest expectants have found unhappy frustration; and to hold long subsistence seems but a scape in oblivion. But man is a noble animal, splendid in ashes, and pompous in the grave, solemnizing nativities and deaths with equal luster, nor omitting ceremonies of bravery in the infamy of his nature.

Life is a pure flame, and we live by an invisible sun within us. A small fire sufficeth for life, great flames seemed too little after death, while men vainly affected precious pyres, and to burn like Sardanapalus; but the wisdom of funeral laws found the folly of prodigal blazes, and reduced undoing fires unto the rule of sober obsequies, wherein few could be so mean as not to provide wood, pitch, a mourner, and an urn.

Five languages secured not the epitaph of Gordianus. The man of God lives longer without a tomb than any by one, invisibly interred by angels, and adjudged to obscurity, though not without some marks directing human discovery. Enoch and Elias, without either tomb or burial, in an anomalous state of being, are the great examples of perpetuity, in their long and living memory, in strict account being still on this side death, and having a late part yet to act upon this stage of earth. If in the decretory term of the world we shall not all die but be changed, according to received translation, the last day will make but few graves; at least quick resurrections will anticipate lasting sepultures; some graves will be opened before they be quite closed, and Lazarus be no wonder. When many that feared to die shall groan that they can die but once, the dismal state is the second and living death, when life puts despair on the damned; when men shall wish the coverings of mountains, not of monuments, and annihilation shall be courted.

While some have studied monuments, others have studiously
declined them: and some have been so vainly boisterous, that
they durst not acknowledge their graves; wherein Alaricus seems
most subtle, who had a river turned to hide his bones at the bottom. Even Sylla, that thought himself safe in his urn, could not
prevent revenging tongues, and stones thrown at his monument.
Happy are they whom privacy makes innocent, who deal so with
men in this world, that they are not afraid to meet them in the
next, who when they die, make no commotion among the dead,
and are not touched with that poetical taunt of Isaiah.

Pyramids, arches, obelisks, were but the irregularities of vain-
glory, and wild enormities of ancient magnanimity. But the
most magnanimous resolution rests in the Christian religion,
which trampleth upon pride, and sits on the neck of ambition,
humbly pursuing that infallible perpetuity, unto which all others
must diminish their diameters, and be poorly seen in angles of
contingency.

Pious spirits who passed their days in raptures of futurity,
made little more of this world, than the world that was before it,
while they lay obscure in the chaos of pre-ordination, and night
of their fore-beings. And if any have been so happy as truly to
understand Christian annihilation, extasis, exolution, lique-
faction, transformation, the kiss of the Spouse, gustation of God,
and ingression into the divine shadow, they have already had
an handsome anticipation of heaven; the glory of the world is
surely over, and the earth in ashes unto them.

To subsist in lasting monuments, to live in their productions,
to exist in their names and predicament of chimeras, was large
satisfaction unto old expectations, and made one part of their
Elysiums. But all this is nothing in the metaphysics of true
belief. To live indeed is to be again ourselves, which being not
only an hope but an evidence in noble believers, 'tis all one to
lie in St. Innocent's churchyard, as in the sands of Egypt: ready
to be anything, in the ecstasy of being ever, and as content with
six foot as the *moles* of Adrianus.

> ——*Tabesne cadavera solvat*
> *An rogus haud refert.*—LUCAN.[1]

---

[1]It matters not whether the corpses are burned on the pyre or decompose with
time. (Duff's trans.)

THE GARDEN OF CYRUS (1658)

Whatever Browne's nominal subject, it soon leads him to his great theme, "O World! O Life! O Time!" Only the confirmed Browneist reads *The Garden of Cyrus*, that wondrous and learned discourse on the quincunx arrangement of trees—and everything else—but only Browne could rise from such a subject to such a conclusion.

But the quincunx of heaven runs low, and 'tis time to close the five ports of knowledge. We are unwilling to spin out our awaking thoughts into the phantasms of sleep, which often continueth precogitations, making cables of cobwebs, and wildernesses of handsome groves. Beside Hippocrates hath spoke so little, and the oneirocritical masters have left such frigid interpretations from plants, that there is little encouragement to dream of paradise itself. Nor will the sweetest delight of gardens afford much comfort in sleep; wherein the dullness of that sense shakes hands with delectable odors; and though in the bed of Cleopatra, can hardly with any delight raise up the ghost of a rose.

Night, which pagan theology could make the daughter of Chaos, affords no advantage to the description of order: although no lower than that mass can we derive its genealogy. All things began in order, so shall they end, and so shall they begin again; according to the ordainer of order and mystical mathematics of the city of heaven.

Though *Somnus* in Homer be sent to rouse up Agamemnon, I find no such effects in these drowsy approaches of sleep. To keep our eyes open longer were but to act our antipodes. The huntsmen are up in America, and they are already past their first sleep in Persia. But who can be drowsy at that hour which freed us from everlasting sleep? Or have slumbering thoughts at that time, when sleep itself must end, and as some conjecture all shall awake again?

JEREMY TAYLOR (1613–1667)

A brief account of Taylor's life is given above (p. 366). *Holy Dying*, his greatest work, was also his most popular, and for many generations in countless households the most richly sensuous devotional book in English stood on the same shelf with the plainest, *Pilgrim's Progress*. For the modern world, no longer concerned with piety, Taylor lives—revived, like so many writers of the period, by Coleridge and his fellows—as a consummate stylist. Without possessing distinctive intellectual power he had imagination, a sense of natural beauty rare in his time, a sensitive and sympathetic heart, and a poet's feeling for words and rhythms. In him, as in many men, the melancholy of the age is draped with purple when the subject of contemplation is death—though Taylor's smooth, controlled ornateness is far from the *macabre* and turbid prose of Donne. His approach to the great theme is partly that of a Christian priest, partly that of a pagan moralist, and *Holy Dying* is full of quotations and echoes of Seneca—and Ovid and Petronius as well, for Taylor was too much of a poet to live wholly among the Fathers. If Browne is the organ among seventeenth-century writers, Taylor is the 'cello.

THE RULE AND EXERCISES OF HOLY DYING
(1651)

CHAPTER I: A GENERAL PREPARATION TOWARDS A HOLY AND BLESSED DEATH, BY WAY OF CONSIDERATION

SECTION I

CONSIDERATION OF THE VANITY AND SHORTNESS OF MAN'S LIFE

A MAN is a bubble, said the Greek proverb; which Lucian represents with advantages and its proper circumstances, to this purpose; saying, that all the world is a storm, and men rise up in their several generations, like bubbles descending *a Jove pluvio*, from God and the dew of heaven, from a tear and drop of man, from nature and Providence: and some of these instantly sink into the deluge of their first parent, and are hidden in a sheet of water, having had no other business in the world but to be born that they might be able to die: others float up and down two or three turns, and suddenly disappear, and give their place to others: and they that live longest upon the face of the waters, are in perpetual motion, restless and uneasy; and being crushed with the great drop of a cloud sink into flatness and a froth; the change not being great, it being hardly possible it should be more a nothing than it was before. So is every man: he is born in vanity and sin; he comes into the world like morning mushrooms, soon thrusting up their heads into the air, and conversing with their kindred of the same production, and as soon they turn into dust and forgetfulness: some of them without any other interest in the affairs of the world but that they made their parents a little glad, and very sorrowful: others ride longer in the storm; it may be until seven years of vanity be expired, and then peradventure the sun shines hot upon their heads, and they fall into the shades below, into the cover of death and darkness of the grave to hide them. But if the bubble stands the shock of a bigger drop, and outlives the chances of a child, of a careless nurse, of drowning in a pail of water, of being overlaid by a sleepy servant, or such little accidents, then the young man dances like a bubble, empty and gay, and shines like a dove's neck, or the image of a rainbow, which hath no substance, and whose very imagery and colors are fantastical; and so he dances out the gaiety of his youth, and is all the while in a storm, and endures only because he is not knocked on the head by a drop of bigger rain, or crushed by the pressure of a load of indigested meat, or quenched by the disorder of an ill-placed humor: and to preserve a man alive in the midst of so many chances and hostilities, is as great a miracle as to create him; to preserve him from rushing into nothing, and at first to draw him up from nothing, were equally the issues of an almighty power. And therefore the wise men of the world have contended who shall best fit man's condition with words signifying his vanity and short abode. Homer calls a man "a leaf," the smallest, the weakest piece of a short-lived, unsteady plant: Pindar calls him "the dream of a shadow": another, "the dream of the shadow of smoke": but St. James spake by a more excellent spirit, saying,

"our life is but a vapor," viz., drawn from the earth by a celestial
influence; made of smoke, or the lighter parts of water, tossed
with every wind, moved by the motion of a superior body, without virtue in itself, lifted up on high or left below, according as it
pleases the sun its foster-father. But it is lighter yet; it is but
"appearing"; a fantastic vapor, an apparition, nothing real: it is
not so much as a mist, not the matter of a shower, nor substantial
enough to make a cloud; but it is like Cassiopeia's chair, or
Pelops' shoulder, or the circles of heaven, $\phi\alpha\iota\nu\acute{o}\mu\epsilon\nu\alpha$, than which
you cannot have a word that can signify a verier nothing. And
yet the expression is one degree more made diminutive: a "vapor,"
and "fantastical," or a "mere appearance," and this but for a little
while neither; the very dream, the phantasm disappears in a
small time, "like the shadow that departeth"; or "like a tale
that is told"; or "as a dream when one awaketh." A man is so
vain, so unfixed, so perishing a creature, that he cannot long last
in the scene of fancy: a man goes off, and is forgotten, like the
dream of a distracted person. The sum of all is this: that thou
art a man, than whom there is not in the world any greater instance of heights and declensions, of lights and shadows, of
misery and folly, of laughter and tears, of groans and death.

And because this consideration is of great usefulness and great
necessity to many purposes of wisdom and the spirit; all the
succession of time, all the changes in nature, all the varieties of
light and darkness, the thousand thousands of accidents in the
world, and every contingency to every man, and to every creature, doth preach our funeral sermon, and calls us to look and
see how the old sexton Time throws up the earth, and digs a
grave where we must lay our sins or our sorrows, and sow our
bodies, till they rise again in a fair or in an intolerable eternity.
Every revolution which the sun makes about the world, divides
between life and death; and death possesses both those portions
by the next morrow; and we are dead to all those months which
we have already lived, and we shall never live them over again:
and still God makes little periods of our age. First we change
our world, when we come from the womb to feel the warmth of
the sun. Then we sleep and enter into the image of death, in
which state we are unconcerned in all the changes of the world:
and if our mothers or our nurses die, or a wild boar destroy our
vineyards, or our king be sick, we regard it not, but during that

state are as disinterest as if our eyes were closed with the clay that weeps in the bowels of the earth.   At the end of seven years our teeth fall and die before us, representing a formal prologue to the tragedy; and still every seven years it is odds but we shall finish the last scene: and when nature, or chance, or vice, takes our body in pieces, weakening some parts and loosing others, we taste the grave and the solemnities of our own funerals, first in those parts that ministered to vice, and next in them that served for ornament, and in a short time even they that served for necessity become useless, and entangled like the wheels of a broken clock.   Baldness is but a dressing to our funerals, the proper ornament of mourning, and of a person entered very far into the regions and possession of death: and we have many more of the same signification; gray hairs, rotten teeth, dim eyes, trembling joints, short breath, stiff limbs, wrinkled skin, short memory, decayed appetite.   Every day's necessity calls for a reparation of that portion which death fed on all night, when we lay in his lap, and slept in his outer chambers.   The very spirits of a man prey upon the daily portion of bread and flesh, and every meal is a rescue from one death, and lays up for another; and while we think a thought, we die; and the clock strikes, and reckons on our portion of eternity: we form our words with the breath of our nostrils, we have the less to live upon for every word we speak.

Thus nature calls us to meditate of death by those things which are the instruments of acting it: and God by all the variety of his providence makes us see death everywhere, in all variety of circumstances, and dressed up for all the fancies and the expectation of every single person.   Nature hath given us one harvest every year, but death hath two, and the spring and the autumn send throngs of men and women to charnel-houses; and all the summer long men are recovering from their evils of the spring, till the dog-days come, and then the Sirian star makes the summer deadly; and the fruits of autumn are laid up for all the year's provision, and the man that gathers them eats and surfeits, and dies and needs them not, and himself is laid up for eternity; and he that escaped till winter only stays for another opportunity which the distempers of that quarter minister to him with great variety.   Thus death reigns in all the portions of our time; the autumn with its fruits provides disorders for us, and the winter's cold turns them into sharp diseases, and the spring brings flowers to strew our hearse, and the summer gives green turf and brambles to bind upon our graves. Calentures and surfeit, cold and agues, are the four quarters of the year, and all minister to death; and you can go no whither but you tread upon a dead man's bones.

The wild fellow in Petronius that escaped upon a broken table from the furies of a shipwreck, as he was sunning himself upon the rocky shore, espied a man rolled upon his floating bed of waves, ballasted with sand in the folds of his garment, and carried by his civil enemy, the sea, towards the shore to find a grave: and it cast him into some sad thoughts; that peradventure this man's wife in some part of the continent, safe and warm, looks next month for the good man's return; or, it may be, his son knows nothing of the tempest; or his father thinks of that affectionate kiss, which still is warm upon the good old man's cheek, ever since he took a kind farewell; and he weeps with joy to think how blessed he shall be when his beloved boy returns into the circle of his father's arms. These are the thoughts of mortals, this is the end and sum of all their designs: a dark night and an ill guide, a boisterous sea and a broken cable, a hard rock and a rough wind, dashed in pieces the fortune of a whole family, and they that shall weep loudest for the accident are not yet entered into the storm, and yet have suffered shipwreck. Then looking upon the carcass, he knew it, and found it to be the master of the ship, who the day before cast up the accounts of his patrimony and his trade, and named the day when he thought to be at home: see how the man swims who was so angry two days since; his passions are becalmed with the storm, his accounts cast up, his cares at an end, his voyage done, and his gains are the strange events of death, which whether they be good or evil, the men that are alive seldom trouble themselves concerning the interest of the dead.

But seas alone do not break our vessel in pieces: everywhere we may be shipwrecked. A valiant general, when he is to reap the harvest of his crowns and triumphs, fights unprosperously; or falls into a fever with joy and wine, and changes his laurel into cypress, his triumphal chariot to a hearse, dying the night before he was appointed to perish in the drunkenness of his festival joys. It was a sad arrest of the loosenesses and wilder feasts of the French court, when their king Henry the Second was killed really by the sportive image of a fight. And many brides have died under the hands of paranymphs and maidens, dressing them for uneasy joy, the new and undiscerned chains of marriage; according to the saying of Bensirah, the wise Jew, "the bride went into her chamber, and knew not what should befall her there." Some have been paying their vows, and giving thanks for a prosperous return to their own house, and the roof hath descended upon their heads, and turned their loud religion into the deeper silence of a grave. And how many teeming mothers have rejoiced over their swelling wombs, and pleased themselves in becoming the channels of blessing to a family, and the midwife hath quickly bound their heads and feet, and carried them forth to burial! Or else the birthday of an heir hath seen the coffin of the father brought into the house, and the divided mother hath been forced to travail twice, with a painful birth, and a sadder death.

There is no state, no accident, no circumstance of our life, but it hath been soured by some sad instance of a dying friend: a friendly meeting often ends in some sad mischance, and makes an eternal parting: and when the poet Æschylus was sitting under the walls of his house, an eagle hovering over his bald head mistook it for a stone, and let fall his oyster, hoping there to break the shell, but pierced the poor man's skull.

Death meets us everywhere, and is procured by every instrument and in all chances, and enters in at many doors; by violence and secret influence, by the aspect of a star and the stink of a mist, by the emissions of a cloud and the meeting of a vapor, by the fall of a chariot and the stumbling at a stone, by a full meal or an empty stomach, by watching at the wine or by watching at prayers, by the sun or the moon, by a heat or a cold, by sleepless nights or sleeping days, by water frozen into the hardness and sharpness of a dagger, or water thawed into the floods of a river, by a hair or a raisin, by violent motion or sitting still, by severity or dissolution, by God's mercy or God's anger; by everything in providence and everything in manners, by everything in nature and everything in chance.

Eripitur persona, manet res;[1]

---

[1] The mask is torn off, the reality is left.

we take pains to heap up things useful to our life, and get our death in the purchase; and the person is snatched away, and the goods remain. And all this is the law and constitution of nature; it is a punishment to our sins, the unalterable event of providence and the decree of heaven: the chains that confine us to this condition are strong as destiny, and immutable as the eternal laws of God.

I have conversed with some men who rejoiced in the death or calamity of others, and accounted it as a judgment upon them for being on the other side, and against them in the contention: but within the revolution of a few months, the same man met with a more uneasy and unhandsome death: which when I saw, I wept, and was afraid; for I knew that it must be so with all men; for we also shall die, and end our quarrels and contentions by passing to a final sentence.

SECTION II

THE CONSIDERATION REDUCED TO PRACTICE

It will be very material to our best and noblest purposes if we represent this scene of change and sorrow a little more dressed up in circumstances, for so we shall be more apt to practise those rules the doctrine of which is consequent to this consideration. It is a mighty change that is made by the death of every person, and it is visible to us who are alive. Reckon but from the sprightfulness of youth, and the fair cheeks and full eyes of childhood, from the vigorousness and strong flexure of the joints of five-and-twenty to the hollowness and dead paleness, to the loathsomeness and horror of a three days' burial, and we shall perceive the distance to be very great and very strange. But so have I seen a rose newly springing from the clefts of its hood, and at first it was fair as the morning, and full with the dew of heaven as a lamb's fleece; but when a ruder breath had forced open its virgin modesty, and dismantled its too youthful and unripe retirements, it began to put on darkness, and to decline to softness and the symptoms of a sickly age; it bowed the head, and broke its stalk, and at night, having lost some of its leaves and all its beauty, it fell into the portion of weeds and outworn faces. The same is the portion of every man and every woman, the heritage of worms and serpents, rottenness and cold dishonor, and our beauty so changed, that our acquaintance quickly knew us not; and that change mingled with so much horror, or else meets so with our fears and weak discoursings, that they who six hours ago tended upon us either with charitable or ambitious services, cannot without some regret stay in the room alone where the body lies stripped of its life and honor. I have read of a fair young German gentleman who, living, often refused to be pictured, but put off the importunity of his friends' desire by giving way that after a few days' burial they might send a painter to his vault, and if they saw cause for it, draw the image of his death unto the life: they did so, and found his face half eaten, and his midriff and backbone full of serpents; and so he stands pictured among his armed ancestors. So does the fairest beauty change, and it will be as bad with you and me; and then what servants shall we have to wait upon us in the grave? what friends to visit us? what officious people to cleanse away the moist and unwholesome cloud reflected upon our faces from the sides of the weeping vaults, which are the longest weepers for our funeral?

This discourse will be useful if we consider and practise by the following rules and considerations respectively:—

1. All the rich and all the covetous men in the world will perceive, and all the world will perceive for them, that it is but an ill recompense for all their cares, that by this time all that shall be left will be this, that the neighbors shall say, "He died a rich man"; and yet his wealth will not profit him in the grave, but hugely swell the sad accounts of doomsday. And he that kills the Lord's people with unjust or ambitious wars for an unrewarding interest, shall have this character, that he threw away all the days of his life, that one year might be reckoned with his name, and computed by his reign or consulship; and many men, by great labors and affronts, many indignities and crimes, labor only for a pompous epitaph and a loud title upon their marble; whilst those into whose possessions their heirs or kindred are entered, are forgotten, and lie unregarded as their ashes, and without concernment or relation, as the turf upon the face of their grave. A man may read a sermon, the best and most passionate that ever man preached, if he shall but enter into the sepulchres of kings. In the same Escurial where the Spanish princes live in greatness and power, and decree war or peace,

they have wisely placed a cemetery where their ashes and their glory shall sleep till time shall be no more; and where our kings have been crowned, their ancestors lay interred, and they must walk over their grandsire's head to take his crown. There is an acre sown with royal seed, the copy of the greatest change, from rich to naked, from ceiled roofs to arched coffins, from living like gods to die like men. There is enough to cool the flames of lust, to abate the heights of pride, to appease the itch of covetous desires, to sully and dash out the dissembling colors of a lustful, artificial, and imaginary beauty. There the warlike and the peaceful, the fortunate and the miserable, the beloved and the despised princes mingle their dust, and pay down their symbol of mortality, and tell all the world, that when we die our ashes shall be equal to kings', and our accounts easier, and our pains or our crowns shall be less. . . .

2. Let no man extend his thoughts or let his hopes wander towards future and far-distant events and accidental contingencies. This day is mine and yours, but ye know not what shall be on the morrow; and every morning creeps out of a dark cloud, leaving behind it an ignorance and silence deep as midnight, and undiscerned as are the phantasms that make a chrisom-child to smile: so that we cannot discern what comes hereafter, unless we had a light from heaven brighter than the vision of an angel, even the spirit of prophecy. Without revelation we cannot tell whether we shall eat to-morrow, or whether a squinzy shall choke us: and it is written in the unrevealed folds of divine predestination that many who are this day alive shall to-morrow be laid upon the cold earth, and the women shall weep over their shroud and dress them for their funeral.

. . . .

3. As our hopes must be confined, so must our designs: let us not project long designs, crafty plots, and diggings so deep that the intrigues of a design shall never be unfolded till our grandchildren have forgotten our virtues or our vices. The work of our soul is cut short, facile, sweet, and plain, and fitted to the small portions of our shorter life; and as we must not trouble our inquiry, so neither must we intricate our labor and purposes with what we shall never enjoy. This rule does not forbid us to plant orchards which shall feed our nephews with their

fruit; for by such provisions they do something towards an imaginary immortality, and do charity to their relatives: but such projects are reproved, which discompose our present duty by long and future designs; such which by casting our labors to events at distance make us less to remember our death standing at the door. It is fit for a man to work for his day's wages, or to contrive for the hire of a week, or to lay a train to make provisions for such a time as is within our eye, and in our duty, and within the usual periods of man's life; for whatsoever is made necessary, is also made prudent: but while we plot and busy ourselves in the toils of an ambitious war, or the levies of a great estate, night enters in upon us, and tells all the world how like fools we lived, and how deceived and miserably we died. Seneca tells of Senecio Cornelius, a man crafty in getting, and tenacious in holding a great estate, and one who was as diligent in the care of his body as of his money, curious of his health, as of his possessions, that he all day long attended upon his sick and dying friend; but when he went away, was quickly comforted, supped merrily, went to bed cheerfully, and on a sudden being surprised by a squinzy, scarce drew his breath until the morning, but by that time died, being snatched from the torrent of his fortune, and the swelling tide of wealth, and a likely hope bigger than the necessities of ten men. This accident was much noted then in Rome, because it happened in so great a fortune, and in the midst of wealthy designs; and presently it made wise men to consider, how imprudent a person he is who disposes of ten years to come, when he is not lord of to-morrow.

4. Though we must not look so far off and pry abroad, yet we must be busy near at hand; we must with all arts of the spirit seize upon the present, because it passes from us while we speak, and because in it all our certainty does consist. We must take our waters as out of a torrent and sudden shower, which will quickly cease dropping from above, and quickly cease running in our channels here below; this instant will never return again, and yet it may be this instant will declare or secure the fortune of a whole eternity. The old Greeks and Romans taught us the prudence of this rule, but Christianity teaches us the religion of it. They so seized upon the present that they would lose nothing of the day's pleasure: "Let us eat and drink, for to-morrow we shall die"; that was their philosophy; and at their solemn

feasts they would talk of death to heighten the present drinking, and that they might warm their veins with a fuller chalice, as knowing the drink that was poured upon their graves would be cold and without relish. "Break the beds, drink your wine, crown your heads with roses, and besmear your curled locks with nard; for God bids you to remember death": so the epigrammatist speaks the sense of their drunken principles. Something towards this signification is that of Solomon: "There is nothing better for a man than that he should eat and drink, and that he should make his soul enjoy good in his labor; for that is his portion; for who shall bring him to see that which shall be after him?" But although he concludes all this to be vanity, yet because it was the best thing that was then commonly known that they should seize upon the present with a temperate use of permitted pleasures, I had reason to say, that Christianity taught us to turn this into religion. For he that by a present and a constant holiness secures the present, and makes it useful to his noblest purposes, he turns his condition into his best advantage, by making his unavoidable fate become his necessary religion.

To the purpose of this rule is that collect of Tuscan hieroglyphics which we have from Gabriel Simeon: "Our life is very short, beauty is a cozenage, money is false and fugitive; empire is odious, and hated by them that have it not, and uneasy to them that have; victory is always uncertain, and peace most commonly is but a fraudulent bargain; old age is miserable, death is the period, and is a happy one if it be not soured by the sins of our life: but nothing continues but the effects of that wisdom which employs the present time in the acts of a holy religion and a peaceable conscience": for they make us to live even beyond our funerals, embalmed in the spices and odors of a good name, and entombed in the grave of the holy Jesus, where we shall be dressed for a blessed resurrection to the state of angels and beatified spirits.

5. Since we stay not here, being people but of a day's abode, and our age is like that of a fly and contemporary with a gourd, we must look somewhere else for an abiding city, a place in another country to fix our house in, whose walls and foundation is God, where we must find rest, or else be restless for ever. For whatsoever ease we can have or fancy here is shortly to be

changed into sadness or tediousness: it goes away too soon, like the periods of our life: or stays too long, like the sorrows of a sinner: its own weariness, or a contrary disturbance, is its load; or it is eased by its revolution into vanity and forgetfulness; and where either there is sorrow or an end of joy, there can be no true felicity: which because it must be had by some instrument and in some period of our duration, we must carry up our affections to the mansions prepared for us above, where eternity is the measure, felicity is the state, angels are the company, the Lamb is the light, and God is the portion and inheritance.

SECTION III

RULES AND SPIRITUAL ARTS OF LENGTHENING OUR DAYS, AND TO TAKE OFF THE OBJECTION OF A SHORT LIFE

1. IN THE accounts of a man's life, we do not reckon that portion of days in which we are shut up in the prison of the womb; we tell our years from the day of our birth: and the same reason that makes our reckoning to stay so long, says also that then it begins too soon. For then we are beholden to others to make the account for us; for we know not of a long time whether we be alive or no, having but some little approaches and symptoms of a life. To feed, and sleep, and move a little, and imperfectly, is the state of an unborn child; and when he is born, he does no more for a good while; and what is it that shall make him to be esteemed to live the life of a man? and when shall that account begin? For we should be loth to have the accounts of our age taken by the measures of a beast: and fools and distracted persons are reckoned as civilly dead; they are no parts of the commonwealth, not subject to laws, but secured by them in charity, and kept from violence as a man keeps his ox: and a third part of our life is spent, before we enter into a higher order, into the state of a man.

2. Neither must we think that the life of a man begins when he can feed himself, or walk alone, when he can fight, or beget his like; for so he is contemporary with a camel or a cow; but he is first a man when he comes to a certain, steady use of reason, according to his proportion: and when that is, all the world of men cannot tell precisely. Some are called at age at fourteen;

some at one-and-twenty; some, never; but all men, late enough; for the life of a man comes upon him slowly and insensibly. But as when the sun approaches towards the gates of the morning, he first opens a little eye of heaven, and sends away the spirits of darkness, and gives light to a cock, and calls up the lark to matins, and by and by gilds the fringes of a cloud, and peeps over the eastern hills, thrusting out his golden horns, like those which decked the brows of Moses when he was forced to wear a veil because himself had seen the face of God; and still while a man tells the story, the sun gets up higher, till he shows a fair face and a full light, and then he shines one whole day, under a cloud often, and sometimes weeping great and little showers, and sets quickly: so is a man's reason and his life. He first begins to perceive himself to see or taste, making little reflections upon his actions of sense, and can discourse of flies and dogs, shells and play, horses and liberty: but when he is strong enough to enter into arts and little institutions, he is at first entertained with trifles and impertinent things, not because he needs them, but because his understanding is no bigger, and little images of things are laid before him, like a cock-boat to a whale, only to play withal: but before a man comes to be wise, he is half dead with gouts and consumptions, with catarrhs and aches, with sore eyes and a worn-out body. So that if we must not reckon the life of a man but by the accounts of his reason, he is long before his soul be dressed; and he is not to be called a man without a wise and an adorned soul, a soul at least furnished with what is necessary towards his well-being: but by that time his soul is thus furnished, his body is decayed; and then you can hardly reckon him to be alive, when his body is possessed by so many degrees of death.

3. But there is yet another arrest. At first he wants strength of body, and then he wants the use of reason: and when that is come, it is ten to one but he stops by the impediments of vice, and wants the strengths of the spirit; and we know that body and soul and spirit are the constituent parts of every Christian man. And now let us consider, what that thing is, which we call years of discretion. The young man is past his tutors, and arrived at the bondage of a caitiff spirit; he is run from discipline, and is let loose to passion; the man by this time hath wit enough to choose his vice, to act his lust, to court his mistress, to talk

confidently, and ignorantly, and perpetually, to despise his bet-
ters, to deny nothing to his appetite, to do things that when he is
indeed a man he must for ever be ashamed of: for this is all the
discretion that most men show in the first stage of their manhood; they can discern good from evil; and they prove their skill
by leaving all that is good, and wallowing in the evils of folly
and an unbridled appetite. And by this time the young man
hath contracted vicious habits, and is a beast in manners, and
therefore it will not be fitting to reckon the beginning of his
life; he is a fool in his understanding, and that is a sad death;
and he is dead in trespasses and sins, and that is a sadder:
so that he hath no life but a natural, the life of a beast or a tree;
in all other capacities he is dead; he neither hath the intellectual
nor the spiritual life, neither the life of a man nor of a Christian;
and this sad truth lasts too long. For old age seizes upon most
men while they still retain the minds of boys and vicious youth,
doing actions from principles of great folly, and a mighty ignorance, admiring things useless and hurtful, and filling up all the
dimensions of their abode with businesses of empty affairs, being
at leisure to attend no virtue: they cannot pray, because they are
busy, and because they are passionate; they cannot communicate
because they have quarrels and intrigues of perplexed causes,
complicated hostilities, and things of the world, and therefore they cannot attend to the things of God: little considering that they must find a time to die in; when death comes, they
must be at leisure for that. Such men are like sailors loosing
from a port, and tossed immediately with a perpetual tempest
lasting till their cordage crack, and either they sink, or return
back again to the same place: they did not make a voyage,
though they were long at sea. The business and impertinent
affairs of most men steal all their time, and they are restless in
a foolish motion: but this is not the progress of a man; he is no
farther advanced in the course of a life, though he reckon many
years; for still his soul is childish, and trifling like an untaught
boy.

If the parts of this sad complaint find their remedy, we have
by the same instruments also cured the evils and the vanity of a
short life. Therefore,

1. Be infinitely curious you do not set back your life in the

accounts of God by the intermingling of criminal actions, or the contracting vicious habits. There are some vices which carry a sword in their hand, and cut a man off before his time. There is a sword of the Lord, and there is a sword of a man, and there is a sword of the devil. Every vice of our own managing in the matter of carnality, of lust or rage, ambition or revenge, is a sword of Satan put into the hands of a man: these are the destroying angels; sin is the Apollyon, the destroyer that is gone out, not from the Lord, but from the tempter; and we hug the poison, and twist willingly with the vipers, till they bring us into the regions of an irrecoverable sorrow. We use to reckon persons as good as dead if they have lost their limbs and their teeth, and are confined to a hospital, and converse with none but surgeons and physicians, mourners and divines, those *pollinctores*, the dressers of bodies and souls to funeral: but it is worse when the soul, the principle of life, is employed wholly in the offices of death: and that man was worse than dead of whom Seneca tells, that, being a rich fool, when he was lifted up from the baths and set into a soft couch, asked his slaves, *An ego jam sedeo*, "Do I now sit?" The beast was so drowned in sensuality and the death of his soul, that whether he did sit or no, he was to believe another. Idleness and every vice is as much of death as a long disease is, or the expense of ten years; and "she that lives in pleasures is dead while she liveth," saith the Apostle; and it is the style of the Spirit concerning wicked persons, "they are dead in trespasses and sins." For as every sensual pleasure and every day of idleness and useless living lops off a little branch from our short life, so every deadly sin and every habitual vice does quite destroy us; but innocence leaves us in our natural portions and perfect period; we lose nothing of our life if we lose nothing of our soul's health; and therefore he that would live a full age, must avoid a sin, as he would decline the regions of death and the dishonors of the grave.

2. If we would have our life lengthened, let us begin betimes to live in the accounts of reason and sober counsels, of religion and the spirit, and then we shall have no reason to complain that our abode on earth is so short: many men find it long enough, and indeed it is so to all senses. But when we spend in waste what God hath given us in plenty, when we sacrifice our youth

to folly, our manhood to lust and rage, our old age to covetousness and irreligion, not beginning to live till we are to die, design-
ing that time to virtue which indeed is infirm to everything and
profitable to nothing; then we make our lives short, and lust
runs away with all the vigorous and healthful part of it, and
pride and animosity steal the manly portion, and crafti-
ness and interest possess old age: *velut ex pleno et abundanti
perdimus*, we spend as if we had too much time, and knew not
what to do with it: we fear everything, like weak and silly
mortals; and desire strangely and greedily, as if we were immortal: we complain our life is short, and yet we throw away
much of it, and are weary of many of its parts; we complain the
day is long, and the night is long, and we want company, and
seek out arts to drive the time away, and then weep because
it is gone too soon. But so the treasure of the capitol is but a
small estate, when Cæsar comes to finger it, and to pay with it
all his legions: and the revenue of all Egypt and the eastern
provinces was but a little sum, when they were to support the
luxury of Mark Antony, and feed the riot of Cleopatra; but a
thousand crowns is a vast proportion to be spent in the cottage
of a frugal person, or to feed a hermit. Just so is our life:
it is too short to serve the ambition of a haughty prince or an
usurping rebel; too little time to purchase great wealth, to
satisfy the pride of a vain-glorious fool, to trample upon all the
enemies of our just or unjust interest; but for the obtaining virtue, for the purchase of sobriety and modesty, for the actions
of religion, God gave us time sufficient, if we make the "out-
goings of the morning and evening," that is, our infancy and old
age, to be taken into the computations of a man. . . .

6. But if I shall describe a living man, a man that hath that
life that distinguishes him from a fool or a bird, that which gives
him a capacity next to angels, we shall find that even a good
man lives not long, because it is long before he is born to this life,
and longer yet before he hath a man's growth. "He that can
look upon death, and see its face with the same countenance with
which he hears its story; that can endure all the labors of his
life with his soul supporting his body; that can equally despise
riches when he hath them and when he hath them not; that is
not sadder if they lie in his neighbor's trunks, nor more brag if
they shine round about his own walls; he that is neither moved

with good fortune coming to him nor going from him; that can look upon another man's lands evenly and pleasedly as if they were his own, and yet look upon his own, and use them too, just as if they were another man's; that neither spends his goods prodigally and like a fool, nor yet keeps them avariciously and like a wretch; that weighs not benefits by weight and number, but by the mind and circumstances of him that gives them; that never thinks his charity expensive if a worthy person be the receiver; he that does nothing for opinion sake, but everything for conscience, being as curious of his thoughts as of his actings in markets and theatres, and is as much in awe of himself as of a whole assembly; he that knows God looks on, and contrives his secret affairs as in the presence of God and his holy angels; that eats and drinks because he needs it, not that he may serve a lust or load his belly; he that is bountiful and cheerful to his friends, and charitable and apt to forgive his enemies; that loves his country, and obeys his prince, and desires and endeavors nothing more than that he may do honor to God"; this person may reckon his life to be the life of a man, and compute his months, not by the course of the sun, but the zodiac and circle of his virtues; because these are such things which fools and children and birds and beasts cannot have; these are therefore the actions of life, because they are the seeds of immortality. That day in which we have done some excellent thing we may as truly reckon to be added to our life as were the fifteen years to the days of Hezekiah.

SECTION IV

CONSIDERATION OF THE MISERIES OF MAN'S LIFE

As our life is very short, so it is very miserable; and therefore it is well it is short. God in pity to mankind, lest his burden should be insupportable and his nature an intolerable load, hath reduced our state of misery to an abbreviature; and the greater our misery is, the less while it is like to last; the sorrows of a man's spirit being like ponderous weights, which by the greatness of their burden make a swifter motion, and descend into the grave to rest and ease our wearied limbs; for then only we shall sleep quietly, when those fetters are knocked off, which not only bound our souls in prison, but also ate the flesh till the very bones opened the secret garments of their cartilages, discovering their nakedness and sorrow.

1. Here is no place to sit down in, but you must rise as soon as you are set, for we have gnats in our chambers, and worms in our gardens, and spiders and flies in the palaces of the greatest kings. How few men in the world are prosperous! What an infinite number of slaves and beggars, of persecuted and oppressed people, fill all corners of the earth with groans, and heaven itself with weeping prayers and sad remembrances! How many provinces and kingdoms are afflicted by a violent war, or made desolate by popular diseases! Some whole countries are remarked with fatal evils, or periodical sicknesses. Grand Cairo in Egypt feels the plague every three years returning like a quartan ague, and destroying many thousands of persons. All the inhabitants of Arabia the desert are in continual fear of being buried in huge heaps of sand, and therefore dwell in tents and ambulatory houses, or retire to unfruitful mountains, to prolong an uneasy and wilder life. And all the countries round about the Adriatic Sea feel such violent convulsions by tempests and intolerable earthquakes, that sometimes whole cities find a tomb, and every man sinks with his own house made ready to become his monument, and his bed is crushed into the disorders of a grave. Was not all the world drowned at one deluge and breach of the divine anger; and shall not all the world again be destroyed by fire? Are there not many thousands that die every night, and that groan and weep sadly every day? But what shall we think of that great evil which for the sins of men God hath suffered to possess the greatest part of mankind? Most of the men that are now alive, or that have been living for many ages, are Jews, heathens, or Turks; and God was pleased to suffer a base epileptic person, a villain and a vicious, to set up a religion which hath filled all the nearer parts of Asia, and much of Africa, and some part of Europe; so that the greatest number of men and women born in so many kingdoms and provinces are infallibly made Mahometans, strangers and enemies to Christ by whom alone we can be saved: this consideration is extremely sad, when we remember how universal and how great an evil it is, that so many millions of sons and daughters are born to enter into the possession of devils to eternal ages. These evils are the miseries of great parts of mankind,

and we cannot easily consider more particularly the evils which happen to us, being the inseparable affections or incidents to the whole nature of man.

2. We find that all the women in the world are either born for barrenness, or the pains of childbirth, and yet this is one of our greatest blessings; but such indeed are the blessings of this world, we cannot be well with nor without many things. Perfumes make our heads ache, roses prick our fingers, and in our very blood, where our life dwells, is the scene under which nature acts many sharp fevers and heavy sicknesses. It were too sad if I should tell how many persons are afflicted with evil spirits, with spectres and illusions of the night; and that huge multitudes of men and women live upon man's flesh; nay, worse yet, upon the sins of men, upon the sins of their sons and of their daughters, and they pay their souls down for the bread they eat, buying this day's meal with the price of the last night's sin.

3. Or if you please in charity to visit a hospital, which is indeed a map of the whole world, there you shall see the effects of Adam's sin, and the ruins of human nature; bodies laid up in heaps like the bones of a destroyed town, *homines precarii spiritus et male hærentis*, men whose souls seem to be borrowed, and are kept there by art and the force of medicine, whose miseries are so great that few people have charity or humanity enough to visit them, fewer have the heart to dress them, and we pity them in civility or with a transient prayer, but we do not feel their sorrows by the mercies of a religious pity; and therefore as we leave their sorrows in many degrees unrelieved and uneased, so we contract by our unmercifulness a guilt by which ourselves become liable to the same calamities. Those many that need pity, and those infinities of people that refuse to pity, are miserable upon a several charge, but yet they almost make up all mankind.

4. All wicked men are in love with that which entangles them in huge varieties of troubles; they are slaves to the worst of masters, to sin and to the devil, to a passion, and to an imperious woman. Good men are for ever prosecuted, and God chastises every son whom he receives, and whatsoever is easy is trifling and worth nothing, and whatsoever is excellent is not to be obtained without labor and sorrow; and the conditions and states

of men that are free from great cares are such as have in them nothing rich and orderly, and those that have are stuck full of thorns and trouble.   Kings are full of care; and learned men in all ages have been observed to be very poor, *et honestas miserias accusant*, "they complain of their honest miseries."

5. But these evils are notorious and confessed; even they also whose felicity men stare at and admire, besides their splendor and the sharpness of their light, will with their appendant sorrows wring a tear from the most resolved eye; for not only the winter quarter is full of storms and cold and darkness, but the beauteous spring hath blasts and sharp frosts, the fruitful teeming summer is melted with heat, and burnt with the kisses of the sun her friend, and choked with dust, and the rich autumn is full of sickness; and we are weary of that which we enjoy, because sorrow is its biggest portion: and when we remember that upon the fairest face is placed one of the worst sinks of the body, the nose, we may use it not only as a mortification to the pride of beauty, but as an allay to the fairest outside of condition which any of the sons and daughters of Adam do possess.   For look upon kings and conquerors: I will not tell that many of them fall into the condition of servants, and their subjects rule over them, and stand upon the ruins of their families, and that to such persons the sorrow is bigger than usually happens in smaller fortunes; but let us suppose them still conquerors, and see what a goodly purchase they get by all their pains, and amazing fears, and continual dangers.   They carry their arms beyond Ister, and pass the Euphrates, and bind the Germans with the bounds of the river Rhine: I speak in the style of the Roman greatness; for nowadays the biggest fortune swells not beyond the limits of a petty province or two, and a hill confines the progress of their prosperity, or a river checks it: but whatsoever tempts the pride and vanity of ambitious persons, is not so big as the smallest star which we see scattered in disorder and unregarded upon the pavement and floor of heaven.   And if we would suppose the pismires had but our understandings, they also would have the method of a man's greatness, and divide their little mole-hills into provinces and exarchates: and if they also grew as vicious and as miserable, one of their princes would lead an army out and kill his neighbor ants, that he might reign over the next handful of a turf.   But then if we consider at what price and

with what felicity all this is purchased, the sting of the painted snake will quickly appear, and the fairest of their fortunes will properly enter into this account of human infelicities. . . .

6. The prosperity of this world is so infinitely soured with the overflowing of evils, that he is counted the most happy who hath the fewest; all conditions being evil and miserable, they are only distinguished by the number of calamities. The collector of the Roman and foreign examples, when he had reckoned two-and-twenty instances of great fortunes, every one of which had been allayed with great variety of evils; in all his reading or experience, he could tell but of two who had been famed for an entire prosperity, Quintus Metellus, and Gyges the king of Lydia: and yet concerning the one of them he tells that his felicity was so inconsiderable (and yet it was the bigger of the two) that the oracle said that Aglaus Sophidius the poor Arcadian shepherd was more happy than he, that is, he had fewer troubles; for so indeed we are to reckon the pleasures of this life; the limit of our joy is the absence of some degrees of sorrow, and he that hath the least of this, is the most prosperous person. But then we must look for prosperity not in palaces or courts of princes, not in the tents of conquerors, or in the gaieties of fortunate and prevailing sinners; but something rather in the cottages of honest, innocent, and contented persons, whose mind is no bigger than their fortune, nor their virtue less than their security. As for others, whose fortune looks bigger, and allures fools to follow it like the wandering fires of the night, till they run into rivers or are broken upon rocks with staring and running after them, they are all in the condition of Marius, than whose condition nothing was more constant, and nothing more mutable; if we reckon them amongst the happy, they are the most happy men; if we reckon them amongst the miserable, they are the most miserable. For just as is a man's condition, great or little, so is the state of his misery; all have their share; but kings and princes, great generals and consuls, rich men and mighty, as they have the biggest business and the biggest charge, and are answerable to God for the greatest accounts, so they have the biggest trouble; that the uneasiness of their appendage may divide the good and evil of the world, making the poor man's fortune as eligible as the greatest; and also restraining the vanity of man's spirit, which a great fortune is apt to swell from a vapor to a bubble; but God

in mercy hath mingled wormwood with their wine, and so restrained the drunkenness and follies of prosperity.

7. Man never hath one day to himself of entire peace from the
things of this world, but either something troubles him, or nothing satisfies him, or his very fullness swells him and makes him
breathe short upon his bed. Men's joys are troublesome, and
besides that the fear of losing them takes away the present pleasure, and a man hath need of another felicity to preserve this,
they are also wavering and full of trepidation, not only from their
inconstant nature, but from their weak foundation: they arise
from vanity, and they dwell upon ice, and they converse with
the wind, and they have the wings of a bird, and are serious but
as the resolutions of a child, commenced by chance, and managed by folly, and proceed by inadvertency, and end in vanity
and forgetfulness. So that as Livius Drusus said of himself, he
never had any play days or days of quiet when he was a boy, for
he was troublesome and busy, a restless and unquiet man; the
same may every man observe to be true of himself; he is always
restless and uneasy, he dwells upon the waters, and leans upon
thorns, and lays his head upon a sharp stone.

SECTION V

THIS CONSIDERATION REDUCED TO PRACTICE

1. THE effect of this consideration is this, that the sadnesses
of this life help to sweeten the bitter cup of death. For let our
life be never so long, if our strength were great as that of oxen and
camels, if our sinews were strong as the cordage at the foot of an
oak, if we were as fighting and prosperous people as Siccius
Dentatus, who was on the prevailing side in a hundred and
twenty battles, who had three hundred and twelve public rewards
assigned him by his generals and princes for his valor and conduct in sieges and sharp encounters, and, besides all this, had his
share in nine triumphs; yet still the period shall be that all this
shall end in death, and the people shall talk of us awhile, good
or bad, according as we deserve, or as they please, and once it
shall come to pass that concerning every one of us it shall
be told in the neighborhood, that we are dead. This we are apt
to think a sad story; but therefore let us help it with a sadder:
for we therefore need not be much troubled that we shall die,

because we are not here in ease, nor do we dwell in a fair condition; but our days are full of sorrow and anguish, dishonored, and made unhappy with many sins, with a frail and a foolish spirit, entangled with difficult cases of conscience, insnared with passions, amazed with fears, full of cares, divided with curiosities and contradictory interests, made airy and impertinent with vanities, abused with ignorance and prodigious errors, made ridiculous with a thousand weaknesses, worn away with labors, loaden with diseases, daily vexed with dangers and temptations, and in love with misery; we are weakened with delights, afflicted with want, with the evils of myself and of all my family, and with the sadnesses of all my friends, and of all good men, even of the whole Church; and therefore methinks we need not be troubled that God is pleased to put an end to all these troubles, and to let them sit down in a natural period, which, if we please, may be to us the beginning of a better life. When the prince of Persia wept because his army should all die in the revolution of an age, Artabanus told him that they should all meet with evils so many and so great that every man of them should wish himself dead long before that. Indeed it were a sad thing to be cut of the stone, and we that are in health tremble to think of it; but the man that is wearied with the disease looks upon that sharpness as upon his cure and remedy; and as none need to have a tooth drawn, so none could well endure it, but he that felt the pain of it in his head: so is our life so full of evils, that therefore death is no evil to them that have felt the smart of this, or hope for the joys of a better.

2. But as it helps to ease a certain sorrow, as a fire draws out fire, and a nail drives forth a nail, so it instructs us in a present duty, that is, that we should not be so fond of a perpetual storm, nor dote upon the transient gauds and gilded thorns of this world. They are not worth a passion, nor worth a sigh or a groan, not of the price of one night's watching; and therefore they are mistaken and miserable persons, who, since Adam planted thorns round about paradise, are more in love with that hedge than all the fruits of the garden, sottish admirers of things that hurt them, of sweet poisons, gilded daggers, and silken halters. Tell them they have lost a bounteous friend, a rich purchase, a fair farm, a wealthy donative, and you dissolve their patience; it is an evil bigger than their spirit can bear; it brings sickness

and death; they can neither eat nor sleep with such a sorrow. But if you represent to them the evils of a vicious habit, and the dangers of a state of sin; if you tell them they have displeased God, and interrupted their hopes of heaven; it may be they will be so civil as to hear it patiently, and to treat you kindly, and first to commend, and then forget your story, because they prefer this world with all its sorrows before the pure unmingled felicities of heaven. But it is strange that any man should be so passionately in love with the thorns which grow on his own ground, that he should wear them for armlets, and knit them in his shirt, and prefer them before a kingdom and immortality. No man loves this world the better for his being poor; but men that love it because they have great possessions, love it because it is troublesome and chargeable, full of noise and temptation, because it is unsafe and ungoverned, flattered and abused; and he that considers the troubles of an overlong garment and of a crammed stomach, a trailing gown and a loaden table, may justly understand that all that for which men are so passionate, is their hurt and their objection, that which a temperate man would avoid, and a wise man cannot love.

He that is no fool, but can consider wisely, if he be in love with this world, we need not despair but that a witty man might reconcile him with tortures, and make him think charitably of the rack, and be brought to dwell with vipers and dragons, and entertain his guests with the shrieks of mandrakes, cats, and screech-owls, with the filing of iron, and the harshness of rending of silk, or to admire the harmony that is made by a herd of evening wolves when they miss their draught of blood in their midnight revels. The groans of a man in a fit of the stone are worse than all these; and the distractions of a troubled conscience are worse than those groans; and yet a careless merry sinner is worse than all that. But if we could from one of the battlements of heaven espy how many men and women at this time lie fainting and dying for want of bread, how many young men are hewn down by the sword of war, how many poor orphans are now weeping over the graves of their father by whose life they were enabled to eat: if we could but hear how many mariners and passengers are at this present in a storm, and shriek out because their keel dashes against a rock, or bulges under them, how many people there are that weep with want, and are mad with oppression, or are desperate by too quick a sense of a constant infelicity; in all reason we should be glad to be out of the noise and participation of so many evils. This is a place of sorrows and tears, of great evils and a constant calamity: let us remove from hence, at least in affections and preparation of mind.

MISCELLANEOUS

THOMAS DEKKER (?1570–1641?)

Dekker seems more at home under "Miscellaneous" than under "Religion," however sincere his prayers. When plays were not in demand he wrote pamphlets, and pamphlets in the Elizabethan tradition had a way of telling most of what the author knew up to the date of publication. Dekker's prose, formless and breathless like so much journalism of his time, has that exuberant verve, those careless vivid felicities of observation and phrase, which make lusty reading as well as valuable social documents. Not Johnson nor Lamb nor Dickens loved London more than Dekker, or had a more "extensive and peculiar" knowledge of its sights and sounds, its gulls and its rogueries. He has more color, more poetry, more variety of tone, than Defoe, for instance; the plague could inspire alike the matchless tale of the tinker, the crawling horrors of the charnel-house, the rich and somber picture of the stage of man's little life, and the "prayer to stay the pestilence." And no one can understand Elizabethan drama without knowing Dekker's account of the trials to be faced by playwrights and players. Dekker was as fond of parentheses as Henry James, and his innumerable brackets are retained in the text.

THE WONDERFUL YEAR (1603)

. . . WHAT an unmatchable torment were it for a man to be barred up every night in a vast, silent charnel-house? Hung (to make it more hideous) with lamps dimly and slowly burning, in hollow and glimmering corners; where all the pavement should, instead of green rushes, be strewed with blasted rosemary, withered hyacinths, fatal cypress and yew, thickly mingled with heaps of dead men's bones; the bare ribs of a father that begat him lying there, here the chapless hollow skull of a mother that bore him; round about him a thousand corses, some standing bolt upright in their knotted winding sheets, others half-mouldered in rotten coffins, that should suddenly yawn wide open, filling his nostrils with noisome stench, and his eyes with the sight of nothing but crawling worms. And to keep such a poor wretch waking, he should hear no noise but of toads croaking, screech-owls howling, mandrakes shrieking—were not this an infernal prison? Would not the strongest-hearted man (beset with such a ghastly horror) look wild, and run mad, and die? And even such a formidable shape did the diseased city appear in. For he that durst (in the dead hour of gloomy midnight) have been so valiant as to have walked through the still and melancholy streets, what think you should have been his music? Surely the loud groans of raving sick men, the struggling pangs of souls departing, in every house grief striking up an alarum, servants crying out for masters, wives for husbands, parents for children, children for their mothers. Here he should have met some franticly running to knock up sextons, there others fearfully sweating with coffins, to steal forth dead bodies, lest the fatal handwriting of death should seal up their doors. And to make this dismal consort more full, round about him bells heavily tolling in one place and ringing out in another. The dreadfulness of such an hour is unutterable. . . .

. . . .

To some the very sound of death's name is in stead of a passing-bell. What shall become of such a coward, being told that the self-same body of his, which now is so pampered with superfluous fare, so perfumed and bathed in odoriferous waters, and so gaily appareled in variety of fashions, must one day be thrown (like stinking carrion) into a rank and rotten grave, where his goodly eyes, that did once shoot forth such amorous glances, must be eaten out of his head, his locks that hang wantonly dangling, trodden in dirt underfoot? This doubtless (like thunder) must needs strike him into the earth. But (wretched man!), when thou shalt see and be assured (by tokens sent thee from heaven) that to-morrow thou must be tumbled into a muck-pit, and suffer thy body to be bruised and pressed with threescore dead men lying slovenly upon thee, and thou to be undermost of all! yea, and perhaps half of that number were thine enemies! (And see how they may be revenged, for the worms that breed out of their putrefying carcasses shall crawl in huge swarms from them and quite devour thee.) What agonies will this strange news drive thee into? If thou art in love with thyself this cannot choose but possess thee with frenzy.

. . . .

[During the plague a Londoner dies suddenly while drinking in a tavern in a country town, and host and townspeople are in a panic.]

The whole village is in danger to lie at the mercy of God, and shall be bound to curse none but him for it; they should do well therefore to set fire on his house before the plague scape out of it, lest it forage higher into the country and knock them down, man, woman, and child, like oxen, whose blood (they all swear) shall be required at his hands. At these speeches my tender-hearted host fell down on his maribones, meaning indeed to entreat his audience to be good to him, but they, fearing he had been peppered too, as well as the Londoner, tumbled one over another, and were ready to break their necks for haste to be gone. Yet some of them (being more valiant than the rest, because they heard him roar out for some help) very desperately stepped back and with rakes and pitchforks lifted the gulch from the ground: concluding (after they had laid their hogsheads together to draw out some wholesome counsel) that whosoever would venture upon the dead man and bury him should have forty shillings (out of the common town-purse, though it would be a great cut to it), with the love of the church-wardens and sidemen during the term of life. This was proclaimed, but none durst appear to undertake the dreadful execution. They loved money well; marry, the plague hanging over any man's head that should meddle with it in that sort, they all vowed to die beggars before it should be chronicled they killed themselves for forty shillings; and in that brave resolution everyone with bag and baggage marched home, barricadoing their doors and windows with fir bushes, fern, and bundles of straw to keep out the pestilence at the stave's end.

At last a tinker came sounding through the town, mine host's house being the ancient watering place where he did use to cast anchor. You must understand that he was none of those base rascally tinkers that with a bandog and a drab at their tails, and a pikestaff on their necks, will take a purse sooner than stop a kettle. No, this was a devout tinker, he did honor god Pan; a musical tinker, that upon his kettle-drum could play any country dance you called for, and upon holidays had earned money by it, when no fiddler could be heard of. He was only feared when he stalked through some towns where bees were, for he struck so sweetly on the bottom of his copper instrument that he would empty whole hives and lead the swarms after him only by the sound.

This excellent egregious tinker calls for his draught (being a double jug). It was filled for him, but before it came to his nose the lamentable tale of the Londoner was told, the chamber door (where he lay) being thrust open with a long pole (because none durst touch it with their hands), and the tinker bidden (if he had the heart) to go in and see if he knew him. The tinker, being not[1] to learn what virtue the medicine had which he held at his lips, poured it down his throat merrily and crying trillill, he feared no plagues. In he stepped, tossing the dead body to and fro, and was sorry he knew him not. Mine host, that with grief began to fall away villainously, looking very ruefully on the tinker, and thinking him a fit instrument to be played upon, offered a crown out of his own purse if he would bury the party. A crown was a shrewd temptation to a tinker; many a hole might he stop before he could pick a crown of it, yet being a subtle tinker (and to make all sextons pray for him, because he would raise their fees), an angel he wanted to be his guide, and under ten shillings (by his ten bones) he would not put his finger in the fire. The whole parish had warning of this presently, thirty shillings was saved by the bargain, and the town likely to be saved too; therefore ten shillings was levied out of hand, put into a rag, which was tied to the end of a long pole and delivered (in sight of all the parish, who stood aloof, stopping their noses) by the headborough's own self in proper person to the tinker, who with one hand received the money and with the other struck the board, crying "Hey, a fresh double pot!" Which armor of proof being fitted to his body, up he hoists the Londoner on his back (like a schoolboy), a shovel and pick-axe standing ready for him. And thus furnished, into a field some good distance from the town he bears his deadly load, and there throws it down, falling roundly to his tools, upon which the strong beer having set an edge, they quickly cut out a lodging in the earth for the citizen. But the tinker, knowing that worms needed no apparel saving only sheets, stripped him stark naked, but first

---

[1]Grosart supplies "unwilling."

dived nimbly into his pockets, to see what linings they had, assuring himself that a Londoner would not wander so far without silver. His hopes were of the right stamp, for from one of his pockets he drew a leathern bag with seven pounds in it; this music made the tinker's heart dance. He quickly tumbled his man into the grave, hid him over head and ears in dust, bound up his clothes in a bundle, and carrying that at the end of his staff on his shoulder, with the purse of seven pounds in his hand, back again comes he through the town, crying aloud, "Have ye any more Londoners to bury, hey down a down derry, have ye any more Londoners to bury?"—the Hobbinols running away from him as if he had been the dead citizen's ghost, and he marching away from them in all the haste he could, with that song still in his mouth.

SEVEN DEADLY SINS OF LONDON (1606)

. . . O LONDON, thou art great in glory, and envied for thy greatness; thy towers, thy temples, and thy pinnacles stand upon thy head like borders of fine gold, thy waters like fringes of silver hang at the hems of thy garments. Thou art the goodliest of thy neighbors, but the proudest; the wealthiest, but the most wanton. Thou hast all things in thee to make thee fairest, and all things in thee to make thee foulest; for thou art attired like a bride, drawing all that look upon thee to be in love with thee, but there is much harlot in thine eyes. Thou sittest in thy gates heated with wines, and in thy chambers with lust. What miseries have of late overtaken thee? Yet (like a fool that laughs when he is putting on fetters) thou hast been merry in height of thy misfortunes.

. . . .

The politician, being thus got into the city, carries himself so discreetly that he steals into the hearts of many. In words is he circumspect, in looks grave, in attire civil, in diet temperate, in company affable, in his affairs serious, and so cunningly does he lay on these colors that in the end he is welcome to, and familiar with, the best. So that now there is not any one of all the twelve Companies in which (at one time or other) there are not those that have forsaken their own hall to be free of his; yea, some of your best shopkeepers hath he enticed to shut themselves up from the cares and business of the world to live a private life; nay, there is not any great and famous street in the city wherein there hath not (or now doth not) dwell someone or other that hold the points of his religion. For you must understand that the politic bankrupt is a harpy that looks smoothly, a hyena that enchants subtilly, a mermaid that sings sweetly, and a chameleon that can put himself into all colors. Sometimes he's a puritan, he swears by nothing but "Indeed," or rather does not swear at all, and wrapping his crafty serpent's body in the cloak of religion he does those acts that would become none but a devil. Sometimes he's a protestant, and deals justly with all men, till he see his time, but in the end he turns Turk. Because you shall believe me, I will give you his length by the scale, and anatomize his body from head to foot. Here it is.

Whether he be a tradesman or a merchant, when he first sets himself up and seeks to get the world into his hands (yet not to go out of the city), or first talks of countries he never saw (upon the Change), he will be sure to keep his days of payments more truly than lawyers keep their terms, or than executors keep the last laws that the dead enjoined them to, which even infidels themselves will not violate; his hand goes to his head to his meanest customer (to express his humility); he is up earlier than a sergeant, and down later than a constable, to proclaim his thrift. By such artificial wheels as these he winds himself up into the height of rich men's favors till he grows rich himself, and when he sees that they dare build upon his credit, knowing the ground to be good, he takes upon him the condition of an ass to any man that will load him with gold; and useth his credit like a ship freighted with all sorts of merchandise by venturous pilots. For after he hath gotten into his hands so much of other men's goods or money as will fill him to the upper deck, away he sails with it, and politicly runs himself on ground, to make the world believe he had suffered shipwreck. Then flies he out like an Irish rebel, and keeps aloof, hiding his head when he cannot hide his shame; and though he have feathers on his back pulled from sundry birds, yet to himself is he more wretched than the cuckoo in winter, that dares not be seen. The troops of honest citizens (his creditors), with whom he hath broken league and hath thus defied, muster themselves together and proclaim open war.   Their bands consist of tall yeomen that serve on foot, commanded by certain sergeants of their bands, who for leading of men are known to be of more experience than the best Low-Country captains.   In ambuscado do these lie day and night, to cut off this enemy to the city, if he dare but come down.   But the politic bankrupt, barricadoing his sconce with double locks, treble doors, invincible bolts, and pieces of timber four or five stories high, victuals himself for a month or so; and then in the dead of night marches up higher into the country with bag and baggage.   Parleys then are summoned, compositions offered, a truce is sometimes taken for three or four years; or (which is more common) a dishonorable peace (seeing no other remedy) is on both sides concluded, he (like the States) being the only gainer by such civil wars, whilst the citizen that is the lender is the loser.   *Nam crimine ab uno disce omnes,*[1] look how much he snatches from one man's sheaf, he gleans from every one, if they be a hundred.

The victory being thus gotten by baseness and treachery, back comes he marching with spread colors again to the city, advances in the open street as he did before, sells the goods of his neighbor before his face without blushing.   He jets up and down in silks woven out of other men's stocks, feeds deliciously upon other men's purses, rides on his ten-pound geldings, in other men's saddles, and is now a new man made out of wax, that's to say, out of those bonds whose seals he most dishonestly hath cancelled.   O velvet-guarded thieves!   O yea-and-by-nay cheaters!   O civil, O grave and right worshipful cozeners!

. . . .

How then dares this nasty and loathsome sin of Sloth venture into a city amongst so many people?   Who doth he hope will give him entertainment?   What lodging (thinks he) can be tain up, where he and his heavy-headed company may take their afternoon's nap soundly?   For in every street carts and coaches make such a thundering as if the world ran upon wheels.   At every corner, men, women and children meet in such shoals that posts are set up of purpose to strengthen the houses, lest with jostling one another they should shoulder them down.   Besides,

---

[1]From one instance of guilt learn what they all are.

hammers are beating in one place, tubs hooping in another, pots clinking in a third, water-tankards running at tilt in a fourth; here are porters sweating under burdens, there merchants' men bearing bags of money, chapmen (as if they were at leap-frog) skip out of one shop into another; tradesmen (as if they were dancing galliards) are lusty at legs and never stand still; all are as busy as country attorneys at an assizes; how then can idleness think to inhabit here?

THE BLACK AND WHITE ROD (1630)

THIS earthly, spacious building in which we dwell (as tenants only for life) is likewise a glorious theatre, full of admirable conveyances and curiosities. The frame or module of it is round, with a silver, moving roof (called the heavens) to cover it by day, and a golden canopy of stars to curtain about it by night.

Instead of arras and tapestry (which commonly do now, and ever have adorned, the old amphitheatres) this is richly hung round about with the element of air.

The beauties of the earth are the stage, furnished bounteously, and set forth in all bravery, with woods full of trees, gardens full of flowers, orchards full of fruit, fields full of standing corn, (like so many spears ready for a battle), mountains high in pride, valleys sweet in pleasure.

Our mother's womb is the tiring-house, where we make us ready, and our cradle the music-room, for there we are sweetly strung with innocence. Nothing (then) puts us out of tune but a peal of crying. And what's that? Only a little note, a little too high, which being mended, the melody is heavenly, for there is no concord without discord.

Upon this goodly stage all sorts of people (men, women, and children) are actors. Some play emperors, some kings, some beggars, some wise men, some fools. The hardest part to play is a good man, and 'tis rare to see a long part given him to study.

On this stage are presented tragedies and comedies. The terriblest tragedy is that of the soul fighting to get off (well) from the body. The best and most pleasing comedy is that of a white conscience and the peace of mind.

Some have plaudits, shouts, and acclamations, and those are

such who have played good parts and played them bravely well. Some go hissed off the stage. And that is for want of being perfect in those good parts which are put into them.

Some play very long parts (and they are old men), some have done in the midst of the play (and they are young men), some, being but in a scene, before they speak are out and lost (and they are children).

Every actor hath his entrance, everyone his exit. As one comes out, another goes off, and sometimes meeting on the stage together they leave the stage together. But in the conclusion, he that can get angels to sit in the galleries of heaven and clap his action with their immortal hands, he is the only Roscius of the time, and one of the best actors that ever stepped on stage.

The sum, upshot, and close of all is this: that, as many men as that walk on that Royal Exchange and seem rich, do often break and are laid in prison, so in this world, when we appear never so strong in body, never so stirring in mind, yet, if health turns bankrupt once, and that the sergeant with the black rod (sickness) arrests us, if either casualties by sea or land, if losses, vexations, misfortunes or miseries, break our hearts, whither then are we carried! To our everlasting prison, the grave.

And so, when in this magnificent theatre we have jetted long on the stage and borne our heads high, yet, our parts being done, we are enforced to put off our gay borrowed garments, and, wrapping ourselves in poor winding sheets, hasten to our own homes, and (still) that's the grave.

THE GULL'S HORN-BOOK (1609)

CHAPTER IV

HOW A GALLANT SHOULD BEHAVE HIMSELF IN PAUL'S WALKS

BEING weary with sailing up and down alongst these shores of Barbaria, here let us cast our anchor, and nimbly leap to land in our coasts, whose fresh air shall be so much the more pleasing to us, if the ninnyhammer (whose perfection we labor to set forth) have so much foolish wit left him as to choose the place where to suck in. For that true humorous gallant that desires to pour himself into all fashions (if his ambition be such to excel even compliment itself) must as well practise to diminish his walks, as to be various in his sallets, curious in his tobacco, or ingenious in the trussing up of a new Scotch hose. All which virtues are excellent and able to maintain him, especially if the old worm-eaten farmer, his father, be dead, and left him five hundred a year, only to keep an Irish hobby, an Irish horse-boy, and himself like a gentleman. He therefore that would strive to fashion his legs to his silk stockings, and his proud gait to his broad garters, let him whiff down these observations. For, if he once get but to walk by the book (and I see no reason but he may, as well as fight by the book) Paul's may be proud of him; Will Clarke shall ring forth encomiums in his honor, John in Paul's Churchyard shall fit his head for an excellent block; whilst all the Inns of Court rejoice to behold his most handsome calf.

Your mediterranean aisle is then the only gallery, wherein the pictures of all your true fashionate and complimental Gulls are and ought to be hung up. Into that gallery carry your neat body, but take heed you pick out such an hour, when the main shoal of islanders are swimming up and down. And first observe your doors of entrance, and your exit, not much unlike the players at the theatres, keeping your decorums, even in fantastic-ality. As for example: if you prove to be a northern gentleman, I would wish you to pass through the north door, more often especially than any of the other: and so, according to your countries, take note of your entrances.

Now for your venturing into the walk, be circumspect and wary what pillar you come in at, and take heed in any case (as you love the reputation of your honor) that you avoid the serving-man's log, and approach not within five fathom of that pillar; but bend your course directly in the middle line, that the whole body of the church may appear to be yours; where, in view of all, you may publish your suit in what manner you affect most, either with the slide of your cloak from the one shoulder,—and then you must (as 'twere in anger) suddenly snatch at the middle of the inside (if it be taffeta at the least) and so by that means your costly lining is betrayed,—or else by the pretty advantage of compliment. But one note by the way do I especially woo you to, the neglect of which makes many of our gallants cheap

and ordinary, that by no means you be seen above four turns;
but in the fifth make yourself away, either in some of the semp-
sters' shops, the new tobacco-office, or amongst the booksellers,
where, if you cannot read, exercise your smoke, and inquire who
has writ against this divine weed, etc.   For this withdrawing
yourself a little will much benefit your suit, which else, by too
long walking, would be stale to the whole spectators.   But howsoever, if Paul's jacks be once up with their elbows, and quarrel-
ing to strike eleven, as soon as ever the clock has parted them,
and ended the fray with his hammer, let not the Duke's gallery
contain you any longer, but pass away apace in open view.   In
which departure, if by chance you either encounter, or aloof off
throw your inquisitive eye upon any knight or squire, being your
familiar, salute him not by his name of *Sir such a one*, or so, but
call him *Ned*, or *Jack*, etc. This will set off your estimation
with great men: and if (though there be a dozen companies between you, 'tis the better) he call aloud to you (for that's most
genteel), to know where he shall find you at two o'clock, tell
him at such an ordinary, or such, and be sure to name those that
are dearest, and whither none but your gallants resort.   After
dinner you may appear again, having translated yourself out of
your English cloth cloak, into a light Turkey grogram (if you
have that happiness of shifting), and then be seen (for a turn or
two) to correct your teeth with some quill or silver instrument,
and to cleanse your gums with a wrought handkercher.   It
skills not whether you dined or no (that's best known to your
stomach), or in what place you dined, though it were with cheese
(of your own mother's making) in your chamber or study.

Now if you chance to be a gallant not much crossed among
citizens, that is, a gallant in the mercer's books, exalted for
satins and velvets, if you be not so much blest to be crossed (as I
hold it the greatest blessing in the world, to be great in no man's
books), your Paul's Walk is your only refuge: the Duke's tomb is
a sanctuary, and will keep you alive from worms and land-rats,
that long to be feeding on your carcass.   There you may spend
your legs in winter a whole afternoon; converse, plot, laugh, and
talk anything, jest at your creditor, even to his face, and in the
evening, even by lamp-light, steal out, and so cozen a whole
covey of abominable catchpoles.   Never be seen to mount the
steps into the choir but upon a high festival day, to prefer the

fashion of your doublet, and especially if the singing-boys seem to take note of you; for they are able to buzz your praises above their anthems, if their voices have not lost their maidenheads. But be sure your silver spurs dog your heels, and then the boys will swarm about you like so many white butterflies, when you in the open choir shall draw forth a perfumed embroidered purse (the glorious sight of which will entice many countrymen from their devotion to wondering) and quoit silver into the boys' hands, that it may be heard above the first lesson, although it be read in a voice as big as one of the great organs.

This noble and notable act being performed, you are to vanish presently out of the choir, and to appear again in the walk: but in any wise be not observed to tread there long alone, for fear you be suspected to be a gallant cashiered from the society of captains and fighters.

Suck this humor up especially. Put off to none, unless his hatband be of a newer fashion than yours, and three degrees quainter: but for him that wears a trebled cypress about his hat, (though he were an alderman's son) never move to him: for he's suspected to be worse than a Gull, and not worth the putting off to, that cannot observe the time of his hatband, nor know what fashioned block is most kin to his head. For, in my opinion, the brain that cannot choose his felt well (being the head ornament) must needs pour folly into all the rest of the members, and be an absolute confirmed fool *in summa totali*.

All the diseased horses in a tedious siege cannot show so many fashions as are to be seen for nothing, every day, in Duke Humphrey's walk. If therefore you determine to enter into a new suit, warn your tailor to attend you in Paul's, who, with his hat in his hand, shall like a spy discover the stuff, color, and fashion of any doublet or hose that dare be seen there, and stepping behind a pillar to fill his table-books with those notes, will presently send you into the world an accomplished man; by which means you shall wear your clothes in print with the first edition. But if fortune favor you so much as to make you no more then a mere country gentleman, or but some three degrees removed from him (for which I should be very sorry, because your London experience will cost you dear before you shall have the wit to know what you are), then take this lesson along with you. The first time that you venture into Paul's pass

through the body of the church like a porter, yet presume not to
fetch so much as one whole turn in the middle aisle, no, nor to
cast an eye to *Si quis* door, (pasted and plastered up with serving
men's supplications,) before you have paid tribute to the top of
Paul's steeple with a single penny.   And when you are mounted
there, take heed how you look down into the yard, for the rails
are as rotten as your great-grandfather; and thereupon it will
not be amiss if you inquire how Kit Woodroffe durst vault over,
and what reason he had for it, to put his neck in hazard of reparations.   From hence you may descend, to talk about the
horse that went up, and strive, if you can, to know his keeper:
take the day of the month, and the number of the steps, and
suffer yourself to believe verily that it was not a horse, but something else in the likeness of one: which wonders you may publish
when you return into the country, to the great amazement of
all farmers' daughters, that will almost swound at the report,
and never recover till their bans be asked twice in the church.

But I have not left you yet.   Before you come down again, I
would desire you to draw your knife, and grave your name (or,
for want of a name, the mark which you clap on your sheep) in
great characters upon the leads, by a number of your brethren
(both citizens and country gentlemen), and so you shall be sure
to have your name lie in a coffin of lead, when yourself shall be
wrapped in a winding-sheet: and indeed the top of Paul's contains more names than Stow's *Chronicle*.   These lofty tricks
being played, and you (thanks to your feet) being safely arrived
at the stairs' foot again, your next worthy work is to repair to
my Lord Chancellor's tomb (and, if you can but reasonably
spell), bestow some time upon the reading of Sir Philip Sidney's
brief epitaph; in the compass of an hour you may make shift to
stumble it out.   The great dial is your last monument: there
bestow some half of the three-score minutes, to observe the sauciness of the jacks that are above the man in the moon there; the
strangeness of the motion will quit your labor.   Besides, you
may here have fit occasion to discover your watch, by taking it
forth and setting the wheels to the time of Paul's, which, I assure
you, goes truer by five notes than St. Sepulchre's chimes.   The
benefit that will arise from hence is this, that you publish your
charge in maintaining a gilded clock; and withal the world shall
know that you are a time-pleaser.   By this I imagine you have

walked your bellyful, and thereupon being weary, or (which rather I believe) being most gentlemanlike hungry, it is fit that I brought you in to the Duke; so (because he follows the fashion of great men, in keeping no house, and that therefore you must go seek your dinner) suffer me to take you by the hand, and lead you into an ordinary.

CHAPTER V

HOW A YOUNG GALLANT SHOULD BEHAVE HIMSELF IN AN ORDINARY

FIRST, having diligently inquired out an ordinary of the largest reckoning, whither most of your courtly gallants do resort, let it be your use to repair thither some half hour after eleven; for then you shall find most of your fashion-mongers planted in the room waiting for meat. Ride thither upon your Galloway nag, or your Spanish jennet, a swift ambling pace, in your hose and doublet (gilt rapier and poniard bestowed in their places), and your French lackey carrying your cloak, and running before you; or rather in a coach, for that will both hide you from the basilisk eyes of your creditors, and outrun a whole kennel of bitter-mouthed sergeants.

Being arrived in the room, salute not any but those of your acquaintance: walk up and down by the rest as scornfully and as carelessly as a gentleman-usher. Select some friend (having first thrown off your cloak) to walk up and down the room with you; let him be suited, if you can, worse by far than yourself, he will be a foil to you: and this will be a means to publish your clothes better than Paul's, a tennis-court, or a playhouse. Discourse as loud as you can, no matter to what purpose; if you but make a noise, and laugh in fashion, and have a good sour face to promise quarrelling, you shall be much observed.

If you be a soldier, talk how often you have been in action; as the Portingale voyage, Cales voyage, the Island voyage, besides some eight or nine employments in Ireland and the Low Countries. Then you may discourse how honorably your Grave used you; observe that you call Grave Maurice, "your Grave"; how often you have drunk with Count such a one, and such a Count, on your knees to your Grave's health. And let it be your virtue to give place neither to St. Kynock, nor to any

Dutchman whatsoever in the seventeen provinces, for that soldier's compliment of drinking. And if you perceive that the untraveled company about you take this down well, ply them with more such stuff, as how you have interpreted between the French king and a great lord of Barbary, when they have been drinking healths together, and that will be an excellent occasion to publish your languages, if you have them: if not, get some fragments of French, or small parcels of Italian, to fling about the table. But beware how you speak any Latin there; your ordinary most commonly hath no more to do with Latin than a desperate town of garrison hath.

If you be a courtier, discourse of the obtaining of suits, of your mistress's favors, etc. Make inquiry, if any gentleman at board have any suit, to get which he would use the good means of a great man's interest with the King; and withal (if you have not so much grace left in you as to blush) that you are (thanks to your stars) in mighty credit, though in your own conscience you know, and are guilty to yourself, that you dare not (but only upon the privileges of handsome clothes) presume to peep into the presence. Demand if there be any gentleman (whom any there is acquainted with) that is troubled with two offices, or any vicar with two church livings; which will politicly insinuate that your inquiry after them is because you have good means to obtain them. Yea, and rather than your tongue should not be heard in the room, but that you should sit (like an ass) with your finger in your mouth, and speak nothing, discourse how often this lady hath sent her coach for you, and how often you have sweat in the tennis-court with that great lord; for indeed the sweating together in France (I mean the society of tennis) is a great argument of most dear affection, even between noblemen and peasants.

If you be a poet, and come into the ordinary (though it can be no great glory to be an ordinary poet) order yourself thus. Observe no man, doff not cap to that gentleman to-day at dinner, to whom, not two nights since, you were beholden for a supper; but, after a turn or two in the room, take occasion (pulling out your gloves) to have some epigram, or satire, or sonnet fastened in one of them, that may (as it were unwittingly to you) offer itself to the gentlemen. They will presently desire it, but, without much conjuration from them, and a pretty kind of counterfeit loathness in yourself, do not read it; and, though it be none of your own, swear you made it. Marry, if you chance to get into your hands any witty thing of another man's that is somewhat better, I would counsel you then, if demand be made who composed it, you may say: "Faith, a learned gentleman, a very worthy friend." And this seeming to lay it on another man will be counted either modesty in you, or a sign that you are not ambitious of praise, or else that you dare not take it upon you, for fear of the sharpness it carries with it. Besides, it will add much to your fame to let your tongue walk faster than your teeth, though you be never so hungry, and, rather than you should sit like a dumb coxcomb, to repeat by heart either some verses of your own, or of any other man's, stretching even very good lines upon the rack of censure. Though it be against all law, honesty, or conscience, it may chance save you the price of your ordinary, and beget you other supplements. Marry, I would further entreat our poet to be in league with the mistress of the ordinary, because from her (upon condition that he will but rhyme knights and young gentlemen to her house, and maintain the table in good fooling) he may easily make up his mouth at her cost, *gratis*.

Thus much for particular men. But in general let all that are in ordinary pay march after the sound of these directions. Before the meat come smoking to the board, our gallant must draw out his tobacco-box, the ladle for the cold snuff into the nostril, the tongs and prining-iron. All which artillery may be of gold or silver (if he can reach to the price of it); it will be a reasonable useful pawn at all times when the current of his money falls out to run low. And here you must observe to know in what state tobacco is in town, better than the merchants, and to discourse of the poticaries where it is to be sold, and to be able to speak of their wines, as readily as the poticary himself reading the barbarous hand of a doctor: then let him show his several tricks in taking it, as the whiff, the ring, etc. For these are compliments that gain gentlemen no mean respect, and for which indeed they are more worthily noted, I ensure you, than for any skill that they have in learning.

When you are set down to dinner, you must eat as impudently as can be (for that's most gentlemanlike). When your knight is upon his stewed mutton, be you presently, though you be but a captain, in the bosom of your goose; and when your justice of peace is knuckle-deep in goose, you may, without disparagement to your blood, though you have a lady to your mother, fall very manfully to your woodcocks.

You may rise in dinner-time to ask for a close-stool, protesting to all the gentlemen that it costs you a hundred pound a year in physic, besides the annual pension which your wife allows her doctor. And (if you please) you may (as your great French lord doth) invite some special friend of yours from the table, to hold discourse with you as you sit in that withdrawing-chamber; from whence being returned again to the board, you shall sharpen the wits of all the eating gallants about you, and do them great pleasure to ask what pamphlets or poems a man might think fittest to wipe his tail with; (marry, this talk will be somewhat foul if you carry not a strong perfume about you); and, in propounding this question, you may abuse the works of any man, deprave his writings that you cannot equal, and purchase to yourself in time the terrible name of a severe critic; nay, and be one of the college, if you'll be liberal enough, and (when your turn comes) pay for their suppers.

After dinner, every man as his business leads him, some to dice, some to drabs, some to plays, some to take up friends in the court, some to take up money in the city, some to lend testers in Paul's, others to borrow crowns upon the Exchange. And thus, as the people is said to be a beast of many heads (yet all those heads like hydras') ever growing, as various in their horns as wondrous in their budding and branching, so, in an ordinary, you shall find the variety of a whole kingdom in a few apes of the kingdom.

You must not swear in your dicing, for that argues a violent impatience to depart from your money, and in time will betray a man's need. Take heed of it. No! whether you be at primero, or hazard, you shall sit as patiently (though you lose a whole half-year's exhibition) as a disarmed gentleman does when he's in the unmerciful fingers of sergeants. Marry, I will allow you to sweat privately, and tear six or seven score pair of cards, be the damnation of some dozen or twenty bale of dice, and forswear play a thousand times in an hour, but not swear. Dice yourself into your shirt; and, if you have a beard that your friend will lend but an angel upon, shave it off, and pawn that, rather than to go home blind to your lodging. Further, it is to be remembered, he that is a great gamester may be trusted for a quarter's board at all times, and apparel provided, if need be.

At your twelvepenny ordinary, you may give any justice of peace, or young knight (if he sit but one degree towards the equinoctial of the salt-cellar) leave to pay for the wine; and he shall not refuse it, though it be a week before the receiving of his quarter's rent, which is a time albeit of good hope, yet of present necessity.

There is another ordinary, to which your London usurer, your stale bachelor, and your thrifty attorney do resort; the price three-pence; the rooms as full of company as a jail, and indeed divided into several wards, like the beds of an hospital. The compliment between these is not much, their words few, for the belly hath no ears. Every man's eye here is upon the other man's trencher, to note whether his fellow lurch him, or no. If they chance to discourse, it is of nothing but of statutes, bonds, recognizances, fines, recoveries, audits, rents, subsidies, sureties, inclosures, liveries, indictments, outlawries, feoffments, judgments, commissions, bankerouts, amercements, and of such horrible matter, that when a lieutenant dines with his punk in the next room, he thinks verily the men are conjuring. I can find nothing at this ordinary worthy the sitting down for: therefore the cloth shall be taken away, and those that are thought good enough to be guests here shall be too base to be waiters at your grand ordinary; at which your gallant tastes these commodities. He shall fare well, enjoy good company, receive all the news ere the post can deliver his packet, be perfect where the best bawdy-houses stand, proclaim his good clothes, know this man to drink well, that to feed grossly, the other to swagger roughly. He shall, if he be minded to travel, put out money upon his return, and have hands enough to receive it upon any terms of repayment. And no question, if he be poor, he shall now and then light upon some Gull or other, whom he may skelder (after the genteel fashion) of money. By this time the parings of fruit and cheese are in the voider, cards and dice lie stinking in the fire, the guests are all up, the gilt rapiers ready to be hanged, the French lackey and Irish footboy shrugging at the doors, with their masters' hobby-horses, to ride to the new

play: that's the rendezvous: thither they are galloped in post.
Let us take a pair of oars, and now lustily after them.

CHAPTER VI

HOW A GALLANT SHOULD BEHAVE HIMSELF IN
A PLAYHOUSE

THE theatre is your poet's Royal Exchange, upon which their
Muses (that are now turned to merchants) meeting, barter
away that light commodity of words for a lighter ware than
words,—plaudities, and the breath of the great beast; which
(like the threatenings of two cowards) vanish all into air.
Players are their factors, who put away the stuff, and make the
best of it they possibly can (as indeed 'tis their parts so to do).
Your gallant, your courtier, and your captain had wont to be
the soundest paymasters, and, I think, are still the surest
chapmen: and these, by means that their heads are well stocked,
deal upon this comical freight by the gross, when your ground-
ling and gallery-commoner buys his sport by the penny, and,
like a haggler, is glad to utter it again by retailing.

Sithence then the place is so free in entertainment, allowing a
stool as well to the farmer's son as to your templar; that your
stinkard has the self-same liberty to be there in his tobacco-
fumes which your sweet courtier hath; and that your car-man
and tinker claim as strong a voice in their suffrage, and sit to
give judgment on the play's life and death as well as the proudest
Momus among the tribe of critic: it is fit that he, whom the most
tailors' bills do make room for, when he comes, should not be
basely (like a viol) cased up in a corner.

Whether therefore the gatherers of the public or private playhouse stand to receive the afternoon's rent, let our gallant
(having paid it) presently advance himself up to the throne of
the stage. I mean not into the lords' room (which is now but the
stage's suburbs): no, those boxes, by the iniquity of custom,
conspiracy of waiting-women and gentlemen-ushers that there
sweat together, and the covetousness of sharers, are contemptibly
thrust into the rear, and much new satin is there damned, by
being smothered to death in darkness. But on the very rushes
where the comedy is to dance, yea, and under the state of
Cambyses himself, must our feathered estridge, like a piece

of ordnance, be planted valiantly (because impudently) beating down the mews and hisses of the opposed rascality.

For do but cast up a reckoning, what large comings-in are pursed up by sitting on the stage. First, a conspicuous eminence is gotten; by which means, the best and most essential parts of a gallant (good clothes, a proportionable leg, white hand, the Persian lock, and a tolerable beard) are perfectly revealed.

By sitting on the stage, you have a signed patent to engross the whole commodity of censure, may lawfully presume to be a girder, and stand at the helm to steer the passage of scenes; yet no man shall once offer to hinder you from obtaining the title of an insolent, overweening coxcomb.

By sitting on the stage, you may (without traveling for it) at the very next door ask whose play it is; and, by that quest of inquiry, the law warrants you to avoid much mistaking. If you know not the author, you may rail against him, and peradventure so behave yourself that you may enforce the author to know you.

By sitting on the stage, if you be a knight, you may happily get you a mistress; if a mere Fleet-street gentleman, a wife; but assure yourself, by continual residence, you are the first and principal man in election to begin the number of "We three."

By spreading your body on the stage, and by being a justice in examining of plays, you shall put yourself into such true (scenical) authority that some poet shall not dare to present his Muse rudely upon your eyes, without having first unmasked her, rifled her, and discovered all her bare and most mystical parts before you at a tavern, when you most knightly shall, for his pains, pay for both their suppers.

By sitting on the stage, you may (with small cost) purchase the dear acquaintance of the boys; have a good stool for sixpence; at any time know what particular part any of the infants present; get your match lighted, examine the play-suits' lace, and perhaps win wagers upon laying 'tis copper, etc. And to conclude, whether you be a fool or a justice of peace, a cuckold, or a captain, a Lord Mayor's son, or a dawcock, a knave, or an under-sheriff; of what stamp soever you be, current or counterfeit, the stage, like time, will bring you to most perfect light and lay you open. Neither are you to be hunted from thence, though the scarecrows in the yard hoot at you, hiss at you, spit at you, yea, throw dirt even in your teeth: 'tis most gentleman-like patience to endure all this, and to laugh at the silly animals. But if the rabble, with a full throat, cry: "Away with the fool!" you were worse than a madman to tarry by it; for the gentleman and the fool should never sit on the stage together.

Marry, let this observation go hand in hand with the rest, or rather, like a country serving-man, some five yards before them. Present not yourself on the stage (especially at a new play) until the quaking prologue hath (by rubbing) got color into his cheeks, and is ready to give the trumpets their cue that he's upon point to enter; for then it is time, as though you were one of the properties, or that you dropped out of the hangings, to creep from behind the arras, with your tripos or three-footed stool in one hand, and a teston mounted between a forefinger and a thumb in the other. For if you should bestow your person upon the vulgar when the belly of the house is but half full, your apparel is quite eaten up, the fashion lost, and the proportion of your body in more danger to be devoured than if it were served up in the Counter amongst the poultry: avoid that as you would the bastone. It shall crown you with rich commendation to laugh aloud in the midst of the most serious and saddest scene of the terriblest tragedy, and to let that clapper (your tongue) be tossed so high, that all the house may ring of it; your lords use it; your knights are apes to the lords, and do so too; your Inn-o'-Court man is zany to the knights, and (many very scurvily) comes likewise limping after it. Be thou a beagle to them all, and never lin snuffing till you have scented them; for by talking and laughing (like a ploughman in a morris) you heap Pelion upon Ossa, glory upon glory. As first, all the eyes in the galleries will leave walking after the players, and only follow you; the simplest dolt in the house snatches up your name, and, when he meets you in the streets, or that you fall into his hands in the middle of a watch, his word shall be taken for you; he'll cry, "He's such a gallant," and you pass. Secondly, you publish your temperance to the world, in that you seem not to resort thither to taste vain pleasures with a hungry appetite, but only as a gentleman to spend a foolish hour or two, because you can do nothing else. Thirdly, you mightily disrelish the audience, and disgrace the author; marry, you take up (though it be at the worst hand) a strong opinion of your own judgment, and enforce the poet to take pity of your weakness, and, by some dedicated sonnet, to bring you into a better paradise, only to stop your mouth.

If you can (either for love or money), provide yourself a lodging by the water-side; for, above the conveniency it brings to shun shoulder-clapping, and to ship away your cockatrice betimes in the morning, it adds a kind of state unto you to be carried from thence to the stairs of your playhouse. Hate a sculler (remember that) worse than to be acquainted with one o' th' scullery. No, your oars are your only sea-crabs, board them, and take heed you never go twice together with one pair; often shifting is a great credit to gentlemen, and that dividing of your fare will make the poor water-snakes be ready to pull you in pieces to enjoy your custom. No matter whether, upon landing, you have money or no, you may swim in twenty of their boats over the river upon ticket. Marry, when silver comes in, remember to pay treble their fare, and it will make your flounder-catchers to send more thanks after you, when you do not draw, than when you do; for they know it will be their own another day.

Before the play begins, fall to cards. You may win or lose (as fencers do in a prize) and beat one another by confederacy, yet share the money when you meet at supper. Notwithstanding, to gull the ragamuffins that stand aloof gaping at you, throw the cards (having first torn four or five of them) round about the stage, just upon the third sound, as though you had lost; it skills not if the four knaves lie on their backs and outface the audience; there's none such fools as dare take exceptions at them, because, ere the play go off, better knaves than they will fall into the company.

Now sir, if the writer be a fellow that hath either epigrammed you, or hath had a flirt at your mistress, or hath brought either your feather, or your red beard, or your little legs, etc., on the stage, you shall disgrace him worse than by tossing him in a blanket, or giving him the bastinado in a tavern, if, in the middle of his play, (be it pastoral or comedy, moral or tragedy) you rise with a screwed and discontented face from your stool to be gone: no matter whether the scenes be good or no; the better they are the worse do you distaste them: and, being on your feet, sneak not away like a coward, but salute all your gentle acquaintance, that are spread either on the rushes or on stools about you, and draw what troop you can from the stage after you. The mimics are beholden to you for allowing them elbow-room; their poet cries, perhaps, "A pox go with you," but care not for that, there's no music without frets.

Marry, if either the company or indisposition of the weather bind you to sit it out, my counsel is then that you turn plain ape; take up a rush, and tickle the earnest ears of your fellow gallants, to make other fools fall a-laughing; mew at passionate speeches, blare at merry, find fault with the music, whew at the children's action, whistle at the songs; and, above all, curse the sharers, that, whereas the same day you had bestowed forty shillings on an embroidered felt and feather (Scotch fashion), for your mistress in the court, or your punk in the city, within two hours after, you encounter with the very same block on the stage, when the haberdasher swore to you the impression was extant but that morning.

To conclude, hoard up the finest play-scraps you can get, upon which your lean wit may most savorly feed, for want of other stuff, when the Arcadian and Euphuized gentlewomen have their tongues sharpened to set upon you; that quality (next to your shittlecock) is the only furniture to a courtier that's but a new beginner, and is but in his A B C of compliment. The next places that are filled, after the playhouses be emptied, are (or ought to be) taverns; into a tavern then let us next march, where the brains of one hogshead must be beaten out to make up another.

FYNES MORYSON (1566–1630)

If Moryson's *Itinerary* is not the most weighty and fruitful of travelers' records, it is not the least amusing. Having gone forth as a young man, in the last decade of Elizabeth's reign, "for to admire an' for to see," Moryson had not lost his zest when in later years he came to the task of composition. Although he devoted much of his voluminous work to the things every tourist ought to see and know, in the following extracts we get closer to the heart of the man. Over a Europe not yet taken under the paternal wing of Thomas Cook, and full of dangers for adventurous English Protestants, Moryson roamed with the apparent desire to get into as many tight places as possible in order to prove his ingenuity in getting out of them. So we find him, tireless and dauntless in his curiosity, investigating all that an Englishman ought not to have seen, and, thanks to his wits and his linguistic talents, emerging with success and modest complacency.

ITINERARY (1617)

THE FIRST PART; THE FIRST BOOK

CHAPTER III

. . . From Stode I passed to Emden, and for the better explaining of that journey, give me leave to prefix the following letter, out of the due place, being written from Emden, and directed

To Ægidius Hoffman, a gentleman of Flanders, my dear friend, student at Heidelberg.

Noble Ægidius, the letters you gave me to deliver at Breme have produced a comical event (such may all the passages be of our love), which you shall understand in a word. When in my purposed journey I came to Stode, more tired with the base companions I had than the way, it happened, whilst I spent some days there with my friends, every man spake of Spanish thieves, vulgarly called freebooters, who, stealing out of their garrisons upon the Low Countries, lay in the villages and upon the highways by which I was to pass in my journey to Emden,

from which city a merchant was newly arrived who terrified me
more than all the rest, affirming that in one day he had fallen
thrice into these cut-throats' hands, and though he were of a
neutral city, yet had paid many dollars for his ransom, adding
that they inquired curiously after Englishmen, promising rewards in the villages to any man should give them notice when
any such passed. I knew not what counsel to take. There was
no less danger from the pirates of Dunkirk, if I passed by sea,
especially in a ship of Hamburg, no other being in the harbor,
and they being like to betray me, out of malice to our nation.
Besides, the weather was very tempestious, and not like to
change. Therefore my obstinate purpose to see the cities upon
this coast made me resolve to go by land. So I bought an old
Brunswick thrummed hat, and made me a poor Dutch suit,
rubbing it in the dust to make it seem old, so as my tailor said
he took more pains to spoil it than to make it. I bought me
linen stockings, and discolored my face and hands, and so,
without cloak or sword, with my hands in my hose, took my
place in a poor wagon. I practised as much as I could Pytha-
gorical silence; but if any asked me who I was, I told him that
I was a poor Bohemian and had long served a merchant at Leip-
zig, who left me to despatch some business at Stode and then
commanded me to follow him to Emden. If you had seen my
servile countenance, mine eyes cast on the ground, my hands in
my hose, and my modest silence, you would have taken me for a
harmless young man. Many pleasant events happened to me
thus disguised, wherewith I will not trouble you, only one I am
tied to impart to you. When I came to Breme I was doubtful
what to do with your letters. I thought not to deliver them, but
keep them till a fitter time, or at least to send them by a messenger. But in so doing I should have broken my promise to
you, have lost the fruit of your recommendation, and the opportunity to see your mother and sisters, without hope hereafter
to see them. Then I thought to deliver them, and because I
was disguised in base apparel, to confess who I was, and wherefore so disguised. But when I looked my face in a glass, I
could not for shame take this course. At last I resolved to
deliver them, and to say I was servant to myself (wherein I lied
not, for I have ever too much obeyed my own affections), and
that my master, meaning to pass from Stode by sea, for fear of

the abovesaid dangers, had sent me by land, with command to stay for him at Leyden. To be brief, I went to your mother's house, where a servant opened me the door, to whom I gave your letters; but when he, scarce looking at me, would have locked the door, I took my letters again, saying I had promised to deliver them with my own hand; and so I entered with him, and gave them into the hands of your mother and sister, who inquired much after you, and so much after my master as I might perceive you had made friendly mention of me in your letters. They entertained me with much courtesy, being thus disguised for my own servant; and when I went away your mother would needs give me six batzen to spend, neither would any refusal prevail, but I must needs take them. So I set a mark upon these pieces, lest I should spend them, and am not out of hope, ere I die, to show them to you. To the purpose; at the door I met your brother, whom I had seen at Frankfort, and was not a little afraid lest for all my disguising he would have known me. Let it not trouble you that I tell you another merry accident I had in the same city of Breme. Disguised as I was I went to the house of Doctor Peuzelius, desiring to have the name of so famous a divine written in my stem-book, with his motto, after the Dutch fashion. He, seeing my poor habit, and a book under my arm, took me for some begging scholar, and spake sharply unto me. But when in my master's name I had respectively saluted him and told him my request, he excused his mistaking, and with all courtesy performed my desire. I will trouble you no longer, but hope by some good occasion to embrace you, and tell you all the other passages of my journey. In the meantime I go forward to Leyden in Holland, you (as you do) ever love me, and as my soul, live and farewell. From Emden the twenty-one of October, 1592. . .

THE SECOND BOOK

CHAPTER I

. . . .

THE MARKET PLACE OF RIALTO [IN VENICE]

THE four-square market place of Rialto is compassed with public houses, under the arches whereof, and in the middle part lying open, the merchants meet. And there is also a peculiar place where the gentlemen meet before noon, as they meet in the place of St. Mark towards evening; and here to nourish acquaintance, they spend an hour in discourses, and, because they use not to make feasts one to another, they keep this meeting as strictly as merchants, lest their friendship should decay. The goldsmiths' shops lie thereby, and over against them the shops of jewelers, in which art the Venetians are excellent. There is the palace of a gentleman, who proving a traitor, the state (for his reproach) turned the same into a shambles, and some upper chambers to places of judgment. The fish market lies by this shambles, a great length along the bank of the great channel, and in the same shambles and fish market, as also in the like of St. Mark, great plenty of victuals, especially of fish, is daily to be sold. A public palace stately built lieth near the bridge of Rialto.

. . . .

CHAPTER II

. . . When we went out of Rome, our consorts suddenly in a broad street lighted from their horses and gave them to the vetturines to hold, and so went themselves to the Holy Stairs, vulgarly called *le scale sante*, that they might there pray for a happy journey; at which time myself and my consorts slipped into the next church, and, going in at one door and out at the other, escaped the worshiping of those holy stairs, and at fit time came to take our horses with the rest.

. . . .

CHAPTER IV

. . . .

WE HAD now scarce entered France when suddenly the mischief fell upon me which my friends at Metz had foretold me. When I had passed half this day's journey I met with some dozen horsemen, whose captain demanded of me my name and country. I answered that I was a Dutchman, and the servant of a Dutch merchant, who stayed for me at Chalons, whither I was then going. He (as it seemed to me), thinking it dishonorable to him if he should himself assault a poor fellow and a stranger, did let me pass, but before I came to the bottom of the hill I might see him send two horsemen after me, who, wheeling about the mountains that I might not know they were of his company, suddenly rushed upon me, and with fierce countenance threatening death, presented their carbines to my breast. I, having no ability to defend me, thought good not to make any the least show of resistance, so they took my sword from my guide, and were content only to rob me of my money. I formerly said that I could not find at Venice any means to exchange my money to Paris, the long civil war having barred the Parisians from any traffic in foreign parts, and that I was forced to exchange my money to Geneva. This money there received I had quilted within my doublet, and when I resolved to go on foot to Paris I made me a base cover for my apparel, which when they perceived they took from me the inward doublet wherein I had quilted the gold, and though they perceived that under my base cover I had a jerkin and hose laid with gold lace, yet they were content to take only the inner doublet, and to leave me all the rest of my apparel, wherein I do acknowledge their courtesy, since thieves give all they do not take. Besides, they took not only my crowns, but my sword, cloak, and shirts, and made a very unequal exchange with me for my hat, giving me another deep greasy French hat for it.

One thing in this misery made me glad. I formerly said that I sold my horse for sixteen French crowns at Metz, which crowns I put in the bottom of a wooden box, and covered them with a stinking ointment for scabs. Six other French crowns, for the worst event, I lapped in cloth, and thereupon did wind divers colored threads, wherein I sticked needles, as if I had been so good a husband as to mend my own clothes. This box and this ball of thread I had put in my hose, as things of no worth, and when in spoiling me they had searched my pockets they first took the box, and smelling the stink of the ointment, they cast it away on the ground; neither were they so frugal to take my ball of thread to mend their hose, but did tread it likewise under their feet. Then they rode swiftly to their companions and I, with some spark of joy in my greater loss, took up the box and ball of thread, thinking myself less miserable that by the grace of God I had some money left, to keep me from begging in a strange country. . . .

Thence we went to Chalons, where my guide brought me to a poor alehouse, and when I expostulated the wrong he did me, he replied that stately inns were not for men who had never a penny in their purses; but I told him that I looked for comfort in that case rather from gentlemen than clowns. Whereupon he willingly obeyed me, and with a dejected and fearful countenance brought me to the chief inn, where he ceased not to bewail my misery and to recount my tragedy, as if it had been the burning of Troy, till the very host, despairing of my ability to pay him, began to look disdainfully upon me. The next morning when he, being to return home and taking his leave of me, I paid him his hire, which he neither asked nor expected, thinking that I had not one penny, and likewise paid my host for my supper and lodging, he first began to talk like a madman, and coming to himself professed that he knew not how I should have one penny, except I were a juggler or an alchemist, or had a familiar spirit. Then, confounded between wonder and joy, he began to triumph with the servants, and would not depart till he had first drunk a quart of wine. . . .

THE THIRD BOOK

CHAPTER I

. . . And no doubt in many things we must follow the opinion of the common people, with which it is better (regarding only men) to be foolish than alone to be wise. I say that I did for the aforesaid causes change my mind; and because I could not make that undone which was done, at least I resolved to desist from that course. Only I gave out one hundred pound to receive three at my return among my brethren and some few kinsmen and dearest friends, of whom I would not shame to confess that I received so much of gift. And lest by spending upon the stock my patrimony should be wasted, I moreover gave out to five friends one hundred pound, with condition that they should have it if I died, or after three years should repay it with one hundred and fifty pound gain if I returned; which I hold a disadvantageous adventure to the giver of the money. Neither did I exact this money of any man by suit of law after my return, which they willingly and presently paid me, only some few excepted, who, retaining the very money I gave them, dealt not therein so gentlemanlike with me as I did with them. And by the great expenses of my journey, much increased by the ill accidents of my brother's death and my own sickness, the three hundred fifty pounds I was to receive of gain after my return, and the one hundred pounds which my brother and I carried in our purses, would not satisfy the five hundred pound we had spent (though my brother died within the compass of the first year), but I was forced to pay the rest out of my own patrimony. . . .

PART III. BOOK I

CHAPTER II

OF PRECEPTS FOR TRAVELERS, WHICH MAY INSTRUCT THE UNEXPERIENCED

. . . Let a traveler observe the underwritten things, and of them some curiously, some slightly, as he shall judge them fit for his purpose. He shall observe the fruitfulness of each country, and the things wherewith it aboundeth, as the mines of metals and precious stones, the chief laws and customs of the workers in those mines, also baths and the quality of the water, with the diseases for the curing whereof it is most proper, the names, springs, and courses of rivers, the pleasant fountains, the abundance or rarity of pastures, groves, wood, corn, and fruits, the rare and precious plants, the rare and proper beasts, the prices of necessary things, and what he daily spends in his diet and horsemeat, and in hiring horses or coaches, the soil of every day's journey, the plenty of fishes or flesh, the kinds of meat or drink, with the sauces and the rarer manners of dressing meats, the country's expense in apparel, with their constancy or fickleness in wearing it, the races of horses, as the jennets of Spain, the coursers of Naples, and the heavy horses of Friesland, and how they manage and feed these horses, the situation of cities and provinces, the healthfulness of the air, the chorography, the buildings, the riches, the magnificence of citizens, their household stuff, and in general all special things, as statues, colosses, sepulchres with the inscriptions, libraries, with the most rare books, theatres, arches, bridges, forts, armories, treasuries, monasteries, churches, public houses, universities, with their founders, revenues, and disputations. To conclude, let him visit the most learned men, and those that excel in military art or any virtue, and let him confer with them, as his ends require. Thus did I visit Beza at Geneva, thus did I visit Bellarmine at Rome (being ready to take horse, and in the habit and person of a Frenchman). Thus in my return did I gladly see Henry the Fourth of Bourbon, King of France, famous for the feats of arms and wisdom; only Lipsius, whom I loved for his book of constancy, and much desired to see for his universal learning, did bereave me of this hope, when I came into the Low Countries, by his inconstant flight to the Spaniards. The traveler shall further observe the policy of each state, and therein the courts of each king or prince, with the courtiers' entertainments, fees or offices, the statutes of the princes, their revenues, the form of the commonwealth, whether the prince be a tyrant, or beloved of the people, what forces he hath by sea or land, the military discipline, the manners of the people, their vices, virtues, industry in manual arts, the constitution of their bodies, the history of the kingdom, and since the soul of each man is the man, and the soul of the commonwealth is religion, he shall observe the disposition of the people, whether it be religious, superstitious, or profane, and the opinions of religion differing from his, and the most rare ceremonies thereof. He shall also observe the traffic of merchants, and therein the commodities which they carry out, and most want, the havens and roads for ships, their skill in navigation, and whether they use subjects or strangers for their mariners. Lastly, the value of the coins in each country, and the several current pieces, and whatsoever he shall think meet to add hereunto.

And because the memory is weak, and those who write much are many times like the clerks that carry their learning in their book, not in their brain, let him constantly observe this, that whatsoever he sees or hears, he apply it to his use, and by discourse (though forced) make it his own. Thus students of rhetoric, at first seeking matter for words, rather than words for matter, at last attain an easy style flowing like a still river, and lay aside the affectation of words. Let nothing worth the knowledge pass his eyes or ears, which he draweth not to his own possession in this sort. In the meantime, though he trust not to his papers, yet for the weakness of memory let him carefully note all rare observations; for he less offends that writes many toys than he that omits one serious thing, and after, when his judgment is more ripe, he shall distil gold (as the proverb is) out of this dung of Ennius. Let him write these notes each day, at morn and at even in his inn, within writing tables carried about him, and after at leisure into a paper book, that many years after he may look over them at his pleasure. But great caution must be had, especially in places of danger, how he carry about him these papers, the subject whereof cannot but in many places be offensive and perhaps dangerous, if once upon suspicion he chance to be searched. Therefore, as he sends his books and heavy things for carriage, half-yearly, either into his own country or to some place in the way by which he is to return, there to be kept for him, he shall do well to write such things in ciphers and unknown characters, being also ready to give a feigned interpretation of them to any magistrate, if need be.

. . . .

There is great art for a traveler to conceal his religion in Italy and Spain, with due wisdom and without offending his conscience. . . .

Myself lived in Italy, and for the space of one year never heard a mass, but daily I went out of my chamber in the morning as if I had gone to the mass. At my very first coming into Italy I presently went to Rome and Naples, and so at my first entrance passed my greatest dangers, that having satisfied my curiosity, if perhaps in my return I should happen to fear any danger, I might more contentedly and speedily escape away. For they who stay at Padua some months, and after go to Rome, may be sure that the Jesuits and priests there are first by their spies advertised, not only of their coming, but also of their condition, and the most manifest signs of their bodies whereby they may be known. Moreover, I being at Rome in Lent time, it happened that some few days before Easter a priest came to our lodging and took our names in writing, to the end (as he told us) that we might receive the sacrament with our host's family. Therefore I went from Rome upon Tuesday before Easter, and came to Siena upon Good Friday, and upon Easter even (pretending great business) took my journey to Florence, where I stayed only Easter day, and thence went to Pisa, and before the end of Easter week returned in haste to Siena, where I had a chamber which I kept when I was at Rome, and where I meant now to abide for a time. Thus by often changing places I avoided the priests' inquiring after me, which is most dangerous about Easter time, when all men receive the sacrament. Yet indeed there is less danger of the Inquisition in the state of Florence than otherwhere, as there is no danger thereof at all in the state of Venice to him that can hold his peace and behave himself modestly.

One thing I cannot omit, that some few days before Easter, when I was ready to come from Rome, I adventured to visit Bellarmine, and that in the Jesuits' College, professing myself to be a Frenchman, and wearing Italian clothes, and that after their manner, which is a matter of no small moment; for if I had not been wary therein, the crafty spies of Rome would easily have known me by some gesture or fashion of wearing my clothes which they know to be proper to the English, as the muffling a man's face with his cloak, or the like. But especially I took heed not to gaze on the College walls, a manifest sign of a stranger, nor to look steadfastly in the face of any Englishman chancing to meet me, whereof some were like to have known me in the University of Cambridge, lest by such beholding of them I might draw their eyes to look earnestly on me, for one look invites another. And with these cautions I did happily satisfy this my curiosity. Also upon good judgment I made myself known to Cardinal Allen when I first came from Naples to Rome, and when he had promised me his protection, holding my peace and abstaining from public offence, I rested thereupon for the worst events, yet withal, to avoid the conversation and familiarity of priests and Englishmen, yea, even of those that were of the Cardinal's family, I first left the common inn, then changed my hired chamber, taking another in a poor house close under the Pope's palace, as a place least like to be searched.

BEN JONSON (1572-1637)

Timber was a commonplace-book, compiled mainly in the period 1620–1635, and perhaps not at first intended for print. Much of it is paraphrased from Cicero, Quintilian, and other ancient and modern authors; the characterization of Bacon as an orator, for example, is derived from Seneca. But the sources of many of Jonson's ideas are much less important than their influence upon him and upon the development of neoclassicism. In the first extract we have in a nutshell the quarrel between ancients and moderns which Daniel had eloquently defined in 1603, and Jonson's classicism, nourished from various roots, repudiates the slavish extravagances of academic humanism as well as the undisciplined waywardness of the Elizabethans. His familiar words on Shakespeare reveal both his strength and his limitations.

TIMBER: OR DISCOVERIES (1641)

[ANCIENTS AND MODERNS]

I CANNOT think Nature is so spent and decayed that she can bring forth nothing worth her former years. She is always the same, like herself; and when she collects her strength is abler still. Men are decayed, and studies: she is not.

I know nothing can conduce more to letters than to examine the writings of the ancients and not to rest in their sole authority, or take all upon trust from them, provided the plagues of judging and pronouncing against them be away, such as are envy, bitterness, precipitation, impudence, and scurrile scoffing. For to all the observations of the ancients we have our own experience, which if we will use and apply we have better means to pronounce. It is true they opened the gates, and made the way that went before us, but as guides, not commanders: *non domini nostri, sed duces fuere.* Truth lies open to all, it is no man's several. *Patet omnibus veritas, nondum est occupata; multum ex illa etiam futuris relicta est.*[1]

[LIBERAL STUDIES]

ARTS that respect the mind were ever reputed nobler than those that serve the body, though we less can be without them: as tillage, spinning, weaving, building, etc., without which we could scarce sustain life a day. But these were the works of every hand, the other of the brain only, and those the most generous and exalted wits and spirits that cannot rest or acquiesce. The mind of man is still fed with labor: *opere pascitur.*

There is a more secret cause, and the power of liberal studies lies more hid than it can be wrought out by profane wits. It is not every man's way to hit. There are men, I confess, that set the caract and value upon things as they love them; but science is not every man's mistress. It is as great a spite to be praised in the wrong place, and by a wrong person, as can be done to a noble nature.

[ON CERTAIN POETS]

NOTHING in our age, I have observed, is more preposterous than the running judgments upon poetry and poets; when we shall hear those things commended and cried up for the best writings which a man would scarce vouchsafe to wrap any wholesome drug in; he would never light his tobacco with them. And those men almost named for miracles, who yet are so vile that if a man should go about to examine and correct them, he must make all they have done but one blot. Their good is so entangled with their bad as forcibly one must draw on the other's death with it. A sponge dipped in ink will do all:

> ——*Comitetur Punica librum*
>   *Spongia.*——
> *Et paulo post,*
>   *Non possunt. . . .   multæ*
>   . . . .   *una litura potest.*[2]

---

[1] Truth lies open to all, the territory has not yet been conquered; much remains even for future generations.

[2] Let a Punic sponge go with the book. . . (and, a little futher on), Many erasures are not enough . . . a single one will do.

Yet their vices have not hurt them; nay, a great many they have profited, for they have been loved for nothing else. And this false opinion grows strong against the best men, if once it take root with the ignorant. Cestius, in his time, was preferred to Cicero, so far as the ignorant durst. They learned him without book, and had him often in their mouths; but a man cannot imagine that thing so foolish or rude but will find and enjoy an admirer; at least a reader, or spectator. The puppets are seen now in despite of the players; Heath's epigrams and the sculler's poems have their applause. There are never wanting that dare prefer the worst preachers, the worst pleaders, the worst poets; not that the better have left to write or speak better, but that they that hear them judge worse—*Non illi pejus dicunt, sed hi corruptius judicant.* Nay, if it were put to the question of the water-rhymer's works against Spenser's, I doubt not but they would find more suffrages; because the most favor common vices, out of a prerogative the vulgar have to lose their judgments and like that which is naught.

Poetry in this latter age hath proved but a mean mistress to such as have wholly addicted themselves to her, or given their names up to her family. They who have but saluted her on the by, and now and then tendered their visits, she hath done much for, and advanced in the way of their own professions (both the law and the gospel) beyond all they could have hoped, or done for themselves without her favor. Wherein she doth emulate the judicious but preposterous bounty of the time's grandees, who accumulate all they can upon the parasite or fresh-man in their friendship; but think an old client or honest servant bound by his place to write and starve.

Indeed, the multitude commend writers as they do fencers or wrestlers, who if they come in robustiously and put for it with a deal of violence, are received for the braver fellows; when many times their own rudeness is a cause of their disgrace, and a slight touch of their adversary gives all that boisterous force the foil. But in these things the unskilful are naturally deceived, and judging wholly by the bulk, think rude things greater than polished, and scattered more numerous than composed. Nor think this only to be true in the sordid multitude, but the neater sort of our gallants; for all are the multitude, only they differ in clothes, not in judgment or understanding.

[OF OUR FELLOW-COUNTRYMAN SHAKESPEARE]

I REMEMBER the players have often mentioned it as an honor to Shakespeare, that in his writing (whatsoever he penned) he never blotted out [a] line. My answer hath been, "Would he had blotted a thousand!" which they thought a malevolent speech. I had not told posterity this, but for their ignorance, who choose that circumstance to commend their friend by wherein he most faulted; and to justify mine own candor, (for I loved the man, and do honor his memory, on this side idolatry, as much as any). He was, indeed, honest, and of an open and free nature; had an excellent fancy, brave notions, and gentle expressions, wherein he flowed with that facility that sometime it was necessary he should be stopped. *Sufflaminandus erat,*[1] as Augustus said of Haterius. His wit was in his own power; would the rule of it had been so too. Many times he fell into those things could not escape laughter, as when he said in the person of Cæsar, one speaking to him, "Cæsar, thou dost me wrong." He replied, "Cæsar did never wrong but with just cause;" and such like, which were ridiculous. But he redeemed his vices with his virtues. There was ever more in him to be praised than to be pardoned.

[DIFFERENCE OF WITS]

IN THE difference of wits, I have observed there are many notes; and it is a little maistry to know them, to discern what every nature, every disposition will bear; for before we sow our land we should plough it. There are no fewer forms of minds than of bodies amongst us. The variety is incredible, and therefore we must search. Some are fit to make divines, some poets, some lawyers, some physicians; some to be sent to the plough and trades.

There is no doctrine will do good where nature is wanting. Some wits are swelling and high; others low and still; some hot and fiery; others cold and dull; one must have a bridle, the other a spur.

There be some that are forward and bold, and these will do every little thing easily—I mean that is hard by and next them,

---

[1]He needed to be checked.

which they will utter unretarded without any shamefastness. These never perform much, but quickly. They are what they are on the sudden; they show presently like grain that, scattered on the top of the ground, shoots up, but takes no root; has a yellow blade, but the ear empty. They are wits of good promise at first, but there is an *ingenistitium*;[1] they stand still at sixteen, they get no higher.

You have others that labor only to ostentation, and are ever more busy about the colors and surface of a work than in the matter and foundation; for that is hid, the other is seen.

Others, that in composition are nothing but what is rough and broken: *quæ per salebras, altaque saxa cadunt*.[2] And if it would come gently, they trouble it of purpose. They would not have it run without rubs, as if that style were more strong and manly that struck the ear with a kind of unevenness. These men err not by chance, but knowingly and willingly; they are like men that affect a fashion by themselves, have some singularity in a ruff, cloak, or hat-band; or their beards, specially cut to provoke beholders and set a mark upon themselves. They would be reprehended while they are looked on. And this vice, one that is in authority with the rest, loving, delivers over to them to be imitated; so that oft-times the faults which he fell into, the others seek for. This is the danger, when vice becomes a precedent.

Others there are that have no composition at all; but a kind of tuning and rhyming fall in what they write. It runs and slides, and only makes a sound. Women's poets they are called, as you have women's tailors.

> They write a verse as smooth, as soft as cream,
> In which there is no torrent, nor scarce stream.

You may sound these wits and find the depth of them with your middle finger. They are cream-bowl or but puddle deep.

Some, that turn over all books, and are equally searching in all papers, that write out of what they presently find or meet, without choice; by which means it happens that what they have discredited and impugned in one work, they have before or after

---

[1] A wit-stand.

[2] That fall over the rough ways and high rocks.

extolled the same in another. Such are all the essayists, even
their master Montaigne. These, in all they write, confess still
what books they have read last, and therein their own folly so
much, that they bring it to the stake raw and undigested; not
that the place did need it neither, but that they thought themselves furnished and would vent it.

Some, again, who after they have got authority, or, which is
less, opinion, by their writings, to have read much, dare presently to feign whole books and authors, and lie safely. For
what never was will not easily be found, not by the most curious.

And some, by a cunning protestation against all reading,
and false vendition of their own naturals, think to divert the
sagacity of their readers from themselves, and cool the scent of
their own fox-like thefts; when yet they are so rank as a man
may find whole pages together usurped from one author; their
necessities compelling them to read for present use, which could
not be in many books; and so come forth more ridiculously and
palpably guilty than those who, because they cannot trace,
they yet would slander their industry.

But the wretcheder are the obstinate contemners of all helps
and arts; such as, presuming on their own naturals (which
perhaps are excellent), dare deride all diligence, and seem to
mock at the terms when they understand not the things; thinking that way to get off wittily with their ignorance. These are
imitated often by such as are their peers in negligence, though
they cannot be in nature; and they utter all they can think
with a kind of violence and indisposition, unexamined, without
relation either to person, place, or any fitness else; and the more
wilful and stubborn they are in it, the more learned they are
esteemed of the multitude, through their excellent vice of judgment, who think those things the stronger that have no art;
as if to break were better than to open, or to rent asunder
gentler than to loose.

It cannot but come to pass that these men, who commonly
seek to do more than enough, may sometimes happen on something that is good and great; but very seldom: and when it
comes, it doth not recompense the rest of their ill. For their
jests, and their sentences (which they only and ambitiously
seek for) stick out, and are more eminent, because all is sordid
and vile about them; as lights are more discerned in a thick

darkness than a faint shadow. Now, because they speak all they can (however unfitly), they are thought to have the greater copy; where the learned use ever election and a mean; they look back to what they intended at first, and make all an even and proportioned body. The true artificer will not run away from nature as he were afraid of her, or depart from life and the likeness of truth, but speak to the capacity of his hearers. And though his language differ from the vulgar somewhat, it shall not fly from all humanity, with the Tamerlanes and Tamerchams of the late age, which had nothing in them but the scenical strutting and furious vociferation to warrant them then to the ignorant gapers. He knows it is his only art so to carry it, as none but artificers perceive it. In the meantime, perhaps, he is called barren, dull, lean, a poor writer, or by what contumelious word can come in their cheeks, by these men who, without labor, judgment, knowledge, or almost sense, are received or preferred before him. He gratulates them and their fortune. Another age, or juster men, will acknowledge the virtues of his studies, his wisdom in dividing, his subtlety in arguing, with what strength he doth inspire his readers, with what sweetness he strokes them; in inveighing, what sharpness; in jest, what urbanity he uses; how he doth reign in men's affections; how invade and break in upon them, and makes their minds like the thing he writes. Then in his elocution to behold what word is proper, which hath ornament, which height, what is beautifully translated, where figures are fit, which gentle, which strong, to show the composition manly; and how he hath avoided faint, obscure, obscene, sordid, humble, improper, or effeminate phrase; which is not only praised of the most, but commended (which is worse), especially for that it is naught.

[FRANCIS BACON, LORD VERULAM]

One, though he be excellent and the chief, is not to be imitated alone; for never no imitator ever grew up to his author; likeness is always on this side truth. Yet there happened in my time one noble speaker who was full of gravity in his speaking; his language, where he could spare or pass by a jest, was nobly censorious. No man ever spake more neatly, more pressly, more weightily, or suffered less emptiness, less idleness, in what he uttered. No member of his speech but consisted of the own graces. His hearers could not cough, or look aside from him, without loss. He commanded where he spoke, and had his judges angry and pleased at his devotion. No man had their affections more in his power. The fear of every man that heard him was lest he should make an end. . . .

My conceit of his person was never increased toward him by his place or honors. But I have and do reverence him for the greatness that was only proper to himself, in that he seemed to me ever, by his work, one of the greatest men, and most worthy of admiration, that had been in many ages. In his adversity I ever prayed that God would give him strength; for greatness he could not want. Neither could I condole in a word or syllable for him, as knowing no accident could do harm to virtue, but rather help to make it manifest.

[A LETTER ON EDUCATION]

It PLEASED your Lordship of late to ask my opinion touching the education of your sons, and especially to the advancement of their studies. To which, though I returned somewhat for the present, which rather manifested a will in me than gave any just resolution to the thing propounded, I have upon better cogitation called those aids about me, both of mind and memory, which shall venter my thoughts clearer, if not fuller, to your Lordship's demand. I confess, my Lord, they will seem but petty and minute things I shall offer to you, being writ for children, and of them. But studies have their infancy as well as creatures. We see in men even the strongest compositions had their beginnings from milk and the cradle; and the wisest tarried sometimes about apting their mouths to letters and syllables. In their education, therefore, the care must be the greater had of their beginnings, to know, examine, and weigh their natures; which, though they be proner in some children to some disciplines, yet are they naturally prompt to taste all by degrees, and with change. For change is a kind of refreshing in studies, and infuseth knowledge by way of recreation. Thence the school itself is called a play or game, and all letters are so best taught to scholars. They should not be affrighted or deterred in their entry, but drawn on with exercise and emu-

lation. A youth should not be made to hate study before he
know the causes to love it, or taste the bitterness before the
sweet; but called on and allured, entreated and praised: yea,
when he deserves it not. For which cause I wish them sent to
the best school, and a public, which I think the best. Your
Lordship, I fear, hardly hears of that, as willing to breed them
in your eye and at home, and doubting their manners may be
corrupted abroad. They are in more danger in your own
family, among ill servants (allowing they be safe in their schoolmaster), than amongst a thousand boys, however immodest.
Would we did not spoil our own children, and overthrow their
manners ourselves by too much indulgence! To breed them at
home is to breed them in a shade, whereas in a school they have
the light and heat of the sun. They are used and accustomed to
things and men. When they come forth into the commonwealth, they find nothing new, or to seek. They have made
their friendships and aids, some to last till their age. They
hear what is commanded to others as well as themselves; much
approved, much corrected; all which they bring to their own
store and use, and learn as much as they hear. Eloquence
would be but a poor thing if we should only converse with
singulars, speak but man and man together. Therefore I like
no private breeding. I would send them where their industry
should be daily increased by praise, and that kindled by emulation. It is a good thing to inflame the mind; and though ambition itself be a vice, it is often the cause of great virtue. Give
me that wit whom praise excites, glory puts on, or disgrace
grieves; he is to be nourished with ambition, pricked forward with
honor, checked with reprehension, and never to be suspected of
sloth. Though he be given to play, it is a sign of spirit and
liveliness, so there be a mean had of their sports and relaxations.
And from the rod or ferule I would have them free, as from the
menace of them; for it is both deformed and servile.

[OF STYLE]

FOR a man to write well, there are required three necessaries—
to read the best authors, observe the best speakers, and much
exercise of his own style. In style, to consider what ought to
be written, and after what manner, he must first think and ex-

cogitate his matter, then choose his words, and examine the weight of either. Then take care, in placing and ranking both matter and words, that the composition be comely; and to do this with diligence and often. No matter how slow the style be at first, so it be labored and accurate; seek the best, and be not glad of the forward conceits or first words that offer themselves to us, but judge of what we invent, and order what we approve. Repeat often what we have formerly written; which beside that it helps the consequence, and makes the juncture better, it quickens the heat of imagination, that often cools in the time of setting down, and gives it new strength, as if it grew lustier by the going back. As we see in the contention of leaping, they jump farthest that fetch their race largest; or, as in throwing a dart or javelin, we force back our arms to make our loose the stronger. Yet, if we have a fair gale of wind, I forbid not the steering out of our sail, so the favor of the gale deceive us not. For all that we invent doth please us in the conception or birth, else we would never set it down. But the safest is to return to our judgment, and handle over again those things the easiness of which might make them justly suspected. So did the best writers in their beginnings; they imposed upon themselves care and industry; they did nothing rashly: they obtained first to write well, and then custom made it easy and a habit. By little and little their matter showed itself to them more plentifully; their words answered, their composition followed; and all, as in a well-ordered family, presented itself in the place. So that the sum of all is, ready writing makes not good writing, but good writing brings on ready writing. Yet, when we think we have got the faculty, it is even then good to resist it, as to give a horse a check sometimes with a bit, which doth not so much stop his course as stir his mettle. Again, whether a man's genius is best able to reach, thither it should more and more contend, lift and dilate itself; as men of low stature raise themselves on their toes, and so oft-times get even, if not eminent. Besides, as it is fit for grown and able writers to stand of themselves, and work with their own strength, to trust and endeavor by their own faculties, so it is fit for the beginner and learner to study others and the best. For the mind and memory are more sharply exercised in comprehending another man's things than our own; and such as accustom themselves and are familiar with the best authors shall ever and anon find somewhat of them in themselves, and in the expression of their minds, even when they feel it not, be able to utter something like theirs, which hath an authority above their own. Nay, sometimes it is the reward of a man's study, the praise of quoting another man fitly; and though a man be more prone and able for one kind of writing than another, yet he must exercise all. For as in an instrument, so in style, there must be a harmony and consent of parts.

[THE DIGNITY OF SPEECH]

SPEECH is the only benefit man hath to express his excellency of mind above other creatures. It is the instrument of society; therefore Mercury, who is the president of language, is called *deorum hominumque interpres*.[1] In all speech, words and sense are as the body and the soul. The sense is as the life and soul of language, without which all words are dead. Sense is wrought out of experience, the knowledge of human life and actions, or of the liberal arts, which the Greeks called 'Ἐγκυκλοπαιδείαν. Words are the people's, yet there is a choice of them to be made; for *verborum delectus origo est eloquentiæ*.[2] They are to be chose according to the persons we make speak, or the things we speak of. Some are of the camp, some of the council-board, some of the shop, some of the sheepcote, some of the pulpit, some of the bar, etc. And herein is seen their elegance and propriety, when we use them fitly and draw them forth to their just strength and nature by way of translation or metaphor. But in this translation we must only serve necessity (*nam temere nihil transfertur a prudenti*),[3] or commodity, which is a kind of necessity: that is, when we either absolutely want a word to express by, and that is necessity; or when we have not so fit a word, and that is commodity; as when we avoid loss by it, and escape obsceneness, and gain in the grace and property, which helps significance. Metaphors far-fet hinder to be understood; and, affected, lose their grace. Or when the person fetcheth his translations from a wrong place: as if a privy councillor should

---

[1] Messenger of gods and men.

[2] Choice of words is the beginning of eloquence.

[3] For the sensible person will not use metaphors heedlessly.

at the table take his metaphor from a dicing-house, or ordinary, or a vintner's vault; or a justice of peace draw his similitudes from the mathematics; or a divine from a bawdy-house or tavern; or a gentleman of Northamptonshire, Warwickshire, or the Midland, should fetch all his illustrations to his country neighbors from shipping, and tell them of the main-sheet and the bowline. Metaphors are thus many times deformed, as in him that said, *Castratam morte Africani rempublicam;*[1] and another, *Stercus curiæ Glauciam,*[2] and *Cana nive conspuit Alpes.*[3] All attempts that are new in this kind are dangerous, and somewhat hard, before they be softened with use. A man coins not a new word without some peril and less fruit; for if it happen to be received, the praise is but moderate; if refused, the scorn is assured. Yet we must adventure; for things at first hard and rough are by use made tender and gentle. It is an honest error that is committed, following great chiefs.

Custom is the most certain mistress of language, as the public stamp makes the current money. But we must not be too frequent with the mint, every day coining, nor fetch words from the extreme and utmost ages; since the chief virtue of a style is perspicuity, and nothing so vicious in it as to need an interpreter. Words borrowed of antiquity do lend a kind of majesty to style, and are not without their delight sometimes; for they have the authority of years, and out of their intermission do win themselves a kind of gracelike newness. But the eldest of the present, and newest of the past language, is the best. For what was the ancient language, which some men so dote upon, but the ancient custom? Yet when I name custom, I understand not the vulgar custom; for that were a precept no less dangerous to language than life, if we should speak or live after the manners of the vulgar: but that I call custom of speech, which is the consent of the learned; as custom of life, which is the consent of the good. Virgil was most loving of antiquity; yet how rarely doth he insert *aquai* and *pictai!* Lucretius is scabrous and rough in these, he seeks them: as some do Chaucerisms with us, which were better expunged and banished. Some words are to be culled

---

[1] The country castrated by the death of Africanus.

[2] Glaucia, the dunghill of the assembly.

[3] (Jove) spits white snow upon the Alps.

out for ornament and color, as we gather flowers to straw houses or make garlands; but they are better when they grow to our style; as in a meadow, where, though the mere grass and greenness delights, yet the variety of flowers doth heighten and beautify. Marry, we must not play or riot too much with them, as in paronomasies; nor use too swelling or ill-sounding words, *quæ per salebras, altaque saxa cadunt*. It is true there is no sound but shall find some lovers, as the bitterest confections are grateful to some palates. Our composition must be more accurate in the beginning and end than in the midst, and in the end more than in the beginning; for through the midst the stream bears us. And this is attained by custom, more than care or diligence. We must express readily and fully, not profusely. There is difference between a liberal and a prodigal hand. As it is a great point of art, when our matter requires it, to enlarge and veer out all sail, so to take it in and contract it is of no less praise, when the argument doth ask it. Either of them hath their fitness in the place. A good man always profits by his endeavor, by his help, yea, when he is absent; nay, when he is dead, by his example and memory: so good authors in their style. A strict and succinct style is that where you can take away nothing without loss, and that loss to be manifest.

JAMES HOWELL (? 1594–1666)

After leaving Oxford, Howell carried his alert eye and mind about the continent—but as a business man, not a young patrician on a grand tour. Returning to England, he held various positions under the Crown. During the Civil War he sojourned in the Fleet Prison as a not particularly uncomfortable martyr—or debtor. The *Epistolae Hoelianae* appeared at intervals from 1645 to 1655, and were deservedly popular. As a journalist Howell belongs to a less robustious and more sophisticated generation than Dekker, and he is a superlative reporter. When he gives such lively entertainment it is hardly fair to scrutinize his veracity, for he was not only a journalist but a Welshman. But he was also an essayist, and he had an essayist's capital, a vivid personality, with abundant quirks and quiddities, and a most infectious light-heartedness.

EPISTOLAE HO–ELIANAE (1645–1655)

SECTION I

I

[THE ART OF LETTER-WRITING]

To Sir J. S. at Leeds Castle

It was a quaint difference the ancients did put 'twixt a letter and an oration, that the one should be attired like a woman, the other like a man. The latter of the two is allowed large side robes, as long periods, parentheses, similes, examples, and other parts of rhetorical flourishes; but a letter or epistle should be short-coated and closely couched; a hungerlin becomes a letter more handsomely than a gown. Indeed we should write as we speak, and that's a true familiar letter which expresseth one's mind, as if he were discoursing with the party to whom he writes in succinct and short terms. The tongue and the pen are both of them interpreters of the mind, but I hold the pen to be the more faithful of the two. The tongue *in udo posita*, being seated

587

in a moist slippery place, may fail and falter in her sudden ex-temporal expressions; but the pen, having a greater advantage of premeditation, is not so subject to error, and leaves things be-hind it upon firm and authentic record. Now letters, though they be capable of any subject, yet commonly they are either narratory, objurgatory, consolatory, monitory, or congratula-tory. The first consists of relations, the second of reprehensions, the third of comfort, the last two of counsel and joy; there are some who in lieu of letters write homilies, they preach when they should epistolize; there are others that turn them to tedious tractates; this is to make letters degenerate from their true nature. Some modern authors there are who have exposed their letters to the world, but most of them, I mean among your Latin epistolizers, go freighted with mere Bartholomew ware, with trite and trivial phrases only, listed with pedantic shreds of schoolboy verses. Others there are among our next trans-marine neighbors eastward, who write in their own language, but their style is so soft and easy that their letters may be said to be like bodies of loose flesh without sinews, they have neither joints of art nor arteries in them; they have a kind of simpering and lank hectic expressions made up of a bombast of words and finical affected compliments only. I cannot well away with such fleecy stuff, with such cobweb compositions, where there is no strength of matter, nothing for the reader to carry away with him that may enlarge the notions of his soul. One shall hardly find an apothegm, example, simile, or anything of philosophy, history, or solid knowledge, or as much as one new-created phrase, in a hundred of them; and to draw any observa-tions out of them were as if one went about to distil cream out of froth; insomuch that it may be said of them what was said of the echo, "that she is a mere sound, and nothing else." . . .

Westminster, July 25th, 1625.

II
[THE OVERBURY CASE]

To my Father upon my first going beyond sea

I should be much wanting to myself, and to that obligation of duty the law of God and his handmaid Nature hath imposed upon me, if I should not acquaint you with the course and quality of my affairs and fortunes, especially at this time that I am upon point of crossing the seas to eat my bread abroad. Nor is it the common relation of a son that only induced me hereunto, but that most indulgent and costly care you have been pleased (in so extraordinary a manner) to have had of my breeding (though but one child of fifteen) by placing me in a choice methodical school (so far distant from your dwelling) under a learned (though lashing) master; and by transplanting me thence to Oxford, to be graduated; and so holding me still up by the chin until I could swim without bladders. This patrimony of liberal education you have been pleased to endow me withal, I now carry along with me abroad, as a sure inseparable treasure; nor do I feel it any burden or encumbrance unto me at all. And what danger soever my person or other things I have about me do incur, yet I do not fear the losing of this, either by shipwreck or pirates at sea, nor by robbers, or fire, or any other casualty ashore; and at my return to England I hope at leastwise I shall do my endeavor that you may find this patrimony improved somewhat to your comfort. . . .

Touching the news of the time, Sir George Villiers, the new favorite, tapers up apace, and grows strong at Court. His predecessor, the Earl of Somerset, hath got a lease of ninety years for his life, and so hath his articulate lady, called so for articling against the frigidity and impotence of her former lord. She was afraid that Coke the Lord Chief Justice (who had used extraordinary art and industry in discovering all the circumstances of the poisoning of Overbury) would have made white broth of them, but that the prerogative kept them from the pot; yet the subservient instruments, the lesser flies, could not break through, but lay entangled in the cobweb. Amongst others, Mistress Turner, the first inventress of yellow starch, was executed in a cobweb lawn ruff of that color at Tyburn, and with her I believe that yellow starch, which so much disfigured our nation and rendered them so ridiculous and fantastic, will receive its funeral. Sir Gervas Elwaies, Lieutenant of the Tower, was made a notable example of justice and terror to all officers of trust; for being accessory, and that in a passive way only, to the murder, yet he was hanged on Tower Hill, and the *caveat* is very remarkable which he gave upon the gallows, that people should be very cautious how they make vows to heaven, for the breach of them seldom passes without a judgment, whereof he was a most ruthful example; for, being in the Low Countries, and much given to gaming, he once made a solemn vow (which he broke afterwards) that if he played above such a sum, he might be hanged. My Lord (William) of Pembroke did a most noble act, like himself; for the King having given him all Sir Gervas Elwaies' estate, which came to above £1000 per annum, he freely bestowed it on the widow and her children. . . .

LONDON, March 1st, 1618.

IV

[SIR WALTER RALEIGH]

To Sir James Crofts, Knight, at St. Osith

. . . . THE news that keeps greatest noise here now is the return of Sir Walter Raleigh from his mine of gold in Guiana, the south parts of America, which at first was like to be such a hopeful boon voyage, but it seems that the golden mine is proved a mere chimera, an imaginary airy mine; and, indeed, His Majesty had never any other conceit of it. But what will not one in captivity, as Sir Walter was, promise, to regain his freedom? Who would not promise not only mines, but mountains of gold, for liberty? And 'tis pity such a knowing, well-weighed knight had not had a better fortune; for the *Destiny* (I mean the brave ship which he built himself of that name, that carried him thither) is like to prove a fatal destiny to him and to some of the rest of those gallant adventurers who contributed for the setting forth of thirteen ships more, who were most of them his kinsmen and younger brothers, being led into the said expedition by a general conceit the world had of the wisdom of Sir Walter Raleigh; and many of these are like to make shipwreck of their estates by this voyage. Sir Walter landed at Plymouth, whence he thought to make an escape; and some say he hath tampered with his body by physic, to make him look sickly, that he may be the more pitied, and permitted to lie in his own house. Count Gondomar, the Spanish Ambassador, speaks high language, and, sending lately to desire audience of His Majesty, he said he had but one word to tell him, His Majesty wondering what might be delivered in one word; when he came before him, he said only, "Pirates, Pirates, Pirates," and so departed.

'Tis true that he protested against this voyage before, and that it could not be but for some predatory design; and that if it be as I hear, I fear it will go very ill with Sir Walter, and that Gondomar will never give him over till he hath his head off his shoulders, which may quickly be done, without any new arraignment, by virtue of the old sentence that lies still dormant against him, which he could never get off by pardon, notwithstanding that he mainly labored in it before he went; but His Majesty could never be brought to it, for he said he would keep this as a curb to hold him within the bounds of his commission and the good behavior.

Gondomar cries out that he hath broke the sacred peace betwixt the two kingdoms, that he hath fired and plundered Santo Thoma, a colony the Spaniards had planted with so much blood, near under the line, which made it prove such hot service unto him, and where, besides others, he lost his eldest son in the action; and could they have preserved the magazine of tobacco only, besides other things in that town, something might have been had to countervail the charge of the voyage. Gondomar allegeth further that, the enterprise of the mine failing, he propounded to the rest of his fleet to go and intercept some of the Plate galleons, with other designs which would have drawn after them apparent acts of hostility, and so demands justice; besides other disasters which fell out upon the dashing of the first design, Captain Remish, who was the main instrument for discovery of the mine, pistolled himself in a desperate mood of discontent in his cabin in the *Convertine.* . . .

LONDON, March 28th, 1618.

SECTION IV

VIII

[THE FALL OF BACON]

To Dr. Prichard

. . . My Lord Chancellor Bacon is lately dead of a long languishing weakness; he died so poor so that he scarce left money to bury him, which, though he had a great wit, did argue no great wisdom, it being one of the essential properties of a wise man to provide for the main chance. I have read that it hath been the fortunes of all poets commonly to die beggars; but for an orator, a lawyer, and philosopher as he was to die so, 'tis rare. It seems the same fate befell him that attended Demosthenes, Seneca, and Cicero (all great men), of whom the two first fell by corruption. The fairest diamond may have a flaw in it, but I believe he died poor out of contempt of the pelf of fortune, as also out of an excess of generosity; which appeared, as in divers other passages, so once when the King had sent him a stag, he sent up for the underkeeper, and having drunk the King's health unto him in a great silver-gilt bowl, he gave it him for his fee.

He wrote a pitiful letter to King James not long before his death, and concludes, "Help me, dear sovereign lord and master, and pity me so far, that I, who have been born to a bag, be not now in my age forced in effect to bear a wallet; nor I that desire to live to study may be driven to study to live." Which words, in my opinion, argueth a little abjection of spirit, as his former letter to the prince did of profaneness, wherein he hoped that as the Father was his creator the Son will be his redeemer. I write not this to derogate from the noble worth of the Lord Viscount Verulam, who was a rare man, a man *reconditæ scientiæ, et ad salutem literarum natus*,[1] and I think the eloquentest that was born in this isle. . . .

LONDON, January 6th, 1625.

SECTION V

VII

[ASSASSINATION OF THE DUKE OF BUCKINGHAM]

To the Right Honorable the Lady Scroop, Countess of Sunderland, from Stamford.

MADAM,

I lay yesternight at the post-house at Stilton, and this morning betimes the postmaster came to my bed's head and told me the Duke of Buckingham was slain. My faith was not then

---

[1] Of profound knowledge, and born for the good of letters.

strong enough to believe it, till an hour ago I met in the way with my Lord of Rutland (your brother), riding post towards London. It pleased him to alight and show me a letter, wherein there was an exact relation of all the circumstances of this sad tragedy.

Upon Saturday last, which was but next before yesterday, being Bartholomew eve, the Duke did rise up in a well-disposed humor out of his bed, and cut a caper or two; and being ready, and having been under the barber's hand (where the murderer had thought to have done the deed, for he was leaning upon the window all the while), he went to breakfast, attended by a great company of commanders, where Monsieur Soubize came to him, and whispered him in the ear that Rochelle was relieved; the Duke seemed to slight the news, which made some think that Soubize went away discontented. After breakfast the Duke going out, Colonel Fryer stepped before him, and stopping him upon some business, and Lieutenant Felton, being behind, made a thrust with a common tenpenny knife over Fryer's arm at the Duke, which lighted so fatally that he slit his heart in two, leaving the knife sticking in the body. The Duke took out the knife and threw it away, and laying his hand on his sword, and drawing it half out, said, "The villain hath killed me" (meaning, as some think, Colonel Fryer), for there had been some difference 'twixt them; so reeling against a chimney, he fell down dead. The Duchess being with child, hearing the noise below, came in her night-gears from her bedchamber, which was in an upper room, to a kind of rail, and thence beheld him weltering in his own blood. Felton had lost his hat in the crowd, wherein there was a paper sewed, wherein he declared, that the reason which moved him to this act, was no grudge of his own, though he had been far behind for his pay, and had been put by his captain's place twice, but in regard he thought the Duke an enemy to the state, because he was branded in Parliament; therefore what he did was for the public good of his country. Yet he got clearly down, and so might have gone to his horse, which was tied to a hedge hard by; but he was so amazed that he missed his way, and so struck into the pastry, where, though the cry went that some Frenchman had done't, he, thinking the word was Felton, boldly confessed 'twas he that had done the deed, and so he was in their hands.

Jack Stamford would have run at him, but he was kept off

by Mr. Nicholas; so being carried up to a tower, Captain Mince tore off his spurs, and asking how he durst attempt such an act, making him believe the Duke was not dead, he answered boldly that he knew he was dispatched, for 'twas not he but the hand of heaven that gave the stroke; and though his whole body had been covered over with armor of proof, he could not have avoided it. Captain Charles Price went post presently to the King four miles off, who being at prayers on his knees when it was told him, yet he never stirred, nor was he disturbed a whit till all divine service was done. This was the relation, as far as my memory could bear, in my Lord of Rutland's letter, who willed me to remember him to your ladyship, and tell you that he was going to comfort your niece (the Duchess) as fast as he could. And so I have sent the truth of this sad story to your ladyship, as fast as I could by this post, because I cannot make that speed myself, in regard of some business I have to despatch for my lord in the way.—So I humbly take my leave, and rest your ladyship's most dutiful servant,

STAMFORD, August 5th, 1628.   J. H.

SECTION VI

IX

[THE OXENHAM BIRD]

To Mr. E. D.

I THANK you a thousand times for the noble entertainment you gave me at Berry, and the pains you took in showing me the antiquities of that place. In requital, I can tell you of a strange thing I saw lately here, and I believe it is true. As I passed by St. Dunstan's in Fleet Street the other Saturday, I stepped into a lapidary or stone-cutter's shop to treat with the master for a stone to be put upon my father's tomb; and casting my eyes up and down, I might spy a huge marble with a large inscription upon it, which was thus to my best remembrance:—

Here lies John Oxenham, a goodly young man, in whose chamber, as he was struggling with the pangs of death, a bird with a white breast was seen fluttering about his bed, and so vanished.

Here lies also Mary Oxenham, the sister of the said John, who died the next day, and the same apparition was seen in the room.

Then another sister is spoke of. Then,

Here lies hard by James Oxenham, the son of the said John, who died a child in his cradle a little after, and such a bird was seen fluttering about his head a little before he expired, which vanished afterwards.

At the bottom of the stone there is,

Here lies Elizabeth Oxenham, the mother of the said John, who died sixteen years since, when such a bird with a white breast was seen about her bed before her death.

To all these there be divers witnesses, both squires and ladies, whose names are engraven upon the stone. This stone is to be sent to a town hard by Exeter where this happened.

Were you here I could raise a choice discourse with you hereupon. So, hoping to see you the next term to requite some of your favors, I rest your true friend to serve you.

WESTMINSTER, July 3rd, 1632.

SECTION VII

XIII

[AN EVENING WITH BEN JONSON]

To Sir Tho. Hawk, Knight

I WAS invited yesternight to a solemn supper by B. J., where you were deeply remembered. There was good company, excellent cheer, choice wines, and jovial welcome. One thing intervened which almost spoiled the relish of the rest, that B. began to engross all the discourse, to vapor extremely of himself, and by vilifying others to magnify his own Muse. T. Ca. buzzed me in the ear that, though Ben had barreled up a great deal of knowledge, yet it seems he had not read the *Ethics*, which among other precepts of morality forbid self-commendation, declaring it to be an ill-favored solecism in good manners. It made me think upon the lady (not very young) who, having a good while given her guests neat entertainment, a capon being brought upon the table, instead of a spoon she took a mouthful of claret and spouted it into the poop of the hollow bird. Such an accident happened in this entertainment, you know: *Proprio laus sordet in ore*—be a man's breath ever so sweet, yet it makes one's praises stink if he makes his own mouth the conduit pipe of it. But for my part I am content to dispense with the Roman infirmity of B., now that time hath snowed upon his pericranium. You know Ovid and your Horace were subject to this humor, the first bursting out into

> *Iamque opus exegi quod nec Jovis ira, nec ignis,*[1] etc.,

the other into

> *Exegi monumentum ære perennius,*[2] etc.

As also Cicero, while he forced himself into this hexameter,

> *O fortunatam natam, me consule Romam !*[3]

There is another reason that excuseth B., which is that if one be allowed to love the natural issue of his body, why not that of the brain, which is of a spiritual and more noble extraction? I preserve your manuscripts safe for you till you return to London. What news the times afford this bearer will impart unto you. So I am, sir, your very humble and most faithful servitor,

WESTMINSTER, April 5th, 1636.   J. H.

SECTION VIII

VII

[IN PRAISE OF TOBACCO]

To Henry Hopkins, Esq.

To USHER in again old Janus, I send you a parcel of Indian perfume, which the Spaniard calls the holy herb, in regard of the various virtues it hath, but we call it tobacco. I will not say it grew under the King of Spain's window, but I am told it was

---

[1] Now I have completed a work which neither the wrath of Jove nor fire ... shall destroy.

[2] I have raised a monument more lasting than bronze.

[3] Happy Rome, dating thy birth from my consulship.

gathered near his gold mines of Potosi (where they report that in some places there is more of that ore than earth), therefore it must needs be precious stuff. If moderately and seasonably taken (as I find you always do), it is good for many things; it helps digestion, taken awhile after meat, it makes one void rheum, break wind, and keeps the body open. A leaf or two being steeped overnight in a little white wine is a vomit that never fails in its operation. It is a good companion to one that converseth with dead men, for if one hath been poring long upon a book, or is toiled with the pen and stupefied with study, it quickeneth him, and dispels those clouds that usually overset the brain. The smoke of it is one of the wholesomest scents that is against all contagious airs, for it overmasters all other smells, as King James, they say, found true when, being once a-hunting, a shower of rain drove him into a pigsty for shelter, where he caused a pipeful to be taken of purpose. It cannot endure a spider or a flea, with suchlike vermin, and if your hawk be troubled with any such, being blown into his feathers it frees him. It is good to fortify and preserve the sight, the smoke being let in round about the balls of the eyes once a week, and frees them from all rheums, driving them back by way of repercussion. Being taken backward, it is excellent good against the colic, and, taken into the stomach, it will heat and cleanse it; for I could instance in a great lord (my Lord of Sunderland, President of York), who told me that he taking it downward into his stomach, it made him cast up an imposthume, bag and all, which had been a long time engendering out of a bruise he had received at football, and so preserved his life for many years. Now to descend from the substance of the smoke to the ashes, 'tis well known that the medicinal virtues thereof are very many, but they are so common that I will spare the inserting of them here. But if one would try a pretty conclusion how much smoke there is in a pound of tobacco, the ashes will tell him, for let a pound be exactly weighed, and the ashes kept charily and weighed afterwards, what wants of a pound weight in the ashes cannot be denied to have been smoke, which evaporated into air. I have been told that Sir Walter Raleigh won a wager of Queen Elizabeth upon this nicety. . . .

Fleet, January 1st, 1646.

XXIII

[WITCHES]

To the Honorable Sir Edward Spencer, Knight

. . . I RETURN you the manuscript you lent me of *Dæmonology*, but the author thereof and I are two in point of opinion that way, for he seems to be on the negative part, and truly he writes as much as can be produced for his purpose.
. . . I will not say that this gentleman is so perverse, but to deny there are any witches, to deny that there are not ill spirits which seduce, tamper, and converse in divers shapes with human creatures and impel them to actions of malice—I say that he who denies there are such busy spirits and such poor passive creatures upon whom they work, which commonly are called witches,—I say again, that he who denies there are such spirits shows that he himself hath a spirit of contradiction in him, opposing the current and consentient opinion of all antiquity. . .

What a multitude of examples are there in good authentic authors of divers kinds of fascinations, incantations, prestigiations, of philtres, spells, charms, sorceries, characters, and suchlike, as also of magic, necromancy, and divinations! Surely the Witch of Endor is no fable, the burning of Joan of Arc, the Maid of Orleans, in Rouen, and of the Marchioness d'Ancre, of late years in Paris, are no fables. . . .

But we need not cross the sea for examples of this kind. We have too many (God wot) at home. King James a great while was loth to believe there were witches, but that which happened to my Lord Francis of Rutland's children convinced him, who were bewitched by an old woman that was servant at Belvoir Castle; but being displeased she contracted with the devil (who conversed with her in form of a cat, whom she called Rutterkin) to make away those children out of mere malignity and thirst of revenge.

But since the beginning of these unnatural wars there may be a cloud of witnesses produced for the proof of this black tenet, for within the compass of two years near upon three hundred witches were arraigned, and the major part executed, in Essex and Suffolk only. Scotland swarms with them now more than ever, and persons of good quality are executed daily.

Thus, sir, have I huddled together a few arguments touching this subject, because in my last communication with you methought I found you somewhat unsatisfied and staggering in your opinion touching the affirmative part of this thesis, the discussing whereof is far fitter for an elaborate large treatise than a loose letter. . . .

FLEET, February 20th, 1647.

IZAAK WALTON (1593–1683)

A few lines about Walton have been given above (p. 163) and it would be only impertinence to say anything here of the one book of the period which is universally known, though perhaps not universally read. Doubtless God could have made a better man than Walton, but doubtless God never did.

THE COMPLETE ANGLER (1653)

EPISTLE TO THE READER

. . . . AND I wish the reader also to take notice that in writing of it I have made myself a recreation of a recreation; and that it might prove so to him, and not read dull and tediously, I have in several places mixed, not any scurrility, but some innocent, harmless mirth, of which, if thou be a severe, sour-complexioned man, then I here disallow thee to be a competent judge; for divines say there are offences given, and offences not given but taken.

And I am the willinger to justify the pleasant part of it, because though it is known I can be serious at seasonable times, yet the whole discourse is, or rather was, a picture of my own disposition, especially in such days and times as I have laid aside business, and gone a-fishing with honest Nat. and R. Roe; but they are gone, and with them most of my pleasant hours, even as a shadow that passeth away and returns not.

And next let me add this, that he that likes not the book, should like the excellent picture of the trout, and some of the other fish, which I may take a liberty to commend, because they concern not myself. . . .

But I think all that love this game may here learn something that may be worth their money, if they be not poor and needy men: and in case they be, I then wish them to forbear to buy it; for I write not to get money, but for pleasure, and this discourse boasts of no more, for I hate to promise much, and deceive the reader.

And however it proves to him, yet I am sure I have found a high content in the search and conference of what is here offered to the reader's view and censure. . . .

When I have told the reader, that in this fifth impression there are many enlargements, gathered both by my own observation, and the communication with friends, I shall stay him no longer than to wish him a rainy evening to read this following discourse; and that if he be an honest angler, the east wind may never blow when he goes a-fishing.

I. W.

THE FIRST DAY

PISCATOR. Sir, I hope you will not judge my earnestness to be impatience: and for my simplicity, if by that you mean a harmlessness, or that simplicity which was usually found in the primitive Christians, who were, as most anglers are, quiet men, and followers of peace; men that were so simply wise as not to sell their consciences to buy riches, and with them vexation and a fear to die; if you mean such simple men as lived in those times when there were fewer lawyers; when men might have had a lordship safely conveyed to them in a piece of parchment no bigger than your hand, though several sheets will not do it safely in this wiser age; I say, sir, if you take us anglers to be such simple men as I have spoke of, then myself and those of my profession will be glad to be so understood: but if by simplicity you meant to express a general defect in those that profess and practise the excellent art of angling, I hope in time to disabuse you, and make the contrary appear so evidently, that if you will but have patience to hear me, I shall remove all the anticipations that discourse, or time, or prejudice, have possessed you with against that laudable and ancient art; for I know it is worthy the knowledge and practice of a wise man.

. . . .

THE THIRD DAY

PISCATOR. Trust me, sir, there is not a likely place for a trout hereabout: and we stayed so long to take our leave of your huntsmen this morning, that the sun is got so high, and shines so clear, that I will not undertake the catching of a trout till evening; and though a chub be, by you and many others, reckoned the worst of fish, yet you shall see I'll make it a good fish by dressing it.

VENATOR. Why, how will you dress him?

PISCATOR. I'll tell you by and by, when I have caught him. Look you here, sir, do you see? (but you must stand very close) there lie upon the top of the water, in this very hole, twenty chubs. I'll catch only one, and that shall be the biggest of them all: and that I will do so, I'll hold you twenty to one, and you shall see it done.

VENATOR. Ay, marry! sir, now you talk like an artist; and I'll say you are one, when I shall see you perform what you say you can do; but I yet doubt it.

PISCATOR. You shall not doubt it long; for you shall see me do it presently. Look! the biggest of these chubs has had some bruise upon his tail, by a pike or some other accident, and that looks like a white spot; that very chub I mean to put into your hands presently; sit you but down in the shade, and stay but a little while; and I'll warrant you, I'll bring him to you.

VENATOR. I'll sit down and hope well, because you seem to be so confident.

PISCATOR. Look you, sir, there is a trial of my skill; there he is, that very chub that I showed you with the white spot on his tail: and I'll be as certain to make him a good dish of meat as I was to catch him: I'll now lead you to an honest ale-house, where we shall find a cleanly room, lavender in the windows, and twenty ballads stuck about the wall; there my hostess (which I may tell you is both cleanly, and handsome, and civil) hath dressed many a one for me, and shall now dress it after my fashion, and I warrant it good meat.

VENATOR. Come, sir, with all my heart, for I begin to be hungry, and long to be at it, and indeed to rest myself too; for though I have walked but four miles this morning, yet I begin to be weary; yesterday's hunting hangs still upon me.

PISCATOR. Well, sir, and you shall quickly be at rest, for yonder is the house I mean to bring you to.

Come, hostess, how do you? Will you first give us a cup of your best drink, and then dress this chub, as you dressed my last, when I and my friend were here about eight or ten days ago? But you must do me one courtesy, it must be done instantly.

Hostess. I will do it, Mr. Piscator, and with all the speed I can.

Piscator. Now, sir, has not my hostess made haste? and does not the fish look lovely?

Venator. Both, upon my word, sir; and therefore let's say grace and fall to eating of it.

Piscator. Well, sir, how do you like it?

Venator. Trust me, 'tis as good meat as I ever tasted. Now let me thank you for it, drink to you, and beg a courtesy of you; but it must not be denied me.

Piscator. What is it, I pray, sir? You are so modest, that methinks I may promise to grant it before it is asked.

Venator. Why, sir, it is, that from henceforth you would allow me to call you master, and that really I may be your scholar; for you are such a companion, and have so quickly caught and so excellently cooked this fish, as makes me ambitious to be your scholar.

Piscator. Give me your hand; from this time forward I will be your master, and teach you as much of this art as I am able; and will, as you desire me, tell you somewhat of the nature of most of the fish that we are to angle for, and I am sure I both can and will tell you more than any common angler yet knows.

.   .   .   .

Venator. On my word, master, this is a gallant trout; what shall we do with him?

Piscator. Marry, e'en eat him to supper: we'll go to my hostess from whence we came; she told me, as I was going out of door, that my brother Peter, a good angler and a cheerful companion, had sent word he would lodge there to-night, and bring a friend with him. My hostess has two beds, and I know you and I may have the best; we'll rejoice with my brother Peter and his friend, tell tales, or sing ballads, or make a catch, or find some harmless sport to content us, and pass away a little time without offence to God or man.

Venator. A match, good master, let's go to that house, for the linen looks white, and smells of lavender, and I long to lie in a pair of sheets that smell so. Let's be going, good master, for I am hungry again with fishing.

PISCATOR. Nay, stay a little, good scholar, I caught my last trout with a worm; now I will put on a minnow, and try a quarter of an hour about yonder trees for another; and so walk towards our lodging. Look you, scholar, thereabout we shall have a bite presently, or not at all. Have with you, sir! o' my word I have hold of him! Oh! it is a great logger-headed chub; come, hang him upon that willow twig, and let's be going. But turn out of the way a little, good scholar, towards yonder high honeysuckle hedge; there we'll sit and sing, whilst this shower falls so gently upon the teeming earth, and gives yet a sweeter smell to the lovely flowers that adorn these verdant meadows.

Look! under that broad beech-tree I sat down, when I was last this way a-fishing; and the birds in the adjoining grove seemed to have a friendly contention with an echo, whose dead voice seemed to live in a hollow tree, near to the brow of that primrose-hill; there I sat viewing the silver streams glide silently towards their center, the tempestuous sea; yet sometimes opposed by rugged roots, and pebble-stones, which broke their waves, and turned them into foam: and sometimes I beguiled time by viewing the harmless lambs; some leaping securely in the cool shade, whilst others sported themselves in the cheerful sun; and saw others craving comfort from the swollen udders of their bleating dams. As I thus sat, these and other sights had so fully possessed my soul with content, that I thought, as the poet has happily expressed it:

> I was for that time lifted above earth;
> And possessed joys not promis'd in my birth.

As I left this place, and entered into the next field, a second pleasure entertained me; 'twas a handsome milkmaid that had not yet attained so much age and wisdom as to load her mind with any fears of many things that will never be, as too many men too often do; but she cast away all care, and sung like a nightingale. Her voice was good, and the ditty fitted for it; 'twas that smooth song which was made by Kit Marlowe, now at least fifty years ago: and the milkmaid's mother sung an answer to it, which was made by Sir Walter Raleigh in his younger days.

They were old-fashioned poetry, but choicely good, I think

much better than the strong lines that are now in fashion in this critical age. Look yonder! on my word, yonder they both be a-milking again. I will give her the chub, and persuade them to sing those two songs to us.

God speed you, good woman! I have been a-fishing, and am going to Bleak Hall, to my bed, and having caught more fish than will sup myself and my friend, I will bestow this upon you and your daughter, for I use to sell none.

MILKWOMAN. Marry! God requite you, sir, and we'll eat it cheerfully. And if you come this way a-fishing two months hence, a grace of God! I'll give you a syllabub of new verjuice, in a new-made haycock, for it. And my Maudlin shall sing you one of her best ballads; for she and I both love all anglers, they be such honest, civil, quiet men. In the meantime will you drink a draught of redcow's milk? you shall have it freely.

PISCATOR. No, I thank you; but, I pray, do us a courtesy that shall stand you and your daughter in nothing, and yet we will think ourselves still something in your debt: it is but to sing us a song that was sung by your daughter when I last passed over this meadow, about eight or nine days since.

MILKWOMAN. What song was it, I pray? Was it "Come, shepherds, deck your herds," or "As at noon Dulcina rested," or "Phillida flouts me," or "Chevy Chace," or "Johnny Armstrong," or "Troy Town"?

PISCATOR. No, it is none of those; it is a song that your daughter sung the first part, and you sung the answer to it.

MILKWOMAN. Oh, I know it now. I learned the first part in my golden age, when I was about the age of my poor daughter; and the latter part, which indeed fits me best now, but two or three years ago, when the cares of the world began to take hold of me: but you shall, God willing, hear them both, and sung as well as we can, for we both love anglers. Come, Maudlin, sing the first part to the gentlemen, with a merry heart; and I'll sing the second, when you have done.

THE MILKMAID'S SONG

Come live with me, and be my love,
And we will all the pleasures prove
That valleys, groves, or hills, or fields,
Or woods, and steepy mountain yields;

Where we will sit upon the rocks,
And see the shepherds feed our flocks,
By shallow rivers, to whose falls
Melodious birds sing madrigals.

And I will make thee beds of roses,
And then a thousand fragrant posies,
A cap of flowers, and a kirtle,
Embroidered all with leaves of myrtle;

A gown made of the finest wool
Which from our pretty lambs we pull;
Slippers lin'd choicely for the cold,
With buckles of the purest gold;

A belt of straw, and ivy-buds,
With coral clasps and amber studs;
And if these pleasures may thee move,
Come live with me, and be my love.

Thy silver dishes for thy meat,
As precious as the gods do eat,
Shall on an ivory table be
Prepared each day for thee and me.

The shepherd swains shall dance and sing
For thy delight each May morning:
If these delights thy mind may move,
Then live with me, and be my love.

VENATOR. Trust me, master, it is a choice song, and sweetly sung by honest Maudlin. I now see it was not without cause that our good Queen Elizabeth did so often wish herself a milkmaid all the month of May, because they are not troubled with fears and cares, but sing sweetly all the day, and sleep securely all the night: and without doubt, honest, innocent, pretty Maudlin does so. I'll bestow Sir Thomas Overbury's milkmaid's wish upon her, "That she may die in the spring; and, being dead, may have good store of flowers stuck round about her winding sheet."

THE MILKMAID'S MOTHER'S ANSWER

If all the world and love were young,
And truth in every shepherd's tongue,
These pretty pleasures might me move
To live with thee, and be thy love.

But Time drives flocks from field to fold,
When rivers rage, and rocks grow cold;
Then Philomel becometh dumb,
And age complains of cares to come.

The flowers do fade, and wanton fields
To wayward winter reckoning yields.
A honey tongue, a heart of gall,
Is fancy's spring, but sorrow's fall.

Thy gowns, thy shoes, thy beds of roses,
Thy cap, thy kirtle, and thy posies,
Soon break, soon wither, soon forgotten,
In folly ripe, in reason rotten.

Thy belt of straw, and ivy-buds,
Thy coral clasps, and amber studs,
All these in me no means can move
To come to thee, and be thy love.

What should we talk of dainties then,
Of better meat than's fit for men?
These are but vain: that's only good
Which God hath blest, and sent for food.

But could youth last, and love still breed,
Had joys no date, nor age no need;
Then those delights my mind might move,
To live with thee, and be thy love.

PISCATOR. Well met, brother Peter! I heard you and a
friend would lodge here to-night, and that hath made me to bring
my friend to lodge here too. My friend is one that would fain be
a brother of the angle; he hath been an angler but this day, and

I have taught him how to catch a chub by daping with a grass-hopper, and the chub he caught was a lusty one of nineteen inches long. But pray, brother Peter, who is your companion?

PETER. Brother Piscator, my friend is an honest countryman, and his name is Coridon; and he is a downright witty companion that met me here purposely to be pleasant and eat a trout, and I have not yet wetted my line since we met together; but I hope to fit him with a trout for his breakfast, for I'll be early up.

PISCATOR. Nay, brother, you shall not stay so long; for, look you! here is a trout will fill six reasonable bellies. Come, hostess, dress it presently; and get us what other meat the house will afford; and give us some of your best barley-wine, the good liquor that our honest forefathers did use to drink of; the drink which preserved their health, and made them live so long, and to do so many good deeds.

PETER. O' my word, this trout is perfect in season. Come, I thank you, and here is a hearty draught to you, and to all the brothers of the angle wheresoever they be, and to my young brother's good fortune to-morrow. I will furnish him with a rod, if you will furnish him with the rest of the tackling: we will set him up, and make him a fisher.

And I will tell him one thing for his encouragement, that his fortune hath made him happy to be scholar to such a master: a master that knows as much both of the nature and breeding of fish as any man; and can also tell him as well how to catch and cook them, from the minnow to the salmon, as any that I ever met withal.

PISCATOR. Trust me, brother Peter, I find my scholar to be so suitable to my own humor, which is to be free and pleasant, and civilly merry, that my resolution is to hide nothing that I know from him. Believe me, scholar, this is my resolution; and so here's to you a hearty draught, and to all that love us, and the honest art of angling.

VENATOR. Trust me, good master, you shall not sow your seed in barren ground, for I hope to return you an increase answer-able to your hopes; but however you shall find me obedient, and thankful, and serviceable to my best ability.

PISCATOR. 'Tis enough, honest scholar! come, let's to supper. Come, my friend Coridon, this trout looks lovely; it was twenty-two inches when it was taken; and the belly of it looked some part of it as yellow as a marigold, and part of it as white as a lily; and yet methinks it looks better in this good sauce.

CORIDON. Indeed, honest friend, it looks well, and tastes well: I thank you for it, and so doth my friend Peter, or else he is to blame.

PETER. Yes, and so I do; we all thank you: and, when we have supped, I will get my friend Coridon to sing you a song for requital.

CORIDON. I will sing a song, if anybody will sing another; else, to be plain with you, I will sing none. I am none of those that sing for meat, but for company: I say,

> 'Tis merry in hall,
> When men sing all.

PISCATOR. I'll promise you I'll sing a song that was lately made, at my request, by Mr. William Basse; one that hath made the choice songs of the "Hunter in his Career," and of "Tom of Bedlam," and many others of note; and this that I will sing is in praise of angling.

CORIDON. And then mine shall be the praise of a countryman's life. What will the rest sing of?

PETER. I will promise you, I will sing another song in praise of angling to-morrow night; for we will not part till then, but fish to-morrow, and sup together, and the next day every man leave fishing, and fall to his business.

VENATOR. 'Tis a match; and I will provide you a song or a catch against then too, which shall give some addition of mirth to the company; for we will be civil and as merry as beggars.

PISCATOR. 'Tis a match, my masters. Let's e'en say grace, and turn to the fire, drink the other cup to wet our whistles, and so sing away all sad thoughts.

Come on, my masters, who begins? I think it is best to draw cuts, and avoid contention.

PETER. It is a match. Look, the shortest cut falls to Coridon.

CORIDON. Well, then, I will begin, for I hate contention.

. . . .

THE FOURTH DAY

PISCATOR. . . . No life, my honest scholar, no life so happy and so pleasant as the life of a well-governed angler; for when the lawyer is swallowed up with business, and the statesman is preventing or contriving plots, then we sit on cowslip banks, hear the birds sing, and possess ourselves in as much quietness as these silent silver streams which we now see glide so quietly by us. Indeed, my good scholar, we may say of angling, as Dr. Boteler said of strawberries, "Doubtless God could have made a better berry, but doubtless God never did"; and so, if I might be judge, God never did make a more calm, quiet, innocent recreation than angling.

.   .   .   .

VENATOR. Marry, and that you shall; and as freely as I would have my honest master tell me some more secrets of fish and fishing, as we walk and fish towards London to-morrow. But, master, first let me tell you, that very hour which you were absent from me, I sat down under a willow-tree by the water-side, and considered what you had told me of the owner of that pleasant meadow in which you then left me; that he had a plentiful estate, and not a heart to think so; that he had at this time many law-suits depending; and that they both damped his mirth and took up so much of his time and thoughts that he himself had not leisure to take the sweet content that I, who pretended no title to them, took in his fields: for I could there sit quietly, and looking on the water, see some fishes sport themselves in the silver streams, others leaping at flies of several shapes and colors; looking on the hills, I could behold them spotted with woods and groves; looking down the meadows, could see, here a boy gathering lilies and lady-smocks, and there a girl cropping culverkeys and cowslips, all to make garlands suitable to this present month of May: these, and many other field flowers, so perfumed the air, that I thought that very meadow like that field in Sicily of which Diodorus speaks, where the perfumes arising from the place make all dogs that hunt in it to fall off and to lose their hottest scent. I say, as I thus sat, joying in my own happy condition, and pitying this poor rich man that owned this and many other pleasant groves and meadows about me, I did thankfully remember what my Savior said, that the meek possess the earth; or rather, they enjoy what the others possess and enjoy not; for anglers and meek quiet-spirited men are free from those high, those restless thoughts, which corrode the sweets of life; and they, and they only, can say, as the poet has happily expressed it,

> Hail! blest estate of lowliness!
>   Happy enjoyments of such minds
> As, rich in self-contentedness,
>   Can, like the reeds, in roughest winds,
> By yielding make that blow but small
> At which proud oaks and cedars fall.

THE FIFTH DAY

VENATOR. . . . This is my firm resolution. And as a pious man advised his friend that, to beget mortification, he should frequent churches, and view monuments, and charnel-houses, and then and there consider how many dead bodies time had piled up at the gates of death, so when I would beget content and increase confidence in the power and wisdom and providence of Almighty God, I will walk the meadows, by some gliding stream, and there contemplate the lilies that take no care, and those very many other various little living creatures that are not only created but fed, man knows not how, by the goodness of the God of Nature, and therefore trust in him. This is my purpose; and so, let everything that hath breath praise the Lord: and let the blessing of St. Peter's Master be with mine.

PISCATOR. And upon all that are lovers of virtue, and dare trust in his providence, and be quiet, and go a-angling.

"Study to be quiet."

GLOSSARY

GLOSSARY[1]

a, he.

accessary, contributing factor, accompaniment.

accompt, account.

adiaphorous, indifferent, immaterial.

admiration, wonder.

advertisement, notice.

advowson, presentation to a benefice.

affect, like, incline toward.

affectate, affected.

affecting, affected; liking, inclination.

affection, feeling, quality, influence.

allay, alloy.

amated, dismayed, daunted.

amercement, fine.

angel, coin worth about 10 s.

annection, addition, adjunct.

anthropophagi, man-eaters.

antic, clown, buffoon; grotesque; grotesque dance.

antimetathesis, inversion of the members of an antithesis.

antiperistasis, heightening by contrast.

appose, question.

arefaction, drying up.

ascendant, in astrology, the point of the ecliptic, or degree of the zodiac, which at any moment (especially, e.g., at the birth of a child) is just rising above the eastern horizon; the horoscope. *The house of the ascendant* includes 5 degrees of the zodiac above this point, and 25 below it. *The lord of the ascendant:* any planet within the house of the ascendant. The ascendant and its lord were supposed to exercise a special influence upon the life of a child then born. (N. E. D.)

aspect, the relative positions of the heavenly bodies as they appear to an observer on the earth's surface at a given time; properly, the way in which the planets, from their relative positions, look upon each other, but popularly transferred to their joint look upon the earth. (N. E. D.)

assay, endeavor, attempt.

bains, baths.

bale, set of dice.

balm-wood, balsam wood.

bandog, mastiff.

bankerout, bankrupt, bankruptcy.

basilisk, fabulous serpent said to kill with a glance; kind of cannon.

bastone, bastinado, flogging on soles of the feet.

batzen, small German coins.

beneplacit, favor, good pleasure.

blacks, mourning garments.

blown (furnaces), blast furnaces.

bovoli, snails or cockles dressed in the Italian manner.

---

[1]It is perhaps needless to say that the glossary omits countless words the meaning of which, though now more or less altered, is explained by the context, and that many of the words included, with archaic or unusual meanings attached, are found in the text bearing their ordinary sense as well.

bravery, boastfulness, display, splendor.

caitiff, mean-spirited, niggardly, base.

calenture, fever, delirium.

callosity, callous spot.

can, know how.

canicular (days), dog days, days of great heat.

cantharides, genus of flies.

caract, mark, character.

card, chart.

careful, full of cares.

carking, anxiety, toiling.

case-divinity, casuistry, study of cases of conscience.

casually, by chance.

cat, cate, cake.

catchpole, sheriff's officer, sergeant.

catena, Biblical commentary in the form of a series of extracts from the Fathers.

cautelous, deceitful.

censure, judgment, opinion, survey; express opinion.

cento, patched garment; patchwork composition.

champaign, open country.

chapless, without the lower jaw.

chapman, merchant.

Chetiv, see Keri.

cheverel, kid leather; pliable, elastic.

chirurgeon, surgeon, physician.

chop, barter.

chorography, description of regions and countries.

chrisom-child, child in first month.

chylus, chyle, milky fluid formed by action of digestive juices on food.

climacter, beginning of period of decay.

coævus, contemporary.

coagulation, experiment in thickening fluids.

cockatrice, mistress.

cockering, pampering.

colosses, large structures.

combust, destruction of a planet's "influence" when it comes within a certain distance of the sun.

commutative (justice), exchange of things profitable for an equivalent.

complement, completeness.

complemental, subsidiary, nonessential.

complexion, constitution, temperament.

compliment, accomplishment.

complimental, accomplished; complimentary.

compost, manure.

conceit, mind, imagination, idea, conception.

conclusion, experiment.

concoction, digestion.

concourse, concurrence, coöperation.

conditions, character, disposition, behavior.

coney, hare; gull, dupe of swindlers.

confectionary, confectioner, apothecary.

congee, bow, leave-taking.

conscience, consciousness.

conscionable, conscientious.

consist, stand firm, agree with.

consort, combination of voices or instruments; companion.

conster, construe.

construction, translation.

contexted, woven together.

conversation, behavior, mode of life.

conveyance, contrivance.

convince, demonstrate error, expose real character.

copia, abundance, fluency.

coranto, lively dance.

cornel, cherry tree.

corpse, body, living or dead.

corpulency, material quality, bodily character.

corse, corpse.

counter-roll, catalogue.

courb, bend, bow.

crabbed, rough, difficult.

crambe, tiresome repetition.

crany, cranium.

crasis, constitution, temperament, resulting from mixture of humors.

cross, mark off debt as paid.

crudity, digestion.

culverkey, wild hyacinth or bluebell.

curious, subtle, careful.

curranto, gazette, news-letter.

cynegetics, hunting, the chase.

dap, fish by letting the bait bob on the water.

dastard, frighten, intimidate.

dawcock, silly fellow.

dearness, affection.

decoct, boil down.

delatory, of the nature of criminative information or accusation. (N. E. D.)

delicate, affected.

demean, manage.

deprave, depreciate.

derive, divert; communicate.

derivation, subsidiary device.

descension, the setting, or descent below the horizon, of a celestial body. (N. E. D.)

determinate, authoritative, final.

determine, end.

digladiation, fighting with swords, strife.

ding, throw.

disinterest, disinterested.

distributive (justice), distribution of rewards and punishments.

ditty, words of a song as distinct from the music.

diuturnity, long duration.

Dominical, concerned with Christ.

donative, gift.

dorado, fish noted for golden color; rich man.

dormitive, sleeping draught.

doublets, old game of tables or backgammon.

dragon, the part of the moon's path which lies south of the ecliptic. (N. E. D.)

ductible, pliable, agreeable.

effront, embolden.

election, selection, choice.

electuary, medicinal conserve or paste.

eleemosynaries, beggars.

elegant, of cultivated taste.

elench, logical refutation.

emaculate, wipe out.

embase, corrupt, debase.

empyreal, of the highest heaven; lofty, rare.

enchiridion, handbook.

engross, monopolize; write in large letters; make bulky.

enlifen, animate, give life to.

enow, enough.

ensure, assure.

entelechia, realization or complete expression of some function; informing spirit, soul. (N. E. D.)

ephemerides, astrological tables, almanacs.

ephori, Spartan magistrates who controlled the kings.

epicycle, in old astronomy, a small circle whose center describes a larger one.

equal, just.

ergo, therefore; conclusion.

estrich, estridge, ostrich.

ethnic, Gentile, heathen.

exarchate, province, state.

excremental, of the nature of an outgrowth or excrescence (N. E. D.)

exercitation, exercise of the faculties, practice.

exhibition, allowance, income.

exolution, (in mystical theology) rapturous faintness.

expatiate, move about freely without limits.

exquisite, careful, choice.

extasis, mystical trance, ecstasy.

extended, intensified, prolonged.

extenuate, made thin.

eyebite, bewitch with the eye.

facility, readiness to be led, pliancy.

factor, agent.

fagioli, French beans.
falling, cadence.
falls, results.
fame, report, common talk.
far-fet, far-fetched.
fashionate, fashionable.
fashions, disease of horses.
feoffments, instruments, deeds.
feral, deadly, fatal.
ferula, cane, rod.
fescue, pointer.
fineness, cunning.
fit, humor, mood.
flashy, tasteless.
fond, foolish.
forelay, lie in wait for, waylay.
fretting, irritation.
froward, perverse.

galliard, lively dance.
galliardize, mirth.
gamut, musical scale.
gatherer, money-taker at door of theatre.
gaud, toy.
genial, fruitful.
gird, sneer.
glister, glitter.
glister, clyster.
glosing, cajoling, speciously representing.
Godamercy, thanks, thanks to.
gomer, Hebrew measure (same as "omer").
graff, graft.
gramercy, thanks.
grandence, greatness.
gulch, glutton.

haggard, (in falconry) wild, untamed.
halieutics, art or practice of fishing.
hazard, game of dice.
hear, be spoken of.
heteroclite, abnormal, eccentric person, oddity.
Hobbinol, rustic.
hobby, small horse.
hockey, the feast at harvest home.

homœomera, the ultimate particles of matter which, according to Anaxagoras, were homogeneous.
house, in astrology, *a.* twelfth part of the heavens as divided by great circles through the north and south points of the horizon; the whole sky, excluding those parts that never rise and set, being thus divided into twelve houses, numbered eastwards, beginning with the *house of the ascendant,* and each having some special signification attached to it. *b. A sign of the zodiac* considered as the seat of the greatest influence of a particular planet; each of the seven planets, except the sun and moon, having two such houses, a *day house* and a *night house.* (N. E. D.)
huke, cloak with a hood.
humor, in ancient and mediæval physiology, one of the four chief fluids of the body (blood, phlegm, choler, and melancholy or black choler), by the relative proportions of which a person's physical and mental qualities and disposition were held to be determined; character, style, whim, vagary. (N. E. D.)
hungerlin, short fur coat introduced from Hungary.
hypostasis, distinct substance.

imbase, corrupt, debase.
imbonities, unkindnesses.
impertinent, irrelevant, foolish.
impleasing, unpleasing.
imposthume, abscess.
imprimis, in the first place; first: originally used to introduce the first of a number of items, as in an inventory or will.
improperation, reproach, taunt.
improve, disprove, disapprove.
incense, kindle, burn.
increpation, reproof.

incurious, careless, indifferent.

induration, experiment in hardening.

infancy, inability or unwillingness to speak, silence.

informity, shapelessness.

ingeminate, repeat.

ingenuity, nobility of character, candor, talent.

ingine, genius.

ingle, friend, male favorite.

iniquity, injustice, unfairness.

inoculate, (of trees) bud.

inquisiturient, eager to act as inquisitor.

insolation, exposing body of substance to the sun.

instauration, restoration, renewal.

institution, training, discipline.

insuavities, surliness, unpleasantness.

intellectuals, mind, judgment.

intend, direct one's course, devote oneself to.

inward, intimate, close.

jacks, automatons which struck the hour.

jet, strut in fine clothes.

keeping, (dark keeping), being kept in the dark.

Keri, in the Hebrew text of the Old Testament, the word, given in the margin, to be substituted in reading for that standing in the text (Kethib) [Chetiv], the latter having been retained, though considered erroneous or unintelligible. (N. E. D.)

kickshaw, fantastical, frivolous person.

last, duration.

leese, lose, loosen.

let, hindrance.

licorous, greedy.

lightly, commonly

like, please.

lin, cease.

listed, stuffed.

lively, keenly, vigorously.

loligo, a genus of cephalopods; one of the genus, a squid. (N. E. D.)

loose, shot of an arrow; issue.

lot, spell.

lurch, cheat, trick.

macaronicon, medley.

maistry, art, craft.

make, mate.

malster, maltster.

mandrake, poisonous plant, having a forked root which was thought to resemble human form, and which was said to shriek when pulled.

maniple, subdivision of Roman legion; handful.

maribone, marrowbone.

mast, fruit of oak, beech, etc.

mate, daunt, subdue.

mediocrity, moderation.

method, formal treatise.

mew, perhaps "to renew by the process of moulting"; some would render "exchanging her mighty youth for the still mightier strength of full age." (N. E. D.)

misted, blurred, dulled.

module, pattern.

moles, mausoleum.

monomachy, combat, duel.

montera, hunting cap with flap for ears.

motion, impulse, suggestion; kind of motion; machine; puppet-show.

motive, movable.

mought, might.

murena, fish of eel family.

mystery, see maistry.

nard, costly ointment.

naturals, natural gifts.

necessited, fixed, unavoidable.

neoteric, new, modern.

niceness, fastidiousness.

ninnyhammer, simpleton.

nominalist, one who holds the scholastic view that universals or abstract concepts are mere names, with no corresponding reality.

numerous, harmonious, rhythmical.

oblige, bind, please.

obnoxious, subject to the authority of another, dependent.

occasionally, for the occasion.

occurrent, occurrence.

omer, *see* "gomer."

omneity, "allness."

one and thirty, card game.

oneirocritical, concerning the interpretation of dreams.

orb, orbit.

ordinary, tavern or eating-house providing public meal at a fixed price.

ossuaries, receptacles for bones of the dead.

painful, painstaking, laborious.

pair (of cards), pack.

palled, weakened.

paneguries, general assemblies.

pantaloon, character in Italian comedy and pantomime.

parænetical, advisory, hortatory.

paranymph, bridesmaid.

paronomasy, play on words which sound alike.

partile, in astrology, of an aspect: exact to the same degree and minute, or, at least, within a degree; e. g. *partile conjunction,* exact conjunction. (N. E. D.)

pasquil, lampoon.

passant, current.

pastry, place where pastry is made.

percase, perchance.

peremptory, dogmatic, arbitrary.

perspective, telescope.

pert, lively.

phytognomy, the alleged art of discovering the qualities of a plant from its appearance. (N. E. D.)

pia mater, the brain; strictly, the innermost membrane.

piscation, fishing.

pismire, ant.

placet, expression of assent.

planed, smoothed.

plausible, deserving of applause.

politician, schemer.

politique, politician.

pomander, ball of mixed aromatic substances carried in a box, bag, etc., as preservative against infection. (N. E. D.)

pompous, splendid, magnificent.

poser, examiner.

posy, motto, inscription in a ring.

poticary, apothecary.

praxis, practice, use.

precisian, puritan.

predicament, situation, condition.

prefer, show off.

pre-occupate, anticipate, forestall.

preposterously, in reverse of right order.

prescious, fore-knowing.

present, represent.

presently, immediately.

pressly, exactly, concisely.

prestigiation, sorcery, magic.

pretend, claim.

prevent, anticipate.

primero, card game.

prining-iron, apparently an instrument for removing burnt tobacco.

prize, fencing match.

prize, cheapen, price.

proairesis, rational choice between right and wrong.

profound, plunge into, plumb.

propending, favorably inclined.

propense, inclined.

prophesying, preaching, public discussions on religious subjects.

propriety, property.

proyning, pruning, cultivating.

pucellage, virginity.

punk, prostitute, mistress.

puny, minor.

quacksalver, quack.
quadragesimal, concerning Lenten fasts.
quaint, fine, fashionable, odd.
quality, profession.
quarrel, reason, pretext.
quartan, recurring every fourth day.
quietus, acquittance, receipt given on payment of account.
quincunx, arrangement in fives, one at each corner of a rectangle, and one in the center.
quotidian, daily.

rash, smooth textile fabric made of silk or worsted.
realist, one who holds scholastic view that universals have an objective or absolute existence (opposite of nominalist).
rebeck, primitive form of violin.
recover, reach.
reins, kidneys.
remarked, noted.
remember, remind.
resorts, sources, beginnings.
returns, money deposited by prospective traveler, to be got back with profit on return.
ring, a mode of taking tobacco, perhaps blowing rings.
rivelled, wrinkled, shrivelled.
rock, distaff (Rock Monday, the Monday after Twelfth Day, when women resumed spinning after the festivities of Christmas).
rodomontado, boast, rant.

sacramentary, person holding "high" doctrines concerning the sacraments.
sad, sober.
sallet, salad.
salve, solve, explain.
scelestique, wicked.
scenical, outward.
sconce, head, fortress.
scornful, contemptible.

secondine, after-birth.
semblably, similarly.
sentence, aphorism, maxim.
septuagenary, too old to beget children.
sharer, holder of share in theatre.
sharp (play at), fight in earnest.
shittlecock, shuttlecock.
shoeing-horn, appetizer, allurement.
shoulder-clapping, arrest.
shroving, merrymaking at Shrovetide.
simple, gather herbs, botanize.
sindon, fine linen cloth.
Si quis, notice, advertisement.
sith, sithence, since.
skelder, swindle.
skill (vb.), matter; have skill, manage.
sol-fa, musical scale.
sounding, playing on a musical instrument.
spectrum, apparition, spectre.
spintrian, obscene, unnatural.
spital, hospital.
squinzy, quinzy.
state, settle, establish in security.
statist, statesman, politician.
steal, conceal.
stem-book, album.
still, always.
stomach, anger, spirit.
stond, hindrance.
strappado, form of punishment (person raised with ropes and allowed to drop part way).
stub, trunk, stump; blockhead.
stupend, stupendous.
suppeditation, usefulness.
supplements, supplies, advantages.
syllabub, cream or milk mixed with wine.
syntagma, orderly compilation.

tables, notebook; old name of backgammon.
tain, taken.
tapist, concealed, in ambush.
tarasse, terrace.

tasker, piece-worker.
tenent, tenet.
tentation, temptation.
tenterbellies, gluttons.
tester, teston, sixpence.
theatre, spectacle, things seen.
thrummed, made of thrums or waste yarn.
tissue, rich cloth.
touchstone, kind of jasper used in testing alloys.
touze, disturb, disorder, harass.
traduce, injure, calumniate.
traduction, propagation.
trillill, drinking term representing sound of flowing liquid.
tropical, figurative.
trunk, tube.

ubi, dwelling place.
unreclaimed, (in falconry) untamed.
usher, assistant master.
utcunque, in any way whatever, however.
utter, sell, dispose of.

velvet-guarded, wearing clothes trimmed with velvet.
venation, hunting.
venditation, display.

veneries, erotic desires.
venery, hunting.
venter, venture, dare to utter.
verjuice, acid liquor made from crab-apples, etc.
vermiculate, intricate, like wriggling of worms.
vespillo, corpse-bearer.
vetturine, driver of carriage.
voider, basket for removing remnants of a meal.
voisinage, neighborhood.

wait, treat with unkindness, cruelty, etc.
weak, weaken.
wearish, sickly, wizened.
whether, whither.
whiff, swallow; in smoking, perhaps "inhale."
wild-fire, inflammable composition.
wit, mind, natural gifts.
witty, able, clever, wise.
wool-ward, wearing wool next the skin.
wretch, miser.

zany, inferior clown who mimics his master.
zeal, zealous person, zealot.

DATE DUE

WITHDRAWN